PHR/SPHR: Professional in Human Resources Certification® Study Guide, Fourth Edition

HRCI Test Specifications

RESPONSIBILITIES	CHAPTER
Business Management and Strategy	
01 Interpret and apply information related to the organization's operations from internal sources, including finance, accounting, business development, marketing, sales, operations, and information technology, in order to contribute to the development of the organization's strategic plan.	3
02 Interpret information from external sources related to the general business environment, industry practices and developments, technological advances, economic environment, labor force, and the legal and regulatory environment, in order to contribute to the development of the organization's strategic plan.	3
03 Participate as a contributing partner in the organization's strategic planning process (for example: provide and lead workforce planning discussion with management, develop and present long-term forecast of human capital needs at the organizational level).	3
04 Establish strategic relationships with key individuals in the organization to influence organizational decision-making. **SPHR only**	3
05 Establish relationships/alliances with key individuals and outside organizations to assist in achieving the organization's strategic goals and objectives (for example: corporate social responsibility and community partnership).	3
06 Develop and utilize business metrics to measure the achievement of the organization's strategic goals and objectives (for example: key performance indicators, balanced scorecard). **SPHR only**	3
07 Develop, influence, and execute strategies for managing organizational change that balance the expectations and needs of the organization, its employees, and other stakeholders.	3
08 Develop and align the human resource strategic plan with the organization's strategic plan. **SPHR only**	3
09 Facilitate the development and communication of the organization's core values, vision, mission, and ethical behaviors.	3
10 Reinforce the organization's core values and behavioral expectations through modeling, communication, and coaching.	3
11 Provide data such as human capital projections and costs that support the organization's overall budget.	3
12 Develop and execute business plans (i.e., annual goals and objectives) that correlate with the organization's strategic plan's performance expectations to include growth targets, new programs/services, and net income expectations. **SPHR only**	3
13 Perform cost/benefit analyses on proposed projects. **SPHR only**	3
14 Develop and manage an HR budget that supports the organization's strategic goals, objectives, and values. **SPHR only**	3
15 Monitor the legislative and regulatory environment for proposed changes and their potential impact to the organization, taking appropriate proactive steps to support, modify, or oppose the proposed changes.	3
16 Develop policies and procedures to support corporate governance initiatives (for example: whistleblower protection, code of ethics). **SPHR only**	3

Sybex®
An Imprint of
🕸 WILEY

03	Develop and implement employee relations programs (for example: recognition, special events, diversity programs) that promote a positive organizational culture.	7
04	Evaluate effectiveness of employee relations programs through the use of metrics (for example: exit interviews, employee surveys, turnover rates).	7
05	Establish, update, and communicate workplace policies and procedures (for example: employee handbook, reference guides, or standard operating procedures) and monitor their application and enforcement to ensure consistency.	7
06	Develop and implement a discipline policy based on organizational code of conduct/ethics, ensuring that no disparate impact or other legal issues arise.	7
07	Create and administer a termination process (for example: reductions in force [RIF], policy violations, poor performance) ensuring that no disparate impact or other legal issues arise.	7
08	Develop, administer, and evaluate grievance/dispute resolution and performance improvement policies and procedures.	7
09	Investigate and resolve employee complaints filed with federal agencies involving employment practices or working conditions, utilizing professional resources as necessary (for example: legal counsel, mediation/arbitration specialists, investigators).	7
10	Develop and direct proactive employee relations strategies for remaining union-free in non-organized locations. **SPHR only**	7
11	Direct and/or participate in collective bargaining activities, including contract negotiation, costing, and administration.	7

Risk Management

01	Ensure that workplace health, safety, security, and privacy activities are compliant with applicable federal laws and regulations.	8
02	Conduct a needs analysis to identify the organization's safety requirements.	8
03	Develop/select and implement/administer occupational injury and illness prevention programs (i.e., OSHA, workers' compensation). **SPHR only**	8
04	Establish and administer a return-to-work process after illness or injury to ensure a safe workplace (for example: modified duty assignment, reasonable accommodations, independent medical exam).	8
05	Develop/select, implement, and evaluate plans and policies to protect employees and other individuals, and to minimize the organization's loss and liability (for example: emergency response, workplace violence, substance abuse).	8
06	Communicate and train the workforce on security plans and policies.	8
07	Develop, monitor, and test business continuity and disaster recovery plans.	8
08	Communicate and train the workforce on the business continuity and disaster recovery plans.	8
09	Develop policies and procedures to direct the appropriate use of electronic media and hardware (for example: email, social media, and appropriate website access).	8
10	Develop and administer internal and external privacy policies (for example: identity theft, data protection, workplace monitoring).	8

Exam objectives are subject to change at any time without prior notice at HRCI's sole discretion. Please visit HRCI's website (www.hrci.org) for the most current listing of exam objectives.

Sybex®
An Imprint of
WILEY

RESPONSIBILITIES	CHAPTER

Human Resource Development

01	Ensure that human resources development activities are compliant with all applicable federal laws and regulations.	5
02	Conduct a needs assessment to identify and establish priorities regarding human resource development activities.	5
03	Develop/select and implement employee training programs (for example: leadership skills, harassment prevention, computer skills) to increase individual and organizational effectiveness.	5
04	Evaluate effectiveness of employee training programs through the use of metrics (for example: participant surveys, pre- and post-testing). **SPHR only**	5
05	Develop, implement, and evaluate talent management programs that include assessing talent, developing career paths, and managing the placement of high-potential employees.	5
06	Develop, select, and evaluate performance appraisal processes (for example: instruments, ranking and rating scales) to increase individual and organizational effectiveness. **SPHR only**	5
07	Develop, implement, and evaluate performance management programs and procedures (includes training for evaluators).	5
08	Develop/select, implement, and evaluate programs (for example: telecommuting, diversity initiatives, repatriation) to meet the changing needs of employees and the organization.	5
09	Provide coaching to managers and executives regarding effectively managing organizational talent.	5

Compensation and Benefits

01	Ensure that compensation and benefits programs are compliant with applicable federal laws and regulations.	6
02	Develop, implement, and evaluate compensation policies/programs (for example: pay structures, performance-based pay, internal and external equity).	6
03	Manage payroll-related information (for example: new hires, adjustments, terminations).	6
04	Manage outsourced compensation and benefits components (for example: payroll vendors, COBRA administration, employee recognition vendors). **SPHR only**	6
05	Conduct compensation and benefits programs needs assessments (for example: benchmarking, employee surveys, trend analysis).	6
06	Develop/select, implement/administer, update and evaluate benefit programs (for example: health and welfare, wellness, retirement, stock purchase).	6
07	Communicate and train the workforce in the compensation and benefits programs, policies and processes (for example: self-service technologies).	6
08	Develop/select, implement/administer, update, and evaluate an ethically sound executive compensation program (for example: stock options, bonuses, supplemental retirement plans). **SPHR only**	6
09	Develop, implement/administer and evaluate expatriate and foreign national compensation and benefits programs. **SPHR only**	6

Employee and Labor Relations

01	Ensure that employee and labor relations activities are compliant with applicable federal laws and regulations.	7
02	Assess organizational climate by obtaining employee input (for example: focus groups, employee surveys, staff meetings).	7

Sybex®
An Imprint of
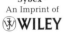 WILEY

17	Participate in enterprise risk management by ensuring that policies contribute to protecting the organization from potential risks.	3
18	Identify and evaluate alternatives and recommend strategies for vendor selection and/or outsourcing. **SPHR only**	3
19	Oversee or lead the transition and/or implementation of new systems, service centers, and outsourcing. **SPHR only**	3
20	Participate in strategic decision-making and due diligence activities related to organizational structure and design (for example: corporate restructuring, mergers and acquisitions [M&A], divestitures). **SPHR only**	3
21	Determine strategic application of integrated technical tools and systems (for example: new enterprise software, performance management tools, self-service technologies). **SPHR only**	3

Workforce Planning and Employment

01	Ensure that workforce planning and employment activities are compliant with applicable federal laws and regulations.	4
02	Identify workforce requirements to achieve the organization's short- and long-term goals and objectives (for example: corporate restructuring, workforce expansion or reduction).	4
03	Conduct job analyses to create and/or update job descriptions and identify job competencies.	4
04	Identify, review, document, and update essential job functions for positions.	4
05	Influence and establish criteria for hiring, retaining, and promoting based on job descriptions and required competencies.	4
06	Analyze labor market for trends that impact the ability to meet workforce requirements (for example: federal/state data reports).	4
07	Assess skill sets of internal workforce and external labor market to determine the availability of qualified candidates, utilizing third party vendors or agencies as appropriate.	4
08	Identify internal and external recruitment sources (for example: employee referrals, diversity groups, social media) and implement selected recruitment methods.	4
09	Establish metrics for workforce planning (for example: recruitment and turnover statistics, costs).	4
10	Brand and market the organization to potential qualified applicants.	4
11	Develop and implement selection procedures (for example: applicant tracking, interviewing, reference and background checking).	4
12	Develop and extend employment offers and conduct negotiations as necessary.	4
13	Administer post-offer employment activities (for example: execute employment agreements, complete I-9/e-Verify process, coordinate relocations, and immigration).	4
14	Develop, implement, and evaluate orientation and on-boarding processes for new hires, rehires, and transfers.	4
15	Develop, implement, and evaluate employee retention strategies and practices.	4
16	Develop, implement, and evaluate the succession planning process. **SPHR only**	4
17	Develop and implement the organizational exit/off-boarding process for both voluntary and involuntary terminations, including planning for reductions in force (RIF).	4
18	Develop, implement, and evaluate an affirmative action plan (AAP) as required.	4
19	Develop and implement a record retention process for handling documents and employee files (for example: pre-employment files, medical files, and benefits files).	4

Sybex®
An Imprint of
🕸 **WILEY**

PHR®/SPHR®
Professional in Human Resources Certification

Study Guide
Fourth Edition

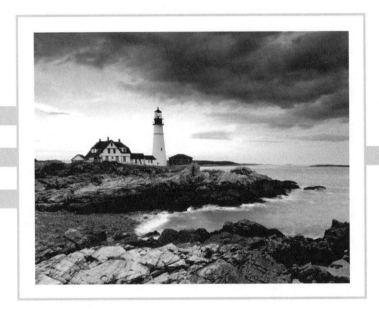

PHR®/SPHR®
Professional in Human Resources Certification

Study Guide
Fourth Edition

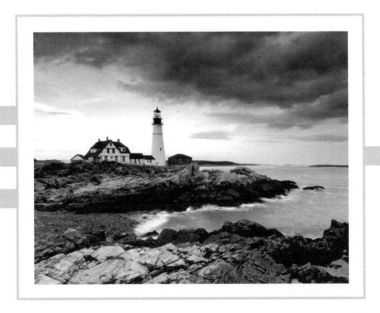

Sandra M. Reed

Anne M. Bogardus

WILEY

John Wiley & Sons, Inc.

Senior Acquisitions Editor: Jeff Kellum
Development Editor: Kim Wimpsett
Technical Editors: Brenda Budke and Tamra Aguinaldo
Production Editor: Christine O'Connor
Copy Editor: Tiffany Taylor
Editorial Manager: Pete Gaughan
Production Manager: Tim Tate
Vice President and Executive Group Publisher: Richard Swadley
Vice President and Publisher: Neil Edde
Media Project Manager 1: Laura Moss-Hollister
Media Associate Producer: Shawn Patrick
Media Quality Assurance: Marilyn Hummel
Book Designers: Judy Fung and Bill Gibson
Proofreader: Josh Chase, Word One New York
Indexer: Robert Swanson
Project Coordinator, Cover: Katherine Crocker
Cover Designer: Ryan Sneed

Dear Reader,

Thank you for choosing *PHR/SPHR: Professional in Human Resources Certification Study Guide, Fourth Edition.* This book is part of a family of premium-quality Sybex books, all of which are written by outstanding authors who combine practical experience with a gift for teaching.

Sybex was founded in 1976. More than 30 years later, we're still committed to producing consistently exceptional books. With each of our titles, we're working hard to set a new standard for the industry. From the paper we print on, to the authors we work with, our goal is to bring you the best books available.

I hope you see all that reflected in these pages. I'd be very interested to hear your comments and get your feedback on how we're doing. Feel free to let me know what you think about this or any other Sybex book by sending me an email at nedde@wiley.com. If you think you've found a technical error in this book, please visit http://sybex.custhelp.com. Customer feedback is critical to our efforts at Sybex.

Best regards,

Neil Edde
Vice President and Publisher
Sybex, an Imprint of Wiley

To my husband Chris, whose three little words never fail to inspire me: "Go for it." To my children, Calvin and Clara, because the best part of me will eternally be each of you. I am filled with love and gratitude for having the three of you in my life.

Acknowledgments

Any acknowledgement in the updating of this book must begin by recognizing the professionalism and intellect of Anne Bogardus. Her thoroughness and attention to detail represented in the previous editions of this work made writing these updates an absolute career highlight.

To the editors Jeff Kellum, Kim Wimpsett, Pete Gaughan, Brenda Budke, Christine O'Connor and Tim Tate, thank you for your professionalism, encouragement, superior organizational skills and insightful additions to the expanded version of this work — it absolutely made for a better final product.

A book like this requires a great deal of time and thought, and nobody felt that more than my clients, co-workers, and support staff who watched me attempt to juggle it all. To TAGS, VWC, and my clients at SBDC, thank you for allowing me a peek into your business, for letting me rattle your cage with strategic "leaps," for picking up the slack when I went underground, and for supporting my crazy schedule—I quite literally could not have done it without you.

Finally, to the students, a brief mention of my own testing experience: I remember sitting in my hotel room the night before my SPHR exam, trying to cram in a few more details, desperate to figure out what I didn't already know. It was around Christmas time, and my youngest child was just 2 years old. Feeling guilty for being away from my family and with my confidence at an all-time low, I wondered if I was really up for the challenge. Then, surrounded by my books and flashcards, I suddenly "got" it. The pieces starting fitting together, the processes had rationale, and the big picture came into clear focus. The next morning, I took a 4-hour exam in just 2 hours and passed it on the first go-round. My excitement about being a part of this project is a reflection of that one "a-ha" moment, representing for me when HR crosses over from just being a job to an intelligent, strategic career choice. My hope is that with each pass through this material, you will get closer to your own enlightened moment when suddenly, you just get it. Many thanks, and good luck in your career—this absolutely can happen for you!

About the Authors

Sandra M. Reed, SPHR,   has more than 17 years of experience in human resources, the last ten of which have been spent in training and instruction. Prior to teaching, she spent much of her work career in the recruiting and risk-management functions of human resources, which evolved into a passion for training through on-boarding and OSHA compliance activities. She obtained her PHR and her SPHR designations through the Human Resource Certification Institute and received her teaching credential in adult vocational education from California State University, San Bernardino. As an independent contractor, she has conducted onsite training for California State University Stanislaus, University of the Pacific, the Small Business Development Center of Stanislaus County, and private employers throughout Northern California. She has authored learning modules and case studies for the Society for Human Resource Management, focusing on educating the emerging workforce and future human resource professionals. She currently is owner of Epoch Resources, a consulting firm located in the Central Valley of California that specializes in the unique HR needs of small businesses. Find her on the Web at http://epochresources.com.

Anne M. Bogardus, SPHR,   began her human resources career in compensation at a public multinational corporation, Castle & Cooke, owner of the Dole food brand, and later at First Nationwide Bank. She also founded and was principal of S.T.A.R. HR in northern California, which specialized in building human resource functions that serve strategic business needs. Her practice included small to medium-sized businesses in a wide range of industries including biotechnology, mortgage lending, high technology, public relations, retail, nonprofit, and construction. Ms. Bogardus is also the author of an introductory book for non-HR business professionals, *Human Resource Jumpstart*, as well as the previous three editions of this book, all published by John Wiley & Sons, Inc.

About the Technical Editors

Brenda G. Budke is the executive director for Sierra HR Partners, Inc., an HR consulting and outsourcing service located in Fresno, California. She is a certified SPHR with over 20 years experience in the human resource field. Prior to joining Sierra HR Partners, Brenda served as the human resources manager for a national communications company, overseeing employment, employee relations, and training. She is founder and dean of a corporate university and has developed curriculum and presented performance-based training at all levels. Ms. Budke holds a Bachelor of Science degree in organizational behavior with a concentration in Human Resource Management from the University of San Francisco. She currently serves on the board of the Central California Employment Round Table (CCERT), working in conjunction with DFEH to prevent harassment and discrimination in the workplace; she is a member of the Society of Human Resource Management (SHRM) and past-president of the Human Resource Association of Central California (HRACC). Most recently she served as deputy director for the California State Council for SHRM.

Tamra Aguinaldo has a background in human resources and education and currently works as an HR consultant in Northern California. She has a Master of Arts degree in Education with an emphasis in Guidance Counseling. Prior to becoming a consultant, she was Director of Professional Development for the Northern California Human Resources Association in San Francisco.

HR is a dynamic profession requiring practitioners to keep up-to-date with current trends and changes to employment law. The PHR/SPHR exams are updated annually to reflect these trends and changes. For information about updates between revisions of this study guide, log on to http://epochresources.com, and click PHR/SPHR Certification to view changes or ask questions about content.

Contents at a Glance

Contents

Introduction

Congratulations on taking the first step toward achieving your Professional in Human Resources (PHR) or Senior Professional in Human Resources (SPHR) certification! The process you're embarking on is rewarding and challenging, and as more than 100,000 of your fellow human resource colleagues have already discovered, it's an excellent opportunity to explore areas of HR management with which you may not work every day. In the next few pages, you'll find some general information about HR certification, some suggestions for using this book, information about what to expect in the following chapters, and a discussion of the organizations involved in certification.

Before we begin, a word about what you should already know. This study guide was designed to serve as a refresher for experienced professionals who have practiced for several years or have been educated in human resources. We assume that those who are pursuing certification have the basic HR knowledge that comes not only from education in human resources but also, more importantly, from exempt-level experience. If your daily work is truly generalist in nature, you likely have touched on many of the topics I cover, but you may not have in-depth knowledge in all of them. Conversely, if you specialize in one or two areas of HR, you probably have extensive experience in those areas but may need to refresh your knowledge in other areas.

The goal of this study guide is to provide enough information about each of the functional areas of HR management to enable candidates in either situation to find what they need to prepare themselves for successfully completing the exam. More than 22,000 books related to human resources are listed on Amazon.com alone, and there is obviously no way we can cover all the aspects of HR in a single book. So, we've organized the information around the test specifications (test specs) established by the Human Resource Certification Institute (HRCI), the certifying body for our profession. We'll talk more about the test specs in Chapter 1, "Certifying Human Resource Professionals," but for now, suffice it to say that the key to success on the exam is a thorough understanding of and ability to apply the test specs when answering questions on the exams.

About Human Resource Certification

What exactly *is* human resource certification? Briefly, let's just say that certification is a way of acknowledging individuals who have met the standard of competency established by HR practitioners as that which is necessary to be considered a fully competent HR professional. To understand whether this book is for you, you'll want to know why you should become certified and how the certification process works.

Who Certifies HR Professionals?

Three organizations are involved in the certification of HR professionals: the Human Resource Certification Institute (HRCI), the Society for Human Resource Management (SHRM), and the Professional Examination Service (PES).

The Human Resource Certification Institute

HRCI is the certifying body for the HR profession. It was formed by the American Society of Personnel Administrators (ASPA) in 1972, when it was known as the ASPA Accreditation Institute (AAI). In its early stages, HRCI was financially dependent on SHRM, but it's now financially independent. Both HRCI and SHRM have individual boards of directors that govern their operations. Although HRCI and SHRM have a long history of affiliation and mutual support, the certification process is a separate and distinct function of HRCI, and SHRM has no more control over or access to the certification process than does anyone else in the profession.

You can find HRCI's organizational mission statement at www.hrci .org/Page.aspx?id=31&terms=mission.

The Society for Human Resource Management

SHRM is the largest organization of HR professionals in the world, representing more than 250,000 members worldwide, with more than 900 affiliated professional and student chapters. From its beginning in 1948 as the American Society for Personnel Administrators (ASPA), SHRM has been a leader in the endeavor to gain recognition for the HR profession. Today's certification program is a direct result of efforts by the first volunteer members of SHRM, who recognized the need for a defined body of knowledge and set about to develop it along with a certification process that evaluates the abilities of practitioners in the field.

Professional Examination Service

PES is a nonprofit organization that conducts license and credential examinations for a wide variety of professions, including psychology, pharmacy, real-estate appraisal, security management, as well as human resources. PES maintains the database of test items developed by HRCI and is responsible for ensuring that applicants for the PHR and SPHR exams meet the eligibility requirements, administering and scoring the tests, and notifying candidates of the results. PES conducts a *practice analysis study* to ensure the continued relevance of the credentialing process to current business practice.

We'll refer to these organizations frequently in Chapter 1 as we discuss the body of knowledge and the certification process.

Why Become Certified?

Over time, the certification offered by HRCI has become the industry standard for determining competence in the field of human resources. There are many reasons that individuals may decide to seek professional certification. Let's talk about just a few of them.

First, certification is an acknowledgement that you have met the standards of excellence determined by other HR professionals to be those that are necessary to be fully competent in the field. Because the standards are developed by working professionals, not just by those who teach and consult in the field, this credential demonstrates that you're a fully competent HR practitioner based on a standard set by your peers.

Second, certification is a way to increase your marketability. In difficult economic times, when there is tough competition for jobs, certification provides an edge that can be advantageous in your job search. With an abundance of job seekers for a limited number of jobs, whatever you can do to set yourself apart from the crowd can give you the edge when potential employers are making the final hiring decision.

Third, those who spend the time to advance their own knowledge and achieve certification have demonstrated their ability to continue learning and growing as times and business needs change. A person who is willing and able to set a significant goal and do what is necessary to achieve it demonstrates characteristics that are in great demand in business today: results orientation, technical competence, commitment, and excellence.

Finally, certification enhances your credibility with co-workers and customers by demonstrating to the people you encounter during your workday that you have proven competence in the field.

Whether your reason for seeking certification falls into one of these categories or you're motivated to do so for some other reason, it can be a great opportunity to validate how much you already know about the practice of human resources as a profession.

How to Become Certified

To become a certified HR professional, you must pass either the PHR or SPHR exam, both of which have been developed by HRCI in a comprehensive process described in Chapter 1.

HRCI uses a computer-based testing (CBT) process during two time periods each year: between the beginning of May and the end of June, and from mid-November through mid-January. One advantage of the CBT process is that exam candidates know before they leave the testing center whether they are certified.

Each exam, PHR and SPHR, consists of 225 questions. Of these questions, 200 are scored to determine whether you pass the exam. The additional 25 questions are being "pretested" in order to determine their reliability and validity for inclusion in future test cycles. You can find a detailed discussion of how the questions are developed and scored in the *HR Certification Institute's 2012 Certification Policies and Procedures Handbook*, which can be viewed and/or downloaded at the HRCI website (www.hrci.org), or you can request a hard copy from HRCI by calling (866) 898-4724. The handbook is an essential guide to all aspects of the exams and includes test dates, application deadlines, fee information, and answers to frequently asked questions about the certification process, as well as the full list of test specifications.

Chapter 1 explains in greater detail how much and what kinds of experience are required for each exam level and how the questions differ on each level.

How This Book Is Organized

We've talked a little about Chapter 1, which provides information about requirements for certification and the testing process. Chapter 1 also provides some suggestions on the best ways to study for the exam.

Chapter 2, "Core Knowledge Requirements for HR Professionals," provides a brief discussion of knowledge with implications in multiple functional areas. Reading this chapter first gives exam candidates a base for understanding topics covered in subsequent chapters.

Chapters 3–8 get down to the specifics of each functional area and discuss the test specifications in detail. Each of these chapters consists of a list of objectives, an overview of the functional area, the federal employment laws applicable to that area, and a discussion of the test specs, including the appropriate court cases.

We have also provided five appendices to facilitate your study. Appendix A, "Answers to Review Questions," provides all of the answers to the questions at the end of every chapter.

Appendix B, "Case Study," gives you an opportunity to pull information from multiple functional areas to solve typical HR challenges in a fictitious company.

Appendix C, "Federal Employment Legislation and Case Law," is a chronological listing of the federal legislation appearing throughout the book, as well as significant court decisions with implications for human resources. This appendix also includes additional court decisions that were not discussed in the chapters but have significance for HR practice and with which you should be familiar, so be sure to review them. They are included in a separate section of the appendix.

Appendix D, "Resources," is just that: a list of additional sources of information about each of the functional areas of human resources.

Appendix E, "About the Additional Study Tools," provides a listing of all the material you can find on the book's companion web site.

Finally, we've included some additional study tools including the Sybex test engine, electronic flashcards, and a PDF of a glossary of terms: an alphabetical listing of all the key terms throughout the book with their corresponding definitions.

For up-to-the-minute updates please see www.epochresources.com; and for directions on where to get the study tools, visit www.sybex.com/go/phr4e.

The Elements of a Study Guide

You'll see many recurring elements as you read this study guide. Here's a description of some of those elements:

Assessment Test   At the end of this introduction is an assessment test that you can use to check your readiness for the exam. Take this test before you start reading the book; it will help you determine the areas on which you may need to brush up. The answers to the assessment test questions appear on a separate page after the last question of the test. Each answer includes an explanation and a note telling you the chapter in which the material appears.

Objective Map and Opening List of Objectives   On the inside front cover of this book is a detailed exam-objective map showing you where each of the exam objectives is covered in this book. In addition, each chapter opens with a list of exam objectives that are covered in that chapter. Use these to see exactly where each of the exam topics is covered.

Summary   The summary is a brief review of the chapter to sum up what was covered.

Exam Essentials   The "Exam Essentials" section at the end of each chapter highlights topics that could appear on one or both of the exams in some form. Although we obviously don't know exactly what will be included in a particular exam, these sections reinforce significant concepts that are key to understanding the functional area and the test specs HRCI has developed.

Chapter Review Questions   Each chapter includes 20 practice questions designed to measure your knowledge of key ideas discussed in the chapter. After you finish each chapter, answer the questions; if some of your answers are incorrect, it's an indication that you need to spend more time studying that topic. The answers to the practice questions can be found in Appendix A. The chapter-review questions are designed to help you measure how much information you retained from your reading and are different from the kinds of questions you'll see on the exam.

The assessment test and chapter-review questions can also be taken via the Sybex test engine. The next section tells you where to get the additional study tools, including the test engine.

Additional Study Tools

We've included a number of additional study tools that can be found on the book's companion site at www.sybex.com/go/phr4e. All of the following gear should be loaded on your computer when you're studying for the test.

The Sybex Test Preparation Software

The test-preparation software helps prepare you to pass the PHR/SPHR exams. In this test engine, you'll find all the chapter-review and assessment questions from the book, plus two additional bonus practice exams that appear exclusively on the test engine: one specifically for PHR candidates and one for SPHR candidates. You can take the assessment test, test yourself by chapter, or take the bonus practice exams.

> Just as on the certification exams, the practice exam questions draw on your experience as an HR professional. Be on the lookout for questions based on your everyday activities in HR and not just on the material in the *PHR/SPHR Study Guide*.

Electronic Flashcards

Sybex's electronic flashcards include more than 200 PHR questions and more than 200 SPHR questions designed to challenge you further for the PHR and SPHR exams. Between the review questions, practice exams, and flashcards, you'll have a wide variety of materials to help you prepare!

Glossary of Terms in PDF

Sybex offers an exclusive glossary of terms in PDF format as part of the additional study tools. Now you can review key terms on your computer or e-reader if you travel and don't want to carry a book or if you just like to read from the computer screen.

> You can get the additional study tools by visiting www.sybex.com/go/phr4e. Here, you'll get instructions on how to download the files to your hard drive.

How to Use This Book and the Additional Study Tools

This book has a number of features designed to guide your study efforts for either the PHR or the SPHR certification exam. All of these features are intended to assist you in doing the most important thing you can do to pass the exam: understand and apply the test specs in answering questions. This book helps you do that by listing the current test specs at the beginning of each chapter and by ensuring that each of them is fully discussed in the chapter.

The practice questions at the end of each chapter and the practice exams included with the study tools (which can be found on the companion site at www.sybex.com/go/phr4e) are designed to assist you in testing your retention of the material you've read to make you aware of areas on which you should spend additional study time. We've provided web links and other resources to assist you in mastering areas where you may require additional study materials. Here are some suggestions for using this book and study tools:

- Take the assessment test before you start reading the material. These questions are designed to measure your knowledge and will look different from the questions you'll see on the exam. They will give you an idea of the areas on which you need to spend additional study time, as well as those areas for which you may just need a brief refresher.

- Review the test specs at the beginning of each chapter before you start reading. Make sure you read the associated knowledge requirements in the *HR Certification Institute's 2012 Certification Policies and Procedures Handbook* because these may help you in your study process. After you've read the chapter, review the requirements again to be sure you understand and are able to apply them.

- Answer the review questions after you've read each chapter. If you miss any of them, go back over the chapter and review the topic, or use one of the additional resources if you need more information.

- Make sure you understand the laws that apply to each functional area, the information covered in each of them, and to which companies or government agencies they apply.

- Download the flashcards, and review them when you have a few minutes during the day.

- Take every opportunity to test yourself. In addition to the assessment test and review questions, there are bonus practice exams. Take these exams without referring to the chapters, and see how well you've done—go back and review any topics you've missed until you fully understand and can apply the concepts.

Finally, find a study partner if possible. Studying for, and taking, the exam with someone else will make the process more enjoyable, and you'll have someone to help you understand topics that are difficult for you. You'll also be able to reinforce your own knowledge by helping your study partner in areas where they are weak.

Assessment Test

1. According to the WARN Act, an employer with 200 employees is required to provide 60 days' notice of a mass layoff when which of the following is true?

    A. The employer is seeking additional funding and will lay off 70 employees if the funding falls through.

    B. A major client unexpectedly selects a new vendor for the company's products, and the company lays off 75 employees.

    C. The employer lays off 5 employees a week for 3 months.

    D. A flood requires that one of the plants be shut down for repairs, and 55 employees are laid off.

2. An employee has come forward with an allegation of quid pro quo harassment by her supervisor. As the HR manager, you are responsible for investigating the complaint. The supervisor in question is someone with whom you have become quite friendly. In this case, who is the best person to conduct the investigation?

    A. You

    B. The corporate attorney

    C. The direct manager of the accused supervisor

    D. A third-party investigator

3. As of July 24, 2009, the federal minimum wage is set at which of the following?

    A. $5.15 per hour

    B. $7.25 per hour

    C. $5.75 per hour

    D. $6.55 per hour

4. During the union-organizing process, how is the bargaining unit determined?

    A. By the union organizers

    B. Jointly, by the union and the employer

    C. By the National Labor Relations Board

    D. By the employees during the election

5. The motivation theory that suggests people are motivated by the reward they will receive when they succeed and that they weigh the value of the expected reward against the effort required to achieve it is known as what?

    A. Vroom's expectancy theory

    B. Adams' equity theory

    C. McClelland's acquired needs theory

    D. McGregor's Theory X and Theory Y

6. What is the most effective method of performance evaluation?

   A. A field-review process

   B. A continuous-feedback process

   C. A forced-ranking process

   D. A behaviorally anchored rating-scale process

7. Which of the following is an example of a nonqualified deferred-compensation plan?

   A. An excess-deferral plan

   B. A target-benefit plan

   C. A money-purchase plan

   D. A cash-balance plan

8. Which of the following is an example of a passive training method?

   A. Vestibule training

   B. Demonstration

   C. Distance learning

   D. Self-study

9. What is the purpose of the OSHA consulting service?

   A. Helps employers identify the OSHA standards that apply to their workplace

   B. Fines employers for violating OSHA safety standards

   C. Does not require compliance with OSHA standards

   D. Acts as a one-time service

10. One purpose of a diversity initiative is to do what?

   A. Increase workplace creativity

   B. Increase the effectiveness of the workforce

   C. Increase the organization's ability to attract customers

   D. All of the above

11. What is an employer's responsibility when workplace conditions pose a threat to an unborn child?

   A. Do nothing. It is up to employees to protect their unborn children.

   B. Move the employee into a different job that does not pose a threat to the unborn child.

   C. Advise the employee of the potential threat, and allow the employee to make the decision.

   D. Allow only sterile employees to work in jobs that pose a threat to unborn children.

12. What does the Health Insurance Portability and Accountability Act do?

   A. Prevents HR from investigating claims issues

   B. Requires continuation of health benefits

   C. Establishes EPO networks

   D. Limits preexisting condition restrictions

13. The concept that recognizes that businesses are social organizations as well as economic systems and that productivity is related to employee job satisfaction is known as what?

   A. Human resource management

   B. Strategic management

   C. Human relations

   D. Human resource development

14. Before selecting an HRIS system, which of the following questions should be answered?

   A. What information will be converted to the HRIS?

   B. Who will have access to the information stored in the HRIS?

   C. How will the HRIS be accessed?

   D. All of the above.

15. The correlation coefficient is a statistical measurement that is useful for which of the following?

   A. Determining whether one variable affects another

   B. Compensating for data that may be out of date

   C. Determining which variables are outside acceptable ranges

   D. Describing standards of quality

16. The process of identifying risks and taking steps to minimize them is referred to as what?

   A. Liability management

   B. Risk management

   C. Qualitative analysis

   D. Risk assessment

17. What is the most effective method to use when an employer wants to obtain insight into employee goals and job satisfaction and provide career counseling to those in the work group?

   A. An employee survey

   B. A skip-level interview

   C. An employee focus group

   D. A brown-bag lunch

18. Which of the following is an example of workplace ethics issues?

   A. Workplace privacy

   B. Conflicts of interest

   C. Whistle-blowing

   D. All of the above

19. Which of the following statements about substance-abuse policies is *not* true?

    A. Substance-abuse policies identify who will be tested.

    B. Federal law requires all employers to implement substance-abuse policies.

    C. An effective policy describes when tests will occur and what drugs will be tested.

    D. An effective policy describes what happens to employees who test positive.

20. Which one of the following statements is true of a hostile work environment?

    A. When a single incident of unwanted touching occurs, a hostile work environment has been created.

    B. A hostile work environment may be created when an individual witnesses the ongoing harassment of a co-worker.

    C. Only a supervisor can create a hostile work environment.

    D. A grievance procedure/policy against discrimination protects employers from hostile work environment claims.

21. An HR audit is designed to help management do what?

    A. Improve employee morale.

    B. Analyze HR policies, programs, and procedures against applicable legal requirements.

    C. Improve HR effectiveness.

    D. All of the above.

22. Which of the following is a productivity type of statistical HR measurement?

    A. Turnover and retention

    B. Cost per hire

    C. Revenue per employee

    D. Job satisfaction

23. Federal legislation does not specifically prohibit disparate treatment of caregivers, but claims of disparate treatment for employees caring for elders, children, or disabled family members increased 450 percent between 1990 and 2005. On what basis are these claims filed?

    A. Title VII

    B. Americans with Disabilities Act

    C. Family Medical Leave Act

    D. All of the above

24. A statement of cash flows is a financial report that tells you which of the following?

    A. The financial condition of the business at a specific point in time

    B. Where the money used to operate the business came from

    C. The financial results of operations over a period of time

    D. How much money is owed to the company by its customers

25. According to the Copyright Act of 1976, which of the following is most likely to be considered a fair use of copyrighted material?

    A. Distributing 30 copies of a chapter in a book to a study group

    B. Copying a book for 10 staff members of a nonprofit organization

    C. Distributing 30 copies of a paragraph in a book to a study group

    D. None of the above

26. A PEST analysis is used during the strategic planning process. What is PEST an acronym for?

    A. Political, environmental, strengths, threats

    B. Political, economic, specific, timely

    C. Political, economic, social, technology

    D. Product, environment, social, technology

27. Which of the following organizational structures is characterized by networks instead of traditional hierarchies?

    A. Seamless organization

    B. Geographic organization

    C. Flat organization

    D. Matrix organization

28. The Occupational Safety and Health Act of 1970 grants employees the right to do all of the following *except* which one?

    A. Be advised of potential safety hazards.

    B. Speak privately to an OSHA inspector during an inspection.

    C. Observe the employer when measuring and monitoring workplace hazards.

    D. View detailed reports of all workplace accidents.

29. Which of the following alternative staffing methods would be *most* appropriate for a company with ongoing yet sporadic needs for a specific job to be done?

    A. Intern program

    B. On-call worker

    C. Seasonal worker

    D. Temp worker

30. A standard employment practice that seems to be fair yet results in discrimination against a protected class is a description of what?

    A. Disparate treatment

    B. Disparate impact

    C. Adverse impact

    D. Unfair treatment

31. Which of the following is required by the Economic Growth and Tax Relief Reconciliation Act of 2001?

A. Requires pension plans to account for employee contributions separately from employer contributions

B. Allows employers to contribute a percentage of company earnings to retirement plans each year

C. Allows employees older than 50 to make catch-up contributions to retirement accounts

D. Requires employer pension contributions to be funded on a quarterly basis

32. Measuring staffing needs against sales volume could be done most effectively by using which of the following techniques?

A. A multiple linear regression

B. A ratio

C. A simulation model

D. A simple linear regression

33. Which of the following points is important to effective lobbying: that is, attempting to influence or persuade an elected official to pass, defeat, or modify a piece of legislation?

A. Learning how the legislative and political process works

B. Beginning by using persuasion to convince the elected official to accept your position

C. Making big financial contributions

D. Letting the elected official choose a solution rather than present a proposal solution

34. The Vietnam Era Veterans Readjustment Assistance Act (VEVRAA) requires which of the following?

A. All contractors must list all job openings with state employment agencies.

B. All employers must list all job openings with state employment agencies.

C. State employment agencies must give preference to Vietnam veterans for senior-level management position referrals.

D. State employment agencies must give preference to Vietnam veterans for positions lasting 3 days or longer.

35. The FLSA requires employers to pay nonexempt employees for time spent where?

A. At home while waiting to be called to work

B. At work reading a book while waiting for an assignment

C. Attending a voluntary training program

D. Commuting to work

36. What provides the framework for collecting information about factors that are relevant to the planning process?

A. A SWOT analysis

B. A PEST analysis

C. An environmental scan

D. An internal assessment

37. A process for reducing the impact of bias during performance reviews by using multiple raters is known as what?

   A. Inter-rater reliability

   B. An MBO review

   C. A rating scale

   D. Paired comparison

38. According to the OSHA inspection priorities, which type of workplace hazard receives first priority for an inspection?

   A. Catastrophes and fatal accidents

   B. Programmed high-hazard inspections

   C. Imminent danger

   D. Employee complaints

39. A lockout occurs when which of the following occurs?

   A. The employees shut down operations by refusing to work.

   B. The employer refuses to allow the union to unionize the workplace.

   C. The employer shuts down operations to keep employees from working.

   D. The employees patrol the entrance to the business.

40. Total quality management focuses all employees on producing products that meet customer needs. This is achieved by doing what?

   A. Eliminating processes that waste time and materials

   B. Developing a high level of expertise in all employees

   C. Sharing information with all levels in the organization

   D. Balancing the needs of all stakeholders in the organization

41. A high-involvement organization is an example of what type of OD intervention?

   A. Human process

   B. Human resource management

   C. Techno-structural

   D. Strategic

42. An employee earning $22,500 per year supervises three employees and spends 35 hours per week on essential job duties that require discretion and independent judgment. Which of the following describes this employee?

   A. Exempt, based on the executive exemption test

   B. Exempt, based on the administrative exemption test

   C. Nonexempt, based on the salary basis requirement

   D. Nonexempt

43. Health and wellness programs are beneficial for employers because they do what?

    A. Increase productivity, reduce medical costs, and attract top-quality job candidates

    B. Provide nutrition counseling, exercise programs, and health education programs

    C. Require employees to lose weight, stop smoking, and avoid substance abuse

    D. Provide on-site opportunities for physical fitness

44. An effective progressive disciplinary process begins with which of the following?

    A. A written warning

    B. A verbal warning

    C. A suspension

    D. Coaching or counseling

45. Which of the following would be considered an extrinsic reward?

    A. Challenging work on a new project

    B. A 10 percent salary increase

    C. A feeling of accomplishment after completing a tough assignment

    D. Recognition by the CEO at a company meeting

46. "Thanks for such a great presentation! You'll always have a job with us." This is an example of what?

    A. The duty of good faith and fair dealing

    B. An express contract

    C. An implied contract

    D. Fraudulent misrepresentation

47. Samantha applied as an outside sales rep for a new sales territory. Part of the selection process included an assessment test that measures successful sales characteristics. Samantha scored particularly high on the test. During the interview, Christopher, the hiring manager, had some concerns about how well Samantha would fit into the company culture, but when he learned how high she scored on the test, he immediately decided to hire her. What bias could be at work in this situation?

    A. Halo effect

    B. Knowledge-of-predictor effect

    C. Cultural-noise effect

    D. Stereotyping effect

48. What is an Excelsior list?

    A. A list of all employees in the bargaining unit provided by the employer to the union within 7 days of the scheduling of an election by the NLRB

    B. A list of the employees who do not want the union to represent them

    C. A list of the employees who have signed authorization cards for the union

    D. A list of all employees in the bargaining unit provided by the union to the employer within 7 days of the scheduling of an election by the NLRB

49. Which of the following activities is *not* a responsibility of the operations function of a business?

   A. Designing the product

   B. Scheduling production runs to coincide with customer demand

   C. Ensuring that products or services meet quality standards

   D. Determining what new products will be produced

50. Which of the following activities does *not* contribute to ergonomic injuries?

   A. Awkward postures

   B. Extended vibrations

   C. Falling down stairs

   D. Contact stress

51. What is a target-benefit plan?

   A. Uses actuarial formulas to calculate individual pension contribution amounts

   B. Requires an actual deferral-percentage test to be performed each year

   C. Provides a means for employees to become owners of the company

   D. Uses a fixed percentage of employee earnings to defer compensation

52. To increase the chances for successful repatriation of employees, the process should include which of the following?

   A. Development of a qualified pool of candidates for global assignments

   B. A formal repatriation program that includes career counseling

   C. Setting expectations for repatriation before employees begin global assignments

   D. All of the above

53. Richard, who works at the customer service counter in an auto-supply store, told his manager that because of chronic back pain, it is difficult for him stand for long periods and asked for an accommodation. The manager isn't sure, based on the essential job functions, how an accommodation can be provided. You advise the manager to begin the interactive process with the employee. What should the manager do to begin this process?

   A. Ask Richard how his back was injured.

   B. Provide a stool for Richard to use at the counter.

   C. Ask Richard whether he has any suggestions for an accommodation.

   D. Ask Richard to meet with HR to resolve the problem.

54. Human resource professionals are likely to use third-party contracts when doing which of the following?

   A. Conducting a job evaluation

   B. Hiring a temporary employee

   C. Writing the employee handbook

   D. Hiring a full-time executive

55. Which of the following is an example of direct compensation?

    A. Variable compensation

    B. Vacation pay

    C. 401(k) matches

    D. Employer Social Security contributions

56. For purposes of developing a security program, an HR manager must assess potential risks and costs related to loss and protection. Which factor must the manager first examine?

    A. Severity of impact of the loss to the organization

    B. Cost of the loss, including a permanent or temporary substitute

    C. Degree of probability that the loss will occur

    D. Availability and cost of insurance to cover the loss

57. A correlation coefficient is an example of a type of what?

    A. Qualitative analysis

    B. Quantitative analysis

    C. Job evaluation

    D. Learning matrix

58. An organizational picket may lawfully take place when which of the following is true?

    A. The union members are unhappy with their current union and ask a new union to represent them.

    B. The union files a representation petition with the NLRB no later than 15 days after picketing starts.

    C. There are fewer than 45 days left before the current collective-bargaining agreement expires.

    D. The union wants to attract employees so they will authorize the union to represent them.

59. Arbitrators chosen by all parties to resolve any disputes arising between them in the future are known as what?

    A. Tripartite arbitrators

    B. Compulsory arbitrators

    C. Ad hoc arbitrators

    D. Permanent arbitrators

60. When the NLRA imposes a voluntary-recognition bar, this means what?

    A. No election will take place for a reasonable period of time.

    B. The NLRB has certified a bargaining representative.

    C. The union withdrew its petition for an election.

    D. A representation election took place in the previous 12 months.

61. Which of the following HR strategies would be most useful in dealing with a workforce that lacks accountability?

    A. Identify training needs through an assessment.

    B. Conduct a skills assessment to determine performance deficiencies.

    C. Begin to gather employee feedback through surveys and exit interviews.

    D. Follow the progressive disciplinary process.

62. Characteristics of high-involvement organizations include all of the following *except* which?

    A. Decision-making from the bottom up

    B. Data-sharing from the top down

    C. Pay-for-performance system that clearly links employee behavior to rewards

    D. Team learning

63. Data integrity, employment practices liability insurance, OSHA, and workplace violence policies are all examples of which of the following HR functions?

    A. EEO

    B. Risk management

    C. Workforce planning and employment

    D. Employee relations

64. For employers with 15 or more employees, records of all job announcements, applications, and resumes must be kept for one year under which of the following acts?

    A. Americans with Disabilities Act

    B. Executive Order 11246

    C. Temporary Employee Records

    D. Title VII of the Civil Rights Act

65. A strategic response to the increasing use of mobile technology in the applicant job search would include all of the following *except* which?

    A. Creating mobile-friendly company websites

    B. Posting current openings online using videos

    C. Using Facebook and LinkedIn for technical job openings

    D. Outsourcing the positions to social-media recruitment firms

66. Which of the following is *false* about the E-Verify program?

    A. It is mandated by certain states for some employers.

    B. Employers must verify all employees after an MOU has been written.

    C. It is a program in which employers may verify the employment eligibility of newly hired workers.

    D. Employees may contest a tentative nonconfirmation.

67. A code of conduct is primarily used by companies that wish to do which of the following?

   A. Establish the framework for a discipline system

   B. Work toward preventing disciplinary action through clearly communicated behavior standards

   C. Provide equal opportunity for all employees

   D. Discourage violations of company policy

68. If a dress-code policy prohibits the use of ethnic clothing, but an employee requests an accommodation based on their religious preference, how should the employer respond?

   A. Modify the dress code unless doing so would create an undue hardship.

   B. Refuse the accommodation based on business necessity.

   C. Allow the employee to dress in ethnic clothing with sufficient advance notice.

   D. Only allow the clothing on casual dress days, when other employees are also allowed to dress outside of policy guidelines.

69. The ability of an employee to use multiple skill sets on the job represents which of the following job-enrichment activities?

   A. Task variety

   B. Task identity

   C. Skill variety

   D. Job rotation

70. A corporate manager regularly participates in discussion boards with a group of peers and one-on-one emails with a development specialist. He is *most* likely engaged in which of the following development activities?

   A. Mentoring

   B. Peer-to-peer coaching

   C. Leadership coaching

   D. Virtual coaching

Answers to Assessment Test

1. **C.** The WARN Act requires employers to provide 60 days' notice when 500 employees or 33 percent of the workforce are laid off, and it requires the number to be counted over a period of 90 days. Five employees a week for 3 months is a total of 65 employees (5 employees times 13 weeks), which is 33 percent of the workforce. The three exceptions are the "faltering company exception" (A) when knowledge of a layoff will negatively impact the company's ability to obtain additional funding, the "unforeseeable business circumstance" (B) when unexpected circumstances occur, and the "natural disaster" (D) exception. See Chapter 4 for more information.

2. **D.** In this case, the organization will be best served by a third-party investigator. The most important consideration in an investigation of sexual harassment is that the investigator is seen as credible and impartial. Because you have become friendly with the accused, it will be difficult to maintain impartiality during an investigation. While the corporate attorney (B) may be selected to conduct investigations, this solution can lead to conflict-of-interest issues. The direct manager of the accused supervisor (C) may not be viewed as impartial by the accuser or by regulatory agencies. See Chapters 2 and 8 for more information

3. **B.** As of July 24, 2009, the federal minimum wage was raised to $7.25 per hour from (D) $6.55 per hour, which became effective on July 24, 2008. The minimum wage in some states and other localities may be different. See Chapter 6 for more information.

4. **C.** The National Labor Relations Board (NLRB) determines which jobs will be included in the bargaining unit based on the "community of interest" shared by the requirements of the jobs. See Chapter 7 for more information.

5. **A.** Vroom explains his theory with three terms: expectancy (the individual's assessment of their ability to achieve the goal), instrumentality (whether the individual believes they are capable of achieving the goal), and valence (whether the anticipated goal is worth the effort required to achieve it). Adams' equity theory (B) states that people are constantly comparing what they put into work to what they get from it. McClelland's acquired needs theory (C) states that people are motivated by one of three factors: achievement, affiliation, or power. McGregor's Theory X and Theory Y (D) explain how managers relate to employees. Theory X managers are autocratic, believing that employees do not want to take responsibility. Theory Y managers encourage employees to participate in the decision-making process, believing that they respond to challenges. See Chapters 2 and 5 for more information.

6. **B.** A continuous-feedback review process is most effective because it provides immediate feedback to employees, enabling them to correct performance issues before they become major problems. In a field review (A), reviews are conducted by someone other than the direct supervisor. Forced ranking (C) is an evaluation method in which all employees are listed in order of their value to the work group. The BARS process (D) identifies the most important job requirements and creates statements that describe varying levels of performance. See Chapter 5 for more information.

7. **A.** An excess-deferral plan makes up the difference between what an executive could have contributed to a qualified plan if there had not been a limit on contributions and how much was actually contributed because of the discrimination test required by ERISA. These plans are nonqualified because they are not protected by ERISA; they are limited to a small group of executives or highly compensated employees. A target-benefit plan (B) is a hybrid with elements of defined-benefit and money-purchase plans. A money-purchase plan (C) defers a fixed percentage of employee earnings. A cash-balance plan (D) combines elements of defined-benefit and defined-contribution plans. See Chapter 6 for more information.

8. **C.** Distance learning is similar to a lecture in that a presenter provides information to a group of participants but does not require active participation. Vestibule training (A) is a form of simulation training. Demonstration (B) is an experiential training method. Self-study (D) is an active training method. See Chapters 2 and 5 for more information.

9. **A.** OSHA consultants provide free services to assist employers in identifying workplace hazards and the standards that apply in their workplaces. The consulting service requires employers to abate any hazards that are identified during the consultation but does not fine them for violations. To receive a free consultation, employers must agree to advise OSHA of changes in operating processes that may require additional consultations. See Chapter 8 for more information.

10. **B.** The purpose of a diversity initiative is to increase the effectiveness of an already diverse workforce by educating the employee population about the benefits of a diverse workforce, which include increased creativity (A) and an enhanced ability to attract customers (C). See Chapter 2 for more information.

11. **C.** The Supreme Court determined in *Automobile Workers v. Johnson Controls, Inc.* that it is the responsibility of prospective parents to protect their unborn children. Although employers must provide information about potential hazards, the employer may not decide for the employee whether to work in a job that poses a risk to an unborn child. See Chapter 8 for more information.

12. **D.** HIPAA prohibits health insurance providers from discriminating on the basis of health status and limits restrictions for preexisting conditions. HIPAA does not prevent HR from investigating claims issues (A) as long as the employee provides written permission. COBRA requires continuation of health benefits (B). EPO networks (C) are established by physicians connected to a hospital. See Chapter 6 for more information.

13. **C.** The concept of human relations was first introduced in the 1920s and challenged previous assumptions that people work only for economic reasons and could be motivated to increase productivity simply by increasing monetary incentives. Human resource management (A) is the business function responsible for activities related to attracting and retaining employees, including workforce planning, training and development, compensation, employee and labor relations, and safety and security. Strategic management (B) is the process by which organizations look for competitive advantages, create value for customers, and execute plans to achieve goals. Human resource development (D) is the functional area of human resources focused on upgrading and maintaining employee skills and developing employees for additional responsibilities. See Chapters 2 and 5 for more information.

14. **D.** A needs analysis will provide answers to these questions, as well as whether the HRIS will be integrated with payroll or other systems and what kinds of reports will be produced. See Chapters 2 and 3 for more information.

15. **A.** The correlation coefficient is useful in determining whether two factors are connected. For example, the correlation coefficient will tell you whether an increase in resignations is related to a change in location of the worksite and, if so, whether the change had a strong impact on resignations. See Chapter 2 for more information.

16. **B.** Risk management identifies areas of possible legal exposure for the organization and reduces those risks with preventive actions. Liability management (A) occurs after a liability is incurred, while risk management seeks to prevent liability. Qualitative analysis (C) covers several subjective tools for analysis. A risk assessment (D) is used to determine how likely it is that an identified risk will actually occur. See Chapters 2 and 8 for more information.

17. **B.** A skip-level interview provides an opportunity for a manager's manager to obtain insight into the goals and satisfaction of employees in the work group. An employee survey (A) is best used to gather information about various issues that can be collated and summarized. A focus group (B) can be used to involve employees in the decision-making process. A brown-bag lunch (D) is an effective way for senior managers to meet with small groups of employees to answer questions about the company goals and mission and to obtain feedback about operations. See Chapter 7 for more information.

18. **D.** Workplace privacy, conflicts of interest, and whistle-blowing are all examples of workplace ethics issues. Ethics are considered a standard of conduct and moral judgment defined by the processes that occur and the consequences of these processes. See Chapter 3 for more information.

19. **B.** The Drug-Free Workplace Act of 1988 requires only federal contractors and subcontractors to establish substance abuse policies. A fair and effective policy will describe which employees will be tested (A), whether it is all or specific job groups. The policy should describe (C) when tests will be done (pre-employment, randomly, on reasonable suspicion, or according to a predetermined schedule), what drugs are included in the process, and the consequences for employees who test positive (D). See Chapter 8 for more information.

20. **B.** A co-worker who witnesses the ongoing harassment of another individual may have an actionable claim of a hostile work environment. A single incident of unwanted touching (A), unless it is particularly offensive or intimidating, will not reach the threshold of a hostile work environment established by the courts. A hostile work environment may be created by any individual in the workplace, including customers, vendors, or visitors, in addition to supervisors or co-workers (C). In the case of *Meritor Savings Bank v. Vinson*, the Supreme Court held that the mere existence of a grievance procedure and antiharassment policy (D) does not necessarily protect an employer from hostile work environment claims. See Chapter 7 for more information.

21. **D.** An HR audit is an organized process designed to identify key aspects of HR in the organization such as employee morale, HR policies, programs and procedures, and HR effectiveness. See Chapter 3 for more information.

22. **C.** There are three types of statistical HR measurements: employee measures, such as turnover/retention (A) and job satisfaction (D); productivity measures, such as revenue per employee and OSHA incident rates; and HR activities measures, such as cost per hire (B) and ratio of total employees to HR staff. See Chapter 3 for more information.

23. **D.** According to guidance published by the EEOC, caregivers are not a protected class, but there are circumstances in which disparate treatment becomes unlawful based on stereotyping prohibited by Title VII, association with disabled individuals prohibited by the ADA, or violations of FMLA caregiving requirements. See Chapter 4 for more information.

24. **B.** A statement of cash flows provides information about the money that flowed through the business. It identifies whether the cash was received from customers, loans, or other sources; how much cash was spent to operate the business; and how much was reinvested in the business. A balance sheet describes the financial condition of the business at a specific point in time (A). The income statement, or profit and loss statement, tells you the financial results of operations over a period of time (C). An accounts-receivable ledger describes how much money is owed to the company by each customer (D). See Chapters 2 and 3 for more information.

25. **C.** Four factors are considered in determining whether the use of published material is a fair use: the purpose of the use, the nature of the work being copied, how much of the work is copied, and what economic effect copying the material will have on the market value of the work. See Chapter 5 for more information.

26. **C.** A PEST analysis is used to scan the political, economic, social, and technological conditions in the external environment to determine what impact those conditions will have on the success of the organization. See Chapter 3 for more information.

27. **A.** A seamless organization replaces traditional hierarchies with networks designed to enhance communication and creativity. These networks are made possible by advanced technology that allows employees to connect from anywhere in the world. See Chapters 2 and 3 for more information.

28. **D.** Employees have the right to review accident reports without information that identifies the employees involved in the accident. See Chapter 8 for more information.

29. **B.** An on-call worker is the best solution for situation in which the employer needs the same job to be done on a sporadic basis. This allows the employer to rely on the same person to do the job, reducing training requirements. An intern program (A) would not be appropriate because it is a short-term training solution. Seasonal workers (C) are generally required only at specific times of the year. Temp workers (D) provided by agencies may not be available when needed because they may be on other assignments. See Chapter 4 for more information.

30. **B.** Disparate impact occurs when an employment practice that seems to be fair unintentionally discriminates against members of a protected class. Disparate treatment (A) occurs when a protected group is treated differently than other applicants or employees. The EEOC defines adverse impact (C) as a substantially different rate of selection in hiring, promotion, or another employment decision that works to the disadvantage of members of a race, a sex, or an ethnic group. Unfair treatment (D) can refer to any perceived difference in how employees are treated. See Chapter 4 for more information.

31. **C.** EGTRRA made changes to pension contribution limits and allows employees older than 50 to make catch-up pension contributions. See Chapter 6 for more information.

32. D. A simple linear regression measures one variable against another. Multiple linear regression (A) measures more than one variable against others. A ratio (B) compares one number to another. A simulation model uses a computer program (C) to predict the possible outcomes of different business scenarios. See Chapters 2 and 4 for more information.

33. A. To be effective, most experts agree that it is best to first do your homework: that is, learn how the legislative and political process works. In this way, you can participate effectively in the process. Persuasive skills (B) are useful in presenting your point of view. (C) Big financial contributions are often used by lobbyists to ensure that elected representatives will listen to their points of view. Lobbyists prefer to present a proposed solution to elected officials (D). See Chapter 3 for more information.

34. D. VEVRAA applies to government contractors and requires that all job openings be listed with state employment agencies *except* those that will be filled from within, are for senior-level management positions, or will last less than 3 days. See Chapter 4 for more information.

35. B. A nonexempt employee who is waiting for an assignment while at work must be paid for the time spent waiting. See Chapter 6 for more information.

36. C. An environmental scan is used to gather the information used to forecast future business conditions. SWOT (A) and PEST (B) analyses are tools used during an environmental scan. An internal assessment (D) is another tool used during strategic planning. See Chapters 2 and 3 for more information.

37. A. Inter-rater reliability seeks to reduce bias by having multiple reviewers rate an individual's performance and averaging the ratings. Management by objectives (B) establishes goals at the beginning of a review period and rates how well the goals were achieved. A rating scale (C) is one method of performance appraisal. The paired-comparison (D) method compares all employees in a group to each other. See Chapter 5 for more information.

38. C. OSHA inspections that will prevent injury or illness receive first priority. An imminent danger is one that has a reasonable certainty of death or serious injury occurring before normal enforcement procedures can occur. Catastrophes and fatal accidents (A) are given second priority. Programmed, high-hazard inspections (B) receive fourth priority, and employee complaints (D) have third. See Chapter 8 for more information.

39. C. A lockout is an action taken by the employer to stop employees from working. A strike occurs when employees refuse to work (A). An employer that refuses to allow the union to conduct an organizing campaign (B) is committing an unfair labor practice. Picketing occurs when employees patrol the entrance to the business (D). See Chapter 7 for more information.

40. A. The TQM concept reviews processes to eliminate waste, relies on teamwork, and involves all members of the organization in meeting customer needs. Personal mastery, a high level of employee expertise (B), is one of the five disciplines of a learning organization. Information sharing is one characteristic of a high-involvement organization (C). The ability to balance stakeholder needs is a requirement of a change agent (D). See Chapter 5 for more information.

41. C. Techno-structural interventions address issues of how work gets done in an organization. A high-involvement organization is one in which employees at all levels are involved in making decisions about how work is accomplished. Human-process interventions (A) are designed to build competencies at the individual level of the organization. HRM interventions (B) focus on HR processes and programs such as selection procedures or performance management that address individual employee needs. Strategic interventions (D) are used to execute changes to an organization's vision, mission, or values. See Chapter 5 for more information.

42. C. Effective in 2004, employees must be paid a minimum of $455 per week to be exempt from FLSA requirements. This employee earns only $432.69 per week. ($22,500/52 weeks = $432.69.) Although D is also correct, the *best* answer is the one that explains why. See Chapter 6 for more information.

43. A. Employers look for benefit programs that add value to the bottom line. Health and wellness programs do this by increasing productivity and reducing costs. These programs are attractive to job candidates and enhance recruiting efforts. See Chapter 8 for more information.

44. D. An effective progressive disciplinary process begins with coaching or counseling, acknowledging good performance, and providing guidance on performance that needs to be changed. Providing ongoing feedback, both positive and negative, reduces the stress level for both employees and supervisors when serious performance issues arise and must be addressed. A written warning (A) is the second step of a formal disciplinary process. A verbal warning (B) is the first step. Suspensions (C) are usually the last step prior to termination. See Chapter 7 for more information.

45. D. Extrinsic rewards are nonmonetary rewards where self-esteem comes from others, such as formal recognition for a job well done. Challenging work on a new project (A) is an intrinsic reward. Salary increases (B) are monetary rewards. A feeling of accomplishment after completing a tough assignment (C) is another type of intrinsic reward. See Chapter 6 for more information.

46. B. An express contract can be oral or written and states what the parties to the contract agree to do. The duty of good faith and fair dealing (A) is a common-law doctrine that parties to an oral or written contract have an obligation to act in a fair and honest manner to facilitate achievement of the contract goals. An implied contract (C) can be created by conduct and doesn't have to be stated explicitly. Fraudulent misrepresentation (D) occurs when an employer makes false statements to entice a candidate to join the company. See Chapter 7 for more information.

47. B. The knowledge-of-predictor effect occurs when an interviewer is aware that a candidate has scored particularly high or low on an assessment test and allows this to affect the hiring decision. The halo effect (A) occurs when the interviewer allows a single positive characteristic of the candidate to overshadow other considerations. Cultural noise (C) occurs when a candidate gives answers they think the interviewer wants to hear. Stereotyping (D) occurs when the interviewer makes assumptions about a candidate based on generalizations about the group the candidate belongs to (for example, women). See Chapter 4 for more information.

48. A. Once an election has been scheduled, the employer must provide a list, known as an Excelsior list, containing the names and address of all employees in the bargaining unit determined by the NLRB. See Chapter 7 for more information.

49. D. Marketing is responsible for determining what new products will be produced based on market research designed to find out what products customers are willing to purchase. See Chapter 3 for more information.

50. C. Ergonomic injuries are caused by repeated stress to a part of the body. A fall down the stairs is a single occurrence and therefore not an ergonomic injury. See Chapter 8 for more information.

51. A. A target benefit plan is a hybrid plan that has similarities to defined-benefit pension plans and money-purchase plans. These plans use actuarial formulas to calculate individual pension contribution amounts. Deferral percentage tests (B) are required each year for 401(k) plans. An ESOP provides a means for employees to become owners of the company (C). A money purchase plan (D) defers a fixed percentage of employee earnings. See Chapter 6 for more information.

52. D. Organizations that are able to successfully repatriate employees after global assignments do so by carefully selecting candidates for those assignments, setting appropriate expectations before the assignment begins, and establishing a formal program to assist employees in reintegrating into the home office after a global assignment. See Chapter 5 for more information.

53. C. To assess the reasonableness of a requested accommodation, employers should ask employees to describe their limitations, how those limitations affect their performance of essential job functions, and whether they have suggestions for an accommodation that would allow them to perform the functions. See Chapter 8 for more information.

54. B. In a third-party contract, some or all of the work is performed by an individual who is not a party to the contract. There are many examples of third-party contracts in business; perhaps the best known for HR professionals is an agreement with a temp agency in which the company agrees to pay the temp agency for services provided by an employee of the agency. See Chapters 2 and 4 for more information.

55. A. Direct compensation is composed of base pay (hourly wage or salary), variable compensation, and pay for performance. Vacation pay (B), 401(k) matches (C), and employer Social Security contributions (D) are examples of indirect compensation. See Chapter 6 for more information.

56. C. The significance of various security issues depends partly on the size of the organization. However, regardless of size, the same considerations go into assessing vulnerabilities and the method for estimating the cost of potential losses. The justification of such a program requires that the potential losses will exceed the cost of the program. See Chapter 8 for more information.

57. B. Qualitative analysis is a form of research that uses mathematical models such as correlation, correlation coefficient, and measures of central tendency to provide solutions to problems. Quantitative analysis attempts to measure historical data (B), a job evaluation measures the relative value of each job within the organization (C) and a learning matrix is a generic term that can be used to identify organizational learning strategies (D). See Chapters 2 and 4 for more information.

58. D. Organizational pickets may take place when no other union is currently representing employees at a company. See Chapter 7 for more information.

59. D. All parties agree that permanent arbitrators are fair, impartial, and able to resolve any issues that arise between them. A tripartite arbitration panel (A) consists of three arbitrators who hear the issues and reach a joint decision. An ad hoc arbitrator (C) is selected to hear a single case. In compulsory arbitration, both parties are mandated to the arbitration process (B). See Chapter 7 for more information.

60. A. The NLRB imposes a voluntary-recognition bar while negotiations take place between the union and an employer that voluntarily recognized the union. See Chapter 7 for more information.

61. C. Employee-engagement activities center around the function of gathering meaningful feedback. Surveys, interviews, and focus groups are just some of the examples of formal feedback systems that can be used to improve organizational outcomes. From this feedback, solutions such as training (A) and targeted performance improvement plans (B, D) can be assessed. See Chapter 7 for more information.

62. D. High-involvement organizations are those in which employees are encouraged to remain active, accountable members of the company. Allowing employees to come up with creative solutions to problems, clearly linking rewards to behavior (C) encouraging decision-making from the ground up (A) and demonstrating management trust through data sharing (B) are other characteristics of HIOs. See Chapters 3 and 7 for more information.

63. B. Risk management has influence that goes beyond the traditional safety role of HR, often influencing other HR functions such as EEO compliance (A), workforce planning (C) and employee relations (D). It revolves around removing or mitigating business risks, whether they are internal or external, or data- or employee-driven. See Chapters 4, 7, and 8 for more information.

64. A. The Americans with Disabilities Act applies to employers with 15 or more employees, and regulates employment practices—including record-keeping and -retention—related to qualified individuals with a disability. EO 11246 (B) and Title VII of the Civil Rights Act (D) established standards for non-discriminatory employment practices. See Chapter 2 for more information.

65. C. The use of Facebook and LinkedIn are effective sources for all positions, but not necessarily the best strategic response to the increase in use of mobile technology. Giving applicants the ability to view open positions remotely requires that a company website is designed to maximize ease of use on these devices (A). Online job posting with video (B) is an example of a tool used in a social-media recruiting campaign, created either in-house or through the use of a professional firm (D). (See Chapter 4 for more information.)

66. B. Enrollment in the E-Verify system is limited to new employees only. E-Verify is a service offered by the United States Citizenship and Immigration Services to help employers verify the employment eligibility of newly hired workers (C), allowing employees to contest a non-confirmation (D). While participation in E-Verify is voluntary for most businesses, some companies may be required by state law (A) or federal regulation to use E-Verify. See Chapter 4 for more information.

67. **B.** A code of conduct is one tool used by employers to clearly communicate company expectations. With regular feedback, employees are given the opportunity to succeed in their jobs based on organizational needs. A code of conduct is not the foundation of a system (A), nor does it focus on providing EEO in employment (C) or discourage violations of company policy (D). See Chapter 7 for more information.

68. **A.** A dress-code policy is generally an accepted employer practice, provided it applies to all employees or employees in certain job categories. There are exceptions, however, based on ethnicity or religious practices. As with any other accommodation, an employer should actively seek a solution that does not result in undue hardship. See Chapter 7 for more information.

69. **C.** Skill variety is one of many job-enrichment activities introduced by J.R. Hackman. Enriching the work of employees can lead to greater job satisfaction and retention. Task variety (A), task identity (B) and job rotation (D) are other job enrichment activities that allow employees to vary their job tasks, identify the whole of the work produced, and be cross-trained in multiple functions. See Chapter 5 for more information.

70. **D.** Virtual coaching is one method of leadership development. Used as part of overall coaching activities, it employs multiple sources of electronic media to reinforce management development. See Chapter 5 for more information. Mentoring (A), Peer to peer (B) and Leadership coaching (C) all primarily take place in a face-to-face setting.

Chapter 1

Certifying Human Resource Professionals

Human resources. Ask 10 different people what human resources (HR) is or does, and you'll get at least 8 different answers. Management advisor, recruiter, talent manager, employee advocate, paper pusher, union negotiator, counselor, policy police, coach, mediator, administrative expert, corporate conscience, strategic business partner, and the dreaded "party planner"—these are just a few of the roles that those both inside and outside of the profession think we play. Some of these descriptions are based on misperceptions from nonpractitioners, others describe the roles we aspire to attain within our organizations, and some describe what we do each day. The *HR Certification Institute PHR/SPHR Body of Knowledge (BOK)* provides the means by which we define ourselves to the larger business community and communicates to them what roles are appropriate for the human resource function in an organization.

This chapter provides you with an overview of HR certification: the growth of human resources as a profession, a little history about the certification process, a discussion of the types of professional HR certification (there are four—PHR, SPHR, GPHR, and CA State Certification), and the required and recommended eligibility standards for each. You'll also learn about the HR body of knowledge and obtain a few tips to assist you in preparing for the PHR and SPHR exams.

For up-to-the-minute updates for this chapter, visit www.sybex.com /go/phr4e.

The Human Resource Profession

By the end of the nineteenth century, the industrial revolution had changed the nature of work—businesses were no longer small organizations that could be managed by a single owner with a few trusted supervisors. As a result, many support functions were delegated to individuals who began to specialize in specific areas. One of these functions became known as *industrial relations* or *personnel* and evolved into what we know today as *human resources*.

As businesses continued to become even larger entities, standards began to develop as practitioners met and shared information about the ways they did their jobs. The need for more formal training standards in various aspects of this new function became apparent, and colleges began to develop courses of study in the field. By the middle of the twentieth century, the personnel function was part of almost every business, and numerous individuals worked in the field. A small group of these individuals got together in 1948 and determined that personnel was developing into a profession and was in need of a national organization to define it, represent practitioners, and promote its interests in the larger business community. Thus, the American Society for Personnel Administration (ASPA) was born.

For the first 16 years of its existence, ASPA was strictly a volunteer organization. By 1964, membership had grown from the small group of charter members in 1948 to more than 3,100—enough to support a small staff to serve the members. With membership growing, the discussion quite naturally turned to the topic of defining the practice of personnel as a profession. Although established professions have similar characteristics, such as a code of ethics, a specific and unique body of knowledge, and an education specific to the profession, there are aspects of most professions that set them apart from each other and personnel was no different. To solicit the contribution of practitioners in this process, ASPA cosponsored a conference with Cornell University's School of Industrial Relations to determine how best to define the characteristics that made personnel a profession. This conference spawned a year of consideration and debate among ASPA members.

The culmination of this process was an agreement on five characteristics that would set personnel/HR apart as a profession:

- HR would need to require full-time practice.

- The HR profession must be defined by a common body of knowledge that defines a course of study at educational institutions.

- There must be a national professional association that represents the views of practitioners in the larger business community and in the legislative process.

- There must be a certification program for HR professionals.

- There must be a code of ethics for the HR profession.

Once ASPA had a clear definition of what was required for the practice of personnel to be considered a profession, the members knew what needed to be done to make this a reality: develop a body of knowledge and a certification program to evaluate the competence of practitioners.

Development of the Human Resource Body of Knowledge

With its goal clearly set, ASPA went about the process of developing a body of knowledge for the profession. ASPA created a task force to study and report on the issues involved and recommend a course of action. The ASPA Accreditation Institute (AAI) was formed in 1975 with a mandate to define a national body of knowledge for the profession and develop a program to measure the knowledge of its practitioners.

As a first step in the process, AAI created six functional areas for the *BOK*:

- Employment, Placement, and Personnel Planning
- Training and Development
- Compensation and Benefits
- Health, Safety, and Security
- Employee and Labor Relations
- Personnel Research (later replaced by Management Practices)

Over time, as personnel evolved into human resources, ASPA changed its name to the Society for Human Resource Management (SHRM) to reflect changes in the profession. At that point, AAI became the Human Resources Certification Institute (HRCI) for the same reason. These associations exist today to represent and certify the profession.

HRCI ensures the continued relevance of the *BOK* to actual practice with periodic codification studies. The first of these occurred in 1979; subsequent studies were conducted in 1988, 1993, 1997, 2000, 2005, and 2012. These reviews enlisted the participation of thousands of human resource experts in ongoing assessments of what a human resource generalist needs to know to be fully competent.

As with all previous codification studies, HRCI began the most current review with the question, "What should a human resource practitioner know and be able to apply to be considered a competent HR generalist?" HRCI commissioned the Professional Examination Service (PES) to conduct a *practice analysis study* to obtain information from a variety of sources on the existing state of human resource practices as well as trends predicted for future needs of the profession. Under the guidance of PES, additional information was collected through the use of critical-incident interviews, subject matter experts, validation surveys, and focus groups. The culmination of this data collection was a comprehensive look at how HR is being practiced in the field and a relevant picture of what the business climate needs from its HR representatives. From this, the exam content was developed.

Clearly, the nomenclature has changed over the past 30 years, yet the basic functional areas of HR have remained fairly stable. Significant changes have occurred, however, within the six functional areas, ensuring the relevance of human resource practice to the changing needs of business in the twenty-first century.

In 2011, HRCI announced another revision to the *BOK* based on the results of the regularly scheduled practice-analysis study. The structure of the exams remained the same and constitutes the current human resource body of knowledge:

- Business Management and Strategy
- Workforce Planning and Employment
- Human Resource Development
- Compensation and Benefits
- Employee and Labor Relations
- Risk Management

Interestingly enough, as the result of previous studies, two functional areas continue to have title changes, indicating a rapid evolution of practical application:

- Functional Area 1: "Management Practices" to "Strategic Management" to "Business Management and Strategy"
- Functional Area 4: From "Compensation and Benefits" to "Total Rewards" back to "Compensation and Benefits"

Entire content changes included the addition of exam questions related to business-plan development and execution, policies addressing electronic media use, executive coaching and talent management, and the process of conducting a cost-benefit analysis of HR projects. Although anticipating the types of questions on an exam such as this can be difficult, there are several areas where we can apply deductive reasoning. Take, for example, the continued explosion of the use of technology in business management. We can anticipate an increase in exam questions related to social-media recruiting, employee privacy issues, and virtual training. Furthermore, changing the name of Functional Area 1 from "Strategic Management" to "Business Management and Strategy" indicates that the content will reflect expanded principles of business. These may include cost-benefit analysis and cross-functional activities such as accounting, business planning, and strategic staffing.

Initially, the certification process was a series of exams, one for each level of certification in each of the six functional areas identified by the AAI task force. A few years later, HRCI added a generalist exam. The intent of the process in this early stage was to serve the needs of both specialists and generalists. Because there were two levels of certification for each functional area, the process was quite cumbersome and a little confusing. Eventually, the popularity of the generalist exam led to elimination of the specialist certifications, which left just two: Professional in Human Resources (PHR) and Senior Professional in Human Resources (SPHR). These are the generalist certification levels in existence today.

As the practice of human resources continues to evolve to meet the needs of international business operations, more emphasis is being placed on the area of global human resources. In response, HRCI developed a new certification, the Global Professional in Human Resources (GPHR). The first GPHR exam was administered in Spring 2004. As of January 2011, more than 1,300 practitioners have been certified in global practices.

In 2007, HRCI implemented the first state certification examination for California. As of January 2011, 700 California practitioners have earned the SPHR-CA or PHR-CA certification.

Currently, and with more and more employers recognizing the value of this exam and the preparation process, more than 115,000 HR professionals have earned a certification as a mark of high professional distinction.

Defining the Functional Areas of the *BOK*

Once HRCI collated the information from the practice-analysis study, test specifications were developed to define each functional area. The test specifications have two parts: responsibilities and knowledge requirements. The *responsibilities* describe areas of practice with which a fully qualified generalist must be familiar. For example, one of the areas of responsibility for Risk Management is to "Develop and monitor business continuity and disaster recovery plans." The *knowledge requirements* describe the information needed to master the responsibilities. Continuing the example from Risk Management, knowledge of "Business continuity and disaster recovery plans (for example, data storage and backup, alternative work locations and procedures)" is needed for full understanding of the Risk Management functional area.

For the 2011 *BOK*, HRCI has identified some responsibilities as "PHR Only" or "SPHR Only" within the functional areas. As you're reading Chapters 2–8, look for these icons in the margins:

Although the body of knowledge is the same for both exam levels (PHR and SPHR), the functional areas in each test are weighted differently to distinguish the different experience requirements of candidates for each level. To understand how this works, let's look at what each functional area covers:

Business Management and Strategy   Looks at the "big picture" of the organization and requires an understanding of overall business operations, basic knowledge of other functional areas in the organization, and the ability to interact and work effectively with those functions. Business Management places a strong emphasis on the cross-functional roles of an organization, paying specific attention to how the organizational (or HR) structure develops the landscape on which to conduct business. Business Management and Strategy ensures that traditional HR activities contribute to and support organization goals through the HR planning process, incorporating change initiatives when needed to move the organization forward and providing tools to measure HR effectiveness.

Workforce Planning and Employment   Covers activities related to planning for and managing entry into and exit from the organization to meet changing business needs. This includes practices for evaluating workforce requirements, recruitment and selection, developing an employer brand, managing records, establishing a succession plan, and exiting employees from the organization.

Human Resource Development   Utilizes training, development, change, and performance management programs to ensure that individuals with the required knowledge, skills, and abilities are available when needed to accomplish organization goals.

Compensation and Benefits   Focuses on the development, implementation, and maintenance of all forms of compensation and benefit systems. This includes the use of employee relations programs (such as recognition and work-life balance) and development programs (such as performance and career-growth opportunities) to drive employee engagement and satisfaction, leading to superior business results.

Employee and Labor Relations   Addresses the practices for building positive employment relationships in both union and nonunion environments. This includes employee relations programs, workplace policies and procedures, dispute-resolution programs, and collective-bargaining activities.

Risk Management   As the name change of this functional area implies, the scope is broadening from traditional programs that reduce or eliminate organizational risks from health, safety, and security issues to encompass other company risks related to programs in other functional areas. This includes risks such as those arising from the failure to train effectively, high turnover issues, the failure to provide for succession planning, and legal noncompliance.

Core Knowledge Requirements of the *BOK*

In addition to the 6 functional areas of the *BOK*, HRCI identified 23 core knowledge requirements for the HR body of knowledge, all of which have implications in all of the functional areas. Among the core knowledge requirements are topics such as needs assessment and analysis, liability and risk analysis, and motivation concepts and applications, to name just a few. We'll discuss each core knowledge topic in more detail in Chapter 2, "Core Knowledge Requirements for HR Professionals."

In the meantime, as an example, let's look at how one of the core requirements, "Communication skills and strategies," applies in each of the six functional areas:

- In the Business Management and Strategy functional area, it means building consensus among senior managers for communicating a reorganization to the workforce.
- In the Workforce Planning and Employment functional area, it means communicating a sexual-harassment policy to new hires.
- In the Human Resource Development functional area, it means introducing a new performance-management process to the workforce.
- In the Compensation and Benefits functional area, it means communicating company benefit plan changes to employees affected by the changes.
- In the Employee and Labor Relations functional area, it means advising management on appropriate responses to a union-organizing campaign.
- In the Risk Management functional area, it means introducing an emergency response plan to the workforce.

As you can see, each of these scenarios requires a different strategy in order to effectively communicate necessary information to the intended audience. These core knowledge requirements can be the basis for exam questions in any of the functional areas, so it's important to be familiar with them in general terms and understand how they apply to each area.

Now that we've introduced the six functional areas in broad terms, let's look at what each exam is intended to measure and how the weightings reflect this in each exam.

HRCI's functional areas, test specifications, and functional-area weightings are subject to change at any time and at the Human Resource Certification Institute's sole discretion. Please visit HRCI's website (www.hrci.org) for the most current information on the exams' content. On the HRCI website, you'll find the *PHR/SPHR/GPHR Certification Handbook*, HRCI's authoritative publication for PHR/SPHR/GPHR certification and requirements, containing the most current version of the test specifications. California practitioners can find information about state certifications in the *2012 Certification Policies and Procedures Handbook,* also available on the HRCI website.

Certification Levels

The questions asked most often by those considering taking the step toward certification are, "Which level should I choose? Is the PHR easier than the SPHR? What is the difference?" Choosing an exam level is an individual choice—if you meet the eligibility requirements (which will be discussed in the next section), the choice is really up to you. As to whether one is easier than another, we doubt that anyone who has taken them would say that either test is easy. They're equally difficult but in different ways. Let's look now at what each of the certifications is intended to measure:

Professional in Human Resources (PHR)   The PHR certification measures a candidate's ability to apply HR knowledge at an operational or technical level, according to the HRCI website. This exam tests a candidate's ability to apply HR knowledge to situations occurring on a day-to-day basis. PHR candidates are skilled in implementing processes and procedures and are knowledgeable in the requirements of employment legislation for problems or situations with a narrow organizational impact. They're able to develop solutions by drawing on a variety of sources and knowledge that apply to a particular situation.

The functional areas in the PHR exam are weighted to reflect its emphasis on the operational, administrative, and tactical application of the elements of the body of knowledge. Table 1.1 shows the functional area weightings for the PHR exam.

On the PHR exam, then, the bulk of the questions are related to operational and tactical application of the responsibilities and knowledge fairly equally distributed between Workforce Planning and Employment with Employee and Labor Relations (44 percent), and Workforce Planning and Employment with Compensation and Benefits (43 percent).

Senior Professional in Human Resources (SPHR)   The SPHR certification measures a candidate's strategic perspective and ability to pull information from a variety of sources to address issues with organization-wide impact. This exam measures the candidate's ability to apply HR knowledge and experience in developing policies that will meet the organization's long-term strategic objectives and impact the entire organization.

The SPHR exam measures a senior-level candidate's strategic ability to integrate HR processes into the big picture of an organization's needs and to develop policies to support the achievement of business goals. Table 1.2 demonstrates how the weightings for the functional areas reflect this.

TABLE 1.1   PHR functional area weighting

Functional Area	Exam Weight
Business Management and Strategy	11%
Workforce Planning and Employment	24%
Human Resource Development	18%
Compensation and Benefits	19%
Employee and Labor Relations	20%
Risk Management	8%

TABLE 1.2   SPHR functional area weighting

Functional Area	Exam Weight
Business Management and Strategy	30%
Workforce Planning and Employment	17%
Human Resource Development	19%
Compensation and Benefits	13%
Employee and Labor Relations	14%
Risk Management	7%

From the weightings in Table 1.2, you see that 49 percent of the questions—almost half of the SPHR exam—are contained in two of the functional areas. The first is related to the senior candidate's ability to develop effective strategic plans for successful business operations (Business Management and Strategy), and the other is the need to effectively plan for and develop the human talent of an organization to respond to the ever-changing market conditions identified through strategic planning (Human Resource Development).

The *PHR/SPHR/GPHR Certification Handbook* contains the most current listing of the HRCI test specs. Because both the PHR and SPHR exams are built around them, we strongly urge those preparing for the test to review the handbook and familiarize themselves with the test specs for each functional area prior to reading the related chapter. The HRCI website (`www.hrci.org`) provides information on downloading or ordering this free publication.

Eligibility Requirements

As we've mentioned, complete information on eligibility requirements for the exams is available in the *PHR/SPHR/GPHR Certification Handbook*, and HRCI, of course, makes the final decision as to whether or not a candidate meets them. In this section, we'll provide a broad overview of the requirements, along with some suggestions based on the experience of successful candidates.

The current eligibility requirements reflect a candidate's education and experience. "Demonstrated professional experience" means that candidates must spend 51 percent of their work time on exempt-level human resource activities. It's important to note that almost all supervisors and managers perform some HR functions as part of their daily requirements, but because these activities aren't usually the major function of the position and constitute less than 51 percent of their time at work, this experience most likely would not meet the requirements established by HRCI. See Table 1.3 for the exam eligibility requirements.

TABLE 1.3   PHR and SPHR eligibility

	Experience	Education
PHR	1 year	Master's degree or higher
	2 years	Bachelor's degree
	4 years	Less than a Bachelor's degree
SPHR	4 years	Master's degree or higher
	5 years	Bachelor's degree
	7 years	Less than a Bachelor's degree

So, the minimum requirements are pretty simple. Let's be realistic for a moment, though. The PHR and SPHR exams don't measure just book knowledge. They measure your ability to apply that knowledge in work situations. The more experience you have in applying knowledge at work, the greater your chances of passing the test. To give candidates an idea of what is needed to be successful (as opposed to what is minimally required),

HRCI recommends PHR candidates have 2–4 years of experience prior to taking the exam; for SPHR candidates, they recommend 6–8 years. HRCI provides profiles of the ideal candidate for each of the exams, which can be found in the *PHR/SPHR/GPHR Certification Handbook* on the HRCI's website www.hrci.org.

Recommendations for PHR Candidates　To summarize the ideal PHR profile, HRCI suggests that candidates have 2–4 years of professional-level, generalist HR experience before they sit for the exam. PHR candidates generally report to a more senior HR professional within the organization and during the course of their daily work focus on implementation of programs and processes that have already been developed. PHR experience focuses on providing direct services to HR customers within the organization.

Recommendations for SPHR Candidates　According to HRCI, the ideal SPHR candidate has 6–8 years of increasingly responsible HR experience. An SPHR needs to be able to see the big picture for the entire organization, not just what works best for the human resource department. This requires the ability to anticipate the impact of policies and decisions on the achievement of organizational goals. SPHR candidates are business focused and understand that HR policies and processes must integrate with and serve the needs of the larger organization. Whereas a PHR's decisions and activities have a more limited effect within narrow segments of the organization, decisions made by SPHR candidates will have organization-wide impact.

Student or Recent Graduate Requirements　As of 2011, students are no longer eligible to take the exams. However, students who took the exam under the former eligibility requirements may apply for conversion once the 2-year exempt-level experience has been satisfied.

Recertification

Until 1996, HRCI awarded lifetime certification to individuals who successfully recertified twice. At that time the policy was changed to reflect the need for professionals to remain current with developments in the field. As a result, the lifetime certification program ended, and, with the exception of those who were awarded lifetime certification prior to 1996, all PHRs and SPHRs are now required to recertify every 3 years.

There are a number of ways to be recertified; they fall into two basic categories:

Recertification by Exam　HR professionals may retake either exam to maintain certification at that level. Information on recertifying by exam is available in the *PHR/SPHR/ GPHR Certification Handbook*.

Professional Development　To recertify on this basis, PHRs and SPHRs must complete 60 credit hours of professional development during the 3-year period. These 60 hours may be accomplished in a variety of ways. One of the more common is through attending continuing education courses, including workshops and seminars related to HR functions. Another way to earn recertification credit is by developing and/or presenting HR courses, seminars, or workshops. Recertification credit for teaching a specific course is awarded only for the first time it's taught.

On-the-job experience can also be the basis for recertification credit: the first time you perform a new task or project that adds to your mastery of the HR *BOK*, you may earn credits for the work if it meets the criteria established by HRCI.

Professionals who take on leadership roles in HR organizations or on government boards or commissions may earn certification for those activities if they meet the criteria established by HRCI.

Finally, certified professionals receive credit for membership in SHRM and other national professional associations or societies, as well as for publishing HR-related articles or blogs. HRCI publishes the *PHR/SPHR/GPHR Recertification Handbook* to provide detailed information on the various methods of recertifying and the amount of credit that can be earned for the different activities. You can download this guide at `www.hrci.org`, or you can request a copy by calling HRCI at (866) 898-4724.

The Test

Now, a little information about the test.

One question frequently asked by candidates preparing for the exam is, "What are the questions like?" The HRCI website provides a very detailed explanation of testing theory and question development. In this section, we've summarized what we think is the most practical information for those preparing to take the exams. If you're interested in the details, you'll find more than you ever wanted to know about it on the HRCI website. Click the HR Certification tab, and then click How Exams Are Developed in the menu on the left; you'll see several sections explaining how HRCI builds the tests.

The questions in these tests are designed to measure whether candidates meet the objectives established by HRCI as the standard required for a minimally qualified human resource professional to achieve certification. The exam questions are designed to assess the depth and breadth of candidates' knowledge and their ability to apply it in practice. Questions at the basic level examine a candidate's ability to not only recall information but comprehend it as well. Questions designed to measure knowledge and comprehension constitute the smallest percentage of questions on both the exams, but there are slightly more of them on the PHR exam. Questions at the next level, application, are more complex and require candidates to apply their knowledge in practical situations that require the ability to differentiate which information is most relevant to the situation and will solve the problem. Questions of this type are most prevalent on both the exams. Questions at the highest level of complexity, synthesis, require candidates to use their knowledge in multifaceted situations by drawing on information from different areas of the body of knowledge to create the best possible result. They require the ability to review actions taken in a variety of situations and evaluate whether the best solution was implemented. This type of question appears on both the exams but is more prevalent on the SPHR.

The exam questions, which HRCI refers to as *items*, are developed by two panels of volunteers, all of whom are SPHR-certified professionals trained to write test items for the exams. These panels meet twice a year to review items that each member has written between meetings. Each volunteer generates about 50 questions annually that are then reviewed by the entire panel. Questions that make it through the item-writing panel process move to an item-review panel for additional consideration. As a question travels through either panel, one of three things can happen to it:

- The item can be rejected as not meeting the criteria for the exam.
- The item can be returned to the writer for additional work.
- The item can be forwarded to the next step in the process.

When an item is accepted by the review panel, it moves on to the pretest process for inclusion as an unscored pretest question.

Each item consists of the *stem*, or premise, and four possible answers: one of these is the correct or best possible answer, and three others are known as *distractors*. There may be two answers that could be technically correct, but one of them is the best possible answer. As part of the item-development process, HRCI requires that the correct answers are documented and takes great care to ensure that the best possible answer is one that is legally defensible.

For the May 2012 exam update, the total number of questions went from 225 to 165. The exam consists of 140 multiple-choice test questions (which are used to determine your score) and 25 pretest items (which aren't scored). The exams are 3 hours long. This means you'll have just over a minute to answer each question. You'll be surprised how much time this gives you to consider your answers if you're well prepared by your experience and have taken sufficient time to study the test specifications. As you answer practice questions in preparation for the exam, be sure to time yourself so you can get a feel for how much time it takes you to answer each question.

Test candidates often ask why the pretest questions are included on the exam, and the answer is simple: these items are included to validate them prior to inclusion on future exams as scored questions. Although the 25 pretest items aren't scored, you won't know which questions are the pretest questions while taking the exam, so it's important to treat every question as though it will be scored.

The more you know about how the questions are designed, the better able you will be to focus your study—which leads us to the next section: some tips on preparing for the exam and what to expect on test day.

If you're anything like the tens of thousands of HR professionals who have taken the certification exam since 1976, you're probably a little nervous about how you will do and the best way to prepare. In this section, we'll provide you with some hints and tips gathered from our experiences as well as from others who have generously shared their experiences in taking these exams.

It's *Experiential* and *Federal*

The most important thing to keep in mind, and this can't be stressed enough, is that these exams are *experiential*. That means they test your ability to *apply* knowledge, not just that you *have* knowledge. For this reason, memorizing facts isn't all that helpful. With a few exceptions, it's far more important to understand the *concepts* behind laws and practices and how they're best applied in real-life situations.

Another crucial factor to keep in mind is that these exams test your ability to apply knowledge of *federal* requirements, so you should be aware of legislation and significant case law that has developed since the 1960s. As experienced professionals are aware, federal law is very often different from the requirements of a particular state. This brings us to our first bit of advice from previous test candidates:

> Do not rely on your past experiences too heavily. Just because you have done it that way at one company doesn't mean it is the right (or legal!) way.
>
> —BECKY RASMUSSEN, PHR

> Don't necessarily think of how you would do it at work. It is possible the way your company is doing it is wrong, so you will answer the question wrong. Look for the most correct answer, and take plenty of practice tests. The more you take, the more familiar you will become with test taking.
>
> —SUSAN K. CRAFT, MS, PHR

These tips apply to several situations: your state requirements may be different from the federal requirements that are the subject of the test, your company practice may not be up-to-date with current requirements, and, in some cases, you may be operating on the basis of a common myth about legal requirements or HR practices that is not, in fact, accurate. One way that HRCI tests candidates' depth of knowledge is to provide one of those commonly held myths as a distractor for a question. It's not really a trick question, but a candidate with minimal experience may not know the difference. As you study, think about why you do things in a particular way, how you got that information, and how sure you are that it's the most current and up-to-date approach. If it is current, great! You're a step ahead of the study game. If you aren't sure it's the most current, do a little research to find out whether it will apply on the exam, whether it's a state requirement, or whether it's possibly misinformation you picked up somewhere along the way.

What the Questions Look Like

As mentioned earlier, the HRCI website goes into a fair amount of detail about the technical aspects of test development. Much of that technical information won't help you in developing a study plan. However, you may find it useful to know the types of questions that the item-writing panels are trained to develop.

In the previous section, we discussed the different parts that make up a test item. Each item begins with a stem, which presents a statement or a question requiring a response. The stems will either ask a question or present an unfinished statement to be completed. Within that context, the stem can be categorized in one of the following ways:

Purpose   To answer these questions, you need to demonstrate that you know the objective of a particular law, regulation, or HR practice.

Ordering   These questions require that you know the sequence of a multipart process or practice. A question may require that you're able to identify what needs to happen before or after any step in the process.

Recognition of Error   These questions require you to be familiar with HR practices and federal laws in order to identify practices or actions that are incorrect and to understand why they are.

Cause and Effect   To answer a question phrased in this way, you will need to understand the consequences of a practice or action.

Similarity   To correctly answer these questions, you must be able to identify the common elements of two or more practices, ideas, or concepts.

Association   These questions require candidates to form a connection between two concepts or ideas.

Definition   These questions may provide a definition and require that you select the correct term, or they may provide a term and provide four possible definitions.

Finally, SPHR candidates in particular should prepare themselves for scenario-type test items. These items are preceded by a short description of a typical HR situation and are followed by two or more questions that relate to the same scenario. These items are well suited to test concepts at the synthesis level of complexity.

> My experience was that the actual test differed from any of the prep materials or sample tests that I had seen. The exam questions were differentiated by nuance rather than clear distinctions. Studying from multiple sources helped me be better prepared for this unexpected approach.
>
> —LYMAN BLACK, SPHR

Preparing for the Exam

A number of options are available to assist candidates in preparing for the exams. One option is a self-study program that you put together for yourself based on the test specifications. Another option, depending on your location, is to attend a formal preparation course. In the past few years, informal online study groups have become popular and effective ways to prepare for the exam. Regardless of the option you choose, the most important step is to know what you already know. Then figure out what you need to learn, and develop a study plan to help you learn it.

Study Options

Several study options are available for exam candidates: study partners, self-study, and formal preparation courses are the most common. Whichever option you choose, be sure to review the *PHR/SPHR/GPHR Certification Handbook*, specifically Appendix A, to ensure that you cover all areas of the test specifications:

Study Partners   No matter which study option works best for you, many have found that partnering with someone else is a critical part of the process. Find one or two others who are studying, develop a group study plan, and meet each week to review the material for that week. Working with a reliable study partner makes the process more enjoyable and helps you stay focused. The ideal study partner is one whose areas of strength coincide with your areas of weakness, and vice versa. One effective technique is to prepare the material and "teach" it to your study partner. Teaching your partner one of your weaker areas results in a deeper understanding than just reading or listening to someone else talk about it.

Online Study Groups   If there is no one local for you to partner with, try an online study group. If you're a member of SHRM, you can find others interested in forming an online study group on the HRCI/Certification bulletin board at www.shrm.org/forums. There are also a number of other online communities where you may find study partners, such as www.workforce.com, www.legalworkplace.com, and others.

> I'd advise anyone to form a study group and meet on a regular basis to read, compare notes, quiz each other, and lend moral support! Not only did I learn a lot from my study partners, I gained some wonderful professional friendships—and we all passed!
>
> —Julie O'Brien, PHR

> Present the material yourself! Don't just listen—participate. If you teach it, you think of it much differently than if you are sitting passively and listening.
>
> —Alicia Chatman, SPHR

> I set up a very small study group: three people. We met once a week until a month before the test, when we met twice a week. It was good to have someone say, "Listen to the question." This made me slow down and review the phrasing and some key words like *most*, *not*, *least*, etc.
>
> —Patricia Kelleher, SPHR

Preparation Materials   Several publications are designed to prepare candidates for the exams. This book (of course!) is an intense, very focused overview of material you may find on the exam.

Other helpful publications include the SHRM Learning System, available online from the SHRM Store at www.shrm.org, and the Human Resource Certification Program (HRCP), available at www.hrcp.com.

In Appendix D of this book, "Resources," you'll find a list of additional materials that focus on specific functional areas, and many other excellent sources are available.

> I think there was a synergistic benefit from applying several approaches rather than using just one technique or single source of information. I used several approaches to prepare: two study guides, a review course, and flash cards. I also found that my kids enjoyed quizzing me during our times driving to school, sports, etc.
>
> —LYMAN BLACK, SPHR

Self-Study   Self-study provides you with the greatest flexibility in deciding what areas to focus on. If you go this route, developing a study plan is crucial in keeping you focused (and be sure to use Appendix A of the *PHR/SPHR/GPHR Certification Guide* when you set up your plan). Equally important for this method is finding a study partner to share questions and ideas.

> Capitalize on your resources. Look to guidance from peers, bosses, consultants, subject-matter experts, textbooks, white papers, and articles, and anyone/anything else you can find that will complement your knowledge. I made my own flash cards on specific topics where my knowledge was weaker. Those helped a lot, too.
>
> —SHIRLEY PINCUS, SPHR

Formal Preparation Courses   A number of organizations sponsor formal preparation courses designed specifically for the exam. These are offered by colleges and universities and by local SHRM chapters in some cases. Contact your local SHRM chapter for information on courses in your area.

Developing a Study Plan

Although many are tempted to jump in and immediately start reading books or taking classes, the best thing you can do for yourself at the outset is to identify where you are right now and what study methods have worked for you in the past, and then develop a study plan for yourself:

> The study technique that worked best for me was simply making preparation for the test a priority! I outlined a realistic study schedule for myself and stuck to it as much as possible. Plus, I studied away from my everyday environment in order to avoid distractions. For me this was a local bookstore cafe, a table covered with notes, a latte in one hand, and a pack of flashcards in the other...and it worked!
>
> —JULIE O'BRIEN, PHR

Where are you right now?   The best way to answer this question is to take the self-assessment test immediately following the introduction to this book. This will help you to see where your strengths and weaknesses lie. Based on the assessment test and on your work experience, make a list of areas you will need to spend the bulk of your time studying (your weaknesses) and the areas in which you simply need a refresher review (your strengths).

What study methods have worked for you in the past?   This may be easy or hard to determine, depending on how long it has been since you took a class. List study methods you have used successfully in the past.

Develop a study plan.   Using your list of strengths and weaknesses and the study methods that work for you, create a study plan:

> **Develop a timeline.**   Decide how much time you need to spend on each functional area of the body of knowledge.
>
> Working back from the test date, schedule your study time according to your strengths and weaknesses. You may want to leave time close to the test date for an overall review—be reasonable with yourself! Be sure to factor in work commitments, family events, vacations, and holidays so you don't set yourself up for failure.
>
> **Get organized!**   Set up folders or a binder with dividers to collect information for each functional area so you know where to find it when you're reviewing the material.
>
> **Plan the work, and then work the plan.**   Make sure you keep up with the plan you have set for yourself.

> > Keep up with the reading; do it every week, faithfully. Take notes on what you don't understand, then ask someone about them.
> >
> > —*Becky Rasmussen, PHR*

> > Make sure you don't cram; at least a week before the test, take some days off or make extra time available to study so that you're not cramming the night before.
> >
> > —*Rose Chang, PHR*

When creating your study plan, did you do the following?

- Assess your strengths and weaknesses by taking the assessment test at the beginning of this book?

- Review the HRCI test specifications?

- Identify study methods that will work for you, such as self-study, working with a study partner, using a virtual (online) study group, or taking a formal preparation class?

- Identify useful study materials such as this study guide and website content, online HR bulletin boards, and current HR books and magazines?

- Develop a study time line?

- Plan to start studying 3 to 4 months before the test?
- Allow more time to study weaker areas?
- Allow refresher time for stronger areas?
- Schedule weekly meetings with a study partner?
- Set up a file or a binder with space for each functional area to store all your study materials, questions, and practice tests?
- Allow time 2 to 3 weeks before the test for a final review of everything you've studied?
- Simulate the test experience by finding a place to study that is free from distractions and giving yourself 1.07 minutes to answer each bonus exam question from this book?
- Challenge yourself further by setting a timer to see how well you do?

Preparation Techniques

To begin with, the best preparation for the exam is solid knowledge of human resource practices and federal employment law combined with broad generalist experience. Because it's experiential in nature, your ability to use HR knowledge in practical situations is the key to success. This isn't a test you can cram for, regardless of the materials you use.

> Rewrite the book in your words! Use your experiences to explain the lesson. It will help you remember the lesson.
>
> —*ALICIA CHATMAN, SPHR*

Preparation materials can help provide an organized way of approaching the material. In many cases, you already have the information; you just need a refresher of where it came from and the reason it's appropriate for a particular situation.

> A friend of mine used the practice tests to give me oral exams on the material. This was very helpful because I was not reading the questions, just listening to them and answering them, marking, of course, the ones that I answered wrong to emphasize my study on that specific topic.
>
> —*MARCELA ECHEVERRIA*

> I found an "SQ3R" technique (Survey, Question, Read, Recite, Review) effective in studying the materials.
>
> —*LYMAN BLACK, SPHR*

Possibly the best advice to give you is this: don't rely on a single source of information in your preparation. If you have a limited budget, check out books about the various functional areas from your public library. If you're financially able and so inclined, take the opportunity to build your personal HR library (and don't forget to read the books while you're at it!). Take a preparation course. Form a study group. Ask questions of your peers at work. Find a mentor willing to answer your questions. Make use of online HR bulletin boards to ask questions and to observe what others ask and the responses they receive.

A word of caution about HR bulletin boards: although they can be a great source of information and provide a wide range of responses, in some cases, the answers provided are *not correct*. If you make these bulletin boards part of your preparation, make sure you verify the information you receive with other sources.

None of the people who create the preparation materials for the PHR/SPHR exams have special access to the test. The best any preparation materials can do is to provide you with a review of HRCI's test specifications. It's to your advantage to utilize as many sources of information as you can to obtain the broadest possible review of the HR body of knowledge.

Answer as many questions as possible! Whether or not they're the same format as the questions on the exam, they will assist you in recalling information, and that will benefit you during the exam. Aside from the practice questions provided with this book, a great source of questions is HRCI's online assessment exams. Because the questions used are retired from actual PHR/SPHR exams, HR professionals have the opportunity to prepare for the style and types of questions they're likely to encounter when taking the actual exam. Additionally, the assessment content is weighted in accordance with the exam requirements, allowing you the opportunity to identify strengths and weaknesses by functional area, resulting in a more meaningful study plan. Purchase the two-exam package, and take one at the beginning of the study period and one before the exam itself for maximum value.

> Knowing the material isn't always enough. Many people sitting for the exam have been away from test taking for a long time. I think it helped me a lot to practice taking tests with time limits. Practice evaluating similar answers and identifying the best of the lot (not always the very best answer, but the best one presented).
>
> —*Judy Wiens, SPHR*

Taking the Exam

One of the comments heard most often by candidates as they leave the test site is that the information in their preparation materials did not bear any resemblance to what was on the test. None of the questions in this book or in any other preparation materials will be exactly like the questions on the exam. The broader your preparation and experience, the greater will be your ability to successfully answer the exam questions.

Knowing the kinds of questions that may be asked, as described earlier in this chapter, can help you focus your study and be as prepared as possible.

One of the best pieces of advice we've heard about getting ready for test day is to stop studying 2 or 3 days before the test. By then, if you've been diligent about your study plan, you will be well prepared. The night before, get a good night's sleep. Allow yourself plenty of time to get to the test site.

Go to bed early the night before and have a light breakfast the morning before the test, so you are alert...unlike me who kept falling asleep during the test!

—*Rose Chang, PHR*

On Test Day

The PHR/SPHR exams are administered as a computer-based test (CBT) by Prometric. This provides candidates with greater flexibility in scheduling the test and has other benefits as well.

Here are some time-tested hints and tips for exam day gathered from many who have gone before you and were willing to share some of what they learned in the process. For the day of the exam, do the following:

- Get a good night's sleep the night before the test.
- Plan to arrive at least 15 minutes before your scheduled test time.
- Bring your ID (your driver's license, your passport, or any other unexpired government-issued photo ID with a signature) and the test admission letter, along with any other required documents.
- Bring only items you must have with you. You won't be able to take anything into the testing area except your ID.
- Don't overeat in the morning or drink a lot of caffeine before the exam.

While taking the exam, do the following:

- Read the entire question carefully; don't skim it. Taking the time to do this can make the difference between a correct and an incorrect answer.

  I am a speed-reader, and missing one little word could change the entire question. Slow down and read every word.

  —*Marie Atchley, SPHR*

- Read all of the answer choices carefully; don't skim them or select an answer before you've read them all.
- If you're unsure of the answer, eliminate as many wrong answers as you can to narrow down your choices. Remember: one of them is correct!
- Very often, your gut instinct about the correct answer is right, so go with it.
- Don't overanalyze the questions and answers.
- Don't look for patterns in the answers. A myth has been circulating for a number of years that the longest answer is the correct one—it's just not true.
- If you don't know the answer to a question, *guess*. If you don't answer, the question will be counted as incorrect, so you have nothing to lose, and you might get it right.

I was not surprised by the test at all. Everyone said it was hard; it was! Everyone said that it was subjective; it was! Everyone said that you will feel like you flunked; I did! (But I actually passed.)

—*Patricia Kelleher, SPHR*

The Aftermath

The best thing about CBTs is that you will have a preliminary test result before you leave the test center. If you pass, knowing immediately relieves you of the anxiety of worrying and wondering about the results for 4–6 weeks until they arrive in the mail. If you don't pass the test, knowing immediately probably won't make you feel any better about it, but there are a couple of consolations:

- The time and work you put into studying has already benefited you by increasing your knowledge about your chosen profession—congratulate yourself for investing in your career.

- Although the test is important to you, put it in its proper perspective—it's only a test about HR; it's not your life. People take tests every day, and not all of them pass on the first attempt.

If you plan to take the test again, review HRCI's advice on retaking the exam at www. hrci.org. Click the HR Certification tab, then click Schedule and Take an Exam, and then click Retaking an Exam. Browse the entire HRCI website—there is a lot of information about how the test is constructed and scored that may help you refine your study plan for better success.

Summary

Certification for HR professionals is a process that has been evolving for more than 50 years. The HR *BOK* was first developed in 1975 to define the profession and provide the basis for certification. Over the years, HRCI has updated the *BOK* to reflect current business needs and trends to ensure its viability in business. Both the PHR and SPHR exams are based on federal legislation and case law and are experiential, meaning that in order to pass them, candidates need to have exempt-level experience in the field.

Questions on the exams are developed by certified HR professionals who volunteer their time to produce 50 questions per year. The questions go through two levels of review prior to inclusion as unscored pretest questions on an exam. A question that is validated in this process goes into the pool of questions available for testing purposes. Questions that don't pass this rigorous process are either discarded or returned to the writer for additional work.

A number of methods can be used to prepare for the exam. The most important preparation methods are to use as many sources of information as possible and to study with a partner or group.

Chapter 2

Core Knowledge Requirements for HR Professionals

THE HRCI CORE KNOWLEDGE REQUIREMENTS COVERED IN THIS CHAPTER ARE:

✓ Needs assessment and analysis

✓ Third-party or vendor selection, contract negotiation, and management, including development of requests for proposals (RFPs)

✓ Communication skills and strategies (for example: presentation, collaboration, sensitivity)

✓ Organizational documentation requirements to meet federal and state guidelines

✓ Adult learning processes

✓ Motivation concepts and applications

✓ Training techniques (for example: virtual, classroom, on-the-job)

✓ Leadership concepts and applications

✓ Project management concepts and applications

✓ Diversity concepts and applications (for example: generational, cultural competency, learning styles)

✓ Human relations concepts and applications (for example: emotional intelligence, organizational behavior)

✓ Ethical and professional standards

✓ Technology to support HR activities (for example: HR Information Systems, employee self-service, e-learning, applicant tracking systems)

✓ Qualitative and quantitative methods and tools for analysis, interpretation, and decision-making purposes (for example: metrics and measurements, cost/benefit analysis, financial statement analysis)

✓ Change management theory, methods, and application

✓ Job analysis and job description methods

✓ Employee records management (for example: electronic/paper, retention, disposal)

✓ Techniques for forecasting, planning, and predicting the impact of HR activities and programs across functional areas

✓ Types of organizational structures (for example: matrix, hierarchy)

✓ Environmental scanning concepts and applications (for example: Strengths, Weaknesses, Opportunities, and Threats [SWOT], and Political, Economic, Social, and Technological [PEST])

✓ Methods for assessing employee attitudes, opinions, and satisfaction (for example: surveys, focus groups/panels)

✓ Budgeting, accounting, and financial concepts

✓ Risk-management techniques

The *HR Certification Institute PHR/SPHR Body of Knowledge (BOK)* consists of six functional areas plus the core knowledge requirements. These core areas have been identified as knowledge and skill capabilities that are essential to competency as a human resources (HR) professional. Because each of these knowledge areas may have implications for practice in two or more of the HR functional areas, the basic concepts are introduced in this chapter. These introductions are brief and designed only to provide a refresher for each of the concepts. At the beginning of Chapters 3 through 8 is a cross-reference to the core knowledge requirements most relevant to that particular chapter.

For up-to-the-minute updates for this chapter, visit www.sybex.com/go/phr4e.

Needs Assessment and Analysis

Needs assessment and *needs analysis* are terms used interchangeably to describe methods for obtaining the information necessary to make decisions that will best accomplish an organization's goals. These methods can measure needs in any area of business; in HR they're often employed in the areas of training and development, staffing projections, and benefit planning, but they can be used to gather information for any program.

There are many models for needs assessment. The common elements involve the following steps:

Step 1: Describe the objective.   This step answers the question, "Where do we want to be?" and looks at the various elements necessary to accomplish that objective. It's important to obtain relevant information from all the possible stakeholders to ensure a full understanding of what is needed, as well as to ensure buy-in when recommendations are presented. In developing the objective, consider elements such as strategic business goals, department goals and objectives, budget constraints, available resources, and any other factors that impact the situation. These include the right people, skills, systems, and materials necessary to meet the objective.

Step 2: Define the current situation.   This step answers the question, "Where are we now?" and looks at each element described in step 1 to determine what is already available in the organization and create an inventory of skills, people, equipment, technology, and other assets already in place.

Step 3: Conduct a gap analysis.   A *gap analysis* compares the objective to the current situation and results in a list of people, actions, or items needed to attain the objective described in step 1. As part of this process, it's important to gather as much information as possible about the gaps so they're clearly understood and to identify any constraints that may inhibit efforts to close them.

Step 4: Set priorities.   In a world of limited resources, it isn't realistic to expect to go out and obtain everything that is needed to fill all the gaps immediately. Prioritizing identifies the gaps most critical to achieving the primary objective and focuses on closing them first.

Step 5: Investigate and develop options.   This step answers the question, "What is the most effective way to fill this gap?" Be as open-minded as possible when developing options, and collect data from as many sources as are available. Involve others in brainstorming sessions as appropriate, and look for ways in which similar needs have been met both inside and outside the organization.

Step 6: Evaluate options, and determine budget impact.   Determine which of the possible options will be the most effective way to fill the gap. A crucial element of this step is the cost of implementation. It's important to consider both direct and indirect costs: the impact on the company's bottom line in the short term, as well as the return on investment (ROI) and long-term costs and savings. Another budgetary consideration is the cost of not implementing the option: in the long run, will it cost more or less to operate without it?

Step 7: Recommend solutions.   Whether you or someone higher in the organization is the final decision maker, it's important to document the reasons for selecting a particular solution.

Third-Party Contract Management

A *contract* is a legally enforceable agreement between two or more parties in which all parties benefit in some way. Generally, one party makes an offer to do or provide something of value (a product or service), and the other agrees to do or provide something in return (payment). Contracts can be formal or informal, oral or written, and implied or explicit. Although oral and implied contracts can be legally enforceable, written contracts provide more clarity and protection for the parties involved.

In a *third-party contract*, some part of the transaction is provided by an entity other than those who have signed the contract. There are many examples of third-party contracts in business; perhaps the best known for HR professionals is an agreement with a temp agency in which the company agrees to pay the temp agency for services provided by an employee of the agency.

As an increasing number of HR functions are outsourced, the need for practitioners to understand the issues involved in effectively managing third-party contractors becomes more important. A critical factor for a successful contractor relationship is a clear understanding of the product or service to be provided, along with clearly defined expectations for quality and service levels. This information is best communicated through a process known as a *request for proposal* (RFP).

In many organizations, the RFP process is handled by a purchasing group or is outsourced to someone who specializes in preparing RFPs, but it's important to understand what information is needed to develop an RFP that satisfies both parties. A well-constructed RFP serves as the basis on which the product or service is obtained, a guide to ensure that the delivery meets the organization's requirements, and a means of evaluation at the end of the project. Although there is no standard RFP format for use in all situations, the elements for developing one are similar:

Conducting a Needs Assessment   Whether you're requesting bids for a one-time project or an ongoing outsource relationship, you must be able to describe your objectives and budget clearly so that vendors will provide an accurate and appropriate proposal.

As part of the needs-assessment process, a client may conduct informal pre-proposal meetings with possible vendors. This is particularly useful when the client has little direct experience with the project or wants to learn more about the product or service in order to describe it more clearly in the RFP. This is sometimes known as *scoping* the project and can become a more formal process with the use of a scoping document that solicits information from a variety of possible vendors before the RFP is written.

Developing the RFP   The format of an RFP varies with each organization. In general, the following components are included:

- A brief description of the organization, including information that will help vendors provide an accurate bid, such as number of employees, locations, and so on.
- An overview of the project summarizing what is needed.
- Administrative details about the process, including submission deadlines, how to request an extension, the format requirements for submissions, and what happens if there are errors or omissions in the RFP. Information about how the proposals will be evaluated should be included here as well (for example, will the project be awarded to the lowest bidder, or will other criteria be more important?). Any penalties for late delivery and how to handle work that is beyond the scope of the RFP are also included in this step.
- A clear, complete, and detailed project description (also referred to as the scope of work, technical description, or project specifications) that contains information significant to the ability of the vendor to prepare a bid and that can be measured during the evaluation phase.
- The name of the contact person for additional information about preparing the proposal.

Proposal Formats   As per step 3, the RFP provides vendors with a format to follow when submitting proposals. This serves two purposes. First, it makes evaluating the proposals easier; and second, it ensures that vendors provide all the relevant information for an evaluation of the project. Although the format will vary between organizations and different projects, the following elements will make it easier to compare and evaluate the proposals:

Executive Summary   A brief overview of the vendor's qualifications to provide the product or service needed by the client.

Vendor Qualifications   Includes references from other clients.

Project Management Plan   Describes specifically how the vendor intends to supply the product or service.

Project Team   Includes personnel who will be supplied by the vendor as well as the client's employees who will be involved.

Roles and Responsibilities   Includes information about members of the project team.

Delivery Schedule   Provides a timeline and milestones for the completion of specific events.

Pricing Information   Includes how the project will be billed and whether the price is based on project completion, time and materials, or completion of specific milestone events. The vendor should also provide pricing information for any requested work that is beyond the scope of the proposal.

Evaluating the Proposals   Once the proposals have been submitted, the evaluation process can begin. There are many factors to consider, including the reputation of the vendor, the qualifications and experience of the project team, the size of the company and whether it has the capability to complete the project, how flexible the vendor can be in terms of schedule or other issues, the proposed cost, whether the schedule submitted meets the needs of the organization, and whether the vendor's approach to the project is compatible with the organization's culture.

Selecting a Vendor   When the evaluation has been completed, notify the successful vendor, along with those whose proposals weren't accepted.

Negotiating the Contract   Formalize the agreement, and sign a contract with the successful vendor. For more information on contract-negotiation techniques, see the discussion on negotiating collective-bargaining agreements in Chapter 7, "Employee and Labor Relations."

Executing the Agreement   Implement the project. Initially, gathering together all the members of the project team, both those who work for the vendor and those who work for the organization, is important to ensure that the project gets off to a good start. It's also important to maintain contact with the vendor during the implementation phase to ensure that it stays on track and meets your expectations.

Evaluating the Project   Whether this is an ongoing outsource function or a one-time project, an evaluation ensures that the project continues to meet organizational needs and provides useful information for future projects.

Communication Skills and Strategies

HR professionals must develop expertise in communicating information to a variety of stakeholders, from top executives to production workers, customers, and vendors. This requires the ability to determine which strategies will most successfully communicate different types of information to these various audiences.

Employee Communication

An effective employee *communication strategy* provides opportunities for top-down communication by management and bottom-up communication from employees. It must balance management's need to ensure the confidentiality of sensitive company information with the need of employees to know, understand, and feel part of what is happening with the company. An effective strategy builds employees' trust in the organization during the communication process by sharing meaningful information with them. The more employees know about the company's vision, goals, and operations, the more engaged and productive they are. Employees who feel connected to the success of the organization become goodwill ambassadors, enhancing the company's reputation in the community and effectively referring qualified candidates for open positions.

There are many options for providing or exchanging information with employees; Table 2.1 lists some of them.

TABLE 2.1   Possible communication delivery methods

Top-Down Communication	Bottom-Up Communication
Intranet	Open-door policy
Public address system announcements	All-hands meetings
Posters	Staff meetings
Newsletters	Brown-bag lunches
Individual letters to employees	One-on-one meetings
Flyers	Email
Bulletin board postings	Webcasts

An effective communication strategy delivers the same information in several ways; determining the best mix of methods begins with a clear picture of what management hopes to achieve. Once the objective is clear, answers to the following questions determine which delivery methods are most appropriate for a particular situation:

- What information will be provided?
- Who is the intended audience?
- Who will provide the information?
- Is the information time sensitive?

To select the best delivery mechanisms for a particular organization and message, it's also important to consider the organization's culture. The most effective strategies are a reflection of the culture, whether it's very formal or informal and laid-back. Another consideration that guides the selection of communication methods is the employee base: is the workforce computer savvy, or are employees accustomed to receiving information from their managers in small group meetings?

Bottom-up communication methods help employees feel that their concerns are heard and addressed, which adds to their investment in the organization's success. There are, of course, many messages that are most appropriately delivered top-down as well, such as changes in policy or new operational directives. Mechanisms to enhance both types of communication will contribute to the effectiveness of the overall strategy.

Professional Communication

Because HR professionals must communicate a variety of messages to differing audiences, it's likely that multiple communication strategies will be developed to ensure that each audience receives necessary information in the way that best meets its needs and that gets the HR message across effectively. To achieve this, HR professionals need skills for a wide variety of purposes, including presentations, collaboration, influencing, diplomacy, and sensitivity.

Documentation Requirements

Documentation requirements fall into two basic categories. The first is the collection and maintenance of required employment records, such as application forms, tax documents, and benefit records. These requirements are described in the "Employee Records Management" section later in this chapter. In that section, Table 2.6 provides a detailed list of most employment documents that must be maintained for legal purposes along with the required retention period required by each federal law.

The second category is the maintenance of appropriate documentation for employment actions.

Documenting Employment Actions

Traditionally, the HR department has been charged with responsibility to ensure that all the "i's are dotted and t's are crossed" when it comes to documenting employment relationships. As the *subject matter experts* (SMEs), HR professionals are those most qualified to ensure the maintenance of proper documentation and to safeguard the privacy of personal employee information. The maintenance of these records is important for two basic reasons: some are required to be maintained to comply with federal, state, or local employment laws, and others provide information necessary for effective management of the organization. In some cases, the records are needed to meet both of those requirements.

Documenting Performance Issues

There are two key considerations in documenting performance concerns. The first is timeliness, which is the need for managers to address performance issues when they occur in order to effectively manage the employees who report to them. All too often, line managers are reluctant to confront employees about performance issues and neglect to advise them of any problems until either the annual performance review or the situation becomes so untenable that the manager's only thought is immediate termination of the employee. In either situation, the employee is taken completely by surprise at the seriousness of the situation and won't have had the opportunity to rectify the problem.

This side of performance management will be fully discussed in Chapter 5, "Human Resource Development."

The other key consideration is creating and maintaining written documentation for disciplinary action taken as appropriate and warranted based on the seriousness of the performance issue. In keeping with the at-will policy, employers can exercise their judgment in administering disciplinary action based on the severity of the situation; however, the following are typical disciplinary actions that can be administered:

Step 1: Verbal Warning   Although it may seem contradictory to state that a written record of a *verbal warning* should be maintained, it isn't. The verbal warning includes specific examples of the unacceptable performance or behavior and notice of the consequences if it doesn't change: that is, further disciplinary action, up to and including termination. The written record of this conversation can be as simple as a contemporaneous note by the supervisor that describes the date and time of the warning, the name of the employee involved, what was discussed, and any agreements that were made about future changes in behavior or performance.

Step 2: First Written Warning   At this stage, the written record becomes more formal. In some companies, forms are provided for managers to fill in with the appropriate information. In companies without specific forms, the *first written warning* is a memo to the employee describing steps that have already been taken, exactly what the performance problem is, steps that need to be taken to avoid future consequences, and any agreements that have been made about performance changes. This document should be signed by the employee. When employees are reluctant to sign a warning with which they disagree, the supervisor can advise them that signing doesn't indicate agreement, merely that the warning has been discussed. If the employee still won't sign, the supervisor can make a note indicating the date and time of the discussion and the fact that the employee refused to sign the document.

Step 3: Final Written Warning   A *final written warning* is similar to the first, with the addition of a statement advising the employee that a continued inability or refusal to make necessary performance changes will result in termination of employment.

Step 4: Decision-Making Day   As a final step prior to termination, some companies provide a decision-making day. Employees are sent home, usually with pay, and asked to think about whether they're willing to make the changes and keep their jobs. If they are, they return to work the next day and make a commitment to make the necessary changes. It is made clear to employees that if the changes aren't made, immediate termination will result without additional disciplinary steps. If they indicate that they aren't willing to conform to the performance requirements, they're terminated without further disciplinary action.

Step 5: Suspension   Some companies take an additional step prior to termination and suspend employees for varying periods of time depending on the seriousness of the offense and other considerations. A *suspension* is accompanied by a written document spelling out all the steps previously taken to resolve the issue, the reason for the suspension, and a statement that continued nonconformance may result in termination.

Step 6: Termination of Employment   At this stage, employees are well aware of the issues leading up to the *termination*. Depending on the circumstances, prior to taking this step it may be advisable to have counsel review the existing documentation and provide guidance for the final termination letter.

Some of the additional documents that must be provided and maintained when employees are terminated include agreements for severance (with accompanying releases) or for compliance with the ADEA (discussed in Chapter 4, "Workforce Planning and Employment"), along with documentation of compliance with COBRA requirements (discussed in Chapter 6, "Compensation and Benefits") and state unemployment documentation (if required).

As experienced HR practitioners are aware, including a disciplinary process in an employee handbook can void the doctrine of at-will employment (to be fully discussed in Chapter 7). This presents a dilemma: without documentation of adverse employment actions, employers are unable to defend against claims of discrimination. With a published disciplinary process, employers are vulnerable to claims of discrimination if the process isn't followed in all cases. To address these conflicting issues, some employment attorneys recommend that this disciplinary process be used as a guideline for managers to follow in addressing performance issues but that it not be published in an employee handbook.

Maintaining contemporaneous records as just described can make the difference between a summary judgment in the employer's favor and a large jury award to a former employee.

Adult Learning Processes and Learning Styles

The concept that adult learning processes were different from those of children was developed in the United States by Eduard Lindeman during the 1920s. Lindeman first promoted the idea that, for adults, the methods of learning were more important than what was being taught. His belief was that the most effective learning for adults took place in small groups where knowledge could be shared based on the life experience of the participants. Malcolm Knowles expanded on Lindeman's theories in the 1970s when he identified characteristics that set adult learning apart from the way children learn. The work of Lindeman and Knowles is the basis for the study of how adults learn known as *andragogy*. The definition of andragogy evolved as researchers sought to further define adult learning; today it has come to mean education in which the learner participates in decisions about what will be taught and how it will be delivered. This approach is in contrast to *pedagogy*, the study of how children learn, which is defined as education in which the teacher decides what will be taught and how it will be delivered.

Much of Knowles' work centered on identifying characteristics of adult learning that would make the process more productive for learners. Knowles promoted the idea that, with maturity, people grow into new ways of learning, described by the following five characteristics, which form the basis of andragogy today:

Self-concept   An individual's self concept moves from dependency on others to autonomy and self-direction.

Experience   An individual builds a wealth of knowledge that grows with each new experience. This information reserve can then be drawn on for further learning.

Readiness to Learn   Individuals become increasingly interested in the relevance of information to specific needs and how directly it applies to their current situations.

Orientation to Learning   The ability to apply information immediately to solve current problems is increasingly important to learners.

Motivation to Learn   The motivation to learn is based more on personal needs and desires than on expectations of others.

When designing training, you must consider adult learning styles, which answer the question, "How do I learn?" There are generally considered to be three types of learners:

Auditory   *Auditory learners* process information by hearing. Individuals who are auditory learners will, for example, recite a phone number out loud several times to memorize it.

Visual   *Visual learners* depend on their visual processing of information. Often described as "thinking in pictures," these learners will write down a phone number to see it, committing the image to memory for future recall.

Tactile/Kinesthetic   *Tactile/kinesthetic learners* are physical learners; they rely on their sense of touch for memory recall. These individuals will "air dial" the phone number, tracing the pattern in the air for future recall of the proper sequence of numbers.

Because all learning styles are represented in the workforce, it's important to incorporate elements of each style when designing training. Other factors to consider include the following:

- These styles are often innate; you can train employees to use multiple styles, but their default method of learning will often yield the best results.

- Trainers often unintentionally discriminate. They design training to their own personal learning style instead of accounting for the blended needs of their audience.

- The study of these categories of learning styles continues to evolve, via the use of music, logic, words, pictures, and simulation.

These basic characteristics of adult learners are important concepts with implications beyond traditional training and development. Learning is, of course, the point of training, so understanding the best ways to provide information in work situations can enhance productivity and job satisfaction for the workforce.

Motivation Concepts

From the beginning of the industrial revolution, business owners have sought the key to improving productivity. This search prompted scientists to study the work environment, businesses, and the relationship of people to organizations. These studies led to many theories about work, some related to the physical environment or organization structures and others that looked at why people work and what motivates them.

The traditional theories of motivation discussed next center either on the need for employees to be self-motivated or on the need for managers to motivate them. They provide a basis for understanding what drives employees to perform at peak levels of productivity, which can help managers understand the reasons for lowered productivity. Each functional area of the *BOK* is impacted by whether employees are motivated or demotivated at work. Incorporating these concepts into the planning stage of HR programs and initiatives can increase the value of the end result.

Abraham Maslow: The Hierarchy of Needs (1954)

Maslow, a behavioral scientist, developed his *hierarchy of needs* to explain how people meet their needs through work. This theory describes needs that begin with the most basic requirements for life—food, shelter, and basic physical comforts—and progresses through stages of growth as people strive to fill higher-level needs. Maslow identified five levels of needs that motivate people:

Physiological Needs   These are the most basic needs. Individuals striving to find enough food to eat or a place to live are motivated by attaining those things. People at this level are motivated by actions that provide the basic necessities of life.

Safety Needs   Once people have food and shelter, they look for ways to ensure that they're safe from physical and emotional harm.

Social Needs   At this level, people are motivated by the desire for acceptance and belonging in their social group.

Esteem Needs   At this level, people are motivated by recognition for their achievements.

Self-actualization Needs   When people are confident that their basic needs have been met, they become motivated by opportunities to be creative and fulfill their own potential. They don't look outside themselves for these opportunities but depend on themselves to find and act on them.

B. F. Skinner: Operant Conditioning (1957)

The results of Skinner's work on *behavioral reinforcement* are more commonly known as *behavior modification*. His basic theory is that behavior can be changed through the use of four intervention strategies:

Positive Reinforcement   Encourages continuation of the behavior by providing a pleasant response when the behavior occurs.

Negative Reinforcement   Encourages continuation of the behavior by removing an unpleasant response to a behavior.

Punishment   Discourages future occurrence of the behavior by providing an unpleasant response when the behavior occurs.

Extinction   Discourages future occurrence of the behavior by ceasing to reinforce it. For example, when a parent praises a child for doing his homework each night and the child starts doing it without being reminded, the parent may stop praising the child. If the child then reverts to the previous behavior of forgetting to do his homework, the behavior has become extinct.

Frederick Herzberg: Motivation/Hygiene Theory (1959)

Herzberg's *motivation/hygiene theory* (also known as the *two-factor theory*) began with a study on job attitudes that he conducted in Pittsburgh in the 1950s. He began the study believing that the causes of job satisfaction would be the opposite of the causes of job dissatisfaction. However, his review of several thousand books and articles on job attitudes didn't prove his premise; in fact, the results were so vague that it wasn't possible to draw any conclusions. This led Herzberg to conduct a study in which he asked the participants to identify the work experiences that resulted in positive feelings about their jobs and the ones that resulted in negative feelings.

The result, as Herzberg himself described it in an interview, was that "What makes people happy is what they do or the way they're used, and what makes people unhappy is the way they're treated" ("An Interview with Frederick Herzberg: Managers or Animal Trainers?" *Management Review*, 1971). Both factors can motivate workers, but they work for very different reasons. The satisfaction (motivation) factors motivate by changing the nature of the work so that people are challenged to develop their talents and fulfill their potential. For example, adding responsibilities that provide learning opportunities for a receptionist performing at a substandard level can result in improved performance of all duties assigned if the poor performance is related to boredom with repetitive tasks. The dissatisfaction (hygiene) factors motivate to the extent that they allow people to avoid unpleasant experiences. For example, as long as employees continue to perform their assignments at an acceptable level, they continue to receive a paycheck. Hygiene factors provide only short-term benefits to employers, whereas factors related to motivation lead to longer-term job satisfaction.

A result of Herzberg's theory is the concept of job enrichment in which the significance of the tasks in a job is increased to provide challenging work and growth opportunities.

Douglas McGregor: Theory X and Theory Y (1960)

McGregor expanded on Maslow's work to describe the behavior of managers in their relationships with their employees. McGregor identified two distinct management approaches, *Theory X* and *Theory Y*.

Theory X managers have a worldview of employees as lazy and uninterested in work and needing constant direction to complete their assignments. Theory X managers believe that employees don't want to take responsibility and are interested in job security above all else. Theory X managers are generally autocratic, utilizing a top-down management style.

In contrast, Theory Y managers believe that, given the opportunity, people will seek out challenging work and additional responsibility if the work is satisfying. Theory Y managers are more likely to invite participation in the decision-making process from their subordinates.

David McClelland: Acquired Needs Theory (1961)

The premise of McClelland's *acquired needs theory* is that experiences acquired throughout their lives motivate people to achieve in one of three areas:

Achievement   Those motivated by achievement take moderate risks to achieve their goals, respond to frequent feedback, and generally prefer to work as sole contributors or with others interested in achieving at the same level.

Affiliation   Individuals who need affiliation look for acceptance in the work group and need regular interaction with their co-workers or customers.

Power   These individuals are looking for either personal power or institutional power. Those interested in institutional power are often effective managers who are motivated by coordinating work groups to achieve organization goals.

J. Stacey Adams: Equity Theory (1963)

The basic concept of Adams' *equity theory* is that people are constantly measuring what they put into work against what they get from work. If their perception is that it's a fair trade, they're motivated to continue contributing at the same level. When they perceive there is an imbalance and they're putting in more than they're getting back, they become demotivated and lose interest in their work, decreasing productivity and quality.

Victor Vroom: Expectancy Theory (1964)

Vroom's *expectancy theory* maintains that people are motivated by the expectation of the reward they will receive when they succeed and that each individual calculates the level of effort required to receive a particular reward to determine whether the reward is worth the effort that is required to attain it. Vroom uses the following terms to explain this theory:

Expectancy According to Vroom's theory, motivation starts with an assessment by individuals about their capabilities to successfully complete an assignment.

Instrumentality If individuals believe they're capable of completing an assignment, they next ask "What's in it for me?"—that is, will their effort to complete the work be the instrument for obtaining a reward for the work?

Valence This is the result of calculations as to whether the possible reward is worth the effort required to successfully complete the work.

Clayton Alderfer: ERG Theory (1969)

The *ERG theory* developed by Alderfer builds on Maslow's work as well. Alderfer identifies three levels of needs:

Existence This relates to Maslow's definition of physiological and safety needs as those that are required to maintain basic life needs.

Relatedness This is similar to Maslow's descriptions of social needs and the esteem we find from others.

Growth This is based on the self-esteem and self-actualization concepts Maslow described.

The premise for Maslow's theory was that people move sequentially through the levels one at a time. Alderfer's theory allows for the possibility that people can work on multiple levels simultaneously. It also describes the concept of frustration-regression, which occurs when an individual falls back to a lower level in frustration at the difficulty of a higher level.

 Real World Scenario

Operant Conditioning in Customer Service

The customer service manager at Wright Sisters, Inc., Susan Sherwood, has a problem employee, David Rogers. David can be charming and has a knack for calming down disgruntled customers on the phone. In fact, his co-workers often rely on him for assistance with unhappy customers who are difficult to please. David has worked for WSI for three years and is for the most part productive and cooperative. At times, however, he has snapped at co-workers, and he is often disruptive in staff meetings. Recently, Susan has observed him being rude to some customers during customer support calls. She has also noticed that co-workers have stopped giving him work that he is supposed be doing; instead, they're doing it themselves to avoid dealing with him. Susan, who has been working on her MBA, just finished a course in industrial psychology and decides to try Skinner's theory of operant conditioning to see whether it will work in a practical application. She comes up with the following interventions to use with David:

Positive Reinforcement   At the end of each meeting in which David exhibits professional behavior, Susan will thank him publicly for his contribution during the meeting.

Negative Reinforcement   When David behaves professionally during the day and doesn't create any disruptions, he won't have to meet with Susan at the end of the day.

Punishment   Whenever David is rude to a customer or co-worker, Susan will reprimand him.

Extinction   Co-workers will no longer do his work for him when David becomes confrontational with them.

Training Techniques

Training techniques are used throughout the HR *BOK* for programs specific to each area, such as the following:

- Business Management and Strategy: Ethics, Sarbanes-Oxley compliance

- Workforce Planning and Employment: New-hire orientation, interviewing

- Human Resource Development: Training delivery such as virtual or on the job, skill development, performance appraisal

- Compensation and Benefits: Salary increase guidelines

- Employee and Labor Relations: Union avoidance, supervisory skills

- Risk Management: Safety training

Training techniques are fully discussed in Chapter 5 along with all other aspects of training and development.

Leadership Concepts

Much has been written about leaders and how they develop: are they born or made? There is little agreement in research about where leaders come from. Does the effectiveness of a leader depend on the situation? Which is more important as a function of leadership—the ability to develop structures or the ability to develop people? One thing is certain: however they do so, effective leaders are able to inspire the people around them to do their best work and influence people to follow them in achieving a common goal. This section introduces some of the theories researchers have developed to explain leadership. As you'll see, none of these theories are able to explain all its aspects. Although some theories are currently more popular than others, all of them are the subject of ongoing study as researchers continue to try to explain leadership ability.

The study of how leaders become leaders was first addressed during the nineteenth century when Thomas Carlyle suggested the "great man" theory: that is, that leaders are born with innate qualities that set them apart from other "mere mortals." It was Carlyle's premise that leadership couldn't be learned but was instead the result of the superior qualities of a few men. Early in the twentieth century, this premise became the basis for trait theories of leadership that look to the personality, intellect, and physical traits of individuals to explain their ability to lead others.

Several drawbacks to trait theories became apparent over time. The first and most significant of these was that each researcher identified different leadership traits, which resulted in multiple lists of relevant traits. The second was that research showed there was little difference between the traits exhibited by leaders and those of followers. For example, traits such as courage and intelligence were found in followers as often as in leaders. Finally, trait theories didn't explain how leaders were successful in different situations using very different methods. As the limitations of early explanations for leadership development became clear, researchers turned to other areas for investigation, including behavioral, situational, and contingency theories of leadership.

Behavioral Theories

During the 1940s, researchers moved to a new area of research and focused on the ability of leadership to be taught: anyone could become a leader with the right information. This view of leadership moved the research focus from personality traits to what leaders did to inspire people to follow them. Two aspects of behavior became apparent in the research. The first was behavior that focused on the structural elements of the job, such as establishing rules and guidelines for employees. The second was behavior that considered the needs of employees, such as standing up for them and explaining decisions. Douglas McGregor's Theory X and Theory Y provide an example of a behavioral theory of leadership.

As with trait theories, there were leadership characteristics that weren't explained by behavioral theories, most notably, how or why a given behavioral aspect worked in one situation but not in others. This led to a new avenue for research: the impact of leadership in different situations.

Situational Theories

Situational theories of leadership seek to explain leader effectiveness in different situations. The elements that are considered in situational theories are how the leader and followers interact and how the work is structured. Several well-known theories fall into this category:

Blake-Mouton Managerial Grid (1968)   Robert R. Blake and Jane S. Mouton developed a grid to explain the characteristics of different leadership styles. The grid considers two aspects of leadership: concern for people and concern for production, as shown in Figure 2.1.

FIGURE 2.1   Blake-Mouton managerial grid

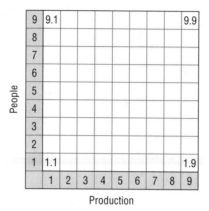

The grid uses nine levels to measure each aspect. Leaders at the lowest extreme (1,1) show no concern for either people or production. At the highest extreme (9,9), leaders show maximum concern for both production and people and, according to Blake and Mouton, are the most effective leaders.

Path-Goal Theory (1971)   The path-goal theory of leadership was developed by Robert House, a professor at the Wharton School of Business. This theory proposes that a leader can impact the behavior of a group by establishing goals and providing direction on reaching those goals. House describes four leadership styles that may be used to accomplish this, based on the specific situation:

- Directive, which specifies what is to be done
- Supportive, in which the leader provides encouragement for the group members
- Participative, in which the leader involves the group in the decision-making process
- Achievement, in which the leader establishes a difficult goal and encourages the group to accomplish it

Hersey-Blanchard Theory (1977)   Paul Hersey and Kenneth Blanchard describe leadership in terms of the maturity level of the followers. In this theory, maturity refers to psychological maturity (or motivation) and job task maturity (or level of experience). The model provides four styles of leadership appropriate in different circumstances:

Telling   When followers are immature or inexperienced, the leader must be more directive by providing guidelines and defining roles for the followers.

Selling   When followers have some experience, the leader is still directing them but in a more general sense. Greater emphasis is placed on encouraging followers who have the motivation but lack sufficient experience to do the job.

Participating   At this level, the followers have progressed in terms of their ability but may lack the necessary motivation and require support to encourage them to act on their own.

Delegating   At this level, followers have both the experience and motivation to accomplish their tasks. The leader identifies the goal, and followers are accountable for producing results.

Although situational theories address issues that were missing in both the trait and behavioral theories, they're criticized for being two-dimensional and not allowing for multifaceted situations that occur in the real world of business. In addition, these theories don't account for differences in culture and gender in explaining leadership.

Contingency Theories

To address some of these criticisms, Fred E. Fiedler developed a model known as Fiedler's Contingency Theory to address the shortcomings of situational theories. Fiedler's theory begins with an assessment of the leader's style. Fiedler uses a method known as the *least preferred co-worker* scale to determine this. Leaders identify the co-worker, past or present, with whom they had the most difficulty working and rate this person on a scale of 1 to 8 on a series of measures such as the co-worker's level of cooperation and friendliness. The result is known as the least preferred co-worker (LPC) score. A high LPC score indicates that the leader has a greater concern for people than for tasks, and a low score indicates a greater concern for tasks. Fiedler proposed that the LPC score could be used to predict the situations in which a leader would have a better chance for success.

Fiedler then describes situations in terms of three aspects:

Leader-Member Relations   The relationships leaders have with members of the group are the key factor in determining the level of influence the leader has in the group.

Task Structure   Jobs that are highly structured provide a leader with greater influence than do those that require less structure.

Position Power   Situations in which a leader has the discretion to assign tasks or to reward or punish members of the group provide the leader with a greater chance of success.

Each of these theories provides a different perspective on leadership and helps explain something about it. They're the basis for many of the discussions in subsequent chapters; in particular, Chapters 3, 5, and 7 consider different aspects of the interactions between employees and managers, and these theories may provide the basis for a deeper understanding of the ways in which managers and leaders are able to influence employees.

Leadership Styles

Everyone has experienced leaders with different styles: the authoritarian leader who tells employees what to do, the democratic leader who involves employees in the process, the laissez-faire leader who abdicates responsibility and leaves employees to figure things out without guidance or support, and the coach who prepares employees to take on additional responsibility. There are different situations when all these styles may be appropriate:

Authoritarian or Directive   *Authoritarian leaders* are effective in situations requiring immediate action or those that are life threatening. When productivity is the highest concern, authoritarian leadership may be the best style.

Democratic   *Democratic leaders* are most effective in environments of highly skilled professional employees who are self-motivated and accomplish tasks on their own. When relationships in the work environment are of primary concern, this style is most effective.

Laissez-faire   *Laissez-faire* leaders allow group members to operate on their own. This leadership style provides no direction or guidance and can lead to chaos if members lack confidence in their abilities. For individuals who are highly motivated and can work independently, this may be an acceptable style. In general, it results in lower levels of productivity.

Coaching   Coaches work with group members to develop skills and abilities so they will be able to operate independently.

There are two other leadership styles to keep in mind:

Transactional   *Transactional leadership* focuses on getting the job done and seeks to do this by offering a reward in exchange for accomplishing organization goals. Transactional leaders manage by exception, either by seeking out areas where rules aren't being followed and making a correction or by taking action when the goal isn't met.

Transformational   *Transformational leadership* focuses on the relationships in the group, building them to achieve organization goals. These leaders set the ideal for the group and act as role models, inspiring excellence in the group and stimulating new ideas and perspectives. Transformational leaders are coaches who work with individuals to develop their skills and abilities and improve their performance.

Project Management Concepts

Project management (PM) describes the process of initiating, planning, executing, controlling, and closing an assignment that is temporary in nature. The assignment may involve designing a new software program, constructing a building, implementing a new marketing strategy, or doing any other activity that isn't part of the ongoing operations of a business. In *Project Management Jumpstart*, Kim Heldman, a certified project management professional (PMP), describes the five phases of a project life cycle:

Initiation   During the initiation phase, project requests are evaluated and selected for implementation. Those who will be affected by the project—the *stakeholders* such as the project manager, sponsor, team members, customers, and others—meet to discuss the proposed project. Once a project is selected, the sponsor creates a project charter to sanction the project and commit resources to its completion. The charter also identifies the goals and appoints the project manager.

Planning   The planning phase is led by the project manager (PM) and lays out how the project will be accomplished. The plan describes the deliverables, budget, and scope of the project and then develops specific activities and identifies the *knowledge, skills, and abilities* (KSAs) required to execute the activities. Finally, a timeline for completing the project is created.

Executing   During this phase, the project plan is implemented. A project team is created, and other resources are acquired. Activities identified in the planning phase are completed during this time, and the PM manages the timeline, conducts status meetings, and disseminates information to the sponsor and other stakeholders as needed.

Controlling   The PM keeps the project on course and on budget by comparing accomplishments to the original plan and making course corrections as needed. As the project progresses, stakeholders may request changes to the original scope, and the PM will review and incorporate them into the project as appropriate.

Closing   The closing phase is the point at which the sponsor/customer acknowledges achievement of the project goals. The PM collects information from stakeholders to improve future projects, stores documentation of project activities, and releases resources for use in other projects or activities.

For HR professionals, the ability to manage projects is critical to success. The following list shows how HR projects can occur in any of the functional areas:

Business Strategy and Management   Integrating the cultures of two organizations after a merger

Workforce Planning and Employment   Developing a new-hire orientation program

Human Resource Development   Creating a career-development program

Compensation and Benefits   Developing a stock-option program

Employee and Labor Relations   Developing an employee handbook

Risk Management   Developing an emergency response plan

Each of these activities is a short-term assignment that will result in a program that will become part of the organization operations when it's complete, but the process of designing the program isn't an ongoing operation.

The Project Management Institute maintains a website with additional information about projects and how they're managed at www.pmi.org.

Diversity Concepts

As businesses become global entities employing individuals with diverse cultural, racial, and ethnic backgrounds, understanding *diversity* in the workplace becomes more critical to organizational success. Organizations implementing programs to increase diversity realize benefits such as improved productivity and bottom-line results for shareholders. There are many other business reasons to make workplace diversity a priority:

A diverse workforce is more creative.   Increasing the variety of perspectives available to an organization brings new points of view to decision-making processes, challenging conventional wisdom and creating an atmosphere that encourages the synergy of ideas.

A diverse workforce reflects the population.   When businesses increase the diversity of their workforces, they increase their ability to attract customers. Customers are attracted to organizations when they feel comfortable with its representatives, and employees who understand and communicate well with customers help increase the customer base for a company's products or services.

A diverse workforce increases the candidate pool.   The Department of Labor (DOL) predicts an increasing shortage of qualified candidates for available positions throughout the next decade. According to the U.S. Bureau of Labor Statistics, more than 25 percent of the working population will reach retirement age by 2012, resulting in a potential shortage of nearly 10 million skilled workers. Increasing the candidate pool by including a wide diversity of applicants will continue to be essential in filling open positions.

Workplace diversity presents challenges that organizations look to HR professionals to address, including the difficulty associated with change and the need to do things in new ways. It's challenging for individual employees to work with people who behave and communicate differently than what is perceived as normal. For example, something as seemingly simple as differences in the amount of personal space that are customary in different cultures can create uncomfortable situations, such as one person backing away from another to increase the space between them while the other moves closer seeking to decrease the space.

In addition, HR professionals should be familiar with *cultural competence*: the ability of a diverse group of people to achieve organizational aims, and a measure of a company's ability to work with individuals from multiple walks of life. Cultural competence is a necessary component of a corporate diversity management program and should focus not only on the operational needs of the workgroup but also on the more subjective realities of cross-cultural needs. HR has a broad influence in developing and assessing an organization's cultural competence. Examples of this influence include addressing cross-cultural conflict, assessing the hiring patterns of managers, sensitivity training efforts, recruitment practices, leave policies, healthcare benefits design, and anti-harassment policy development.

Diversity Concept: Cultural Competence

According to the U.S. Department of Health and Human Services Office of Minority Health: "Culture refers to integrated patterns of human behavior that include the language, thoughts, communications, actions, customs, beliefs, values, and institutions of racial, ethnic, religious, or social groups. Competence implies having the capacity to function effectively as an individual and an organization within the context of the cultural beliefs, behaviors, and needs presented by consumers and their communities."

Based on Cross, T., Bazron, B., Dennis, K., and Isaacs, M., (1989). *Towards a Culturally Competent System of Care Volume I.* Washington, D.C.: Georgetown University Child Development Center, CASSP Technical Assistance Center.

Difficulties also arise for employees whose backgrounds are dissimilar to the group. They may feel uncomfortable in situations requiring them to make major adjustments in order to be accepted by a group whose culture or demographic is different from their own, such as when managing a multigenerational workforce, for example. The workforce of today spans more generations than at any other time in history, with an average age-span difference ranging between 20 to 30+ years and many older workers unable or unwilling to retire. Although this is a boon in terms of talent availability based on work and life experiences, the result is a generational division that plays out in the hallways of the corporate landscape. Differing values, expectations, and cultural identities are the hallmarks of the type of factors influencing a company's ability to manage a multigenerational workforce. Examples of the HR factors that must be considered include training design, benefits utilization, and diversity management programs.

The comfort level for all involved can be improved with *diversity training*, which seeks to educate all groups about the cultures, needs, and attitudes of other groups in the workforce to ensure the inclusion of all groups in workplace activities.

A *diversity initiative* seeks to increase the diversity of the workforce or to increase the effectiveness of an already diverse workforce. As with any company-wide objective, top management support is essential for success of the initiative, as is a clear picture of the challenges the initiative will address. Communicating the purpose of the initiative and providing feedback mechanisms for employees to ask questions will help ease any fears about the changes taking place in the organization. The initiative may begin with training designed to educate employees about the need for and benefits of diversity for the organization and to explain the benefits of diversity to them as individuals. As with any HR program, an evaluation of its effectiveness should be conducted at an appropriate time.

Human Relations Concepts

The concept of human relations covers a broad spectrum of ideas that concentrate on the importance of the human element at work, including interpersonal characteristics and organizational behavior.

This approach to workplace relationships, introduced in the 1920s, challenged traditional assumptions that people work only for economic reasons and that monetary incentives provided sufficient motivation for increased productivity. Human relations theories recognized that businesses are social as well as economic systems and looked at the impact of formal (management) and informal (work group) social connections in the workplace and the impact these connections have on work processes. For the first time, there was recognition that employees are complex individuals, motivated at different times by different factors, and that increased productivity could be tied to employee job satisfaction.

Human relations theories classify intelligence into several types; of interest here are the two types of personal intelligence: intrapersonal and interpersonal. *Intrapersonal* intelligence refers to self-knowledge or how well individuals know themselves. *Interpersonal* intelligence refers to emotional intelligence and social aptitude. *Emotional intelligence* (EI) is characterized by individuals who are aware of their emotions and are able to control how they react to them. Emotionally intelligent individuals are able to motivate themselves to achieve goals and are sensitive to the emotion of others and able to manage relationships with them.

Over time, a number of tests have been developed to identify how individuals react in different situations; for example, are they confrontational, or do they attempt to mediate situations? These tests are used in some organizations to help employees work together more effectively. For example, the *Myers-Briggs Type Indicator* inventory identifies personality types with four-letter codes; the explanation of the code provides a description of the individual's personality. These tests are used in organizations to improve organizational effectiveness and increase understanding between co-workers.

HR Ethics and Professional Standards

Both the Society for Human Resource Management (SHRM) and the Human Resource Certification Institute (HRCI) have developed standards for professional behavior for the human resource profession.

The SHRM Code of Ethical and Professional Standards in Human Resource Management consists of six core principles summarized here:

Professional Responsibility   HR professionals represent their profession to their organizations. As such, they must hold themselves accountable for their decisions and ensure that their actions further the credibility of the profession.

Professional Development   HR professionals are expected to continuously expand their knowledge of the profession and the organizations in which they work.

Ethical Leadership   HR professionals are expected to model ethical behavior in their organizations and act as an example and guide to develop other ethical leaders.

Fairness and Justice   HR professionals bear a responsibility to ensure that all those with whom they come in contact and all those in their organizations are treated with dignity and respect and afforded equal employment opportunities.

Conflicts of Interest   To maintain trust in their organizations, HR professionals must avoid even the appearance of conflicts of interest and prevent situations where they appear to or actually do receive personal gain from their positions.

Use of Information   HR professionals are privy to confidential information related to their organizations and the employees who work for those organizations. As such, HR professionals have a responsibility to protect this information from inappropriate uses.

The complete text of the SHRM Code of Ethics is available at `www.shrm.org/about/Pages/code-of-ethics.aspx`.

HRCI's Model of Professional Excellence sets a high standard of professional integrity and excellence for practitioners with expectations for honesty, reliability, fairness, and cooperation at all times. The complete text is in the *PHR/SPHR/GPHR Certification Handbook*.

Human Resource Technology

With the reams of paper generated during the course of an employment relationship, the advent of the *human resource information system* (HRIS) was a clear benefit for HR professionals. An HRIS serves two purposes: first, as a repository of information, and second, as an aid to effective decision making.

HRIS Systems

As a repository of information, the HRIS provides an electronic means of storing employment documents, thereby reducing the need to maintain physical files. In firms with multiple locations, both national and global, the ability for employees to access information through the company's intranet or via the World Wide Web reduces delays in payroll-processing tasks and ensures instant access to the information for those with the authority and need to access it. For companies required to produce reports for the Equal Employment Opportunity Commission (EEOC) or the Office of Federal Contract Compliance Programs (OFCCP), electronic access to the data needed to compile reports has increased accuracy and reduced the time required to produce them.

As an effective decision-making tool, the HRIS provides access to a wealth of information needed to make strategic decisions, such as analyzing turnover trends, creating succession plans, and projecting staffing needs.

Selecting an HRIS

As with any project, the first step in selecting an HRIS is to conduct a needs analysis and identify the following:

- What information will be converted to the HRIS, and how is it currently maintained? Table 2.2 lists some uses to consider for an HRIS.

TABLE 2.2 Uses for HRIS

Applicant Tracking	COBRA Administration
Automated benefit administration	EEO/AA reporting
Tracking recruitment efforts	Administering training programs
Eliminating duplication of data entry	Compensation administration
Tracking service awards	Tracking time and attendance
Sharing payroll information with the finance department	

- Will the system need to integrate or share data with other company systems?
- Who will have access to the information, and how many levels of access will be needed (for example, to view and change individual records, view and change workgroup records, view payroll information, and so on)? Table 2.3 displays what a typical access hierarchy could look like.
- What kinds of reports will need to be produced based on the information?
- Will the HRIS be accessible via the intranet or the Web? If so, what security will be in place to protect the privacy of employees and prevent identity theft?

Once this information has been collected, research can begin on the availability and cost of a system that fulfills the requirements. This analysis should include the purchase cost for the system with a comparison to the cost of continuing to use the current system.

Implementing an HRIS

Once the HRIS installation project has been approved, some practical considerations need to be worked into the implementation schedule. If the HRIS software vendor or a third party will be handling the implementation phase, the RFP should include information about this phase of the project. If the implementation is to be done with internal IT staff, it's important to establish a timeline that works for both departments and allows the organization's HR information needs to be met during this stage.

TABLE 2.3   Typical HRIS access hierarchy

HR Access (Global Information)

Maintain employee records	Coordinate payroll administration
Administer employee benefits	Administer labor-relations programs
Post jobs	Administer safety programs
Administer compensation plan	Administer employee relations
Administer FMLA leaves	Manage recruiting
Track attendance/vacation time	Complete EEO/AAP reports
Track applicants	Administer training programs
Manage relocations	

Payroll Access (Restricted Information)

View payroll information	Administer payroll

Management Access (Restricted to Work Group)

View budget/forecast reports	Manage performance
View succession plans	Administer service awards
Track attendance/vacation time	View compensation
Manage training needs	View recruiting status
Change emergency contact, address, telephone numbers, and family status	Change payroll tax withholding
View company policies	View attendance/vacation tracking
View benefit enrollment information	Open enrollment benefit changes
Bid for internal job openings	Obtain and view paycheck stubs

When implementation is complete and the system has been tested to ensure that it's functioning correctly, the new service can be rolled out to those who will be using it. If an employee self-service component is included, this means providing the necessary level of training for all employees. Using some of the training methods described in Chapter 5 could mean this happens via small group trainings with demonstrations, with self-study computer-based test (CBT) training, or by some other means that ensures those who will need to access the system are able to do so.

Employee Self-Service

Employee self-service (ESS) allows employees to access their own records through some type of automated system. This could be through a company intranet, the Internet, an automated phone system, or a computer kiosk. Providing employees with the ability to access and make changes to routine information frees HR staff to perform other mission-critical functions and gives employees 24/7 access to their information.

Table 2.3, shown previously, identifies the kinds of access typically provided in employee self-service applications. ESS systems are evolving as technical capability continues to improve and the workforce becomes increasingly knowledgeable about computer and Web use. Access to information such as skills profiles, learning opportunities, and goal-setting guidelines empowers employees and their managers to take charge of their personal development and career planning, and facilitates successful communication in these important relationships. Advances in ESS technology also reduce repetitive administrative HR tasks, freeing professionals to concentrate on other important tasks and projects.

Applicant Tracking Systems

An *applicant tracking system* (ATS) provides an automated method for keeping track of job applicants from the time they first apply to an organization to the point when the position is filled—and beyond, if the database is searched as new openings occur. These systems range from Excel spreadsheets to sophisticated database systems that track applicant qualifications, are easily searchable based on different criteria, and provide reports that can be used for annual EEO-1 reports or Affirmative Action Plans (AAPs). Table 2.4 presents the types of information typically captured in an ATS.

Hiring Management Systems

If ATS systems ease the administrative burden of the hiring process, *hiring management systems* (HMSs) take the technology to the next level. An HMS uses technology to carry the employer brand throughout the application process. It integrates with corporate recruiting websites to simplify the candidate's experience by moving data directly from candidate input to the database. This reduces errors and improves relationship management with faster response times. HMS systems can prescreen by providing questions that will help candidates self-screen out of the process if they don't meet minimum qualifications, thus reducing the time recruiters spend reviewing resumes of unqualified candidates.

An HMS also provides additional recruiter support with templates to standardize candidate communication and facilitate communication between recruiters in large organizations. Most HMS systems include customizable report writers that can be used to answer questions about specific jobs or the recruiting system in general.

TABLE 2.4 Typical ATS capabilities

Applicant Information	Open Positions	Recruiter Needs
Resume upload	List of open positions	Applicant contact information
Application upload	Job descriptions	Search by applicant information
Applicant profile	Hiring manager access	Search by qualifications
Applicant auto-response	Job posting	Information security
Comments		EEOC report information
Link resume to profile		Report generator

Learning Management Systems

A *learning management system* (LMS) streamlines the administration of employee training programs. The components included in an LMS depend on organization size and the complexity of training needs. These systems can be used to automatically enroll students in required courses (such as safety trainings required by OSHA) and notify managers when employees don't attend. The programs can provide managers with access to approve training requested by employees and to identify skill-development needs in their departments or for individual employees. An LMS can maintain curriculum for required (or optional) courses and provide access on an individual, functional, or organizational basis. Other administrative functions performed by LMS programs include course calendars, facility assignments, pre- and post-testing, and report generation. An LMS can also include self-service functions that eliminate tedious administrative chores from daily HR tasks, such as registering employees, notifying participants, obtaining approvals, and maintaining waitlists. Table 2.5 summarizes the functions available in an LMS system.

TABLE 2.5 LMS system functions

HR Tasks	Training Tasks	User Benefits
Streamline process (automate recordkeeping, notices, and reminders)	Manage resources: facilities, instructors, and equipment	Employees: self-registration, Web access, online learning
Automatic enrollment for mandated courses	Manage course calendar	Managers: approve employee requests, access to online assessment tools, plan department trainings
Verify qualifications	Self-registration	
Manage waiting lists	Web-based delivery	
Generate reports	Deliver/score tests, including pre- and post-tests Score and record course work	

An LMS is capable of managing the organization's learning tasks in a wide range of situations, from tracking attendance, maintaining training calendars, and generating reports to delivering Web-based content to participants, administering and scoring tests, and providing planning tools for managers.

The next step in LMS development seems to be Learning and Performance Management Systems (LPMSs) that incorporate functions for managing performance (including 360-degree assessments, self-evaluations, succession planning, and manager feedback) and that track individual rewards. These functions improve a manager's ability to assess performance, assign training to address areas of improvement, and prepare employees for the next level in their career growth.

Organizations that develop their own content use Learning Content Management Systems (LCMSs) to create, deliver, and modify course content. These systems allow trainers to develop content, often in a module format so a single module can be used in multiple training courses. For example, a geographically dispersed organization may create an orientation program with different modules for corporate information, employee benefit options, expense reporting, and other information common to employees throughout the organization, along with modules for each geographic location. This allows an HR professional in a regional office to provide a customized orientation that includes information specific to that office along with relevant information about the corporation at large.

Qualitative and Quantitative Analysis

Making business decisions requires accurate and reliable information; without it, for example, a decision can result in excess inventory rather than increased profits because demand for the product was less than projected. Because there are no crystal balls in the boardroom, business leaders must rely on the judgment of experienced managers and an analysis of historical data to predict possible future trends.

There are two types of research: primary and secondary. *Primary research* is original, meaning that the researcher has performed the research. *Secondary research* is based on information that has been collected or reported by others, such as books or articles by primary researchers, industry standards, or analysis of trends in an organization.

One very formal method of primary research is known as the *scientific method*, and although it isn't generally identified as such in analyzing business problems, the process is similar to the way in which business problems are analyzed prior to making decisions. There are five steps to the scientific method. Using a common business problem, absenteeism, the following analysis shows how these steps can be used in solving HR problems:

1. Identify a problem:

   Absenteeism is too high.

2. Create a hypothesis:

   The absentee rate is higher with new employees.

3. Decide how to test the hypothesis:

   A correlation analysis of length of employment and attendance data will confirm or not confirm the hypothesis.

4. Collect data to verify the hypothesis:

   Review employee files and attendance records. Correlate hire date and number of absences for each employee.

5. Draw conclusions/analyze the data:

   Does the correlation analysis verify or not verify the hypothesis?

The result of the analysis will either prove the hypothesis, that absences are higher among new employees, or disprove it. Sometimes, the process of analyzing data may shed light on other factors that contribute to the problem.

Another issue to consider is whether there will be a control group in the test. Using a control group tells the researcher whether the hypothesis being tested causes the result or whether the result is the same with both the group being tested and the control group.

In many situations, secondary research also provides valuable insights for HR professionals looking for ways to solve problems in their organizations. For example, the SHRM website offers a variety of white papers and toolkits created by practitioners to solve problems encountered in specific organizations. Accessing these tools provides insight into how other professionals have solved various problems common to many organizations and can be used to develop solutions without reinventing the wheel.

Data Collection

Collecting data is an important element of the analysis process; if the proper data isn't collected, any decision based on it, regardless of the method of analysis used, won't be an accurate decision. So, how do you find reliable data to use in analyzing HR problems? Here are some sources to consider:

Personnel Records   Personnel records provide information used for analyzing trends. For the absentee example, personnel records describe how long each employee has worked for the company as well as how often the employee is absent from work.

Observations   The hypothesis for the absentee example could have been based on the observation of a general manager who noticed that several new employees were frequently absent.

Interviews   Interviews provide direct information about problems. The HR department can interview some new employees to find out how often they're absent and why. This data-collection method can provide more information than records, but its relevance depends on the frankness of the people being interviewed and their willingness to share information. In addition, interviews are time-consuming and may not be cost effective for that reason.

Focus Groups   Focus groups are often used to find out how people feel about products or advertisements. They can also be an effective method for gathering information for HR analysis, but again, they're subject to the willingness of participants to open up. In a focus group, this willingness may be inhibited by the presence of co-workers or supervisors.

Questionnaires   Questionnaires can be an effective means of gathering information from large groups of geographically dispersed employees but are limited in the types of data that can be collected.

Once data has been collected, there are two basic categories of data-analysis tools: quantitative analysis methods based on mathematical models and qualitative analysis methods based on the best judgment of experienced managers or SMEs.

Analysis Tools

A number of different tools are available for data analysis, and they fall into two basic categories: quantitative tools and qualitative tools. Both types of analysis have benefits and drawbacks; relying on a single method may not provide the most comprehensive analysis. Using several different tools helps minimize errors.

Quantitative Analysis

Quantitative analysis tools are based on mathematical models for measuring historical data. Several of these measures provide useful data for HR decisions. Some quantitative analyses commonly used to analyze HR and other business data include the following:

Correlation   A *correlation* measures two variables to determine whether there is a relationship between them. For example, if the HR department posts a quarterly reminder of the referral bonus that is paid for new hires, a correlation analysis could be used to determine whether there is an increase in referrals in the weeks after the reminder.

Correlation Coefficient   The *correlation coefficient* describes the relationship between two variables and is stated as a number between –1.0 and +1.0.

For example, say the HR department wants to find out what factors contribute to absenteeism in the company. One of the factors they decide to analyze is length of time at the company, so one hypothesis they might use is "The absentee rate is higher with new employees."

To analyze this, they would collect two numbers for each employee: how many months employed and how many days absent. The numbers are then plotted on a graph for analysis.

If this hypothesis is correct, they would expect to see a *negative* correlation coefficient; that is, the shorter the length of time employed, the higher the absentee rate. This would be reflected by a negative number: for example, –.2. Figure 2.2 shows how this looks.

FIGURE 2.2   Negative correlation

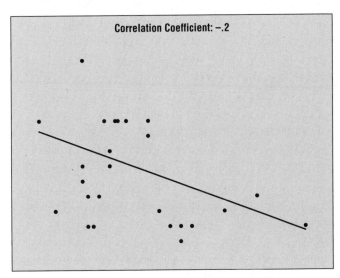

A *positive* correlation coefficient would tell HR that the opposite is true—that the absentee rate is actually higher when employees have longer tenure with the company. This would be reflected by a positive number, such as +.8. Figure 2.3 shows what this would look like.

If there were no correlation at all—that is, if length of employment had nothing to do with absenteeism—the correlation coefficient would be 0.0, as shown in Figure 2.4.

FIGURE 2.3 Positive correlation

FIGURE 2.4 No correlation

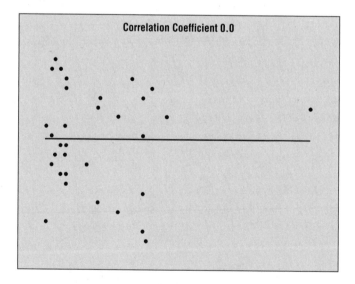

The steeper the trend line (the higher the absolute number), the greater the connection between the two variables. In the absentee example, the positive correlation (+.8) reflects a stronger connection between a longer amount of time with the company and more absences than the example of negative correlation (−.2).

Measures of Central Tendency   Central tendency is often referred to as the *average*. Several measures can be used in analyzing data:

Mean Average   The *mean average* is the sum of the values in a set of numbers, divided by the number of values in the set.

Mode   The *mode* is the number that occurs most frequently in a set of numbers.

Median   The *median* can be found by putting the numbers in a set in sequential order. The median is at the physical center, so half the numbers are below it and half are above it.

Moving Average   Sometimes called a *rolling average*, the *moving average* is used to calculate an average for a specific period: for example, to calculate the average number of new hires each month for the past 12 months. As the number for the most recent month is added, the oldest number is dropped.

Weighted Average   A *weighted average* is used to compensate for data that may be out of date; the more current data is multiplied by a predetermined number to better reflect the current situation.

Weighted Moving Average   The *weighted moving average* calculation assigns more weight to current data with the use of a predetermined number and drops the oldest data when new data is added.

Time-Series Forecasts   Several *time-series forecasts* exist that can be used to measure historic data and provide a basis for projecting future requirements. One example of how HR uses these tools is in the area of staffing levels; but they're useful in analyzing many other areas as well, including benefit utilization, compensation trends, and the effectiveness of a recruiting system. For purposes of discussion, staffing-level analysis is used to demonstrate how each of the following tools is used:

Trend Analysis   *Trend analysis* compares the changes in a single variable over time; over a period of years, they generally move upward or downward. For example, this tool can reveal information about seasonal staffing requirements, which are periods of time within a one-year period that regularly vary from the general trend. *Cycles*, periods of time during which a pattern of performance is shown (growing, peaking, declining, and plateauing at the lower level), also become apparent in a trend analysis.

Simple Linear Regression   *Simple linear regression* measures the relationship between one variable (for example, staffing) against another variable (such as production output) and allows prediction of one variable from the other. For example, measuring the number of units produced against the number of employees producing the units over a period of years would allow the analyst to forecast the number of employees needed to meet an increase in demand.

Multiple Linear Regression   *Multiple linear regression* measures the relationship between several variables to forecast another. An application of this model in workforce planning would be to determine whether there is a relationship between lower staffing levels, absenteeism, and production output.

Simulation Models   Simulation models allow several possible plans to be tested in abstract form. For example, an organization that wants to know the predicted results of different staffing alternatives can use a simulation model to determine which is the most cost effective.

Ratios   Ratios provide a benchmark based on the historic relationship of one variable to another. For example, the average HR staffing ratio is generally considered to be 1:100. As an organization's workforce increases or decreases, this ratio can provide an estimate of the number of staff required to provide services for the general employee population.

Qualitative Analysis

Qualitative analysis tools are subjective evaluations of general observations and information and include various types of judgmental forecasts. These tools can be as simple as an estimate made by a knowledgeable executive (for example, an experienced sales manager may be able to predict quite accurately by the end of the first month of a quarter whether the sales goal will be met). In other situations, the tools can be as involved as formalized brainstorming using a Delphi or nominal group technique.

The *Delphi technique* obtains input from a group of individuals who provide their expertise in succeeding rounds of questions about an issue or problem. After each round, the results are collated, prioritized, and returned to the participants in the form of additional questions for further analysis until a consensus is reached. An important factor of the Delphi technique is that the participants never meet but provide their input in written form. This technique has several benefits, including the fact that it's a viable alternative when participants are geographically separated and that it encourages a wide variety of ideas that might otherwise not be considered.

The *nominal group technique* is a structured meeting format designed to elicit participation from all members of the group in order to arrive at the best possible solution to the problem at hand. The process requires a facilitator and begins with a period of time for individuals to think about and write down all their ideas about the issue. After that, each participant presents one idea, which is recorded by the facilitator for later discussion. When all the ideas have been presented, the process of prioritizing and consensus building takes place until a resolution has been agreed on.

Choosing appropriate tools for data analysis provides the HR professional with a comprehensive view of what is needed to accomplish department and organization goals.

Metrics: Measuring Results

Metrics provide a standard of measurement that can be used to compare results over time. The value of this measurement for HR is that it can be used to quantify activities and programs to demonstrate the value added to the organization. The most important factor to consider in determining which metrics to use in a specific organization is a simple one: measure what is relevant and meaningful to management and what will add value to the decision-making process.

Determining which specific metrics will add value to any particular organization is best done by those who work in the organization and know how it operates and what metrics will be useful to assess past experience and project future needs. Two types of metrics are useful for HR professionals: those that measure business impact and those that measure tactical accountability. At the end of each of the following chapters, a section titled "HR Metrics: Measuring Results" provides some commonly used metrics for that functional area:

Business Impact Measures   Business impact measures demonstrate how a particular HR program or activity adds value to the bottom line. Two metrics that are useful in measuring business impact are ROI and cost/benefit analysis:

Return on Investment   One of the most commonly used business metrics is *return on investment* (ROI). ROI is calculated by dividing the benefits realized as a result of a program by the total related direct and indirect costs.

Cost/Benefit Analysis   A *cost/benefit analysis* (CBA) compares all costs of a proposed program to the benefits that will be realized if it's implemented and forecasts the net impact on the bottom line. CBA can be used to evaluate the cost effectiveness of several alternatives and recommend a preferred course of action. The difference between CBA and ROI is that CBA includes soft costs in the calculation, whereas ROI generally includes only hard costs.

Tactical Accountability Measures   Tactical accountability measures provide relevant information for evaluating the effectiveness of specific HR programs. These measures identify how well programs for workforce management issues, productivity, and other HR activities are working. Some measures commonly used for this purpose include the following:

- Job satisfaction
- Organizational commitment and involvement
- Training cost per employee
- Cost per hire
- Turnover and retention
- Absenteeism and sick-leave use and frequency
- Grievance rates
- Terminations as a percent of population

Building a Business Case   A business case is used to evaluate the possible consequences of taking (or not taking) a particular action, such as implementing an HRIS system, for example. A business case identifies what criteria will be used to determine success, proposes alternative ways to execute the action, and describes possible risks that could result from implementing or not implementing the proposal. An extended timeline demonstrates the impact of the program on cash flow, identifying where cost reductions or gains are to be expected. An important element is the description of the basis for quantifying benefits and costs so that those reviewing the proposal clearly understand the assumptions that led to the final recommendation or decision.

Change Management

Change management is another concept that will be more fully developed in Chapter 5. Its reason for inclusion as a core knowledge requirement is simple: change is everywhere. Processes change constantly to meet changing business needs. People change jobs. Economies change. Government regulations change. All these changes and many others must be addressed with HR programs that are flexible enough to take in the changes while continuing to serve the needs of people in the organization.

Major changes in an organization occur as the result of restructuring, mergers or acquisitions, "right-sizing," and workforce expansions. All these changes require the workforce to adjust to new ways of operating.

For example, when mergers or acquisitions occur, two organizations, two sets of processes, two cultures, and two groups of people doing similar jobs must acclimate to each other to ensure the success of the business. The process is stressful for employees because, almost inevitably, some people will lose their jobs as the organization eliminates redundancy from its operations. Maintaining morale and productivity during this process often presents a monumental challenge for organizations and HR professionals.

A key element of managing change is ensuring that employees receive current information as soon as possible. Although management is often tempted to "wait until we have all the answers," the absence of information creates added stress and apprehension that hinders the acceptance of change by employees. Keeping employees abreast of a situation in flux, even by telling them that all decisions haven't been made yet, builds trust that they won't be left in the dark about what is happening.

In general, people resist change for many reasons, some of which can be explained by the motivational theories discussed earlier in this chapter. Change removes the underlying sense of safety and impacts the social structures people create around them in organizations. This makes it difficult for them to accept change, particularly when there is a lack of certainty about the future. Balancing the organization's need to continually adapt to changes in the business environment with the employee's need for clarity and direction presents challenges for every functional area of human resources.

As with any other operational theory, change management is a process that can be mapped out in a logical sequence of events when working with the end in mind. Starting with the desired outcome, an HR professional can select and apply the appropriate change management theory (CMT) for their specific needs. Total quality management (TQM), business process reengineering (BPR), and Six Sigma are examples of CMTs that are explored in more detail in Chapter 5.

For the exam, it isn't enough to have some basic knowledge of these types of theories. The *BOK* specifies that the student will have an understanding of the theory, methods, and application of change management.

Job Analysis and Description

Job analysis and job descriptions provide the foundation for much of what happens in the employment relationship. The job description compiles all the information collected during the job analysis into a document that is used for multiple purposes in the organization, beginning with the hiring process:

- Based on the job description, the recruiter screens applicants to ensure that their KSAs are appropriate for the position.
- The applicants for the position use the job description to find out what they will be required to do if the position is offered to them.
- The job description is the basis for performance management and appraisal.
- The job description is the basis for determining the appropriate level of pay for the work that is done.
- The job description includes the essential job functions and provides a guideline for employees who request reasonable accommodation for disabilities.

Job descriptions are also used to determine competitive compensation, to classify employees properly for equal-opportunity and affirmative-action reports, and for many other aspects of employment. It's essential, therefore, that these processes produce full and complete information about the jobs in the organization.

Job Analysis

The purpose of job analysis is to define a job so that it can be understood in the context of accomplishing organizational goals and objectives. To do this, information that describes the work to be done must be collected. Information can be collected during the job analysis process in several ways:

- Interview the incumbent if available.
- Interview the supervisor or a group of co-workers.
- Complete a structured or an open-ended questionnaire.
- Complete a task inventory.
- Observe incumbents and make notes.
- Use work logs kept by incumbents.

The information gathered during the analysis is summarized in a job description that is used for the various purposes described previously.

Job Descriptions

Job descriptions are written documents that contain information about a job. The description includes the following information:

Identifying Information   The job description is identified with the title of the position, department, supervisor's title, Fair Labor Standards Act (FLSA) exemption status, salary range or grade, and the date it was created.

Supervisory Responsibilities   If the position has responsibility for supervising others, a description of those leadership responsibilities is listed in this section.

Position Summary   The summary provides a brief overview of the job and its primary purpose, usually two to five sentences.

Essential Functions   *Essential job functions* are the reason the job exists and must be performed by the incumbent. This information is required to comply with the Americans with Disabilities Act (ADA), to be discussed in Chapter 4. Each function should include a description of the level of complexity and the frequency of tasks. As appropriate, the functions describe relationships that the incumbent will have, including supervisory, with co-workers in the work group, with co-workers in other departments of the company, and any external relationships with vendors or customers, and the level of interaction that will take place in these relationships.

Nonessential Functions   *Nonessential job functions* are those that could be performed as part of another job in the organization. For ADA purposes, these functions could be moved into other jobs as a reasonable accommodation for a disabled employee who is fully qualified to perform the essential job functions.

Equipment Operated   This section lists tools or equipment that will be used and the frequency of use. This includes use of the computer, telephone, and production equipment; any hazardous equipment or tools that will be used; and protective gear or uniforms that will be required.

Job Specifications   Job specifications state the minimum qualifications needed for successful performance. Depending on the job, some or all of the following may be required specifications:

> **Education, Licenses, or Certificates Required**   Minimum required qualifications are described in this section. The requirements must be related to the essential job functions to comply with the ADA.

Communication Skills Required   A description of the level of communication skills necessary to do the job is included in this section. Will the position be writing reports, making presentations internally or externally, or communicating orally?

Experience Required   The minimum level of experience required to successfully perform the position is identified.

Skills   Any skills necessary for successful job performance are included in this section.

Physical Requirements   Any physical requirements must be described to comply with the ADA. The physical requirements must be related to the essential job functions.

Mental Requirements   For ADA purposes, describe the level of mental acuity required to perform essential job functions.

Work Environment   The work environment is described, whether it's in an office setting or includes any hazardous equipment or locations that will impact the employee. If stairs or ladders must be used or the job will require work in confined spaces, this must be included as well.

Approvals   The job description should be signed by the manager to verify its accuracy.

During the job analysis process, it's important to keep in mind that the analysis focuses on the *job*, not the *person*. Particularly when a high-performing employee has been in a particular job for any length of time, it can be difficult to separate what the employee brings to the job from the job's main purpose.

Employee Records Management

Not surprisingly, mounds of paperwork are generated in the employment process; resumes, applications, references, government forms, and performance evaluations are just a few of the many documents created for each employee. In enacting employment legislation, Congress has mandated retention requirements for various documents that, unfortunately, aren't consistent. In addition, many state and local governments have retention requirements that differ from federal requirements.

Table 2.6 lists federal document-retention requirements for the PHR/SPHR exams; these may be different from the state and local requirements where you practice, so keep that in mind while you're studying. As with any other conflicting requirements, documents should be retained in accordance with the strictest requirement.

TABLE 2.6 Federal employment document-retention requirements

Federal Law or Regulation	Document(s) Covered	Retention Period	Covered Employers
Title VII of the Civil Rights Act of 1964 (Title VII)	Records of all employment actions: employment applications, resumes, hires, rehires, layoffs, recalls, terminations, promotions, demotions, transfers, compensation	1 year	15+ employees
	Apprentice selection records Name, address, Social Security number, gender, date of birth, occupation, job classification Compensation records (direct and indirect), tax forms, records of hours worked, benefit payments, tax deductions Current EEO-1 Report	1) 2 years or period of apprenticeship, whichever is longer, or 2) 1 year from date of report	
Title VII of the Civil Rights Act of 1964 (Title VII)	Personnel records related to discrimination charges	Required: until resolution	15+ employees
Americans with Disabilities Act (ADA)		Best practice: 7 years after employee leaves (for use in future litigation)	15+ employees
Age Discrimination in Employment Act of 1967 (ADEA)	Personnel records related to discrimination charges	Required: until resolution Best practice: 7 years after employee leaves (for use in future litigation)	20+ employees

Federal Law or Regulation	Document(s) Covered	Retention Period	Covered Employers
Rehabilitation Act of 1973 (RA)	Personnel records related to discrimination charges	Required: until resolution Best practice: 7 years after employee leaves (for use in future litigation)	Federal contractors and subcontractors with contracts of $10,000+
Americans with Disabilities Act (ADA) of 1990; Americans with Disabilities Act Amendments Act (ADAAA) as amended in 2008	Job announcements, advertisements, and job orders sent to agencies or unions Records of all employment actions: applications, resumes, promotions, transfers, demotions, layoffs, terminations Reasonable accommodation requests Name, address, Social Security number, gender, date of birth, occupation, job classification Compensation records (direct and indirect), tax forms, records of hours worked, benefit payments, tax deductions	1 year	15+ employees
Age Discrimination in Employment Act of 1967 (ADEA)	Compensation records (direct and indirect), tax forms, records of hours worked, benefit payments, tax deductions Name, address, Social Security number, gender, date of birth, occupation, job classification	3 years	20+ employees

TABLE 2.6 Federal employment document-retention requirements *(continued)*

Federal Law or Regulation	Document(s) Covered	Retention Period	Covered Employers
Age Discrimination in Employment Act of 1967 (ADEA)	Job announcements, advertisements, and job orders sent to agencies or unions Records of all employment actions: applications, resumes, promotions, transfers, demotions, layoffs, terminations Pre-employment records for temp positions Employment test results Physical examination results Training records	1 year	20+ employees
Age Discrimination in Employment Act of 1967 (ADEA)	Employee benefit plans Written merit plans	1 year after plan ends	20+ employees
Age Discrimination in Employment Act of 1967 (ADEA)	Temporary employee records	90 days	20+ employees
Consolidated Omnibus Budget Reconciliation Act (COBRA)	Written COBRA procedures Payment records and correspondence Documentation that COBRA notices are sent within specified time period	6 years (required by Employee Retirement Income Security Act [ERISA])	20+ employees

Federal Law or Regulation	Document(s) Covered	Retention Period	Covered Employers
Davis-Bacon Act	Name, address, Social Security number, gender, date of birth, occupation, job classification	3 years from end of contract	Federal construction contractors and subcontractors with contracts of $2,000+
	Compensation records (direct and indirect), tax forms, records of hours worked, benefit payments, tax deductions		
Employee Polygraph Protection Act (EPPA)	Reason for test administration	3 years	All employers
	Test results		
Employee Retirement Income Security Act of 1974 (ERISA)	Dated and signed documentation of employee receipt of plan reports and disclosures	Indefinitely	All employers except churches and governments
	Beneficiary designation and distribution elections—beneficiary distribution		
	Documentation for eligibility determinations: age, length of service record, marital status		
Employee Retirement Income Security Act of 1974 (ERISA)	Copies of summary plan descriptions and annual reports, COBRA notices, and other plan reports	6 years after filing date	All employers except churches and governments
	Wage and hour records used to determine retirement benefits		
Employee Retirement Income Security Act of 1974 (ERISA)	Beneficiary designation and distribution elections—participant distribution	3 years	All employers except churches and governments

TABLE 2.6   Federal employment document-retention requirements *(continued)*

Federal Law or Regulation	Document(s) Covered	Retention Period	Covered Employers
Equal Pay Act (EPA)	Date of birth for employees younger than 19 Gender Occupation Payroll records: time cards, wage/salary rate, deductions, explanation for difference between rates for men and women	3 years	All employers
Executive Order 11246	AAP and supporting documents	2 years	Federal contractors and subcontractors with 50+ employees and contracts of $50,000+
Fair Labor Standards Act (FLSA)	Collective bargaining agreements Individual employment contracts Sale and purchase records Date of birth for employees under 19 Payroll records, including record of name, birth date, gender, occupation Basis for salary calculations for exempt employees Written training agreements, job and selection criteria, records of minority and female applicants	3 years	All employers

Federal Law or Regulation	Document(s) Covered	Retention Period	Covered Employers
Fair Labor Standards Act (FLSA)	Regular pay rate Beginning of work week, start time Straight time and overtime earnings calculations (day/week) Total wages for pay period Pay deductions Pay period and date of payment Basis for payment of wages Work schedules	2 years	All employers
Fair Labor Standards Act (FLSA)	Job announcements, advertisements, and job orders sent to agencies or unions	1 year	All employers
Fair Labor Standards Act (FLSA)	Certificate of age	Until termination	All employers
Family and Medical Leave Act (FMLA)	Basic employee information: name, address, title, compensation, employment terms, hours worked, wage deductions Employee notices and description of policy Records of leave dates and hours of intermittent leave Benefit premium payments Documentation of disputes about FMLA leave	3 years	50+ employees within a 75-mile radius
Federal Insurance Contributions Act (FICA)	Income tax withholding information	4 years	All employers

TABLE 2.6 Federal employment document-retention requirements *(continued)*

Federal Law or Regulation	Document(s) Covered	Retention Period	Covered Employers
Federal Unemployment Tax Act (FUTA)	Income tax withholding information	4 years	All employers
Immigration Reform and Control Act (IRCA)	I-9 signed by employee and employer	3 years from hire date *or* 1 year after termination (whichever is longer)	4+ employees
National Labor Relations Act (NLRA)	Collective bargaining agreements Individual employment contracts Sale and purchase records Written training agreements, job and selection criteria, records of minority and female applicants	3 years	All employers
National Labor Relations Act (NLRA)	Straight time and overtime earnings calculations (day/week) Basis for payment of wages Total wages for pay period Pay deductions Pay period and date of payment Work schedules	2 years	All employers
National Labor Relations Act (NLRA)	Certificate of age	Until termination	All employers
Occupational Safety and Health Act (OSHA)	Safety and health training records	3 years	11+ employees

Federal Law or Regulation	Document(s) Covered	Retention Period	Covered Employers
Occupational Safety and Health Act (OSHA)	Illness and injury logs Supplementary injury and illness records Employer records of adverse reaction to chemical substances	5 years	11+ employees
Occupational Safety and Health Act (OSHA)	Medical exam records for exposures to toxic substances Medical exam records for exposures to blood-borne pathogens Hazardous material exposure records	30 years	11+ employees
Rehabilitation Act of 1973 (RA)	Job announcements, advertisements, and job orders sent to agencies or unions Records of all employment actions: applications, resumes, promotions, transfers, demotions, layoffs, terminations Employment test results Physical examination results Training records Name, address, Social Security number, gender, date of birth, occupation, job classification Compensation records (direct and indirect), tax forms, records of hours worked, benefit payments, tax deductions	Retain for 2 years (1 year if less than 150 employees)	Federal contractors and subcontractors with contracts of $10,000+

TABLE 2.6   Federal employment document-retention requirements *(continued)*

Federal Law or Regulation	Document(s) Covered	Retention Period	Covered Employers
Service Contract Act (SCA)	Name, address, Social Security number, gender, date of birth, occupation, job classification Compensation records (direct and indirect), tax forms, records of hours worked, benefit payments, tax deductions Wages and tax deductions	3 years from end of contract	Federal service contractors and subcontractors with contracts of $2,500+
Social Security Act	Employee name and ID number Social Security number Employee home address with ZIP code	4 years from tax due date	All employers
Toxic Substance Control Act (TSCA)	Documentation of hazardous material exposures Documentation of significant adverse reactions to work environment Claims of occupational disease or health problems	30 years from report date	Manufacturers, importers, processors, and distributors of toxic chemicals
Uniform Guidelines on Employee Selection Procedures (UGESP)	Applicant race and sex Employee race and sex Veteran status Disability status	2 years for 150+ employees; 1 year if less	Employers subject to Title VII, EO 11246, and other EEO laws (ADEA and RA are exempt)

Federal Law or Regulation	Document(s) Covered	Retention Period	Covered Employers
Vietnam Era Veterans' Readjustment Assistance Act (VEVRAA)	AAP for current and prior year	2 years	Federal contractors and subcontractors with contracts of $25,000+
	Documentation of good faith effort to comply with AAP		
	Job announcements, advertisements, and job orders sent to agencies or unions		
	Records of all employment actions: applications, resumes, promotions, transfers, demotions, layoffs, terminations		
	Employment test results		
	Physical examination results		
	Training records		
	Name, address, Social Security number, gender, date of birth, occupation, job classification		
	Compensation records (direct and indirect), tax forms, records of hours worked, benefit payments, tax deductions		
Walsh-Healey Public Contracts Act (PCA)	Name, address, Social Security number, gender, date of birth, occupation, job classification	3 years from end of contract	Federal contractors and subcontractors with contracts of $10,000+
	Compensation records (direct and indirect), tax forms, records of hours worked, benefit payments, tax deductions		

Interrelationships Among HR Activities

It has become increasingly important for HR practitioners to understand how individual HR programs, processes, policies, and functions interact with each other. Particularly for SPHR candidates, the ability to link together various aspects of best practices and legal requirements from a variety of functional HR areas, along with being able to evaluate the impact of these activities as a whole, is crucial to exam success. The Real World Scenario "Changing the Compensation Plan" demonstrates how the functions interact.

Probably the best example of the way HR programs and activities connect to each other is the area of talent management. This activity unites the HR functions that build, retain, develop, and manage a workforce capable of taking an organization into the future. The talent-management approach incorporates several human resource activities—planning for future workforce needs; recruiting, retaining, and developing employees; managing their performance; and creating a positive and supportive culture.

 Real World Scenario

Changing the Compensation Plan

Wright Sisters Inc. (WSI) manufactures garden equipment and employs about 3,000 people, most of whom work on the production line. WSI prides itself on the quality of its products and the loyalty and dedication of its workforce. For many years, WSI has been considered one of the best places to work in the community; as a result, the company was able to be selective about who it hired. About six months ago, a new plant opened in the area, and WSI now faces unaccustomed competition in the labor market. Candidate quality has declined noticeably in recent months, and line managers are having some problems maintaining product quality. Senior management is considering a number of options to solve the problem.

Although the pay being offered by the other company is about the same as WSI's pay plan, the new plant is located in a new building with many amenities that WSI's building doesn't offer. Making changes to the building would require a lengthy remodeling process, and WSI's management wants to take some immediate steps to increase the quality of the candidates WSI is attracting. As a result, management has decided to increase the starting pay for new hires. At the same time, management is unwilling to make any changes to pay rates for current workers. As the Vice President of HR (VP) contemplates this decision, she foresees some problems:

- Because management isn't willing to consider a change to the pay ranges even though they're increasing the starting pay, compression will become an issue in a very short period of time.

- Once word gets out that new employees are making more than employees with more seniority, the VP foresees an increase in employee relations issues, most notably morale problems among the production workers. As she is well aware, morale problems generally lead to decreases in productivity and quality.

- Although WSI's workforce has remained loyal to this point, with only a very few defections to the new plant, the VP is concerned that there will be an increase in turnover when employees feel their loyalty isn't appreciated.

- Management has always been very open and responsive to employee concerns, so employees haven't been susceptible to union-organizing efforts. The VP is concerned that this change will open the door for an organizing campaign.

- Finally, the VP is concerned about possible claims of discrimination, because much of WSI's workforce is older than the average age of applicants for these positions.

As she considers these issues, the VP begins work on a presentation for management to ensure that they understand all the implications of this change prior to its implementation; although this change may temporarily solve the recruiting issue, it could easily lead to increased costs in a number of areas.

Chapter 4 describes how workforce planning, including recruitment and retention, is used to attract individuals with the right skills. One of the tools used to retain key employees is development, discussed in Chapter 5. Another element of talent management discussed in Chapter 5 is an effective performance-management program that provides ongoing feedback to employees so they can continue to improve their skills and knowledge. Chapter 7 discusses the importance of a positive organization culture and the impact it has on the retention of qualified, productive employees.

There are two schools of thought about which employees should be included in talent-management initiatives. Some organizations take a very narrow view, and talent management focuses on high-potential employees being groomed for leadership positions. Other organizations take a broader view, recognizing the need to retain talented individuals at all levels. Although it's crucial to have talented, effective individuals at senior organization levels, front-line employees are often more visible to customers, and the impact these individuals have in one-on-one interactions affects organization success. Management philosophy and budget constraints have an impact on which philosophy is embraced in different organizations.

Data collection is critical in assessing the need for HR activities across departments. Taking part in the strategic planning process allows HR to anticipate interventions, plan for training and development programs, and reallocate resources depending on the needs of the strategic initiative. For example, a company that plans to expand overseas will need the help of HR to consider offshoring business functions, remote talent-management plans, compensation structures, and cultural implications. The development of new products or services is another example of a strategic initiative that would require the aid of HR. Analyzing the new work, assessing the talent availability of the internal and external labor force, and reviewing potential safety issues are examples of how HR can influence the success of this type of organizational strategy.

Understanding the impact of individual programs on the HR function, as well as on the organization as a whole, is key to increasing the strategic value of HR to organizations. As you study the material in this book, keep in mind the possible impact of the various principles, theories, laws, and regulations on HR activities and programs. In this way, you'll gain a better understanding and appreciation of their role in HR.

Organizational Structures

Keeping a large group of people with different perspectives and assignments moving in the same direction is a challenge for organizations. *Organizational structures* were designed to provide a framework that keeps information flowing to the functions and employees who need it to keep the organization moving forward. Some structures are more successful at this than others, and over time, as the business environment changed, different structures were developed to solve the shortcomings of traditional structures. In some cases, organizations may use different structures in different business units. For example, the vice president of sales in an organization with a functional structure reports to the CEO, but the sales organization may be organized with a geographic or product structure for the most efficient management of the sales operation:

Functional Structure   The *functional organization structure* is represented by the traditional pyramid-shape organization chart with which most people are familiar. It's a hierarchical structure in which communication moves from the top down and from the bottom up. These structures are more formal and rigid than some other structures and are appropriate for businesses with a single product line where specialization is an advantage. In this structure, each functional area reports to the CEO. Functional organizations are generally very centralized. Figure 2.5 depicts the traditional functional structure.

FIGURE 2.5   Functional organization structure

Product-Based Structure   A *product-based organization structure*, also known as a *customer-oriented structure*, is organized by product line and is appropriate when the company has well-defined product lines that are clearly separate from each other. In this structure, each product line reports to the CEO; these structures lend themselves to either centralized or decentralized decision-making processes. Figure 2.6 displays a product-based structure.

FIGURE 2.6   Product-based organization structure

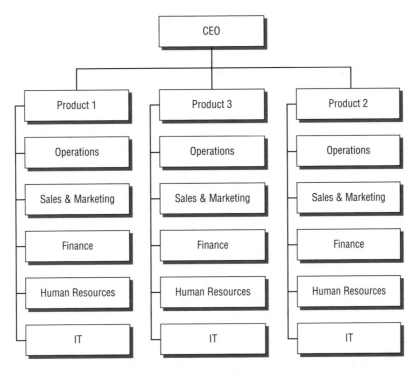

Geographic Structure   In a *geographic organization structure*, executives of regional areas are responsible for all the business functions in their assigned region; the regional executives report to the CEO. Structuring an organization in this way is appropriate when there are common requirements in the region that are different from the requirements in other regions. Geographic structures are decentralized, with most decisions being made at the local level. Figure 2.7 depicts a geographic structure.

Divisional Structure   A *divisional organization structure* has characteristics similar to that of the geographic structure, but the divisions may be based on criteria other than geography, such as the market or industry. Like the geographic structure, divisional structures are characterized by decentralized decision making. Figure 2.8 shows a sample division structure.

FIGURE 2.7   Geographic organization structure

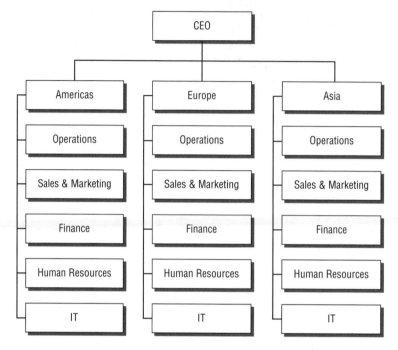

FIGURE 2.8   Divisional organization structure

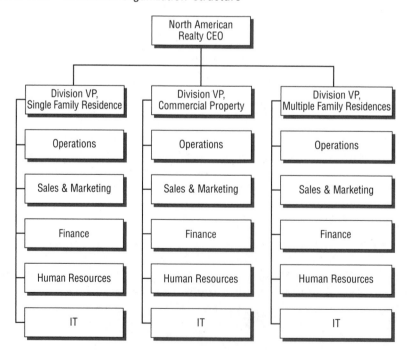

Matrix Structure   In a *matrix organization structure*, employees report to two managers. Generally, one manager is responsible for a product line, and the other has functional responsibility. For example, the VP of marketing and the production manager for a specific product would both supervise the marketing coordinator who is creating collateral for the product. A matrix organization is advantageous because it encourages communication and cooperation; it requires a high level of trust and communication from employees at all levels to ensure that contradictory instructions are minimized. Figure 2.9 depicts a matrix structure.

FIGURE 2.9   Matrix organization structure

Seamless Organization   A *seamless organization* is one in which the traditional hierarchies don't exist—it's a horizontal organization connected by networks instead of separated by the boundaries that characterize other organization structures. The purpose of this structure is to enhance communication and creativity. Seamless organizations wouldn't be possible without the technology that allows employees to connect with each other via email and the Internet from anywhere in the world. This technology enables employees to meet with co-workers who have specialized knowledge without the expense of traveling.

Environmental Scanning Concepts

To develop a strategic plan and set the future direction of a company or develop human resource programs to support its growth, leaders need to know what is going on in the organization, in the industry, and in the marketplace, and they need to know how technological developments will affect operations. An *environmental scan* provides the framework for collecting information about factors relevant to the decision-making process and can help management make decisions that take advantage of existing opportunities and avoid pitfalls. There are two elements to the scanning process: internal assessment and external assessment. A number of planning tools are available to collect the information.

Conducting a comprehensive environmental scan can be a challenge; a great deal of information is available from many sources, and finding the information that is relevant to the specific business can be time-consuming. In addition to the information available from industry associations, government agencies, and trade organizations, customers and suppliers are excellent sources of information for a specific business. Many business-focused cable television channels present in-depth program segments on pertinent topics such as unemployment and inflation (among others), and business publications also provide in-depth examination of some topics. A wealth of information is available—the challenge comes in finding what is most appropriate for a specific organization's needs.

Environmental Scanning Tools

A number of tools are available for use in the scanning process. Let's take a look at some that are commonly used:

Statistical Models   A number of quantitative analysis models that can be used to identify trends were described earlier in this chapter. These are useful internally (to analyze turnover rates, for example) and externally (to analyze customer buying habits).

SWOT Analysis   A *SWOT analysis* looks at the strengths, weaknesses, opportunities, and threats that are facing the organization. Strengths and weaknesses are internal factors that can be controlled by the organization; opportunities and threats are external factors that may impact an organization's plans:

> **Strengths**   Strengths are internal factors that will support the organization's plans. These can include people, such as a workforce that is highly trained in a unique skill not available to other businesses in the market. Machinery and equipment can be a strength: for example, when a recent upgrade of manufacturing equipment allows the company to produce more high-quality products at a lower cost. Developments in technology, such as a state-of-the-art order-processing system, and other factors that give the organization an edge in the marketplace are also considered strengths that contribute to organizational success.

> **Weaknesses**   Weaknesses are also internal factors, but these represent obstacles to the organization. Weaknesses can include workforce issues such as poorly trained workers, old machinery or equipment that is inefficient and costly to operate, outdated technology, and any other factors that make it difficult for an organization to achieve its goals.

> **Opportunities**   Opportunities are external factors that will aid the organization in the marketplace. These can include a wide variety of factors such as economic upswings, demand for the product, a competitor whose product quality has declined, and other factors that are discussed more fully in the next section.

Threats   External factors that the organization must overcome or turn to an advantage are threats to its ability to achieve success. These can include strong product competition, economic problems, low unemployment rates, and other factors that make it more difficult for the organization to compete.

PEST Analysis   A *PEST analysis* (also sometimes referred to as a *STEP analysis*, depending on how the words are arranged) scans the external environment to identify opportunities and threats as part of the SWOT analysis. PEST is an acronym for political, economic, social, and technological factors. PEST is discussed in more detail in the "External Assessment" section.

Porter's 5 Forces   *Porter's 5 Forces* is an analytical tool created by Michael E. Porter, PhD, a professor at Harvard Business School who has written extensively on business planning and strategy. In his book *Competitive Strategy: Techniques for Analyzing Industries and Competitors*, first published in 1980 by Free Press, he described five forces that are found in all industries. These forces include new competitors, suppliers, buyers, alternative products available to consumers, and the type and level of competition in the industry. The importance of these factors in strategic planning is discussed more fully in the "External Assessment" section.

Internal Assessment

Leaders need a firm grasp of the talent and resources currently available in the organization. Some areas to consider in an assessment of strengths and weaknesses include the following:

Credibility of executive team	Market penetration
Strength of management team	Customer service reputation
Organization culture	Market share
Workforce diversity	Customer loyalty
Current product quality	Level of sales
Time to market	Employee loyalty
State of technology	Turnover rate

The areas to be reviewed depend to a certain extent on the nature of the business but should include an assessment of performance in every function of the business.

This information can be collected in a number of ways: questionnaires, qualitative analyses, focus groups, surveys (of customers, suppliers, and employees), stakeholder interviews, and other information-collection techniques as discussed earlier in this chapter.

External Assessment

Scanning the external environment presents more challenges than does an internal assessment because the vast amounts of information available must be sought in a wide variety of locations. Tools such as the PEST analysis and Porter's 5 Forces analysis can assist in narrowing down what kind of information needs to be collected. The PEST analysis provides a guide for collecting information related to the general business environment:

Political   The political environment includes such things as increased government regulations and events that influence them, such as massive business frauds. A recent example of this is the impact of the Sarbanes-Oxley Act of 2002 (SOX), enacted by Congress in response to the Enron and WorldCom scandals. Less spectacular but equally important considerations for business planning purposes include changes in employment regulations such as the changes to overtime regulations proposed by the DOL in 2003–2004 and changes to the FMLA regulations that took effect on January 16, 2009.

For multinational corporations, consideration must be given to political situations in each country of operation, including the stability of the government in some countries, restrictive trade policies, and the friendliness of the government to foreign investment.

All countries and businesses are now faced as well with the threat of terrorism that has negatively impacted sales in the travel industry; however, products related to security have a wider market in this situation.

Economic   The most obvious example of economic concerns has to do with the strength of the economy—can customers afford the organization's products? The unemployment rate is a key factor here, along with interest rates, inflation, and changes in fiscal policy.

For investment and expansion purposes, the stock market impacts the ability of a business to raise capital, and the price of real estate can add to the cost of purchasing or leasing new facilities. The strength of the dollar and the rate of inflation must both be considered when creating a long-term strategy.

Social   The demographics of the target market must be considered in long-term planning as well. If an organization's products are targeted at young adults, for example, and that population is static or decreasing, the organization must either change its products or find new markets for them. For multinational corporations, analyzing the social factors of widely diverse markets around the world can prove challenging, but it's essential to ensure that the long-term planning will result in a strategy that increases the success of the business.

Technological   The rate of change in technology varies in different industries, as does the cost of purchasing new technology. Technology affects the level of automation in an organization, and that impacts the overall cost of products. From cell phones to handheld computers and robotics on production lines, advances in technology affect how work is done and must be considered in the environmental scanning process.

Although the PEST analysis provides a guide for scanning the general business environment, Porter's 5 Forces analysis hones in on issues specific to the industry in which the organization operates. It's critical to understand these industry-specific factors and address them during the planning process. The following questions gather the information necessary to conduct the analysis:

How likely is it that new competition will enter the market?   A market with great demand for a product that is inexpensive to produce and requires little initial investment will encourage new competition. This puts pressure on the organization to maintain a competitive price or to differentiate its product on some basis to maintain market share.

How reliant is the organization on its suppliers?   When an organization produces a product requiring a unique part that can be obtained from only one supplier, the organization may find itself at the mercy of the supplier should it decide to raise the price of the part, discontinue it, or change it substantially.

How diverse is the organization's customer base?   A company reliant on one or only a few customers may find itself being pressured to lower prices, particularly if the product is easy to obtain from other sources.

Are comparable replacement products available to customers at a reasonable cost?   A serious threat to the organization's customer base will be present if a product is generic and similar products made by competitors are easy to obtain at a similar or lower price.

What is the level of competition in the marketplace?   The level of competition in the market will, to a certain extent, limit the strategies available to an organization wanting to enter that market. A market dominated by one or two large competitors holding the bulk of the market share presents quite a different challenge than a new, untapped market with a few small competitors.

You can find a more detailed discussion of Porter's 5 Forces at `www.quickmba.com/strategy/porter.shtml`.

Employee Attitude Assessment

Gathering information about employee attitudes and opinions provides insight into how well the organization is meeting employee needs and the level of engagement in the employee population. An employee attitude assessment also provides input for changes to a benefit package or other HR programs. Employee attitudes impact productivity, and conducting an assessment can help an organization diagnose what is causing low productivity or morale. Once problems are identified, programs can be designed to address the issues and improve productivity. Various methods are used to collect this information, including surveys, interviews, and focus groups:

Employee Surveys   Employee surveys can be used to gather information on any number of issues and are effective for large numbers of employees. Surveys can be developed in-house or outsourced to companies that specialize in developing and conducting them regularly.

Outsourcing a survey can result in more honest feedback because the identity of participants can be protected.

Interviews   One-on-one interviews are used to gather in-depth information about individual attitudes and perspectives. This method of collecting information is best for collecting detailed information about, for example, a complex work process. When information must be gathered from large groups of employees, however, interviews are an inefficient and time-consuming method.

Employee Focus Groups   When it's impractical to solicit input from all employees, a focus group consisting of a cross section of employees from various departments and levels in the organization can be used to solicit employee input.

Whichever method is selected, it's important to give all employees an opportunity to be heard and to collect information on a wide variety of topics, from the effectiveness of individual managers to organizational climate and specific policies. Employees must feel safe to provide honest feedback, and this is most often accomplished by making the survey anonymous. The most important result of employee attitude assessment is the ability to identify trends that are affecting morale and productivity.

Basic Budgeting and Accounting

The finance function is responsible for creating and maintaining accounting records and managing organization budgets. HR professionals at the management level are often expected to participate in the budgeting process not only for HR-specific expenses but also by providing compensation and benefit information that is incorporated in the overall organization budget. Although closely related, accounting and budgeting activities have different goals.

Accounting

The accounting function creates reports to summarize the results of business activity, including the balance sheet, income statement, and statement of cash flows. All accounting reports are produced at the end of accounting periods, which are generally monthly, quarterly, and annually. The annual reporting period can be defined as any 12-month period and doesn't necessarily coincide with a calendar year (January through December). An annual reporting period that is different from a calendar year is known as a *fiscal year*. Many companies, for example, have fiscal years that begin on July 1 and end on June 30 of the following calendar year.

The *balance sheet* is a picture of the financial condition of the organization on a specific day, usually the last day of the accounting period. Information on the balance sheet includes the company's assets, liabilities, and equity. This report is known as a balance sheet because the total of the liabilities and the equity must equal the total of the assets as represented by the balance sheet formula:

Assets = Liabilities + Equity

The *income statement*, sometimes referred to as the *profit and loss statement* (P&L), provides information about the financial results of operations during the reporting period. The report informs readers how much revenue was produced from various sources, how much it cost to produce the goods or services, what the overhead expenses were, and what the profit or loss for the period was.

The *statement of cash flows* provides important facts about the money that flowed through the business during the accounting period: where it came from and what it was used for. This statement shows how much cash was a result of sales, how much was spent to produce the products that were sold, how much money was borrowed or came in as a result of new capital investments, and how much was invested in assets.

HR professionals need to understand some basic accounting terminology and be able to read and understand financial reports in order to be effective strategic partners in their organizations. Table 2.7 provides definitions for some common accounting terms.

TABLE 2.7 Common accounting terms

Term	Definition/Description
Accrued expense	Expenses, such as vacation leave, that have been incurred but not yet paid
Accounts payable	Money owed by the business to its suppliers
Accounts receivable	Money owed to the business by customers
Assets	Tangible or intangible items of value owned by the business
Audited financial statements	Financial statements that have been examined by an independent auditor (not affiliated with the company) to determine whether they fairly represent the financial condition of the business
Budget	A projection of revenue and expenses used to control actual expenses
Cost of goods sold	Money spent on supplies and labor to produce goods or services
Equity	Value of the business to owners after all liabilities have been paid

TABLE 2.7 Common accounting terms *(continued)*

Term	Definition/Description
Expense	Money spent to operate the business
Generally accepted accounting principles (GAAP)	Standards established by the Financial Accounting Standards Board (FASB) for recording financial transactions
Gross profit	Sales revenue less cost of goods sold
Liability	Money owed by the business to others, such as lenders or the government (for payroll taxes withheld), or to employees (for unused vacation time)
Net profit	Gross profit less operating expenses
Profit	Money earned by the business after all expenses have been paid
Retained earnings	Net profits that aren't distributed to owners but remain in the business as equity
Revenue	Money received from customers for products or services

Budgeting

The budgeting process determines how many and what kind of resources will be required to accomplish goals and objectives generated by the strategic plan. Whether the plan requires additional employees, funds to outsource elements of the plan, new technology, or new equipment, these elements determine how much cash is needed to achieve the goal. There are two basic ways to create a budget; the first is based on historical budget information, and the second is known as *zero-based budgeting* (ZBB):

Budgets Based on Historic Information A historic budget bases the current budget on the prior year's budget. Past budgets and expenditures are reviewed and the new budget is based on the historical trends. In some cases, the amounts in the budget are increased by a flat percentage rate, based on inflation or anticipated salary increases. This method assumes that operationally, nothing will change from the last budget.

Zero-Based Budgeting (ZBB) The concept behind ZBB is very simple: assume you're starting from scratch, and determine what is needed to achieve the goals. How many people will be required? How much will you need to spend on outsourcing? What will be the cost of new technology or equipment? Unlike the historic budget process, ZBB requires that the need for each expenditure be justified in terms of the new goals and action plans.

As part of a zero-based budget planning process, HR examines all the programs offered to employees to determine whether they're still adding value to the organization. Programs that no longer add value are dropped and replaced with those that do add value; or, if cost cutting is required, are dropped and not replaced.

Regardless of the way in which the budget is developed, it can be created from the top down, from the bottom up, or with a combination approach:

Top-Down Budgeting   The *top-down budget* is created by senior management and imposed on the organization. Managers with operating responsibility have little input on how much money they will have to achieve their goals. This process is advantageous to senior management because they have complete control of how and where the money is spent. The disadvantage is that those creating the budget are generally far removed from actual operations and may not have full knowledge of what will be needed to achieve the goals they establish. This method often results in political battles as mid- and lower-level managers lobby senior management for additional funds for their particular departments.

Bottom-Up Budgeting   The *bottom-up* budget includes all managers with budget responsibility in the budget-creation process. Managers with direct operating responsibility for achieving goals develop a budget based on their knowledge of operating costs and provide the information to senior managers who have a view of the big picture for the organization. One advantage of this process is the commitment of operating managers to a budget they helped to create. Disadvantages include the amount of time required, the lack of awareness of the organization's big picture on the part of operating managers, and initial budget requests that may be unrealistic.

Parallel Budgeting   A *parallel* budget includes elements of both the top-down and bottom-up approaches: senior management provides broad guidelines for operating managers to follow in creating budgets for individual departments. This approach gives operating managers a context for developing individual budgets that are more realistic.

The end result of the budget process is a projection of expected revenue and costs needed to generate the revenue. Budget reports also include a cash flow projection that is used to prepare for short- or long-term shortfalls of cash, such as might occur in a seasonal business when the cash that comes in during the sales period (such as Christmas or Mother's Day) must support expenses that occur over a longer period of time. A separate report, known as a *capital budget*, is used to project asset purchases, such as buildings, machinery and equipment used in manufacturing, or computers.

Risk Management

Each day, business owners and managers take risks; some of the most successful businesses in existence today are the result of someone moving ahead in spite of an uncertain outcome. In some ways, business is all about taking risks of one kind or another. Some risks have positive results (Steve Jobs took a risk when he returned to lead Apple Computer after several years of absence and reinvented the Mac). Other risks have the potential to threaten not only business results but lives (a tire manufacturer that cuts corners during the production process, resulting in deaths when the tires fail at high speed on a freeway).

Businesses can choose to manage risk on an ad hoc basis, dealing with issues in a reactive way, sometimes known as the *fire drill* or *crisis management* method. In this situation, risks are either unrecognized or ignored until a problem occurs, and then they're dealt with by having employees stop other work to resolve the crisis. This lowers productivity and can create a stressful work environment for employees if it's a regular occurrence. Another reactive way that companies manage risk is to address risks as soon as they're recognized and before they grow into crises. This approach also disrupts workflow and can reduce productivity.

A proactive method for addressing business risks is a systematic approach known as *risk management*. There are four basic steps to managing risk:

Identifying the Business Assets Subject to Threats   Risks to an organization come in many forms, including such events as accidents, product failures that harm customers, natural disasters, failure to comply with government regulations, inadequate internal controls, and others.

In the human resource function, risks are often in the form of liability for questionable employment actions. Liability is a legal term that refers to a duty or responsibility owed by one party to another. A *liability* can result from an agreement or a contract or can be created through a tort. A *tort* is another legal term that describes an action that injures someone. Torts aren't related to laws or contracts but can result in legal action: the party who has been injured is able to sue the wrongdoer and collect damages for the injury that has been done.

Other human capital related risks to the business may involve nonlegal issues such as high turnover of key talent, failure to plan for executive or key position succession, or lack of qualified talent to achieve strategic goals.

Assessing/Analyzing the Types of Possible Threats   A risk analysis looks at each asset and the possible threats to it. For example, cash is subject to embezzlement, the assembly line could be negatively affected by equipment failure, or an HR policy could become noncompliant after a change to an employment law.

The risk analysis makes it possible for a risk assessment to take place. The risk assessment examines each risk identified in the risk analysis and considers the probability that each risk will occur and the consequences to the company if it does occur. The level of risk involved can be measured with the following formula:

Risks = Probability × Consequences

The formula expresses the level of risk as a function of how likely (probable) the risk will occur against the cost to the business (consequences) if it did occur.

For example, a typical risk for HR is the filing of an employee lawsuit because of noncompliance with an employment law that could lead to a judgment or settlement for the plaintiff. If an employment attorney reviews company policies on a regular basis, the probability of the risk occurring falls, and the consequences (amount of the possible settlement) are lowered.

Managing Threats Through Prevention or Mitigation   When all asset risks have been identified and prioritized, company management can decide to manage the risks in one of four ways:

- *Risk mitigation* means steps are taken to reduce the risk. In the previous example, having employment policies reviewed on a regular basis mitigates the risk of an employee lawsuit.

- *Risk acceptance* means the company is aware that the risk could occur, but because there is a lower probability or consequence, management takes the risk that it either won't occur or will be easily managed if it does occur.

- *Risk avoidance* means the company takes steps to avoid the risk. For example, in a unionized environment during contract negotiations, the risk of sabotage to production equipment increases. This risk could be avoided by adding security guards to the facility until the new contract is accepted by both parties.

- *Risk transfer* is usually accomplished by purchasing insurance. With regard to HR risks, an important policy for businesses to maintain is *employment practices liability insurance* (EPLI). EPLI protects employers against lawsuits brought by current or former employees. During the application process, an insurance company evaluates the employer's human resource policies and any lawsuits or claims filed by employees or former employees. These factors, along with considerations of the employer's operations and size, are used to determine whether an EPLI policy may be issued and the amount of the premium to be paid.

A cost-benefit analysis for each risk provides a basis for deciding which risks will be mitigated, accepted, avoided, or transferred based on the resources available.

Review/Monitor   With changing circumstances and operating processes, risk-management decisions need to be monitored on a regular basis to ensure that resources continue to be allocated appropriately to maximize risk-management benefits.

As will be discussed in Chapter 7, liability for wrongful actions in employment relationships costs businesses millions of dollars in judgments for many different types of torts, from wrongful termination to sexual harassment and discrimination. In their risk-management role, HR professionals inform managers of the legal exposure that may result from making adverse employment decisions. When senior managers understand the possible consequences, including the costs of defending a lawsuit, they can take steps to mitigate, avoid, or transfer the risk.

Many HR risks can be managed by educating managers about the exposure created by unlawful practices or inconsistent application of policy in an organization:

- Identify possible exposures to legal action (for example, inconsistent policy application).

- Audit the organization's employment practices.

- Educate managers on the possible costs that could result from unlawful employment actions or inconsistent policy application.

- Develop a plan to reduce the risks, and obtain top management support.

- If losses related to employment issues have occurred in the past, develop a way to present a plan to top management for reducing the costs of these losses.

Summary

This chapter provided an overview of the core HR knowledge requirements, which have implications in all the HR functional areas and are the basis for understanding responsibilities in those areas.

Each of these requirements is the subject of many books, articles, and seminars, and some are even the basis for entire professional associations or certification programs in their own right. If, after reading this chapter, you feel the need for additional information about any of these topics, the Internet or your local library will provide additional resources to enhance your knowledge. Appendix D, "Resources," toward the end of this study guide also provides some resources that may be helpful.

Keep in mind that it's most important to understand the concepts introduced in this chapter and the way they apply to the functional areas of the body of knowledge.

Exam Essentials

Be able to describe how HR programs interact.   It's important to understand the ways programs or policies developed for one functional area impact others. For example, the compensation policy will affect the quality of candidates attracted by the company, turnover rates, the ability of the company to maintain union-free status, and employee job satisfaction.

Be able to describe the needs assessment and analysis process.   Needs assessment/analysis is a process used to obtain information about what a business needs to meet its goals. There are seven steps in a needs assessment: describing the objective, defining the current situation, conducting a gap analysis, setting priorities, developing options, determining the costs, and recommending the solution.

Understand the uses of a third-party contract.   Third-party contracts are used for various functions in the HR department. Choosing a third-party contractor begins with a needs assessment to determine how best to serve the needs of the organization. The RFP process provides an organized way to select the best option for the needs of the business.

Be able to describe communication strategies.   To ensure that the right information is provided to employees when they need it and that there is a mechanism for senior management to hear from employees, a communication strategy must be developed based on what information is needed, who needs to hear it, who will provide it, and when it will be delivered.

Understand the basic concepts associated with andragogy (adult learning theory) and adult learning styles.   Andragogy, also known as adult learning theory, is built on concepts that say adults are autonomous, self-directed, goal-oriented, relevancy-oriented, and practical, and that they need respect. Also, adults build new knowledge on a foundation of life experiences. Adult participants react either positively or negatively to training as a result of the presence or absence of these characteristics. Adult learning styles include auditory, visual, and tactile/kinesthetic.

Be able to recognize and describe various motivation theories.   Motivational theories help HR professionals and managers understand why employees behave the way they do and develop programs that result in highly motivated, productive workers.

Understand the uses for qualitative and quantitative analysis methods.   Quantitative analysis is based on mathematical models, such as correlation and measures of central tendency. Qualitative analysis is based on more subjective judgments based on secondary research.

Be able to describe the benefits of workplace diversity.   A diverse workforce is more creative and better reflects the customer population. Increasing diversity in the workforce provides access to more qualified candidates; this is important because of the projected shortfall of qualified workers over the next decade.

Understand the HR Code of Ethics.   The HR Code of Ethics developed by SHRM requires HR professionals to maintain standards of professional responsibility and development, provide ethical leadership in their organizations, ensure fairness and justice in their organizations, avoid the appearance of conflicts of interest, and use confidential information appropriately.

Understand the difference between job analysis and job descriptions.   Job analysis is the process used to identify and determine duties associated with a particular job; job descriptions are the end product. Typically, job descriptions document a job's major functions or duties, skill and physical requirements, and working conditions.

Understand metrics and how they're used in HR practice.   Metrics provide a means for quantifying HR programs and activities to exhibit the value added to organizations. The best metrics are those that provide relevant information to management and add value to the decision-making process.

Review Questions

You can find the answers in Appendix A.

1. A department manager advises you that the productivity of his data-entry operators is unsatisfactory and asks you to develop a training program to improve their data-entry skills. What is your first step?

   A. Conduct a needs assessment.

   B. Develop a lesson plan.

   C. Talk to other managers to validate the situation.

   D. Select a training method.

2. For several months, the management team has been struggling to come to grips with the need for a formal succession plan. About 30 percent of the workforce will reach retirement age within 10 years, and little has been done to prepare for the loss of knowledge in key roles that will occur as employees begin to retire. The team has come to a consensus that what is needed is a comprehensive plan, one that includes a mentor program for each of the key positions, identification of key skills that will need to be replaced, a recruiting strategy that attracts qualified candidates who are looking for longevity, and creating a more open culture. Which of the following can be used to accomplish these goals?

   A. Create a succession plan.

   B. Create a knowledge-management program.

   C. Create a talent-management program.

   D. All of the above.

3. Based on an analysis of the industry and labor market trends, a VP of Human Resources has determined that the best course of action for her company is to change from a narrow to a broadband salary structure. The current structure has been in place for more than 15 years, and the VP is anticipating strong resistance to making the change. Which of the following tools should the VP use to convince the executive team to make the change?

   A. Calculate the return on investment.

   B. Build a business case.

   C. Calculate the cost-benefit analysis.

   D. Conduct a SWOT analysis.

4. Maslow's hierarchy of needs does *not* include the following need:

   A. Social

   B. Safety

   C. Growth

   D. Self-actualization

5. Rachel has worked in accounting for six years. She has always been a steady performer, but recently she has made several costly errors in her work. The accounting manager, Rachel's boss, has talked to her several times, but no improvement has taken place. What is the most appropriate action the manager should take?

    A. First written warning

    B. Verbal warning

    C. Decision-making day

    D. Coaching

6. What is the purpose of a diversity initiative?

    A. To educate all employees about other groups in the workforce

    B. To increase the diversity of the workforce

    C. To increase organizational creativity

    D. To increase the comfort level of employees

7. Which of the following is *not* an appropriate use of an HRIS?

    A. Tracking applicant data for the EEO-1

    B. Tracking time and attendance

    C. Tracking employee expense reports

    D. Maintaining employee records

8. The middle value when values are arranged in order from high to low is which of the following?

    A. Mean

    B. Median

    C. Mode

    D. Moving average

9. Which of the following is a basic principle behind job analysis?

    A. The analysis focuses on the job, not the person.

    B. The analysis focuses on the person doing the job, not the job.

    C. The analysis is limited to task inventories and questionnaires.

    D. The required qualifications should include everything the manager would like the employee to have.

10. After conducting a risk assessment, what can you do to protect the company against any identified risks?

    A. Identify policies that are applied inconsistently throughout the organization.

    B. Obtain employment practices liability insurance.

    C. Develop a plan to reduce the risks.

    D. Present management with a plan for reducing the risks.

11. Offering training in cross-cultural conflict management is one example of what?

    A. An industry best practice

    B. Generational diversity effort

    C. Cultural competence

    D. Qualitative analysis

12. The best way for HR to contribute to the development of an organization's strategic plan using internal business operational factors is to do which of the following?

    A. Interpret and apply internal operational information such as the relationships between departments

    B. Scan the legal and regulatory environment

    C. Analyze industry changes

    D. Stay informed of technological developments

13. Which of the following is *not* a benefit of hiring a multigenerational workforce?

    A. A multigenerational workforce increases the availability of different perspectives for use in management decision-making.

    B. Recruiting for a multigenerational workforce increase the applicant pool from which to choose employees.

    C. A multigenerational workforce is a reflection of the population, considering the large number of baby boomers who are reaching retirement age.

    D. A multigenerational workforce increases an organization's productivity.

14. Computer-based training, web-based training, and virtual learning are all examples of what?

    A. Mobile learning

    B. Self-directed learning

    C. Electronic learning

    D. Asynchronous training

15. Gathering information about employee attitudes and opinions through surveys and focus groups provides _____ employee levels of engagement.

    A. Intuition about

    B. Instruction for

    C. Individual measurement of

    D. Insight into

16. Which of the following is another term for a profit and loss statement?

    A. Income statement

    B. Statement of cash flow

    C. Balance sheet

    D. Fiscal year summary

17. Which of the following organizational structures would be *most* effective for a company with three distinct commodities for sale?

A. Functional structure

B. Product-based structure

C. Divisional structure

D. Flat-line structure

18. According to the Toxic Substance Control Act, documentation of hazardous material exposures must be kept on file for how many years?

A. 5

B. 15

C. 25

D. 30

19. Why is a job analysis important?

A. It provides the supervisory responsibilities necessary to accomplish organizational goals.

B. It allows for proper training and development of key personnel.

C. It provides the foundation from which all other HR activities are designed.

D. It ensures compliance with EEO laws.

20. Which of the following methods of quantitative analysis would be most effective for an organization with data that is out of date?

A. Trend analysis

B. Weighted average

C. Simple linear regression

D. Mode

Chapter 3

Business Management and Strategy

THE HRCI TEST SPECIFICATIONS FROM THE BUSINESS MANAGEMENT AND STRATEGY FUNCTIONAL AREA COVERED IN THIS CHAPTER INCLUDE:

✓ Interpret and apply information related to the organization's operations from internal sources, including finance, accounting, business development, marketing, sales, operations, and information technology, in order to contribute to the development of the organization's strategic plan.

✓ Interpret information from external sources related to the general business environment, industry practices and developments, technological advances, economic environment, labor force, and the legal and regulatory environment, in order to contribute to the development of the organization's strategic plan.

✓ Participate as a contributing partner in the organization's strategic planning process (for example: provide and lead workforce planning discussion with management, develop and present long-term forecast of human capital needs at the organizational level). **SPHR ONLY**

✓ Establish strategic relationships with key individuals in the organization to influence organizational decision-making.

✓ Establish relationships/alliances with key individuals and outside organizations to assist in achieving the organization's strategic goals and objectives (for example: corporate social responsibility and community partnership).

✓ Develop and utilize business metrics to measure the achievement of the organization's strategic goals and objectives (for example: key performance indicators, balanced scorecard). **SPHR ONLY**

✓ Develop, influence, and execute strategies for managing organizational change that balance the expectations and needs of the organization, its employees, and other stakeholders.

✓ Develop and align the human resource strategic plan with the organization's strategic plan. **SPHR ONLY**

✓ Facilitate the development and communication of the organization's core values, vision, mission, and ethical behaviors.

✓ Reinforce the organization's core values and behavioral expectations through modeling, communication, and coaching.

✓ Provide data such as human capital projections and costs that support the organization's overall budget.

✓ Develop and execute business plans (i.e., annual goals and objectives) that correlate with the organization's strategic plan's performance expectations to include growth targets, new programs/services, and net income expectations. **SPHR ONLY**

✓ Perform cost/benefit analyses on proposed projects. **SPHR ONLY**

✓ Develop and manage an HR budget that supports the organization's strategic goals, objectives, and values. **SPHR ONLY**

✓ Monitor the legislative and regulatory environment for proposed changes and their potential impact to the organization, taking appropriate proactive steps to support, modify, or oppose the proposed changes.

✓ Develop policies and procedures to support corporate governance initiatives (for example: whistleblower protection, code of ethics). **SPHR ONLY**

✓ Participate in enterprise risk management by ensuring that policies contribute to protecting the organization from potential risks.

✓ Identify and evaluate alternatives and recommend strategies for vendor selection and/or outsourcing. **SPHR ONLY**

✓ Oversee or lead the transition and/or implementation of new systems, service centers, and outsourcing. **SPHR ONLY**

✓ Participate in strategic decision-making and due diligence activities related to organizational structure and design (for example: corporate restructuring, mergers and acquisitions [M&A], divestitures). **SPHR ONLY**

✓ Determine strategic application of integrated technical tools and systems (for example: new enterprise software, performance management tools, self-service technologies). **SPHR ONLY**

The current business environment, with its emphasis on the ability to compete in global markets and respond to rapidly changing conditions, requires more of its leaders and managers than ever before. They must seek and develop a competitive advantage in their marketplaces and continuously create new processes, products, and services to meet the ongoing challenges presented in a global business setting. As each challenge is met, successful managers are already forecasting the next challenge on the horizon, looking for an advantageous market position. This ongoing process of innovation, advantage, value creation, and reassessment is known as *strategic management*. Human resources (HR) professionals seeking certification must understand what strategic management means, how the process impacts HR policies and practices, and how HR can add value in the organization's quest for market advantages, aligning itself to organization strategy through the human capital management plan.

This chapter examines the elements of strategic management for HR professionals. Beginning with a look at the general business environment in relation to individual organizations, the chapter investigates internal structures and business functions. Moving on to business strategy, the chapter reviews the strategic planning process and the development of human capital management plans and HR budgets, which leads into a review of strategic management. That section discusses change management, technology impacts, risk management, and the importance of HR interactions with other functional areas and in the community. The following section on the legislative environment reviews corporate governance, core values, and organizational ethics. The chapter concludes by discussing the application of metrics to HR practice, as well as the effect of globalization on HR practitioners.

As you begin this chapter, be sure to refer to the knowledge requirements for Business Management and Strategy in the HR Certification Institute PHR/SPHR Body of Knowledge (BOK) described in the introduction to this book. In addition, several sections in Chapter 2, "Core Knowledge Requirements for HR Professionals," have particular relevance here: a review of the discussions of needs assessment, development of Request For Proposals (RFPs), communication strategies, leadership concepts, HR ethics and professional standards, technology, quantitative and qualitative analysis tools, change management, employee records management, types of organizational structures, environmental scanning, employee attitude assessment, basic budgeting, and risk-management techniques will enhance your review of the material in this chapter.

For up-to-the-minute updates for this chapter, go to www.sybex.com/go/phr4e.

Organizations

Since ancient times, people have formed groups to achieve goals that they were unable to achieve on their own. Whether it was for protection, shelter, food, or profit, organizing gave people the means to achieve more than they could by acting alone. With the advent of the Industrial Revolution in the late eighteenth century, organizations grew larger and more complex as the goals to be achieved became more complex. As the production of goods moved from a single worker creating an entire product to multiple workers completing pieces of a single product, the need for control over the production process became greater. The modern organization evolved to coordinate the many different activities that are needed to produce the goods or services necessary to achieve its goals.

Because organizations consist of people, the HR function is impacted by everything that affects an organization, whether it's an external development (such as a competitor's technological development) or a change in a business process (such as a product design change). Whatever the impact, HR professionals are called on to implement the resulting changes.

External Business Environment

Many organizational changes occur as the result of forces outside an organization's control, and HR professionals must understand how these forces impact existing organizational strategies as well as the effect of those forces on HR processes. These external forces affect other organizations as well, and how different organizations respond to these forces plays a role in determining whether they succeed in the new environment:

Technological Developments   Historically, developments in technology have driven the growth and decline of organizations. Family farms have largely been replaced by corporate farms as a result of improved techniques and equipment, for example. Typewriters and mimeograph machines have been replaced by computers and plain-paper copy machines. Organizations that make a point of keeping abreast of these types of developments thrive, while others deteriorate when they ignore or dismiss the changes as insignificant.

Industry Changes   Technological developments often lead to industry changes. For example, the methods used to distribute goods have evolved over the past 100 years or so from animal power (horse-and-wagon) to railcars, trucks, and airplanes. Very few companies that began distributing goods using horse-drawn wagons were able to adapt to these changes. One company that did, the West Motor Freight Company, successfully transitioned from horse-and-wagon deliveries to a regional delivery service, celebrating 100 years of continuous operation in 2007 because it has been able to embrace industry changes.

Economic Environment   The economic environment impacts all organizations and individuals. When the economy is growing, there is a greater demand for business goods and services, and many companies are able to thrive and grow. When the economy is shrinking, companies survive, or may even prosper, when they're able to keep expenses in line with declining income. In this environment, tightly run companies (those able to eliminate redundancy and waste) are more likely to succeed.

Many factors impact economic conditions. Higher taxes mean customers have less cash to spend on goods and services and are more selective about their purchases. Stricter government regulations mean organizations must spend more of their money on mandated expenses, such as reducing the pollution created by manufacturing processes. In the United States, the availability of cash is affected by decisions of the Board of Governors of the Federal Reserve System (the Fed). When the Fed raises interest rates, organizations and individuals pay more to borrow money, which means less money is available to spend on goods and services.

Labor Pool   Another significant aspect of the general business environment that affects organizations is the availability of skilled labor. This topic is covered in detail in Chapter 4, "Workforce Planning and Employment."

Legal and Regulatory Activity   Finally, the external business environment is affected by activities of federal, state, and local governments. These activities are covered in detail later in this chapter in the "Legislative and Regulatory Processes" section.

As important as the general business environment is to the health of an organization, it's equally affected by internal business operations.

Internal Business Operations

Every organization is unique in how it organizes itself, but some basic functions and structures are common to all of them. HR professionals who are focused on strategic contributions to their organizations must understand how organizations function.

All businesses in the United States are organized into one of the following four basic structures:

Sole Proprietorships   This business structure is the most basic and easy to organize. The owner is a single (sole) person who is the final authority for all decisions in the business. Any profits earned by the business belong to the owner, and the owner has unlimited personal liability for all business decisions and activities.

Partnerships   A partnership is owned by two or more people who share final authority for all business decisions and are jointly liable for the actions of the business. Partners are liable not only for their own individual actions but for the actions taken by their other partner(s) as well. The profits of the business are split according to the ownership shares established at the beginning of the partnership (most often equal shares, but ownership can be any arrangement agreed on by the partners). There are several types of partnership arrangements:

- In a *general partnership* (GP), the partners share responsibility for managing the business based on the partnership agreement.

- In a *limited partnership* (LP) or a *limited liability partnership* (LLP), most of the partners are involved only as investors and have little input into daily operations of the business. These forms are commonly used for medical clinics, accounting practices, law firms, and other service businesses.

- A *joint venture* (JV) is similar to a GP but is formed to manage a specific project or for a limited time frame.

Corporations   Corporations are entities defined by four characteristics:

- Liability is limited to assets owned by the corporation.
- The life of the corporation can extend beyond the life of its original owner/founder.
- There is a central management structure.
- Ownership may be transferred freely by selling stock.

Corporations sell stock to raise the funds necessary to operate the business. Owners of the stock, known as *stockholders* or *shareholders*, are free to sell the stock they own to other investors at any time. These stockholders can be individuals or other entities, and for the most part they aren't involved in the daily operation of the business. They elect a board of directors to represent their interests with the senior management team in making decisions about the strategic direction of the company. Because corporate liability is limited to the assets owned by the corporation, stockholder/owner liability is generally limited to the amount of stock owned by individual investors; there are exceptions for corporate officers who may be held personally liable for any wrongdoing or negligence.

Corporations are legal entities and may incur debts, sign contracts, and be sued in the same way that individuals may be. This is the most common form of business for large enterprises in the United States.

Limited Liability Company   A limited liability company (LLC) is a cross between a general partnership and a corporation and provides its owners with the liability protection of a corporation with fewer operating restrictions. An LLC exists for a finite period of time defined when it's organized, and it can be extended by a vote of the owner/members when it expires. An LLC may have only two of the four characteristics of a corporation; otherwise, the entity must become a corporation.

Regardless of an organization's legal form, three aspects of organizations must be considered by HR professionals in developing plans and programs: structures, functions, and life cycles. Chapter 2 discussed various structures. The next section describes organization functions and life cycles.

Organization Functions

Every business has some common components: production and operations, sales and marketing, research and development, finance and accounting, information technology, and, of course, the people who make everything happen. Regardless of whether the business is simple or complex and whether it has one employee or hundreds of thousands, these components are all necessary for success.

Production and Operations

The terms *production* and *operations* are, in many cases, used interchangeably. When used separately, *production* generally refers to the process by which businesses create the product or service they offer to customers. Traditionally, this meant manufactured goods, but with the growth of service and information businesses, it has come to include services as well.

The *operations* function encompasses all the activities necessary to produce the goods or services of the business. These can include such activities as the following:

Capacity   This includes determining how much of a product or service is able to be produced with the available materials, labor, and equipment (known as *inputs*) as well as what changes in inputs are required by fluctuating customer demands.

Production Layout   This is the way in which the goods or service will be produced: for example, the design of an assembly line or, in the case of a service, the process to be used in providing it, such as a model plan or protocol for a financial audit.

Scheduling   Scheduling activities make sure the products or services are available at times of peak customer demand.

Quality Management   Quality assurance (QA) ensures that the product or service meets acceptable standards.

Inventory Management   Operations managers must balance two conflicting needs related to inventory: the cost of maintaining a large inventory and the need to satisfy customers by filling orders promptly. *Just-in-time* (JIT) inventory-management systems attempt to do this by purchasing smaller amounts of supplies more frequently to reduce inventories and ensure a steady supply of products for distribution.

Technology   Increasing the use of technology can improve product quality and the amounts that are produced.

Facility Location   Evaluating the best places to locate production facilities involves many considerations: the cost of labor, distribution systems, and government regulations, to name a few.

Cost Control   As with all business functions, operations must provide products or services that meet the quality standards set by the organization at the lowest possible cost.

Sales and Marketing

Sales and marketing are closely related activities involved with creating a demand for the company's products and moving them from the company to the customer.

The *sales* function includes the near-term activities involved in transferring the product or service from the business to the customer.

Marketing incorporates longer-term functions necessary to promote and distribute products in the marketplace, provides support for the sales staff, conducts research to design products that customers will be interested in purchasing, and determines the appropriate pricing for the products. Marketing begins with an identification of the target market for the organization's product or service. Once that has been identified, decisions about the four *p*'s of marketing (product, price, placement, and promotion) can be made:

Product   This can be a physical product, a service, or, in some cases, both. Product development includes making decisions about what the product will do, how it will look, what kind of customer service is needed, whether a warranty or guarantee is appropriate, and how the product will be packaged to attract customers.

Price   Setting the correct price point for a product is an important marketing function. The price must attract the customer, compete with other similar products, and return a profit. Pricing looks not only at the list price but also at any discounts or allowances that will be offered.

Placement   Also referred to as *distribution*, this is where decisions are made about where the customer will find the product. Having an in-depth description of the target customer is helpful in this step: How does the customer shop? On the Internet? At the mall? By phone? These and similar questions must be answered to appropriately place the product.

Promotion   Products are promoted in many different ways including advertising, public relations, personal selling, and providing incentives for customers to buy. Incentives such as discounts, rebates, and contests are techniques commonly used to market products and services.

Research and Development

The research and development (R&D) function is charged with designing new product offerings and testing them to make sure they do what they're designed to do before they're offered to the public. R&D develops new products and redesigns old ones to meet changing market demands, often developing products to create demand where none previously existed. R&D works closely with marketing and production in this process. Marketing provides information it gathers from customers about their needs, whereas production provides input on the ability of the production process to create the product or the need for new processes.

In some organizations and industries, such as automobile manufacturing and pharmaceuticals, R&D is a separate function. In other organizations, it may be shared by the marketing and operations functions.

Finance and Accounting

Finance and accounting are closely related functions and include all the activities related to moving money into and out of the organization.

The *finance* function is responsible for obtaining credit to meet the organization's needs, granting credit to customers, investing and managing cash for maximum return on investment (ROI), and establishing banking relationships for the organization. The finance function also provides technical expertise for the analysis of current operations or proposals for new business directions and the projection of future financial needs.

Financial analysts work with all functions of the organization in a variety of ways. For the operations function, an analyst can provide models to predict the number of employees needed at different production levels, along with the budget impact of those different levels. Working with personnel in the operations and marketing functions, analysts compile cost data, profit margins, and pricing information to provide accurate profitability forecasts at different sales volumes and pricing levels. HR practitioners may work with analysts to project needed staffing levels or benefit costs for budget planning purposes.

The *accounting* function is responsible for activities that record financial transactions within an organization.

 Basic accounting activities are described in more detail in Chapter 2.

Transactions related to product sales and the costs related to creating the product are known as *cost accounting*; this information is critical for the operations function to manage production costs. Other accounting activities include the processing of various transactions such as payroll, expense reimbursements, and accounts receivable and payable, and the establishment of internal controls to ensure compliance with government regulations, standards set by the Financial Accounting Standards Board, and generally accepted accounting principles. The accounting function is also responsible for preparing the budget reports managers use to maintain control of operating costs.

Under the Securities Exchange Act of 1934, Congress gave statutory authority for establishing reporting standards for publicly held companies to the Securities and Exchange Commission (SEC). In 1939, the American Institute of Certified Public Accountants (AICPA) established a committee to develop accounting standards and reports for the private sector. This committee developed generally accepted accounting principles (GAAP) for use by accounting professionals. In 1972, an independent body, the Financial Accounting Standards Board (FASB), was created by the AICPA to take over responsibility for setting accounting standards. FASB standards are officially recognized by the SEC as the authority for accounting practices. These standards are essential to the efficient functioning of the economy because they enable investors, creditors, auditors, and others to rely on credible, transparent, and comparable financial information.

In 2008, the SEC began to consider allowing U.S. companies to use international accounting rules developed by the International Accounting Standards Board (IASB) instead of GAAP rules when preparing and filing their financial reports. The International Financial Reporting Standards (IFRS) would provide consistency for global financial reporting, but because this would be a fundamental change in the way financial reports are prepared, any final changes would take place over an extended period of time.

Information Technology

Information technology (IT) is the area of the business responsible for managing systems such as voicemail, computer networks, software, websites, and the Internet as well as the data collected by these systems.

As technology has become more prevalent and sophisticated, the use of IT systems has expanded from the original data storage and retrieval function. For example, the ability of new systems to increase the accuracy of scheduling requirements for operations managers by providing real-time sales and inventory tracking makes the IT function a strategic advantage in organizations. As a result, IT plays a growing role in the strategic management of organizations.

People/Employees

Whether it's a one-person operation or a company with hundreds of thousands of employees throughout the world, the people who do the work *are* the business. With appropriate and effective human resource strategies, employees drive business results and are satisfied, productive goodwill ambassadors for the company. Conversely, low productivity, lower revenue, higher costs, and poor customer service are by-products of ineffective HR strategies. The connection between these differing results and the level of employee engagement in an organization was made by the Gallup Organization in research conducted over a period of years and presented in the book *First, Break All the Rules: What the World's Greatest Managers Do Differently* by Marcus Buckingham and Curt Coffman (Simon and Schuster, 1999). Buckingham and Coffman identified four factors that contribute to an engaged workforce:

- Identify the best fit for employees.

- Concentrate on individual employee strengths.

- Clearly establish desired results.

- Look for talent as well as knowledge, skills, and abilities (KSAs) when selecting employees.

So, what does it take to build employee engagement in a workforce? To an extent, the specifics of an engaged workforce are unique in each organization; but generally speaking, employees who see a connection between their daily responsibilities or tasks, their personal development, and the organization's goals are more engaged in its success. Three themes have emerged in research on engagement:

Leadership   The most important connection for employees is the one they have with their direct manager or supervisor, and how this relationship is managed directly affects their level of engagement. Chapter 5, "Human Resource Development," includes a discussion of the importance of *emotional intelligence*, the ability of managers to create personal connections with those they supervise. This personal connection, combined with a manager's enthusiastic support for the organization and its goals, is necessary for employees to develop a level of trust. Trust is reinforced by managers who do what they say they will do by following through on their commitments to employees. Leadership is also demonstrated when managers communicate effectively about organizational goals and the workgroup's role in achieving those goals. Further, clearly communicating individual employee expectations within the context of organizational goals helps keep them focused on what is important for the organization. A key factor to engaging employees is making this an interactive communication by listening to employees and acting on their suggestions whenever possible.

Professional Development   Professional development begins with the selection process when employers hire talented candidates who demonstrate potential for, and interest in, professional growth opportunities. Employees are engaged by managers who not only talk about development but who also "walk the talk" and actively groom subordinates for higher-level responsibilities or improve/enlarge their capabilities in their current role. Chapter 5 goes into more detail on professional development.

Employee Recognition   It's human nature for employees to respond positively to recognition for achievements or for performing above and beyond normal expectations. Recognition can take many forms, both monetary and nonmonetary, and knowing what form appeals most to a particular individual is crucial. It's also important that the recognition, whatever form it takes, be genuine and gratefully expressed.

Organization Life Cycles

As organizations are established and grow, they move through four distinct phases: startup, growth, maturity, and decline. Organizations approach each of these stages with different expectations and needs:

Startup   During the startup phase, organization leaders struggle to obtain funding so the organization can survive. Because employees hired during this phase must wear many different hats, there is little time for training, so they're usually fully qualified for their positions, and base pay is very often below the market rate. At this stage, outsourcing can be a cost-effective alternative for specialized functions that don't require full-time employees. There are generally few layers of management, which allows employees to work closely with the founders and leaders.

Growth   In the growth phase, the founder isn't able to manage the organization alone, so additional management personnel are brought into the company. This can lead to morale issues when employees who once had access to organization leaders lose the daily contact common in the startup phase. As the organization becomes more successful, funds are available to provide competitive compensation and benefits to attract and retain qualified employees. From an operation standpoint, the growth phase presents challenges when it exceeds the ability of the infrastructure to handle it, sometimes necessitating the outsourcing of some functions to meet needs.

Not all organizations are able to make it through the growth phase and instead collapse under the weight of their good fortune or are acquired by larger entities with the infrastructure to support operations.

Maturity   At the maturity phase, the organization has enough resources to provide planning and standardize policies and procedures. In this stage, it's possible to become bureaucratic and unwieldy, making it difficult for the company to change direction as rapidly as may be necessary to remain competitive. From an HR standpoint, the relative stability of this phase means that it's possible to hire less experienced personnel and provide them with training and development so that they're able to take on additional responsibilities. The compensation and benefits for executives are often enhanced during this stage.

Decline   A declining organization is characterized by inefficiency and bureaucracy. To remain viable, leaders may implement workforce reductions, close facilities, and take other cost-cutting measures. The organization's products may be outdated and unable to compete, resulting in a downward sales trend.

Organizations in the declining phase of the life cycle will need to reinvigorate themselves in order to survive. This may happen with the development of new product lines or with the redesign of existing products to bring them up to current competitive standards. When this doesn't occur, the organization may be acquired by a competitor or may cease to exist.

From this discussion, it's clear that all organizations consist of similar components. Why, then, do some organizations succeed while others either stumble along at a mediocre level or fail completely? The difference lies in how well the organization is able to position itself to take advantage of market opportunities and avoid the pitfalls present in the business environment. The strategic planning process provides a framework within which organizations are able to do this.

HR's Role in Organizations

The role of human resources in organizations is characterized by change. Not long ago, HR practitioners were expected to contribute to the organization in an advisory capacity, provide services to employees and others, and control employment policies and procedures in their organizations. As advisors, we were asked to provide information and guidance for managers to deal with employee issues. As service providers, HR professionals were required to answer questions and provide information for a wide range of constituents, from government agencies to candidates for employment and senior management. In the control role, HR was expected to enforce policies and ensure compliance with federal, state, and local employment regulations and laws.

Today, although the roles are still in flux, they have begun to evolve into strategic, administrative, and operational roles.

Strategically, HR professionals contribute to decisions that build on employee strengths to meet corporate goals. Establishing recruiting and retention plans to attract the best-qualified employees and keep them in the organization is a key contribution that HR is uniquely qualified to make. Developing performance-management systems to motivate employees and providing continuous development opportunities are other areas that provide strategic advantage to organizations. Managing change and leading or participating in reengineering or restructuring programs to ensure the retention of key employees furthers the organization's ability to meet its goals.

Administratively, HR manages compliance issues related to government regulations, maintains employee and benefit records, and ensures the confidentiality of employee information.

Operationally, HR professionals manage the employee relations and recruiting functions that require daily attention to maintain a productive work environment.

Strategy

What is business strategy, and how does it impact HR professionals? For business applications, *strategy* defines organizational goals and the methods to be used in achieving those goals—strategic planning and strategic management.

A business strategy is developed by the executive management team led by the Chief Executive Officer (CEO), president, or other leader of an organization. The purpose of the strategy is to clearly identify the goals to be achieved by the organization, create an implementation plan, and distribute assets and other resources needed for success. HR professionals contribute to business strategy as the subject matter experts (SMEs) for attracting, retaining, and managing a workforce qualified to implement the strategy and achieve organization goals.

SPHR ONLY Strategic Planning

Global competition requires business leaders to use many tools to give them an advantageous position in the marketplace. One such tool is known as *strategic planning*. Broadly defined, strategic planning is a systematic way of setting the direction for an organization and developing tactics and operational plans to ensure its success. Strategic planning is a dynamic process—it's not something an organization does one time to produce an attractively bound booklet that sits on the shelf gathering dust. By its very nature, strategic planning requires that organizations constantly revisit the plan to make sure it's still viable in the face of changes within the organization and in the marketplace. The strategic planning process answers four essential questions:

- Where are we now?
- Where do we want to be?
- How will we get there?
- How will we know when we arrive?

Because strategic planning has been a popular topic for business writers, consultants, and academicians during the past decade, there are a number of planning models from which to choose.

The specific model selected for use in an organization will depend on the structure and culture of that organization. The elements of all the models fall into four very broad categories: environmental scanning, strategy formulation, strategy implementation, and strategy evaluation.

You should be aware of how all these elements contribute to the strategic planning process. Figure 3.1 illustrates a typical strategic planning process.

The steps are described here in a logical sequence. In real life, the process may not occur in a straight-line progression; if new information that will affect results is uncovered at any stage, previous steps may be revisited so the information can be incorporated into the plans and goals.

Planning to Plan

Very often, a strategic planning initiative is led by a consultant experienced in the process. This is helpful for many reasons, not least of which is that during the course of determining the future of the organization, disagreements about the long-term direction of the company may surface, and these are more readily resolved with a neutral third party who is better able to facilitate a resolution and move the process forward than someone with a vested interest in the outcome. When a consultant is used, the preplanning process is generally part of the service they provide.

The *preplan* includes decisions about who will be invited to participate and at what stages in the process, a time frame for completing the plan, and a determination of the tools to be used in collecting data for the plan. Spending this additional time at the beginning of the process could prevent costly errors or omissions from being made and can assist in making the resulting strategic plan more accurate and meaningful.

The result of this stage should be an agreement about the process to be followed, a list of those who will be involved at various stages in the process and the type of information they will be asked to provide, the timeline for completing the plan, and a list of the planning tools to be used in gathering information to be used in the planning process.

Let's begin by defining the terms that will be used to discuss the strategic planning process:

- A *strategy* uses the strengths of a business to its competitive advantage in the marketplace.

- A *goal* describes the direction the business will take and what it will achieve. Goals are set at the corporate and business-unit levels of the organization.

- An *objective* is a specific description of the practical steps that will be taken to achieve the business goals. Objectives are set at the functional level of the organization.

To effectively determine the future direction of a company, it's necessary to know what is going on within the organization, industry, and marketplace and to know what the technology developments will mean for operations. Beginning the strategic planning process with this information can help to focus management on a plan that will avoid pitfalls and take advantage of existing opportunities.

Environmental Scanning

As discussed more fully in Chapter 2, an *environmental scan* is the framework for collecting information to create a successful plan for future growth. Information gathered during the scan is used to forecast future business circumstances so that the organization can take advantage of the strengths and opportunities presented by the marketplace while reducing the negative impact of its weaknesses and external threats. The forecasting process is particularly crucial when organizations are in the midst of rapid change. For example, the forecast allows management to be proactive by redesigning products that will comply with regulations being proposed by federal or state governments so that they're available when the regulations take effect.

During the forecasting process, management must consider the impact of changes that are anticipated to take place over the long term, mid term, and short term. *Long-range plans* set the organization's direction for 3 to 5 years, *midrange plans* can be accomplished in 1 to 3 years, and *short-range plans* will be achieved within 6 to 12 months. Plans that incorporate the information gathered during the environmental scan are developed during the next planning phase, which is strategy formulation.

FIGURE 3.1   Elements of the strategic planning process

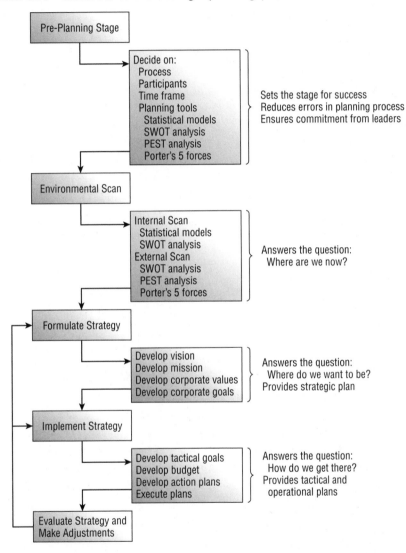

Interpreting the information from the environmental scan is one of the many contributions made by HR through the strategic planning process. An environmental scan and its corresponding activities are methods used to identify the following:

General Business Environment   Who is hiring, what price points are selling, trends, and the culture

Industry Practices and Developments   Changes in the industry, as well as an evaluation of the competition

Technological Advances   Technology related to streamlining practices, automation, and database management

Economic Environment   Economic indicators, product positioning, and new product needs

Changes in the Labor Force Population   The unemployment rate, availability of labor by skill set, and demographic shifts

Legal and Regulatory Environment   Compliance with new regulations or regulations that have been triggered by employment numbers

Strategy Formulation

Having scanned both the internal and external environments and gathered data relevant to the strategic planning process, the executive team is ready to create the vision, mission, and core value statements, which guide the organization over the long term. Once these long-term guidelines have been established, corporate goals are developed to provide direction during the implementation phase:

Vision Statement   A vision statement should inspire the organization and inform customers and shareholders, describing what will carry the organization into the future and what it will accomplish. In a very concise way, the vision statement should communicate what the company does, for whom it does it, and what long-range success will look like.

Mission Statement   The mission statement gets a bit more specific, describing how the organization will achieve the vision. Effective mission statements describe the company, what it does, where it's going, and how it's different from other organizations. The message of the mission statement is generally directed at employees in the organization, and it should tell them where the company is headed in the mid to long term.

Core Competencies   During the formulation of a strategic plan, organizations often identify their *core competencies*: the parts of their operations that they do best and that set them apart from the competition. Many organizations believe that focusing on these core competencies makes it possible to expand their revenue streams. Competencies can be related to the technology used in operations, customer relationship management, product characteristics, manufacturing processes, knowledge management, organization culture, or combinations of these or other organizational aspects that work together synergistically and are difficult for others to replicate. When core competencies are identified, organizations can focus their strategy on ways to build related products or services instead of moving into unrelated areas.

Corporate Values Statement   A statement of corporate values is a way for the executive team to communicate their standards for how the organization will conduct business.

The values chosen for this purpose should be those that will be true regardless of changes in product lines or business processes. A question to ask in selecting an organization's values is whether the value would hold true if the organization changed its focus entirely and began doing business in a completely different way. Values such as integrity, excellence, teamwork, customer service, and mutual respect are some of those that remain constant regardless of changes in business operations.

These beliefs about the organization are usually reflected in its culture. When identifying corporate values, it's important to look not only at what the management team would like to see in the way of behaviors in the organization but also at the values being demonstrated in the course of business each day. When there are discrepancies between the stated, formal values and the informal values demonstrated by the workforce, the strategic plan can include goals designed to align the two.

Once the vision and mission statements have defined why the organization exists, corporate goals are needed to describe how the organization will get there in the mid to long term. Effective corporate goals follow the SMART model:

Specific The goal should be descriptive enough to guide business-unit managers in developing action plans that will accomplish the goal.

Measurable The goal must include a method for determining when it has been met.

Action-Oriented Goals must describe the actions that will be taken.

Realistic The goal must be high enough to challenge the organization or individual but not so high that it's unachievable.

Time-Based Goals must include a time frame for completion.

Once identified, these elements are combined into one strategic document, often called a *business plan*. The contents of a business plan may vary, but ultimately, it must match the purpose identified through the strategic planning process. Identifying performance targets, recommending new products or services to use the existing talent, and defining net income expectations are examples of HR activities that are represented in a business plan. It's from this document that implementation begins.

Strategy Implementation

The strategy implementation phase further defines the corporate goals for implementation at the business-unit and functional levels of the organization. It's at this stage that most of the short-range goals are developed:

Develop Tactical Goals Whereas the strategic goal broadly defines direction, the tactical goal describes what will be accomplished to achieve the strategy.

Develop Action Plans The action plan breaks down the tactical goal into steps to be taken by an individual, a team, or an operating group to accomplish the tactical goal.

Real World Scenario

Wright Sisters, Inc. Strategic Plan

As you recall from Chapter 2, Wright Sisters Inc. (WSI) is a fictional company with 3,000 employees that has been recently challenged by the appearance of a new manufacturing plant in the small Midwestern city where it's located. The unexpected impact of this seemingly small change in the external environment has made senior management and the board of directors realize how unprepared they are to respond rapidly to changes in their business sector. They've decided to be proactive and implement a strategic planning process to discover what other unexpected changes could be lurking in the future.

Over the years, there have been many changes in the market for WSI's products, both technological and demographic. Because WSI has always maintained strong relationships with the hardware stores that distribute its products, WSI has been able to meet the changing needs of its customer base.

As a result of the strategic planning process, the WSI board has settled on the following statement of their vision for the company:

> "Bringing the joy of gardening to new generations of gardeners."

To accomplish this vision, WSI has developed a mission to guide its operations over the next five years:

> "We are the home-gardening source. The quality of our products allows busy families to enjoy gardening together. Our gardening education programs grow 'gardeners for life' by teaching adults and children to make gardening easier and more enjoyable."

Based on the company's history and its vision and mission statements, the board created a corporate value statement to set expectations for how employees and managers interact:

> "WSI values integrity and excellence in its products and its people. We treat ourselves, our customers, and our suppliers with dignity and respect. We believe in and encourage new ideas to make our products better and help our business grow, and we acknowledge and reward those who present these ideas. We are accountable for our actions and, when mistakes occur, we focus on preventing future errors and moving forward. We are passionate about achieving our goals, and we are passionate about gardening."

As a result of the environmental scan, the WSI board learned that one of its underutilized strengths is the popularity of "Ask Lydia," a gardening column written by one of its founders, Lydia Wright. Because of this, they have decided to capitalize on Lydia Wright's knowledge of and passion for gardening. To do this, they have developed the following corporate goal:

"Within three years, create a nationally recognized gardening education program based on the 'Ask Lydia' columns."

In order to accomplish this midrange goal, the marketing department has developed a short-range tactical goal and action plan:

Tactical goal: "Increase the number of newspapers in which 'Ask Lydia' appears by 25 by the end of the fiscal year."

The marketing action plan looks like this:

1. Identify newspapers to target.

2. Create a sales pitch.

3. Contact editors.

4. Draw up contracts.

5. Submit weekly columns.

With the goals in place, the marketing department is now able to develop a budget and implement the plan.

SPHR ONLY Develop a Budget

Once the action plans are developed, it's possible to determine how many and what kind of resources will be required to implement the strategy. The plan may require additional employees, funds to outsource some components of the plan, or the purchase of new technology or new equipment; if so, these elements determine how much cash is required to achieve the desired goal. At this point, those involved in the planning process have the information necessary to analyze the cost of achieving the goals against the potential benefits before committing resources to implement the strategy.

Refer to Chapter 2 for a more detailed discussion of the budget development process.

SPHR ONLY Strategy Evaluation

The ability of a company to accomplish its mission and conduct business in accordance with its core values largely depends on the behavior modeled by upper management. Employees are quickly able to observe any disconnect between what the employer says and what the employer does. Reinforcing values through corporate behavior is accomplished by modeling value-based behavior, communicating successful missions (celebrating success), and coaching employees using the mission, vision, and values as performance benchmarks. These activities help the organization achieve positive outcomes while reinforcing its strategic plan.

Evaluating the strategy tells the planners whether the organization is achieving the desired goals and moving the strategy forward. This stage is important because if the action plans aren't working or if conditions in the marketplace change, the organization must be prepared to respond immediately and adjust the tactical goals and action plans. In some cases, the corporate goal may need to be revisited and adjusted to adapt to the change in conditions. One method of evaluation is the balanced scorecard discussed later in this chapter.

Human Capital Management Plans

During the strategic planning process, HR, along with all other business functions, develops tactical goals and action plans designed to meet the needs of the organization. For HR, the result is known as a *human capital management plan (HCMP)*. Also known as a *strategic HR plan*, an HCMP answers the same four questions addressed during the strategic planning process previously described:

- Where are we now?
- Where do we want to be?
- How will we get there?
- How will we know when we arrive?

To be effective and credible, the HCMP must align with the corporate strategy and goals and help achieve the desired business results. So, the answer to the question "Where do we want to be?" is based on the human capital requirements of the goals in the organization's strategic plan. From there, the HCMP lays out the HR contribution to those goals. The most impactful HCMP is as critical as any marketing plan or R&D road map—something that creates a competitive advantage for the organization.

The specific requirements of an HCMP will differ in various organizations, but some common components need to be addressed, as described in Table 3.1.

TABLE 3.1   Human capital management plan

Component	Description
HR statement of strategic direction	The HR team gathers information from the organization's strategic plan, external sources (such as labor market demographics), and internal sources (other functional areas of the organization), and so on, to clearly understand the workforce requirements for organization goals, what resources are available to achieve those goals, and the timing of deliverables.
Desired results or goals	Broadly stated, what will the HR function contribute to the organization's strategic goals? For example, "Attract and retain skilled workers to assemble the new product line."
Objectives	What, specifically, will HR do to achieve its goals? For example, "Reduce time to hire."

Component	Description
Action plans	Identify the steps to be taken to achieve the objectives. For example, "Hire contract recruiter with expertise in sourcing candidates with required skills."
Communication plan	If necessary to achieve the objective, describe how HR will notify the organization of changes. For example, "Conduct workshop for production supervisors on hiring for retention."
Measurement	The means used to measure success of the HCMP coincide with other measures used by the organization. For example, if the technical workforce in the production department needs to be increased to accommodate a new product line, a hiring target of x number of employees can be used. For other types of objectives, metrics such as retention rate, ROI, and so on, may be more appropriate.

Information developed during the HCMP is necessary for creating the HR function budget—the basic budgeting elements covered in Chapter 2 are used in creating this as well as the organization budget process. As with any functional area budget, some standard expense items are under the control of the head of the HR functions, such as the following:

- Salaries
- Payroll taxes
- Benefits
- Equipment and supplies
- Repairs and maintenance
- Training and development (for HR team)
- Travel
- Professional services
- Outsourced services (HRIS, payroll, and so on)

The budget may also include expenses that are allocated from budgets created in other functional areas, such as the following:

- Liability insurance (often managed by the accounting or finance function)
- Software (often purchased through the IT function)
- Computer hardware (often purchased through the IT function)

In some organizations, the HR function creates budget items that are then allocated to other functional business units, such as the following:

- Training and development
- Employee awards

- Performance increases
- Temporary replacements
- Recruiting fees

Positioning HR as a strategic partner also requires scrutiny of current HR practices with an eye toward streamlining them to increase organizational productivity and to provide better service to internal customers. This could mean replacing the HR department head count with outsourced services, implementing an employee self-service system, or implementing an HRIS that provides managers with access to information about their direct reports. These and similar process changes can reduce HR department costs and free professionals to spend more time on other organization issues.

Human Capital Projections

The "human" in human resources refers to the people getting the work done on behalf of the organization. *Human capital projecting* is a budgetary activity in which HR attempts to measure the value of these resources. These projections take into account the elements of the HCMP, creating depth by identifying the current competencies of the existing internal workforce. Further creating the competitive advantage, the process analyzes the skill set of the current employees and matches it to the skill sets necessary to accomplish the strategic objectives. From here, the gap is documented, and a plan is created to develop the competencies necessary to meet performance targets. These projections take into account the following:

- The necessary skill set of the workforce to achieve both short-term and long-term objectives as communicated through the strategic plan
- The current skill set of the workforce, measured through the performance management system
- The creation of a plan to address any deficiencies
- The decision to build or buy/develop the talent in-house or hire from the external labor force
- The cost of implementation
- The return on the investment in the human resource

One example of a strategic consideration related to human capital management is the national unemployment rate. It's often a great moment to "buy" talent from outside the organization in times of high unemployment, because the surplus of available labor and knowledge resources allows companies to compete at far less cost than in a healthy economic climate. Although it may seem at first glance that freezing hiring in times of economic stress is a good strategy, HR must make the argument for hiring when the right conditions exist, calculate the ROI, and align the hiring behavior with the organizational objectives.

Finally, with the shift of U.S. labor output from manufacturing to service, it has become necessary to measure knowledge and mind competencies rather than quantifiable or objective physical output. See Chapter 5 for more information on knowledge management.

Strategic Management

As organizations developed and grew ever larger, the need for controlling large numbers of workers in geographically diverse locations presented a challenge for business owners, who responded by creating bureaucracies to ensure that operations were conducted in accordance with the direction set by senior management. These bureaucracies, developed by American businessmen in the mid-nineteenth century, enabled the dominance of American products throughout the world for 100 years and were emulated by businesses in other countries. As long as the demand for products was greater than the number of products available, this model, in which business dictated what it would produce to the customer, worked extremely well.

When business conditions changed and customers became more demanding, this "one size fits all" approach was not as successful. Japanese manufacturers gave customers an alternative, and customers responded by purchasing those companies' products. American businesses, because of their bureaucratic methods, were slow to respond. The need for constant innovation to satisfy changing customer needs was a difficult transition, and it continues to affect American business.

It's up to management to ensure that the strategies and plans developed to meet changing customer needs are implemented and accomplished. Four basic management functions are used for this purpose: planning, organizing, directing, and controlling. These functions ensure that organization resources are used in the best way to achieve corporate goals. The planning function has been covered extensively; let's talk briefly now about the other functions:

Organizing   Managers are responsible for providing a structure within which employees are able to complete their work. Many factors must be considered, including what work needs to be done, how employees interact and with whom, the decision-making process in the organization, and how work is delegated. Issues to be considered in developing an organization structure are whether management is centralized or decentralized, the nature of the functions, and the span of control for each manager.

A *centralized organization* is one in which the decision-making authority is concentrated at higher levels in the organization; in a *decentralized organization*, the decision-making authority is delegated to lower levels.

Business functions are classified as either *line functions*, such as operations and sales, which make decisions about operating needs, or *staff functions*, such as human resources and finance, which don't make operating decisions but do advise line managers.

Finally, *span of control* refers to the number of employees that one manager can directly supervise. Depending on the nature and complexity of the task, this number varies. Managers responsible for very complex tasks requiring closer supervision are able to supervise fewer employees than managers responsible for those performing less complex tasks.

The five basic organization structures—functional, product-based, geographical, divisional, and matrix—are described in Chapter 2, as is the emerging seamless organization. Each is appropriate for different situations, as described in that chapter.

Directing   Managers must establish relationships with the employees they supervise to encourage and support them in accomplishing their goals. Management style contributes to the development of these relationships. Chapter 2 discusses different management styles in detail.

Controlling   The control function is used by managers to ensure that the strategies, tactics, and plans developed during the planning process are implemented. As discussed earlier in "Strategy Evaluation," this is an ongoing process. In addition to evaluating individual goals and action plans as described in that section, management must have a "big picture" view of overall progress.

There are other methods for controlling operations, such as Six Sigma, total quality management (TQM), and management by objectives (MBO). These are also used as organizational development strategies and are discussed in Chapter 5.

Another management responsibility is managing risk to protect the organization's assets and ensure continuity of operations in extreme conditions, discussed later in this chapter and in Chapter 8, "Risk Management."

Strategic Relationships

If the purpose of business strategy is to plot the course for organizational success, what is meant by a *strategic relationship*? For HR professionals, strategic relationships are those that advance the contribution of the HR function toward achieving organization goals. Strategic relationships reflect the business plan and are important enough to make any strategic-planning tool succeed or fail. Strategic relationships are built between individuals defined as *stakeholders*, who are the employees, the management hierarchy, the shareholders, and the community. In addition, these relationships create a subculture of the very identity of the brand—both internally from the perspective of the management team and their employees and externally, driven by the forces of the business climate.

It could be argued that the success of any strategic or business planning outcomes depends on the quality of the internal and external relationships:

Internal Relationships   Internal relationships that move HR toward the accomplishment of organization goals are built over time as the HR function establishes its credibility with the executive team, management, employees, and vendors. Credibility is established when the HR function provides solutions to organization workforce problems at all levels. Often identified through an organizational chart, the relationships that exist within the corporate framework reflect both personal and professional connections. The ability of individuals to work with each other helps create the culture that drives business outcomes and often is the target of HR efforts defined under the function of employee and management relations. These individual relationships are further enhanced when they're built on the shared responsibilities and outcomes of the business departments described at the beginning of the chapter. Communication, goal-setting, and project-management skills are representative of the types of behaviors that can be addressed through strategic employee relations activities.

These labor-management relationships are at the core of many of HR's responsibilities, because HR defines the structure from which management takes employment-related action. The following are examples of the HR activities that define these relationships:

- Creating policies, procedures, and rules

- Complying with legal and regulatory directives

- Analyzing jobs from which job descriptions and performance metrics are developed

- Employing strategic HCMPs to ensure that the workforce has the appropriate skill set to achieve the corporate objectives identified through the strategic planning process

External Relationships   A network of individuals whose work influences or intersects with an organization's goals brings long-range benefits to HR professionals. Frequently, the ease with which you can obtain information about the best service providers, find employees with critical skills, or build partnerships that add value to human resource programs and influence the bottom line is enhanced when relationships are established before they're needed.

In addition, identifying reliable, high-quality service providers for organization workforce needs, such as recruiting agencies, benefit brokers, and others with expertise in areas of importance to the organization, ensures the availability of needed services when they're required.

 Outsourcing HR Functions   In some cases, it may be strategically advantageous for an organization to outsource individual HR systems such as payroll and benefit administration, to outsource the entire function to an HR *business process outsource* (BPO) provider, or to lease employees through a *professional employer organization* (PEO). When this is the case, selecting the appropriate vendor for an organization is crucial to establishing a successful relationship with services that meet the organization's needs. As with any other strategic decision, the first step is to clearly define the services required of the provider as well as the organization's service expectations to ensure that business needs are met. It's also important to identify the responsibilities of both parties so that there is a framework for addressing situations that aren't specifically covered in the agreement. This is most commonly done using the request-for-proposal process described in Chapter 2.

Considering that virtually all HR processes have the potential to affect every member of an organization, it's crucial that HR ensures a smooth transition to the provider and clearly communicates process changes to the organization.

Corporate Responsibility

Corporate responsibility (CR) is a business behavior that is focused on building external strategic relationships. Identifying the CR goals and resulting behaviors used for future decision making is an element of the strategic planning process.

CR activities are interdependent on multiple department responsibilities, thus linking the external environment to the internal environment. Achieving the CR objectives often requires the active participation and commitment of the entire organization.

The emerging stakeholders with an investment in the outcomes of CR activities are often identified as those with a need for deeper participation and activity on the part of their business leaders (employees and the community), social initiatives, and the global landscape. These stakeholders typically are represented at a local, national, or global level. Starbucks CEO Howard Schultz had this to say about corporate responsibility:

> Values increasingly drive consumer and employee loyalties. Money and talent will follow those companies whose values are compatible with their own.
>
> *From "Invest in Communities to Advance Capitalism" by Howard Schultz. Harvard Business Review blog, 17 October 2011: http://blogs. hbr.org/cs/2011/10/ceos_should_invest_in_communit.html*

How does an organization identify which CR objectives to address? The same forces described by Porter (as discussed in Chapter 2) drive the need for CR efforts. The local economy, the skill set of the national labor force, and the global marketplace are all examples of these forces that create the direction of this strategic effort (see Table 3.2).

TABLE 3.2   Using five forces to identify corporate responsibility initiatives

Porter's 5 Forces	Examples of Corporate Responsibility Considerations	Strategic Benefit	Operational Outcomes
Political/Legal	American Labor Laws	Global positive brand recognition	Fair wages and working conditions at facilities outside of the United States
Economic	Skill set of the labor force population	The ability to define the skill sets of future labor to create or sustain a qualified workforce	Training of the existing workforce; supplying tools to classrooms
Social	Often driven by trends such as: Sustainability Disaster response Corporate governance	Increased efficiencies, risk management, cultural perception of the brand	Engage in best practices, partner with local emergency-response teams, have a corporate ethics officer or conduct committee. These responses can all vary based on the current social trend or need.

Porter's 5 Forces	Examples of Corporate Responsibility Considerations	Strategic Benefit	Operational Outcomes
Technology	Worker privacy, data protection, security of confidential information	Risk management, consumer and employee confidence	Investment in proper tools and programs, training of the workforce, policy development
Competition	The global marketplace, quality vs. production costs, the values of the suppliers	Profit, market share, customer loyalty, trust	Supply-chain management, managing the cost of production, continued scanning of the external environment

Sustainability

Sustainability is defined as behavior that doesn't deplete the resources used to achieve an outcome. These resources include time, labor, and finances, all three of which have a significant impact on the long-term health of a corporation. Sustainability first became a widely recognized principle as the result of "green" initiatives, and companies now understand that the financial benefit of sustainable business practices is a long-term strategic solution that influences factors far beyond their environmental footprint.

CR and sustainability are the responsibility of all departments, with HR being no exception. Figure 3.2 shows examples of HR behaviors that support corporate responsibility and accountability efforts.

FIGURE 3.2   HR's role in CR efforts

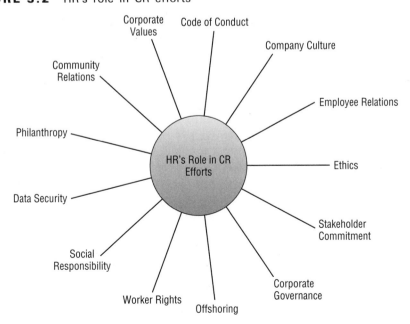

Change Management

One possible result of a strategic planning process can be structural changes to an organization. Although, intellectually, many people understand the need for these changes, how they're personally affected has a direct impact on employee morale and productivity. There are two aspects to the change process: structural changes (covered in this chapter) and individual behavior (covered in Chapter 5). The discussion of methods and how they can be used to effect organizational change occurs in Chapter 5, along with the discussion of the impact of changes on individuals in the organization. This section provides a brief look at the structural changes that significantly affect workforce populations today:

Reengineering   Reengineering involves looking at the entire organization to simplify or eliminate unnecessary processes with the goal of increasing customer satisfaction through improvements in efficiency.

Corporate Restructuring   Corporate restructuring looks at individual units in the organization to reduce or eliminate redundancy or bureaucratic processes in order to reduce costs and increase production.

Workforce Expansion   Workforce expansions create their own type of stress in an organization. When a large number of employees enter an organization within a short period of time, it can be difficult for them to assimilate into the existing culture and climate. The resulting clashes of operating styles (face-to-face vs. email communication, team orientation vs. individual contributors, or authoritarian vs. laissez-faire management style, for example) can create mistrust and reduce productivity.

Workforce Reduction   Workforce reductions, also known as *reductions in force* (RIFs), *downsizing*, or *rightsizing*, are used to decrease expenses by reducing the size of the workforce. One way RIFs are used is to lower expenses for short-term improvements in net profits in order to meet previously stated earnings targets for stock-market analysts.

 Mergers and Acquisitions   Mergers and acquisitions (M&A) have similar results—the combining of two organizations into one—but they happen for different reasons and in somewhat different ways. A *merger* occurs when two or more organizations are combined into a single entity with the goal of leveraging the assets of both into a more successful entity. One well-known recent merger was that between Sirius Satellite Radio and XM Satellite Radio in 2008.

An *acquisition* occurs when one organization, generally a corporation, purchases or trades stock to gain controlling interest in another. Acquisitions can be hostile, when the management and board of directors of the company being acquired object to the takeover. Hostile takeovers are usually antagonistic, with the acquiring company purchasing shares on the open stock market. This type of acquisition can negatively affect employee morale as rumors about mass layoffs circulate among the staff of the target organization. For example, in 2011, after a friendly bid by International Paper for Temple-Inland was rejected by Temple-Inland's board of directors, International Paper went directly to the shareholders with a $3.31 billion offer. This offer was 46 percent more than what Temple-Inland stock was trading for in the days leading up to the offer.

Go online to see a Bloomberg video of International Paper's CEO discussing its takeover attempt for Temple-Inland at www.bloomberg.com/video/70556482/.

In a friendly takeover, the management and board of the targeted company agree to terms offered by the acquiring organization, generally a cash purchase of stock or a predetermined number of shares in the acquiring company. An example of an acquisition was the purchase of Siebel Systems in 2005 by its competitor, Oracle Corporation.

HR professionals participate in the due-diligence process prior to a merger or an acquisition. There are many aspects to review in order to obtain a complete picture of the employment practices of the target company. The types of information to be collected as part of the due-diligence process include the following:

Documents

- Names of all employees and their locations
- Offer letters
- Employment contracts
- I-9 forms and visa documentation
- Benefit plans

Compensation

- Hourly wage rates by job
- Salary schedules
- Number of employees in each position

Policies and procedures

- Policy manual
- Employee handbook
- Supervisor/manager handbook

Equal opportunity compliance

- EEO-1 reports
- Affirmative Action Plans (if required)
- Government notices of compliance activity

Legal compliance

- COBRA notices and participants
- Active FMLA leaves
- WARN compliance
- OSHA compliance

Labor relations

- Collective bargaining agreements
- Ongoing negotiations
- Union activity
- Grievance history and outstanding grievances

Legal exposure

- Pending or resolved sexual-harassment claims
- Termination disputes
- Violations of state or federal laws
- Active workers' compensation claims

HR professionals also work to facilitate the successful integration of the two workforces in a merger or an acquisition. To begin with, an analysis of the workforce of the two organizations provides information on how to best utilize people in the new entity. This may result in transferring employees into different positions or reducing the workforce as redundant operations are identified and streamlined. Development of strategies to retain key employees is an important task, particularly during the initial period of uncertainty. In the longer term, one of the most difficult transitions is combining the two cultures into a cohesive environment that enhances productivity.

SPHR ONLY **Divestitures**   In a divestiture, a company asset such as a product line, a division, or another part of an organization is sold or somehow disposed of. This may occur as the result of a strategic decision to focus on core competencies or because the asset has greater value as a stand-alone operation than as part of the original organization. In some cases, there will be little change to day-to-day operations for employees because the organization remains intact with a new ownership structure.

Offshoring and Outsourcing Decisions and Management   Offshoring is the process of moving production or service processes to other countries to realize cost savings. For example, India has become a popular offshore site for U.S. service processes, such as customer support call centers.

Outsourcing contracts internal business services to outside organizations that specialize in the specific process, such as payroll processing, IT, or janitorial services.

Either decision generally results in a reduction in staff for employees who previously did the work that will now be done externally. In some cases, an outsource firm may hire those employees, who will continue to do the same work as members of the new organization.

No matter the cause, even employees who remain in the company after a change occurs are affected by it. A key contribution to be made by HR during change is to be sure the decision makers understand the difficulties that employees will face during and after the change and how those difficulties affect productivity. HR can put programs into place that mitigate the negative effects of the change as much as possible. It's simply not possible to overcommunicate in such situations. Some steps that can help reduce employee anxiety include the following:

- Keep employees in the loop about the actual situation.

- If there are actions that employees can take to remedy the situation, tell them what they can do.

- When talking to employees, be honest and truthful. Don't hide the facts.

Good or bad, the way companies handle change will be remembered long after employees have adjusted to the new way of doing business. The long-term impact of including employees in the change process through open and honest communication is to increase loyalty and productivity. If the organization has a habit of being brutal in its change processes, long-term productivity suffers, and it will be more difficult to attract and retain the quality of employees needed for future success.

Enterprise Risk Management

Enterprise risk management (ERM) is a practice of forecasting possible risks to the organization and taking steps to mitigate their impact on operations. The first step in ERM is to identify the risks; for HR, that means conducting an audit of HR practices to identify areas of potential loss.

SPHR ONLY HR Audits

An *HR audit* identifies areas that may be out of compliance with legal requirements or are in need of updating because of strategic changes within the organization, and it defines elements that are working well. First identifying the exposure factors and then developing an audit system to measure the current levels based on behaviors and outcomes (not the intent) are important contributions of HR within the scope of ERM.

Once possible risks are identified and analyzed, options to mitigate the risks are reviewed, and recommendations for handling the risk are made. Depending on the level of risk and its possible impact on operations, decisions can be made about how to handle each risk. When a risk has been identified, the following are examples of the types of audits HR can use to minimize exposure and to demonstrate a good-faith effort toward compliance:

Hiring Statistics at All Levels of Employees   What percentage of your management team are protected-class individuals?

Recruiting Sources   Which recruiting sources offer the most diverse pool of qualified applicants?

Data Security   Review components such as the security of confidential information, breaches in the process, and the validity of control measures.

I9 Audits   Verify procedures, and conduct a review to reduce penalties associated with improperly completed forms.

Harassment Claim Management   Review training records, conduct an employee survey to ensure that claims are taken seriously, and review the policy to ensure compliance with both state and federal laws.

An experienced HR professional is capable of identifying the elements that should be audited and monitoring the process. A complete audit will include a review of policies and practices in all the functional areas of HR, including hiring, compensation, benefits, training and development programs, employee relations, records management, legal and regulatory compliance, and safety. HR audits can use a variety of methods to obtain the information needed for an assessment, including checklists or questionnaires, surveys of employees and managers, and interviews.

Insurance Policies

For some risks, the purchase of an insurance policy will adequately protect the organization. Employment practices liability insurance (EPLI) provides protection for employers to help them reduce the potential loss associated with various employment-related claims. Sexual harassment, discrimination, and wrongful discipline are some examples of the types of protection EPLI offers. In cases where the risk is low, a plan for self-insuring—that is, to pay out-of-pocket should the risk occur—may make sense. It may be possible to reduce the level of risk for some practices, such as unsigned I-9 forms, by implementing checklists or reviewing procedures. The potential exposure from other risks may be so high that eliminating the practice would provide the best protection for the organization.

Employee Handbooks

An employee handbook can be an organization's first step toward compliance with labor laws that require or recommend written policies as part of compliance efforts. A well-written policy can protect the employer against potentials risks from the following: sexual harassment, reasonable accommodations of employees with a disability, safety, wage and hour laws, and at-will employment statements and leave laws. An employee handbook should include the company's expectations, the employees' rights, and the company's legal obligations to the employees. For a more in-depth discussion regarding employee handbooks, see Chapter 7, "Employee and Labor Relations."

Litigation Statistics

Another way to identify an organization's risk is to identify current trends based on litigation statistics. For example, the Equal Employment Opportunity Commission (EEOC) compiles a list of all charges filed with the agency related to adverse employment actions. Although a charge filed with the EEOC doesn't by default mean that a company is guilty of an illegal practice, the burden of proof rests firmly with the employer. A company must dedicate the resources necessary to defend a charge once filed. See Table 3.3 for the types of EEOC charges filed from 2006 through 2010.

In late 2011, the EEOC issued its Performance and Accountability Report for 2011, reporting nearly 100,000 new charges of discrimination—the most new charges filed in any year in the agency's nearly 50-year history. View the report in its entirety at www.eeoc.gov/eeoc/plan/upload/2011par.pdf.

TABLE 3.3 Types of EEOC charges filed from 2006 through 2010

	FY 2006	FY 2007	FY 2008	FY 2009	FY 2010
Total Charges	75,768	82,792	95,402	93,277	99,922
Race	27,238	30,510	33,937	33,579	35,890
	35.9%	37.0%	35.6%	36.0%	35.9%
Sex	23,247	24,826	28,372	28,028	29,029
	30.7%	30.1%	29.7%	30.0%	29.1%
National Origin	8,327	9,396	10,601	11,134	11,304
	11.0%	11.4%	11.1%	11.9%	11.3%
Religion	2,541	2,880	3,273	3,386	3,790
	3.4%	3.5%	3.4%	3.6%	3.8%
Retaliation - All Statutes	22,555	26,663	32,690	33,613	36,258
	29.8%	32.3%	34.3%	36.0%	36.3%
Retaliation - Title VII only	19,560	23,371	28,698	28,948	30,948
	25.8%	28.3%	30.1%	31.0%	31.0%
Age	16,548	19,103	24,582	22,778	23,264
	21.8%	23.2%	25.8%	24.4%	23.3%
Disability	15,575	17,734	19,453	21,451	25,165
	20.6%	21.4%	20.4%	23.0%	25.2%
Equal Pay Act	861	818	954	942	1,044
	1.1%	1.0%	1.0%	1.0%	1.0%

Source: Equal Employment Opportunity Commission. Sourced on October 28, 2011 at http://eeoc.gov/eeoc/statistics/enforcement/charges.cfm

NOTE

In Table 3.3, the Total Charges number reflects the number of individual charge filings. Because individuals often file charges claiming multiple types of discrimination, the number of total charges for any given fiscal year is less than the total of the eight types of discrimination listed.

The data are compiled by the Office of Research, Information, and Planning from data reported via quarterly reconciled Data Summary Reports and compiled from the EEOC's Charge Data System and, from FY 2004 forward, the EEOC's Integrated Mission System.

Other

Other examples of risk-management trending and forecasting include the following:

- Unemployment rates by geographic location

- Safety standards (for example, ergonomics and heat-illness prevention)

- Updates to labor laws referencing cultural or technological trends (such as religious discrimination post September 11, 2001; disaster preparedness in response to Hurricane Katrina; or Office of Federal Contract Compliance Programs [OFCCP] regulations for defining an "Internet applicant")

SPHR ONLY **HR Technology**

As mentioned earlier in this chapter, the human resource role in organizations has evolved over the years. One area most changed by this evolution is the administrative function. Because of technological developments, there are many opportunities to reduce the amount of time required by HR staff to perform these types of tasks. Table 3.4 describes some of the functions that are more easily and accurately accomplished with the use of technological tools such as human resource information systems (HRIS) and applicant tracking systems (ATS).

TABLE 3.4   HR technology applications

Wage and Hour	HR Management	Benefit Administration
Timekeeping	Recruiting	Eligibility
Payroll	Employee records	COBRA administration
Tax payments	Workforce planning	Annual open enrollment
Attendance	EEO compliance	
Work schedules	Compensation management	
Garnishment orders	Performance management Succession planning	

In addition to automating repetitive tasks and more accurately maintaining records, technological advances also provide opportunities to improve the accuracy of information and accessibility for employees and managers by providing them with direct access to the information they need. For employees, this could mean the ability to access and update personal information such as address and dependent status changes (referred to as *employee self-service*). For managers, this could take the form of access to performance-management or training records. Even candidates can benefit through the ability to input their resumes or applications directly into the applicant-tracking system.

Legislative and Regulatory Processes

The human resource profession can play a key role in the development of legislation and regulations affecting the employment relationship between an organization and its employees. HR professionals should be aware of the ways in which they, as individual citizens and as business leaders, can affect these processes. Because the PHR/SPHR exam is based on federal laws, this section will discuss how proposed legislation or regulation is handled by the federal government. A similar process is followed by state and local governments, and involvement at any level of government can benefit business organizations.

Legislative Process

The federal legislative process begins when someone has an idea. This idea can come from a senator or congressman, an individual, a business, a church, or a professional association. Ideas for particular types of legislation may also come from citizen's groups, lobbyists, or special-interest groups interested in solving a particular problem. If the idea comes from someone other than a member of Congress (MOC), it must be presented to a member of the U.S. House of Representatives or U.S. Senate to begin the process of becoming a law. The steps in the process are as follows:

1. When an MOC agrees to sponsor a bill and presents it to the full body of the House or the Senate, it's assigned to a committee for study.

2. The committee first determines the likelihood that the bill will be able to pass a vote in the full body; if the determination is made that it isn't likely to pass, no further action is taken, and the bill effectively dies in the committee.

3. Bills that are deemed likely to pass a vote of the full body are studied by a subcommittee, and hearings are conducted to obtain input from government representatives, subject-matter experts, and citizens with points of view for or against the bill.

4. Once the bill has been studied, the subcommittee may make changes, a process known as *marking up* the bill. The subcommittee then votes on whether to return the bill to the full committee with a recommendation for further action. A bill that isn't reported back to the committee dies in the subcommittee.

5. Bills that are returned to the full committee may be subjected to further study, or the committee may vote to accept the subcommittee recommendations and "order the bill reported" to the full body.

6. When the committee votes to report a bill to the full body, a written report of the findings and recommendations of the committee is prepared, including dissenting views of members who voted against the bill.

7. Bills that are reported out of committee are placed on the legislative calendar and scheduled for a vote by the full body.

8. Members of the full body are able to present their views about passage of the bill prior to a vote. During the debate period, members may offer amendments that will take effect if the bill is passed.

9. When debate is completed, a vote is conducted.

10. If the full body passes the bill, it must go to the other body and usually begin the process again; in some cases, the other body may vote to pass the bill as it was presented. During the review process, the second body may vote it down, table it, or change the bill. Bills that are rejected or tabled at this stage are considered dead and won't become laws.

11. If the bill passes the second body, any major differences between the two bills are reconciled in a conference committee. If the conference committee can't agree on the form of the bill, it will die and not become a law. If the committee recommends a conference report incorporating the changes, both houses of Congress must vote to approve the conference report before the bill is forwarded to the president for signature.

12. When the president receives the bill, he has three choices: he may sign it into law, veto it, or fail to sign it. If the bill is vetoed, Congress may override the veto by a two-thirds vote of a quorum in each house, in which case the bill will become a law in spite of the veto.

   If the president simply fails to sign a bill, one of two things will happen. When Congress is in session, a bill that remains unsigned for 10 days will become law without the president's signature. If Congress adjourns before the 10-day period is up, the bill won't become law. This is known as a *pocket veto*.

Administrative Law

In addition to the laws passed by Congress and signed by the president, HR professionals should be aware of the process by which administrative law is developed. Three types of administrative law impact employment relationships: agency rules and regulations, agency orders, and executive orders.

Much of the legislation passed by Congress empowers and requires federal agencies to develop enforcement regulations. An example of this is the Occupational Safety and Health Act of 1970, in which Congress established the Occupational Safety and Health Administration (OSHA) and required that it develop regulations to improve the safety of American workplaces. In developing these regulations, the agencies follow an established process.

First, they develop rules or regulations and publish them in the *Federal Register* (the official daily publication for rules, proposals, and notices of federal agencies and the Office of the President) and give the public an opportunity to comment on the proposals. Once the comment period has been completed, the agency publishes final rules that take effect no less than 30 days after the date of public notice.

Some federal agencies, such as the National Labor Relations Board (NLRB) and the EEOC, have the power to order compliance with federal laws in courts known as *administrative law courts*. The orders issued by an administrative law judge (ALJ) in these cases have the effect of law, and many of these decisions are published in the Federal Register as well.

The final type of administrative law with which HR professionals should be familiar is the executive order (EO). EOs are issued by the president of the United States and become law after they have been published in the Federal Register for 30 days.

Lobbying

Lobbying is an activity in which anyone can participate when they want to influence new laws and regulations. HR professionals can contribute as individuals or as part of the HR profession. The Society for Human Resource Management (SHRM) has legislative affairs committees (LACs) on the national and local levels that monitor and provide information on proposed changes to employment-related legislation and regulation in addition to coordinating lobbying efforts.

HR professionals who want to influence the legislative or regulatory processes should first make sure they fully understand the topic and are able to provide sound justifications for the position they take. It's also important to gather as much support as possible—legislators are more likely to be responsive when a large number of voters feel the same way. To be an effective lobbyist, it's also important to find a senator or a congressman who will guide you through the process and introduce you to other legislators.

There are many avenues for contacting elected officials or regulators. The House of Representatives has a website, www.house.gov, which provides information about contacting representatives; the Senate has a similar site at www.senate.gov.

HR professionals who want to stay abreast of legislative activity can find information on pending legislation in many places. In addition to the LACs mentioned previously, information about pending legislation is available at the House and Senate sites just mentioned and on the SHRM website at www.shrm.org.

SPHR ONLY Corporate Governance

Corporate governance refers to the various influences and processes that impact the way a corporation is managed and the relationship among its stakeholders, principally the shareholders, board of directors, and management. Other groups, including employees, vendors, customers, lenders, and members of the general public are affected by the way decisions are made in the process of governance. Let's look at the roles of each of the key stakeholders:

Shareholders   Shareholders are the owners of the corporation.

Board of Directors   Members of the board of directors (BOD) are elected by the share-holders to represent the shareholders' interests with management. There are two types of directors: inside and outside. An *inside director* is a person with operational responsibilities who is employed by the organization, such as the CEO, the CFO, or another officer of the corporation. An *outside director* is someone who isn't employed by the corporation and doesn't have operational responsibilities.

Management   Management includes the officers of the corporation, such as the CEO, Chief Financial Officer (CFO), Chief Operating Officer (COO), and other executives who make day-to-day decisions about company operations.

As discussed at the beginning of this chapter, a corporation is a legal entity that has rights and obligations. Although a corporation itself can't make decisions, those at top levels in the organization must make decisions on behalf of its owners. They have a *fiduciary responsibility*, or obligation to act in the best interests of the shareholders by making decisions that benefit the organization over decisions that benefit them personally. Recent events have demonstrated that this responsibility is sometimes ignored by those at the highest corporate levels. The failures of corporate executives at Enron, WorldCom, Tyco, and other public corporations to appropriately perform their fiduciary responsibilities led to the enactment of the Sarbanes-Oxley Act (SOX) in 2002.

Two of the major factors that determine how a corporation is run are the values and ethics of those who have fiduciary responsibility.

Organization Values and Ethics

Business organizations have a responsibility, and sometimes a legal requirement, to interact with employees, shareholders, and the community at large in a trustworthy and ethical manner. These responsibilities range from making appropriate decisions about pollutants that are released into the environment; to treating employees, customers, and other stake-holders honestly and fairly; to working with and training disadvantaged individuals to become productive members of society. This section describes ways to approach some of the issues in these areas.

Since the Enron scandal erupted in December 2001, the issue of business ethics has come to the forefront of discussions about the behavior of corporate executives, auditors, attorneys, and board members. Subsequent revelations about possible accounting irregu-larities at other multinational corporations such as AOL, WorldCom, and Global Crossing made it clear that this was not simply a case of one company that ran amok, but a pervasive problem at the top levels of major corporations. SOX made many of the practices that occurred in these companies illegal and provided penalties for violations. These are some of the changes made by Sarbanes-Oxley:

- Established the Public Company Accounting Oversight Board (PCAOB) and required all public accounting firms to register with the board, which conducts periodic inspections to ensure their compliance with audit standards.

- Established new standards to ensure the independence of auditors relative to the businesses they audit, including restrictions on non-audit-related services such as book-keeping, management, human resource consulting, or other similar services; rotation of audit partner assignments at least every five years; and a requirement that the audit report and recommendations to the management team be delivered directly to the audit committee of the BOD.

- Established standards for corporate responsibility, holding the chief executive of a public company accountable for the fairness and accuracy of financial reports filed with the Securities and Exchange Commission (SEC).

- Required CEOs and CFOs to reimburse the company for incentive- or equity-based compensation in the event of a material restatement of financial reports to the SEC caused by misconduct.

- Prohibited insider trading of stock during pension fund blackout periods when employees aren't able to trade the stock in their pension accounts.

- Established ethical requirements for senior financial officers.

- Took steps to ensure the fairness, accuracy, and independence of stock analysis.

- Established criminal penalties for management officials who defraud shareholders, destroy documents, or obstruct justice.

- Protected employees who report conduct that they reasonably believe violates SEC regulations or federal laws related to shareholder fraud.

Ethical behavior begins at top levels in the organization. The BOD must demand it of the executive team, and the executive team must model it for all others in the organization. It would seem that this should be a pretty simple thing to do; after all, at the end of the day, ethical behavior occurs when people do the right thing. But because the values people hold are different depending on the culture they grew up in, their family background, and their personal experiences, the right thing can mean different things to different people. That is why the executive team must set the standard of behavior, communicate it, model it, and enforce it if they're serious about maintaining an ethical workplace.

Companies that are committed to ethical practices often create behavior codes as guidelines for employees to follow. In most cases, the terms *code of ethics* and *code of conduct* are used to describe these guidelines, but some organizations use other terms, such as *code of practice* or *code of professional standards*. In practice, the terms *code of ethics* and *code of conduct* are interchangeable, but each has a different purpose. A code of ethics is a statement of ideal standards that the organization is committed to uphold in its business practices. A code of conduct is a statement of behaviors that the organization expects from employees; inherent in the conduct is the idea that disciplinary action would be the result of violating the behavioral standard. In some cases, the two statements are combined, and each topic (honesty, conflict of interest, and so on) consists of the ethical statement followed by a description of expected behavior. For example, a business might write a conflict-of-interest statement in this way:

Ethical/Value Statement   It is the intent of our company to comply not only with regulatory requirements, but also to act in the best interest of our stakeholders. Our employees have a duty to disclose any real or perceived conflict of interest or financial interest when exercising their corporate responsibilities.

Conduct Statement   In the event that a conflict, or the possibility of a conflict, arises between the interests of an employee and those of the business, the employee should report the conflict to the manager or ethics officer for guidance before proceeding.

A corporate values statement created during the strategic planning process can begin to set the stage for ethical behavior, but the code of conduct, or code of ethics, is a useful tool that can inform people in the organization about what behavior is expected and what is unacceptable. Some topics to consider when creating a code of ethics could include those discussed next:

Honesty   The code of ethics should set an expectation of honesty in the workplace. As with all other aspects of an ethics code, the executive team must model honesty in the representations they make to employees, customers, suppliers, and all other stakeholders in order for the message to be taken seriously within the company.

Integrity   *Integrity* is defined as a firm adherence to a code of moral values. Integrity is demonstrated when an individual does the right thing, even when that "thing" is unpopular.

Confidentiality   In most companies, confidential information can be found in every department: marketing plans, new product development, financial statements, personal employee information, and email accounts can all contain highly confidential information. In HR, professionals work every day with confidential employee information and are sometimes pressured to share this information for one reason or another. However, information collected during the employment process such as an employee's age, religion, medical condition, or credit history, may not be used to make employment decisions such as promotions, transfers, discipline or selection for training. HR professionals and other employees with access to confidential information have a duty to maintain its confidentiality.

Conflicts of Interest   As mentioned at the beginning of this section, employees must put the interests of the organization before their own. Any time an employee stands to gain personally from an action taken by the employer, there is a conflict of interest (except, of course, for payment of the employee's salary). At a minimum, these situations must be disclosed to the employer, or employees should remove themselves from the situation. The ethics statement should make it clear that even the appearance or perception of a conflict of interest is damaging to the company and should be avoided.

Insider Information   Although insider information is most commonly associated with trading securities on the stock exchange, it can also apply to other areas. Insider information is any information that an employee has access to or comes into contact with that isn't available to the general public. Using this information in stock exchanges is illegal and can result in criminal prosecution and civil penalties.

The prohibitions against using insider information with regard to stock transactions apply to an employee who overhears the information as much as they apply to decision makers in the organization. Federal law requires that those with access to insider information may not act on it until the information is made public.

Gifts   An ethics policy should address the issue of gift exchanges with customers, vendors, and employees. It should describe under what circumstances gifts are acceptable and define limitations on the amounts if they're to be allowed. When the receipt of a gift unfairly influences a business decision, the gift becomes unethical and should be refused.

For companies operating outside the United States, this can be a difficult issue because in some cultures exchanging business gifts is a standard and expected practice, and the failure to do so can be seen as an insult. The Foreign Corrupt Practices Act of 1977 was enacted by Congress in response to revelations by multinational corporations of the bribes that were paid to obtain business in some foreign countries. The act prohibits the payment of bribes and requires accounting practices that preclude the use of covert bank accounts that could be used to make these payments.

Personal Use of Company Assets   A code of ethics should clearly state what the employer considers to be an appropriate and acceptable use of company assets. In some organizations, the receipt of any personal telephone calls or emails is considered inappropriate, whereas in other companies a limited number is acceptable. Copying and distributing copyright material from newspapers, books, magazines, CDs, or other company assets may also violate patents or copyrights, and employees should be made aware of the consequences if they use any of these assets inappropriately.

Workplace Privacy   Some employers feel the need to install surveillance cameras in work areas. This happens for a variety of reasons. For a retail store open late at night, for example, this practice provides a measure of security for employees. In other situations, concerns about productivity or pilferage can spur an employer to install a surveillance camera in a distribution warehouse. Whatever the reason, the employer must balance the need to manage its workforce with an individual employee's expectation of privacy.

Advances in technology have made it possible for employers to monitor Internet, email, and voicemail usage, and some employees see this as an invasion of privacy. Employers who plan to monitor employee communication and Internet usage should develop and distribute a policy clearly stating what information is subject to monitoring and under what conditions.

The code of ethics should include a statement about the use of surveillance and monitoring to reduce the risk for claims of invasion of privacy.

Fairness   Actions taken by employers have the ability to significantly impact the lives of their employees. Whether decisions are being made about hiring or layoffs, or accusations of malfeasance or inappropriate behavior are being made, employers have an obligation to treat employees fairly in all their actions. Employees who have the power to make decisions, such as selecting suppliers or evaluating employee performance, have an equal responsibility to handle these decisions fairly.

A real test of an organization's fairness occurs when an employee makes a complaint to a federal agency, claiming that illegal activity has occurred. A person who does this is known as a *whistle-blower*. Some federal statutes, such as the Occupational Safety and Health Act, Railroad Safety Act, Safe Drinking Water Act, and Toxic Substances Control Act provide protection for employees who "blow the whistle" on their employers. Even so, it's a true ethical test to see how the whistle-blower who continues to work for the company is treated in the workplace once the complaint has been made.

As important as a code of ethics is, it's equally important to be aware of situations where conflicting needs and desires make doing the right thing less clear-cut. As those responsible for maintaining the confidentiality of personal employee information, HR professionals make ethical decisions on a regular basis and are in a position to model ethical behavior in the way they respond to inappropriate requests for information.

Whistle-Blower Protection

The Sarbanes-Oxley Act requires violations of securities laws or breaches of fiduciary responsibility to be reported to either the chief legal officer or CEO of the company by in-house attorneys or outside counsel; if resolution doesn't occur, attorneys must report the concerns to the audit committee of the BOD. Section 806 of SOX provides broad protection for employees who initiate reports of what they reasonably believe are company actions in violation of SEC regulations or federal securities laws. Enforcement of these whistle-blower protections is delegated to the Department of Labor's OSHA. In 2004, OSHA issued final regulations for administering the whistle-blower protections. The regulations apply to employees who provide information, assist someone else in providing information, or assist in an investigation of alleged violations of mail, wire, bank, or securities fraud, or violations of SEC regulations or federal laws protecting shareholders from fraud.

Prior to issuance of the final rules, business groups including the United States Chamber of Commerce and SHRM expressed concerns that the statute's vague description of wrongful conduct, the lack of meaningful deterrents for frivolous accusations, and its ambiguity on the question of whether the regulations applied to foreign employees of U.S. corporations or other foreign companies would lead to the filing of unwarranted claims. OSHA concluded that the regulations proposed were aligned with language in SOX and that it didn't have the authority to expand those definitions.

OSHA rules state that employers may not take unfavorable employment actions against employees in any of the terms and conditions of employment, such as laying off or terminating, demoting, blacklisting, denying benefits, failing to hire or rehire, intimidating, reassigning, reducing hours or pay, disciplining, and others. Employees who believe that their employment status has been unlawfully affected by the filing of an allegation must file a written complaint including their name, the name of the company that allegedly retaliated against them, and *prima facie* evidence of the violation. A *prima facie* violation includes the following four elements:

1. The employee was engaged in a protected activity.
2. The employer knew or suspected that the employee was engaged in the protected activity.
3. The employee suffered an unfavorable employment action.
4. Sufficient circumstances existed to infer that a contributing factor to the unfavorable action was the employee's participation in the protected activity.

Employees must file retaliation complaints within 90 days of the retaliatory action by the employer, and if OSHA doesn't issue a final order within 180 days of filing, the employee may file suit in a U.S. district court. If OSHA finds that retaliation occurred, it first seeks to reach a settlement between the parties. If that isn't possible, OSHA has authority to order reinstatement of the employee with back pay, restore benefits, and order other actions that make the employee whole, including paying interest on back wages and compensation for attorney's fees and litigation costs. If company officials are found guilty of retaliation, they're subject to criminal penalties, including up to 10 years in prison.

OSHA has the authority to issue a *preliminary order of reinstatement* prior to conducting a hearing on the claim if it reasonably believes a violation occurred. If the employee has become a security risk and preliminary reinstatement isn't appropriate, OSHA may require economic reinstatement; that is, it may require the company to pay the employee at full pay and benefits even though the employee doesn't return to work.

BOD audit committees have the responsibility to establish processes to facilitate confidential reports of possible violations. The elements of an effective process include the following:

- A clear policy statement or code of business conduct identifying specific steps for employees to follow if they discover unlawful or unethical activity.

- Training for employees to help them recognize the difference between lawful and unlawful activity.

- Training for managers on how to handle employee reports, maintain confidentiality, and prevent retaliation.

- A system for tracking complaints, maintaining records of investigations, verifying follow-up activities, and resolving the complaint.

- Development of an investigative process before it's needed. By identifying in advance whether the company will use internal or external investigators, how evidence will be gathered and maintained, how interviews will be conducted, specifics on maintaining confidentiality, a process to receive anonymous reports, and the range of disciplinary actions to be taken if wrongdoing is identified, investigations can begin almost immediately upon receiving a report. The process should also describe what kind of reports will be made, if any, to employees or others who report concerns.

- A record-retention system for documents gathered during an investigation, to comply with SOX requirements for full and complete access in any legal action related to SOX.

Whether an employer is publicly held and bound by SOX requirements or is a midsized, privately held company, some attorneys recommend the establishment of a formal channel for reporting possible unethical or fraudulent activities. Employees are often in a better position to observe questionable actions of co-workers and supervisors than are their managers whose multiple responsibilities may distance them from day-to-day operations. The Association of Certified Fraud Examiners reported in 2008 that 46 percent of frauds are initially detected by tips provided by employees, vendors, customers or other stakeholders, compared to 19 percent discovered through an internal audit process. A well-planned and publicized process provides an avenue for employees and others to make confidential reports of unethical or unlawful activity. This builds employee morale and establishes credibility in the marketplace.

Ethics Officers

Businesses serious about establishing meaningful ethics programs have appointed ethics officers or facilitators charged with the responsibility to ensure that the organization adheres to the ethical standards set by the executive team. Ethics officers advise employees at all levels in an organization on ethical issues and manage programs designed to allow confidential reporting of ethical concerns by employees, customers, shareholders, or others, and they also investigate allegations of wrongdoing. Ethics officers provide periodic reports for the executive team to keep them apprised of ethical issues in the organization.

 Real World Scenario

Whistle-Blowing in the Wake of the Enron Scandal

In the wake of the Enron scandal, and particularly during the month when congressional hearings into the bankrupt corporation's activities were televised each day, the SEC saw a marked increase in complaints, from an average of 365 per day in 2001 to 525 per day for the month of January 2002. On February 27, 2002, Katie Fairbank of the *Dallas Morning News* also reported an increase in whistle-blower complaints at the Department of Justice, from 33 in 1987 to 483 in 1999.

Sherron Watkins, who is credited with blowing the whistle on the Enron accounting practices that eventually led to its bankruptcy in December 2001, may have inspired the increased reports. Ms. Watkins followed a path typical of whistle-blowers by meeting with Enron CEO Ken Lay long before she went to regulators. Her desire was to advise him of the wrongdoing so he could put an end to it. That unfortunately did not happen, and the company filed for bankruptcy a few months after their meeting.

Although some whistle-blowers have statutory protection from retaliation, courts are divided on just what whistle-blowing activity is protected; those who go to regulators are often unable to work in their chosen profession after taking the action.

One whistle-blower who paid the price for his actions is Dr. Jeffrey Wigand, a former tobacco executive who was fired by Brown & Williamson Tobacco Corporation in 1993 after the company refused to remove a known carcinogen from its cigarette products. After his termination, Dr. Wigand testified against tobacco companies in civil lawsuits and appeared in an interview on the television show *60 Minutes*; his former employers launched a campaign to discredit him. Dr. Wigand was a key witness in the lawsuit brought by 46 states against tobacco companies that was settled when they agreed to pay $206 billion to reimburse the states for medical expenses related to smoking.

▣ HR Metrics: Measuring Results

Chapter 2 includes a discussion of two of the best measures of HR results: ROI and cost-benefit analysis (CBA). Other useful metrics for the Strategic Management functional area of the BOK include the following:

Business Impact Measures   The business impact of HR plans created to support an organization's strategic plans and goals can be difficult to measure because it's hard to isolate the effect of the HR support from other factors. However, it's easier to measure whether HR achieved its specific goals; for example, if the marketing department staffing plan was to hire three marketing analysts and three were hired, HR met its target for that objective. The impact of HR initiatives designed to improve productivity, such as an engagement initiative, can be measured by using metrics such as revenue per employee or units produced per employee.

There are other ways to measure how HR is adding value, such as how well risk is being managed, measured by the presence or absence of employee complaints, injuries, or lawsuits. If functions such as benefit administration or payroll are outsourced, an analysis of employee satisfaction with service levels and cost savings realized from outsourcing vs. performing the service in-house can be used to measure business impact.

Balanced Scorecard   Developed by Robert Kaplan, PhD, and David Norton, PhD, the *balanced scorecard* is a management tool that ties the outcomes of each department together in one measurement system. When used properly, it improves communication between departments and measures the progress of operational outcomes that are in alignment with the strategic objectives developed through the planning process.

Kaplan and Norton found that because traditional business measurements focused only on financial results, other key elements that impacted business success weren't included in strategic management decisions. To address this shortcoming, the balanced scorecard tracks information in four key areas: financial results, customer results, key internal processes, and how people are hired and trained to achieve organization goals. The Balanced Scorecard Institute provides a complete discussion of the concept at `www.balancedscore-card.org/basics/bsc1.html`.

Other methods for controlling operations include Six Sigma, TQM, and MBO. These are also used as organizational development strategies and are discussed in Chapter 5.

Tactical Accountability Measures   Meaningful measures of tactical accountability for strategic management include the following:

HR Expenses as a Percent of Operating Expenses   This metric is calculated by totaling all the direct and indirect HR costs and dividing them by the total operating expenses.

HR Expenses as a Percent of Total Revenue   This metric is calculated by totaling all the direct and indirect HR costs and dividing them by the total revenue.

Ratio of Total Employees to HR Staff   The total number of HR staff is divided by total employees in the organization to calculate this ratio.

HR Department Expenses per Employee   As the organization grows, this metric can help HR maintain costs in line with other expenses. Total direct and indirect HR department expenses are divided by the total number of employees to obtain the ratio.

The data collected from these measures over a period of time can be examined to identify and compare internal practices to market data in similar industries or for similar activities. The results can indicate problems on the horizon and allow HR to be proactive in addressing those issues. Not only is this information important as part of the internal scanning process, but it also provides ongoing controls for HR during the strategy-evaluation phase of the strategic planning process.

Global Considerations

Deciding to open a facility in a new country requires that thought be given to a variety of issues, including the employment laws unique to each country, the business culture in the region, the legal form of the entity, and others that may be unique to specific countries or regions of the world. Some of the more common issues include the following:

- The rate of pay for the new hire
- Offer letters or employment contracts that comply with foreign and U.S. laws
- The impact of foreign tax structures on the corporate income statement
- Details of starting operations in a new country for the first time, such as complying with payroll-processing regulations, understanding foreign stock-option rules, and creating intercompany agreements
- How day-to-day support will be delivered
- Corporate tax filings

In addition, there are very real cultural and practical differences in the ways business is done in the United States vs. other countries. For example, the United States is a *low-context culture*, in that Americans take their cues from what others say to them. In a country with a *high-context culture* like Japan, the opposite is true: people rely more on nonverbal clues and relationships to discern what is meant. Acclimating to this difference presents unique challenges to operating globally.

Summary

The role of HR in the twenty-first century is changing into one that is more strategic and involved with planning the future direction of the organization and driving the achievement of business results. As a result, it's crucial for HR professionals to have a working knowledge of other functional areas of the business in order to provide the operational and administrative support necessary to attract and retain qualified employees in each area.

Strategic management occurs as the result of a planning process that reviews internal and external factors affecting the ability of an organization to successfully achieve its goals. This process requires that all business functions provide their expertise in both the planning and implementation of goals, objectives, and action plans.

The strategic planning process begins with an environmental-scanning process to gather information from internal and external sources. Based on the scanning results, long-range, midrange, and short-range forecasts can be created to provide the information necessary for developing the vision, mission, and goals for the organization, which are needed by functional area managers to set tactical goals and action plans for their business units. Based on the organization's strategic plan, a human capital management plan describes the contribution HR will make to achieve organizational goals.

As change becomes increasingly prevalent in business, HR plays a role in advising management and counseling employees to reduce the stress that accompanies change and maintain productivity during the process.

HR professionals are expected to act ethically and handle their organizational responsibilities with care and respect. Employees rely on HR practitioners to carry out their responsibilities in a professional manner, assuming a moral responsibility to preserve the integrity and personal nature of employee information they handle. The organization relies on HR to protect its best interests by maintaining a high standard and adhering to a professional code of ethics.

Through active involvement in the development of legislation at the federal, state, and local levels, HR professionals can influence the course of proposed laws and regulations, thus providing a benefit to their employers, their employees, and the profession.

Exam Essentials

Understand different business functions.   HR professionals must understand the purpose of different business functions and how they interact with each other and with HR. Understanding the unique needs of production and operations, sales and marketing, finance, accounting, and information technology and how each contributes to the organization's success allows HR to be more effective in providing services to the organization.

Understand the strategic planning process.   The strategic planning process consists of four broad elements: scanning the environment; formulating the corporate strategy with the vision, mission, values, and corporate goals; implementing the strategy with tactical goals, action plans, and budgets to accomplish organization goals; and evaluating the strategy to ensure that it can be adjusted to accommodate changes in the organization or the external environment.

Be able to describe a human capital management plan, including projections and costs that support the organization's overall budget.   HR creates an HCMP to describe how it will contribute to achieving the organization's strategic plan. The HCMP clearly describes the strategic direction for the HR function, states the desired results to be achieved, states the objectives for achieving the results, creates action plans, and describes how the goals will be communicated and measured.

Understand the importance of change management and HR's role in managing change.   Change is a fact of life in organizations; reengineering, restructuring, and downsizing occur often as a result of strategic decisions and changes in the marketplace. HR can develop programs that provide a means for communication, both top-down and bottom-up, to ease the process and reduce stress in the work environment.

Understand HR's role in the organization.   The role of HR is evolving into one that provides strategic, administrative, and operational services for the organization.

Be able to describe the steps involved in the legislative process.   A bill can originate in the House of Representatives or in the Senate, where it's referred first to a committee for consideration and then, if it's reported out of committee, is ready for full floor consideration. After all debate is concluded, the bill is ready for final passage. It must pass both bodies in the same form before it can be presented to the president for signature. The president may sign the bill; veto it and return it to Congress; let it become law without signature; or at the end of a session, pocket-veto it.

Review Questions

You can find the answers in Appendix A.

1.   HR participates in the strategic planning process by doing which of the following?

   A.   Formulating the strategy

   B.   Scanning the environment

   C.   Providing expertise

   D.   Identifying strategic goals

2.   Restructuring is used to do which of the following?

   A.   Remove redundant operations

   B.   Assimilate employees into the organization

   C.   Simplify processes to increase customer satisfaction

   D.   Purchase stock to gain controlling interest in a competitor

3.   A statement that describes what an organization does that is different from others is a:

   A.   Values statement

   B.   Corporate goal

   C.   Vision statement

D.   Mission statement

4.   Which of the following options is one characteristic of an organization during the growth phase?

   A.   Executive benefit packages are upgraded.

   B.   New hires may have less experience.

   C.   The compensation package is competitive.

   D.   Employees work closely with founders.

5.   Improvements in technology have had their greatest effect on which of the following?

   A.   Employee morale

   B.   Productivity

   C.   Cost of living

   D.   Management's span of control

6.   To which of the following does the balanced scorecard concept *not* apply?

   A.   Tie objectives to specific performance measures.

   B.   Eliminate unnecessary processes to increase customer satisfaction.

   C.   Measure how objectives contribute to organization goals.

   D.   Set targets for meeting objectives.

7.   Which of the following is an appropriate use for an HR audit?

   A.   To determine which employees no longer have the skills needed by the organization

   B.   To determine the employee productivity and turnover rates

   C.   To determine whether the employee handbook is in compliance with current government regulations

   D.   To determine the timeline for changes that are necessary in the HR department

8.   The four *p*'s summarize the marketing function. Which of the following is not one of the *p*'s?

   A.   Perception

   B.   Price

   C.   Placement

   D.   Promotion

9.   Which of the following is one of the elements of a SMART goal?

   A.   Action-oriented

   B.   Strength

   C.   Technology

   D.   Threat

10. What is a pocket veto?

   A. The president vetoes a bill from Congress. Congress holds a vote, but the bill does not pass.

   B. Congress submits a bill to the president and then adjourns. The president does not sign the bill within 10 days.

   C. The president vetoes a bill from Congress. Congress holds a vote but does not have a quorum.

   D. Congress submits a bill to the president, but the president does not sign the bill within 10 days.

11. Which of the following is *not* a method used by organizations (not possessive) to communicate expected behavior to employees?

   A. Written policies

   B. Executive behavior modeling

   C. Mentor programs

   D. Employee coaching

12. Which of the following risk management tool or activity is *not* required by law?

   A. Employee handbooks

   B. Employer practice(s) prohibiting harassment

   C. The reporting of securities law violations

   D. EEO-1 reporting

13. An HR audit enables an employer to do which of the following?

   A. Evaluate the effectiveness of current HR practices in alignment with strategic goals

   B. Identify exposure factors and the employer's potential risk due to compliance failures

   C. Conduct a knowledge assessment of the current workforce

   D. All of the above

14. What are corporate programs that focus on behaviors that minimize the depletion of time, money, and labor called?

   A. Viability programs

   B. Sustainability efforts

   C. Corporate governance

   D. Strategic planning

15. Ethics, offshoring, data security, and philanthropy are all examples of HR's role in which of the following functions?

   A. Strategic planning

   B. Workforce planning

   C. Technology development

   D. Corporate responsibility

16. A decision about outsourcing specialized labor would most likely be made at which stage of the organizational life cycle?

   A. Startup

   B. Growth

   C. Maturity

   D. Decline

17. What is the purpose of an HR budget?

   A. To determine how much cash is required to achieve a goal

   B. To hold departments accountable for outcomes

   C. To ensure that the outcomes match the strategic plan

   D. To evaluate the effectiveness of HR strategy

18. What element of an inventory-management system is defined by "purchasing smaller amounts of supplies more frequently"?

   A. Inventory allocation

   B. Just-in-time inventory

   C. Distributive inventory

   D. Blanket orders

19. Which of the following statements about whistle-blower protection is false?

   A. Whistle-blower protection is provided under Sarbanes-Oxley.

   B. Attorneys must report concerns of securities law violations to the CEO or CLO and are protected under whistle-blower law.

   C. An employee must be engaged in a protected activity such as reporting a violation to qualify for protection.

   D. The employee does not have to have suffered an unfavorable employment action to qualify for protection.

20. Salaries, payroll taxes, and benefits are all examples of which of the following HR activities?

   A. Conducting a business impact measure

   B. Creating an HR budget

   C. Creating a compensation strategy

   D. Analyzing the cost of recruiting

Chapter

4

Workforce Planning and Employment

THE HRCI TEST SPECIFICATIONS FROM THE HUMAN RESOURCE DEVELOPMENT FUNCTIONAL AREA COVERED IN THIS CHAPTER INCLUDE:

- ✓ Ensure that workforce planning and employment activities are compliant with applicable federal laws and regulations.

- ✓ Identify workforce requirements to achieve the organization's short- and long-term goals and objectives (for example: corporate restructuring, workforce expansion or reduction).

- ✓ Conduct job analyses to create and/or update job descriptions and identify job competencies.

- ✓ Identify, review, document, and update essential job functions for positions.

- ✓ Influence and establish criteria for hiring, retaining, and promoting based on job descriptions and required competencies.

- ✓ Analyze labor market for trends that impact the ability to meet workforce requirements (for example: federal/state data reports).

- ✓ Assess skill sets of internal workforce and external labor market to determine the availability of qualified candidates, utilizing third party vendors or agencies as appropriate.

- ✓ Identify internal and external recruitment sources (for example: employee referrals, diversity groups, social media) and implement selected recruitment methods.

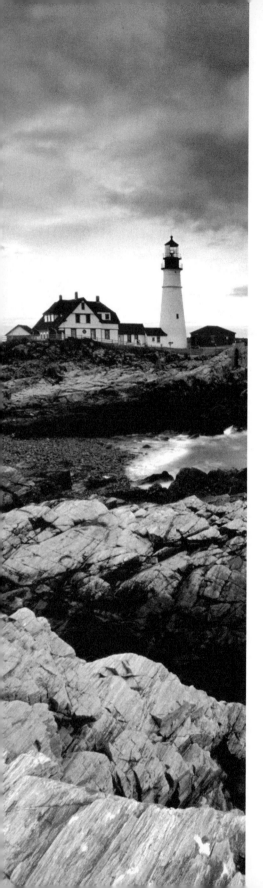

✓ Establish metrics for workforce planning (for example: recruitment and turnover statistics, costs).

✓ Brand and market the organization to potential qualified applicants.

✓ Develop and implement selection procedures (for example: applicant tracking, interviewing, reference and background checking).

✓ Develop and extend employment offers and conduct negotiations as necessary.

✓ Administer post-offer employment activities (for example: administer drug/alcohol and fitness for work testing, execute employment agreements, complete I-9/E-Verify process, coordinate relocations, and immigration).

✓ Develop, implement, and evaluate orientation and on-boarding processes for new hires, rehires, and transfers.

✓ Develop, implement, and evaluate employee retention strategies and practices.

✓ Develop, implement, and evaluate the succession planning process. **SPHR ONLY**

✓ Develop and implement the organizational exit/off-boarding process for both voluntary and involuntary terminations, including planning for reductions in force (RIF).

✓ Develop, implement, and evaluate an affirmative action plan (AAP) as required.

✓ Develop and implement a record retention process for handling documents and employee files (for example: pre-employment files, confidential/medical files, and benefits files).

In today's fast-paced business environment, human resource (HR) professionals must be able to "turn on a dime," adjusting workforce plans and employment activities to meet the changing needs of their organizations. Workforce Planning and Employment (WFP) is the functional area of the human resource body of knowledge (BOK) that tests your knowledge of workforce planning and the associated employment activities of staffing, retaining, and exiting employees from the organization. The workforce planning process identifies skills and timelines for acquiring the employees needed to achieve organization goals; staffing is the process by which HR professionals work with line management to locate, hire/transfer, and integrate new employees into existing workgroups. Once employees are hired, activities include ensuring that talented individuals in the organization are identified, developed, and retained so they're available to move into positions of greater responsibility as organizational needs evolve. The final function of WFP, organizational exits, includes voluntary exits (those due to resignations or retirements) and involuntary exits (those occurring due to mergers, outsourcing, terminations for cause, and so on). This chapter reviews the PHR and SPHR responsibility and knowledge requirements for WFP, including the impact of federal legislation, regulation, and case law on these activities.

Let's begin with the federal laws and regulations that govern employment relationships.

As you begin this chapter, be sure to refer to the knowledge requirements for WFP in the HR Certification Institute PHR/SPHR Body of Knowledge (BOK) described in the introduction to this book. In addition, several sections in Chapter 2, "Core Knowledge Requirements for HR Professionals," have particular relevance here: a review of the discussions on needs assessment, communication strategies, development of Request For Proposals, quantitative and qualitative analysis tools, job analysis and description methods, organizational documentation requirements, and employee-records management will enhance your review of the material in this chapter.

For up-to-the-minute updates for this chapter, visit www.sybex.com/go/ phr4e or visit my website at www.epochresources.com.

Federal Employment Legislation

Over the years, all three branches of the federal government have participated in regulating the ways employers interact with their employees. Congress has enacted legislation, the Executive Branch has promulgated regulations, and the courts have adjudicated cases to clarify the legislation and regulation created by the other two branches. Table 4.1 describes the types of employment activities covered by some form of federal regulation. Understanding these various laws, regulations, and cases is a key element in the development and implementation of compliant workforce plans and activities.

TABLE 4.1 Federal legislation governing WFP activities

Type	Enforcement agency	Chapter reference
Civil rights	Equal Employment Opportunity Commission (EEOC) and/or Office of Federal Contract Compliance Programs (OFCCP)	4
Executive Orders	OFCCP	4
Fair Credit	Federal Trade Commission (FTC)	4
Immigration	U.S. Citizenship and Immigration Services (USCIS)	4
Mass layoffs	Department of Labor (DOL)	4
Military service	DOL and/or OFCCP	7
Polygraph	DOL	4
Privacy	Department of Justice (DOJ)	4
Sexual harassment	EEOC	7

The following sections describe the civil rights legislation and executive orders that affect employment activities. Other government requirements listed are reviewed in the section or chapter where they're most relevant to daily HR practice.

Civil Rights Legislation

Although several pieces of civil rights legislation were enacted between 1866 and 1963, the Civil Rights Act of 1964 is regarded as the milestone for modern equal employment opportunity. This sweeping legislation impacted many areas of American life, and Title VII of the act was dedicated to providing equal employment opportunities for all Americans. Title VII has been amended several times to expand coverage to areas not covered in the original act of 1964.

Title VII of the Civil Rights Act of 1964

Title VII of the Civil Rights Act of 1964 introduced the concepts of *protected classes* and *unlawful employment practices* to American business. Unlawful employment practices are those that have an adverse impact on members of a protected class, which is a group of people who share common characteristics and are protected from discriminatory practices. Title VII established the basis for two types of unlawful practices, disparate treatment and disparate impact. *Disparate treatment* happens when employers treat some candidates or employees differently, such as requiring women to take a driving test when they apply for a job but not requiring men to take the test when they apply for the same job. Practices that have a *disparate impact* on members of protected classes seem fair on their face but result in adverse impact on members of protected classes, such as requiring all candidates for fire-fighter positions to be a certain height. Although the requirement applies to all candidates equally, Asian and female candidates who might otherwise qualify for the position are eliminated because they're generally shorter than male candidates of other races.

The act identified five protected classes: race, color, religion, national origin, and sex. It also defined the following unlawful employment practices:

- Discriminatory recruiting, selection, or hiring actions
- Discriminatory compensation or benefit practices
- Discriminatory access to training or apprenticeship programs
- Discriminatory practices in any other terms or conditions of employment

Legitimate seniority, merit, and piece-rate payment systems are allowable under Title VII as long as they don't intentionally discriminate against protected classes.

Title VII allowed for limited exceptions to its requirements, some of which are listed here:

- *Bona fide occupational qualifications* (BFOQs) occur when religion, sex, or national origin is "reasonably necessary to the normal operation" of the business.
- Educational institutions weren't originally subject to Title VII.
- Religious organizations may give preference to members of that religion.
- A potential employee who is unable to obtain, or loses, a national security clearance required for the position isn't protected.
- Indian reservations may give preference to Native Americans applicants and employees living on or near the reservation.

Title VII created the Equal Employment Opportunity Commission (EEOC) with a mandate to promote equal employment opportunity, educate employers, provide technical assistance, and study and report on its activities to Congress and the American people. The EEOC is the enforcement agency for Title VII and other discrimination legislation.

 You can view the full text of Title VII at www.eeoc.gov/policy /vii.html.

Amendments to Title VII

Title VII was amended in 1972, 1978, and 1991 to clarify and expand its coverage.

Equal Employment Opportunity Act of 1972

Created in 1972, the Equal Employment Opportunity Act (EEOA) provides litigation authority to the EEOC in the event that an acceptable conciliation agreement can't be reached. In those cases, the EEOC is empowered to sue nongovernmental entities, including employers, unions, and employment agencies.

The EEOA extended coverage of Title VII to entities that had been excluded in 1964:

- Educational institutions
- State and local governments
- The federal government

In addition, the EEOA reduced the number of employees needed to subject an employer to coverage by Title VII from 25 to 15 and required employers to keep records of the discovery of any unlawful employment practices and provide those records to the EEOC on request.

The EEOA also provided administrative guidance for the processing of complaints by providing that employers be notified within 10 days of receipt of a charge by the EEOC and that findings be issued within 120 days of the charge being filed. The EEOC was empowered to sue employers, unions, and employment agencies in the event that an acceptable conciliation agreement couldn't be reached within 30 days of notice to the employer. The EEOA also provided protection from retaliatory employment actions for whistleblowers.

Pregnancy Discrimination Act of 1978

Congress amended Title VII with the Pregnancy Discrimination Act (PDA) of 1978 to clarify that discrimination against women on the basis of pregnancy, childbirth, or any related medical condition is an unlawful employment practice. The act specified that pregnant employees should receive the same treatment and benefits as employees with any other short-term disability.

To read the text of the PDA, go to

http://www.eeoc.gov/laws/statutes/pregnancy.cfm.

Civil Rights Act of 1991

The Civil Rights Act (CRA) of 1991 contained amendments that affected Title VII, the Age Discrimination in Employment Act (ADEA), and the Americans with Disabilities Act (ADA) in response to issues raised by the courts in several cases that were brought by employees based on Title VII. The CRA is discussed later in this chapter, as are the cases that led to this legislation.

Age Discrimination in Employment Act of 1967

According to the preamble, the purpose of the ADEA is to "promote employment of older persons based on their ability rather than age; to prohibit arbitrary age discrimination in employment; to help employers and workers find ways of meeting problems arising from the impact of age on employment."

The ADEA prohibits discrimination against persons 40 years of age or older in employment activities including hiring, job assignments, training, promotion, compensation, benefits, terminating, or any other privileges, terms, or conditions of employment. The act applies to private businesses, unions, employment agencies, and state and local governments with more than 20 employees. As with Title VII, the ADEA provides for exceptions to the act:

- BFOQs that are reasonably necessary to business operations
- The hiring of firefighters or police officers by state or local governments
- Retirement of employees age 65 or older who have been in executive positions for at least 2 years and are eligible for retirement benefits of at least $44,000 per year
- Retirement of tenured employees of institutions of higher education at age 70
- Discharge or discipline for just cause

The act also provides that any waiver of rights must be written in an understandable manner and refer specifically to the waiver requirements contained in the ADEA. Any waiver of rights is valid only if valuable consideration, usually some form of payment, is exchanged and must include the following elements:

- Advice to consult with an attorney before signing the agreement
- A period of not less than 21 days to review and consider the agreement
- A period of no less than 7 days during which the agreement may be revoked

Additional requirements are needed for waivers made in connection with exit incentives or other termination programs, such as a reduction in force or layoff that involves more than one employee. In addition to the preceding requirements, the waiver must provide protected individuals with no less than 45 days to consider the agreement and

- A list of the eligibility factors for the group or individuals affected by the employment action
- A list of the job titles and ages of all individuals participating in the program as well as those who weren't selected for the program

Individuals who think they have been subjected to an unlawful employment practice must file charges with the EEOC, which has federal enforcement responsibility for the ADEA, or with the state equal employment agency (if one exists for the location where the incident occurred). Timely filing of charges is essential for complainants, because the EEOC won't investigate charges that aren't made according to the guidelines described in this chapter.

Visit http://www.eeoc.gov/laws/types/age.cfm to view the additional information regarding the ADEA.

Real World Scenario

Discrimination Claim Filing Requirements

One of the changes made by the EEOA was increasing the period of time individuals have to file discrimination complaints. These time limits apply to all laws enforced by the EEOC except the Equal Pay Act (discussed in Chapter 6, "Compensation and Benefits"). Some states have enacted EEO legislation and established agencies, known as Fair Employment Practices Agencies (FEPA), to enforce the laws in their states. In those states, individuals may file EEO complaints with either the state agency or the EEOC. Either agency receiving the complaint may "dual file" with the other agency to protect the complainants' rights under the other law. In addition,

- In states without a FEPA, an individual must file a charge with the EEOC within 180 days of the incident.

- In states with a FEPA, a charge must be filed within 300 days of the incident or, if the charge was initially filed with the state enforcement agency, within 30 days after receiving written notice from the state that the investigation was terminated. (For ADEA complaints, only state laws extend the filing limit to 300 days.)

- If the EEOC doesn't file a civil suit or enter into a conciliation agreement within 180 days of the initial charge, the complaining individual is notified and may file a civil suit within 90 days of receiving that notification.

- Once an individual has filed a charge with the EEOC, there is a 60-day waiting period before the individual may request a right-to-sue letter. This request ends the EEOC investigation and requires the individual to file a civil action within 90 days or lose the right to pursue this claim in the future.

The EEOC also enforces EEO laws and executive orders for federal employees. The time limits and procedures for these complaints are somewhat different than those for private employers or nonfederal government employees. Information about those guidelines is available at www.eeoc.gov/facts/fs-fed.html.

Americans with Disabilities Act of 1990

The Americans with Disabilities Act (ADA) of 1990 was based in large part on the Rehabilitation Act of 1973 (discussed in the section "Federal Contractors, Subcontractors, and Agencies" later in this chapter), and it extended protected-class status to qualified persons with disabilities. Employment discrimination is covered by Title I of the act and identifies covered entities as employment agencies, labor unions, joint labor-management committees, and employers with 15 or more employees (including those who work on a part-time or temporary basis) for each working day in each of 20 weeks in the current or previous calendar year. Excluded from coverage are the federal government and 501(c) private-membership clubs. The ADA prohibits discrimination in job application procedures; the hiring, advancement, or discharge of employees; employee compensation; job training; and other terms, conditions, and privileges of employment.

The ADA requires covered entities to make *reasonable accommodation* to develop employment opportunities for qualified persons with disabilities in two areas:

- Facilities should be accessible to persons with disabilities.
- Position requirements may be adjusted to accommodate qualified persons with disabilities.

The ADA allows that accommodations constituting an *undue hardship* to the business aren't required and defines undue hardships as an accommodation that places an excessive burden on the employer. The act identifies the factors to be considered in determining whether an accommodation is an undue hardship by looking at the cost, the financial resources of the organization, the size of the organization, and other similar factors.

In 2008, Congress enacted the ADA Amendments Act of 2008, which took effect on January 1, 2009. According to language in the amendment, Congress took the action to clarify the intention of the original legislation, which was to make the definition of "disability" consistent with the way the courts had defined the term under the Rehabilitation Act of 1973. In fact, court interpretations under the ADA had "narrowed the broad scope of protection" originally intended. The amendment more clearly describes the intent of Congress in the following areas:

Broadly Defines "Disability"   A disability is a physical or mental impairment that causes *substantial limitation* to one or more *major life activities* for an individual, a record of impairment for an individual, or an individual who is regarded as being impaired.

Defines "Major Life Activity"   The amendment defines major life activities in two areas: general activities and major bodily functions. Table 4.2 lists activities Congress cites in the law as examples but isn't meant to be a complete list.

Ignores Mitigating Measures   Congress directs that, except for "ordinary glasses or contact lenses," mitigating measures such as medication, prosthetics, hearing aids, mobility devices, and others may not be used to limit the definition of disability for an individual.

Clarifies the Definition of "Regarded As"   This amendment requires that individuals who are able to demonstrate that they have been the subject of prohibited activities under the ADA, whether or not they actually have some type of impairment, are protected by its requirements.

Explicitly Authorizes the EEOC to Regulate Compliance   The amendment mandates the EEOC to develop and implement regulations and guidance for employers to follow, specifying the inclusion of a definition for "substantially limits" that is consistent with the intent of Congress in the legislation.

Prohibits "Reverse Discrimination" Claims   The amendment clearly states that individuals without disability may not use the ADA to file claims of discrimination when disabled individuals receive favorable employment actions.

A key element of ADA compliance is the requirement to engage in an interactive process with disabled individuals requesting a reasonable accommodation that will enable them to perform essential job functions. This process is described in Chapter 8, "Risk Management."

TABLE 4.2   Major life activities

General Activities	Major Bodily Functions
Caring for oneself, performing manual tasks, seeing, hearing, eating, sleeping, breathing, learning, reading, concentrating, thinking, communicating, working	Functions of the immune system, normal cell growth, and functions of the digestive, bowel, bladder, neurological, brain, respiratory, circulatory, endocrine, and reproductive systems

At this writing, the EEOC is evaluating the impact of the 2008 amendment on its regulation and enforcement. You can find the text of the ADA, along with current information on the availability of regulatory and enforcement changes, at http://www.ada.gov/.

Civil Rights Act of 1991

The purpose of the Civil Rights Act (CRA) of 1991, as described in the act itself, is fourfold:

- To provide appropriate remedies for intentional discrimination and unlawful harassment in the workplace

- To codify the concepts of "business necessity" and "job related" articulated by the Supreme Court in *Griggs v. Duke Power Co.* and in other Supreme Court decisions prior to *Wards Cove Packing Co. v. Atonio*

- To confirm statutory authority and provide statutory guidelines for the adjudication of disparate impact suits under Title VII of the Civil Rights Act of 1964

- To respond to recent decisions of the Supreme Court by expanding the scope of relevant civil rights statutes in order to provide adequate protection to victims of discrimination

Amendments contained in the CRA affected Title VII, the ADEA, and the ADA. One of the issues addressed is that of *disparate impact*, first introduced by the *Griggs v. Duke Power* case in 1971. Disparate impact occurs when an employment practice, which appears on its face to be fair, unintentionally discriminates against members of a protected class. The CRA places the burden of proof for discrimination complaints on the complainant when there is a job-related business necessity for employment actions. When an individual alleges multiple discriminatory acts, each practice in itself must be discriminatory unless the employer's decision-making process can't be separated, in which case the individual may challenge the decision-making process itself. The CRA also provides additional relief for victims of intentional discrimination and harassment, codifies the concept of disparate impact, and addresses Supreme Court rulings over the previous few years that had weakened equal employment opportunity laws.

The CRA made the following changes to Title VII:

- Provided punitive damages when employers engage in discriminatory practices "with malice or with reckless indifference"
- Excluded back-pay awards from compensatory damages
- Established a sliding scale for compensatory and punitive damages based on company size, as shown in Table 4.3
- Provided that any party to a civil suit in which punitive or compensatory damages are sought may demand a jury trial
- Expanded Title VII to include congressional employees and some senior political appointees
- Required that the individual alleging an unlawful employment practice is in use prove that it results in disparate impact to members of a protected class
- Provided that job-relatedness and reasonable business necessity are defenses to disparate impact and that if a business can show that the practice doesn't result in disparate impact, it need not show the practice to be a business necessity
- Provided that business necessity isn't a defense against an intentional discriminatory employment practice
- Established that if discrimination was a motivating factor in an employment practice it was unlawful, even if other factors contributed to the practice
- Allowed that if the same employment decision would have been made whether or not an impermissible motivating factor was present, there would be no damages awarded
- Expanded coverage to include foreign operations of American businesses unless compliance would constitute violation of the laws of the host country

TABLE 4.3　CRA limits for total punitive and compensatory damages

Number of employees*	Maximum damage award
15–100	$50,000
101–200	$100,000
201–500	$200,000
501+	$300,000

*Number of employees in each of 20 or more weeks in the current or preceding calendar year.

Visit http://www.eeoc.gov/laws/statutes/cra-1991.cfm

for more information regarding the CRA.

Genetic Information Nondiscrimination Act of 2008

When research into the use of human genomic information made it possible to identify genetic predisposition to particular diseases, many people became uncomfortable with the idea of information so personal being made available to insurance companies or employers that could use it for discriminatory purposes. For more than 10 years, Congress worked on legislation that would prevent that from happening. President George W. Bush signed the resulting legislation, the Genetic Information Nondiscrimination Act (GINA), into law in May 2008.

GINA prohibits employers from unlawfully discriminating against employees or their family members in any of the terms or conditions of employment included in Title VII. The act defines genetic information as the results of genetic tests for employees and their family members or as information about genetic diseases or disorders revealed through genetic testing.

The act makes it unlawful for employers to request, require, or purchase genetic information but doesn't penalize them for inadvertently obtaining the information. GINA allows employers to obtain the information for wellness or health programs they offer when the employee authorizes access to the information in writing. In those cases, the information obtained through genetic testing may be provided only to health-care professionals or board-certified genetic counselors providing services to employees. This information may be provided to employers only in aggregate form that doesn't identify specific employees.

Employers may request the information as required by the Family and Medical Leave Act (FMLA) or similar state laws but may use it only as required by those laws. Employers can also use genetic information if federal or state laws require genetic monitoring of biological effects from toxic substances in the workplace, but only if the employee receives written notice and provides informed, written consent to the monitoring and the monitoring complies with federal and state laws. Any test results may be provided to employers only in aggregate form without identifying individual information.

The DOL issued a request for comments on the implementation of GINA prior to beginning the rule-making process. The submission period ended in December 2008, and the DOL began evaluating regulatory needs with the Department of Health and Human Services and the Treasury Department because aspects of the law impact agencies in those departments as well.

Information about the DOL rule-making process for GINA is posted on the DOL website as it becomes available: www.dol.gov. Visit www .govtrack.us/congress/billtext.xpd?bill=h110-493 to view the full text of the bill.

Federal Contractors, Subcontractors, and Agencies

The employment legislation described in previous sections doesn't always apply to agencies of the federal government, but discrimination in these entities is prohibited by executive orders and other legislation.

Rehabilitation Act of 1973, Sections 501, 503, and 505

The Rehabilitation Act of 1973 was enacted to expand the opportunities available for persons with physical or mental disabilities. The employment clauses of the act apply to agencies of the federal government and federal contractors with contracts of $10,000 or more during a 12-month period. Section 501 addresses employment discrimination, while section 505 details the remedies available for those who have been subjected to unlawful employment practices. The EEOC has enforcement responsibility for section 501. Under section 503, individuals with disabilities who think a federal contractor has violated the requirements of the Rehabilitation Act may also file complaints with the DOL through the Office of Federal Contract Compliance Programs (OFCCP).

For an overview of the Rehabilitation act visit http://www.dol.gov/compliance/laws/comp-rehab.htm.

Vietnam Era Veterans' Readjustment Assistance Act of 1974

EEO and affirmative action protection for veterans who served during the Vietnam War are provided by the Vietnam Era Veterans' Readjustment Assistance Act (VEVRAA), which applies to federal contractors or subcontractors with contracts of $25,000 or more. The act requires federal contractors to list all job openings with state employment agencies unless they are for senior-level management positions, positions that will be filled from within, or positions lasting 3 days or less. State employment agencies are required to give priority to Vietnam-era veterans when providing referrals to these openings.

A Vietnam-era veteran is one who meets specific criteria related to having served on active duty between August 5, 1964, and May 7, 1975. The act provides additional protections for special disabled veterans who have disabilities rated at 10, 20, or 30 or more percent who are entitled to compensation from the Department of Veterans Affairs.

View an overview of DOL compliance requirements at http://www.dol.gov/compliance/laws/comp-vevraa.

Executive Orders

Executive orders (EOs) are presidential proclamations that, when published in the Federal Register, become law after 30 days. EOs have been used to ensure equal employment opportunities are afforded by federal agencies and private businesses that contract or subcontract with those agencies. Executive orders relating to equal employment issues are enforced by the OFCCP:

Executive Order 11246   This EO, established in 1965, prohibits employment discrimination on the basis of race, creed, color, or national origin and requires affirmative steps be taken in advertising jobs, recruiting, employing, training, promotion, compensation, and terminating employees.

Executive Order 11375   Created in 1967, EO 11375 amended EO 11246 and expanded coverage for protected classes to include discrimination on the basis of sex.

Executive Order 11478   This order, written in 1969, again expanded the scope of EO 11246 by adding handicapped individuals and persons 40 years of age or older to the list of protected classes.

Executive Order 12138   In 1979, with the implementation of EO 12138, the National Women's Business Enterprise policy was created. This EO also required federal contractors and subcontractors to take affirmative steps to promote and support women's business enterprises.

Executive Order 13087   This EO from 1998 expanded coverage to include sexual orientation.

Executive Order 13152   This EO added "status as a parent" to the list of protected classes first identified in EO 11246. Written in 2000, it protects those who must care for an "individual who is under the age of 18 or who is 18 or older but is incapable of self-care because of a physical or mental disability" from employment discrimination. The order broadly defines a parent as a biological, adoptive, foster, or stepparent; a legal custodian; one who is acting as a parent; or one actively seeking legal custody or adoption of a child.

Executive Order 13279   This EO limited the impact of EO 11246 on faith-based and community organizations providing social services as federal contractors or subcontractors.

The National Archives provides a list of all EOs, searchable by president, number, and year, at www.archives.gov/federal-register/executive-orders/disposition.html.

Two levels of compliance are required by EOs. The first level, which prohibits employment discrimination and requires contractors to take affirmative action in employment actions, applies to contracts totaling $10,000 or more in a 12-month period.

The second level of compliance, for contractors with 50 or more employees who have contracts of $50,000 or more, requires that a written Affirmative Action Plan (AAP) be developed within 120 days from the origination of the contract with the OFCCP, the agency charged with enforcing EOs.

Annual EEO Survey

Working together, the EEOC and the OFCCP developed a reporting format designed to meet statistical reporting requirements for both agencies. This form, known as the EEO-1, must be filed on or before September 30 of each year using employment data from any pay period during July, August, or September of that year. All employers who meet the following criteria must complete the report:

- Private employers subject to Title VII with 100 or more employees, *except* the following:
    - State and local governments
    - Primary and secondary school systems
    - Institutions of higher education
    - Indian tribes
    - Tax-exempt private membership clubs (other than labor organizations)

- All federal contractors or subcontractors with more than 50 employees, which
    - Have contracts, subcontracts, or purchase orders of $50,000 or more or
    - Are depositories of government funds in any amount or
    - Are financial institutions issuing and paying U.S. savings bonds and notes

Report Types

EEO-1 reports may be submitted electronically or on paper. Employers with operations at a single location or establishment complete a single form, but for those who operate multiple locations, employment data is reported on multiple forms:

Headquarters Report   Employment data for the principal office of the organization is reported on the Headquarters Report.

Locations with 50 or More Employees   A separate Establishment Report is required for each of these locations.

Locations with Fewer Than 50 Employees   Locations with fewer than 50 employees may be reported on an Establishment Report or on an Establishment List. The Establishment List provides the name, address, and total number of employees for each location with fewer than 50 employees along with an employment data grid combining this data by race, sex, and job category.

Consolidated Report   Data from all the individual location reports is combined on the Consolidated Report. The total number of employees on this report must be equal to data submitted on the individual reports.

Parent corporations that own majority interest in another corporation report data for employees at all locations, including those of the subsidiary establishments.

Race and Ethnicity Categories

Revisions to the race and ethnicity reporting categories were effective with the reports due on or after September 30, 2007. Prior reports required employees to be reported in one of five categories; the revision expanded this to seven:

- Hispanic or Latino
- White (not Hispanic or Latino)

- Black or African-American (not Hispanic or Latino)
- Native Hawaiian or Other Pacific Islander (not Hispanic or Latino)
- Asian (not Hispanic or Latino)
- American Indian or Alaska Native (not Hispanic or Latino)
- Two or More Races (not Hispanic or Latino)

The OFCCP prefers that whenever possible, employees should be encouraged to self-identify their race and ethnicity. This normally occurs during the application/interview process, and the information is kept confidential from hiring managers and other interviewers. If a company hasn't included this in its application process but has grown to 100 or more employees and needs to complete its first EEO-1, it may ask its current employees to voluntarily self-identify and add such forms to the application process going forward. If applicants or employees choose to not self-identify, the employer is allowed to make a good-faith selection.

Job Categories

The EEO-1 report requires employers to group jobs into job categories based on the average skill level, knowledge, and responsibility of positions within their organizations. These categories were also revised for reporting periods beginning in 2007:

- Executive/Senior Level Officials and Managers
- First/Mid-Level Officials and Managers
- Professionals
- Technicians
- Sales Workers
- Administrative Support Workers
- Craft Workers
- Operatives
- Laborers and Helpers
- Service Workers

Data Reporting

To assist employers in categorizing their employees for the report, the EEOC describes each of the revised race/ethnicity and job categories at http://www.eeoc.gov/employers/eeo1/qanda-implementation.cfm. For each job category, employers report the total number of male and female employees according to their ethnicity and race. Figure 4.1 shows a sample of the revised EEO-1 form.

FIGURE 4.1 EEO-1 report from 2007

Section D – EMPLOYMENT DATA

Employment at this establishment—report all permanent full- and part-time employees including apprentices and on-the-job trainees unless specifically excluded as set forth in the instructions. Enter the appropriate figures on all lines and in all columns. Blank spaces will be considered as zeros.

Job Categories		Number of Employees (Report employees in only one category)														Total Col A – N
		Race/Ethnicity														
		Hispanic or Latino		Not-Hispanic or Latino												
				Male						Female						
		Male	Female	White	Black or African American	Native Hawaiian or Other Pacific Islander	Asian	American Indian or Alaska Native	Two or more races	White	Black or African American	Native Hawaiian or Other Pacific Islander	Asian	American Indian or Alaska Native	Two or more races	
		A	B	C	D	E	F	G	H	I	J	K	L	M	N	O
Executive/Senior Level Officials and Managers	1.1															
First/Mid-Level Officials and Managers	1.2															
Professionals	2															
Technicians	3															
Sales Workers	4															
Administrative Support Workers	5															
Craft Workers	6															
Operatives	7															
Laborers and Helpers	8															
Service Workers	9															
TOTAL	10															
PREVIOUS YEAR TOTAL	11															

1. Date(s) of payroll period used: _____ (Omit on the Consolidated Report.)

As previously mentioned, information collected on the EEO-1 report is the result of collaboration between the EEOC and OFCCP. The EEOC uses the race/ethnicity and job categories for statistical analysis; they also form the basis for the information in AAPs submitted to the OFCCP.

Affirmative Action Plans

The components of an AAP are determined by the OFCCP and, in a revision effective December 13, 2000, include the items described in Table 4.4.

TABLE 4.4 Components of an AAP

AAP Component	Description
Organizational profile	Employers choose the format that works best: organizational display (traditional organization chart) or workforce analysis (listing of job titles from lowest to highest paid)
Job group analysis	Places job titles with similar duties and responsibilities into groups for analysis
Placement of incumbents in job groups	Lists percentages of minorities and women in each job group
Determination of availability	Reports demographic data on the labor pool for each job group
Comparison of incumbency to availability	Compares protected classes employed in each job group with availability of protected classes in the labor pool
Placement goals	Sets reasonable goals to address underrepresentation of protected classes in the workforce
Designation of the person responsible for implementation within the business	Assigns responsibility for achieving placement goals in the AAP to a person with access to the executive team in the business
Identification of problem areas	Requires analysis of employment processes to determine where barriers to equal opportunity exist
Action-oriented programs	Requires modification of current employment practices to remove barriers to opportunity
Periodic internal audits	Requires periodic review of employment activity with management and reports to executives on actions taken to improve results

It may be helpful to refer to the sample while reading the following explanations of the various components:

Organizational Profile The organizational profile looks at how employees are placed in specific job titles and may be presented as a traditional organization chart or as a workforce analysis. The workforce analysis lists job titles from the lowest to the highest paid within each department or work unit. For each title, the wage rate or salary grade is identified, along with the EEO-1 category, job group, and total number of employees holding that title. The analysis also breaks down the total number of employees into the number of males and females of the seven EEO-1 racial/ethnic descriptions (Hispanic, White, Black or African-American, native Hawaiian or other Pacific Islander, Asian, American Indian or Alaska native, and two or more races).

Job Group Analysis The job group analysis organizes jobs into groups established for the EEO-1 report. For this report, employers list all of their job titles that fall into each job group, as well as the number of employees in the job group, and identify the associated EEO-1 category.

Placement of Incumbents in Job Groups This report lists each job group with the total number of incumbents in each group. The total is broken down into the number and percentage of females and the number and percentage of minorities in each group.

Determination of Availability For each job group, the AAP shows how many minorities or women with the required skills are available externally (within a "reasonable recruiting area") and the percentage of minorities or women available internally for promotion, transfer, or training into the job group. This report identifies the source used to gather the information (most often the most recent Census data for external hires and the internal source for promotable employees), the weight placed on the source, the reason for the weighting, and the statistics adjusted based on the weight assigned.

Comparison of Incumbency to Availability This information is most easily presented as a chart showing each job group with the percentage of female and minority incumbents compared to the availability.

Placement Goals Placement goals are required if the comparison of incumbency to availability indicates that women and/or minorities are underrepresented in a job group. Underrepresentation is determined by the 80 percent rule, described in the section "Uniform Guidelines on Employee Selection Procedures" later in this chapter.

Designation of Responsibility for Implementation This section of the AAP provides the titles of employees with affirmative action responsibility and details the scope of responsibility for each title.

Action-Oriented Programs   Problem areas are identified and corrective actions planned by the employer are described as part of the Action Oriented Program section of the AAP. The action plans include specific steps to be taken along with timelines to correct the identified problem areas.

Periodic Internal Audits   The last section of the AAP describes how the responsibilities detailed in the Designation of Responsibility for Implementation section will be monitored within the organization.

Strategic Workforce Planning

The goal of strategic workforce planning is to ensure that qualified employees are available when the organization needs them. An effective workforce planning process is based on the following:

- Workforce goals and objectives that forecast the organization's future workforce needs
- Job analysis and description that identifies the knowledge, skills, and abilities needed to meet the future needs
- Identification of qualified employees beginning with the organization's current workforce demographics
- Translating the goals and objectives into tactical staffing plans to build the future workforce

The workforce plan resulting from this process provides the framework for targeting and prioritizing future staffing requirements, remaining flexible enough to allow HR to respond rapidly to changing business needs.

Workforce Goals and Objectives

During the strategic planning process discussed in Chapter 3, "Business Management and Strategy," organization leaders make decisions about how to achieve business goals and objectives that provide a competitive advantage, improve the level of business performance, and add value to stockholders. Chapter 3 discussed organizational design decisions that occur as part of the strategic planning process. Depending on the goals established by the plan, these decisions affect workforce planning in different ways:

Reengineering   The goal of reengineering is to realign operations in a way that adds value to customers. For workforce planning, this may mean eliminating jobs in some areas and adding jobs in others.

Corporate Restructuring   Corporate restructuring looks at individual units in the organization to reduce or eliminate redundancy or bureaucratic processes in order to reduce costs and increase production. For workforce planning, this means reducing the workforce or reassigning employees to new jobs.

Mergers and Acquisitions   In some cases, business leaders make a decision to acquire products and market share by purchasing other companies instead of building them internally. One result of a merger or an acquisition is reducing labor costs as economies of scale allow jobs to be combined or eliminated.

Divestitures   When the strategic plan includes a decision to divest an operating unit, this can mean eliminating jobs or transferring employees to a new operating entity. The effect on workforce planning can be twofold: reducing the workforce in the divesting organization and, if appropriate, performing due diligence to determine whether to transfer employees to the new entity.

Offshoring/Outsourcing   In most cases, *offshoring* or outsourcing decisions result in a workforce reduction or transfer of employees to other jobs. When employees are acquired by an outsource provider, they're terminated from the organization and hired by the new company.

Workforce Expansion   An organization may decide to expand its workforce in order to accomplish business objectives. For example, if the strategic plan calls for increasing sales by 15 percent, leaders may determine that achieving that goal requires increasing the sales force.

Workforce Reduction   Whether necessitated by a restructuring, a merger, an acquisition, or in response to loss of market share, reducing labor costs is a painful result of some business decisions. There are many examples of workforce reductions in the business environment, including the job losses that occurred during the dot-com bust of 2000–2001 and the financial market meltdown beginning in 2008.

One thing is certain: human resource professionals must be ready to respond rapidly to changes in business workforce requirements with a road map that produces employees who possess the talent needed by the business to achieve its goals. This road map is built on the jobs that need to be performed and the individuals who will perform those jobs.

Job Analysis and Description

As described in detail in Chapter 2, job analysis provides the foundation for identifying the knowledge, skills, and abilities (KSAs) needed to achieve specific results in an organization. Historically, HR professionals compile this information into job descriptions, which are then used to identify individuals who possess the needed KSAs for different positions. The strategic selection process begins by identifying the qualifications necessary to do each job in the organization. A successful recruitment and selection process is dependent on this process from which the hiring criteria is established, pre-employment tests are written, and proper hiring decisions can be made. The HR department's ability to influence the decision-making process based on person-to-job fit is critical and, when combined with the knowledge of the employee(s) currently doing the work and their supervisor, a powerful and relevant resource.

Retention and promotion opportunities are also identified through the job analysis process. Creating depth in each position allows for the advancement of employees who are potentially overqualified to do their current jobs or who desire career advancement in their chosen field. Retention is improved when employees are properly compensated for the type of work they're doing. For example, a pay imbalance can occur when evolved job duties aren't properly accounted for. Conducting a skills inventory of the internal workforce and matching it to the current requirements of the job(s) will allow for the proper application of the existing talent and/or the development of current employees through education, on-the-job training (OJT) experience, or training.

In the staffing process, more information is always better. Hiring managers and potential candidates make decisions that are more effective when all the particulars about a job are known. In addition to the information in Chapter 2, the following criteria have particular relevance for the staffing process:

Job Competencies Job competencies guide interviewers in formulating questions that elicit information beyond specific tasks and responsibilities assigned to a specific job. This information helps determine how well a candidate will fit into a particular work group and contribute to organization goals. Core competencies may be developed for traits the organization values and would like to see in all its employees, such as teamwork, communication, or customer focus. Job-specific competencies are related to a specific role in the organization. For example, a job with management responsibilities may include competencies for developing subordinates, leadership, and strategic thinking.

Essential Job Functions Well-defined essential job functions are important in the recruiting process to ensure that the organization complies with equal employment opportunities for all candidates, particularly those with disabilities.

Job Specifications Job specifications are another tool for interviewers, helping to further define expectations for performance. Candidates also use them to evaluate their interest in the position and assess how well they will be able to perform if hired.

The ability to update the job competencies, essential functions, and job specifications should be a post-analysis function that is properly planned for and maintained. For example, some companies update the competencies, functions, and specifications each time the position becomes open or on an annual basis sorted by department. These types of processes account for changes or updates to job duties and outputs without having to complete an organization-wide job analysis all at once, which can be time-consuming and disruptive to day-to-day operations.

Qualified Employees

Organizations have three options for locating the talent they need to achieve business goals: internal transfers or promotions, external hires, and alternative staffing methods. HR professionals evaluate the options by deciding which option is best in a given situation. Are there sufficient skills within the organization that can be redirected to the new requirements through transfers or promotions? Is it best to bring in full-time employees? Will some other staffing alternative provide the best solution? Let's take a brief look at these alternatives and discuss the strategic implications of each source.

Internal Talent

The first place to look for qualified employees to fill future needs is among those who already work for the organization. There are a number of advantages to filling jobs internally or "promoting from within." Management has an opportunity to evaluate candidates and determine their suitability for advancement over an extended period of time as they perform current duties, and the possibility of future promotion can encourage employees to maintain a high level of performance. Investing in employees through learning and development and then providing advancement opportunities for them communicates to employees that the organization values and rewards their contributions. When promotion from within is an organization policy, most external hiring is done at the entry level; this allows employees to become acclimated to the organization culture and operating procedures early in their careers, leading to greater success when they move into positions with greater responsibility.

Of course, some disadvantages are associated with relying solely on promotion from within to fill positions of increasing responsibility:

- There is the danger that employees with little experience outside the organization will have a myopic view of the industry.
- Although the morale of those promoted will be high, employees who have been passed over or lost out on promotions may have lower morale and be less motivated in performing their jobs.
- When several people are being groomed for promotion, the competition can lead to a breakdown in teamwork and jockeying for political position.
- If the organization lacks diversity in its workforce, overreliance on promoting from within can perpetuate the imbalance.
- Reduced recruiting costs will be offset by an increase in training costs to prepare employees for positions with increased technical responsibilities or for supervisory or management positions.

External Talent

At some point, organizations need to look outside for new employees. Even if the organization has a policy or practice of promotion from within, entry-level positions must be filled as employees are promoted or transferred. There are, of course, advantages to bringing new people into the organization:

- Experienced professionals bring new ideas with them and can revitalize operations.
- It's usually easier and more cost-effective to hire individuals with highly specialized skills than it is to develop them within the organization.
- If there is an urgent need for someone with particular skills, it's usually faster to hire those skills than to provide on-the-job training.
- Looking outside the organization to fill positions provides opportunities to increase the diversity of the workforce.

Looking outside the organization also has several disadvantages:

- Current employees who have been passed over for promotion will very likely have lower morale.
- It's always difficult to know how someone from outside the organization will fit into an existing team.

- The new hire is an unknown. Until the person begins doing the job, it's very difficult to know what their performance level will be.

Alternative Staffing Methods

To expand the pool of available candidates with the desired skills, it's often wise to consider alternative staffing methods. A wide range of alternatives provides varying levels of flexibility to the organization. Particularly when staffing needs require specialized skills or when the labor market is tight, these methods can provide access to highly qualified candidates who might otherwise be unavailable to the organization:

Telecommuting   Due to advances in technology, *telecommuting*, which allows employees to work at home and connect to the office electronically, has become a viable solution for individuals who don't want to commute or who have other reasons to work at home. Aside from the benefits telecommuting employees enjoy, reducing the number of employees required to be at the office each day can allow employers to reduce overhead costs as well as contribute to reductions in energy consumption and traffic congestion.

Job Sharing   *Job sharing* is an alternative that allows two people with complementary skills to share the duties and responsibilities of a full-time position.

Part-Time Employees   *Part-time employees* are those who work less than a regular workweek. This staffing strategy can be a cost-effective solution for organizations needing particular skills on an ongoing but not full-time basis.

Internships   *Internship programs* are usually designed to give students opportunities to gain experience in their chosen fields prior to graduation. Successful programs provide meaningful work and learning experiences for the students, including opportunities to meet with senior executives. The student gains a valuable learning experience, and the organization benefits by developing low-cost access to employees and the chance to observe the intern's performance prior to making an offer for full-time employment.

Temporary Workers   The temporary worker category covers a wide range of flexible staffing options:

> **Traditional**   In a traditional arrangement, an individual is employed by an agency that screens and tests candidates prior to sending them to a work site for variable periods of time, from short, one-day assignments to assignments lasting for long periods of time. Under certain circumstances, these assignments can be converted to a regular, open position. These arrangements allow organizations to observe and evaluate a worker's performance prior to making an offer of full-time employment.

> **On-Call Workers**   *On-call workers* are employed by the organization, available on short notice, and called to work only when they're needed.

> **Payrolling**   *Payrolling* allows the organization to refer to an agency those individuals they want to hire. The agency hires the individuals to work for the organization and provides payroll and tax services for either a fixed fee or a percentage of the salary, which is generally less than a traditional temp agency fee.

Seasonal Workers   *Seasonal workers* are hired only at times of the year when the workload increases, such as the Christmas shopping season or when it's time to harvest agricultural products.

Contract Workers   *Contract workers* provide another solution for acquiring talent. There are two types of contract workers:

Independent Contractors   *Independent contractors* are self-employed individuals who work on a project or fee basis with multiple customers or clients. Both federal and state governments have guidelines to determine the difference between an independent contractor and an employee. Misclassifying an employee as an independent contractor can result in substantial penalties to the employer, so it's important to ensure that the guidelines are followed.

Contingent Workforce   A *contingent workforce* is made up of non-traditional workers, including part time and seasonal as well as temporary or leased employees. Employment agencies or brokers will typically act as the employer of record on behalf of many contract workers, providing payroll, mandated benefits, and other services to this classification of workers.

Professional Employer Organization   A *professional employer organization* (PEO) operates as the organization's HR department. The PEO becomes the employer of record and then leases the employees back to the organization. PEOs provide full-service HR, payroll, and benefit services and can provide a cost-effective solution that enables smaller companies to offer benefits comparable to those offered by much larger organizations.

Outsourcing   *Outsourcing* moves an entire function out of the organization to be handled by a company specializing in the function. For example, *human resource outsourcers* (HROs) may be used for one or more HR functions, such as benefits administration or recruiting. This solution can be beneficial by allowing the organization to focus on its basic business operations and potentially reduce costs.

 Real World Scenario

Employee or Independent Contractor?

The Internal Revenue Service (IRS) has established guidelines for determining whether an individual can be considered an independent contractor or an employee. Recently, the IRS clarified the factors it uses to determine the appropriate status for an individual. These standards fall into three categories:

- *Behavioral controls* establish whether the organization has the right to direct and control tasks completed by the worker, including the following:

    - Instructions given by the organization to the worker as to when and where the work is done, the tools or equipment used, whether the worker must perform the task or may hire others to assist, the order or sequence of tasks, and who must perform specific tasks.

- Organizations train employees to perform services in a particular manner, whereas independent contractors determine their own methods.

- *Financial controls* establish whether the organization controls the business aspects of the individual, including the following:

  - The extent to which business expenses are *not* reimbursed

  - The extent of investment made by the worker in the business

  - The extent to which the worker makes services available to the relevant market versus a single business

  - How the worker is paid

  - The extent to which the worker can realize a profit or loss

- The *type of relationship that exists between the parties* is demonstrated by the following:

  - The existence of a written contract

  - The existence of benefits such as insurance, a pension, and vacation and sick pay

  - The permanency of the relationship: that is, an indefinite period of time (employee) or a specific project or period of time (contractor)

  - The extent to which the services performed are a key aspect of the regular business of the organization

Additional information about the IRS guidelines is available at www.irs.gov /pub/irs-pdf/p15a.pdf.

Many states have established their own rules for determining the appropriate status for workers. As with all employment laws and regulations, the highest standard is the one with which employers must comply, so be sure to familiarize yourself with the standards for the state(s) in which you practice.

Translating Organization Goals into Staffing Plans

Translating strategic workforce goals and objectives into a tactical action plan is accomplished with the use of a *staffing needs analysis*. This tool is used to determine the numbers and types of jobs forecasted in the organization's strategic plan. Figure 4.2 depicts a typical staffing needs assessment.

FIGURE 4.2   Staffing needs analysis

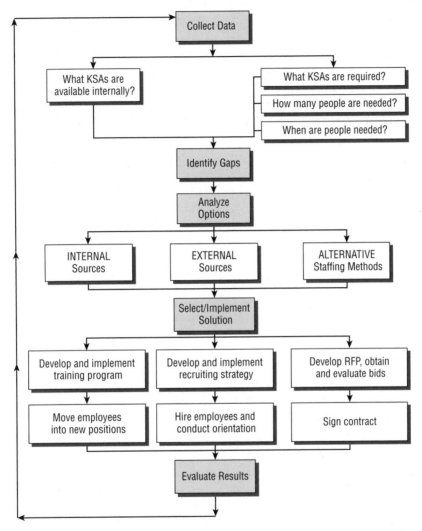

The strategic plan identifies two key pieces of information for HR: the work that needs to be done and how many people are needed to do it. That information forms the objective for the staffing needs analysis and identifies the information to be collected:

Collect Data   Workforce planning provides an opportunity for HR professionals to build key relationships within their organizations, demonstrating the value they can add to the business. Business-unit managers are the ones, of course, who establish the goals and objectives for their individual work groups. During this planning phase, HR can assist these managers to identify the KSAs that will be needed to execute those objectives as well as the number and timing of people required.

At this time, HR also collects information about current employees who may be ready to assume new tasks and responsibilities and any training needed to prepare them for new roles. Organizations fortunate enough to have a robust human resource information system (HRIS) can use that tool to further analyze the current workforce.

Identify Gaps   Building on the data collected from individual business-unit managers, HR develops a comprehensive list of the KSAs required to meet future needs for the organization. Factored into this list should be contingencies for retirements or unexpected resignations of current employees based on prior history of turnover, transfers, and promotions. Comparing the required KSAs with the current capabilities of the workforce identifies the gaps that will need to be filled and provides the data needed to analyze the best way to fill those needs, whether internally, externally, or by using alternative staffing methods.

Analyze Options   Once the list of numbers, types, and timing of future openings is available, HR identifies options for filling the positions, whether from internal transfers or promotions, external hires, or the use of alternative staffing methods.

Select/Implement Solutions   Conducting a cost/benefit analysis of the options identified in the previous step provides a means for comparison between the available options.

Evaluate Results   After the solution has been implemented, an evaluation of its success is conducted to ensure that it meets the needs of the organization.

Labor Market Analysis

Conditions in the labor market affect the ability of an organization to hire the qualified individuals it needs. A labor market analysis looks at various economic indicators and other factors that impact the availability of those individuals:

Economic Indicators   A variety of economic measures are used in labor market analysis. The Bureau of Labor Statistics (BLS) collects data from employers throughout the United States and makes this information available on its website. Some of the measures useful in analyzing the labor market include the unemployment rate, occupational outlook, demographics, and wages by area and occupation. In 2001, BLS introduced the Job Openings and Labor Turnover Survey (JOLTS), which analyzes open positions, hiring statistics, and terminations.

Industry Activity   Another important factor to consider in a labor market analysis is the industry situation. Are new competitors entering the market? Is an existing competitor ramping up to produce a new product? Is a competitor losing market share and laying off employees? Activity within an industry affects an organization's ability to obtain qualified individuals to fill job openings.

Labor Market Categories   Depending on specific job requirements, the labor market most often falls into one of three broad categories:

Geographic   This labor market can be local, regional, national, or international and contains individuals with a wide variety of technical and professional skills and levels of education. Selection of the geographic labor market depends on the availability of candidates with the necessary skills for the position. For example, the pool of candidates for an entry-level customer service representative opening could be quite large in the local labor market, whereas obtaining a sufficient pool of candidates to fill an open CEO position could require looking at the national or international labor market.

Technical/Professional Skills   This labor market contains individuals with expertise in a specific skill or discipline, such as accounting or information technology. These skills are often transferable between industries and can expand the available pool of candidates for openings.

Education   This labor market includes individuals with similar levels of education. In some professions, such as teaching, medicine, or science, an advanced degree may be required to fill a position.

A useful labor market analysis for a particular organization includes data that is relevant to the needs of the organization and the types of employees and skills it's seeking to hire.

Staffing Programs

The workforce plan and staffing needs analysis have identified the jobs to be filled, when they're needed, where they're located, and the KSAs and competencies needed for successful performance. The job descriptions and specifications for successfully recruiting qualified candidates are in place. A review of internal demographics indicates if past recruiting efforts have resulted in a diverse workforce or whether it's necessary to explore alternative ways to promote diversity in the organization. Armed with this information, the process of finding qualified candidates for open positions can begin. The question now becomes where to find the appropriate people to fill the gaps.

Sourcing and Recruiting Candidates

The sourcing and recruiting of qualified candidates to fill open positions is critical to the success of any organization. Sourcing and recruiting functions may be combined into one position or, in large organizations or during periods of intense hiring, may be split. *Sourcing* provides names and contact information for potential candidates in the active and passive markets. Active job seekers are seeking work and often attracted through traditional advertising methods (see the section "External Recruiting"). Passive candidates are those who aren't currently looking for work, so locating them requires additional research, such as identifying professional associations or organizations that are likely to employ individuals with similar skills. *Recruiting* is the process of creating interest about open positions in an organization and seeking candidates who possess the necessary qualifications to successfully fill them.

Recruiting Strategies

An effective recruiting strategy is ongoing. Even during times when few positions are open, continuing to communicate with potential candidates, educational institutions, search firms, and other sources can help shorten the time needed to fill positions when they do occur and result in better service to internal customers.

Employer Brands

Defining the employer's brand identity sets the stage for many aspects of the recruiting process. Each organization has a brand identity in the marketplace, whether or not it has been consciously developed. The reputation established with employees, current and former, along with the way the organization presents itself in the general marketplace, contribute to the brand. Because the information is out there, HR can take a leading role in defining the brand so that it's an accurate reflection of where the company wants to be and can be used in the recruiting process.

Simply developing a catchy PR campaign isn't enough to make an effective employer brand. For a brand to be useful in attracting high-quality employees to the organization, it must first match the reality of working in the organization and describe what is unique about it. When that happens, every employee becomes an ambassador, creating interest among friends, neighbors, former colleagues, or others in working for the organization.

Building an employer brand begins with identifying unique elements of the organization culture. What values are important to the company? How are employees treated? Is the company on the leading edge in its industry? Is risk-taking encouraged or frowned on? Are employees involved in the decision-making process? Is the performance-management process perceived to be fair? Do employees receive regular feedback? How does the company respond to economic downturns? These are some of the considerations that become part of the brand. An accurate brand message gives candidates an idea of what it would be like to work in the organization and positively influences retention. If the employer has differentiated its organization as an employer of choice with a clearly defined message about the benefits of working there, then attracting the quality of candidates desired by the organization becomes less difficult. It's critical, however, that the "official" brand message is an accurate reflection of the organization. To ensure that this is the case, an employee survey can be conducted to find out whether current employees perceive the organization the way the brand portrays it. If there is a discrepancy, the organization can choose whether to adjust the brand message or make operational changes that address the differences between employee perceptions and the branding message.

An effective employer brand that accurately portrays the organization culture benefits the organization in any economic climate. During times of economic growth when high-quality employees are in great demand, the brand both attracts and retains them. In an economic downturn, the brand becomes a vehicle for fostering communication and improving morale.

Total Reward Packages

An organization's total rewards philosophy affects its ability to attract qualified candidates. This strategy is a key element in the organization's recruiting strategy because it directly affects how well it will be able to attract and retain employees with the KSAs it needs. Chapter 6 discusses the philosophies in detail, but in general terms, organizations interested in acquiring the "best and brightest" candidates, or candidates with unique and highly desirable skills, employ a philosophy of leading the market, paying a premium to attract candidates. This philosophy, of course, may require the financial ability to pay at a premium. Organizations that may not be financially able to pay a premium but want to hire qualified employees compete with a philosophy of meeting the market, meaning they pay the average market rate. Some organizations decide to lag the market by paying below the market rate. This may be a financial necessity (such as an early-stage company or a nonprofit organization) or a conscious decision on the part of management if, for example, jobs require little or no skill or training and employees are easily replaced.

Recruiting Methods

During the process of creating job competencies, descriptions, and specifications, HR works with line managers to ensure that the job requirements are accurately presented. In the recruiting process, HR works with line managers to create a candidate profile so that applicants who go through the selection process fit the requirements of the position. In developing this profile, line managers often want to describe an "ideal candidate" who possibly even exceeds the requirements of the position. It's up to HR to work with line managers in developing candidate profiles that are realistic, given the working conditions and salary range offered for the position. At the same time, it's also effective to work with line managers to develop alternatives to the candidate profile, possibly substituting years of experience for education requirements or lowering experience requirements if the experience is in the same industry. This expands the pool of available candidates and increases the chances of success in the recruiting process.

With the job description and candidate profile in hand, HR is able to determine the best sources for qualified candidates. Choosing appropriate sources for candidates depends on how available the specific KSAs are in various labor markets, along with workforce diversity issues that need to be addressed in the hiring process. In general terms, the labor market used to recruit candidates depends in large part on the scarcity of the KSAs needed—the scarcer the KSAs, the larger the labor market to reach and the greater the recruiting budget.

Internal Recruiting

Once the organization has decided to fill positions internally, there are several methods for communicating information about the openings to employees. A *skills inventory* is an HR management tool used to collect and store a wealth of information that would otherwise be obtained only after many hours of research by HR staff. An effective skills inventory collects information on special skills or knowledge, performance appraisals, fluency in foreign languages, educational qualifications, previous experience in or outside of the company, credentials or licenses that may be required, and any continuing education employees have obtained through training classes, seminars, or educational institutions. When collecting this information is one of the functions of an automated HRIS system, obtaining a report with detailed information about the internal talent pool can be accomplished in minutes. When replacement and succession plans are in place, conversations with potential candidates can take place over a period of time, often during performance reviews and goal-setting sessions.

Once possible internal candidates for openings are identified using the skills inventory, replacement chart, or succession plan (both described shortly), two methods are used to publicize current openings throughout an organization:

Job Posting   A *job posting* is an internal job announcement that provides basic information about the opening, including the title; a brief description of the competencies, duties, responsibilities, and specifications; the salary range; and the application procedure.

Job Bidding   *Job bidding* provides a means by which interested employees express interest in a position before it's available. This gives the supervisor and HR department an opportunity to review the job qualifications with the employee, provide training opportunities, let the employee gain additional experience if needed to meet the position requirements, and add the employee's name to the replacement or succession plan as appropriate.

SPHR ONLY Succession Planning

A well-thought-out *succession plan* identifies individuals in the organization who have the talent and ability to move into management and executive positions in one to five years. Once these individuals are identified, development plans are created to ensure that they're mentored and have opportunities to obtain education, training, and experience in areas that will enhance their ability to move into senior positions when the organization needs them.

Organizations might also choose to develop, implement, and use a *replacement chart*. This tool is useful at all organization levels and helps HR and line managers identify staffing needs by categorizing current employees in one of four categories:

Ready for Promotion   Employees in this category demonstrate the KSAs to assume additional responsibilities and are ready to move forward in the organization.

Develop for Future Promotion   This group includes employees who are proficient in their current positions and, with additional training opportunities and experience, will be ready to move forward in the organization.

Satisfactory in Current Position   These employees are proficient in their current positions but don't demonstrate the KSAs or interest to assume greater responsibility in the organization.

Replace   Employees are placed in this category for a variety of reasons, such as transfer or promotion, impending retirement, short-term disability, or unsatisfactory performance.

External Recruiting

Once it has been decided that the appropriate method for filling positions is to hire from outside, a number of factors must be considered. Particularly when the skills needed by the organization are in short supply in the labor market, the organization must find ways to effectively publicize its openings to appropriate candidates.

A variety of recruiting methods can be considered for finding new employees. The appropriate method depends on the type of employee needed by the organization in a particular situation. This means that a number of methods may be used in a single organization at any given time:

Media Sources   Until the advent of Internet job boards, the most prevalent means for recruiting was newspaper advertising; for some jobs it's still the preferred method.

Advertising jobs on the radio is used much less often than newspaper ads, but it can be effective if a company is trying to fill a large number of positions in a short period of time. Television advertising is rarely used to advertise individual positions; when used, it's most often by agencies that accomplish a dual purpose with the ads—attracting candidates and soliciting clients.

Internet Job Boards and Community Sites   Advertising open positions on Internet job boards has become prevalent in recent years, particularly for positions in high-technology companies. Its popularity as a recruiting source is growing because it's often more cost-effective than traditional media advertising. A downside for employers using this method is that some job seekers are indiscriminate when responding to posted jobs, which results in a large number of resumes from unqualified applicants that must be sorted through to find appropriate candidates.

Social-Media Recruitment   Social media is quickly becoming a cost-effective way to recruit for many staff positions. A Society for Human Resource Management (SHRM) research spotlight reported that in 2011, more than 50 percent of the companies polled were using social media sites to recruit. In another report, the popular Internet job board CareerBuilder stated that its mobile device career site had a 400 percent growth rate in 2010, with a 350 percent increase of applicants who stored their resumes on their iPhones. This same CareerBuilder study reported that organizations that posted a short video with the job information had a 34 percent higher application rate than those who posted jobs without video.

These behaviors indicate that the current and future workforce continues to be online and mobile, marking a need for HR to respond. One example of a type of corporate response is the use of an applicant-tracking system. This outsourced activity involves hiring a social-media recruiting service that tracks how many times an employee refers a job through their personal network. The originating employee and the final referring "friend" both share a referral bonus. Other examples of social-media recruiting and selection activity include the use of the following:

- School alumni sites
- Personal networks used to mine passive and active job seekers, such as LinkedIn, Facebook, and Twitter
- Corporate social-media campaigns
- Search engine optimization (SEO) ranking, brand management, and career sections on web pages
- Mobile technology
- Job alerts and mobile-friendly web pages
- Videos
- Job postings with video
- Virtual interviewing
- Skype and GoToMeeting

To review the additional findings of the SHRM report, visit www.shrm.org/research, and search for the "SHRM Research Spotlight: Social Networking Websites and Staffing" research paper. To view the additional statistics from CareerBuilder, visit www.careerbuilder.com/JobPoster/Resources/page.aspx?pagever=ReportsAndeBooks& sc_cmp2=JP_THS_Reports.

Company Websites   Most companies with a web presence have a "career" or "opportunities" page on their websites where they post current openings. When combined with recruiting software that requires applicants to enter their own information into the recruiting database, this recruiting method can greatly reduce the time spent wading through resumes from applicants who don't qualify for positions.

Colleges and Universities   Colleges and universities are a good source for entry-level hires in areas such as accounting, engineering, and human resources. An effective college recruiting program capitalizes on school ties by sending alumni to the campus as recruiters. Recruiters are carefully chosen for their enthusiasm about the students as well as for the company. Key factors for recruiting success are delivering informative presentations about the organization and being honest about the job opportunities currently available in the organization. College recruiting has become a reliable source for locating minority applicants in recent years.

Job Fairs   Job fairs are events designed to bring employers and job seekers together in a single location. This format gives employers a chance to meet many potential job applicants in a short period of time. Including line managers and other employees with HR reps in the booth gives job seekers an opportunity to talk directly to hiring managers and find out about the organization without going through a formal interview process.

Alumni Employees   Building and maintaining professional relationships with former employees who left in good standing and on good terms can be a cost-effective, worthwhile source for re-recruiting. Particularly if they enjoyed their experience in the organization, they may be enticed to return if an appropriate opportunity presents itself, and they can be good sources for referrals.

Previous Applicants   Often during the recruiting process, a recruiter may remember a candidate who wasn't the best fit for one position but left an impression as someone who would be good elsewhere in the organization. Maintaining professional contact with such individuals can pay off when an appropriate position becomes available.

Employee Referrals   Current employees are a great resource for potential candidates. Recommendations from this source can result in long-term hires, because employees will remain longer with a company where they have established a social network. Moreover, a referral program that provides nominal cash awards after the new hire has remained with the company for a specific period of time (normally 90 to 180 days) encourages such referrals and keeps cost per hire under control.

Vendors and Suppliers   Individuals who provide goods or services to the company are often aware of potential candidates for openings. Particularly when there has been a long-term relationship, the vendor is aware of the organization's culture and needs and may prove to be a good source for applicants.

Labor Unions   In union environments, the union hiring hall can be a good source for qualified employees.

Professional Associations   Relationships developed in connection with attendance at professional association functions or conferences often provide leads for qualified applicants. In addition, many associations provide job-posting opportunities on websites or sell job advertisements in their publications.

Employment Agencies   Each state has an agency dedicated to providing services to job seekers, including job counseling and training opportunities. There is no charge for employers to list job openings with the agency, which then screens, tests, and refers appropriate candidates. Contingent employment agencies generally focus on jobs in a specific profession or job category, such as accounting professionals or administrative employees. Fees, paid by the employer only when a candidate is hired, are usually based on a percentage of the first year's salary and vary widely with different agencies. The fee is often negotiable. Retained employment agencies are often referred to as *headhunting firms* or *executive search firms*. When these agencies are engaged by an organization, a fee for recruiting services is paid whether or not any of the candidates are hired. A *retained search firm* is generally used for executive-level positions; these firms specialize in sourcing candidates from the passive labor market.

Walk-in Candidates   Candidates may come into the business in person to fill out applications and apply for jobs.

Where you search for candidates depends on your analysis of the availability of the specific KSAs in the various labor markets. Where you look for candidates also affects the cost of the recruiting effort as well as how much you must pay to attract the right candidate.

Uniform Guidelines on Employee Selection Procedures

The Uniform Guidelines on Employee Selection Procedures (UGESP) were jointly developed by the EEOC, the Civil Service Commission (CSC), the OFCCP, and the DOJ to assist employers in complying with requirements of Title VII, EO 11246 (as amended), and other federal EEO legislation. Specifically exempted from the UGESP are requirements under the ADEA and the Rehabilitation Act. The UGESP states that any selection tool that has an adverse impact against a protected class is discriminatory unless the employer can show that the tool is both job-related and a valid predictor of success in the position. The UGESP directs that if employers have access to more than one selection tool, the tool that has the least adverse impact is the one to be used. Records are to be kept by sex, race, and ethnic group, using categories consistent with the EEO-1 report (Hispanic, White, Black or African-American, native Hawaiian or other Pacific Islander, Asian, American Indian or Alaska native, and two or more races) and EEO reporting purposes.

One report required by the UGESP is a determination of whether selection procedures have an adverse impact on one or more protected groups. An *adverse impact* occurs when the selection rate for a protected class is less than 4/5ths, or 80 percent, of the selection rate for the group with the highest selection rate. This is often referred to as the 4/5ths rule or the 80 percent rule. Table 4.5 illustrates an adverse-impact calculation.

TABLE 4.5 Calculating adverse impact

Group	Applicants	Hired	Selection rate	4/5 of highest rate
Males	255	48	19%	15%
Females	395	52	13%	
Total	650	100		

In this example, the company advertised 100 openings. Applications were received from 255 males and 395 females for the position. Adverse impact is calculated as follows:

1. For each group, divide the number of applicants hired by the total number of applicants:

    Males: 48 ÷ 255 = 19%

    Females: 52 ÷ 395 = 13%

2. Multiply the highest selection rate by 80%:

    Males: 19% × 80% = 15%

3. Compare the selection for the other group(s) to determine whether adverse impact has occurred:

    Females: 13%

    Males: 15%

In this example, female applicants were adversely impacted by the selection process.

Applicant Tracking

The UGESP require employers to keep records of individuals who apply for open positions based on their sex and race/ethnicity as previously described for the EEO-1 report. In 1974, the UGESP defined an applicant as "...a person who has indicated an interest in being considered for hiring, promotion, or other employment opportunities. This interest might be expressed by completing an application form or might be expressed orally, depending on the employer's practice."

As the Internet grew into an increasingly important factor in the recruitment and selection of new employees, it became clear that an additional definition was needed. In October 2005, the UGESP were amended to include the definition of an Internet applicant as meeting these criteria:

- The employer has acted to fill a particular position.

- The individual has followed the employer's standard procedures for submitting applications.

- The individual has indicated an interest in the particular position.

Candidate Selection Tools

The result of the recruiting phase of the employment process should be resumes and application forms from job seekers hoping to be selected for the position. Screening these hopeful candidates to find those who best meet the needs of the position begins with establishing procedures that ensure equal employment opportunities.

Communicating with Applicants

HR departments are often criticized for ignoring job applicants. Although a large volume of applications makes it difficult to personally contact each person who expresses interest in a position, many companies use an "autorespond" email to acknowledge receipt of electronic resumes and applications and let candidates know that they will be contacted if selected for the interview process. Mail or in-person applications can be similarly acknowledged with preprinted postcards carrying the same message.

Recruiters need to stay in contact with candidates who move forward in the process until they have been removed from consideration, and then a final, respectful communication that they're no longer being considered is appropriate. These communications can be made in writing, but candidates who have made it to the final round of interviews deserve a personal call. This allows job seekers to move forward in their job searches and leaves them with a favorable impression of the HR department and the organization.

Screening Tools

The goal of the assessment process is to narrow the candidate pool into a manageable group including those candidates most qualified for a position. A variety of tools are used to assess candidate qualifications.

Resumes

Many organizations rely on candidate resumes as a first step in the assessment process. Although they generally contain relevant information, it can be difficult to compare qualifications of different candidates because of the lack of uniformity of style and content. Resumes generally present information about the applicant in the most favorable light and don't always contain all the information necessary to determine whether the applicant is qualified for the position. For those reasons, having all applicants complete an employment application is a good practice.

Employment Applications

Because application forms are considered employment tests by the EEOC, employers must be certain that the information requested on them is both job related and a valid predictor of success in the position. A key benefit to using a standard application form is the inclusion of a statement signed by the applicant stating that the information contained in the document is true and complete. This statement can be useful in the event that an employer becomes aware of misstatements or discrepancies subsequent to hiring a candidate.

There are four basic types of application forms to consider using; one will suit the needs of the specific position or organization:

Short-Form Employment Application   As its name implies, the short-form application is less extensive than other application forms. The term *short* is relative—it describes application forms that range from one to five pages. Short-form applications are often used by employees who are applying for transfers or promotions and are useful for prescreening candidates or for positions with minimal skill requirements.

Long-Form Employment Application   The long-form application provides space for additional information related to the job requirements, such as advanced degrees and longer employment histories.

Job-Specific Employment Application   If the organization hires a substantial number of employees for positions with similar requirements, the application form can be designed to gather specific information related to the position or profession. This type of form would be appropriate for teaching, scientific careers, or volume hiring in similar professions.

Weighted Employment Application   The weighted application form was developed to assist recruiters in evaluating candidate qualifications. The form is developed using the job description; aspects of the job that are more important for success are given higher weights than other, less critical requirements. Weighted applications tend to reduce bias in the screening process, but they're expensive to maintain because they must be redesigned whenever job requirements change.

Screening Interviews

After reviewing the application forms and choosing those applicants who meet the job specifications and candidate profile, the recruiter conducts screening interviews to decide which candidates will be forwarded to the hiring manager. The purpose of these interviews is to both discover facts about the candidate and provide information about the position. The recruiter can assess the candidate's interest in the position and begin the process of determining which candidates are the best fit for the requirements. Screening interviews may be conducted by telephone or in person, and are relatively short, lasting from 15 to 30 minutes.

Selection Tools

Once HR has screened the applicants for a position and narrowed the candidate pool to those who meet job requirements and fit the candidate profile, the next step in the process of selecting the best candidate for the position begins. This may include several elements, such as an in-person interview, a realistic job preview, an in-box test, or participation in an assessment-center process. By far the most common selection tool is an in-depth interview conducted by hiring managers and others who know what the successful candidate will need to do in the position. The best interview process begins with an interview strategy.

The purpose of an interview strategy is twofold. First, it ensures that everyone on the interview team knows the candidate profile as well as what requirements the hiring manager has for the job. Second, when several interviewers will be interviewing candidates for a position, it ensures that everyone is using the same criteria to evaluate candidates. During the strategy-development phase, HR professionals work with hiring managers to decide the appropriate type of interview for the position.

Conducting Effective Interviews

Job interviews are stressful situations for interviewers and candidates alike. The interviewer has a very short period of time to determine whether the candidate is the best choice for the position, and the candidate wants to make a good impression with the ultimate goal of obtaining a job offer. To reduce the stress and improve the chances of obtaining the information needed to make the best hiring decision, preparing for the interview is essential. HR can assist interviewers in this process by providing advice on structuring an effective interview and developing an interview strategy:

Select the Interview Team   HR's role in selecting the interview team is to work with the line manager to ensure that everyone who needs to be involved in the interview process is involved. In a team environment, it may be appropriate for all members of the team to participate; in other situations, employees from other business units who have frequent contact with the person in the position may be invited to participate in the process, along with employees who are knowledgeable about the work to be done.

Hold a Pre-interview Strategy Meeting   Conducting a pre-interview strategy meeting with the interview team provides an opportunity for the hiring manager to share what will be required of the successful candidate and to ensure that all interviewers are on the same page for the interviews. Topics for discussion can include the job description, specifications, and competencies. At this time, a discussion of the type of interview to be conducted and of common interview biases is also appropriate. This is a good opportunity for HR to share best interview practices with interviewers, such as not making notes on the application form or resume, and to review appropriate interview questions.

Complete Candidate Evaluation Forms   During the pre-interview strategy discussion, HR can review the candidate evaluation form with the interview team. This form provides consistency in the interview process by providing interviewers with a list of topics to cover during the interview. The form is useful in rating candidates on job requirements and acts as a reminder of what to discuss during the candidate-evaluation phase of the selection process.

Conduct Interviews   Interviewers should prepare to meet the candidates by reading the application forms or resumes and making notes of any items that need explanation. During the interview, the candidate should be treated with dignity and respect, beginning with starting the interview on time and giving full attention to the candidate during the course of the interview. Setting the candidate at ease in the first few minutes will set the stage for a productive and informative interview. Providing a clear explanation of the organization's mission, values, and culture; details concerning the position; and what will be expected of the successful candidate early in the interview gives prospective employees a context in which to answer questions. Listening carefully to the candidate's answers, taking notes as appropriate, and following up on points that need clarification indicate a genuine interest in what is being said and encourage an open and honest exchange. Be honest with candidates about the workplace environment, and give them time to ask their own questions. End the interview with an explanation of the next steps in the process.

Evaluate Candidates   When everyone on the interview team has met with all of the candidates, a final meeting takes place. During this meeting, the interviewers review the candidate-evaluation forms and share their thoughts on each candidate.

Types of Interviews

Several types of interviews are available for selecting candidates. Not all of them are appropriate for every situation, and it's up to HR to counsel the hiring manager on what will work best in each situation:

Behavioral Interviews   These interviews are based on the premise that past behavior is the best predictor of future behavior. This interview type asks candidates to describe how they have handled specific situations in previous jobs or life experiences. Candidates are expected to be able to describe a situation or problem, the actions they took to resolve it, and what outcome resulted. Interviewers skilled in this type of questioning are able to drill down into the answers to determine the candidate's depth of experience.

Directive Interviews   As the name implies, a directive interview is very much controlled and guided by the interviewer, with a predetermined set of questions asked of all candidates.

Nondirective Interviews   In this interview style, the interviewer asks broad questions and allows the candidate to guide the conversation. This style may produce a great deal of information relating to the candidate's qualifications; but it's difficult to ensure consistency in questions for all candidates, and that can become a problem during the candidate-evaluation phase, as well as in substantiating or defending the final hiring decision.

Patterned Interviews   A patterned interview is structured to cover specific areas related to the job requirements. The interviewer covers each area with all candidates but may ask different questions of them.

Panel Interviews   In a panel interview, several interviewers interview the candidate at the same time.

Structured Interviews   A structured interview is similar to a directed interview: a list of questions is prepared in advance and used for all candidates.

Stress Interviews   In some positions, such as airline pilots, law enforcement officers, and astronauts, employees encounter highly stressful situations on a regular basis. A stress interview subjects candidates to an intimidating situation to determine how they will handle stress in the position.

Question Guidelines

Equal opportunity legislation and regulations described earlier in this chapter require that questions asked of candidates during the selection process be constructed to obtain only job-related information. Some topics may never be a consideration in a selection decision, such as race. Others, such as age, are BFOQs that may be asked in a nondiscriminatory manner (for example, state laws may require that a bartender be at least 21 to serve alcoholic beverages). Table 4.6 illustrates appropriate and inappropriate ways to obtain job-related information in an interview.

TABLE 4.6   Appropriate and inappropriate job-related questions

Inappropriate Interview Questions	Appropriate Interview Questions
Affiliations	
What clubs or social organizations do you belong to? Do you go to church?	Do you belong to any professional or trade associations or other organizations that you think are relevant to this job?
Age	
How old are you? When did you graduate from high school?	Are you 18 or older? Can you, after employment, provide proof of age?
Arrest Record	
Have you ever been arrested?	Have you ever been convicted of _____? (Name a crime that is plausibly related to the job in question.)
Disabilities	
Do you have any disabilities? Have you had any recent or past illnesses or operations? If yes, list them and give dates when these occurred. How's your family's health? When did you lose your vision/arm/hearing? How did it happen?	After reviewing the job description, are you able to perform all the essential functions of the job, with or without accommodation? Any job offer will be made contingent on a medical exam. Are you willing to undergo one if we offer you a job?
Marital/Family Status	
What is your marital status? With whom do you live? What was your maiden name? Do you plan to have a family? When? How many children will you have? What are your child-care arrangements?	Are you willing to relocate?* This job requires frequent travel. Are you willing and able to travel when needed?* Is there anything that will prevent you from meeting work schedules?*

TABLE 4.6   Appropriate and inappropriate job-related questions *(continued)*

Inappropriate Interview Questions	Appropriate Interview Questions
Military Service	
Were you honorably discharged? What type of discharge did you receive?	In what branch of the armed services did you serve? What type of training or education did you receive in the military?
National Origin/Citizenship	
Are you a U.S. citizen? Where were you/your parents born? What is your race? What language did you speak in your home when you were growing up?	Are you authorized to work in the United States? What language(s) do you read/speak/write fluently? (Acceptable if related to essential functions.)
Personal	
How tall are you? How much do you weigh? Would working on weekends conflict with your religious beliefs?	This job requires the ability to lift a 50-pound weight and carry it 100 yards. Are you able to do that? This job will require work on the weekends. Are you able to do so?

*Acceptable if asked of every candidate.

Interviewer Bias

Any interviewer may bring preconceived ideas or biases into an interview situation; these can have an unintended impact on the hiring decision. The following list includes some of the types of interview bias that can occur. Once interviewers are aware of these, it's possible to reduce their impact on the selection process:

Average/Central Tendency   The *average bias* becomes apparent when the interviewer has difficulty deciding which candidate is best and rates them all about the same.

Contrast   The *contrast bias* occurs when an interviewer compares candidates to each other or compares all candidates to a single candidate. For example, if one candidate is particularly weak, others may appear to be more qualified than they really are.

Cultural Noise   *Cultural noise bias* occurs when candidates answer questions based on information they think will get them the job—what they think the interviewer wants to hear. For example, a candidate who has been an individual contributor may tell an interviewer that they prefer working as part of a team if the interviewer stresses teamwork as a key job requirement.

First Impression   This bias can work either for or against a candidate, depending on the interviewer's *first impression*. A candidate who is very nervous and stutters during the first few minutes of the interview may be viewed as less qualified even if during the remainder of the interview they're poised and well spoken.

Gut Feeling   The *gut feeling bias* occurs when the interviewer relies on an intuitive feeling that the candidate is a good (or bad) fit for the position without looking at whether the individual's qualifications meet the criteria established by the job specifications and candidate profile.

Halo Effect   The *halo effect bias* occurs when the interviewer evaluates a candidate positively based on a single characteristic. For example, a candidate's self-confident attitude may overshadow a lack of experience in a particular requirement.

Harshness/Horn Effect   *Harshness bias*, or the *horn effect*, occurs when the interviewer evaluates a candidate negatively based on a single characteristic.

Knowledge-of-Predictor   *Knowledge-of-predictor bias* occurs when the interviewer is aware that a candidate scored particularly high (or low) on an assessment test that has been shown to be a valid predictor of performance.

Leniency   *Leniency bias* occurs when an interviewer tends to go easy on a candidate and give a higher rating than is warranted, justifying it with an rationalization.

Negative Emphasis   The *negative emphasis bias* occurs when the interviewer allows a small amount of negative information to outweigh positive information.

Nonverbal Bias   *Nonverbal bias* occurs when an interviewer is influenced by body language. For example, a candidate who frowns when answering questions could be rated negatively even though the answers were correct.

Question Inconsistency   *Question inconsistency bias* occurs when an interviewer asks different questions of each candidate. Although this is acceptable to a certain extent in order to delve more deeply into each candidate's qualifications, there is no baseline for comparison if there are no questions that were asked of all candidates.

Recency   The *recency bias* occurs when the interviewer recalls the most recently interviewed candidate more clearly than earlier candidates.

Similar-to-Me   The *similar-to-me bias* occurs when the candidate has interests or other characteristics that are the same as those of the interviewer and cause the interviewer to overlook negative aspects about the candidate. For example, an interviewer who played college football may select a candidate who did so even though the candidate's qualifications aren't the best for the position.

Stereotyping   The *stereotyping bias* occurs when the interviewer assumes a candidate has specific traits because they are a member of a group. For example, an interviewer may assume that a woman would not be able to successfully perform in a job that requires frequent lifting of packages weighing 50 pounds.

In-depth interviews are the cornerstone of the selection process, used in virtually all hiring decisions. However, interviews aren't the only tool available for candidate selection. Equally important information that adds different perspectives to candidates can be obtained by using realistic job previews, in-box tests, and assessment centers.

Realistic Job Preview

A *realistic job preview* (RJP), designed to give candidates an accurate picture of a typical day on the job, provides an opportunity for them to self-select out if the job isn't what they expected it would be. This increases the chances for success on the job, thereby reducing turnover. Depending on the type of job, the RJP can take many forms, including observing a current employee doing the job (as in a call center environment, for example), a simulated experience of the job, or a video presentation about the organization, work environment, and co-workers. A tour of the workplace is another way to provide candidates with an idea of what it would be like to work in the organization. These techniques, either singly or in some combination, can provide candidates with realistic expectations of the job and the organization.

In-Box Test

An in-box test provides candidates with a number of documents describing problems that would typically be handled by an employee in the position, with instructions to prioritize the problems and/or decide how the problems should be handled. Candidates are evaluated on the appropriateness of their decisions as well as on the length of time it takes for them to complete the test.

Assessment Centers

Assessment centers are characterized by multiple tests designed to measure different aspects of the job. Generally used to assess candidates for management potential and decision-making skills, they have been demonstrated to be valid predictors of success on the job. Used extensively by state and local governments and large organizations for assessing internal candidates for promotion, their use is limited due to the high cost of conducting them. Typical assessments include interviews, testing and problem-solving skills, in-basket tests, leaderless group discussions, and role-playing exercises.

Candidate Testing Programs

The use of pre-employment tests has become more prevalent in recent years. These tests take many forms and have a variety of purposes. The key issue to keep in mind with regard to employment tests is the requirement that they must be job-related and, should they be challenged by an EEOC complaint, defensible as valid predictors of success in the position. Candidates for PHR/SPHR certification should be aware of the following types of selection tests:

Aptitude Tests   These tests are designed to measure an individual's knowledge and ability to apply skills in various areas, such as mathematics, typing, language, and reasoning. Properly constructed aptitude tests have been shown to be valid predictors of job success.

Cognitive Ability Test (CAT)   CATs measure an individual's ability to analyze and solve problems and draw conclusions from a set of facts. They also measure an individual's potential for learning, thinking, and remembering.

Personality Test   Personality or psychometric tests assess how a candidate will "fit" into a specific job. If, for example, an employer uses a personality test that has shown particular characteristics to be valid predictors of success in sales positions, and an applicant doesn't reflect those characteristics when tested, the test would indicate an area to be explored with the candidate prior to making the hiring decision.

Integrity Tests   Also known as *honesty tests*, integrity tests assess a candidate's work ethic, attitudes toward theft and drug and alcohol use, and similar traits. According to the EEOC, professionally developed integrity tests don't create an adverse impact for protected classes as long as the tests are administered equally to all candidates.

Psychomotor Assessment Tests   A psychomotor assessment tests an individual's coordination and manual dexterity.

Physical Assessment Tests   Physical assessment tests are used to determine whether candidates are physically capable of performing specific job duties. The tests generally require that tasks be completed within a predetermined period of time and most often simulate activities that regularly occur on the job. A common physical assessment test is one that is given to potential firefighters to ensure that they're capable of lifting and carrying heavy weights for predetermined periods of time in a variety of circumstances.

As previously discussed, a key requirement for selection tools is that they be both related to specific job requirements and valid predictors of successful job performance. To determine whether a specific employment test meets those criteria, employers must ensure that tests are both reliable and valid.

 Real World Scenario

The Courts Address Employment Tests

Once Title VII was enacted, employees who thought they had been subjected to unlawful employment discrimination were able to initiate lawsuits to resolve their grievances. Pre-employment testing practices were the subject of a number of cases, the most prominent of which are described here.

1971: Griggs v. Duke Power Co.   Duke Power Company, located in North Carolina, employed 95 workers in its Dan River Steam Station in 1964. There were five departments at the plant: Labor, Coal Handling, Operations, Maintenance, and Laboratory and Test. The Labor Department was the lowest-paid department in the company; in fact, the highest-paying job in the department paid less than the lowest-paying job in the other four. In 1955, the company began to require that employees in all departments except Labor have a high-school diploma, but prior to that time employees could be hired into any of the departments without one. On July 2, 1965, the effective date of Title VII, Duke added a requirement that all new employees must pass two aptitude tests and that an employee wanting to transfer from Labor to another department needed a high-school diploma.

Willie Griggs was one of 14 black employees working in the Labor Department at the plant. There were no black employees in any of the other departments. Mr. Griggs filed a class-action lawsuit on behalf of himself and 12 of the black employees, alleging that the requirement for a high-school diploma and satisfactory scores on the aptitude tests discriminated against them. The district court that first heard the case dismissed it. The court of appeals found that Griggs had not shown that there was a discriminatory purpose to the requirements and that a discriminatory purpose was required to show discrimination. The Supreme Court granted *certiorari* (agreed to review the case) and heard oral arguments in December 1970.

Because a number of the white employees who didn't have high-school diplomas had been hired prior to the requirements for the diploma or the aptitude tests, and those employees performed well on the job, it was clear that the requirements didn't predict job performance, and Duke Power didn't dispute this fact. The Supreme Court found that "good intent or absence of discriminatory intent" in the face of a job requirement that adversely impacts a protected class isn't a sufficient defense against discrimination. The job requirement must be shown to be job related in order to be lawful, and it's up to the employer to prove this.

The HR significance of *Griggs v. Duke Power Co.* is that discrimination doesn't need to be intentional to exist. It's up to employers to prove that job requirements are related to the job.

1975: Albemarle Paper v. Moody In 1966, a group of current and former black employees at Albemarle Paper's mill in Roanoke Rapids, North Carolina, filed a lawsuit against both their employer, Albemarle Paper, and the union representing them with the company. The group asked the court for an injunction against "any policy, practice, custom, or usage" at the mill that was in violation of Title VII. When the case dragged on for several years, a demand for back pay was added to the injunction request in 1970. One of the policies in question was the employment testing practice used by Albemarle Paper. The district court denied the claim for back pay and refused to consider the testing procedure, saying that the tests had been validated.

The court of appeals reversed the ruling, finding that the absence of bad faith wasn't sufficient grounds to deny back pay and that the validation process had four serious flaws:

- It had not been used consistently.
- It had compared test scores to the subjective rankings of supervisors, which couldn't be tied to job-related performance criteria.

- The tests were validated against the most senior jobs and not entry-level positions.

- The validation study used only experienced white employees, not the new job applicants, who were mostly nonwhite.

The HR significance of *Albemarle Paper v. Moody* is that test validation must be in accordance with the Uniform Guidelines on Employee Selection Procedures. Subjective supervisor rankings aren't sufficient for criterion validation; the criteria must be able to be tied to the job requirements.

1975: Washington v. Davis In 1970, two applicants for the police department in Washington, D.C., filed suit against the city, claiming that the written personnel test given to applicants had an adverse impact on black applicants. The Supreme Court upheld the district court's finding that the test was a valid predictor of successful performance in the police-training program.

The HR significance of *Washington v. Davis* is that tests that have an adverse impact on a protected class are lawful if they're valid predictors of success on the job.

Reliability and Validity

The UGESP requires that selection tests be reliable and valid predictors of success on the job.

Reliability

Reliability measures whether a test or other measurement produces consistent results so that, over time, the scores won't vary greatly. Test reliability is enhanced by several factors, including wording instructions and test questions clearly. Providing optimal conditions for administering the test contributes to its reliability, as does making sure it's long enough to accurately test the candidate's knowledge.

Validity

Validity considers the characteristics being measured by a test and whether the test is measuring the characteristic accurately:

Content Validity   *Content validity* is the simplest of the three validation measures. Job analysis is a key element of the content-validity process, which confirms that a selection procedure samples significant parts of the job being tested. For example, a driving test given to a delivery person who would drive a truck 80 percent of the time if hired for the job is a test with content validity.

Construct Validity   *Construct validity* determines whether a test measures the connection between candidate characteristics and successful performance on the job. According to the DOL, construct validity is a method of testing that measures an applicant's abstract future behaviors. In order for a test to be legally defensible, it must show that it measured the proper characteristic, and that it accurately predicted future success on the job.

Criterion Validity   A criterion is a trait or work behavior that is predicted by a test. *Criterion validity* is established when the test or measure either predicts or correlates the behavior:

Predictive Validity   *Predictive validity* compares the test scores of a test given at the beginning of a job before new employees have experience to the same criterion collected at some future time. When the employees have had some experience (for example, 6 months or 1 year) with the job, the manager evaluates their performance. The original test scores are then measured against the criterion (the evaluation ratings), and the test is validated if they're similar.

Concurrent Validity   The process for determining *concurrent validity* is similar to that of determining predictive validity. The difference is that the criterion measurement occurs at the same time the test is given and not at a later time.

To read an excellent (and easy-to-understand) explanation of testing, assessment, reliability, and validation, go to http://www.onetcenter. org/dl_files/empTestAsse.pdf.

Pre-employment Inquiries

Pre-employment inquiries or background checks cover a range of activities designed to ensure that candidates who receive employment offers are who they represent themselves to be during the selection process. Information collected during these processes should be protected from inappropriate dissemination and, at the appropriate time, disposed of in a way that ensures its security. Pre-employment inquiries verify information collected from candidate resumes and/or interviews during the selection process. Some of the information is relatively easy to verify, such as educational degrees and previous employment, and provides insight into earlier educational and employment experiences.

 Real World Scenario

Validity in Action

What does all this validity stuff have to do with HR? Federal courts look to validation studies to determine whether specific job requirements discriminate against protected classes. A professionally developed validation test serves as proof in court that the employment requirement is a valid predictor of successful performance on the job. The following are some ways that companies can use forms of validity in various situations.

Imagine that a company needs to hire business analysts who will spend 95 percent of their time analyzing sales trends and predicting future sales. The company would want to administer a test that measures a candidate's ability to reason. In this case, a test that measures a candidate's ability to reason would have *construct validity*.

In another example, an accounting firm that has had significant turnover in its entry-level accounting positions in the past few years wants to put some measures in place that will result in new hires with a better chance of success in their positions. As a result, the HR director commissioned a test to measure analytical ability, to use in the hiring process. The firm recently hired 100 recent college graduates with accounting degrees as entry-level accountants, none of whom has ever worked in the accounting field. On their first day of work, all 100 accountants took the new test. Six months later, the accountants were evaluated by their supervisors, and the results of the evaluation ratings (the criterion) were compared to the test results. The accountants who were highly rated by their supervisors had high scores on the test, and those who scored poorly on the test had lower evaluation ratings. The test has *predictive validity*.

Here's an example to illustrate the use of concurrent validity. The owner of CAD-Serv, a computer-aided design service bureau, recently won a large contract for design work with a nationally known real-estate developer. The project will require that CADServ hire at least 20 more CAD operators within a few months. The owner would like to bring in some entry-level operators but needs to be sure they will be successful on the job. The owner contracts with a testing firm to administer an abstract-reasoning test to the candidates but wants to be sure it will be accurate. The owner decides to have the 30 CAD operators who already work at CADServ take the test. The test is given around the same time as the annual review cycle, and when the test results come in, they're similar to the ratings received by the employees—those who received high test scores also received high performance ratings. The test has *concurrent validity*, and CADServ will use it in the hiring process for the new operators.

Pre-employment inquiries may also include a check of the candidate's financial records, driving record, and any previous criminal behavior, depending on the type of job. Any background or reference check conducted by a third party is considered to be a consumer report and is therefore subject to requirements of the Fair Credit Reporting Act (FCRA). When employers conduct their own reference checks, those requirements don't apply.

Reference Checks

An organization may ask for several types of references from potential employees. Types of references may include the following:

Employment References   To make an informed decision about a potential employee, employers should obtain all the information they can from previous employers. Information collected during the reference-checking process includes previous employment history, dates, job titles, and type of work performed. Many employers are reluctant to provide more information than this for privacy reasons, but as long as the information is factual and given in good faith, most states consider it "qualifiedly privileged," which protects the employer from legal action. It's desirable to obtain additional information about the employee's work habits and interpersonal skills and find out if the employee is eligible for rehire.

Educational References   Depending on the position applied for and the length of time since graduation, some employers request high-school, college, and post-graduate transcripts to verify the accuracy of information presented during the selection process.

Financial References   Financial references are generally used only when candidates will be handling large sums of cash. As with all other selection tools, a financial reference must be shown to be job related *and* a valid predictor of success in the position. When required, financial references, generally provided by credit-reporting agencies, are subject to requirements of the federal FCRA.

The Fair Credit Reporting Act of 1970

The FCRA was first enacted in 1970 and has been amended several times since then, most recently with the Fair and Accurate Credit Transactions Act (FACT Act) in 2003. Enforced by the Federal Trade Commission (FTC), the FCRA requires employers to take certain actions prior to the use of a consumer report or an investigative consumer report obtained through a consumer reporting agency for use in making employment decisions.

Familiarity with three terms is valuable for understanding why these consumer-protection laws are important for HR practitioners:

- A *consumer reporting agency* (CRA) is an individual, a business, or a nonprofit association that gathers information about individuals with the intent of supplying that information to a third party.

- A *consumer report* is a written document produced by a CRA containing information about an individual's character, reputation, lifestyle, or credit history for use by an employer in determining that person's suitability for employment.

- An *investigative consumer report* is a written document produced by a CRA for the same purpose as a consumer report but is based on information gathered through personal interviews with friends, co-workers, employers, and others who are acquainted with the individual.

The FCRA established the following process for employers to follow when using CRAs to perform background investigations:

1. A clear and conspicuous disclosure that a consumer report may be obtained for employment purposes must be made in writing to the candidate before the report is acquired.

2. The candidate must provide written authorization for the employer to obtain the report.

3. Before taking an adverse action based in whole or in part on the credit report, either the employer must provide the candidate with a copy of the report and a copy of the FTC notice "A Summary of Your Rights Under the Fair Credit Reporting Act," or, if the application was made by mail, telephone, computer, or similar means, the employer must notify the candidate within 3 business days that adverse action has been taken based in whole or in part on the credit report. This notice must provide the name, address, and telephone number of the CRA and indicate that the CRA didn't take the adverse action and can't provide the reasons for the action to the candidate. If a candidate requests a copy of the report, the employer must provide it within 3 days, along with a copy of the FTC notice just described.

4. Candidates must be advised of their right to dispute the accuracy of information contained in the report.

When an employer requests an investigative consumer report on a candidate, it must comply with these additional steps:

- Provide written disclosure of its intent to the candidate within 3 days of requesting the report from a CRA.

- Include a summary of the candidate's FCRA rights with the written notice.

- Advise the candidate that they have a right to request information about the type and extent of the investigation.

- If requested, provide complete disclosure of the type and extent of the report within the period of 5 days of the request or receipt of the report.

The FACT Act amendment provided relief for employers who used a third party to investigate employee misconduct; these rules are explained in Chapter 8.

Finally, FACT Act established rules to protect consumers from identity theft. Most of these rules apply to merchants, but employers that use consumer reports to make hiring or promotion decisions must dispose of the reports appropriately. FACT Act describes "reasonable measures" for destroying these reports, depending on the medium:

- Paper documents must be shredded, pulverized, or burned in a way that prevents them from being reassembled.

- Electronic files or media must be erased in a way that prevents them from being reconstructed.

- Either type may be destroyed by an outside vendor once the employer has conducted due-diligence research to ensure that the vendor's methods are reliable.

You can view the FCRA in its entirety at www.ftc.gov/os/statutes/fcra.htm#603.

Criminal Record Checks

Criminal record checks can uncover information about substance abuse, violent behavior, and property crimes such as theft and embezzlement. Because private employers don't have access to a central database that collects information from every level of government (federal, state, county, and local), it can be difficult to do a comprehensive check. When applicants have lived or worked in several states, counties, or municipalities, records in each jurisdiction must be checked to ensure completeness.

Negative information obtained through criminal record checks should be carefully reviewed on a case-by-case basis, considering all of the relevant information:

- How does the type of crime relate to the position applied for?
- How recent was the conviction?
- How old was the applicant when the conviction occurred?
- What is the level of risk to customers, co-workers, and others in the workplace if the applicant is hired?

Criminal record checks are considered consumer investigations and must comply with related FCRA requirements.

When an employer considers making an adverse hiring decision based on negative information received in an investigative consumer report, the applicant must be notified in writing and given a chance to respond. Should the negative information be the result of a mistake, the applicant can provide information to clear the record. If the employer decides to proceed with the adverse action, the applicant must receive a second written notice stating that the adverse action has been taken.

The Privacy Act of 1974

The Privacy Act of 1974 was an attempt by Congress to regulate the amount and type of information collected by federal agencies and the methods by which it was stored in an effort to protect the personal privacy of individuals about whom the information had been collected. The act requires written authorization from an individual prior to releasing information to another person. The act doesn't currently apply to private employers.

First, the act provides individuals with the right to know what kind of information is being collected about them, how it's used and maintained, and whether it's disseminated. The act prevents this information from being used for purposes other than that for which it was collected, and it allows individuals to obtain copies of the information, review it, and request amendments to inaccurate information. The act requires the government to ensure that information collected isn't misused. Except under specific circumstances covered by the Privacy Act, such as law enforcement or national security needs, the information collected by one agency may not be shared with another. Damages for violation of these requirements may be sought in federal district court and, if found by the judge to be warranted, are subject to reimbursement of attorney's fees and litigation costs, as well as a fine for actual damages incurred by the individual of up to $1,000 paid by the federal government.

Negligent Hiring

Negligent hiring occurs when an employer knew or should have known about an applicant's prior history that endangered customers, employees, vendors, or others with whom the employee comes in contact. Employers can prevent negligent-hiring lawsuits by carefully checking references and running background checks for all candidates. Once an employer finds out about such a history, the employer is obligated to safeguard others who come in contact with the individual during the workday by taking whatever action is necessary to maintain a safe work environment.

To defend themselves against claims of negligent hiring, employers can demonstrate that they exercised due diligence in the hiring process by taking the following steps:

- Conducting reference checks with previous employers
- Obtaining reports from the Departments of Motor Vehicles in the states where the applicant has lived or worked
- Verifying the validity of the applicant's Social Security number
- Conducting criminal record checks
- Verifying the validity of any government-issued licenses, such as a medical or engineering license issued by a state
- Conducting drug-screening tests

Polygraph Tests

The use of polygraph tests in the employment process is limited by the Employee Polygraph Protection Act (EPPA).

The Employee Polygraph Protection Act of 1988

The EPPA prohibits private employers from using polygraph tests in making employment decisions except under very limited conditions. The act applies to private employers but not federal, state, or local governments and is administered by the Wage and Hour Division of the DOL. Violations of its provisions may result in fines of up to $10,000 against an employer.

The EPPA allows polygraph tests to be administered to employees of federal contractors or subcontractors with national defense, national security, or FBI contracts; to prospective employees of armored car or security services; and to prospective employees who would have access to the manufacture, storage, distribution, or sale of pharmaceutical products. The act also allows the use of polygraph tests during an ongoing investigation of an economic loss to the employer if an employee had access to the property in question. Under these limited circumstances, polygraph tests may be administered by individuals licensed by the state in which the test takes place.

Medical Examinations

As with all other assessment tools, medical examinations are allowable after extending a job offer or conditional job offer if their purpose is job related and they're required of all candidates. These exams are used to ensure that the employee will be fully capable of performing the requirements of the job and, in some cases, may be part of an employer's health and safety program. Under the ADA, employers may make a job offer conditional on a medical examination before the candidate begins working as long as all applicants for positions in the same job category must undergo the exam. If the offer is rescinded as a result of the medical exam, the employer must be able to demonstrate that the job requirement eliminating the candidate from consideration is related to a business necessity.

Drug-Screening Tests

Studies conducted by the Occupational Safety and Health Administration (OSHA) indicate that drug-screening programs reduce job-related accidents. Substance abuse is also linked to reduced productivity.

Drug-screening tests are specifically excluded from the ADA's medical-examination requirement and may be required prior to extending an offer.

Employment Offers

The post-interview strategy meeting has been concluded, the references have been checked, and results of the pre-employment tests are in. The hiring decision has been made, and it's time to extend an offer. After discussion with HR, the hiring manager contacts the successful candidate and extends a verbal offer; or, in some organizations, HR may be responsible for extending verbal offers. When the verbal offer is accepted, a written offer agreement is prepared.

Employment Agreements and Contracts

Employment relationships in many states are subject to the common law concept of *employment-at-will,* meaning that the relationship can be ended at any time by either party with or without a reason (more information about employment-at-will and other common law concepts is included in Chapter 7, "Employee and Labor Relations"). As a result, few employees today work under employment contracts. In most cases, the relationship is defined in an offer letter that is composed after negotiations are complete.

Making and Negotiating Offers

One of the goals of the selection process is to collect information from candidates about their expectations for cash compensation, benefits, and other terms and conditions of employment that may be appropriate to the position. When it's time to make an offer, these expectations are incorporated into the decision-making process of crafting the offer. Prior to making the offer, any required approvals are obtained, along with approval for any "wiggle room" should the candidate come back with a request for a higher salary or increased benefits. Once the verbal negotiations are complete, the written agreement can be completed.

Offer Letters

The offer letter should be prepared immediately upon acceptance of the verbal offer by the candidate. The standard offer letter should be reviewed by the corporate attorney to ensure that its provisions don't compromise the organization and that it contains the terms of the offer as well as any contingencies that apply, such as a medical exam, a background check, or proof of the right to work in the United States. The salary offer should be stated in an hourly or monthly amount. The offer should state clearly that the organization is an at-will employer and that only the terms and conditions of the offer contained in the offer letter are valid. Finally, there should be a reasonable time frame for returning a signed acceptance of the offer.

Care should be taken to ensure that any promises of benefits or special conditions agreed on by the hiring manager are included in the offer letter so there is no ambiguity about the complete offer.

Employment Contracts

An employment contract binds both parties to the agreements contained in the contract. Contracts are generally reserved for senior-level managers and professionals such as doctors and teachers, and can cover a wide range of topics. Any areas of the employment relationship not specifically covered in the contract are subject to common law. Some standard clauses seen in employment contracts include the following:

Terms and Conditions of Employment   This clause covers the start date and duration of the contract and, if the contract is for a set period of time, includes any automatic extension agreements.

Scope of Duties   General and specific duties and responsibilities are covered by this clause. The duties can be part of the contract, or the job description may be incorporated into the agreement as an addendum. Expectations for performance are included here as well.

Compensation   The compensation package is described in this clause, which includes the base salary, any bonus and incentive agreements, auto or telephone allowance, company car, or other agreements.

Benefits and Expense Reimbursements   Items covered by this clause include disability and health insurance benefits and retirement plans. The extent of and conditions for expense reimbursements are also described here.

Nondisclosure of Proprietary Information   Requirements for the maintenance of confidentiality with regard to proprietary information are included here, along with noncompete language and requirements for the return of company property when the employment relationship ends.

Nonsolicitation Agreement   This clause sets forth agreements that limit the employee's ability to solicit customers, vendors, and employees during the course of the contract and for an agreed-on period of time after the contract ends.

Advice of Counsel   A clause advising the employee to seek legal counsel prior to signing the contract is often included.

Disability or Death   The employer can include a clause that states what happens to the agreement in the event of the disability or death of the employee.

Termination Clause   The termination clause sets forth conditions that would lead to a termination for cause, such as inability to perform, neglecting the duties of the position, misconduct, violations of company policy, or other egregious acts.

Change of Control   A change of control clause protects the employee's job and compensation in the event of a reorganization, an acquisition, or a merger, for a specified period of time.

Post-offer Employment Activities

When the offer has been accepted, the transition from candidate to employee begins. At this stage, employees form their first impressions about what it will be like to work in the organization. During this time, employers can take steps to begin the relationship positively by including employees in special events that may be scheduled prior to their first day, and providing them with information that will help them become productive more quickly and begin assimilating into the work group.

Relocation Practices

In some circumstances, employers may be willing to pay the costs of relocating an employee or an applicant. When that occurs, HR may manage the process. Elements of relocation packages that can be negotiated include a company-paid trip for the spouse and family to see the area and look for a new home, assistance with selling the old and/or purchasing the new home, payment of moving expenses, assistance with a job search for the spouse in the new area, and a guarantee of the sale price of the old house if it doesn't sell.

Relocation is an activity that lends itself to outsourcing. Some organizations contract with moving companies that include relocation assistance as part of the moving package, and there are also professional organizations that manage the entire process for the organization and the family. These companies can provide property-management services, home inspections, real-estate attorneys or title companies, home appraisals, moving companies, and, in some cases, corporate living situations for short-term job assignments. This can be a cost-effective solution that saves time for in-house staff.

Immigration Processes

In 2003, enforcement responsibility for the Immigration and Nationality Act (INA) of 1952 and its amendments was transferred to the U.S. Citizenship and Immigration Services (USCIS), an agency of the Department of Homeland Security. The INA and its amendments control immigration policy for the United States established by the following:

INA of 1952 and Amendment of 1965   The purpose of the INA was to simplify the multiple laws that previously governed U.S. immigration policy. As established by previous legislation, immigration quotas continued to be set on the basis of national origin.

Following the trend of equal opportunity established by the Civil Rights Act of 1964, the 1965 amendment eliminated national origin, race, and ancestry as bars to immigration and changed the allocation of immigrant visas to a first-come, first-served basis. The amendment also established seven immigration categories with the goals of reunifying families and giving preference to those with specialty skills that were needed in the United States.

Immigration Reform and Control Act (IRCA) of 1986   IRCA was enacted in 1986 to address illegal immigration into the United States. The law applied to businesses with four or more employees and made it illegal to knowingly hire or continue to employ individuals who weren't legally authorized to work in the United States. Unfair immigration-related employment practices were defined as discrimination on the basis of national origin or citizenship status.

Employers were required to complete Form I-9 for all new hires within the first 3 days of employment and to review documents provided by the employee that establish identity or employment authorization or both from lists of acceptable documents on the Form I-9. IRCA requires employers to maintain I-9 files for 3 years from the date of hire or 1 year after the date of termination, whichever is later, and allows, but doesn't require, employers to copy documents presented for employment eligibility for purposes of complying with these requirements. The act also provides that employers complying in good faith with these requirements have an affirmative defense to inadvertently hiring an unauthorized alien. Substantial fines for violations of both the hiring and recordkeeping requirements were provided in the law. Failure to maintain acceptable Form I-9 records is subject to fines of not less than $110 (per USCIS) or more than $1,100 for each employee without a completed form available upon request to an authorized agent of the USCIS. In addition for penalties assessed for missing or incomplete I-9 forms, IRCA established fines for unauthorized employees. Table 4.7 outlines the fines for hiring violations under IRCA.

TABLE 4.7 IRCA fines

Violation	Amount of Fine
First	Not less than $375 or more than $3,200 for each unauthorized employee
Second	Not less than $3,200 or more than $6,500 for each unauthorized employee
Third	Not less than $4,300 or more than $16,000 for each unauthorized employee

In addition to the fines listed, employers who knowingly hire unauthorized workers are subject to fines of $3,200 per employee and/or 6 months imprisonment.

Until 2005, IRCA required employers to store I-9 forms on one of three types of media: paper, microfilm, or microfiche. Passage of HR 4306, which was signed into law by President George W. Bush, allows employers to store I-9 forms in PDF files or other electronic formats.

E-Verify   E-Verify is a free service offered through the USCIS. It's a tool that helps employers comply with IRCA's requirement that employers must verify the identity and employment eligibility of new employees. The employer accesses E-Verify through the Internet, inputs basic information gleaned from the Form I-9, and receives a near-instant "employment authorized" or "tentative nonconfirmation" (TNC) reply from the website. The employer then prints the results. A TNC result gives the employee more information about the mismatch and a statement of their rights and responsibilities under the law. It's important to note that an employer may not terminate an employee for the initial TNC; it's only when they receive a final nonconfirmation that an employer may terminate under E-Verify.

To get started in the program, employers must first enroll their company, sign a Memorandum of Understanding (MOU) reviewing their obligations and acknowledging their understanding of the terms of enrollment, and commit to using E-Verify for every new employee at the affected hiring site. Under federal law, employers may designate the use of E-Verify to certain locations, although this may be restricted under some state laws.

The USCIS provides several webinars designed to educate employers and employees about the E-Verify process. Visit their home page at www.uscis.gov/portal/site/uscis and follow the instructions to these free webinars.

Immigration Act of 1990   The Immigration Act of 1990 made several changes to IRCA, including adding the requirement that a prevailing wage be paid to H-1B immigrants to ensure that U.S. citizens didn't lose jobs to lower-paid immigrant workers. The act also restricted to 65,000 annually the number of immigrants allowed under the H-1B category and created additional categories for employment visas, as shown in Table 4.8. In 1996, the number and types of documents to prove identity and eligibility to work were reduced.

TABLE 4.8   Employment visas

Visa	Classification
	Visas for Temporary Workers
H-1B	Specialty occupations, DOD workers, fashion models
H-1C	Nurses going to work for up to three years in health professional shortage areas
H-2A	Temporary agricultural worker
H-2B	Temporary worker: skilled and unskilled
H-3	Trainee

Visa	Classification
	Visas for Temporary Workers
J-1	Visas for exchange visitors
	Visas for intracompany transfers
L-1A	Executive, managerial
L-1B	Specialized knowledge
L-2	Spouse or child of L-1
	Visas for Workers with Extraordinary Abilities
O-1	Extraordinary ability in sciences, arts, education, business, or athletics
	Visas for Athletes and Entertainers
P-1	Individual or team athletes
P-1	Entertainment groups
P-2	Artists and entertainers in reciprocal exchange programs
P-3	Artists and entertainers in culturally unique programs
	Visas for Religious Workers
R-1	Religious workers
	Visas for NAFTA Workers
TN	Trade visas for Canadians and Mexicans

Illegal Immigration Reform and Immigrant Responsibility Act (IIRIRA) of 1996   This act reduced the number and types of documents allowable to prove identity, employment eligibility, or both in the hiring process and established pilot programs for verification of employment eligibility.

Visit www.uscis.gov, and click on their "Laws" tab to view the full text of INA and its amendments.

Employee On-Boarding and Orientation Programs

Formal on-boarding and orientation programs are composed of two elements: a general introduction to the organization as a whole and a job-specific orientation. HR often has responsibility to provide the organization orientation, including information about the mission, goals, and values, and answering general questions. The job-specific orientation is conducted or overseen by the hiring manager and provides information specific to the department and position, sets performance expectations, and ensures that the new hire knows where to go for assistance when needed. These programs are an important part of a new hire's introduction to the organization. In many organizations, daily events move so quickly that new employees are sometimes left to fend for themselves without understanding what they're supposed to do or how to get help when they need it. The on-boarding and orientation programs help ensure that new employees have the support they need to be successful. HR helps to bridge the gap between the more administrative orientation activities to the more robust introduction that make up the activities of on-boarding.

Orientation An example of a short-term objective within the scope of on-boarding is the *new-hire orientation*. An orientation typically includes paperwork completion, compliance training, and an introduction to policies, procedures, and rules through a review of the employee handbook. It may also include an expanded tour of the facility and email welcome to all staff. Many organizations provide benefit information and application forms with the written offer so the employee has time to review them, make appropriate selections, and include their spouses in those decisions.

On-boarding On-boarding refers to a system of organizational behaviors at the time of hire focused on the retention of new employees. It consists of both short-term and long-term behaviors that help to integrate employees into their new work environment. On-boarding programs exist to reduce the length of time it takes new employees to become productive team members.

An example of a long-term on-boarding activity is *socialization*. This includes efforts such as the assignment of an internal mentor or peer-to-peer support for training. Buddy programs are sometimes used to provide additional, informal support to new employees. Buddies are employees in good standing with enough time on the job to be familiar with how things work in the organization and can answer questions or direct the new employee to a person with the answers.

As with any successful HR program, scheduled follow-up to measure successful entry is an important component of the on-boarding process. Functional follow-up may include completion of enrollment in a benefits plan or the verification of receipt of an identification badge or working phone extension. A less functional but no less important follow-up activity may be to schedule a meeting within the first 30 days to discuss how the job is matching with the employee's initial expectations. The most effective on-boarding activities take place over an extended period of time with regularly scheduled follow-ups that provide opportunities to check in with the employee and provide support as needed.

Organization Exit/Off-Boarding Processes

Organization exits happen in one of two ways: employees choose to leave of their own volition (resignations and retirements), or they're asked to leave in one way or another (termination, downsizing, or layoff). Organization exits are stressful. Even when the employee has chosen to leave and is exiting on good terms, issues arise for the organization in replacing the employee or allocating duties to remaining co-workers. Co-workers can be affected by the change as well, so developing an exit process that reduces stress and builds a smooth transition will pay off in many ways. Most significant for HR is the positive message a smooth transition sends to employees who remain in the organization.

Voluntary Exit Processes

Employees voluntarily exit the organization by either resigning or retiring. Resignations occur when an employee decides to leave the organization and pursue other opportunities. For HR, resignations present few legal issues, but they do require decisions about replacement or reassignment of work that may lead to promotions or transfers of other employees, all of which affect the workforce planning process. Resignations require HR to ensure that any outstanding loans or advances are repaid to the organization or arrangements are made for that to happen. If the employee provided 72 hours notice, final payment of all wages due, including any unused accrued vacation or PTO, must be paid at the time of departure. In addition, Consolidated Omnibus Budget Reconciliation Act (COBRA) and Health Insurance Portability and Accountability Act (HIPAA) notices must be provided for departing employees. (COBRA and HIPAA requirements are covered in detail in Chapter 6.)

Planned retirements occur when an employee decides to stop working full time and pursue other interests. HR can provide preretirement counseling to prepare employees for the transition from the structure provided by full-time work to unstructured time for pursuing other activities in leading a full and rewarding life. Employee Assistance Programs (EAPs) are excellent sources for this type of counseling and assistance. (EAPs are covered in detail in Chapter 6.)

Before an employee leaves the company, an exit interview should be conducted to gather relevant feedback. An effective exit interview provides an opportunity for employees to communicate information to the organization about why they decided to leave, what improvements the organization could make to enhance the employment experience, and any specific issues that need to be addressed. If the employee is one who has been a significant contributor and whom the organization would consider rehiring in the future, this would be the time to leave the door open for that possibility. Ideally, a third party conducts exit interviews so that employees feel free to be candid. A number of organizations provide this service, most often as a telephone or online interview. Collecting and evaluating this data over time will help identify possible problem areas that, if resolved, can reduce unwanted and costly turnover.

Involuntary Exit Processes

Involuntary exits occur as the result of either performance problems or changing business needs. Performance problems and terminations resulting from those issues are discussed in Chapter 7. This chapter discusses issues related to downsizing, which occurs as businesses change strategic direction or react to economic situations. There are a number of issues to consider in this process, beginning with legal notice requirements.

Worker Adjustment and Retraining Notification (WARN) Act of 1988

The WARN Act was passed by Congress in 1988 to provide some protection for workers in the event of mass layoffs or plant closings. The act requires that 60 days advance notice be given to either the individual workers or their union representatives. The intent of Congress was to provide time for workers to obtain new employment or training before the loss of their jobs occurred. The WARN Act is administered by the DOL and enforced through the federal courts.

Employers with 100 or more full-time employees or those with 100 or more full- *and* part-time employees who work in the aggregate 4,000 hours or more per week are subject to the provisions of the WARN Act. The employee count includes those who are on temporary leave or layoff with a reasonable expectation of recall.

The WARN Act established that a *mass layoff* occurs when either 500 employees are laid off or 33 percent of the workforce and at least 50 employees are laid off. A *plant closing* occurs when 50 or more full-time employees lose their jobs because a single facility shuts down, either permanently or temporarily. In cases where the employer staggers the workforce reduction over a period of time, care must be taken that appropriate notice is given if the total reductions within a 90-day period trigger the notice requirement.

The WARN Act also established rules on notice. For instance, notice is required to be given to all affected employees or their representatives, the chief elected official of the local government, and the state dislocated worker unit. Notice requirements vary according to which group they're being sent to, but they must contain specific information about the reasons for the closure, whether the action is permanent or temporary, the address of the affected business unit, the name of a company official to contact for further information, the expected date of closure or layoff, and whether bumping rights exist.

The WARN Act provides for three situations in which the 60-day notice isn't required, but the burden is on the employer to show that the reasons are legitimate and not an attempt to thwart the intent of the act:

- The *faltering company* exception applies only to plant closures in situations where the company is actively seeking additional funding and has a reasonable expectation that it will be forthcoming in an amount sufficient to preclude the layoff or closure and that giving the notice would negatively affect the ability of the company to obtain the funding.

- The *unforeseeable business circumstance* exception applies to plant closings and mass layoffs and occurs when circumstances take a sudden and unexpected negative change that couldn't have reasonably been predicted, such as the cancellation of a major contract without previous warning.

- The *natural disaster* exception applies to both plant closings and mass layoffs occurring as the result of a natural disaster, such as a flood, an earthquake, or a fire.

Once the organization has determined whether compliance with WARN Act requirements is necessary, decisions regarding a reduction in force (RIF)—also commonly referred to as a *layoff*—can be made. Planning and conducting an RIF is stressful for managers, who must decide which employees will be asked to leave the organization, and even more so for employees, who usually figure out that layoffs are coming long before the management announcement. Maintaining productivity in a workforce that is waiting to find out whether they will have jobs is a challenging prospect. During these times, honest communication with employees is essential, and management should provide as much information as possible before actual layoff decisions are complete. Once the layoff has occurred, open and honest communication is still essential, because remaining employees struggle with feelings of anger that their co-workers had to leave the company, "survivor guilt" because they're still employed, and dissatisfaction or work overload if they're now asked to take on the work of the employees who left the company.

Some states have enacted WARN Acts with more stringent requirements than the federal WARN Act. Be sure to know the federal requirements when you take the exam.

Making Layoff Decisions

As managers struggle with decisions about who will go and who will stay, the focus of those decisions must be on what is necessary for the business. Documenting the business reason for the decision clearly and unambiguously is essential in case the decision is challenged on the basis of disparate impact or other equal opportunity requirements.

Managers often look to layoffs as a way to remove low performers. If this is the route taken, documentation of the method used to determine who these employees are is necessary. Performance appraisals are often used for this purpose.

Severance   Offering a severance package to departing employees helps ease the shock of unemployment. Severance packages must be consistent, based on a rationale that ensures equity to all departing employees. Severance amounts can be based on seniority, employee classes, or some combination of the two.

Outplacement   *Outplacement* services are used to transition employees who are leaving the company, most often as the result of a downsizing or layoff. These services assist employees with updating resumes, preparing for interviews, and searching for new jobs. They're often provided in a group-seminar setting for individuals who have been terminated as part of a mass layoff.

Real World Scenario

Taxman v. Board of Education of Piscataway (1993)

In 1989, the Piscataway Board of Education found it necessary for budgetary reasons to reduce the faculty. According to state law, the board was required to conduct the layoffs based on seniority. Two teachers had the least seniority: Sharon Taxman and Debra Williams. Both had been hired on the same day in 1980, had equivalent educational qualifications, and had received equally outstanding evaluations. In essence, the board felt they were both equally qualified to be retained. In making previous layoff decisions in similar cases when there were no differences in qualifications, the board had drawn lots to determine which teacher to lay off. In this case, however, there was one difference between the teachers that the board considered: Taxman was white, and Williams was black. The board decided it was in the interest of the school to demonstrate the importance of diversity in the workplace and retained Williams because she was black.

There was no evidence of past discrimination that needed to be rectified based on an Affirmative Action Plan; in fact, blacks were employed in the school district at about twice the rate of the applicable labor pool. Sharon Taxman sued the school board for racial discrimination in violation of Title VII. The federal district court that heard the case found in favor of Taxman, and the school board appealed to the Third Circuit Court of Appeals, which also found in favor of Taxman. The school board then appealed to the U.S. Supreme Court but agreed to settle the case before the Supreme Court hearing.

State or local unemployment offices, as well as Workforce Investment agencies, may provide outplacement assistance as well, including on-site meetings with impacted employees.

Executive outplacements may occur as the result of a merger or an acquisition and may include additional benefits, such as headhunting services and one-on-one counseling. Providing outplacements for other employees can be a great help in finding new jobs or in coping with the change in circumstances. Continuing the EAP for a finite period of time for laid-off workers is another way to assist them in coming to terms with a job loss.

Unemployment Insurance   If the RIF or layoff meets WARN notice thresholds, the state unemployment office will be aware of the pending layoff. Whether or not that is the case, HR should ensure that employees are clear about their eligibility for unemployment benefits and how to apply for them. Most states provide pamphlets explaining the requirements, which are distributed at the time of the layoff.

Conducting the Layoff Meeting

During the layoff meeting, managers should communicate the message unambiguously and with compassion. If the layoff decision is a permanent one, employees should be advised that they won't be called back to work; if there is a possibility for rehire, they should be advised of the time frame in which that may occur. Employees should be given adequate time to gather personal items prior to leaving but shouldn't be allowed to hang around indefinitely, because this negatively impacts productivity and is hard on the morale of employees who will be staying with the organization. Once the termination meetings have been conducted, it's important that management meet with the remaining employees to answer questions and provide reassurance.

Easing the Transition

Whether a termination decision will affect a single employee or a group, it's one of the most difficult decisions managers face. Even so, the difficulty and discomfort experienced by management is far less than that of the employees who are losing their jobs and wondering how long it will take to find a new job and how they will make ends meet in the meantime.

Many state governments provide programs through the agencies designated to provide employment or reemployment services. The federal government contributes to these efforts with funding for training or retraining displaced workers. Two of these programs are the result of the Workforce Investment Act and the Trade Adjustment and Assistance Act:

Workforce Investment Act (WIA)   The creation of WIA was a collaborative effort between the DOL and Congress, resulting in a job-training program designed to improve worker skills for jobs in the twenty-first century. WIA programs are designed to achieve three goals:

- Improve workforce quality
- Enhance national productivity and competitive ability
- Reduce reliance on welfare

The foundation of the program is its One-Stop service-delivery centers, which were established to provide a full range of services for workers and employers. These centers can include education services, skills assessment and training, job-search counseling and support, mentoring, and access to job-search information, and are generally managed by state and local governments.

Trade Adjustment Assistance (TAA)   In 2002, Congress established the Trade Adjustment Assistance (TAA) program to assist workers who lose their jobs as the result of an increase in imported goods. Eligibility for the program requires a group of three or more workers to submit an application to the DOL Division of Trade Adjustment Assistance (DTAA). DTAA determines whether the group meets eligibility requirements and, if so, issues a certification. The group must meet three requirements to be certified:

- Workers must have been laid off or had their hours and pay reduced by 20 percent or more.
- The employer's sales and/or production levels must have declined.
- The loss of jobs must be due in large part to increased imports.

Once the DTAA certifies that a group is eligible for the program, individual workers may apply for services and benefits that are available at one of the local One-Stop service centers established by WIA. Retraining and reemployment services available under the TAA program include up to 104 weeks of training, trade readjustment allowances (TRAs) for up to 52 weeks of training after unemployment benefits are exhausted, reimbursement of job-search expenses, and relocation allowances.

Records Management: The Life Cycle

Every employment-related activity in the scope of human resources receives or generates a record. The specific retention, storage, and destruction of these records make up the *records life cycle.*

Establishing the Policy

An effective records-management policy should be focused on defining controls. This includes controlling the creation, access, legibility, retrieval, use, retention, and destruction of each record.

A records-retention policy should include a description of the employment documents covered by the policy (defining what is a record), a control system for limiting access and ensuring availability upon demand or need (description of maintenance or use), and a schedule for retention and eventual destruction by record type.

An HR professional should have a firm understanding of theory and application related to developing and implementing a records-retention process. In addition to being a best practice, records retention is required by several federal laws. For example, the Civil Rights Act of 1964 requires that employers with at least 15 employees must retain applications and other personnel records relating to hires, rehires, tests used in employment, promotion, transfers, demotions, selection for training, layoff, recall, terminations, and discharge for 1 year from making the records or taking the personnel actions. See Table 4.9 for more examples of the types of records that are generated by functional area of HR.

Proper Disposal

In June 2005, the FTC issued a disposal rule related to the destruction of consumer information. This rule covers employment records related to sensitive personal information (Social Security numbers, medical history), consumer credit, references, and background searches. It directs affected companies to destroy covered records in a manner that protects against "unauthorized access to or use of the information." The FTC describes the following as acceptable methods for compliance. Employers may:

- *Burn, pulverize, or shred papers containing consumer report information so that the information cannot be read or reconstructed;*

- *Destroy or erase electronic files or media containing consumer report information so that the information cannot be read or reconstructed;*

- *Conduct due diligence and hire a document destruction contractor to dispose of material specifically identified as consumer report information consistent with the Rule...*

TABLE 4.9   Types of records generated by HR

Functional Area of HR	Examples of Types of Records Created or Received	Laws or Rules Governing Recordkeeping or Retention Requirements
Equal Employment	Medical certifications, training selection procedures, applicant tracking, Affirmative Action Plans/ results	FMLA ADA ADEA EPA CRA 1964 VEVRAA Uniformed Services Employment and Reemployment Rights Act (USERRA)
Staffing	Applications, pre-employment test results, selection notes, EEO-1 reports, I-9 forms, job postings, reference check information, credit reports, basic employee data	IRCA CRA 1964 ADA UGESP FCRA Federal Unemployment Tax Act (FUTA)
Compensation and Benefits	Payroll records, tax records, benefits administration records, summary plan descriptions, leave of absence (LOA) records, copies of employee notices describing benefits, records of insurance premium payments	Employee Retirement Income Security Act (ERISA) HIPAA FMLA PDA Fair Labor Standards Act (FLSA) IRS tax code
Training and Development	Participant records, description of tools used in training	OSHA ADA
Employee Relations	Performance reviews, adverse employment actions, investigative reports	CRA 1964 ADA ADEA
Risk Management	Workplace injury and illness records, records of exposure to hazardous material	OSHA

You can find the final Rule in its entirety on the FTC's website:

www.ftc.gov/os/2004/11/041118disposalfrn.pdf

Electronic Storage

Technology has influenced many HR practices, not the least of which is records retention. Before deciding to electronically store records, an HR professional must consider the specific regulatory requirements of the law(s) governing record retention, security, access, and legibility. A good example of the considerations for the electronic storage of records is given by the USCIS related to storing the Form I-9 electronically:

> Instructions from the U.S. Citizen and Immigration Services
>
> Employers may use a paper system, an electronic system or a combination of paper and electronic systems to store Form I-9 records. An electronic storage system must:

- *Include controls to ensure the integrity, accuracy and reliability of the electronic storage system.*

- *Include controls to detect and prevent the unauthorized or accidental creation of, addition to, alteration of, deletion of or deterioration of an electronically stored Form I-9, including the electronic signature, if used.*

- *Include controls to ensure an audit trail so that any alteration or change to the form since its creation is electronically stored and can be accessed by an appropriate government agency inspecting the forms.*

- *Include an inspection and quality assurance program that regularly evaluates the electronic generation or storage system, and includes periodic checks of electronically stored Form I-9s, including the electronic signature, if used.*

- *Include a detailed index of all data so that any particular record can be accessed immediately.*

- *Produce a high degree of legibility and readability when displayed on video display terminal or reproduced on paper.*

Metrics: Measuring Results

WFP functions lend themselves more readily to measurement than some other areas of HR:

Business Impact Measures   In addition to the return on investment (ROI) measures discussed in Chapter 2, employee productivity is a key measure for business impact in the WFP function. Productivity metrics are calculated by dividing total output (expressed in revenue dollars or [in manufacturing industries] by a measure of inventory output) by the number of employees. This metric can be calculated for the whole organization or by work groups, depending on specific information needs.

Tactical Accountability Measures   A number of established metrics can be used to measure HR's tactical accountability in WFP. Some of the more common include the following:

Accession Rate   The accession rate measures the number of new employees against the total number of employees. This measurement is useful for determining the types of HR programs needed to manage and support the workforce. Accession rate is calculated by dividing the total number of new employees by the number of employees at the end of the previous measurement period.

Quality of Hire   To calculate a quality-of-hire metric, HR must first develop criteria to identify what constitutes a quality hire. This information includes accurate job descriptions, assessment tools that accurately identify the best-qualified candidates, clear communication of expectations to new hires, and pre-established criteria to measure performance. The measurement is often based on performance ratings made by hiring managers after observing employees on the job.

Cost per Hire   Cost per hire is a common metric but is often calculated without including all the costs associated with a hire. For example, a meaningful cost-per-hire calculation includes costs for advertising; in-house recruiter time to review resumes and screen candidates, and/or recruiter fees; HR staff salary; salaries for hiring managers and other members of the interview team; assessment tests; pre-employment inquiries; administrative costs; and any other costs involved in hiring a new employee. The metric is calculated by dividing the total costs by the number of hires for the measurement period.

Time to Hire   The time-to-hire metric is calculated from the date a job is posted to the date a job is accepted by the new employee.

Replacement Cost   Replacement cost per employee can be an eye-opener for managers and executives. In addition to the costs calculated for the cost-per-hire metric, this measurement also includes costs for training, lost productivity, temporary replacements, overtime for employees who fill in while the position is vacant, and others. These costs can easily reach 300 percent of annual salary for the position.

Turnover Analysis   One of the most commonly used metrics, *turnover analysis*, is calculated by dividing the average number of total employees for the measurement period by the number of employees who exited the organization. This measurement can be calculated in a variety of ways to meet specific organization needs. Some variations include calculating on a monthly or annual basis and calculating turnover for voluntary separations only or for different business units in the organization.

SPHR ONLY Global Considerations

As businesses of all sizes become increasingly global, American companies find themselves employing all or part of their workforce in positions overseas. In addition to the planning steps discussed previously, there are a number of additional factors to consider for an international workforce, beginning with determining in which labor market(s) the company will recruit its employees. There are three possible areas:

- The home or parent country is the domicile of the company, where its corporate head-quarters are located. Employees who originate from the home country are known as *expatriates* or *parent-country nationals* (PCNs). Employees returning from a host country assignment are called *inpatriates*, often requiring acclimation and reorientation to their home country workplace.

- The host country is the country wherein the corporation is operating, or is planning to operate, a business unit. Employees originating from the host country are known as *host-country nationals* (HCNs). Although this may seem to be a solution with few problems, there can be many unexpected issues to resolve, including those related to compensation and cultural differences.

- Employees from any country other than the home or host country are known as *third-country nationals* (TCNs). Experienced TCNs who are familiar with the organization's culture and business practices are most often used to set up a new business unit in a neighboring country. This can be an advantageous situation for the business because it's less expensive than relocating an expatriate.

It's important to understand the international staffing strategies that can be used in building the global workforce. Multinational corporations use four basic strategies in making these decisions:

Ethnocentric   The *ethnocentric* approach is one in which all key management positions are filled by expatriates. The benefits of an ethnocentric approach include the ability of the organization to maintain control of its business units and ensure that business is conducted in accordance with corporate mandates. Communication with the home office is made easier because the expatriate is familiar with the organization's culture and business practices. International assignments also provide opportunities to develop individuals who are part of the succession plans for senior management roles.

This approach is often taken during the startup phase of a business unit to ensure that organizational standards are maintained or when there is a real or perceived lack of management talent available in the host country labor market. Although this approach encourages a cohesive culture throughout the organization, it focuses on the home country/parent organization and doesn't take into consideration local customs and business practices. This can lead to misunderstandings and create ill will between the local government and the company.

Polycentric   A *polycentric* approach fills corporate positions in the home country with expatriates, whereas management positions in the host country are filled by HCNs. This approach can have a positive impact by showing a commitment to the host country and generating goodwill for the business, but it doesn't afford upward mobility for top managers in the host country. The business benefits, because it's less expensive to hire local employees—even at top dollar—than it is to fill international positions with expatriates. However, it can also limit communication between business units in the different locations and result in animosity between the home and host country business units because of differences in cultural practices and compensation levels between countries.

Regiocentric   A *regiocentric* approach takes a somewhat larger operational view than does the polycentric. It covers a trade region such as the European Union and has managers move between business units in different countries in the region.

Geocentric   The *geocentric* approach seeks to place the best-qualified person into each position, regardless of their country of origin. As a result, the business builds an international management team whose members are able to move into and address issues in any geographic area.

Once the company has decided which approach best suits its strategic goals and culture, HR has many complex issues to address. There are a myriad of laws, customs, and local practices to be dealt with that often conflict with home-country practices, and it's important to understand the impact of these issues when evaluating international workforce needs.

Expatriate issues in workforce planning fall into three main categories:

Cost   The costs of sending employees to work in foreign countries can be substantial, in some cases as much as three times the annual salary. The additional costs are the result of factoring in expenses for moving families and minimizing the cultural adjustment for employees and their families. Another contributory cost comes from adjustments to pay that may be needed to keep employee salaries whole and retain their equity in the company. In addition, it's often necessary to subsidize schooling costs, taxes, and housing costs.

Foreign Business Practices   The way business is done in foreign countries can be significantly different from the way business is done in the United States. Candidates for expatriate jobs must receive training on the culture and practices of the country to which they will be assigned to be successful in their positions and to avoid unintentionally offending those with whom they're working, thereby straining business relationships. It's important as well to provide training on laws governing U.S. business practices in foreign countries, particularly the Foreign Corrupt Practices Act (FCPA), which prohibits American businesses from proffering bribes in order to obtain contracts or encourage foreign bureaucrats to get things done in a timely fashion.

Cultural Acclimation   Cultural acclimation can be difficult not only for the employee but also for the employee's spouse and children, and often results in the resignation of the employee or insistence on transfer back to the home country. Another issue is that although women are accepted in business leadership positions in the United States and other countries, cultural difficulties can be encountered in countries that are unaccustomed to viewing women in leadership roles. This issue alone can become a huge conflict, with EEO requirements to provide equal access to training and upward mobility at odds with the ability to do business in a country unaccustomed to dealing with women in powerful positions.

As evidence of the increasing significance of human resource expertise in global work environments, HRCI has developed a certification specifically for professionals who manage global HR needs on a regular basis. The Global Professional in Human Resources (GPHR) Exam certifies professionals with expertise in this area in greater detail than the

SPHR exam. SPHR candidates can expect to be tested on their general knowledge of international HR practices and the impact of a global workforce on organization needs.

 Find more information about the GPHR at hrci.org/hrcertification.

Summary

When strategically tied to the organization's vision, mission, and goals, planning for workforce needs is a key element of success. HR professionals must provide expertise for management in deciding whether to aggressively develop current employees for future growth in the organization, hire candidates from the outside, or use alternative staffing methods to accomplish the work that needs to be done. Understanding the implications of each approach allows HR to guide management in making decisions that best suit the organization's needs, culture, and values.

Identifying candidates who not only have the best KSAs for the job but whose personal goals, ambitions, and qualities also complement the needs of the organization requires HR professionals to be keenly aware of the organization's strategic direction. Providing opportunities to all qualified candidates opens up the labor pool available to the organization and includes candidates with a great deal to offer who might not have been considered in the past.

An effective hiring process begins with using sources that produce a pool of candidates with diverse backgrounds who have the required KSAs, continues with screening the candidates with a fair and equitable process designed to find the best match for the organization, and concludes by welcoming them with orientation programs that assist them in becoming productive members of the team. Having an effective organizational exit process in place eases the transition for employees who remain with the company as well as for those who are leaving. When downsizing decisions are made fairly and equitably, voluntary exits are treated with respect, and terminations for poor performance are handled with due process, remaining employees respond with greater loyalty and commitment to organizational goals.

HR professionals can show that they understand the fundamental needs of business by making recommendations and decisions based on quantifiable measures. Being able to show, for example, how much a bad hiring decision costs the organization in terms of the direct and indirect costs of hiring, training, and replacing employees demonstrates to management that effective HR management has a positive effect on the bottom line.

Exam Essentials

Be able to develop and implement a strategic workforce plan.   A strategic workforce plan provides a framework for HR professionals to ensure that the right people with the right qualifications are available at the right time to achieve the organization's goals.

Be able to conduct a staffing needs assessment.   A staffing needs assessment determines which KSAs are needed to meet future strategic goals and where training efforts (if filling jobs internally) or recruiting efforts (if hiring from the outside) should be focused.

Be able to develop a succession plan.   A succession plan identifies high-performing individuals in the company who have the capability to take on positions at the senior and executive management levels. Once the individuals have been identified, they're coached, mentored, and provided with training opportunities to prepare them for greater responsibility.

Understand the Affirmative Action Plan process.   An AAP is required to be filed by companies with federal contracts of $50,000 or more per year and 50 employees. The plan identifies how many incumbents in different job classifications are members of protected classes and compares that information to the availability of protected classes in the labor market.

Be able to develop job requirements from a job analysis.   A job analysis provides the information to develop the job competencies, job descriptions, and test specifications necessary to both identify what needs to be done on a daily basis and recruit effectively for the best candidate to fill the position.

Be able to identify recruitment methods.   Depending on the level of experience and skill being sought, there are a variety of methods to consider in the recruiting process. HR professionals must understand which methods will produce the candidates who are most appropriate to fill positions at different levels.

Be able to establish and implement selection procedures.   Effective selection procedures help ensure that candidates selected for the organization meet all the job requirements and are the best fit for the position. Interviewing, testing, realistic job previews, and assessment centers help organizations determine whether the candidate is the right fit for the job. Reference checks ensure that the candidate has performed successfully in previous positions.

Understand the implications of federal immigration policy.   Immigration laws were designed to protect American workers while encouraging the immigration of highly educated and skilled workers for jobs requiring high-level KSAs. Employers may hire noncitizens only when they can demonstrate that no American citizens with the necessary qualifications are available. When noncitizens are hired, they must be paid the prevailing wage for the position.

Be able to conduct post-hire activities.   HR activities conducted during the post-hire phase have implications for the long-term success of new hires. It's important to understand the ramifications of employment offers and ensure that the new employee has all the necessary information to be successful. An effective orientation will make new employees feel welcome, introduce them to the company, and provide information on company policies.

Be able to create the organization exit process.   HR professionals must develop fair and equitable processes for downsizing and laying off employees and be aware of legal notice requirements that must be followed when applicable. Resignations and retirements require that HR conduct exit interviews and create processes that provide for timely replacement of exiting employees.

Review Questions

You can find the answers in Appendix A.

1. The marketing director needs to hire a replacement for the marketing coordinator, who is being promoted. The position has changed quite a bit since the last time the job was advertised, and the director is looking to HR to assist in redefining the job requirements so the recruiting process can begin. Which of the following would *not* be used in determining the job requirements?

    A. Job competencies

    B. Job description

    C. Job specifications

    D. Candidate profile

2. Which of the following is *not* a BFOQ?

    A. A synagogue hiring a new rabbi requires that the rabbi be Jewish.

    B. A lingerie catalog hires only female models.

    C. A retail store in a predominantly Asian neighborhood advertises for Asian clerks.

    D. A swimming club requires that the men's changing-room attendant be male.

3. The court case that identified adverse impact as an unlawful employment practice was which of the following?

    A. *Griggs v. Duke Power Co.*

    B. *Albemarle Paper v. Moody*

    C. *Washington v. Davis*

    D. *Taxman v. School Board of Piscataway*

4. To determine the numbers and types of jobs necessary to realize business goals, HR must assess the KSAs available within the organization during a staffing needs analysis. What other factor is necessary to complete the assessment?

    A. The KSAs needed to achieve future goals

    B. The tasks, duties, and responsibilities for the work

    C. The KSAs available in the local labor market

    D. The organization's core competencies

5. Your New Orleans plant has an opening for a controller, and four candidates have been selected for interviews. Jack, the son of a plant employee, worked as an accountant for two years to put himself through the Wharton Business School and recently earned his MBA. Richard is a CPA with eight years of experience in a public accounting firm. Susan also has a CPA and has worked as an accounting manager in the corporate office of a large corporation in the same industry. Jane does not have a CPA or MBA but has worked as controller of a smaller local competitor for eight years. After interviewing all four candidates, the general manager told you that he wants to hire Jack because he shows promise. You know from previous conversation with the GM that he also worked his way through college. Which of the following biases could be influencing the GM's decision?

A. Knowledge-of-predictor

B. Halo effect

C. Similar-to-me

D. Gut feeling

6. Please refer to the following table for this question. A company advertised for 100 sales representative positions. They received 650 applications and hired the 100 employees as follows:

Group	Applicants	Hired
Black	140	23
Asian	120	21
Hispanic	145	19
Caucasian	230	35
Native American	15	2
Total	650	100

Which group has the highest selection rate?

A. Black

B. Asian

C. Caucasian

D. Hispanic

7. Please refer to the following table for this question. A company advertised for 100 sales representative positions. They received 650 applications and hired the 100 employees as follows:

Group	Applicants	Hired	Selection Rate	4/5 of Highest Rate
Black	140	23	16%	
Asian	120	21	18%	14%
Hispanic	145	19	13%	
Caucasian	230	35	15%	
Native American	15	2	13%	
Total	650	100		

In which groups has adverse impact occurred?

A. Hispanic and Caucasian

B. Caucasian and Black

C. Hispanic and Native American

D. Native American and Black

8. An Affirmative Action Plan must be completed by employers that meet which criteria?

A. Private employers with 25 or more employees

B. Government contractors and subcontractors with contracts of $10,000 or more in a 12-month period

C. Government contractors with contracts of $2,500 or more in a 12-month period

D. Government contractors with 50 or more employees and contracts of $50,000 or more each year

9. When a reduction in force occurs, the ADEA allows that protected employees may waive their rights under some circumstances. For the waiver to be valid, the protected employee must be allowed how long to review and consider the agreement?

A. 7 days

B. 21 days

C. 45 days

D. 180 days

10. Which of the following is *not* required by IRCA?

A. That an I-9 form be completed for all new hires within 3 days of hire

B. That employers comply with IRCA in good faith

C. That I-9 forms be maintained for all employees

D. That copies of documents presented for employment eligibility be maintained

11. In a self-audit of your employee's I-9 forms, several errors were found. These errors included incomplete sections, questionable documents accepted for verification, and over-documentation. Of the following corrective and prevention strategies, which should you recommend to your employer?

    A. Training for employees

    B. Recertification of all I-9 forms

    C. Enrollment in E-Verify

    D. Requesting updated documents from affected employees

12. Electronic storage of records must include specific controls to ensure which of the following?

    A. Online retrievability on demand

    B. No unauthorized access

    C. Ease of use

    D. Collaboration with an HRIS system

13. Strategic recruitment activities include all of the following except which one?

    A. Labor market analysis

    B. The design of total rewards packages

    C. Employee referral programs

    D. Defining the employer brand

14. Which of the following is a requirement of the Uniform Guidelines on employee selection procedures?

    A. Any selection tool that results in discrimination based on a protected class characteristic is unlawful.

    B. All selection tools must be job related and valid predictors of future success.

    C. Application forms must be the same for all employment classifications within the organization.

    D. Internet recruiting efforts are excluded from applicant-tracking requirements.

15. Which of the following acts requires federal contractors or subcontractors with contracts of $25,000 or more to list all nonsenior management job openings with state employment agencies?

    A. The Rehabilitation Act of 1973

    B. Executive Order 11375

    C. Executive Order 11246

    D. The Vietnam Era Veterans' Readjustment Assistance Act of 1974

16. Within the first 90 days of his employment, a security guard physically assaulted an alleged shoplifter. Upon investigation, it was found that he had been previously convicted of a violent crime, but the employer failed to conduct a background check. This is an example of which of the following?

   A.   A violation of the Privacy Act of 1974

   B.   Negligent hiring

   C.   Failure to report

   D.   A criminal act

17. Which of the following is the correct definition of "a major life activity" under the Americans with Disabilities Act?

   A.   A physical or mental impairment

   B.   Any activity that cannot be mitigated

   C.   General activities and major bodily functions

   D.   A physical or mental impairment that require the use of supplemental medication or prosthetics

18. Professionals, craft workers, and laborers/helpers have what in common?

   A.   They are all job categories on the EEO-1 report.

   B.   They are all classifications for defining exempt workers.

   C.   They are all examples of types of labor unions.

   D.   They are all examples of protected-class individuals.

19. Which of the following definitions is correct for the term *job bidding*?

   A.   An internal job announcement

   B.   Allowing contractors to submit requests for proposals

   C.   The means by which internal employees can express interest in a job prior to it becoming available

   D.   Ranking job applicants based on their comparative qualifications

20. Which of the following interview questions is unlawful?

   A.   If you were an animal, what kind of animal would you be?

   B.   Are you a U.S. citizen?

   C.   Tell me about a time you disagreed with your boss about a course of action.

   D.   Any job offer made will be contingent on a medical exam. Are you willing to undergo one if we offer you the job?

Chapter 5

Human Resource Development

THE HRCI TEST SPECIFICATIONS FROM THE HUMAN RESOURCE DEVELOPMENT FUNCTIONAL AREA COVERED IN THIS CHAPTER INCLUDE:

✓ Ensure that human resources development activities are compliant with all applicable federal laws and regulations.

✓ Conduct a needs assessment to identify and establish priorities regarding human resource development activities.

✓ Develop/select and implement employee training programs (for example: leadership skills, harassment prevention, computer skills) to increase individual and organizational effectiveness.

✓ Evaluate effectiveness of employee training programs through the use of metrics (for example: participant surveys, pre- and post-testing). **SPHR ONLY**

✓ Develop, implement, and evaluate talent management programs that include assessing talent, developing career paths, and managing the placement of high-potential employees.

✓ Develop, select, and evaluate performance appraisal processes (for example: instruments, ranking and rating scales) to increase individual and organizational effectiveness.

✓ Develop, implement, and evaluate performance management programs and procedures (includes training for evaluators).

✓ Develop/select, implement, and evaluate programs (for example: telecommuting, diversity initiatives, repatriation) to meet the changing needs of employees and the organization. **SPHR ONLY**

✓ Provide coaching to managers and executives regarding effectively managing organizational talent.

Human resource development (HRD) is the functional area of human resources (HR) that seeks to affect the behavior of employees so the organization can achieve its goals. This chapter explores organization development (OD), talent management, training, and performance management.

Chapter 3, "Business Management and Strategy," examined the structural, procedural, and technological aspects of an organization's systems and discussed the vision, mission, and value statements that result from the strategic planning process. Building on that information, this chapter looks at ways organizations implement the changes necessary to accomplish their missions and the strategies they use to align employees with the vision, mission, and goals developed by their leaders.

This chapter begins with a review of the federal legislation that impacts HRD activities. It then examines several different approaches to an organization's development and the ways these approaches positively impact organizational culture and climate. That discussion is followed by a review of techniques for developing employees, managers, and leaders as well as a systems model for use in developing training programs.

HRD doesn't occur in a vacuum; it occurs in the context of how the organization sees itself, how it conducts business, and how it views its employees. Every organization makes determinations about these issues, whether consciously, as part of an OD process, or unconsciously, as a result of the way its leaders operate on a day-to-day basis. Effective organizations are those in which values and beliefs are shared at all levels and are reflected in the behavior of individuals throughout the organization.

Be sure to review the *HR Certification Institute PHR/SPHR Body of Knowledge (BOK)* knowledge requirements for HRD as you begin this chapter. Several sections in Chapter 2, "Core Knowledge Requirements for HR Professionals," have particular relevance here: a review of the discussions on needs assessment, adult learning processes, training techniques, diversity, leadership, organization structures, job descriptions, and employee attitude assessment will enhance your review of the material in this chapter.

For up-to-the-minute updates for this chapter, visit www.sybex.com/go/phr4e.

Federal Employment Legislation

Candidates for the PHR/SPHR certifications should understand the effects of federal civil rights legislation and executive orders on HRD activities. These legal requirements were reviewed in Chapter 4, "Workforce Planning and Employment." Civil rights legislation covers all the terms and conditions of employment, which means that members of protected groups must be provided with equal opportunity to participate in workplace training and development programs. In addition, the use of original works created by others, whether they're authors, composers, inventors, or other individuals, is protected by copyright and patent laws. Table 5.1 summarizes federal legislation for HRD activities.

TABLE 5.1   Federal legislation governing HRD activities

Type	Enforcement Agency	Chapter Reference
Civil rights	Equal Employment Opportunity Commission (EEOC) and/or Office of Federal Contract Compliance Programs (OFCCP)	4
Executive orders	OFCCP	4
Copyright	Civil litigation	5
Patent	Civil litigation	5

Copyright Act of 1976

The use of musical, literary, and other original works without permission of the owner of the copyright is prohibited under most circumstances. The copyright owner is, for the most part, the author of the work. There are two exceptions to this. The first is that an employer who hires employees to create original works as part of their normal job duties is the owner of the copyright because the employer paid for the work to be done. The second exception is that the copyright for work created by a freelance author, artist, or musician who has been commissioned to create the work by someone else is owned by the person who commissioned the work. These exceptions are known as *work-for-hire* exceptions.

For trainers who want to use the work of others during training sessions, there are two circumstances that don't require permission. The first is related to works that are in the *public domain*. Copyrights protect original works for the life of the author plus 70 years; after that, the works may be used without permission. Works-for-hire are protected for the shorter of 95 years from the first year of publication or 120 years from the year of creation.

Other works in the public domain include those produced as part of the job duties of federal officials and those for which copyright protection has expired. Some works published without notice of copyright before January 1, 1978, or those published between then and March 1, 1989, are also considered to be in the public domain.

The second circumstance for use of published works without permission is known as the *fair use doctrine*. The act specifies that use of a work for the purposes of criticism, commentary, news reporting, or teaching (including multiple copies for classroom use, scholarship, or research) isn't an infringement depending on four factors:

- The purpose and character of the use: Is it to be used for a profit or nonprofit educational purpose?

- The nature of the work itself: Is it a work of fiction? Or is it based on facts? How much creativity did it require?

- The amount of work: How much of the work (1 copy or 50?) or what portion (a paragraph or an entire chapter?) of the work will be used?

- The effect: What effect will the use of the material have on the potential market value of the copyrighted work?

Permission for the use of copyright-protected material that is outside the fair use exceptions can generally be obtained by contacting the author or publisher of the work.

U.S. Patent Act

A *patent* allows inventors exclusive rights to the benefits of an invention for a defined period of time. Patent laws in the United States define three types of patents:

Design Patents   *Design patents* protect new, original, and ornamental designs of manufactured items. Design patents are limited to 14 years.

Utility Patents   *Utility patents* protect the invention of new and useful processes, machines, manufacture or composition of matter, and new and useful improvements to the same. Utility patents are limited to 20 years.

Plant Patents   Plant patents protect the invention or discovery of asexually reproduced varieties of plants for 20 years.

Organization Development

Organization development (OD) is a systematic method of examining an organization's technology, processes, structure, and human resources, and developing action strategies to improve the way it achieves desired business results. These action strategies are known as *OD interventions* and may be directed toward structures, processes, technology, individuals, groups of individuals, or entire organizations. This section focuses on organization-wide changes to structure, process, and technology.

This sharing of values and beliefs and the behavior related to them is known as the *organizational culture*. The culture of an organization, combined with leadership and management styles and the level of bureaucracy, creates a work environment or climate that will either inspire and motivate employees to achieve the corporate mission or inhibit employees' motivation and enthusiasm for their jobs, thereby limiting the success of the organization. Organizational culture and climate determine the level of employee involvement in the decision-making process and provide the unwritten ground rules on which decisions can be based in the absence of relevant policies. You can find more information about organizational culture and climate in Chapter 7, "Employee and Labor Relations."

Although it's possible for businesses to earn a profit without considering the needs of their employees (and some do), the results of job-satisfaction surveys consistently show that employees are motivated to perform at a high level of productivity by a variety of factors that can be influenced by culture and climate. Challenging work and respect are very often of equal or greater importance to employees than the amount of money they earn in determining their level of satisfaction, commitment, and productivity. Although it's important to keep in mind that businesses exist to earn a profit, rather than to merely provide a satisfying work experience for employees, organizations that are able to create atmospheres including trust, respect, and challenging work are generally rewarded with higher rates of productivity and increased revenue and profits than are organizations focused only on cost reduction and efficiency. The OD process provides a method for developing strategies to accomplish this.

When the culture and climate tend to inhibit goal achievement instead, an OD intervention can be implemented to correct the problem. In their text *Organization Development and Change* (South-Western College Pub, 9th Edition, 2008), Thomas Cummings and Christopher Worley identify four categories of interventions: strategic, techno-structural, human process, and human resource management. As is evident by the category names, interventions can remove obstacles in strategy, technology, structure, process, and management. The following sections concentrate on interventions and strategies in each category that relate to human resource development and the ways they can influence the organizational culture and climate.

Strategic Interventions

Strategic OD interventions are often used to implement changes made to the vision, mission, and values of the organization during a strategic planning process, as discussed in Chapter 3. These interventions are designed to align various elements in the organization with the new direction or focus established by the leaders. Some examples of strategic OD interventions are change management, knowledge management, and learning organizations.

Change Management

The result of any OD process is a change in the way things are done in an organization. Whether it's a new technology, a more efficient process, or a different reporting structure, the resulting change will have to be implemented by people—and no matter how difficult it is to create the new operating plans, implementing them successfully will be even more difficult because the people in the organization must embrace the change and be motivated and committed to making the change work.

Change Process Theory

An early model of *change process theory*, developed by a social psychologist named Kurt Lewin, described three stages for change:

Unfreezing   This stage creates the motivation for change by identifying and communicating the need for the change. In this stage, it's important to create a vision for the outcome of the change and a sense of urgency for getting to the new outcome.

Moving   During this stage, resistance is examined and managed, and the organization is aligned with the change. Communication remains an integral part of the process.

Refreezing   In the final stage of the theory, the change becomes the new norm for the organization, the outcome is evaluated, and additional changes occur to adjust the actual outcomes to those that are desired.

Human resource professionals can use change process theory to aid employees through a stressful work change. Let's take a look at some other ways HR can help employees deal with change.

Tools for Successful Change

People dislike change for a variety of reasons: change moves them out of the comfort zone to which they have become accustomed, and they may be fearful of the unknown. The politics of the organization may make change undesirable in one group or another, and employees may perceive that they will lose status or control. Changes fail most often because the people who are expected to implement them aren't prepared to do so. Organizations can take steps to ensure the success of change initiatives, including the following:

Prepare for Change   The only constant in the current business environment is change. Organizations must be aware of situations developing in the industry or geographic areas in which they operate so they can be ahead of the curve in developing strategies that will effectively handle changes in the environment.

Communicate   To enhance the likelihood of a successful implementation, leaders must communicate effectively and repeatedly with employees well in advance of any planned implementation. Soliciting ideas from those who are closest to operations may provide insight into better solutions and increase buy-in when it's time to implement the change. Communication at every stage of the process will enable employees to get used to the idea of the change gradually, increase the level of acceptance, and build commitment for the process.

Develop a Plan   A comprehensive plan that clearly defines the goals of the change, addresses all of its implications, and includes tools for evaluating its success is essential. Scheduling training for employees who may need to upgrade skills, integrating processes from different areas of the organization, upgrading equipment, and developing a plan to address resistance to the change and reduce stress will increase the chances for successful implementation.

Have an Executive Sponsor   The CEO or another senior executive who is committed to and enthusiastic about the change must be able to inspire employees to commit to the implementation.

Motivate Direct Supervisors   Employees want to know how their supervisors feel about changes and will be influenced by what the supervisors say about the change. When direct supervisors and managers are motivated to implement a change, employees will be more likely to accept it.

Recruit Unofficial Leaders   Every organization has unofficial leaders who are able to influence co-workers; obtaining their commitment to the change will influence others.

Implement   Put the change into action. Ensure that employees have the tools needed to successfully implement the change, whether that is new equipment, facilities, training, or support.

Evaluate   Compare results to the evaluation criteria developed during the planning stage to determine whether the change was successfully implemented.

HR professionals are in a unique position to act as change agents during this process. A *change agent* must be able to balance the needs of various stakeholders in the process, listen to their concerns, and move them toward acceptance of and commitment to the change.

Knowledge Management

During the course of business each day, organizations generate data (such as sales figures) and review it to glean useful information (such as trends). Individual employees then interpret the information based on past experiences with similar circumstances and draw conclusions that are used to move the organization forward. These conclusions are referred to as *knowledge*. Although data and information can be easily replicated by other employees with the right skills, the knowledge that comes from past experiences isn't always so easily repeated. The process of attempting to retain this ability is known as *knowledge management* (KM). This term, while still evolving, generally encompasses activities related to the creation, retention, and distribution of organizational knowledge.

Much of the knowledge that an individual acquires over time in an organization disappears when that person leaves the organization. Whether because of layoffs, outsourcing, or the retirement of key employees, the loss of critical knowledge negatively impacts organizations.

Real World Scenario

Using KM to Solve Administrative Problems

Over time, an experienced executive assistant (EA) learns shortcuts and details that enhance an executive's ability to operate more effectively by eliminating administrative concerns. Some of these details are personal preferences for individual executives, but many are useful for any executive in an organization, such as which IT support person is best at long-distance troubleshooting, or out-of-town businesses that can provide quality services in an emergency, such as printing presentation materials on short notice if they aren't delivered on time.

Sharing this information among EAs usually occurs on an ad-hoc basis, but this requires that individuals with specific knowledge be available when an emergency occurs. A better solution for long-term benefits is the creation of a knowledge management database or manual that the EAs update as they learn new information that can help executives achieve organization goals and objectives.

Executives benefit because they're able to accomplish more, and the EAs benefit because they save time, whether it's locating the best travel deals, identifying restaurants that provide appropriate venues for client meetings, finding the co-worker who can be counted on to solve urgent problems, or handling other administrative details that allow the executives they support to be more effective in their jobs.

Organizations use different methods to retain and institutionalize knowledge so it's easily accessible for improving processes and increasing profits. These methods can be categorized in one of the following ways:

Expert Registers   An expert register or directory collects the names and areas of expertise of employees and is made available to all employees, who are then able to contact internal experts to discuss problems and find solutions.

Best-Practice Standards   The term *best practice* is often used to describe methods or practices that have been demonstrated to produce desired results over a period of time. In the KM context, best practices are those that have been used in an organization by one group of employees to achieve particular results and are codified for distribution to other employees in similar jobs or groups throughout the organization with the idea that the results will be duplicated.

After-Action Evaluations   An after-action evaluation is sometimes referred to as a *postmortem* and is a review conducted at the end of a project or other group endeavor. The purpose of the evaluation is to share in the group what worked, what didn't work, and what knowledge can be retained for use in future projects.

Communities of Practice   A *community of practice* (CoP) is an informal means of learning what works well in environments characterized by open communication and trust. CoPs may be spontaneous and self-organized or sponsored by the organization. In either case, they consist of people with common work interests or needs who are willing to share experiences and expertise with co-workers. These groups benefit individuals by enhancing skills, satisfaction, and productivity; benefit the work group with increased trust and learning opportunities; and benefit the organization with improvements in sales, improved product development, reduced time-to-market lead times, and, ultimately, improved market share because of improved customer satisfaction.

Technology Solutions   The information technology (IT) group can play a large role in facilitating KM initiatives. As the organization function for communication infrastructure, IT implements database management and other IT tools that encourage knowledge sharing among employees.

Knowledge Management Systems   Some business functions lend themselves to the use of a *knowledge management system (KMS).* These systems support and collect the creation, capture, storage, and dissemination of organizational knowledge and information. The goal of a KMS is to provide employees with easy access to information that has been collected from various sources, verified for accuracy, and organized for retrieval to answer questions or solve problems. An example of an effective KM program with which many people have had some experience is customer relationship management (CRM). Customers often complain about the frustration they experience when calling a customer support or help line and having to repeat all the details of a problem with a product to each new customer service representative (CSR) who comes on the line. An effective KMS has each CSR enter facts about customer problems into a database so that, when the customer calls back, the next CSR to answer the call knows everything that has already transpired between the customer and the company. The customer doesn't need to repeat information, and the CSR can avoid going back to step one in the problem-solving process.

Learning Organizations

Learning organizations are innovative environments in which knowledge is originated, obtained, and freely shared in response to environmental changes that affect the ability of the organization to compete. The atmosphere in a learning organization is one in which employees are able to solve problems by experimenting with new methods that have been observed outside the organization or that have been experienced in other parts of the organization.

Peter Senge, author of *The Fifth Discipline*: *The Art and Practice of the Learning Organization* (Crown Business, revised edition, 2006), identifies five disciplines, or guiding principles, that enable organizations to increase their ability to realize desired results, cultivate new ways of thinking, expand on individual ideas, and encourage continuous lifelong learning in the organization. These disciplines include the following:

Systems Thinking   *Systems thinking* describes the ability of individuals and organizations to recognize patterns and project how changes will impact them.

Personal Mastery   *Personal mastery* describes a high level of expertise in an individual's chosen field and a commitment to lifelong learning.

Mental Models   *Mental models* refer to the deep-seated beliefs that color perceptions and can affect how individuals see the world around them and react to it.

Building a Shared Vision   Stretching beyond the corporate vision statement and building a *shared vision* encourages the organization to plan for a future that inspires commitment on the part of all individuals in the organization.

Team Learning   *Team learning*, as defined by Senge, refers to the ability of a team to share and build on their ideas without holding anything back.

Techno-Structural Interventions

OD interventions that fall into the techno-structural category address issues of how work gets done in the organization by examining the level of employee involvement and redesigning work processes. *Total quality management* (TQM), a process that focuses all resources in the organization on providing value for customers, is an example of a techno-structural intervention, as is Six Sigma. Another intervention that is used in this category is known as a high-involvement organization.

Total Quality Management

TQM is a long-term intervention requiring employees at all levels in an organization to focus on providing products that meet customer needs. A successful TQM implementation requires the commitment of top management to lead the process. Because TQM is focused on customer needs, market research and product development are key components of the system. Processes are reviewed to eliminate wasted time as well as materials that either don't contribute or are obstacles to producing the end product. Teamwork is an essential function in a TQM environment; all members involved in the product or service, from front-line workers to suppliers and sales managers, must work together to solve problems for customers.

There have been a number of leaders in the quality movement; the following are four who have made significant contributions:

W. Edwards Deming   The quality movement originated in the 1940s with the work of W. Edwards Deming, who proposed that quality is defined by the consumer. Deming developed a 14-point plan that placed the burden of quality on management because they're able to control the systems in the organization. Although American business was initially cool to the quality concept, Deming's theories were warmly received in Japan during the 1950s. In 1951, the Japanese named their quality award the Deming Prize, after him.

Joseph M. Juran   Another early proponent of the quality movement was Joseph M. Juran, who, like Deming, believed that quality begins with defining customer needs. Unlike Deming, Juran proposed that once customer needs were identified, they should be translated into the "language" of the business in order to deliver a product or service that met the needs of both customers and the business. He developed the Juran Trilogy, which identified three phases in the process: quality planning, quality control, and quality improvements. *Quality planning* initiates programs by addressing quality concerns during the product- or service-development process. *Quality control* ensures conformance to the parameters established in the planning phase during the operations phase. *Quality improvements* are used to continually improve operations and reduce waste.

Dr. Kaoru Ishikawa   Dr. Kaoru Ishikawa made significant contributions to the quality movement. He provided a collection of analytical tools to use in the workplace and developed the cause-and-effect diagram that bears his name. The following list explains some of these tools and provides examples:

Check Sheet   *Check sheets* are the simplest analysis tools, requiring only a list of items that might be expected to occur. In an HR setting, a check sheet might be used to keep track of the reasons people resign from their positions. Figure 5.1 is an example of a check sheet used for that purpose. When an item occurs, a check or tick mark is placed next to it on the list. The data collected with a check sheet may be graphically represented in a histogram to facilitate analysis.

FIGURE 5.1   Sample check sheet

Reason	Number of Occurrences	Total
Lack of advancement	𝍫𝍫	5
Lack of recognition	𝍫𝍫 𝍫𝍫 ||||	14
Long commute	\\	1
Low pay	\\\\	2
Poor supervision	𝍫𝍫 𝍫𝍫 𝍫𝍫 |	16
		38

Histogram   *Histograms* provide a way of looking at random occurrences to find out whether there is a pattern. Using the data from the previous check sheet, a histogram provides a visual image of the reasons for resignations, as illustrated by Figure 5.2.

FIGURE 5.2   Histogram

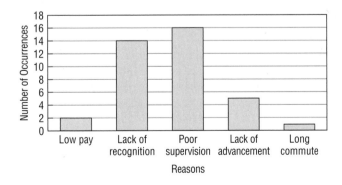

Pareto Chart   The *Pareto chart* provides a graphical representation of the 80/20 rule: 80 percent of the problems are caused by 20 percent of the causes, a principle established by an Italian economist named Vilfredo Pareto. The Pareto chart points out which areas of concern will provide the greatest return when corrected. The difference between a Pareto chart and a histogram is that the Pareto chart arranges the data in descending order and includes a cumulative percentage on the right side of the chart. Figure 5.3 uses the Pareto chart to identify the most significant causes of resignations. In this case, poor supervision and a lack of recognition cause 80 percent of the resignations.

FIGURE 5.3   Pareto chart

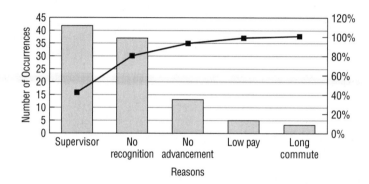

Cause-and-Effect Diagram   A *cause-and-effect diagram* aids in organizing information during brainstorming sessions. This quality-analysis tool is also known as the *Ishikawa diagram* or *fishbone diagram*. Figure 5.4 analyzes what PHR/SPHR candidates can do to maximize their chances for success on the exam.

Stratification   *Stratification charts* show the individual components of a problem in addition to the total or summary. This aids in identifying possible strategies for correcting problems. Figure 5.5 is an example of a stratification chart. In the resignation example, the shorter bars represent components of each category, and the taller bar is the total amount. For example, the poor-supervision reasons could be broken down into categories for poor management skills and the inability to delegate. This kind of chart aids in the development of appropriate programs to solve the individual problems that make up a whole.

Scatter Chart   Also known as an *XY chart*, a *scatter chart* provides a graphical representation for the relationship between two sets of numbers. Information presented on a scatter chart is used for various forms of statistical analysis. Chapter 2 provides more information about data analysis and the concept of correlation.

FIGURE 5.4   Cause-and-effect diagram

FIGURE 5.5   Stratification chart

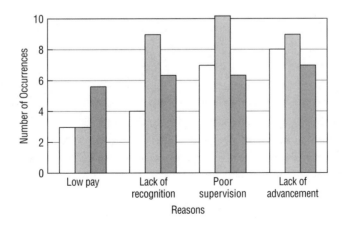

Process-Control Chart   *Process-control charts* provide a graphical representation of elements that are out of the acceptable range by setting parameters above and below the range. This tool is most effective for determining variances in production processes over time. Although this tool is generally used in a production context, to help you understand how it works, let's look at how it could be applied in an HR context. Let's say your department has established that open positions will be filled within 30 days from the date of notification to the HR department, with a 5-day grace period. The sample process-control chart in Figure 5.6 shows you that two positions were out of the normal range: one took less than 25 days, and the other took more than 35 days. Both of these are considered to be "out of control" and warrant investigation to determine what caused the variance.

FIGURE 5.6   Process control chart

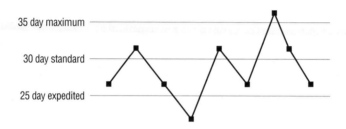

35 day maximum

30 day standard

25 day expedited

Philip B. Crosby   Philip B. Crosby's approach to quality, unlike that of Deming and Juran, focused on management as the key factor. His approach was based on strategic planning as the means to accomplish a high level of quality. Crosby advanced four absolutes of quality:

Conformance to Requirements   Crosby believed that once management clearly described what was required, quality could be determined by whether the product met the standard.

Prevention   "Do it right the first time" is a phrase Crosby associated with this absolute.

Performance Standards   *Zero defects* is another term Crosby came up with to describe the quality standard that should be met.

Measurement   In Crosby's view, quality should be measured by the additional cost of not producing zero-defect products the first time.

Although TQM originated in manufacturing environments, its concepts translate easily to service and other industries. For example, a public accounting firm can establish standards and then develop checklists and templates for accountants to follow when providing client services. By emphasizing the importance of accuracy and measuring how many corrections must be made, the firm can quantify the work of its accountants to ensure that it's up to the standards the company established.

Six Sigma

Six Sigma is a quality philosophy developed by engineers at Motorola during the 1980s, when they were looking for a more precise way to measure process defects. The Six Sigma quality standard is measured on a "defects per million" basis unlike previous standards measured on a "defects per thousand" basis. The Six Sigma methodology is referred to as DMAIC: Define, Measure, Analyze, Improve, and Control:

Define   The first step is to define the customer and issues of importance to them, along with the process and project parameters.

Measure   Once the process is defined, data about defects and other measures is collected and then compared to the original parameters to identify underperformance.

Analyze   An analysis of the data is made to identify gaps between the goal and actual performance, explain why the gaps occurred, and rank possible improvements.

Improve   Based on the analysis, solutions are created and implemented.

Control   During the control phase, systems are revised to incorporate the improvements, and employees are trained in the new processes. The goal of this phase is to prevent backsliding into the previous process by ongoing monitoring.

A significant component of Six Sigma is the quality team structure used to develop, implement, and manage initiatives. In these organizations, employees who are trained and certified in the Six Sigma methodology work full-time on quality initiatives. There are requirements for certification at each level in the structure, including a specific curriculum and requirements for demonstrating effectiveness by working on quality initiatives. In addition, candidates must pass a written test prior to certification. The team structure's levels are as follows:

Quality Leader/Manager   The quality leader in an organization generally reports to the CEO or president in order to remain objective. This role represents customer requirements and focuses on continually improving operations.

Master Black Belt   Master black belts generally work with a single function, such as marketing or accounting. They work closely with process owners to implement the DMAIC methodology and ensure that projects stay on track.

Process Owner   Process owners are individuals responsible for a specific process in the organization; for example, the highest-level HR employee in the organization would be the process leader for HR initiatives.

Black Belt   Black-belt employees work full-time on quality initiatives, coaching green belts to improve their quality skills.

Green Belt   Green belts have received Six Sigma training and participate on project teams part-time while continuing to work in another role for the balance of their time.

High-Involvement Organizations

In *high-involvement organizations* (HIOs), employees are involved in designing their own work processes, are empowered to take the actions necessary to complete their work, and are accountable for the results. HIOs are characterized by broadly defined jobs in flat hierarchies in which continuous feedback is provided and information flows between and among self-directed work teams.

Edward E. Lawler III, founder of the Center for Organizational Effectiveness at the University of Southern California and author of numerous books on organizational effectiveness, identified four elements needed to create an HIO:

Power   Traditional organization structures are built on a "command and control" model in which decisions are made at the top with little or no input from lower levels in the hierarchy. HIOs grant decision-making power down to the employees assigned to carry out the decision and hold them accountable for the results.

Information   "Information is power," and in traditional organizations that often means individuals hold on to information that could be used to improve results instead of sharing it with the individuals who could use it to make improvements. In an HIO, a variety of information (production statistics, sales, expenses, profits, customer feedback, and so on) is disseminated so that everyone can use it to direct their efforts toward improving results.

Knowledge   Increasing the knowledge, skills, and abilities (KSAs) available in the organization enhances the ability of all employees to contribute to bottom-line success. Providing training and development opportunities increases the organization's capability for making decisions and taking actions that improve operating effectiveness.

Rewards   Tying pay to performance compensates employees according to the level of effort they expend to accomplish their goals and objectives and contribute to organizational success. When employees know that their contributions will be recognized, they're encouraged to go "above and beyond" normal job requirements. These rewards can be based on individual or team contributions and are discussed in more detail in Chapter 6, "Compensation and Benefits."

The return on the investment for HIOs is significant. They include higher levels of reported customer satisfaction, reduced turnover, and reduced employee complaints. To view a discussion on the value of engaged employees, watch the panel discussion via Hay Group's video *Fortune World's Most Admired Company* at www.haygroup.com/ww/media/details.aspx?id=27674&c=10.

Human Process Interventions

Human process interventions are directed at developing competencies at the individual level in the organization. Common interventions in this area include team-building activities, conflict resolution, management by objective programs, leadership and management development (discussed later in this chapter), supervisory training (also discussed later in this chapter), and developing an understanding of the impact emotional intelligence has on organizational success.

Team-Building Activities

For a team to function effectively, the members must know the goals they're working toward and what is expected of them as team members. Team-building exercises build relationships in the team to communicate expectations and to involve team members in developing creative and effective ways of accomplishing their goals. Team-building activities run the gamut from expensive events staged by consultants, such as wilderness adventures, to games devised by managers in their individual work groups. The goal of any team-building activity is to put team members in unusual situations that require them to rely on each other to solve a problem. These activities can be fun and effective methods for starting the process, but to be fully effective, the team spirit built or lessons learned must be reinforced when team members are back in the normal routine. The ultimate goal for the organization, of course, is to improve results. Team-building activities can boost productivity by enhancing communication within the group and encouraging collaboration.

Although game-based team-building programs are still used in some organizations, recent research into their effectiveness indicates that the results may not last for the long term. Some organizations have turned to personality inventory models, such as the Myers-Briggs Type Indicator and the Keirsey Temperament Sorter, that help team members understand themselves, provide insight into differences in how others view experiences, and build communication skills. Other team-building methods involve role-playing situations related to actual business problems the team faces and allow team members to work through a collaborative solution together. These experiences can then be drawn on when regular challenges occur back in the real world of work.

Conflict Resolution

Conflict occurs whenever people work together; it can affect relationships between individuals or groups and cover a wide range of intensity levels. *Conflict resolution* is a process of developing strategies for resolving issues and maintaining or rebuilding effective working relationships. These interventions can be conducted by a direct supervisor or manager, an HR professional, or, in some cases, a consultant who specializes in this process. The nature and intensity of the conflict will determine which solution will be most effective in a specific case.

Real World Scenario

Process Council and Facilitators

When organizations get employees involved with team building, leadership, and process improvement, the result can improve organizational processes as well as morale.

One San Francisco Bay Area organization has given the responsibility of process updating and building to the Process Council. Process Council members are specifically chosen for their leadership abilities, experience at the organization, and knowledge of how the organization operates as a whole. When a process issue is identified, the Process Council decides whether a team is needed to tackle the problem. With the help of upper management, the Process Council recommends team members, a team leader, and a facilitator and provides the leader with a charter outlining the council's expectations for the team. The Process Council meets quarterly to discuss process issues, appoint new teams, and discuss teams in progress.

The organization appoints several facilitators to help the Process Council teams meet their goals. Facilitators are chosen for their leadership abilities, their work with various employees across the organization, and their energetic personalities. Facilitators are specifically trained to provide a safe, objective environment in which team members can discuss the process issue at hand without judgment or criticism. Facilitators guide team members by asking pointed questions, politely interrupting "time robbers" (those who talk incessantly with no relevance to the team goal), and keeping members on track to solve the issue in a timely manner.

The Process Council and facilitators have tackled several cross-departmental problems and have even been involved with two reorganizations that occurred as a result of Process Council team decisions. Because facilitators and Process Council members are also employees who will be affected by Process Council results, they have a vested interest in team success. They're also trained to tackle day-to-day problems that may not need a team discussion.

Management by Objectives

A *management by objectives* (MBO) intervention aligns individuals with organization goals and measures the successful attainment of objectives as well as the quality and/or quantity of performance. Because it's an effective way of tying results to goals, MBO is often used as a performance appraisal tool. Its application and acceptance results, at least in part, from its philosophy that rewarding people for what they accomplish is important.

The MBO process is built on the concepts of mutual involvement in setting performance goals, ongoing communication during the performance period (usually one year), measurement, and reward for accomplishments at the end of the period. The process identifies and clarifies expectations and provides for a broad assessment of individual performance. It usually begins in the first quarter of each fiscal year when the supervisor and the employee agree on a few significant business objectives, such as sales volume, new business development, completion of specific projects, or achievement of other specific goals. Utilizing the SMART goal process, described in Chapter 3, will result in goals that clearly communicate what is expected.

The use of an MBO process to tie individual goals to corporate goals and objectives has value but must consider the rapid pace of change in the current business environment and use goals that are broad enough to be meaningful for the entire review period or that allow for revision as business objectives change.

Emotional Intelligence

Emotional intelligence (EI or EQ) describes how people deal with their feelings and how they perceive and interact with others. On an individual level, understanding yourself and why you react to others the way you do increases your ability to work well with others in general. In an organizational setting, individuals who understand how their feelings impact their thought processes can increase their ability to collaborate with co-workers and influence relationships in the organization.

An EQ intervention seeks to improve individual interactions and increase individual effectiveness. Individuals who are able to influence and motivate others are able to move the organization more rapidly toward successful accomplishment of its goals. Although EI isn't particularly necessary in organizations characterized by strictly authoritarian management methods, it's a necessary component for business environments seeking to manage with more facilitative models. EI competencies, although not a substitute for technical expertise, are essential in growing and developing successful organizations.

Human Resource Management Interventions

Human resource management (HRM) interventions focus on individuals in the organization. The following are some examples of these types of interventions:

- Developing hiring and selection procedures that attract people with the KSAs needed by the organization (as discussed in Chapter 4)

- Designing jobs that increase employee satisfaction

- Developing performance-management systems that develop individuals for future needs in the organization

- Developing diversity programs that blend employees from various backgrounds into cohesive work units for the organization

- Developing reward systems (discussed in Chapter 6) that provide incentives for employees who exceed expectations

Whether a strategic, techno-structural, human process, or HRM intervention is the appropriate choice for any particular organization or situation depends on the needs and goals required to achieve results that enable the organization to move forward.

Talent Management

Chapter 2 describes *talent management* as a way of viewing all the activities in those HR functions that attract and retain employees with the skills needed by the organization to move forward in the marketplace. One of the key elements of a talent-management program is development: of employees, managers, leaders, and the high-potential employees being groomed to lead the organization into the future. To effectively develop employees for growth opportunities, organizations need a means of identifying current levels of skill as well as the potential of individual employees. This is accomplished with a process known as *talent assessment*. The ultimate goal of a talent assessment process is to align the organization workforce with *key business initiatives* (KBIs). This includes identifying those employees whose skills and abilities are of particular interest to the organization in achieving KBIs.

Many of the methods used to assess talent for current employees are also used in the selection process covered in Chapter 4. These include personality assessments, aptitude tests, and cognitive ability tests. Assessing current employees can also include other tools such as an *interest assessment* that can be used to retain valuable employees by providing the organization with an understanding of development opportunities that will keep them interested and engaged with the organization. Another useful tool that can be created as part of the assessment process is a *career portfolio*, which gathers information about an individual's education, skills, job-related training, completed development programs, performance appraisals, awards, noteworthy accomplishments, and samples of work. This tool provides the information needed to plan development opportunities, and it helps employees focus on long-term career goals and strategies to achieve those goals. Talent-assessment programs are of particular benefit to organizations that use a staffing strategy of promotion from within and that develop employees to equip them with the KSAs they need to move forward and take on additional responsibilities. Some commonly used development opportunities include the following:

Job Design   One of the factors to consider as part of the job-analysis process described in Chapter 2 is how the tasks, duties, and responsibilities needed by the organization can be combined for use as a development tool. There are two common methods for designing jobs: job enrichment and job enlargement.

Job Enrichment   When an employee shows potential and is interested in growth opportunities, employers use *job enrichment* to assign new responsibilities or tasks that challenge the employee to use existing skills and abilities in new ways or to develop new ones as they tackle new assignments. Beginning with Frederick Herzberg, many social scientists have built behavior models that help incorporate job enrichment activities into job design. This strategy is based on the theory that when certain job factors are present, positive outcomes such as improved attendance, increased productivity, and greater levels of job satisfaction are the result. These job factors include the following:

Skill Variety   The ability of the employee to use multiple skill sets to complete a task.

Task Identity   The concept that the effort applied by the worker produces a whole identifiable unit or outcome, as opposed to a single part.

Task Significance   The inherent or perceived value of a job either internally to co-workers or externally to society.

Autonomy   The degree of independence or discretion allowed on the job.

Feedback   Communication to the employee by management related to how well the employee performs his or her duties.

Job Enlargement   *Job enlargement* is when additional tasks are added to the job without increasing the level of responsibility or skill. Job enlargement may be viewed positively by employees when it reduces job boredom by increasing the variety of tasks assigned. In other cases, employees may view this job design negatively if they perceive they're doing more work without a corresponding increase in pay.

Skills Training   Skills training provides employees with specific information that is needed to do their jobs. In some cases, skills training is job-specific: for example, to teach accounting staff how to use new accounting software, or to provide a software engineer with training in a new language that will be needed to develop a product. Training in soft skills is often used to assist employees; for example, training on meeting management might be provided to reduce the amount of time spent in meetings and make them more productive. Training for communication and time-management skills are other examples of soft skills training. Another type of skills training is provided for employees who are moving into supervisory or management positions for the first time.

Supervisory Training   When the organization is successful in advancing employees, very often they end up in positions with supervisory responsibility. Some organizations make the mistake of assuming that a person who excels in a technical area will automatically be able to supervise employees in that area, but that is rarely the case. Providing training for new supervisors gives them the tools they need to succeed at their new responsibilities.

Supervisory training usually involves topics related to interactions with employees, such as performance management, progressive discipline, performance appraisals, workplace safety, interviewing, and training. New supervisors also benefit from training on topics such as legal requirements for employers (such as exemption status, leave policies, equal employment opportunity [EEO], the Americans with Disabilities Act [ADA], the Family and Medical Leave Act [FMLA], and so on) and policies and procedures specific to the organization. Other topics that help supervisors accomplish more through others include the following:

- Effective management skills
- Conflict management
- Team building
- Influence and negotiation skills
- Communication skills

- Time management
- Interview skills
- Delegation
- Planning
- Motivation skills

Supervisors must understand that different employees are motivated by different approaches and be able to adjust their techniques to encourage each individual to excel.

Career Development   The workforce planning process identifies the skills, knowledge, individuals, and positions that are critical to organizational success. Some of the individuals identified as future organization leaders in this process are known as *high-potential employees* (HiPos) and are provided with extensive training opportunities to prepare them for future roles. Identifying HiPos can be difficult, because future performance can't always be predicted from current performance (as described in *The Peter Principle*, a book written in 1968 by Dr. Lawrence Peter that describes how organizations tend to promote people until they rise to their level of incompetence and leave them in that position). Many of the selection procedures described in Chapter 4 are used to screen candidates for the HiPo track, including assessment centers, behavioral interviews, and observation. In addition, personality inventories such as the Myers-Briggs Type Indicator, the Keirsey Temperament Sorter, and others can be useful in evaluating individuals for a HiPo development program.

The results of these types of assessments highlight the characteristics representative of HiPo performers such as having a capacity to learn and incorporate new ideas and concepts into daily performance, using feedback to improve skills and performance, and having a commitment to continuing career development. Potential HiPos are also able to assess and take risks. These individuals demonstrate a high EQ, understanding how to inspire, influence, and motivate others, qualities that are essential in effective leaders.

Once identified, HiPos receive assignments that challenge their abilities and allow them to take risks. Organizations that create succession plans as part of the workforce planning process factor HiPos into the plan. Very often they're paired with senior-level executive mentors to guide them as they take on assignments with increasing levels of difficulty. Job rotation, which moves HiPos through various divisions, departments, and functions, provides them with a broad view of the organization's needs that will be necessary at the most senior levels.

Mentoring Programs   In a business context, a *mentor* is generally an experienced individual who acts as a teacher, guide, counselor, or facilitator and provides personalized feedback and guidance to a more junior colleague. In many cases, a mentor is someone who takes an interest in an employee's career and acts as a sponsor for them, providing a sounding board for issues and decisions. Traditionally, the mentor relationship is based more on an informal personal interest than on a formal program. *Mentoring programs* formalize this concept and ensure that the benefits of mentoring are available to a diverse group of employees who demonstrate leadership potential.

Formal mentors are those approved by an organization to take on protégés after being screened to ensure that only those who are best suited for mentor relationships enter the program. Mentors in formal programs receive training to develop skills in mentoring, and both mentors and mentees receive training to ensure that everyone understands what to expect from the relationship.

A relatively new feature of mentoring is the *reverse mentor*. These are young individuals who help older co-workers understand technology and the culture of the younger generation.

Executive and Management Coaching   A *coach* is typically a specialist who becomes involved, often at the organization's expense, in developing an employee in a particular area: for example, to hone leadership skills or to improve communication skills. Some coaches can offer guidance in many areas. They differ from mentors in that they focus on skills rather than the employee's career development.

Coaching programs can be tailored to suit many management and executive needs and are especially beneficial to HRD for training management and executives in effectively managing organizational talent. Too often, employees with strong operational skills but very little leadership skill are promoted into management. Yet with the changing workforce and increased demands on employees, the ability to influence others is rapidly becoming a benchmark of effective management techniques. Identifying strengths and weaknesses, discovering latent talent or aptitudes, personal development, and recognizing elements of the job that are most enjoyable to the individual are outcomes from successful coaching methods. Other more technical outcomes of these programs include the analysis of orientation toward learning, EI scores, cognitive processing skills, and measuring levels of motivation.

Non-skill or work-related deficiencies that are unrelated to an employee's skill set can also be addressed through the coaching process. These include issues such as work burnout, career plateaus, lack of personal accountability, and struggles with work/family balance. Coaching is a viable alternative to traditional training that can be quite effective in addressing some of these more difficult influences on management performance.

As with all training design, a needs assessment should first be conducted to evaluate the specific deficiencies to be addressed. Depending on the need, various approaches to coaching can then be applied in an effort to modify and strengthen a leader's ability. The decision of how to deliver the coaching process—internally, externally, or virtually—must then be made:

Internal Sources   Internal sources for coaching and mentoring can be effective for several reasons. Peer-to-peer coaching is useful when the values or behaviors desired are shared within a work group or management tier. For example, some organizations create training initiatives that focus on the achievement of strategic aims such as increasing retention or forecasting growth. Having an internal peer network that can identify with the unique company culture is helpful for managers who are having difficulty achieving specific organizational objectives. Furthermore, assigning a mentor or creating a peer group provides the opportunity for career depth and gives the participant a safe place to brainstorm when the relationships are built on trust and credibility. The facilitator chosen to lead these types of teams or groups should be someone proficient in adult learning styles and who has the ability to address specific company cultural issues such as a highly politicized work group, entrenched employees, or navigating a period of rapid growth or restructuring.

External Sources   External coaching sources are appropriate when the need is for a one-on-one experience or the focus of the coaching is highly technical/psychological in nature. The individual seeking the executive coaching may have a need to hone one or two specific skill sets, and the organizational hierarchy doesn't have an internal source or tools to provide meaningful, real-time feedback and analysis.

Having an objective viewpoint of the manager's knowledge, skills, and abilities in addition to the organizational roadblocks *as perceived by the participant* is often necessary to modify a manager's behavior. Quite often, a perspective change is all that is necessary to get the manager/executive to the next level of performance. Dr. Seuss was once quoted as saying, "Sometimes the questions are complicated and the answers are simple." Furthermore, multiple external resource specialists can be engaged to assess the abilities of the participant in areas such as learning assessments, career aptitudes, or personality tests. They can further be retained to analyze the manager's subordinate group to identify sources of potential conflict or miscommunication. Reaching outside the organization can provide the fresh perspective, personalized attention, and creative problem solving that is at the core of successful coaching programs.

Virtual Coaching   Virtual coaching techniques combine the concepts of self-paced learning with typical coaching outcomes. The mode of delivery varies and can include a combination of email relationships, telephone consulting, videoconferencing, webinars, tests that simulate workplace experiences and measure reactions, discussion boards, and industry-specific forums.

An important element in a coaching relationship is the trust factor, and virtual coaching can fall short of this critical facet. And, as with many other virtual training tools, participant satisfaction rates and successful outcomes can be diminished when there is little to no face-to-face interaction. With this in mind, virtual coaching should be viewed as a tool to augment personalized coaching sessions, not replace them.

Management Development

A *management development* program seeks to upgrade skills for managers who are accountable for achieving results through others. The skills and abilities required for successfully managing people were described previously with regard to supervisory skills training. In addition, management development programs include exposure to financial and technology management, internal controls, and the basic management skills described in Chapter 2. Chapter 2 described the various styles of management in some detail, from the authoritarian Theory X to the opposite participative management styles.

Although formal training can be useful in providing information for managers, one of the best ways to develop them is by assigning a mentor or coach.

Management skills are different from leadership skills. While managers must keep people on track, leaders must inspire; while managers must implement plans, leaders must innovate and set the direction for others to follow.

Leadership Development

Chapter 2 reviewed various leadership theories used to explain how a leader becomes a leader. However that happens, effective leaders are crucial to the success of organizations. They're responsible for inspiring everyone in the organization to achieve the goals they set, and leaders who do this well are rewarded with a motivated and committed workforce. Leaders must be creative individuals who are able to project future needs and aim the organization in a direction that will be successful for the long term. They must be able to inspire trust and confidence and challenge others to put forth their best efforts.

Leaders must also be able to balance the needs of the various constituencies in the organization, from the board of directors who represent the owners, to the management team that is responsible for implementing organizational goals, to the employees who are on the front line of the organization working with customers to achieve the goals.

A *leadership development* program seeks out employees who show promise as potential leaders. Leadership development programs can be a combination of classroom training in specific areas, sponsorship of an advanced degree program such as an MBA, and hands-on training with a mentor or coach. It may mean experience- or exposure-based development such as time spent in company operations outside the country, in different divisions within the country, or on a cross-functional team. Leaders who are exposed to multiple facets of the organization are better able to understand the various needs and challenges of these areas and thus are more effective in the leadership role.

Individuals often reach leadership positions based on their success in their business function, such as an outstanding sales record or significant technical accomplishments. For that reason, not all leaders have developed leadership skills. When the employee has other skills that are essential for success, organizations may implement an *executive coaching program* to assist the employee in developing those skills.

Employee Training Programs

Training is an effective tool for improving productivity and increasing operational efficiency, but it isn't the answer to every organizational problem. Training can solve problems related to employee skills or knowledge about a specific process, but it can't solve problems caused by structural or system issues. Before developing a training program, it's important to find out what is causing the problem and whether training is the appropriate solution.

For example, if customer service representatives are expected to handle an average of 20 calls per hour and they're handling an average of 12, it's important to find out why. One possibility is that the CSRs aren't familiar enough with the products to answer the questions easily, so they must look up answers in a manual. Another possibility is that the call volume has tripled since the call center phone system was installed and it can no longer handle the load, so it's frequently offline. The first possibility can be resolved with training, but the second can't.

Training may take place at one of the following three levels:

Organizational   *Organizational-level training* may encompass the entire organization or a single division or department. At this level, training is focused on preparing for future needs. Analyzing indicators that suggest a decline in the effectiveness of organizational operations can indicate the need for a training intervention. Some indicators that training is needed could include an increase in the number of accidents, a change in strategic direction, or the addition of a new product line. Metrics indicating a negative trend, such as a decline in employee satisfaction or productivity measures, are indicators that training is needed at this level.

Task   *Task-level training* involves processes performed in a single job category. The need for training at this level may be indicated by low productivity for a single process or poor-quality results.

Individual   *Individual-level training* involves a review of performance by individual employees and can be indicated by poor performance reviews or requests for assistance by the employee.

Although development programs address long-term organizational needs, training programs are designed to address short-term needs. Training activities are more technical in nature and include such topics as new-hire orientation, safety, and skill development, among others. The design and development of training programs follows an instructional design model known as the *ADDIE model*. ADDIE is an acronym that describes the five elements of instructional design:

- Analysis
- Design
- Development
- Implementation
- Evaluation

The ADDIE model is discussed here in the context of training at the task level, but the principles of the model can be used to develop training programs at the organizational or individual levels as well.

Training needs are often identified by managers who notice a problem in their departments and determine that training is needed to correct it. This determination may be based on a drop in the production rate, installation of new machinery or equipment, or the addition of a new line of business. Once the need for training has been identified, a needs assessment determines whether training will solve the problem and, if it will, proposes possible solutions.

Finding a Way to Pay for Training

It can sometimes be difficult to convince senior management of the benefits of training. As with any other HR initiative, it's important to demonstrate how a training program will add value to the bottom line. As part of the Workforce Investment Act (WIA) mentioned in Chapter 4, the federal government funds training programs that are managed by state workforce agencies. Some states use these funds to reimburse training costs to employers who want to hire, retain, or upgrade the skills of employees. In Maine, for example, the governor's initiative reimburses employers who provide technical, on-the-job, or workplace safety training to workers, in addition to higher education, high performance skills, or competitive retooling training programs. Employers must submit a comprehensive application to be approved for participation in the program and maintain accurate, detailed documentation to receive reimbursement. Implementation of a learning management system (discussed in Chapter 2) can simplify the reporting and is an effective use of HR technology.

Analysis

The generic needs assessment process described in Chapter 2 provides the basis for analyzing the need for training. Figure 5.7 demonstrates how the generic needs assessment model is modified for use in assessing training needs. Using the model, the following process will provide the information to determine what type of training is necessary to solve the problem:

1. Identify goal.

    The needs assessment begins by identifying the desired outcome. In the preceding example, the customer service manager determined that the CSRs should handle an average of 20 calls per hour, which is the desired outcome. The desired outcome forms the basis for several other steps in the analysis process, including what data is collected, the identification of instructional goals, and development of solutions.

2. Gather and analyze data.

    Once you know the desired outcome, you can begin to collect relevant information that will be used to determine the cause of the problem. Information may be gathered in a number of ways from a variety of sources:

    Review Documents   Many types of documents can be used to gather information about training needs. These include measures of organizational effectiveness such as production records and records of customer complaints, a review of the human resource succession plan to determine what training is needed to prepare individuals for future needs based on skills inventories and performance-appraisal forms, and an analysis of the organizational climate based on HR metrics such as turnover rates and the results of exit interviews.

FIGURE 5.7   Training needs assessment model

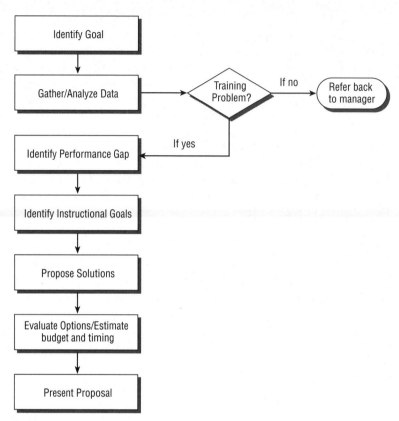

Labor Law Review   Compliance with various labor laws often involves the training of supervisors and workers to the standards. For example, in establishing an affirmative defense against a sexual harassment claim, employers must demonstrate not only that they had a written policy, but that employees and supervisors were properly trained to the requirements. Understanding which labor laws apply to an employer is a necessary component to establishing both short and long term training needs.

Ask Employees   Training often is a function of reaction: reacting to changing market demands, poor performance, or the demands of legal compliance. While all three of those examples are necessary to analyze when assessing training needs, it is also helpful to ask your employees what types of training or development opportunities would be most beneficial. Clearly defining the outcome is necessary in order to ensure the most relevant response from employees. When the data has been gathered and analyzed, a determination can be made as to whether training is the appropriate solution. If it is, the needs analysis continues; if not, HRD can report the results of the analysis to the requesting manager with a recommendation for an appropriate solution.

3. Identify the performance gap.

   Once all the data has been gathered, it's possible to compare where the organization is to where it wants to be. At this stage, the HRD professional begins to have a sense of the type of training that will be required.

4. Identify instructional goals.

   The performance gap is the starting point for identifying the corrections that need to be put into place.

5. Propose solutions.

   At this stage in the needs assessment, all possible means for filling the gap should be identified and considered to find the solution that best meets the organization's needs.

6. Evaluate options, and estimate the budget impact and training timeline.

   Once a comprehensive list of possible solutions is available, it's possible to conduct a cost-benefit analysis (described in Chapter 2) to estimate the cost of implementing each of them and the benefits that will result from the training. It's important to include both direct and indirect costs associated with the program in the estimated budget. This includes the cost of the trainer, facility, preparation of materials, use of equipment, transportation, meals and lodging, wages and salaries of the participants for the time they spend training and in traveling to the training, lost production time due to the training, and incidental office support. It's also important to consider potential savings from increased productivity, reduced errors, higher product quality, and other similar gains that will result from the training and, finally, what it will cost the organization if the training doesn't occur.

   At the same time, an estimate of the time required to implement the solution can be made.

The result of the needs assessment is a proposal that describes the desired outcome, the current situation, and the gap between the two. The proposal should include as many alternative solutions as is feasible, with an estimate of the cost and time needed to implement each of them and HRD's recommended solution.

During the assessment phase, a key consideration is whether the program will be created internally, whether a prepackaged program will be used, or whether the process will be outsourced. These decisions are based on a variety of factors unique to every organization and include the size of the organization, the training expertise and availability of in-house staff, the uniqueness of the subject matter, and the availability of prepackaged programs on the topic. For example, sexual-harassment training may be best conducted by a trainer specializing in the subject matter who is able to answer in-depth legal questions and "what-if" scenarios. Conversely, a training program that is specific to a proprietary manufacturing process may be better developed in-house.

Design

When the appropriate decision-makers concur that training is the appropriate solution for the problem, the design phase begins. During this phase of a training project, the program begins to take shape. The data gathered during the needs analysis phase will be useful in this stage as well:

1. Compile a task inventory.

   To complete the design process, the trainer must know what tasks are required for the job in question. A *task inventory* lists all tasks included in the job. Each task description should contain an action verb, an object, and a function: for example, "Answer phone to assist customers."

   The inventory can be compiled from information collected during the needs-assessment process, or additional information can be acquired during the design phase. The inventory may also be gleaned from a job description if it was written as a result of a job analysis.

2. Identify the target audience.

   Knowing who will be attending the training will be of great use in designing a program that will keep the audience interested. Preparing a training program about the proper completion of expense reports for a group of middle managers from the accounting department will look very different from the same presentation to the sales force.

   In identifying the audience, it's important to keep in mind the three learning styles that impact an individual's ability to learn:

   - *Visual learners* retain information better when they can see or read it.
   - *Auditory learners* retain information more easily when they hear it.
   - *Kinesthetic learners* retain information best when they're able to have a hands-on experience during training.

   Incorporating elements of all three learning styles in a training program helps ensure that all individuals attending the program will benefit from the information presented.

3. Develop training objectives.

   Training objectives are statements that describe a measurable outcome of the training and are developed based on the target audience and task inventory. Objectives help the HRD professional during the development process and during implementation communicate to employees what they will learn. They're also useful during the evaluation phase to determine whether the training was successful.

   A useful training objective is a precise description of what is to be accomplished in normal job circumstances. For example, a training program for carpenters may include a session on how to build straight walls. The objective begins with a description of a normal job situation, uses an action verb to describe a measurable behavior, describes the conditions under which the behavior will occur, and finally describes the criteria that will be used to measure the results. An objective that includes all these elements could be something like this: "Given the necessary materials and tools, build a wall that is perfectly plumb."

   This objective leaves no doubt about what is to be accomplished and includes the basis for determining whether the training was successful.

4. Develop the course content.

   Based on the training objectives, the trainer can begin to design the course, identifying what material should be included to best prepare the attendees to take the information back to their jobs and begin using it immediately.

   An important consideration for this aspect of training design is the learning curve associated with various subjects. A *learning curve* is a graphical representation of the rate of learning over time. Let's look at some examples of various learning curves:

   Negatively Accelerating Learning Curve   A *negatively accelerating learning curve* is characterized by rapid increases in learning at the beginning that taper off as the learner becomes more familiar with the process or task. Negative learning curves are representative of routine tasks, such as operating a cash register. Figure 5.8 provides an example of this learning curve.

FIGURE 5.8   Negatively accelerating learning curve

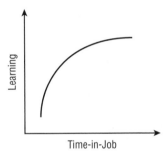

   Positively Accelerating Learning Curve   A *positively accelerating learning curve* is characterized by a slow start in learning that increases as the learner masters different aspects of the process or task. Positive learning curves are representative of tasks that are complex, such as a junior accountant learning to use an accounting software program. The accountant must first know basic accounting practices in order to become proficient in using the program. Figure 5.9 shows a positive learning curve.

FIGURE 5.9   Positively accelerating learning curve

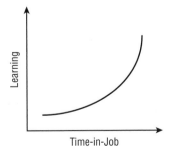

S-Shaped Learning Curve   The *S-shaped learning curve* is a combination of positive and negative learning curves. It begins with a slow learning process that accelerates over time and then slows again. This learning pattern can be found in software-conversion projects. Learners must understand how the new system works before they're able to become as proficient at it as they were with the older system. Figure 5.10 is an example of an S-shaped learning curve.

FIGURE 5.10   S-shaped learning curve

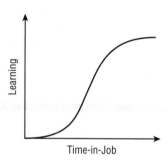

Plateau Learning Curve   A *plateau learning curve* begins with a rapid increase in knowledge that levels off after a period of time, and no additional progress occurs for an extended period of time. A plateau curve might occur when an employee performs a task irregularly, not often enough to become proficient. Figure 5.11 shows a plateau learning curve.

FIGURE 5.11   Plateau learning curve

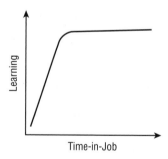

5.   Develop evaluation criteria.

Now is the time to develop the evaluation criteria for the program. The initial evaluation will be based on whether the trainees are able to perform the task described by the objective within the parameters that it sets forth. The real evaluation of training effectiveness is whether the trainees are able to maintain the level of proficiency that was developed during the training and improve operating results.

Development

During the training development phase, the program design is translated into the presentation format. Keeping in mind the characteristics of adult learners described in Chapter 2, the program developer creates a strategy for the presentation, deciding on the materials, instructional techniques, and program-delivery methods that will be used. The trainer may conduct a pilot presentation during this phase to work out the kinks and, if necessary, will revise the program based on the results of the pilot.

Training Materials

One of the activities occurring during the development phase of the training process is the collection of appropriate training materials. It's often tempting to use work created by others, particularly if the material is perfectly suited to the topic of the training. The two federal laws protecting the rights of writers, artists, and inventors with regard to unauthorized use of their original works, the Copyright Act of 1976 and the U.S. Patent Act, are discussed at the beginning of this chapter.

Aside from considerations related to the use of copyrighted material, training materials created in the development phase should be appropriate to the subject matter and the needs of the participants. Some types of materials to consider include the following:

Leader Guide   When more than one trainer will be presenting the training sessions, a leader guide ensures consistency in the presentations. These guides may provide notes to assist the trainer in presenting the material, timing information, and questions for use in facilitating discussion during the session. The guide provides a basic road map for the presentation.

Manuals   Manuals can provide a reference to assist in reinforcing the information covered during the training session when participants return to their jobs. In addition to an agenda or a schedule, they can contain handouts and copies of slides for note-taking purposes as participants follow along during the presentation.

Handouts   Handouts may be used in place of a manual or included with the manual. For presentations that don't require a manual because they're relatively straightforward, a handout can help keep participants focused and provide a place to take notes. In addition, handouts can provide additional information that isn't covered during the presentation but is related to the topic. When the material being covered is technical in nature, a handout can make it easier for participants to follow along and may also be used as a handy reference when employees return to their jobs.

Instructional Methods

There are a variety of instructional methods to choose from when designing a training program, and selecting the appropriate one for a given situation can add to the success of the training:

Passive Training Methods   *Passive training methods* are those in which the learner listens to and absorbs information. These methods are instructor focused and require little or no active participation from the learner:

Lecture   *Lectures* are used to inform and to answer questions, often in combination with other training methods such as demonstrations.

Presentation   A *presentation* provides the same information to a group of people at one time.

Conference   *Conferences* are generally a combination of lecture or presentation with question-and-answer sessions involving the participants.

Active Training Methods   *Active training methods* are those in which the learning experience focuses on the learner:

Facilitation   Facilitation is a moderated learning situation led by a facilitator who leads a group to share ideas and solve problems. Facilitators generally have skills in moderating group discussions and may be experts in the subject of discussion.

Case Study   A *case study* reproduces a realistic situation that provides learners with the opportunity to analyze the circumstances as though they were encountered in the course of business. Case studies let learners investigate, study, and analyze the situation and then discuss possible solutions with the group. Solutions are developed and presented to fellow learners.

Simulation   *Simulation training* is an interactive training method that provides the learner with opportunities to try new skills or practice procedures in a setting that doesn't endanger the inexperienced trainee, co-workers, or the public.

Vestibule   *Vestibule training* is a form of the simulation method. It allows inexperienced workers to become familiar with and gain experience using equipment that either is hazardous or requires a level of speed that can be attained only with practice. Vestibule training is commonly used to train equipment operators in the construction industry and to help retail clerks gain speed at the checkout counter.

Socratic Seminar   Socratic seminars are based on the method of instruction used by the Greek philosopher Socrates in which ideas are examined in a question-and-answer format. A question may be posed by the seminar leader at the beginning of the seminar and discussed by participants to gain a full understanding of the topic.

Experiential Training Methods   *Experiential training methods* provide experience in real-time situations:

Demonstration   The *demonstration* method of training can be used as part of an on-the-job training program or combined with a lecture program. The method involves the trainer explaining the process or operation, demonstrating it on the equipment, and then having the learner perform it under the guidance of the trainer.

One-on-One   In *one-on-one training*, an inexperienced worker is paired with an experienced supervisor or co-worker who uses a variety of techniques to provide the worker with the information and hands-on experience necessary to do the job.

Performance   *Performance-based training* (PBT) is most often used to correct performance problems in highly technical or hazardous professions. The trainee is provided with opportunities to practice and demonstrate the necessary skill or knowledge until the required level of proficiency is mastered.

Program Delivery Mechanisms

Devising suitable delivery methods for training programs is subject to a number of factors, including what information is to be covered, who will be attending the training, the experience level of the participants, the availability of technology, and so on:

Classroom   Classroom training provides the same content to a group of employees in a classroom setting. It's effective for small groups when providing the same information to everyone in the group.

Self-Study   A program of self-study is directed entirely by the learner, who determines what, when, and where learning will occur. It may be based on a defined program and involve a trainer or mentor, but it's controlled by the learner.

Programmed Instruction   *Programmed instruction*, also referred to as *self-paced training*, is the forerunner of computer-based training (CBT). In this method, the learner progresses from lesson to lesson in a predesigned course of instruction as mastery of the objectives is attained. This method allows learners to progress at their own rate. Programmed instruction is effective for disseminating facts and concepts, refreshing previously learned skills, or expanding a learner's knowledge in a field that is already familiar.

Virtual Training (VT)   Deciding whether to conduct training in a classroom setting through the use of virtual tools or use the tried and true on-the-job training (OJT) is one of the first steps taken in training design. In response to the advance of technology and the generational preferences of the emerging workforce, virtual learning is evolving into a viable method for training delivery.

The virtual classroom has grown in importance in many areas, not the least of which has been in the application of training. As one technique in the category of electronic learning (e-learning), virtual classrooms or virtual reality systems are gaining in popularity despite their expense. Other e-learning tools include web-based training (WBT), CBT, self-directed learning (SDL), mobile learning (m-learning), videoconferencing, simulation, multimedia and social networking sites, and discussion boards. These techniques can be *synchronous* (occurring at the same time with the instructor) or *asynchronous* (self-paced), depending on the content, the training goals, and an analysis of training barriers.

E-learning encompasses several types of electronically based training delivery systems that are generally cost-effective, self-directed methods for training employees:

Electronic Performance Support Systems   An electronic performance support system (EPSS) is a training tool integrated in the computer system used by employees on the job. It allows instant access to information that helps them complete tasks more effectively.

Computer-Based Training   *Computer-based training* is an interactive training method that combines elements of the lecture, demonstration, one-on-one, and simulation methods, thus allowing the learner to have a real-world learning experience. Well-designed CBT programs ensure consistency of training across a company that is geographically dispersed. CBT is based on the programmed instruction method.

Distance Learning   Sometimes referred to as a *virtual classroom*, this is similar to lectures and allows simultaneous training to occur in geographically dispersed multiple locations. *Distance learning* provides participants with the ability to communicate with presenters and participants at other locations.

Blended Learning   Blended learning uses multiple delivery methods to enhance the learning experience. The term is currently used to describe different ways of combining delivery methods, such as multiple web-based learning methods, a combination of instructor-led delivery with some form of technology, or combining learning technology with the performance of actual job tasks.

Online Bulletin Boards   Online bulletin boards allow trainees to post questions and share information with each other. They may be supervised or facilitated by a leader who is knowledgeable in the subject matter and acts as a resource for the participants.

One successful example of virtual reality training is the Bus Ride, a VT tool developed by Janssen Pharmaceuticals, Inc. This simulation gave mental health professionals a glimpse into a schizophrenic episode from a patient's perspective. The use of headphones, auditory recordings, and video were developed using years of research and descriptions by psychiatrists and their patients. The goal of this tool was to help practitioners in the diagnosis and treatment of the illness and its symptoms. Other high-profile uses of virtual reality training include military field training, flight simulations, and training for surgeons through the use of highly realistic performance-based training and multisensory learning tools.

According to one report referenced by the American Society for Training and Development, U.S. companies spent $16.7 billion in 2009 on self-paced e-learning. For the human resource professional, this means the ability to demonstrate the return on investment for e-learning initiatives such as VT is a critical stage in the development of strategic training solutions.

Implementation

Implementation is the phase of training where all the preceding work comes together for the presentation. The trainer or facilitator sets up a program schedule, creates the agenda, and notifies participants about the training. At this time, it may be necessary to conduct "train the trainer" sessions to ensure that those who will implement the trainings are themselves fully trained to proceed.

The process begins with selection of the facility and trainers or facilitators:

Facility   The facility selected for the training will depend on the type of training to be conducted, the number of participants attending, and the amount budgeted for the program. Although individual-level training may best be conducted at the employee's workstation, training for larger groups of people is best conducted away from the distractions of the workstation. A conference room at the work site may provide an adequate training facility if the size of the group is small (or the room is large enough). It may be necessary for a variety of reasons to conduct the training offsite. Although the cost will be greater to rent a facility, the reduction of distractions may result in a more effective training experience with longer-lasting results.

The amount of space needed for the training depends largely on what training activities will take place. Passive training that requires little more of participants than listening requires the least amount of space. More space is required for situations in which participants will be taking notes or practicing work activities. Figure 5.12 through Figure 5.17 depict some of the more common seating styles for trainings and the types of training for which each is most appropriate.

FIGURE 5.12   Theater-style seating

Theater-style seating is best for training when lectures, films, or video presentations are used. This seating style accommodates the largest number of people in any space.

FIGURE 5.13   Classroom-style seating

Classroom-style seating is best for training situations when participants will be listening to presentations, using manuals or handouts, and taking notes.

FIGURE 5.14   Banquet-style seating

Banquet-style seating is best for training situations in which participants will be taking part in small group discussions and interacting with each other in addition to participating in activities as a single group.

FIGURE 5.15   Chevron-style seating

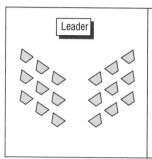

The chevron arrangement is appropriate for training situations in which participants will be interacting with the instructor and each other. This seating style is able to accommodate larger groups than some other seating styles. Useful for situations in which participants will be engaged in several activities: lectures, films, or video presentations, in addition to interacting with others in the room. Chevron-style seating can be used with tables or without, depending on the particular training and space available.

FIGURE 5.16   Conference-style seating

Conference-style seating is used when participants are of equal status and the training is led by a facilitator instead of an instructor. This arrangement provides for maximum interaction between individuals, but is not conducive to the use of visual aids.

FIGURE 5.17   U-shaped-style seating

U-shaped-style seating is an effective seating style for collaborative training situations when presentations and discussions will take place. The center area may be used for additional seating or for role-playing.

Another very important step in preparing the facility is to ensure that the physical environment is conducive to learning. For example, the room temperature should be comfortable for most people, sufficient restroom facilities should be available to accommodate the number of participants, and beverages and/or food should be available as appropriate.

Trainers   Trainers may be selected based on their mastery of the subject matter or for their ability and skill in training. This decision will be based largely on the nature of the training being conducted.

Schedule   The training schedule is affected by many factors, including the feasibility of shutting down operations entirely for the length of the training session so that all employees are trained at the same time or whether it's more cost effective to conduct multiple sessions in order to maintain operations. Sessions may need to be broken into segments and scheduled over a period of days or weeks to accommodate operational needs.

The selection of program-delivery mechanisms and instructional methods for various types of training needs are related to the size of the group, type of training needed, and geographic location of the participants.

Evaluation

Training evaluation occurs both before and after the training takes place and is based on criteria established in the assessment phase. The ultimate goal of the training is to improve performance on the job. This is known as *transfer of training*, and it takes place when learning occurs away from the regular work environment and must then be applied to the real job situation. It's obviously important that the investment made in training employees provides a return in increased productivity, quality, or safety (whatever the subject of the training) on the job. A failure of training to transfer to the job can occur when the new skill isn't applied in the work environment and therefore isn't reinforced. A technique that can overcome this problem is the development of an action plan to be implemented after training. This approach requires trainees to visualize and describe how they plan to apply the training when they're back on the job so they're more likely to use their new skills. An effective evaluation will include provisions for measuring job performance for a period of time after the training has been completed to ensure that the new skills have been transferred to the job.

Formative Evaluation

Formative evaluation is a process used in the design phase of training. It involves testing or previewing the content prior to final delivery to ensure that it will result in the desired behaviors. Designed primarily to elicit feedback from participants, it's a useful tool when used to modify design elements and content prior to the actual delivery. Formative evaluations are designed to identify what the participants want, know, and need. Examples of strategies used in the formative evaluation process include the following:

Needs Assessment   This is a review of who needs the program, what elements must be addressed, and the best method of delivering the message. Asking potential participants for their wants and needs will help to ensure a program designed toward effective transfer of training.

Asking People   There are many methods for gathering information from people, including observations; interviews with employees, supervisors, or subject matter experts (SMEs);

attitude surveys; questionnaires; focus groups; and advisory committees. See Chapter 2 for more information on these techniques.

Analyzing Jobs   In some cases, it may be necessary to conduct a full job analysis as described in Chapter 2 to determine where training is needed.

Pilot Test   Pilot tests are used once the training design and content have been developed. They involve a focus group of participants used to evaluate the relevance of the content and delivery methods to the stated training objectives, followed up by their feedback and influence on the final delivery.

Pre-Test   A pre-test can be used to measure participant knowledge prior to the design of the training. In addition to content-specific questions, it should also ask for feedback related to "the muddiest point"— the content that seems most unclear to the end user. Other options for testing employee knowledge include assessment centers, knowledge tests to measure what people know, and practical tests to determine whether they're able to apply what they know.

Summative Evaluation

A common model for summative training evaluation was developed by Donald Kirkpatrick. He proposed four levels of evaluation for training programs: reaction, learning, behavior, and results. Measurements at each level are based on the objectives developed during the design phase:

Reaction   The *reaction evaluation method* measures the initial reaction of the participants. This is most commonly determined by a survey completed by participants at the end of the training. Although this level of evaluation doesn't measure the organization impact, it does provide feedback for the trainer in terms of the presentation of the information.

Learning   The *learning evaluation method* uses a test to measure whether the participants learned the information that was presented. Although this level of evaluation provides more information about the effectiveness of the training, it still doesn't provide feedback about the application of the information on the job.

In some cases, learning evaluation uses an experimental design known as the *pretest/posttest comparison*:

1.   A group of employees is selected for training.
2.   The employees are randomly assigned to two different groups.
3.   An identical pretest is administered to both groups of employees.
4.   One group receives the training, also known as a *treatment*.
5.   An identical posttest is administered to both groups of employees.
6.   The results are compared to see whether the training resulted in improved performance.

The pretest/posttest comparison is appropriate when an organization wants to isolate the impact of training on productivity. To make a legitimate comparison, all other factors that could affect performance must be equalized. For example, all employees in the group should have similar KSAs, be using similar equipment, and have access to similar resources. If other factors are dissimilar, it isn't possible to isolate the training impact on performance.

Experimental design evaluation requires three criteria:

- More than one group created for the purpose of the comparison
- A measurable outcome common to both groups
- Random assignment of group members

For any number of reasons, it isn't always possible to satisfy these criteria. In those cases, a quasi-experimental design may be used. The evaluation may be made between two groups with dissimilar backgrounds, a posttest only may be used, or a time-series evaluation (in which several tests are administered over a period of time) may take place.

Behavior   The *behavior evaluation method* measures job performance between six weeks and six months after the training. This follow-up evaluation can be based on observations, interviews, tests, or surveys and tells the trainer whether the new skills were successfully transferred to the job.

Results   The *results evaluation method* provides the feedback most meaningful to the business: did the training have an impact on business results? The measurement compares an objective statement, such as "This training will reduce product defects by 20 percent in 12 months," to the actual product results at the end of the 12-month period to determine its success.

Performance-Management Programs

Performance management is an ongoing process of providing feedback for employees about their performance to develop them into increasingly productive contributors to the organization. A key element of a talent-management program, *performance management* ensures that employees are on the right track for completion of their goals, that individual goals are aligned with organization goals, and that employees receive the support they need to be successful. The performance-management process provides for an employee's professional development in the context of organizational needs.

Effective performance management must be based on an agreement between the manager or supervisor and the employee about what the job requires. This information comes from the organization's strategic plan, the manager's goals and objectives, and the employee's essential job functions as contained in an accurate job description. With these elements, the parties can develop individual goals and objectives and agree on the standards of performance to be used in measuring results.

Meaningful feedback that can be used to improve performance is specific, describing the behavior so the employee is clear about what is being done correctly or incorrectly. For example, instead of saying "Good job," you can tell an employee, "The way you handled

Bob Kent's complaint yesterday was professional and effective. I was impressed with how quickly you were able to calm him down by remaining calm yourself and solving his problem." Feedback should also focus on behaviors, not personal attributes. Telling an employee "You have a bad attitude" is open to interpretation and doesn't help them to see where they need to improve. Instead, say, "Sally, I noticed that you were scowling at your desk this morning, and when Joe asked you a question, you told him to find the manual himself. That isn't an appropriate way to respond to questions. Part of our job is to assist our co-workers in finding the reference materials we maintain." This response provides actionable information for the employee. It's also important for the feedback to be as timely as possible and at least within the same day as the observed behavior.

Corrective feedback should be given privately to avoid embarrassing the employee—the point of feedback is to improve behavior, not to alienate the employee. The employee should also be able to respond, explain, or ask for clarification.

On the other hand, positive feedback given more publicly can motivate the recipient and observers to repeat the positive behavior and receive additional recognition.

Performance management isn't a once-a-year proposition—for maximum effectiveness, it must be an ongoing process that enables a manager to intervene in the early stages if an employee is getting off track.

Performance Appraisal

One important aspect of performance management is the *performance appraisal, performance evaluation,* or *performance review* process. These three terms are used interchangeably to describe the process of reviewing how well employees perform their duties during a specified period of time. The appraisal process has the potential to be a powerful tool for building the important relationship between supervisors and their direct reports.

When used well, appraisals provide a structured means for communication, helping to build working relationships. This structure provides for positive performance feedback, recognition of accomplishments during the review period, honest discussion of areas for improvement, and development opportunities for the future. You can find more information about this in the section "Training Performance Evaluators" later in this chapter.

Another important function of the performance-appraisal process is the documentation it provides for employment decisions—positive or negative. For example, appraisals that document a history of achievement and positive contribution provide the basis for promotion decisions or inclusion in a HiPo development program. Conversely, appraisals that document a history of mediocre or below-average performance are crucial when making adverse employment decisions. Contemporaneous performance documentation can be essential in defending employment actions at either end of the spectrum if challenged by disgruntled employees.

Three factors in the appraisal process are important to understand: the elements included in an appraisal process, the timing of review cycles, and the methods used.

Elements of Performance Appraisal

Several elements should be included as part of an effective annual review:

Supervisor Assessment   The supervisor's assessment begins with a review of the goals and objectives set at the beginning of the review cycle and whether the anticipated results were achieved. The supervisor must then evaluate whether any deficiencies occurred because of inadequate performance by the employee or whether they were the result of circumstances outside the employee's control, such as a change in the organization's direction. The supervisor must then develop a plan to address the discrepancies.

Employee Self-assessment   Because this process is meant to be a two-way conversation, employees should be asked to assess their own performance as part of the appraisal. Giving employees advance notice of the scheduled review meeting allows time for reflection about their past performance as well as goals they may have for the future and areas of professional development that are of interest to them.

Assessment from Others   It's important for supervisors to obtain feedback from those with whom the employee has contact each day to find out whether there are areas of concern or outstanding performance about which the supervisor may not be aware. When this is part of the formal review process, it's known as a 360° review and includes feedback from co-workers, internal and external customers, vendors, and subordinates.

Goal Setting   A key component of the review is planning for the future using changes to the strategic plan and the supervisor's goals and objectives to help plan the employee's goals. It's important for employees to participate in the setting of their own goals to facilitate their commitment to achieving them.

Development Goals   As part of the review, supervisors can provide development opportunities for employees to address any areas of deficiency or to prepare them for the next level.

Timing Performance Appraisals

Performance appraisals can be conducted either on employee anniversary dates or during an organization-wide focal review period. In organizations that time reviews to coincide with employee anniversary dates, managers conduct individual reviews throughout the year. The advantage of this process is that there are fewer reviews to conduct at one time; disadvantages occur when awarding salary increases and when using comparative appraisal methods. Managers who don't plan adequately for salary increases or other compensation awards may find that rewards for high performers don't exceed—or, worse, are lower than—what average performers received earlier in the year. It's also difficult to use comparative appraisal methods when appraisals occur on individual employee anniversary dates because the manager will need to consider the performance of employees not up for review at the same time.

During a *focal review period*, all employees in the organization are reviewed at the same time. This is more difficult for managers, as well as for HR, because of the sheer volume of reviews that must be completed. On the other hand, the focal process provides managers with an opportunity to allocate salary increases, equity grants, bonuses, and other rewards in a way that appropriately reflects individual performance levels. Comparative appraisal methods are more easily conducted during a focal review, as well.

Performance-Appraisal Methods

Employee performance appraisal may be based on quantitative data, such as whether specific goals were accomplished, or on more qualitative factors. There is currently much discussion in the HR field about the effectiveness of traditional performance-appraisal processes. Some HR texts suggest that appraisal systems be abolished and replaced with more effective methods of providing feedback and developing employees.

A number of methods have been developed for use in evaluating employee performance; all of them can be placed in one of four basic categories: comparison, rating, essay, and behavioral.

Comparison Methods

Comparison appraisal methods compare the performance of individuals or employees to each other. The most common methods of comparison are ranking, paired comparison, and forced ranking:

Ranking In the *ranking* method, employees are listed in order from the highest to the lowest performer. This method works well for small groups of employees but becomes increasingly difficult as the size of the group increases.

Paired Comparison In the *paired comparison* method, all employees in the group are compared to one employee at a time. For example, if there are three employees in the work group—Susan, Jack, and Rachel—then Susan's performance is compared to Jack's and Rachel's, Jack's performance is compared to Susan's and Rachel's, and finally, Rachel's performance is compared to Susan's and Jack's.

Forced Ranking Also known as *forced distribution* or *forced choice, forced ranking* requires managers to rank employees according to the bell curve, rating a small group of employees at the high end, a small group at the low end, and the bulk of the employees in the average range. This appraisal tool can be used as part of any of the appraisal methods to reduce the effects of the leniency or harshness biases discussed in detail in Chapter 4.

Rating Methods

Common rating methods for performance appraisal include the use of rating scales and checklists:

Rating Scales Rating scales may be numeric, with scales of from 3 to 10 ratings to differentiate levels of performance, or may use phrases such as "exceeds expectations," "meets expectations," or "does not meet expectations." Rating scales attempt to quantify what is a very subjective process, but because of the different ways in which the descriptors are interpreted by raters, these scales aren't as objective as they may appear at first glance.

Checklists   A performance checklist is a list of statements, phrases, or words that describe levels of performance, such as "always finishes work on time." The reviewer checks off those that best describe the employee. The various descriptions may be weighted and used to calculate a rating score.

Narrative Methods

Narrative methods of appraisal require managers to describe the employee's performance. These include critical incident, essay, and field reviews:

Critical Incident   The *critical incident review* process requires that during the review period supervisors make notes of successful and unsuccessful performance issues for each employee. At the time of the review, the supervisor is able to review these critical incidents and present them to employees in a written narrative.

Essay   An *essay review* requires the reviewer to write a short description of each employee's performance during the year. This format provides maximum flexibility for managers to cover areas they see as most important to improving employee performance.

Field Review   A *field review appraisal* may be conducted by someone other than the supervisor. This can be an HR practitioner or someone from outside the organization.

Behavioral Methods

The best-known behavioral review method is the *behaviorally anchored rating scale* (BARS). The BARS method uses the job description to create dimensions that represent the most important requirements of the job. For each dimension, anchor statements are created to represent varying levels of performance behaviors that describe rating numbers on a scale. For example, a job dimension for a receptionist might be greeting customers. Table 5.2 shows the anchors that could be used to measure the behaviors associated with this job dimension.

TABLE 5.2   Sample BARS anchor statements

Rating	Anchor Statement
5	Greets customers warmly and makes them feel welcome
4	Pleasant to customers and answers their questions
3	Courteous to customers
2	Finishes other work before greeting customers
1	Rude to customers when they approach the desk

Regardless of the review method used in an organization, raters should be aware of the various biases that can impact the fairness of a review. It's also important to keep in mind that the same bias and errors described in Chapter 4's discussion of interviewer bias, such as the halo/horn effect, leniency, harshness, and similar-to-me errors, can influence a review. Supervisors should be cognizant of this when preparing the review. When bias is a concern, organizations can use a process known as *inter-rater reliability*, which uses multiple raters to reduce the possibility of rating errors due to bias. The scores of all raters are averaged, with the goal of providing a review that is as free from bias as possible.

Training Performance Evaluators

It's unfortunate that the performance-appraisal process is disliked by so many supervisors and employees, because when well used it provides a structure for building positive, productive working relationships. One of the concerns many employees have about the appraisal process is their perception of its fairness, or lack of fairness. Some employees may think their boss is much tougher than other managers, and some managers have developed reputations for being "easy graders." Those perceptions may never go away entirely, but providing training for those who conduct appraisals will at least ensure that everyone is beginning from the same place. Evaluators should be made aware of the purpose of performance evaluations (it's not just for wage increases), the methods of providing feedback (formal and informal), the behaviors being rated (and how to tell the difference between employees), and the common rater errors such as leniency and bias that can affect the appraisal process (as discussed in Chapter 4).

The training should provide information for activities before, during, and after the actual appraisal meeting.

Before the Meeting

Preparation prior to meeting with employees helps alleviate some of the stress and discomfort that many evaluators feel, particularly when they're new to providing feedback. The goal of the process is to make sure employees know they're valued team members and to motivate them to continue positive performance and improve any areas in which they may be deficient:

- Schedule the meeting for a mutually convenient time, and allow sufficient time for an open conversation. Give the employee advance notice—ideally one week minimum. Don't schedule the meeting for a time when other pressures, such as deadlines or other commitments, will be a distraction.

- Provide the employee with a self-appraisal form or questionnaire to complete prior to the finalizing the evaluation to ensure that the employee's input is considered; at least one day before the meeting, provide the employee with a copy of the completed appraisal. If reviewing multiple employees in the same job category, use the same appraisal criteria for all of them.

- Prepare for the meeting by reviewing the job description, performance standards, goals set during previous appraisals, and the critical-incident log or other notes about specific performance issues (positive and negative) that occurred during the review period.

- Complete the review form using specific, job-related comments to describe positive and negative performance issues. This helps the employee see what to continue doing that is successful, and how to improve other areas as needed.

- Make sure the appraisal is balanced. Keep in mind that few employees are all good or all bad; in most cases, even those with serious performance deficiencies are usually doing some things right, and outstanding performers can improve in some area.

- Whenever possible, use quantitative measurements, such as on-time project completions, missed deadlines, production data, and so on. Describe how the behaviors impacted the organization.

- If improvements are needed in some areas, provide specific information on what is expected from the employee and how feedback will be given. Don't sugarcoat problems—appraisals that neglect to document performance problems make future adverse employment actions difficult and expose the organization to litigation.

- Arrange a private area to conduct the meeting; even if the evaluator has an office, the use of a conference room may be advisable to eliminate interruptions and create a neutral atmosphere conducive to open dialogue.

During the Meeting

Adequate preparation is essential and demonstrates that the supervisor values the employee. It's equally important for evaluators to make full use of that preparation during the meeting. This is an opportunity to communicate about issues that are important to both participants—feedback, expectations, goals, and, in some cases, rewards.

Most employees enter an appraisal meeting wanting to know how they're doing, what the supervisor expects from them, and what their reward for previous performance will be. Some will approach the meeting as though it were a guillotine, while others see it as an opportunity to learn the positive and negative information provided to continue developing their careers.

The evaluator's goal during the meeting is to acknowledge the employee's value to the organization and provide them with constructive feedback to enhance their productivity. Training for evaluators should include the following information:

- Set a tone of mutual respect. It's up to evaluators to ease anxiety by creating an open atmosphere and giving employees their full attention.

- Discuss the appraisal forms that were exchanged prior to the meeting. If there are areas of disagreement, seek to understand the employee's perspective; be willing to revise the appraisal if warranted due to any oversights or misunderstanding of the facts. Don't, however, change an appraisal to avoid confrontation about accurate facts.

- Discuss training options and development needs. Find out what career direction the employee wants to take, and provide realistic guidance about how that may be achieved.

- Set goals for the next review period. Make sure to include the employee in developing the goals instead of merely assigning them. Keep in mind that the goal of the appraisal is to enhance performance; giving employees a voice in setting their goals helps them to feel invested in the outcome.

- Communicate expectations clearly. If attendance or tardiness is an issue, say so flat out—don't leave anything to interpretation.

- Give the employee an opportunity to ask questions about the appraisal, expectations, or goals so that when they leave the meeting they're clear about any next steps.

- Once the appraisal part of the meeting is completed, in many organizations the discussion turns to rewards, whether that is a salary increase, a bonus, a promotion, or another reward.

- Have the employee sign any necessary paperwork required for the appraisal or reward.

After the Meeting

Provide information to supervisors about how to complete the appraisal process. In most cases, this will include submitting paperwork to HR for retention and processing salary changes. In addition, encourage supervisors to make continuous feedback part of their daily interaction with employees. This reduces the level of stress involved in annual appraisals because the feedback becomes a regular part of the daily routine instead of an annual review of what should have been done differently during the year. An appraisal with no surprises is easier on supervisors and their employees.

Training those individuals who conduct appraisals is one way to make the experience, if not pleasant, at least more effective.

Nonsupervisory Evaluators

Evaluators are generally supervisors or managers, but in the case of 360° appraisal systems, co-workers may be asked to provide feedback as well. These evaluators should receive training on the organization's appraisal process and the importance of keeping the feedback related to job activities. They should also be made aware of the biases that can affect the appraisal process.

SPHR ONLY Unique Employee Needs

Employees are people with needs and concerns about areas of their lives other than just work. Although some employers would like to think that what happens outside the workplace doesn't affect performance, sometimes even the best performers may be hindered by personal situations or points of view. To maintain productivity levels and retain otherwise high performers, organizations sometimes find it necessary to provide programs that deal with unique situations. Three common activities in this category include diversity initiatives, flexible work arrangements, and repatriation of global employees.

Real World Scenario

Pitfalls of Diversity Training

When engaging a diversity trainer or designing an in-house program, some trainers use the approach of identifying stereotypes currently held by employees, but this may not be the best solution. Aside from the fact that it can serve to create division instead of bring employees together, there can be legal consequences as well. In the case of *Stender v. Lucky Stores*, a diversity trainer asked employees to describe attitudes or comments attendees had heard in the workplace. These were some of the comments expressed:

- "Women won't work late shifts because their husbands won't let them."

- "Women don't have much drive to get ahead."

- "Women are not the breadwinners."

Members of the HR team were present and took notes during the training.

Sometime later, female employees filed a lawsuit, citing gender discrimination claiming they had been denied promotions because they were women. The court used the notes as "evidence of discriminatory attitudes and stereotyping of women," which led to a settlement in the tens of millions of dollars.

Organizations want to make sure the diversity training they provide accomplishes the intended result—building understanding and teamwork—without creating resentment or division and without providing evidence for discrimination claims. Here are some guidelines to follow:

- Make sure the focus is on positive, respectful, relationship-building information, and eliminate references to past behavior that embarrass members of protected classes.

- Screen trainers prior to engaging them. Check their references, and review presentations and handouts. Make sure they're aware of possible legal issues and are familiar with current company policy.

- Set guidelines to prevent trainers or participants from making comments that will intimidate or embarrass other participants or create a hostile environment.

- Insist that trainers immediately respond to any hostile conduct or comments that occur during the training by clearly discussing why it's inappropriate, what company policy is being violated, and the legal consequences of the behavior.

- If, during the course of the training, participants inform the trainer of ongoing or past situations in the organization, make sure the trainer informs the HR team so that they can conduct a prompt and thorough investigation.

Diversity Initiatives

Discussed in more detail in Chapter 2, diversity programs are designed to ensure that all members of the organization are treated equitably and to facilitate understanding between employees with widely divergent cultural backgrounds. Diversity programs can be used as a human resource management intervention to help individuals feel more connected within the company and promote understanding and tolerance among employees.

Flexible Work Arrangements

The need for employers to consider the impact of family issues on an employee's performance has been increasing in the United States, because of pressure from dual-income families, child-care responsibilities, an aging population, and government regulations. Employers respond to this in different ways. At one end of the spectrum are employers who comply with legal requirements but don't provide any additional leeway for employees who must deal with family issues. At the other end of the spectrum are companies such as SAS, a software company in North Carolina that provides onsite childcare, an eldercare information and referral program, wellness programs, recreation and fitness facilities, and other benefits designed to assist employees in managing the balance between their work and the rest of their lives. These types of programs provide resources for employees so that they're better able to stay focused on work needs while they're at work. Making resources available onsite, or through an Employee Assistance Program (EAP), also reduces the need for employees to take time off to deal with family or other personal needs.

Repatriation

As businesses become more globally oriented, issues of expatriating and repatriating employees will continue to grow. Issues of expatriate training were discussed in Chapter 4, but of equal concern to employees returning from expatriate assignments is how their careers will be impacted after having been away from the home office for an extended period. A comprehensive process for reacquainting repatriates with the home office culture, workgroup processes, and department expectations aids retention of employees returning from assignments in countries where operating procedures differed from the home office.

As with all issues related to employee relations, it's crucial that appropriate expectations be set before employees begin their expatriate assignments, including the issue of what types of assignments will be available to them when they return to the home office. As business conditions at the home office change, the expatriate should be kept advised of any possible changes to the expectations for return assignments. Employees who expect to return to a position of equal or greater authority, responsibility, and pay but find themselves in a position they see as a demotion are understandably demotivated and provide a negative report to their co-workers of their experience, making global assignments less desirable to other employees. Repatriates encountering undesirable assignments on returning to their country of origin may simply resign shortly after returning to their home country, taking the company's investment in their development to another organization that realizes the benefits of their experience. A formal repatriation program that includes a component of career-planning services can assist employees in making the transition back to the home office.

The manager responsible for the repatriate plays a key role in the integration process by reacquainting the repatriate with corporate policies and politics. An effective repatriation-management process includes the following components:

- A one-on-one debrief between the manager and repatriate. This should include an open-door policy to listen to the needs of the repatriate and the repatriate's family throughout the transition, and a discussion about both the employer's and employee's expectations throughout the re-entry process.

- Assistance in managing the transition back to the home country. This includes family relocation needs, locating schools, and, as applicable, job search assistance for the returning spouse/domestic partner.

- Assistance in managing the employee's professional transition. Career planning for employees with international experience is an important step in the repatriation process, and it should begin even before the employee leaves the home country. Clearly defining their role before the assignment and again upon return can aid in retention and ensure the effective transfer of knowledge.

- Effective repatriate knowledge management. Repatriates have a unique skill set that can be used to effectively compete in the increasingly global marketplace. It can also be used to train existing employees on issues related to doing business overseas.

For many companies, repatriation management and career planning are keys to developing global leadership in the long term. Returning expatriates can be a valuable resource for others entering expatriate assignments, and ensuring that the experience is a positive one adds value to the organization. With formal repatriation-management and career-planning strategies in place, companies will more effectively manage assignees' career expectations on repatriation, retain their valuable international experience, and, as a result, maximize the return on investment for both the individual assignee and the organization as a whole.

SPHR ONLY Metrics: Measuring Results

The most important measure for human resource development is how (or whether) an intervention affected business results. For example, if a training program was implemented to improve call center response times, did that occur? If so, was the result immediate, or did improvement occur more slowly as CSRs gained confidence from experience implementing the training?

Business Impact Measures   Metrics that validate the impact of training programs on results are the ones that provide useful information to management. Depending on the situation, some of these metrics may be appropriate:

Production Measures   Metrics that provide measures taken prior to training and several months after training takes place demonstrate how well the program solved the business issue. There are many applications of this for production issues, such as increased speed, number of rejected items, and increased output. A similar measure can be used for other types of training. For example, measuring the number of incidents of sexual harassment prior to training and then again 6 months to 1 year after training occurs demonstrates whether the training was effective.

Return on Investment   As discussed in Chapter 2, ROI is a key measurement for any HR function. Measuring the ROI of HRD programs provides objective information about how they're increasing productivity or providing other benefits to the organization that justifies investing in them.

Tactical Accountability Measures   A number of established metrics are used to measure HR's tactical accountability in HRD. Some of the more common include the following:

Training Cost per Employee   Training cost per employee is calculated by collecting all costs related to training, including design and development, materials, equipment rentals, time spent by HR staff and managers or others who aided in development, participant time to attend the training, facilities, beverages, food, and so on. The total cost is then divided by the number of full-time equivalent employees.

Employee Satisfaction Surveys   Employee satisfaction surveys can provide general information about the effectiveness of HRD programs, such as whether employees are satisfied with the amount and types of training and development provided. This question can be tailored to individual organizations by making it specific with regard to programs provided.

Learning Surveys   Surveying attendees 30, 60, or 90 days after training can provide significant information about how many of the training skills they actually applied in their daily jobs, how impactful such training has been, what was helpful, and what skills were never used.

Global Considerations

Operating in a global marketplace presents unique challenges for the HRD function. Some of these challenges are logistical, such as scheduling the delivery of an organization-wide OD intervention so that all employees have access to the same information as close to simultaneously as possible and that employees are able to hear it in their native languages. Other challenges in an OD context, for example, necessitate presenting business initiatives in a way that is sensitive to the cultures of the different regions and nations in which the organization has facilities. In putting together presentations that will be delivered globally, HRD must keep in mind societal norms that will affect how the presentations are interpreted.

Teamwork in a global organization presents another challenge, although in some ways it's similar to working with virtual teams in the United States. Adding to the inherent possibilities for misunderstandings when the majority of team communication occurs via email is the additional possibility for misinterpretation when this informal communication tool is read from the perspective of different cultural experiences.

Understanding cultural differences is equally important to motivating employees. Specifically, the motivation techniques that work in Western cultures may have little or no meaning for employees in other regions of the world. To motivate employees in different cultures, it's important to first understand the cultural norms and values that are meaningful to those employees. At the same time, the techniques used should meet some common organization requirements.

Summary

Human resource development (HRD) is tied closely to organization development (OD). HRD is more often tied to organizational "software" issues of change management, leadership and management development, and performance management, whereas OD is generally used to address the "hardware" issues of the organization: developing its strategy, technology, and structure.

HRD/OD interventions address organizational challenges with such programs as learning organizations, total quality management, and management by objectives that are designed to align the workforce with the leaders and the organization strategy. These programs must be selected to fit in with the culture and strategy of the organization to be successful.

Talent-management or employee-development programs prepare talented individuals to accept positions of greater responsibility and authority in the organization and aid the retention of individuals who are key to its long-term success.

Training is an important aspect of HRD. The ADDIE model is used to develop training programs that address the needs of the organization and of individuals in the organization.

The continuous feedback provided by effective performance-management programs encourages and assists employees. Ongoing feedback helps to maintain the positive aspects of daily performance and to address areas that need improvement. The performance-appraisal process provides documentation for employment decisions such as promotions and terminations.

Finally, HRD programs that address the unique needs of some employees can be implemented to increase goodwill and attract and retain quality employees.

Exam Essentials

Understand and be able to describe a talent-management program.   Talent-management programs tie together the elements needed to attract and retain key employees. To do this, organizations must assess employees for future growth, develop the skills they will need in the future, and provide opportunities that keep them engaged.

Be able to conduct training-needs analysis.   The needs assessment or analysis first identifies areas in which development is needed and then establishes implementation priorities that are in alignment with KBIs. A training-needs analysis begins with an identification of the goal, the current level of training, and the performance gap. The analysis then identifies instructional goals, proposes solutions, estimates their budget impact, and recommends the preferred solution.

Understand and be able to describe the ADDIE model.   The ADDIE model is an instruction design tool used in creating training programs and stands for Analysis, Design, Development, Implementation, and Evaluation.

Be able to identify the four types of training evaluation.   The four types of evaluation are reaction, which measures immediate feedback; learning, which measures what was learned through testing; behavior, which measures job performance six months or more after training; and results, which measures whether the training had a positive impact on the bottom line.

Understand the difference between performance management and performance appraisal.   Performance management is the process of constantly working with employees to enhance their ability to perform their jobs productively. This begins with understanding job requirements, aligning individual goals to KBIs, and providing regular feedback. Performance appraisal is a structure for documenting individual performance and can contribute to productive relationships between employees and their supervisors.

Understand the connection between change management and OD.   OD *is* change management. It seeks to address issues that prevent organizations from becoming fully effective and introduces interventions to align the workforce with the organization strategy.

Review Questions

You can find the answers in Appendix A.

1. _____ is one of several learning organization characteristics.
   - **A.** An assessment center
   - **B.** Massed practice
   - **C.** Systems thinking
   - **D.** Programmed instruction

2. Which of the following should be included in a supervisory training program?
   - **A.** Conflict-resolution skills
   - **B.** Budgeting
   - **C.** Rotation through various divisions
   - **D.** Internal controls

3. In the evaluation phase, the _____ evaluation method focuses on how well the training resulted in learning new skills and competencies.
   - **A.** Reaction
   - **B.** Learning
   - **C.** Behavior
   - **D.** Results

4. Which of the following factors can adversely affect transfer of training?
   - **A.** The trainer's expertise
   - **B.** A lack of job reinforcement
   - **C.** The subject of the training
   - **D.** None of the above

5. A _____ learning curve begins slowly, with smaller learning increments, but increases in pace and with larger increments as learning continues.
   - **A.** Positively accelerating
   - **B.** Negatively accelerating
   - **C.** S-shaped
   - **D.** Plateau

6. The most common reason for the failure of organizational-change initiatives is which of the following?
   - **A.** The strategic plan was not communicated to employees.
   - **B.** Organization leaders did not support the change.

C. There was no training system in place.

D. Employees were not prepared for the change.

7. The best quality tool to use for gathering information about a specific problem is which of the following?

A. A Pareto chart

B. An Ishikawa diagram

C. A stratification chart

D. A histogram

8. Which employee growth and assessment program is characterized by performance objectives?

A. Behavioral-based performance assessment

B. Skills-based performance assessment

C. Management by objectives (MBO)

D. Continuous-feedback program

9. Which performance appraisal method would be used most effectively in a large, geographically dispersed organization with many similar jobs?

A. Critical incident

B. Forced ranking

C. Behaviorally anchored rating system

D. Field review

10. Mentoring involves which of the following?

A. Someone who monitors an employee's performance in doing their job

B. Someone whose goal is to develop an employee in a particular area

C. Someone who takes a personal interest in an individual's career and who guides and sponsors the individual

D. Someone who provides training in areas of interest to an employee

11. Melissa recently facilitated company-wide diversity training through a series of webinars. Prior to designing the training, she surveyed a sampling of employees to identify their experiences in the organization related to harassment, promotion opportunities, and equitable treatment. This is an example of which of the following?

A. Summative evaluation

B. Knowledge banking

C. Attitude assessment

D. Formative evaluation

12. Wine Cellar Barrels recently became aware of several negative reviews online related to the company's customer service. Management has tasked HR with designing a strategic training initiative to address the interpersonal skills of the call center staff. HR's first step should be which of the following?

    A. Design the training.

    B. Conduct a needs assessment.

    C. Identify training participants.

    D. Schedule the training.

13. Task identity, task significance, and feedback are all examples of what?

    A. Job enrichment

    B. Job enlargement

    C. Key productivity indicators

    D. Performance appraisal criteria

14. Which of the following statements is *most* true about rater bias?

    A. Rater bias exists in all exchanges of performance feedback.

    B. Performance feedback bias is similar to interview bias.

    C. Rater bias nullifies the positive outcomes of providing meaningful performance feedback.

    D. Rater bias is illegal.

15. Participants in a training program are asked to log in to a website at their convenience, watch a video lecture, and take a quiz. This is an example of which of the following types of training?

    A. Vestibule

    B. Mobile learning

    C. Asynchronous

    D. The Delphi technique

16. Which of the following types of evaluations are designed to identify what the participants want, know, and need?

    A. Reaction summaries

    B. Formative evaluations

    C. Summative evaluations

    D. Trainer evaluations

17. People Logistics recently began scheduling offsite meetings for its management team to review the operational realities of implementing elements of the strategic plan. This is an example of which of the following development activities?

A. Peer-to-peer coaching

B. Assigning a mentor

C. Hiring an executive coach

D. Strategic planning

18. Calculate the training cost per employee using the following data: $2,000 for the training design and facilitator; $2,500 for the facility; 20 full-time employees (40 hours per week) and 10 part-time employees (20 hours per week).

A. $150

B. $180

C. $200

D. $300

19. A training session involved asking a group of participants to answer questions related to how Aflac Insurance used a duck to successfully launch its brand. This was an example of which of the following types of training?

A. Vestibule

B. Case study

C. Facilitation

D. Socratic seminar

20. Which of the following is *not* an example of the comparative style of performance review?

A. Ranking

B. Paired

C. Forced

D. Narrative

Chapter

6

Compensation and Benefits

THE HRCI TEST SPECIFICATIONS FROM THE COMPENSATION AND BENEFITS FUNCTIONAL AREA COVERED IN THIS CHAPTER INCLUDE:

✓ Ensure that compensation and benefits programs are compliant with applicable federal laws and regulations.

✓ Develop, implement, and evaluate compensation policies/ programs (for example: pay structures, performance-based pay, internal and external equity).

✓ Manage payroll-related information (for example: new hires, adjustments, terminations).

✓ Manage outsourced compensation and benefits components (for example: payroll vendors, COBRA administration, employee recognition vendors).

✓ Conduct compensation and benefits programs needs assessments (for example: benchmarking, employee surveys, trend analysis).

✓ Develop/select, implement/administer, update and evaluate benefits programs (for example: health and welfare, wellness, retirement, stock purchase).

✓ Communicate and train the workforce in the compensation and benefits programs, policies and processes (for example: self-service technologies).

✓ Develop/select, implement/administer, update, and evaluate an ethically sound executive compensation program (for example: stock options, bonuses, supplemental retirement plans).

✓ Develop, implement/administer and evaluate expatriate and foreign national compensation and benefits programs.

Understanding total rewards programs and their impact on the strategic objectives of an organization is a basic component of human resource (HR) management. For HR professionals, knowledge of federal employment laws governing both aspects of total rewards—compensation and benefits—is essential. It's important to keep in mind that these federal laws and regulations may differ from state and local requirements, so be certain you understand the differences between them for the exams. Table 6.1 summarizes federal legislation that governs employment activities in the compensation and benefits functional area.

TABLE 6.1 Federal legislation governing Compensation and Benefits activities

Type	Enforcement Agency	Chapter Reference
Civil rights	Equal Employment Opportunity Commission (EEOC) and/or Office of Federal Contract Compliance Programs (OFCCP)	4
Compensation	Department of Labor (DOL), Employment Standards Administration	6
Family medical leave	DOL, Employment Standards Administration	6
Health and welfare	DOL, Employee Benefits Security Administration (EBSA); EEOC (older worker benefits)	6
Payroll	Internal Revenue Service (IRS); DOL, Wage and Hour Division	6
Pensions	DOL, Employment Standards Administration; Internal Revenue Service	6

Because this area of human resources is closely tied to the accounting function, understanding accounting practices as they relate to payroll, compensation calculations, and benefit reporting is required. Exam candidates must understand how to develop and implement fair pay practices using job-evaluation methods to price jobs and set pay structures for the organization. HR professionals must also be conversant with executive compensation needs and programs and understand noncash compensation methods.

The *HR Certification Institute PHR/SPHR Body of Knowledge (BOK)* core knowledge requirements that will be particularly helpful in understanding this functional area include the following: needs assessment and analysis, third-party contract negotiation and management, project management, communication skills, HR technology, employee surveys, and basic budgeting concepts. PHR/SPHR candidates should also understand how compensation and benefits programs relate to and affect HR programs in other functional areas.

Finally, with the continuing globalization of business organizations, SPHR candidates need a basic understanding of international compensation and benefit laws as they apply to expatriates, host-country nationals, and third-country nationals, including mandated benefit programs.

For up-to-the-minute updates for this chapter, visit www.sybex.com/go/ phr4e.

Total Rewards Defined

At the broadest level, compensation and benefits, also referred to as *total rewards*, can be described as an exchange of payment from an employer for the services provided by its employees. In today's global economy a competitive total rewards program is vital to attracting, retaining, and motivating employees. In many organizations, compensation and benefits costs are the single largest operating expense and therefore an extremely important component of the human resource program. A total rewards package includes all forms of rewards, which are generally categorized into one of two components: monetary and non-monetary compensation. Let's look now at what goes into each of these components:

Monetary Compensation   Monetary compensation includes any costs the organization incurs for the benefit of employees, such as all forms of cash compensation, 401(k) matching, medical care premiums, pension plans, and paid time off. Other kinds of rewards include benefits that support the organization's culture such as stock options, Employee Stock Ownership Programs (ESOPs), and incentive plans.

Nonmonetary Compensation   It's important to recognize that just as monetary rewards are a critical component of a global total rewards program, so are nonmonetary rewards. This chapter focuses primarily on tangible rewards, but providing an environment that supports intrinsic and extrinsic nonmonetary rewards is a very important part of the total rewards package.

An *intrinsic reward* is one that encourages individual employee self esteem, such as satisfaction from challenging and exciting assignments. An *extrinsic reward* is one in which esteem is achieved from others, such as fulfillment from working with a talented team of peers.

The relationship employees have with their supervisors, recognition of accomplishments, development and career opportunities, and teamwork are a few examples of nonmonetary rewards. Nonmonetary rewards also include nontraditional work-life balance benefits such as telecommuting, on-site childcare, and flex time. The motivational theories discussed in Chapter 2, "Core Knowledge Requirements for HR Professionals," help explain how these nonmonetary rewards can be used effectively in organizations. Theories such as Maslow's hierarchy of needs and McClelland's acquired needs theory help clarify how an individual's drive to achieve nonmonetary rewards such as belonging, esteem, and self-actualization can be impacted with these reward systems.

Other terms used throughout this chapter are direct and indirect compensation:

Direct Compensation   *Direct compensation* includes payments made to employees that are associated with wages and salaries. This includes base pay, variable compensation, and pay for performance.

Indirect Compensation   *Indirect compensation* consists of any employee payments not associated with wages and salaries. This includes fringe benefits such as vacation, sick, and holiday pay; insurance premiums paid on behalf of employees; leaves of absence; 401(k) or other pension plans; and government-mandated benefits such as Social Security or Family and Medical Leave Act (FMLA) and other benefits.

The mix of components included in a total rewards package is unique to the compensation and benefits philosophy, strategic direction, and culture of each organization. Ultimately, the goal of a total rewards package is to maximize the return on investment (ROI) of resources spent on employee rewards.

Compensation and Benefits Philosophy

The *Total Rewards philosophy* is a high-level mission statement used to guide the development and implementation of compensation and benefit programs that attract, motivate, and retain employees. Typically, HR works closely with the executive management team to develop and implement the organization's TR philosophy.

During the development or revision of a TR philosophy, the HR management team facilitates the process by gathering input from and building consensus with key stakeholders such as members of the executive team and, in organizations governed by a board of directors, may involve members of the board's compensation committee in the process as well. Creating a TR philosophy in this way provides an opportunity to look at the whole package offered to employees and analyze which combination of programs will best achieve the organization's hiring and retention objectives. In smaller organizations or new startups that may not take the time to proactively define a TR philosophy, one may develop over time as a result of compensation programs implemented to meet specific needs and decisions made for individual employees. The danger in relying on this type of de facto philosophy in the long term is that it isn't likely to provide a framework that supports organization-wide goals and objectives as the organization grows. Instead, business units may develop total rewards practices designed to satisfy their individual needs but that conflict with programs implemented by other units. Finally, as with any other HR function, the *development* of the program is equally as important as the *evaluation* of the program. Identifying whether the TR philosophy is resulting in the desired outcomes requires a long-term focus and strategy.

The challenge in developing a compensation philosophy comes from balancing the diverse conditions faced by the organization as a whole in a way that is consistent with the organizational culture. These conditions can be split into two categories: internal and external.

Internal Conditions

Internal conditions affect an organization's willingness and ability to pay. In some cases, financial constraints or poor business results prevent an organization from following through with a generous bonus program, for example. Products and services that are cost-sensitive to industry competition, and competing priorities in an organization impact its ability to introduce new rewards programs and maintain existing ones. Another internal consideration with impact on the TR philosophy is how the organizational culture combines with the types of products and services offered by the organization. This combination determines the pecking order for certain positions—and is different in every organization. Consciously or unconsciously, organizations identify the jobs that are the most valuable for achieving their goals and objectives. Differentiating jobs is an important aspect of the TR philosophy. For example, implementing an organization-wide incentive program may not be feasible because of cost considerations. In that case, the organization might choose to include jobs with the highest impact on the organization's success in an incentive program, while jobs with less impact would be ineligible.

Another internal condition that impacts TR philosophy is organizational structure. Organizations that answer to a parent company or corporate headquarters have additional constraints to consider when making total rewards decisions, such as the need to conform to the compensation and benefits philosophy of the parent corporation. The compensation committee of the board of directors for a publicly traded company also has significant input and in many cases must give approval for several types of total rewards programs, including stock option grants, executive compensation in general, pension plans, and so on.

Another condition is the concept of organizational justice in compensation as it relates to the establishment of pay equity. Equity in compensation ensures that what an employee brings to the job (inputs) and what the employee receives (outcomes) are fair and equitable when compared to both the internal factors and external conditions. Examples of inputs are employee knowledge, skills, and abilities; examples of outcomes are base pay, variable pay, and benefits:

Procedural Justice   This is how fair the internal process and procedures in determining pay scales are perceived to be. Considerations include how pay rates are determined, how bonuses are distributed, and who is responsible for making those decisions.

Distributive Justice   This relates to how closely pay reflects actual performance. If, for example, an employee with a high rate of productivity is paid at the same hourly rate as an employee with a lower level of productivity, the perception of the pay system will be that it's unfair.

Pay Openness   This refers to the degree of secrecy that exists around pay issues. In some states, it's illegal to prohibit employees from disclosing their pay rates or amounts of increases. For purposes of internal equity, organizations that allow open conversations about base pay, increases, and pay for performance criteria will have a more positive degree of perceived fairness in the administration of their pay systems. This, of course, assumes that management is able to adequately justify its pay systems to job-related criteria and external market conditions.

External Conditions

The executive team must decide whether the organization's compensation and benefits programs will lead, meet, or lag the market. If the organization's TR philosophy is to lead the market, it will provide compensation and benefit programs above the market rate. If an organization wants (or finds it necessary for financial reasons) to lag the market, its total rewards programs will be below the market rate. If an organization wants to compete at a level equivalent to its competitors, it will meet the average market rate. This strategy is a key element in the organization's TR philosophy because it identifies the equity conditions that must be considered in the development of salary structures, merit budgets, bonus programs, benefit offerings, and other total rewards programs.

Organizational Culture

Organizational culture (discussed in Chapter 7, "Employee and Labor Relations") is rooted in the values and beliefs advocated by an organization's leadership and the ways in which members of the organization behave. It's important that the TR philosophy reflect these values and beliefs to reinforce the culture. The TR philosophy determines whether pay is based on merit/performance (a performance-based culture) or on seniority (an entitlement culture) and how the total compensation package is divided among base salary, variable pay, equity pay, and benefits. To a certain degree, the culture of an organization dictates how the components are allocated in the rewards package:

Performance-Based Philosophy   Organizations with a *performance-based philosophy* use compensation to shape a key component of the corporate culture, employee behavior, by rewarding performance or behavior that moves the organization closer to achieving the goals established by its leaders.

In a performance-based culture, compensation programs use what is known as line of sight. *Line of sight* occurs when employees know that their performance, good or bad, impacts their pay. This provides an increased consciousness for associating behavior with a reward. If employees are aware that their performance impacts their rewards, both monetary and nonmonetary, a high-performance culture can be created.

Entitlement Philosophy   An *entitlement philosophy* rewards seniority or employee longevity. When pay is based on seniority, performance will be secondary to time with the company or time in a particular job. Rewarding seniority creates loyalty to the company; ideally, benefits such as pension plans, stock options, and vacation accrual can reinforce the importance of seniority.

An effective TR philosophy complements the organizational culture, provides rewards for those who contribute to achieving organizational goals, and addresses internal and external conditions.

Compensation Strategy

Most organization leaders have to make choices about how to best use limited resources. A *compensation strategy* is used to determine how the resources available for rewards programs can be used to best advantage in attracting, motivating, and retaining employees. As organizations grow, the compensation strategy can be modified to reflect changing needs. Table 6.2 describes how strategy could change in a growing organization. As sales generate the resources necessary to fund compensation and benefit programs, the strategy evolves to meet the changing needs of the organization.

In the early years, when cash is tight, the organization lags the competition in compensation and benefits; it then meets the competition and adds medical insurance for employees when sales increase. In Year 3, when sales have increased and staffing has doubled, stock options are provided to reward employees while conserving cash. In Year 4, salary increases are possible, and additional benefits are added. Sales slow in Year 5, so a low-cost benefit is added. When the company is acquired in Year 6, all employees receive large cash payouts for their options. In Year 7, the new parent company implements a long-term incentive bonus to retain employees and provides a discount for employee stock purchases.

TABLE 6.2 Evolving total rewards strategies

Phase	Sales	Employees	Total Rewards Strategy
Year 1 (startup)	$750,000	2	Base salaries lag competition.
Year 2	$6,800,000	32	Base salaries meet competition. Add medical insurance.
Year 3	$10,800,000	63	Add stock options for all employees.
Year 4	$18,360,000	70	Salary increases for all employees. Add 401(k). Add dental and vision insurance. Add bonus opportunity for some employees.
Year 5	$20,000,000	70	Add on-site massage therapy.
Year 6	$21,300,000	90	Company acquired—all employees receive cash payouts for options.
Year 7	$28,700,000	90	Stock purchase in parent company at 15 percent discount.

These strategies change attract, motivate, and retain employees who are able to achieve organizational goals and objectives.

Chapter 4, "Workforce Planning and Employment," discussed the importance of an employer brand in attracting and retaining employees, and a compensation and benefits strategy is a key element of the brand. Based on the corporate philosophy, a carefully crafted strategy reinforces the brand. For example, if the brand tells prospective employees that the organization places a high value on teamwork but actually rewards employees for individual contributions, the practice will eventually undermine the teamwork element of the brand.

Budgeting and Accounting for Total Rewards

HR professionals work closely with line managers and finance professionals to build the total rewards budget for the organization. Compensation and benefit budgets are projected during the annual budget process and must consider increases to base salaries as well as adjustments to the salary structure to keep salary ranges competitive with current labor market trends. At this time, budgets are also projected for incentive pay programs and planned promotions. Salary surveys are particularly helpful in forecasting changes to base salaries and salary structure adjustments.

In addition to the information on accounting and budgeting provided in Chapter 2, the TR function has additional requirements, particularly with regard to executive compensation. The Securities and Exchange Commission (SEC) and the Financial Accounting Standards Board (FASB) promulgate rules for financial reporting that affect total rewards decisions.

Executive compensation decisions in particular are subject to reporting and other requirements of the SEC, as are stock options, employee stock ownership plans, and other performance-based executive compensation awards. The SEC requires public companies to fully disclose compensation for the top five executives. In 2007, new rules were issued to provide consistency for investors to use when reviewing and comparing proxy statements. The SEC reports include descriptions of various aspects of the executive compensation program, such as the following:

- Description of compensation objectives
- Existence of employment contracts or severance agreements
- Equity grant practices and awards
- Share ownership guidelines

In addition to the descriptions of compensation philosophy and practices, annual compensation information for the top five executives is reported. This includes information such as the following:

- Cash compensation: base salary and bonuses
- Long-term performance awards
- Deferred compensation
- Executive pensions

Based on the SEC regulations, FASB establishes generally accepted accounting principle (GAAP) standards to be used in preparing financial statements. HR participates in these reporting requirements by maintaining accurate and accessible records. (See the "Executive Compensation" section later in this chapter for more information.)

> You can find additional information about IRS requirements, FASB and its requirements, and the SEC at www.irs.gov, www.fasb.org, and www.sec.gov, respectively.

Fiduciary Responsibility

The dictionary defines *fiduciary responsibility* as one that requires confidence or trust. HR professionals who have responsibility for advising, managing, and/or administering total rewards programs find themselves in a role that requires the confidence and trust of both management and employees to be effective.

In a legal context, a fiduciary relationship has one of the highest, if not the highest, standards of care imposed on the individual acting on behalf of another individual or entity. In the context of compensation and benefits, this most often applies to activities related to pensions and other benefit programs (discussed later in this chapter). Although the legal standard may not be as high in other TR functions, such as establishing salary ranges, recommending salary offers, or establishing merit budgets, these activities require HR professionals to act ethically and with integrity on behalf of their organizations. To establish and maintain a high level of trust and confidence, care must be taken to avoid even the appearance of conflicts or favoritism.

An HR professional could breach this responsibility in three ways:

- *Acting in your own self-interest*—HR professionals must always act in the best interest of the entire organization, not simply their own or their department's interest.

- *Conflicting duties*—In some situations, an HR professional may need to give equal priority to two responsibilities. For example, when placing an HR position into a salary range, responsibility to the HR team may mean placing a new position in a higher salary grade to attract better-qualified candidates. The conflicting responsibility is to ensure the integrity of the salary ranges across the organization as a whole, which could mean paying the position less. Relying on market data to make these and similar decisions can help eliminate such conflicts.

- *Profiting from your HR role*—It may be tempting to take advantage of the unique access to survey and other information HR is privy to, but doing so to ensure personal gain destroys the trust of management and employees in the HR function.

Let's look now at the compensation options available for total rewards packages.

Compensation

Deciding how best to compensate employees for the work they do is based on various factors including internal value (the importance of jobs relative to each other), external value (economic factors, such as supply and demand), and the knowledge, skills, and abilities (KSAs) individual employees demonstrate on the job.

Organizations must be aware of a variety of external factors when developing programs and administering compensation, including economics, the labor market, competition in the product market, and other pressures such as those related to tax and accounting requirements and government legislation and regulations:

Economic Factors The ability of an organization to find qualified employees is affected by a number of economic factors at the local, national, and global levels including economic growth, inflation, interest rates, unemployment, and the comparative cost of living. These factors influence the *cost of labor*, or the cost to attract and retain individuals with the skills needed by the organization to achieve its goals. Organizations recruiting employees with a particular skill set create a competitive environment for individuals with those skills, resulting in an increase in the cost of labor. For example, when two large companies in the same metropolitan area are hiring large numbers of experienced manufacturing technicians, the supply of individuals with this skill set is in demand, and the availability of qualified individuals decreases. This combination of increased demand and decreased availability raises the competitive compensation rate for this skill set, thereby increasing the cost of labor.

With the increasingly competitive global economy, many industries are constantly assessing how to increase quality, accelerate time to market, and improve productivity. This increased intensity has resulted in a creative approach to organizing and redesigning work that, in turn, affects the skill sets needed by the organization and the cost to employ individuals with those skills.

Labor Market Organizations may need to revise their compensation programs to meet the demands of changing labor markets. The *labor market* is made up of any sources from which an organization recruits new employees; a single organization may find itself recruiting from several different labor markets depending on the availability of skills for different positions. Ultimately, the combination of supply and demand for a certain skill set in the labor market impacts what the employers competing for those skills must pay to individuals who possess them. For example, during the unprecedented growth of the late 1990s, intense competition for software-engineering skills led to upwardly spiraling levels of compensation for individuals who possessed those skills. Because the U.S. labor market wasn't producing enough college graduates to meet the demand for qualified candidates, the labor market expanded to include candidates from other countries. This resulted in an increase in the annual immigration quota for the year 2000 to meet the demand of U.S.-based companies for employees with these technical skills.

Labor markets vary by region and industry. In urban areas, there is a greater pool of candidates with a wider set of skills from which to select. Because there are more businesses in urban areas competing for this pool of candidates, urban environments may be more competitive, leading to an increase in the cost of labor. As a result, the cost of labor for a single skill set may vary widely between the areas in which an organization operates. To offset these differences, many companies use regional pay structures to reflect the market conditions of the different areas in which they have business locations. For example, a company that is headquartered in the southeast may have a different pay structure for their regional offices in New York City and in the Silicon Valley in California to reflect the higher cost of labor in those areas.

Over the years, the way people look at pay has changed because of the increased mobility of the workforce, the shift from a manufacturing economy to a knowledge-based economy, and fluctuating economic conditions. During the technology boom of the late 1990s, job hopping and generous compensation packages were prevalent, particularly for individuals with sought-after technological skills. Organizations recruited at a national level and were willing to relocate candidates because the labor market was so competitive. When the technology bubble burst and the unemployment rate increased, organizations were able to recruit for many positions locally, reducing the cost of labor. As the economy improved, competition for talented employees again led to increased labor costs. As this cycle repeats over time, HR professionals must be aware of changing economic factors that impact the labor market and adjust compensation strategies in their organizations to maintain their competitive edge in the labor market.

Product Market Competition   Competitive product markets place financial pressure on an organization and challenge its ability to attract and retain qualified employees. Increased competition creates pressure to do everything faster, better, and cheaper. These added pressures place a strain on the employee population. In a climate epitomized by strong competition between organizations accompanied by a decrease in demand, issues related to the financial health of an organization will likely surface. Some of the repercussions of these pressures for employees can include wage freezes, which may result in skipping a merit-review process, eliminating promotions, and/or not paying incentives. In a strong economy, increased competition can mean growth for the organization because of increasing demand resulting in increased financial rewards for employees. HR professionals must be aware of the implications of changes in the competitive environment to ensure that the programs they propose are in line with these pressures.

Tax and Accounting   Several external factors affect compensation and benefit decisions: in addition to the SEC regulations and the FASB's GAAP standards already described in this chapter, the IRS affects compensation and benefits issues through its enforcement of federal tax legislation, such as Social Security and Medicare taxes, pension regulation, and enforcement of rules about some benefit programs (these will be discussed later in this chapter in the "Benefits" section). When an organization wants to make changes to compensation or benefit programs, it may want to find out how the IRS will view the changes for tax purposes before it makes them. In some situations, it may be beneficial to request a *private letter ruling* from the IRS before the changes are made. These rulings apply only to the specific taxpayer and circumstances included in the request and are used to find out what the tax implications of a complex or unusual financial transaction will be.

Of course, the major government impact on the TR function comes from legislation that regulates pay and benefit practices. Compensation legislation is discussed in the next section. Benefits legislation is discussed later in the chapter.

Federal Employment Legislation

The federal government first began regulating compensation practices during the Great Depression. Initially, legislation affected only those private employers who did business with the government, but a few years later the Fair Labor Standards Act (FLSA) expanded coverage to include virtually all employers in the United States. These laws were designed to protect workers from unfair pay practices and other abuses by employers and are administered by the Wage and Hour Division of the Department of Labor, Employment Standards Administration:

Davis-Bacon Act (1931)   The *Davis-Bacon Act* was the first federal legislation to regulate minimum wages. This act required that construction contractors and their subcontractors pay at least the prevailing wage for the local area in which they're operating if they receive federal funds. Employers with federal construction contracts of $2,000 or more must adhere to the Davis-Bacon Act.

> More information and a link to the full text of the Davis-Bacon Act are available at http://www.dol.gov/WHD/contracts/dbra.htm.

Walsh-Healey Public Contracts Act (1936)   The *Walsh-Healy Public Contracts Act* requires government contractors with contracts exceeding $10,000 (for other than construction work) to pay their employees the prevailing wage for their local area as established by the Secretary of Labor.

> More information and a link to the full text of the Walsh-Healey Act are available at www.dol.gov/compliance/laws/comp-pca.htm.

Service Contract Act (1965)   The McNamara-O'Hara Service Contract Act of 1965 (SCA) requires any federal service contractor with a contract exceeding $2,500 to pay its employees the prevailing wage and fringe benefits for the geographic area in which it operates, provide safe and sanitary working conditions, and notify employees of the minimum allowable wage for each job classification, as well as the equivalent federal employee classification and wage rate for similar jobs.

The SCA expands the requirements of the Davis-Bacon and Walsh-Healey Acts to contractors providing services to the federal government, such as garbage removal, custodial services, food and lodging, and the maintenance and operation of electronic equipment. Federal contractors already subject to the requirements of Davis-Bacon, Walsh-Healey, or laws covering other federal contracts, such as public utility services or transportation of people or freight, are exempt from the SCA.

> More information and a link to the full text of the Service Contract Act are available at www.dol.gov/compliance/laws/comp-sca.htm.

Fair Labor Standards Act (1938)

Enacted in 1938, the FLSA today remains a major influence on basic compensation issues for businesses in the United States. FLSA regulations apply to workers who aren't already covered by another law. For example, railroad and airline employers are subject to wage and hour requirements of the Railway Labor Act, so the FLSA doesn't apply to their employees.

Two categories of employers are subject to the requirements of the FLSA: enterprise and individual. *Enterprise coverage* applies to businesses employing at least two employees with at least $500,000 in annual sales and to hospitals, schools, and government agencies. *Individual coverage* applies to organizations whose daily work involves interstate commerce. The FLSA defines interstate commerce so broadly that it includes those who have regular contact by telephone with out-of-state customers, vendors, or suppliers; on that basis, it covers virtually all employers in the United States.

The FLSA established requirements in five areas relevant to the PHR/SPHR exams:

- It introduced a minimum wage for all covered employees.

- It identified the circumstances in which overtime payments are required and set the overtime rate at one and one half times the regular hourly wage.

- It identified the criteria for determining what jobs are exempt from FLSA requirements.

- It placed limitations on working conditions for children to protect them from exploitation.

- It identified the information employers must keep about employees and related payroll transactions.

Exemption Status

Employers are required to define the pay status of all positions within the organization. This means determining whether the position is exempt from certain components of the FLSA. For example:

- The FLSA covers all employees except those identified in the law as *exempt* from the regulations. All other employees are considered *nonexempt* and must be paid in accordance with FLSA requirements.

- Positions may be exempt from one or all of the FLSA requirements (minimum wage, overtime, or child labor). For example, police officers and firefighters employed by small departments of fewer than five employees are exempt from overtime requirements but not exempt from the minimum wage requirement. On the other hand, newspaper delivery jobs are exempt from the minimum wage, overtime, and child labor requirements. Determining the job responsibilities or duties of a position for purposes of defining exemption status is known as the *duties test*.

- The DOL defines a salary as a regular, predetermined rate of pay for a weekly or less frequent basis (for example, biweekly, semimonthly, monthly, and so on). With the exception of outside sales employees, teachers, practicing attorneys, and medical doctors, employees must be paid a minimum salary of $455 per week, or $23,660 per year, to be classified as exempt. Employees who otherwise qualify for exemption as computer professionals may be paid $455 per week on a salary basis or at an hourly rate of $27.63. This is known as the *salary level test*.

- Finally, the *salary basis test* is used to determine exemption status. It requires that salaried employees receive a predetermined amount of payment on a regularly set schedule, that the employee's compensation cannot be reduced because of the variations in the quantity or quality of work, and the employee must be paid for a full salary for a week in which any work is performed. The employee does not have to be paid for a week in which no work was performed, for example, for a company-wide, week-long furlough.

The determination of exemption status is often misunderstood by both employers and employees. Employers often think that they will save money by designating jobs as exempt and paying incumbent employees a salary. Employees often see the designation of a job as exempt as a measure of status in the company. Neither of these perceptions is accurate, and jobs that don't meet the legal exemption requirements can have costly consequences for employers.

For purposes of the PHR/SPHR exams, candidates should be familiar with exemption requirements for the more commonly used exemptions—those for white-collar jobs (executive, administrative, professional, and outside sales) and computer professionals.

For more information on the definitions of exemptions by the Department of Labor, visit this website: www.dol.gov/whd/regs/compliance/fairpay/fs17a_overview.pdf.

Minimum Wage

The FLSA regulates the federal minimum wage, which is set at $7.25 per hour as of July 24, 2009. Some states, such as Alaska, California, and Massachusetts, have set the minimum wage at a higher rate than the federal government; when this is the case, the state requirement supersedes the federal minimum wage. In other states, such as Arkansas, Georgia, and Minnesota, the state minimum is lower than the federal rate. In those states, the federal minimum wage supersedes state requirements. The DOL provides a useful map showing current minimum wage requirements by state at www.dol.gov/whd/minwage/america.htm.

Nonexempt employees must be paid at least the minimum wage for all *compensable time*. The FLSA defines compensable time as the time an employee works that is "suffered or permitted" by the employer. For example, a nonexempt employee who is permitted to continue to work on an assignment after the end of the business day to finish a project or make corrections must be paid for that time. For this reason, many employers enforce a policy requiring that all overtime must be preauthorized.

Maximum Hours and Overtime

The FLSA defined the maximum work week for nonexempt employees as 40 hours per week and required overtime to be paid for any compensable time that exceeds the maximum. The FLSA defined *overtime* for nonexempt workers as one and one half times the regular hourly wage rate for all compensable time worked that exceeds 40 hours in a work week (also commonly known as *time-and-a-half*).

Although double-time, or two times regular pay, isn't required by the FLSA, it may be required by some states or may be part of a labor agreement. Candidates for the PHR/ SPHR exams must be aware of the difference between the federal requirements that will appear on the test and state requirements and other practices that are more stringent.

While the FLSA doesn't require payment of overtime for exempt employees, it also doesn't prohibit overtime payments for them. Employers who choose to compensate exempt employees for hours worked exceeding the regular work week are free to do so without risking the loss of exemption status. As long as overtime payments are in addition to the regular salary, exemption status isn't affected. Exempt overtime can be paid at straight time, at time-and-a-half, or as a bonus.

Public employers may compensate employees with what is known as *compensatory time off*, or *comp time*, instead of cash payment for overtime worked. For example, a road maintenance worker employed by a city government may work 20 hours of overtime during a snowstorm. Instead of being paid time and a half for the overtime hours, the employee may receive 30 hours of additional paid time off (1.5 times 20 hours) to be used as paid vacation or sick leave. From time to time, initiatives to expand comp time to private employers are presented in Congress, but at this time, the FLSA doesn't permit private employers to use comp time.

Overtime calculations are based on time actually worked during the week. For example, in a week with a paid holiday, full-time nonexempt employees will actually work 32 hours even though they're paid for 40 hours. If some employees then work 6 hours on Saturday, for a total of 38 actual hours worked during the week, those hours are paid at straight time, not time-and-a-half (unless, of course, a state law or union contract requires otherwise). This requirement also applies when employees use paid vacation or sick leave or some other form of paid time off (PTO).

To accurately calculate overtime payments, it's necessary to understand the difference between compensable time—hours that must be paid to nonexempt employees—and noncompensable time. The FLSA defines several situations for which nonexempt employees must be paid, such as the time spent in preparing for or cleaning up after a shift by dressing in or removing protective clothing. Other types of compensable time include the following:

Waiting Time   Time spent by nonexempt employees waiting for work is compensable if it meets the FLSA definition of *engaged to wait*, which means that employees have been asked to wait for an assignment. For example, a marketing director may ask an assistant to wait for the conclusion of a meeting in order to prepare a Microsoft PowerPoint presentation needed for a client meeting early the next morning. If the assistant reads a book while waiting for the meeting to end, that time is still compensable.

Time that is spent by an employee who is *waiting to be engaged* isn't compensable. For example, time spent by an employee who arrives at work 15 minutes early and reads the newspaper until the beginning of a shift isn't considered to be compensable.

On-Call Time   The FLSA doesn't require employees who are on call away from the worksite to be paid for time they spend waiting to be called. These employees may be required to provide the employer with contact information. If, however, the employer places other constraints on the employee's activities, the time could be considered compensable.

Employees who are required to remain at the worksite while waiting for an assignment are entitled to on-call pay. For example, medical interns required to remain at the hospital are entitled to payment for all hours spent at the hospital waiting for patients to arrive.

Rest and Meal Periods   Although rest and meal periods aren't required by the FLSA, if they're provided, that time is subject to its requirements. Commonly referred to as *breaks*, short periods of rest lasting less than 20 minutes are considered compensable time. Meal periods lasting 30 minutes or longer aren't compensable time unless the employee is required to continue working while eating. For example, a receptionist who is required to remain at the desk during lunch to answer the telephone must be paid for that time.

Lectures, Meetings, and Training Programs   Nonexempt employees aren't required to be paid to attend training events when all four of the following conditions are met:

- The event must be outside normal work hours.
- It must be voluntary.
- It may not be job related.
- No other work is performed during the event.

Travel Time   Regular commute time (the time normally spent commuting from home to the regular worksite) isn't compensable. There are, however, some situations in which the FLSA requires that nonexempt employees receive payment for travel time:

Emergency Travel from Home to Work   Any time an employee is required to return to work for a consumer emergency after working a full day, the employee must be compensated for travel time.

One-Day Offsite Assignments   When nonexempt employees are given a one-day assignment at a different location than their regular worksite, any travel time beyond their normal commute is considered compensable.

Travel Between Job Sites   Nonexempt employees (such as plumbers or electricians) who are required to drive to different worksites to perform their regular duties must also be paid for the driving time between worksites.

Travel Away from Home   Travel away from home is defined as travel that keeps employees away from their homes overnight. When nonexempt employees must travel overnight, the FLSA considers the travel time during regular work hours as compensable time. This includes time traveled on nonworkdays (weekends, for example) when it occurs during the employee's regular work hours. The DOL excludes the time spent as a passenger on an airplane, train, boat, bus, or automobile from compensable time calculations.

Real World Scenario

Paid or Unpaid Time?

Geoffrey is a marketing assistant who works for an industrial ceramics manufacturer. The company is introducing an innovative new product at the industry's most significant trade show, and as a result, Geoffrey, who usually provides support from the corporate office only, will be traveling to the trade show to set up the booth and assist the sales team during the show. Geoffrey usually works Monday through Friday from 9 a.m. to 5 p.m. with a one-hour lunch period.

The vendor exhibition hall opens at noon on Monday. But setting up the booth and making sure the video presentation runs flawlessly will take several hours, which means Geoffrey will need to be at the hall by 7 a.m. Monday morning; so, he will arrive at the hotel on Sunday afternoon. There are two options for Geoffrey's travel:

- Option 1: Geoffrey will fly to the trade show, leaving his home at 1:30 p.m. on Sunday, changing planes at an airline hub, and arriving at the trade show hotel around 7 p.m. Sunday evening.

- Option 2: Because there have been some problems with the shipping companies making on-time deliveries of critical sales materials to other trade shows recently, the marketing director is considering asking Geoffrey to drive the company van with the critical materials to ensure everything arrives on time. This would mean an eight-hour drive for him.

Is there any difference in how Geoffrey would be paid for each of these options?

Because Geoffrey would be airline passenger in option 1, he would be paid only for 3-1/2 hours of travel time on Sunday but not for the time between 5 p.m. and 7 p.m. This is because the DOL, as a matter of policy, doesn't consider time traveling as a passenger on an airplane, train, boat, bus, or automobile compensable work time when it occurs outside of normal working hours.

In option 2, Geoffrey would be driving the van, so if all 8 hours took place between 9 a.m. and 5 p.m., he would be compensated for all the hours he was driving. If he decided to leave at noon, he would be paid for 5 hours (from noon to 5 p.m.) but not for the hours between 5 p.m. and his arrival at the hotel.

Salary Deductions   A key element of the new regulations is the definition of permissible deductions for exempt employees that don't affect exemption status. The DOL defines permissible deductions as the following:

- Absence for one or more full days for personal reasons other than sickness or disability

- Absence for one or more full days because of sickness or disability if the deduction is made in accordance with a bona fide plan, policy, or practice of providing compensation for salary lost due to illness

- To offset amounts employees receive for jury or witness fees or military pay

- For good-faith penalties imposed for safety rule infractions of major significance

- Good faith, unpaid disciplinary suspensions of one or more full days for infractions of workplace conduct rules

- During the initial or terminal weeks of employment when employees work less than a full week

- Unpaid leave under the Family and Medical Leave Act

Employers who have an *actual practice* of improper deductions risk the loss of exemption status for all employees in the same job classification, not just for the affected employee. The loss of exemption status will be effective for the time during which the improper deductions were made.

Actual Practice   The DOL looks at a variety of factors to determine whether employers have an actual practice of improper deductions from exempt pay. These factors include the following:

- The number of improper deductions compared to the number of employee infractions warranting deductions

- The time period during which the improper deductions were made

- The number of employees affected

- The geographic location of the affected employees and managers responsible for the deductions

Safe Harbor   The DOL provides a safe-harbor provision for payroll errors that could affect exemption status. The safe harbor applies if all of the following are met:

- There is a clearly communicated policy prohibiting improper deductions that includes a complaint mechanism for employees to use.

- The employer reimburses employees for improper deductions.

- The employer makes a good-faith commitment to comply in the future.

Employers who meet these criteria won't lose exemption status for the affected employees unless they willfully violate the policy by continuing to make improper deductions after receiving employee complaints.

Executive Exemption   Employees who meet the salary-basis requirement may be exempt as executives if they meet all of the following requirements:

- They have as their primary duty managing the organization or a business unit.

- They customarily and regularly direct the work of at least two other full-time employees.
- They have the authority to hire, fire, promote, and evaluate employees or to provide input regarding those actions that carries particular weight.
- Employees who own at least a 20 percent equity interest in the organization and who are actively engaged in management duties are also considered bona fide exempt executives.

Administrative Exemption   Employees who meet the salary-basis requirement may qualify for the administrative exemption if they meet all of the following requirements:

- The primary duty is to perform office work directly related to management or general business operations.
- The primary duty requires discretion and independent judgment on significant matters.

Professional Exemption   The DOL identifies two types of professionals who may qualify for exemption:

Learned Professional Exemption   Employees who meet the salary-basis requirement may qualify for exemption as learned professionals if they also meet all of the following criteria:

- They have advanced knowledge in a field of science or learning acquired through a prolonged course of intellectual instruction.
- The primary duty requires the use of this advanced knowledge for work that requires the consistent use of discretion and judgment.

Creative Professional Exemption   Employees who meet the salary-basis requirement may qualify for exemption as creative professionals if they also meet this criterion:

- The primary duty requires invention, imagination, originality, or talent in a recognized field of artistic or creative endeavor.

In addition to these specific exemption requirements, highly compensated employees (those making $100,000 or more if at least $455 per week of that amount is paid on a salary or fee basis) may also be considered exempt. To meet this exemption requirement, employees must perform office or nonmanual work and, on a customary and regular basis, at least one of the duties listed earlier for the executive, administrative, or professional exemption.

Computer Employee Exemption   Employees who either meet the weekly salary requirement of $455 or are paid an hourly rate of at least $27.63 may qualify for the computer employee exemption if they perform one of the following jobs:

- Computer systems analyst
- Computer programmer
- Software engineer
- Other similarly skilled jobs in the computer field

and if they perform one or more of the following primary duties as part of the job:

- Apply systems-analysis techniques and procedures, including consulting with users, to determine hardware, software, or system functional specifications.
- Design, develop, document, analyze, create, test, or modify computer systems or programs, including prototypes, based on and related to user or system design specifications.
- Design, document, test, create, or modify computer programs related to machine operating systems.
- A combination of the previously described duties, at a level requiring the same skill.

Specifically excluded from this exemption are employees engaged in manufacturing or repairing computer hardware or related equipment and those such as engineers, drafters, or computer-aided designers who rely on computers and software programs to perform their work.

Outside Sales Exemption   Unlike the other white-collar exemptions, there is no salary requirement for outside sales personnel. To qualify for this exemption, employees must meet both of the following requirements:

- The primary duty of the position must be making sales or obtaining orders or contracts for services or for the use of facilities for which a consideration will be paid by the client or customer.
- The employee must be customarily and regularly engaged away from the employer's place of business.

Child Labor

The FLSA states that a child must be at least 16 years old to work in most nonfarm jobs and 18 to work in nonfarm jobs that have been identified as hazardous either in the law or by the Secretary of Labor.

Children 14 and 15 years of age can work in nonfarming, nonmining, and nonhazardous jobs outside of school hours if they work the following hours:

- No more than 3 hours a day or 18 hours in a work week
- No more than 8 hours on a nonschool day or 40 hours in a nonschool work week

During the school year, youths can work between 7 a.m. and 7 p.m. During the summer months, June 1 through Labor Day, the workday can be extended to 9 p.m.

Record Keeping

There are two common methods for reporting time worked: *positive time reporting*, in which employees record the actual hours they're at work along with vacation, sick, or other time off, and *exception reporting*, in which only changes to the regular work schedule are recorded, such as vacation, sick, or personal time. Although the DOL regulations accept either method, in general the positive time method is best for nonexempt employees because it leaves no doubt as to actual hours worked by the employee and protects both the employee and the employer if there is ever a question about overtime payments due. Exception reporting is more appropriate for exempt employees because their pay isn't based on hours worked.

The FLSA doesn't prevent employers from tracking the work time of exempt employees. These records may be used for billing customers, reviewing performance, or for other administrative purposes, but they may not be used to reduce pay based on the quality or quantity of work produced. Reducing the salary invalidates the exemption status and subjects the employee to all requirements of the FLSA.

The FLSA requires the maintenance of accurate records by all employers. The information that must be maintained includes the following:

- Personal information including name, home address, occupation, and sex. Date of birth is also required if the employee is younger than 19 years old.
- The hour and day when the work week begins.
- The total hours worked each workday and each work week.
- The total daily straight-time earnings.
- The regular hourly pay rate for any week including overtime.
- Total overtime pay for the work week.
- Deductions and additions to wages.
- Total wages paid each pay period.
- The pay period dates and payment date.

These FLSA records are usually maintained by the payroll department.

Penalties and Recovery of Back Wages

It isn't uncommon for an employer to make an inadvertent error in calculating employee pay. In most cases when that happens, the employer corrects the error as soon as the employee points it out or the employer catches the error in some other way. Although distressing for employees, employers who make a good-faith effort to rectify the error in a timely manner remain within FLSA requirements.

In other cases, employers intentionally violate FLSA regulations by either paying employees less than the minimum wage, not paying overtime, or misclassifying employees as exempt to avoid overtime costs. These and other employee complaints about wage payments are investigated by state or federal agencies. If the complaints are justified, the employers are required to pay retroactive overtime pay and penalties to the affected employees. The investigation of a complaint by a single employee at an organization can trigger a government audit of the employer's general pay practices and exemption classification of its other employees and may result in additional overtime payments and penalties to other employees if they're found to be misclassified.

Employees whose complaints are verified can recover back wages using one of the four methods the FLSA provides. The least expensive cost to the employer requires payment of the back wages:

- The Wage and Hour Division of the DOL can supervise the payment of back wages.

- The DOL can file a lawsuit for the amount of back wages and liquidated damages equal to the back wages.

- Employees can file private lawsuits to recover the wages, plus an equal amount of liquidated damages, attorney fees, and court costs.

- The DOL can file an injunction preventing an employer from unlawfully withholding minimum-wage and overtime payments.

There is a 2-year statute of limitations for back-pay recovery unless the employer willfully violated the FLSA. In those cases, the statute extends to 3 years. Employers may not terminate or retaliate against employees who file FLSA complaints. Willful violators of the FLSA may face criminal prosecution and be fined up to $10,000; if convicted a second time, the violator may face imprisonment. A civil penalty of up to $1,100 per each violation may be assessed against willful or repeat violators. Employers may also be subject to a civil money penalty (CMP) of up to $11,000 for each employee who is the subject of a child labor violation.

FLSA Amendments

The FLSA has been amended numerous times since 1938, most often to raise the minimum wage to a level consistent with changes in economic conditions.

Two significant federal amendments have been added to the FLSA since 1938, the Portal-to-Portal Act and the Equal Pay Act:

Portal-to-Portal Act (1947)   The Portal-to-Portal Act clarified what was considered to be compensable work time and established that employers aren't required to pay for employee commute time. This act requires employers to pay nonexempt employees who perform regular work duties before or after their regular hours or for working during their lunch period.

Equal Pay Act (EPA) (1963)   The Equal Pay Act, the first antidiscrimination act to protect women, prohibits discrimination on the basis of sex. Equal pay for equal work applies to jobs with similar working conditions, skill, effort, and responsibilities. The EPA applies to employers and employees covered by FLSA and is administered and enforced by the EEOC. The EPA allows differences in pay when they're based on a bona fide seniority system, a merit system, a system that measures quantity or quality of production, or any other system that fairly measures factors other than sex. Prior to the EPA, the comparable-worth standard was used by the U.S. government to make compensation decisions. When Congress passed the EPA, it deliberately rejected the comparable-worth standard in favor of the equal-pay standard.

You can view the text of the EPA at http://www.eeoc.gov/laws/statutes/epa.cfm.

FLSA can be complicated, and compliance is critical to protecting both the organization and the employee population.

Types of Compensation

Compensation comes in many forms. The topic of this section is all forms of direct compensation, from base pay to differentials, variable-pay plans, and other types of special incentives. The backbone of a compensation program is base pay: the salary or hourly wage paid to employees for the work they do.

Base Pay

Whether paid as a salary or as an hourly wage, *base pay* is the amount of compensation that the employer and the employee agree will be paid for the performance of particular job duties. Base pay correlates closely to the company's compensation philosophy because it reflects the internal value of jobs while striving to recognize their external market value.

HR professionals take a variety of factors into consideration when making base-pay determinations: the KSAs employees bring to the job, previous earnings, and internal equity are all part of the decision-making process. Once an employee is hired, changes in base pay may be based on various factors, including performance in the job, seniority, and increased skills.

Base pay is typically evaluated on an annual basis, through a merit- or seniority-based process, discussed in more detail later in this section. When employees take on new roles and responsibilities, base pay can increase through the promotion process. Other changes in base pay can occur as the result of demotions or changes in job duties.

When determining a new hire's base pay, the length and type of previous experience are key factors to consider. Years of experience in a certain profession, a certain industry, or total experience may be relevant to the job. Type of experience may also be relevant to a certain position. How well the new hire will perform in the job is an unknown variable and will be taken into account once the employee begins work.

The company's compensation philosophy drives the type of compensation program that is used. These are categorized as either performance-based or seniority-based programs.

Performance-Based Compensation

Performance-based pay programs, which may include merit increases or promotions, are based on how well individual employees perform against the company's process for measuring performance (as discussed in Chapter 5, "Human Resource Development"). The performance ratings earned by employees determine the eligible range of increase for the review period.

Differentiating pay based on performance means the base salaries of employees in the same classification or salary range may vary from one another. When using a performance-based compensation system, it's important to keep accurate records that justify the reasons for disparity in salaries between employees in the same positions. This documentation will be useful in defending against claims of unfair pay practices should they occur.

Seniority-Based Compensation

Organizations that use *seniority-based compensation* systems make pay decisions based on the length of time employees have been in a position and on years of related experience. A seniority-based compensation system is representative of an entitlement compensation philosophy, discussed earlier in this chapter.

A good example of seniority-based compensation is an organization with a union representing its workers. In a union context, long-term and short-term compensation decisions are the result of negotiations between the union and the employer. Because of this, they aren't necessarily driven by an organization's compensation philosophy. In a union environment, annual increases are typically determined by seniority.

Pay Differentials

Some organizations use pay differentials to encourage employees to perform work that is uncomfortable, out of the ordinary, inconvenient, or hazardous. Pay differentials serve as incentives for employees to work on tough assignments or to be available to respond at inconvenient times. A *pay differential* provides additional pay for work that is considered beyond the minimum requirements of the job. For example, multinational employers who require employees to travel and work in potentially dangerous parts of the world may use hazard pay to make those jobs more attractive to employees.

Examples of pay differentials include overtime, shift pay, on-call pay, call-back pay, reporting pay, hazard pay, and geographic pay.

Overtime

Although the FLSA requires payment only for overtime exceeding 40 hours in a week, some states have overtime laws that exceed federal requirements, and employees are paid at the more generous state rate. Federal law allows employers to require unlimited overtime as long as employees are paid at the required wage rate. It isn't common practice to pay overtime to exempt employees, but doing so isn't prohibited by the FLSA; however, doing so by definition requires employees to keep track of their hours. As discussed previously, requiring exempt employees to keep track of their time isn't prohibited by the FLSA as long as it doesn't result in a reduction of their pay based on the quality or quantity of work produced.

It's important for employers to take a leadership position in managing overtime costs. To prevent abuse, it's ideal for overtime work to be approved in advance. Employers may also want to develop a process or policy when scheduling overtime work for large groups of employees, such as scheduling employees for overtime based on their skill sets, seniority, or shift, depending on the needs of the employer. Overtime is an area that is commonly cut when employers face financial and/or economic challenges.

Shift Pay

The days and hours of a typical work week vary by industry—the most common work schedule is one in which employees work Monday through Friday. A *shift* is any scheduled block of time during the work week when employees perform job-related duties. Shifts have a specific start and end time and are most applicable to nonexempt employees but can also affect exempt employees. There are three commonly recognized shifts: the day shift, with hours from 8 a.m. to 4 p.m.; the evening or *swing shift*, with hours from 4 p.m. to 12 a.m.; and the *graveyard shift*, with hours from 12 a.m. to 8 a.m. Shift work is necessary in industries with 24-hour operations, such as hospitals, airlines, law enforcement, and some manufacturing operations.

In some cases, employers pay more than what is required by the state or federal government for shifts or other time spent at work, such as paying employees for rest or meal periods. Compensating employees in excess of FLSA requirements typically reflects common practice in an industry or market segment. Employers may decide to pay for these items in order to maintain a competitive advantage to more effectively attract, motivate, and retain employees.

A *shift premium* is additional compensation provided for employees who work other than the day shift. Shift premiums may be paid as a percentage of base pay or may be factored into the hourly rate. For example, in high-tech manufacturing, it's common to pay a 10 percent shift premium for shifts that overlap 6 p.m. to midnight and 15 percent for shifts that overlap the midnight to 6 a.m. time period. Although it's most common for nonexempt employees to be paid shift premiums, they may also be paid to exempt employees.

Shift-premium calculations can be a little tricky. Here's an example: Laura works as a nonexempt manufacturing technician at MonoCorp, working an 8-hour shift, 5 days a week, resulting in a 40-hour work week; she makes $10 an hour. Laura also works some hours on the second shift, from 4 p.m. to midnight, Monday through Friday. The second shift at MonoCorp pays a 10 percent shift premium. Table 6.3 illustrates the base pay and overtime costs for Laura's work.

TABLE 6.3 Laura's schedule: hours worked

Day	Shift/Scheduled Hours	Overtime
Monday	8	0
Tuesday	8	2
Wednesday	8	0
Thursday	8	2
Friday	8	2
Total hours worked	40	6

As you can see, Laura worked a full 40-hour week and put in 6 hours of overtime. Table 6.4 illustrates Laura's pay based on her $10/hour salary and her 10 percent shift premium.

TABLE 6.4   Laura's pay schedule

Category	Hours	Pay
Regular	40	$400
Overtime at 1.5 times regular rate	6	$90
Subtotal	46	$490
Shift Premium @ 10 percent		$9
Total		$499

On-call Pay

Although the FLSA establishes minimum requirements for on-call time, employers may decide to provide *on-call pay* that is more generous. Employees who are required to respond to work-related issues on short notice, typically emergencies, and who must be available via pager, telephone, or email, may be paid an hourly or daily premium. In certain professions, being on call is part of the job, and on-call premiums aren't paid.

Call-back Pay

Some companies may provide *call-back pay* to employees who are called to work before or after their scheduled hours. Nonexempt employees who are called into the facility or who work from home are paid their regular rate of pay and any other applicable premiums.

Reporting Pay

When an employee is called into work and there is no work available, the employer may be required by state law or employment agreements to pay for a minimum number of hours of work. This is called a *reporting premium* and ensures the employee receives compensation for showing up for their regular shift or when called to the worksite.

Hazard Pay

Hazard pay is additional pay for dangerous and/or extremely uncomfortable working conditions. Hazard pay may be needed to attract candidates to jobs that require contact with hazardous elements such as radiation, chemicals, or extreme conditions. Firefighters commonly receive hazard pay, because they deal with extreme conditions and physically demanding duties. Examples of other professions that may receive hazard pay include medical positions that work with infectious diseases, police officers, and federal employees who are posted to assignments in countries that are considered dangerous because of wars and/ or active hostilities. Although certain jobs may have risks, they may not provide a hazard pay premium, and their compensation is instead reflective of the labor market. FLSA doesn't require hazard pay, but it does require employers who provide hazard pay to factor it into overtime calculations.

Geographic Pay

Organizations use *geographic pay* to ensure that employees in different locations are paid at rates competitive in the labor market for specific jobs and locations. Geographic structures are put into place to make sure the employees are paid competitively and aligned with the organization's compensation philosophy. It's common to find nonexempt pay structures that vary by city and/or state because of the local cost of labor.

Exempt structures may be adjusted by region to reflect regional labor markets. Having an exempt salary structure specific to the Northeast, Pacific Northwest, or Southeast may be appropriate for some labor markets. As an example, if a manufacturing organization is headquartered in the Silicon Valley in Northern California and has manufacturing plants in San Francisco, St. Louis, and Boston, it would be appropriate to have a salary structure specific to each location.

Variable Compensation

Increasingly, organizations are designing compensation programs that include individual or group incentives as a significant component of the total compensation package. According to several salary surveys, almost two-thirds of U.S. companies include some sort of variable compensation in the pay packages offered to employees. Known as *variable compensation*, *incentive pay*, or *pay for performance*, these programs reward employees for individual and/or organizational results. When aligned with the organization's compensation philosophy, this form of compensation can help shape or change employee behavior or organizational culture by rewarding behaviors that are valued by the organization. An effective variable-pay program motivates employees to achieve business objectives by providing a line of sight between desired performance and the reward.

Another reason incentive pay has become a key component of compensation packages is that the broad spreading of merit dollars may not always reinforce performance. Merit budgets have become smaller, on average, which can make it difficult to provide meaningful rewards that differentiate between levels of performance. Providing meaningful rewards to employees through the merit process, given the average merit budget, requires many employees to be passed over for annual merit increases so the dollars can be spent on top performers.

Once an organization determines the type of employee performance or behavior it wants to encourage, an appropriate incentive plan can be selected. Whether the incentive plan is based on individual or group performance, or on some type of special incentive, depends on the organization's specific needs.

Individual Incentives

Individual incentives reward employees who achieve set goals and objectives and can be powerful tools for motivating individual performance. Incentives are prospective in that they state specific objectives that need to be achieved over designated periods of time and include payout targets stated either as a percentage of base pay or as a flat dollar amount.

Successful incentive-plan programs have three critical phases:

Plan Design　Plan design should be kept simple and should make it as easy and convenient as possible for employees to understand and recall performance goals (for instance, an employee or group needs to increase production by 10 percent or decrease defective parts by 5 percent). Complicated incentive plans tend to create confusion and distrust and may not produce the desired results.

Research on incentive programs has found that a minimum bonus target of 10 percent is required to influence and change behavior. Bonus targets of less than 10 percent of base pay may not provide sufficient motivation for employees to put forward the effort or spend the additional time to achieve the plan objectives and as a result may not produce the desired results.

Review Process   Typically, bonus review and payment corresponds to the end of the organization's fiscal year. In some cases, incentives may be paid more frequently if employees have a direct influence on revenue generation. As with most compensation programs, the *ability to pay* (the company affordability factor) is critical to any incentive program. Many bonus-based incentive programs define desired financial metrics that must be achieved before incentives are paid.

Communication and Implementation   Individual incentive-plan objectives are ideally communicated before or at the beginning of the review period. For example, annual, calendar-based plans are usually communicated in January. Targets for incentive plans are commonly part of an offer package but can be modified as needed. When bonus targets are modified, whether they're increased or decreased, great care should be taken in communicating the rationale. Legal counsel and/or local HR representatives should be involved in making these changes to ensure legal compliance with state and local law, particularly in global environments when modifying bonus targets may require new employment contracts.

Communication of an incentive-plan program is key to ensuring that employees understand the metrics of the plan. As part of a communication strategy, some organizations may choose to create and publish a plan document that describes the incentive program in detail.

Organization or Group Incentives

Organization incentives or *group incentives* have many of the same characteristics as individual incentives. A sure step to a successful organization or group incentive plan is that the plan objectives align with the organization's compensation philosophy. Organization or group incentives are commonly used to increase productivity, foster teamwork, and share financial rewards with employees. Benefits that are common to all group incentives include increased awareness of and commitment to company goals. As the name implies, group incentives aren't used to reward individual performance. There are several types of group incentives, including the following:

Gainsharing   *Gainsharing* programs involve employees and managers in improving the organization's productivity and sharing the benefits of success. The key components of gainsharing include the following:

- Employees and management work together to review organizational performance.

- When measurable improvements are achieved, employees and managers share the success.

- The organization and the employees share the financial gains.

Some of the organizational benefits derived from gainsharing include the following:

- Teamwork, sharing knowledge, and cooperation
- Increased motivation
- Employee focus and commitment to organizational goals
- Greater employee acceptance of new methods, technology, and market changes
- Perceived fairness of pay, which results in increased productivity at all levels

Improshare *Improshare* was developed in the 1970s by Mitchell Fein. It's differentiated from other group incentive plans because a key part of the program is the establishment of a baseline for organization productivity and a baseline for productivity costs. The difference between the baseline productivity and the new output is used to calculate the group's or organization's performance.

Scanlon Plan The *Scanlon Plan* is one of the earliest pay-for-performance plans. In the 1930s, Joseph Scanlon created his plan to increase productivity and decrease costs through employee involvement. Employees receive a portion of cost savings achieved through productivity gains and cost savings. This type of group incentive requires the disclosure of financial information and productivity metrics to employees. Scanlon Plans are administered by committees that are representative of the employee population.

Profit Sharing Very similar to the Scanlon Plan, profit sharing is an incentive-based program that shares company profits. Profit-sharing plans are typically qualified plans found across many industries and available to employees at all levels, from individual contributors to senior management. Profit-sharing plans distribute pretax dollars to eligible employees, typically based on a percentage of an employee's base salary. Distribution of profit-sharing dollars typically occurs annually, after the close of the fiscal year. The set formula for a profit-sharing plan defines individual contributions and distributions. It's typical for the plan to have a vesting schedule, described in the plan document. The document details when and how distributions occur and what happens at milestone events, such as employee termination, leave of absence, death, retirement, and so on. Because most profit-sharing plans are a form of defined-contribution plan, they're covered by regulations of the Employee Retirement Income Security Act (ERISA). Additional information on those requirements is provided in the "Defined-Contribution Plans" section of this chapter.

Employee Stock Ownership Plans (ESOPs) An ESOP is a defined-contribution plan that allows employees to own company stock. An employer sets up a tax-deductible trust that accepts tax-deductible contributions made by the company. Employee eligibility can be based on a formula that may include base salary, length of service, or other factors. At the time of termination, retirement, or death, employees are able to receive the vested portion of their ESOP, which becomes taxable at the time funds are distributed. Additional information is also provided in the "Defined-Contribution Plans" section of this chapter.

Employee Stock Purchase Plans (ESPPs) ESPPs allow employees to use after-tax payroll deductions to purchase company stock at a discounted price. Typically, there is an offering period in which the employee deductions are accumulated until the purchase date, when the money is used to purchase company stock at a discounted rate of up to 15 percent. These types of benefits programs serve a culture of employee ownership, help develop employee loyalty, and can provide a direct line of sight from employee inputs to rewards.

Special Incentives

In some cases, an organization may decide to provide incentive plans to address specific circumstances. For example, as part of an acquisition, the acquiring company may want to make sure specific executives or other key employees from the company being acquired stay with the new organization long enough to ensure a smooth transition. A financial incentive, often referred to as a *retention bonus*, is one way to do this. Retention bonuses are generally structured so that the full bonus is paid if the employee remains with the company through a certain date, but the entire amount is forfeited if the employee leaves before that date. Retention bonuses are also used in situations when an organization is closing its doors. Some employees, such as an accounting manager, will be needed to complete final tasks, and a retention bonus can be used to make sure those employees don't accept new jobs until the necessary tasks are completed.

Special incentive plans can also be included as part of executive compensation packages to reward top executives for achieving established financial goals, such as a percentage of increased sales, a predetermined stock price increase, and other performance goals established by a board of directors.

Commissions and Sales Bonuses

Commissions provide incentives to sales employees by paying them a percentage of the sale price for products and services sold to a customer. Commissions may serve as the entire cash compensation package, or they may be used in combination with a base salary. When sales employees receive a base salary, it's usually a portion of their target cash compensation. The incentive or variable component is intended to drive sales objectives. Compensation for sales employees paid on a commission-only basis must meet at least the minimum wage.

An alternative to a commission plan is a sales bonus plan, in which a percentage of base pay compensates the employee for sales targets achieved. The difference between commission and bonus plans is the method of calculation, and this has many implications for the design of sales compensation programs. For example, Joaquin sells new cars and has an annual quota of 100 cars. For every car Joaquin sells over 100, he receives a bonus of 1 percent of his base salary.

When performance targets are clearly communicated, commissions and bonuses are an excellent way to motivate sales employees to perform desired behaviors and achieve desired results.

Bonus Plans

A *bonus* is additional compensation for performance above and beyond expectations and is paid in addition to an employee's base salary or hourly rate. Unlike incentive plans communicated when an assignment is made and conditional upon successfully completing the assignment, most bonuses are considered discretionary. This means the bonus is optionally offered and isn't based on established objectives. An example of a *bonus plan* is the holiday bonus that some organizations distribute at the end of the year. It's up to the employer to decide whether a bonus will be paid each year, which employees are eligible to participate, and how much each individual receives. Another example is a spot-bonus plan, which provides an immediate reward for outstanding performance, such as an employee who makes sure a critical customer proposal is completed in time to make the delivery cut-off schedule. Bonuses also take the form of a sales-performance bonus paid to sales people who exceed their quotas, employee-referral bonuses paid to employees who refer candidates hired for open positions, patent awards, employee-of-the-month rewards, and so on.

Traditional Pay Structures

Traditional pay programs have existed relatively unchanged for more than 50 years. The way an organization develops pay structures and uses them to administer pay on a day-to-day basis is known as *salary administration*, *compensation administration*, or *pay administration*. Figure 6.1 represents the steps in this process.

FIGURE 6.1 Salary administration

Each step in this process is aligned with the organization's compensation philosophy, and a description of the process may be kept in its policy manual. The first step in salary administration is the job-analysis process described in Chapter 2. As you recall from that discussion, job analysis is the process used to collect information about jobs and create job descriptions. Accurate job descriptions are an essential element of the job-evaluation process.

Compensation administration includes concepts and tools used on a regular basis to manage compensation decisions. These include job evaluation, job pricing, comparable worth, designing a pay structure aligned with organization goals, conducting salary surveys, and salary administration.

Job Evaluation

Job evaluation is the process used traditionally to determine the value of jobs relative to each other in the organization. It's an inexact science that attempts to remove subjectivity from the process as much as possible by replacing opinions and preconceived ideas with more objective criteria. Job evaluations are normally conducted when a job is developed, when the job duties change, or as part of a routine job-evaluation process. HR professionals partner with line management when conducting job evaluations; defined job-evaluation methods allow for a repeatable process for this key component of the compensation system.

Job-evaluation methods identify and define the compensable factors of each job that are most relevant for the organization. *Compensable factors* are characteristics that define and distinguish jobs from one another. For instance, a junior-level engineer's compensable factors might include the following:

- Bachelor's degree in electrical engineering
- Two years of industry-related experience
- Two years of experience testing products for quality and reliability

The two methods discussed in this chapter for job evaluation include the ranking method and classification method. Let's examine each of these in greater detail.

Ranking Method

The *ranking method* requires evaluators to compare the value of jobs to one another. Because this is a subjective method for evaluating jobs, evaluators can be influenced by any preconceptions they may have about different positions or job duties, and this impacts the way in which jobs are ranked. Although ranking is a simple and cost-effective method for use in small organizations, it can become a very complicated process in a complex organization with many positions to evaluate. In this method, it's also difficult to compare unrelated jobs.

Here is an example of the ranking method in action: SkyLine Healthcare uses the ranking method to compare Judy, an administrative assistant, to Leonard, a file clerk. Both Judy and Leonard are administrative-level employees. Judy's job requires higher or more advanced qualifications and experience than Leonard's; therefore, Judy's position is ranked higher than Leonard's.

Classification Method

The *classification method* involves identifying key *benchmark positions*. Benchmark positions are jobs common to organizations regardless of size or industry, such as accountants or administrative assistants. Once a job is matched to a benchmark position, it may be classified according to value on a vertical scale. Benchmark positions are then associated with a grade on a hierarchical salary structure. Positions with similar characteristics are slotted into the same grade or level, which are identified by a similar level of knowledge, skills, and abilities.

To use the classification method, companies must determine *internal equity*, or the value of jobs to each other relative to their value to the organization. There are several ways to measure and assess internal equity, including broadbanding (discussed in the section "Nontraditional Pay Structures" later in this chapter), the point-factor method, and the HAY system:

Point Factor   The *point-factor method* provides organizations with a system of points that are assigned to the position being evaluated. Based on the total number of points a position receives, a pay grade/range is assigned to the position. Each company that uses this complicated method for evaluating jobs may have abstract or very specific factors that broadly fall under five categories: education, skill, effort, responsibility, and working conditions.

HAY System   In 1943, Edward Hay, founder of the Hay Group, a professional services organization and consulting agency, developed the *HAY system*, a classification method that uses a complex point-factor system. Jobs are evaluated using three factors: knowledge, problem solving, and accountability. Using the points from the evaluation, the jobs are matched to a profile.

Job Pricing

Job pricing occurs when a new job is created or an existing job has undergone changes and is a common practice when administering compensation. Many organizations, especially those going through high-growth periods, use job pricing to ensure pay is competitive. A four-step process is used to determine the appropriate pay level for a position:

1. Review the job description, and understand the level and scope of the job and its required responsibilities and skills.

2. Select a salary survey (salary surveys are discussed in the next section). When selecting a salary survey, it's important to consider the type and number of survey participants. For example, if you're pricing a job in Austin, Texas, it may not be appropriate to use data from a salary survey if most of the participants are located in Silicon Valley. Most compensation managers like to see several competitors or other premier employers as part of the survey so the data is perceived as valid.

3. Review compensation components, such as base pay, variable pay, equity pay, and so on. At this time it's also important to review a number of matches for a certain position. The more matches, the better, because the data will be more reliable and less

likely to be skewed by outliers (jobs that are paid significantly above or below the average).

4. Recommend a salary range. The recommendation should be in alignment with your organization's compensation philosophy of leading, matching, or lagging the market. In addition to a salary range, it may be appropriate to recommend incentive pay or special pay programs.

It's important for HR professionals to review job-pricing results with management to validate that the survey positions and data match the job. Once a job is priced, it's appropriate to slot the job into the appropriate pay range and grade.

Salary Surveys

Salary surveys allow organizations to gather compensation and benefits data that reflects current trends in the labor market. Surveys are often provided by professional services vendors or compensation consulting firms. The vendor provides a confidential data-collection process by administering the survey and compiling data into a usable, aggregated format. Salary surveys identify trends in labor costs and are integral in ensuring that compensation and benefits programs continue to attract, retain, and motivate employees. There are different types of salary surveys for an organization to consider; these include the following:

Employee Surveys   Polling the internal workforce is one method companies can use to gauge employee satisfaction with their pay structures, measure perceptions of pay equity, and identify the needs of the current workforce as it relates to compensation and benefit offerings.

Government Surveys   A great source for compensation data is the Bureau of Labor Statistics (BLS), an independent national statistical agency whose mission is to collect, analyze, and distribute statistical data. The BLS is a statistical resource to the DOL as well as a source for salary survey data.

Industry Surveys   For certain jobs, it may be important to consider industry-specific salary surveys for greater validity. For example, the high-tech and hospitality industries are two that provide specific surveys for companies in their sectors.

Commissioned Surveys   Many organizations operate in industries with very specific skill requirements that may be difficult to match in readily available surveys, or they may want to find out how their compensation practices stack up against several specific competitors. This information can sometimes be collected by commissioning a third party to conduct a survey, aggregate the data, and supply the results to the participating organizations. Commissioning a survey can be very costly and time-consuming but may provide the best data for building a competitive salary structure.

An alternative way to collect some of this data is to use an informal process where HR professionals exchange information on pay practices with their counterparts in other organizations. Another informal option is to work with a local/regional HR or compensation association and have the group facilitate the collection of pay practice data from participating members.

When conducting or participating in a salary survey, one of the first decisions to be made is which jobs will be priced in the survey. The most accurate data would be obtained by including all the organization's jobs, but this may not be practical. Generally, including 65 to 70 percent of organization jobs in a survey provides a solid base for use in creating a salary structure.

It's important for HR professionals and employees to keep salary survey data confidential in order to comply with legislative mandates. Over the years, there have been a number of lawsuits against organizations and individuals who shared salary data inappropriately.

Salary Structure Development

A salary structure provides an organized, systematic way of identifying base pay for employees in different jobs throughout the organization. The structure consists of a specified number of salary grades with a range of compensation attached to each. Developing a salary structure requires an analysis of both internal equity and external labor market conditions obtained through the job-pricing process. Jobs are grouped using the data collected during job evaluation and pricing. During the pricing process, job descriptions are matched to comparable benchmark positions that provide a market range for each.

In most cases, the market median or fiftieth percentile is used as the data-comparison point for each job. There may be times when an organization decides to use a higher point of comparison for some jobs (highly skilled positions that are in short supply in the labor market, for example) or for all jobs (if the compensation philosophy is to lead the market). Jobs are grouped according to the data points established by the survey. These groups of jobs with similar market levels provide the basis for determining the number of job grades to include in the structure.

Using the grouped jobs as a starting point, midpoints are established for each job grade. The *midpoint progression*, or difference between the midpoints of consecutive grades, is generally narrower for lower grades and increases for higher grades. Typically, the midpoint progression ranges from 12–15 percent at lower grades to 25 percent at higher grades. Once grades are established, a pay range is developed for each grade.

A *pay range* (also known as a *salary range*) is the spread between the minimum and maximum pay for the job grade. Ranges can be stated as an hourly amount for workers paid on an hourly basis or a monthly, semimonthly, biweekly, or annual amount for salaried workers. The spread of traditional pay ranges is typically narrow and varies depending on level. At entry-level grades, ranges are the narrowest based on the assumption that employees in those grades will gain KSAs and progress to higher job grades. At the highest grades, the spread is quite wide to provide salary progression for highly valued employees who remain in positions for longer periods of time. The spread for entry-level job grades usually begins at 15 percent and can go as high as 25–30 percent for the highest job grades. The spread is calculated based on the midpoint established by the market.

For example, the pay grade for a group of midlevel professional positions might have an 18 percent spread. At a midpoint of $50,000, the minimum would be 82 percent of the midpoint, or $41,000, and the maximum would be 118 percent of the midpoint, or $59,000.

Placing Jobs in Grades

Initially, jobs are placed in pay grades based on the grouping done to develop the grades. If market data was collected only for benchmark positions, the rest of the jobs will need to be placed in the ranges based on internal equity with the benchmark positions. At this point, the placements are reviewed with senior management to make sure they make sense in the context of the organization's strategic direction. By providing a chart or spreadsheet that shows the jobs in each job grade by business unit, executives can determine whether changes are necessary. Once agreement is reached, the structure is finalized and communicated to employees.

 Real World Scenario

Comparable Worth

Comparable worth, or *pay equity*, describes the concept of minimizing pay disparities between jobs traditionally held by women, such as teachers, with higher-paying jobs traditionally held by men, such as carpenters. This concept suggests that jobs with similar duties and responsibilities requiring similar levels of knowledge, skill, and ability should be paid similarly. Comparable worth doesn't reflect supply and demand in the labor market because it's about the inherent value of the job's content to society. The issue is complex because value is a subjective measure and how jobs are valued often depends on who is valuing them. Those opposed to this concept argue that the price of a particular job in the labor market is based on the supply and demand for its skills and that social engineering isn't an appropriate role for business.

Communicating the Structure

The goal of the communication plan is to have buy-in at all levels of the organization so that the salary structure accomplishes what it needs to do: provide a fair and equitable structure for making pay decisions. To do this, communication about the pay structure takes place at two levels: employee and manager. Employees need to understand how the structure was developed so they feel fairly compensated for their work and have a line of sight from their performance to their compensation. Explaining how the structure was created should alleviate any concerns about political influence or favoritism in the decision-making process.

Managers need to understand how the salary structure can be used to influence behavior in a way that encourages employees to accomplish their goals and objectives. They need to be well versed in how the structure works so they can effectively explain pay decisions to employees.

Administering the Compensation Plan

Once a pay structure is created, managers must have the tools they need to administer pay for their work units. Compiling a salary-administration handbook helps managers throughout the organization apply the system consistently. A typical handbook contains the following kinds of information:

- The organization's compensation philosophy
- The roles played by HR, line managers, and executives in salary administration
- Basic information about pay increases
- A description of how salaries or wages for new hires are determined

If variable compensation is part of the compensation mix, information about bonuses and other incentives is included as well.

Range Placement

Up to this point, the pay-structure discussion has concentrated on jobs, not on the employees in the jobs. The focus now turns to using the pay structure to make decisions for individual employees. One of the key factors to consider when making individual pay decisions is the employee's place in the pay range. Table 6.5 illustrates how ranges are used to make individual pay decisions.

TABLE 6.5   Using ranges in pay decisions

Placement	Use For
Minimum	Entry-level employees
	Employees new to the organization or the position
	Employees performing below standard
Midpoint	Fully proficient employees
Maximum	Employees highly valued by the organization based on:
	• Technical skill level
	• Company-specific experience
	• Consistently outstanding level of performance

When changes are made to an existing salary structure, pay for some employees may fall outside the new range. Pay that falls below the minimum of the salary range is referred to as a *green circle* rate of pay. Employees may also be green-circled because their experience and/or skills don't meet the requirements of the position or as a result of performance issues. Conversely, *red-circle* pay refers to employees whose pay falls above the maximum of the salary range. This may occur when an employee is demoted without a corresponding decrease to base pay, because of a transfer, or for some other unusual circumstance.

Wage Compression

Wage compression occurs when new employees are hired at a rate of pay greater than that earned by incumbent employees for similar skills, education, and experience. These situations are usually the most challenging during high-growth economic times or when there is high demand for certain skill sets. Compression may also occur if the organization's pay practices, merit increases, and promotional budgets aren't in line with the market. One way to reduce compression is to provide salary adjustments for the incumbent population.

Compa-ratios

A *compa-ratio* is a simple calculation that compares an employee's base pay to the midpoint of the pay range. This measure is commonly used for comparison against a group of employees and is especially useful when providing recommendations for pay increases for promotions, merit increases, and so on.

Here's the formula for finding the compa-ratio:

Base Salary ÷ Midpoint of Salary Range × 100

Here's an example of a compa-ratio in action:

120,000 base salary ÷ 100,000 midpoint × 100 = 120

A compa-ratio of 100 percent indicates that the base pay equals the midpoint of the salary range. For example, an HR manager, Elena, is evaluating the new base pay for Joseph, an executive who is about to be promoted to the next pay grade. Elena determines that incumbents in the new position have an average compa-ratio of about 110 percent. Because Joseph is entering this level for the first time, a compa-ratio of less than 100 percent may be most appropriate for him.

Increases to Base Pay

Base pay can be increased for a variety of reasons: cost-of-living adjustments, annual reviews, and promotions are some of the most common.

Cost-of-Living Adjustments (COLAs)

Cost-of-living adjustments are generally used during periods of high inflation to reduce the effects of wage compression. These adjustments happen more often in public-sector jobs than in the private sector, which generally relies on survey data to maintain compensation at a level that is competitive with the appropriate labor market, whether at the local or national level.

Annual Reviews

Calculating increases for annual reviews can be simple or complex. In a seniority-based compensation system where increases are based on time in the job, the calculation is relatively simple—the most common methods use a fixed dollar amount or percentage of base pay. In a performance-based system, where *merit increases* are based on demonstrated performance, the calculation is usually more complex.

Merit programs are often aligned with a performance-management system. When this is the case, an annual performance rating is the key determining factor for the amount of a merit increase. Reviews may be conducted on an employee's anniversary date or during a *focal review* period when all employees are reviewed at the same time.

A merit matrix is commonly developed by HR as a tool for managers to use in planning increases for their work units. A merit matrix combines a performance rating with the employee's position in the salary range to recommend the amount of increase. The matrix shown in Table 6.6 demonstrates that in addition to differentiating employees based on performance, it's also important to differentiate based on their positions in the salary range. For example, employees at the midpoint of the salary range are considered to be fully trained and able to perform all job duties. Employees on the low end of the salary range who are moving up the learning curve quickly may warrant a higher merit increase than an employee at the midpoint or maximum of the salary range.

TABLE 6.6   Merit increase matrix, assuming 5 percent annual merit budget

Performance/position in range	Minimum	Midpoint	Maximum
Exceeds expectations	8–10 percent	6–8 percent	3–6 percent
Meets expectations	5–7 percent	4–6 percent	0 percent
Doesn't meet expectations	0 percent	0 percent	0 percent

There are several things to consider before giving a merit-based salary increase:

Employee's Position in the Salary Range   Before providing a merit increase, consider the employee's current salary and where it fits into the range for the job title. For example, Tanya and Maurice are both customer service representatives. They perform the same job equally well. Tanya is at the high end of the salary range, and Maurice is on the low end. In order to keep Tanya and Maurice within the same range, Maurice, with his salary on the low end, should receive a higher merit increase than Tanya. Typically, the midpoint of the salary range is the ideal place in the salary range for a fully trained, solidly performing employee.

Tenure in Position (Hire Date/Date of Last Promotion)   It's important to consider how long an employee has held a job, the amount of time since the employee's last promotion, and the date of the last increase. For example, an employee who was recently promoted may still be learning a position and not performing all job requirements at a fully qualified level. The impact of this situation on the amount of increase would be to reduce the amount of the award so that the employee's salary is between the low and midpoints of the salary range. This would reflect the level of performance being delivered.

Skill Set and Performance Compared to Peer Group   HR managers and supervisors should be aware of the marketable skills and current compensation of an employee relative to the employee's peers. Employees have access to market data via the Internet, and many are very aware of their worth in the marketplace. From the employer's perspective, this places employees at risk for recruitment by competitors if they believe their pay is substandard.

In addition to merit matrices, some organizations require managers to use some sort of forced-distribution calculation when awarding merit increases. This helps to manage the salary increase budget and forces managers to differentiate between varying levels of performance by employees in their work units. To reward outstanding performers with a meaningful increase, increases for poor performers are minimal or nonexistent. This approach is designed to send a message to employees in both categories.

Managers should understand how to connect merit increases to performance and explain the connection between the two to employees. When it's unclear, employees can begin to view merit increases as COLAs. Connecting the two will help managers avoid an atmosphere of entitlement in their work units.

Promotions

Promotions occur when employees are moved into new positions with different duties and greater responsibilities or when they develop a level of experience and skill enabling them to assume added responsibilities in their current positions. Typically, a promotion is accompanied by a change in title and salary level. In organizations with traditional pay structures, this also means an increase in salary grade.

When determining how much of an increase to provide for a promotion, several factors are considered. These include how long the employee has been in the current position, how recently a merit increase was awarded, whether the new position is in the same area of the organization or a different one, and where the new salary will place the employee in the new salary range. Generally speaking, an increase of 10–15 percent is provided for promotions.

Nontraditional Pay Structures

In the more than 50 years that traditional pay structures have been used, significant changes in the way businesses operate have taken place, and many compensation professionals think that traditional, job-based systems don't serve current employer needs. Some organizations may strongly consider skill sets as determining factors for pay decisions, awarding increases to employees who possess skills that are critical to the organization's success. Other organizations may provide additional compensation for the development and acquisition of new skills. An example of this can commonly be found in manufacturing environments, where an entry-level operator who acquires additional skills for the position receives additional compensation for these skills. One method for doing this is competency-based compensation.

Although traditional pay programs focus on job requirements, a *competency-based compensation* program focuses on employee KSAs, tying individual pay to increased ability. Competency-based pay programs place responsibility for advancement on each employee: the greater the level of competence, the higher level of pay is available. The underlying concept for organizations is that as employees gain competence in their jobs, fewer employees are needed to achieve organizational goals, and employers can afford to pay them more.

As the information and knowledge economies replaced the industrial economy, many organizations found the bureaucracy of traditional pay programs an impediment to the rapid changes necessary for responding to changing market conditions. Instead of conducting a job analysis and evaluation so that a new job description can be created each time an employee's duties change, competency-based programs encourage employees to hone their current KSAs and develop new ones, rewarding them for their increased abilities instead of for specific job duties that may change over time.

Competency profiles replace job descriptions in these programs. A competency profile consists of 10–12 key competencies identified by those who know the job requirements best—in most cases, job incumbents who are performing at a high level. A career ladder then identifies specific levels of competency required at various stages (usually three or four, beginning at entry level and advancing to a senior, highly skilled level). The profile describes the level of fully functional competence expected from employees at each stage and the corresponding pay for each level. Competency profiles include technical skills specific to individual jobs and softer skills identified as valuable to the organization, such as communication skills, teamwork, or adaptability. Because competency-based compensation doesn't reward performance in the way traditional programs do, it's often combined with cash incentive programs to reward desired performance.

Competency-based compensation is used most effectively with broadband salary ranges to maximize flexibility as employees attain greater levels of competence in current KSAs or add new ones. Range levels are generally tied to the different stages of the competency profile.

This type of pay program communicates organizational focus to employees by selecting competencies that support strategic goals. For example, creating competencies that reward teamwork will help to change the culture from highly competitive to one that is more team based by rewarding those employees who work effectively in teams. Clearly defined competencies help employees see that increased competence results in higher compensation and places responsibility for advancement on individual employees.

Traditional salary structures don't support the needs of competency-based pay, so some organizations have used broadbanding in conjunction with this pay program. *Broadbanding* splits positions in the company into just a few specific pay ranges. Each range includes a variety of jobs. For example, a broadband classification structure may have four levels, such as individual contributor, manager, director, and VP. All jobs in the company fit into one of the four classifications. Broadbanding helps organizations remain flat and facilitates lateral career movement. In contrast, narrowbanding or traditional pay classifications have many levels and are organized in a hierarchical and vertical fashion. Narrowbanding may not facilitate lateral movement and can create an employee focus on the organizational structure rather than job responsibilities. One benefit of broadbanding is that it can lead to greater collaboration by limiting employee focus on hierarchical differences between jobs.

Benefits

Employee benefit programs are an integral part of a company's total compensation plan and represent a significant cost to employers. Of equal importance to compensation in the total rewards mix, employee benefit programs are varied and designed to meet specific employee needs. There are two basic types of benefit programs: those that are legally mandated and those that are voluntary. The purpose of this section is to explore how HR professionals, working with senior management, can determine the mix of benefits that will attract and retain the type of employees needed by the organization to achieve its goals.

When most employees think about their benefit packages, they think of medical and dental insurance, vacation and sick leave, and the retirement plan; however, employers provide many other benefits that employees often overlook. These include nonmonetary benefits such as the location of their facilities, the length of the daily commute for employees, "dress down" days, and monetary benefits such as salaries that are competitive with the industry and profession. These are all factors taken into consideration by candidates when determining whether to accept an offer. However, without specific effort on the part of employers, employees are often unaware of the value of the benefits provided for them because they rarely consider these costs when they think about their total income. Decisions about these facets of the employment relationship in each company can either help or hurt the efforts of the organization to attract and retain employees.

Two main categories of benefits may be offered: those that are legally mandated and those that are voluntary. Legally mandated benefits are relatively straightforward. They include Social Security, Medicare, unemployment insurance, family and medical leave (eligibility based on number of employees in the organization and individual hours worked), workers' compensation, and COBRA benefit continuation.

The kinds of benefits that organizations may voluntarily provide are significantly more complicated. Table 6.7 provides some examples of voluntary benefits.

TABLE 6.7 Voluntary employee benefits

Types of Benefits	Benefit Details
Deferred compensation	Qualified pension plans
	Nonqualified pension plans
Health and welfare benefits	Medical insurance
	Dental insurance
	Vision insurance
	Life insurance
	AD&D insurance
	Short-/long-term disability insurance
	Prescription coverage
Long-term care insurance	Vacation leave
Work-life balance	Sick leave
	Paid time off
	Paid holidays
	Childcare
	Fitness
	Elder care

Types of Benefits	Benefit Details
Other voluntary benefits	Employee assistance plans Relocation assistance Tuition reimbursement Flexible spending accounts Cafeteria plan Adoption assistance Section 529 plans Commute assistance

Let's begin our discussion with a brief review of the benefits that are mandated by the federal government. Once again, keep in mind that legal requirements in your state may differ in some respects from the federal requirements. For the PHR/SPHR examinations, you must be familiar with the federal requirements.

Involuntary Benefits

The first involuntary, or legally mandated, employee benefits were introduced as part of President Franklin Delano Roosevelt's (FDR) New Deal programs during the mid-1930s to aid the millions of Americans who lost their jobs and were unable to find work during the Great Depression. Unemployment reached 25 percent at the low point of the Depression in 1933, leaving many families destitute, homeless, and living in shantytowns throughout the nation. In response to this economic crisis, when FDR was elected in 1932, he set about creating protections for American workers to provide a safety net during economic downturns.

Social Security and Medicare

A key piece of the legislation introduced by FDR that has had an enduring impact on employers was the Social Security Act of 1935 (SSA). The SSA introduced *Old Age, Survivors, and Disability Insurance* (OASDI) that is to be paid to qualified workers upon retirement or disability or to their surviving dependents in the event of a worker's death. In addition to these social welfare benefits, the SSA established unemployment insurance (UI) for workers. The constitutionality of both the OASDI and UI was challenged in court, and in 1937, the U.S. Supreme Court ruled that both were valid and constitutional.

In the early 1960s, Presidents John F. Kennedy and Lyndon B. Johnson committed themselves to raising the standard of living among poor and elderly Americans; in his State of the Union message in 1965, President Johnson presented a report to Congress recommending what became the Medicare program. This program was created by the Social Security Amendments of 1965 and provided medical and hospital insurance benefits for the elderly.

Taxes to support the OASDI and Medicare programs are paid equally by employers and employees. The original legal basis for the tax was contained in the SSA of 1935, but in 1939 Congress repealed the tax sections of the SSA and enacted the Federal Insurance Contributions Act (FICA) to replace them. The FICA transferred responsibility for collecting these taxes to the IRS, which remains the taxing authority for OASDI and the Medicare program.

There have been many changes in both the tax rates and the wage base over the years as a result of changes in the economy. The tax rates for both programs are set by statute and reviewed as needed by Congress to ensure the fiscal viability of the programs. The wage base for Social Security tax is revised each year according to a formula set by statute; there is no maximum wage base for Medicare tax. Table 6.8 shows the changes in the taxable rate over several years. Note that in 2011 the OASDI employee tax rate *decreased* for the first time in decades.

TABLE 6.8 OASDI and Medicare tax rates for 1937–1958 and 2005–2008

Year	OASDI Rate	Maximum Wage	Medicare Rate
1937–49	1.000	$3,000	—
1950	1.500	3,000	—
1951–53	1.500	3,600	—
1954	2.000	3,600	—
1955–56	2.000	4,200	—
1957–58	2.250	4,200 *data cut*	—
2005	6.200	90,000	1.450
2006	6.200	94,200	1.450
2007	6.200	97,500	1.450
2008	6.200	102,000	1.450
2010	6.200	106,800	1.450
2011	4.200	106,800	1.450

The complete table of OASDI and Medicare tax rates is available on the DOL website at www.ssa.gov/OACT/ProgData/taxRates.html.

Employees must receive a statement of all taxes withheld from their paychecks each pay period. Depending on the payroll system that is selected, the deduction for Social Security tax may be listed on paychecks as OASDI, FICA, or SSA. Deductions for the Medicare tax are listed separately and are generally easier to identify because they're usually referred to as Medicare withholdings.

Another change in the OASDI program that affects employers is the age at which workers may receive maximum benefits. An increase in the retirement age was necessary because of improvements in healthcare and the resulting increased longevity of older Americans. This, combined with the impending retirement of employees born during the Baby Boom (people in the United States born between 1946 and 1964 are considered part of the Baby Boom) required Congress to take action to ensure the continued viability of the fund. In 1983, amendments to the SSA gradually increased the age at which workers are eligible to receive full retirement benefits based on a worker's year of birth. Table 6.9, based on data prepared by the Social Security Administration, shows the gradual increase for workers born in different years.

TABLE 6.9   Changes in full retirement age

Year of Birth	Full Retirement Age
1937 or earlier	65
1938	65 and 2 months
1939	65 and 4 months
1940	65 and 6 months
1941	65 and 8 months
1942	65 and 10 months
1943–1954	66
1955	66 and 2 months
1956	66 and 4 months
1957	66 and 6 months
1958	66 and 8 months
1959	66 and 10 months
1960 and later	67

These increases in the retirement age mean that Americans will be part of the workforce for longer periods of time. As discussed in Chapter 4, just as employers must consider these demographic changes when forecasting their needs for employees, an aging workforce also affects benefit programs with increased healthcare costs.

The complete table of retirement benefits by year of birth is available on the SSA website at www.ssa.gov/retire2/agereduction.htm.

Unemployment Insurance

Recall that the SSA of 1935 established the first federal unemployment insurance program. The SSA confers on the states the responsibility for UI administration and distributes federal unemployment insurance funds to them for that purpose. Each state develops its own UI program, so eligibility requirements for *state unemployment insurance* (SUI) vary between states, as do the SUI tax rates. The state rates vary between employers as well, because states increase or decrease the amount of tax based on the number of employees terminated during the year.

When Congress moved taxing authority for OASDI to the IRS in 1939 by creating FICA, it also created the Federal Unemployment Tax Act (FUTA), moving unemployment taxing authority to the IRS as well. The FUTA tax rate is set by statute as a percent of workers' salaries. Effective July 2011, the rate was decreased from 6.2 percent to 6.0 percent of the first $7,000 earned by each worker during the year. All employers who make their SUI payments in full and on time receive a credit of 5.4 percent toward their FUTA taxes, which means the effective FUTA tax rate is .6 percent for them.

Although unemployment is administered by the states, FUTA mandates minimum requirements for them to follow, as described next.

Employers Subject to FUTA

Amendments to FUTA have changed the definition of which employers are subject to FUTA since the law was first enacted. Currently, employers subject to FUTA include those who pay employees who aren't farm workers or household workers. Those employers who paid wages of $1,500 or more in any calendar quarter in either 2010 or 2011 or who employed one or more employees for a portion of a day in any 20 or more different weeks during the previous year or the current year to date are also subject to FUTA.

Employers of farm workers are subject to FUTA if they paid $20,000 or more to the workers during a calendar quarter in the previous year or the current year to date. FUTA is also collected if 10 or more farm workers were employed during some part of a day (not necessarily at the same time) during any 20 or more different weeks during the previous year or the current year to date.

Employers of household workers are subject to FUTA tax if they pay $1,000 or more per calendar quarter to those who work in private homes, college clubs, or chapters of college sororities and fraternities.

Employee Eligibility for Unemployment Benefits

As previously mentioned, each state determines SUI eligibility requirements within its jurisdiction. With few exceptions, unemployment compensation is typically paid for a maximum of 26 weeks, during which the recipient must be actively pursuing employment. When the unemployment rate is very high, Congress will submit a bill to the president extending this time period. If the president signs the bill, compensation will be extended. As of January 2012, the maximum total weeks of UI benefits remains extended to 99 weeks.

Reducing Unemployment Tax Rates

As previously mentioned, employers are able to reduce the SUI tax rate by carefully managing their employment processes. There are a number of ways to do this, beginning with an effective hiring process that appropriately screens candidates to ensure that whoever is selected has all the qualifications for the position. Particularly in very large organizations, establishing a means of communicating between divisions and departments to avoid hiring new employees when employees in other areas of the organization with the necessary skills and experience are being laid off will make better use of the organization's investment in training and reduce the SUI tax rate. An effective performance-management program in which employees are regularly coached and counseled about their performance so that they have an opportunity to improve will also reduce the need to terminate employees. When employees must be terminated for cause, maintaining accurate records of the reasons for termination will provide the basis for aggressively fighting claims that aren't justified. Finally, the HR department must be diligent in contesting ineligible unemployment claims to ensure that unjustified claims are challenged.

Family and Medical Leave Act

In 1993, President Bill Clinton signed the Family and Medical Leave Act (FMLA), which was created to assist employees in balancing the needs of their families with the demands of their jobs. In creating the FMLA, Congress intended that employees not have to choose between keeping their jobs and attending to seriously ill family members.

In 2008, the DOL ended a multiyear fact-finding and public review process with the issuance of final regulations for changes to FMLA. The final rule changes address court rulings that had invalidated some of the previous regulations and incorporate military family-leave provisions passed by Congress in the 2008 National Defense Authorization Act (NDAA). DOL also solicited public comment about the previous FMLA regulations from a variety of stakeholders, including employer groups, HR advocacy groups, labor unions, and healthcare providers. Some of these comments were incorporated into the final rules as well.

In addition to protecting employees from adverse employment actions and retaliation when they request leave under FMLA, the act provides three benefits for eligible employees in covered organizations:

- 12 weeks of unpaid leave within a 12-month period (26 months for military caregiver leave)

- Continuation of health benefits

- Reinstatement to the same position or an equivalent position at the end of the leave

Designation of FMLA Leave   Employers are responsible to designate leave requests as FMLA-qualified based on information received from employees or someone designated by employees to speak on their behalf. When the employee doesn't provide enough information for the employer to determine if the leave is for a reason protected by FMLA, it's up to the employer to request additional information. FMLA regulations don't require employees to specifically request FMLA leave, but they must provide enough information to allow the employer to determine if the request is protected by FMLA. If leave is denied based on a lack of information, it's up to the employee to provide enough additional information for the employer to ascertain that the leave is protected by FMLA.

The regulations allow employers to retroactively designate leave as FMLA-qualified, as long as sufficient notice is given to the employee and the retroactive designation doesn't cause harm or injury to the employee. The retroactive designation can be made by mutual agreement between the employee and employer. When an employer fails to appropriately designate that leave is FMLA-qualified at the time of the employee's request, the employee may be entitled to any loss of compensation and benefits caused by the employer's failure. This can include monetary damages, reinstatement, promotion, or other suitable relief.

Failure to Designate Timely One of the 2008 changes incorporated the Supreme Court ruling in *Ragsdale v. Wolverine Worldwide, Inc.,* a case that addressed what happens when an employer fails to designate a leave as FMLA-qualified in a timely manner. (See the sidebar for more information on this case.) Prior to the *Ragsdale* case, some employees interpreted the regulations in a way that required employers to provide more than the 12 weeks of unpaid leave required by FMLA. The regulations now state that, if an employer neglects to designate leave as FMLA, employees who are harmed may be entitled to restitution for their losses.

Waiver of Rights Prior to the 2008 changes, DOL required any settlement of past claims, even those mutually agreeable to both parties, to be approved by either the DOL or a court. The 2008 final rules amend this, allowing employers and employees who mutually agree on a resolution to settle past claims between them, avoiding costly and unnecessary litigation. However, the regulations don't permit employees to waive their future FMLA rights.

Substitution of Paid Leave DOL regulations permit employees to request, or employers to require, the use of all accrued paid vacation, personal, family, medical, or sick leave concurrently with the FMLA leave. Eligible employees who don't qualify to take paid leave according to policies established by their employers are still entitled to the unpaid FMLA leave.

Perfect-Attendance Awards Employers may now deny perfect-attendance awards to employees whose FMLA leave disqualifies them, as long as employees who take non-FMLA leave are treated the same way.

Light-Duty Assignments Some courts interpreted light-duty assignments following a FMLA leave as a continuation of the leave. The 2008 final rules stipulate that light-duty work assignments aren't counted against an employee's FMLA entitlement. In addition, the employee's job restoration rights continue until the employee is released to full duty or until the end of the 12-month FMLA leave year.

Recordkeeping Requirements FMLA leave records must be kept in accordance with recordkeeping standards established by the FLSA and may be maintained in employee personnel files. FMLA doesn't require submission of FMLA leave records unless requested by the DOL, but they must be maintained and available for inspection, copying, or transcription by DOL representatives for no less than 3 years. The DOL may not require submission more than once during any 12-month period without a reasonable belief that a violation has occurred.

 Real World Scenario

Ragsdale v. Wolverine

In 2002, the U.S. Supreme Court affirmed a U.S. District Court decision that affects FMLA leave designations by employers.

Wolverine Worldwide, Inc. is a global footwear manufacturer headquartered in Rockford, Michigan. In 1996, Wolverine granted 30 weeks of medical leave to Tracy Ragsdale after she was diagnosed with a serious illness, but the company didn't designate the leave as FMLA. At the end of 30 weeks, Ms. Ragsdale requested a 30-day extension of the leave, which was denied by Wolverine. When she didn't return to work, Wolverine terminated her employment. Ms. Ragsdale filed a lawsuit against Wolverine claiming that it had violated a DOL regulation that if "the employer doesn't designate the leave as a FMLA leave, the leave taken doesn't count against an employee's FMLA entitlement." The lawsuit claimed that she should be eligible for an additional 12 weeks of leave.

Wolverine filed a motion for summary judgment that was granted by the District Court in a finding that the DOL regulation was invalid because it would have required Wolverine to provide more than 12 weeks of FMLA leave to Ms. Ragsdale in one 12-month period. The Supreme Court upheld the District Court in a 5-4 decision. Writing for the majority, Justice Anthony M. Kennedy stated that the DOL regulation "imposes a high price for a good-faith but erroneous characterization of an absence as non-FMLA leave, and employers like Wolverine might well conclude that the simpler, less generous route is the preferable one."

Final regulations issued by the DOL in 2008 incorporated this decision into FMLA.

Employers Covered

FMLA applies to all public agencies and schools, regardless of their size, and to private employers with 50 or more employees working within a 75-mile radius. The law provides detailed descriptions on how employers determine whether these requirements apply to them:

50 or More Employees Employers must comply with FMLA when they employ 50 or more employees for each working day during each of 20 or more calendar work weeks in the current or preceding year. The statute doesn't require the work weeks to be consecutive.

Guidelines in FMLA specify that the number of employees at a worksite is determined by the number of employees on the payroll for that site.

Employers remain subject to FMLA rules until the number of employees on the payroll is less than 50 for 20 nonconsecutive weeks in the current and preceding calendar year. This means that if employers with 50 employees on the payroll for the first 20 weeks in 2011 reduce the number of employees for the rest of 2011 and remain at the reduced level throughout 2012, they must continue to comply with FMLA through the end of 2012.

Worksites Within a 75-Mile Radius The number of employees at each worksite is based on the employees who report to work at that site or, in the case of outside sales representatives or employees who telecommute, the location from which their work is assigned.

This can be either a single place of business or a group of adjacent locations, such as a business park or campus.

A worksite may also consist of facilities that aren't directly connected if they're in reasonable geographic proximity, used for the same purpose, and share the same staff and equipment.

Employees such as construction workers or truck drivers who regularly work at sites away from the main business office are counted as employees in one of the three following ways:

- At the business site to which they report
- At the worksite that is their home base
- At the site from which their work is assigned

However, these employees may not be counted at a worksite where they may be temporarily deployed for the duration of a project.

Notice Obligations The 2008 final rule consolidates notice requirements for employers to clear up confusion created by conflicting requirements and time frames in the previous rules. Employers have two notice obligations for FMLA: the first obligation is to inform employees of their FMLA rights, and the second requires specific information to be provided in response to an FMLA leave request:

Informational Notice Upon hire, employers must provide employees with a general informational notice in two formats. DOL provides a poster (WH Publication 1420) explaining FMLA rights and responsibilities. Employers must post this information in an area frequented by employees.

Employers must also provide information about employee rights and responsibilities in the employee handbook, collective bargaining agreement (CBA), or other written documents. When an employer doesn't have a handbook or CBA, DOL provides *Fact Sheet #28*, a four-page summary of FMLA that the employer may distribute to employees.

Notice in Response to Leave Request Once an employee requests FMLA leave, the final rules require employers to respond within 5 business days. At this time, employers must inform employees of their eligibility, rights, and responsibilities for FMLA leave, and designate the leave as FMLA. DOL provides two forms for this purpose: WH-381 and WH-382.

The eligibility, rights, and responsibilities notice (form WH-381) informs employees of the following:

- The date of leave request, and beginning and ending dates of the leave
- The reason for the leave (birth or adoption of a child or serious health condition of the employee or a family member)
- Employee rights and responsibilities under FMLA
- That employee contributions toward health insurance premiums continue and whether the employee will be required to reimburse the employer for premiums paid if the employee doesn't return to work after the leave
- Whether the employer will continue other benefits
- Whether they're eligible for FMLA leave
- Whether the employee is designated as a *key employee* and therefore may not be restored to employment upon the end of the leave
- Whether the employer requires periodic reports on the employee's status and intention to return to work

The designation notice (form WH-382) informs employees of the following:

- Whether the requested leave will be counted against their FMLA leave entitlement
- Whether a medical certification is required
- Whether the employer requires them to use their accrued paid leave for the unpaid FMLA leave; if not required, whether the employee chooses to substitute accrued paid leave for all or part of the FMLA leave
- Whether the employer requires a fitness-for-duty certificate prior to the employee's return to work

Employers aren't required to use the DOL forms, but if a substitute form is used, it must include all information required by the regulations.

Employers may not revoke an employee's eligibility, once confirmed. Similarly, if an employer neglects to inform an employee that they're ineligible for FMLA leave prior to the date the leave begins, the employee is considered eligible to take the leave, and the employer may not deny it at that point.

Employees Eligible for FMLA

FMLA also provides guidelines for determining which employees are eligible for leave. This includes employees who

- Work for an employer who is subject to FMLA as described previously.
- Have been employed by the employer for at least 12 months, which need not be consecutive. Time worked prior to a break in service of 7 or more years doesn't need to be counted, unless the service break was to fulfill a military service obligation. Employees who received benefits or other compensation during any part of a week are counted as having been employed for that week.

- Worked at least 1,250 hours during the 12 months immediately preceding the leave, based on the FLSA standards for determining compensable hours of work. If accurate time records aren't maintained, it's up to the employer to prove that the employee didn't meet the requirement; if this isn't possible, the law provides that the employee will be presumed to have met the requirement.

The determination of whether an employee meets the requirement for 1,250 hours of work within the past 12 months is counted from the date the leave begins.

Key Employee Exception

FMLA leave is available to all employees of covered organizations who meet the FMLA eligibility requirements. FMLA includes a provision that key employees may be denied reinstatement to the position they held or an equivalent position if the employer demonstrates that the reinstatement would cause "substantial and grievous economic injury" to its operations. A key employee is defined by FMLA as a salaried employee among the highest-paid 10 percent of employees at the worksite as defined previously. The law requires that the determination of which employees are the highest paid is calculated by dividing the employee's year-to-date earnings (base salary, premium pay, incentive pay, and bonuses) and dividing the total earnings by the number of weeks worked. Whether an employee meets the definition of a key employee is to be determined at the time leave is requested. The employee must be advised of this status, either in person or by certified mail, as soon as possible. The employer must also explain why restoring the employee's job will cause substantial and grievous economic injury.

If the employee decides to take the leave after being informed of the implications of key employee status, the employee may still request reinstatement upon return to work. The employer must review the circumstances again and, if substantial and grievous economic injury would still occur under the circumstances at that time, notify the employee in writing in person or by certified mail that restoration is denied.

Key employees continue to be protected by FMLA unless they notify their employers that they won't return to work, or until the employer denies reinstatement at the end of the leave.

Employee Notice Requirement

One FMLA requirement that caused difficulty for employers was an interpretation of previous rules that employees had up to 2 full days after a FMLA-qualifying event occurred to notify their employers of the need for FMLA leave. This made it difficult for employers to meet production schedules and ensure necessary coverage of critical work needs.

The 2008 final rule eliminated this language and clarified the timing of employee notices for two situations: foreseeable and unforeseeable leaves. In either case, employees must provide verbal notice so that the employer is aware of the need for FMLA-qualified leave, the expected timing and length of the leave, and information about the medical condition described in the section "Reasons for FMLA Leave." Employees aren't required to specifically request FMLA leave or mention FMLA for the first occurrence of a qualified event, but they're required to answer reasonable questions about the need for leave so that employers can determine whether the leave is qualified under FMLA:

Foreseeable Leave   When the need for leave is foreseeable, FMLA rules require employees to notify their employers at least 30 days prior to the anticipated start date of leaves such as for the birth of a child, adoption, placement of a foster child, or planned medical treatment for a serious health condition. If the circumstances surrounding the planned leave change (such as a child being born earlier than expected), notice must be given as soon as practicable. This means as soon as both practical and possible, on the same day or the next business day. In these circumstances, a family member or someone else representing the employee may provide notice.

If the leave is foreseeable more than 30 days in advance and an employee fails to provide notice at least 30 days in advance without a reasonable excuse for delaying, the employer may delay FMLA coverage until 30 days after the date the employee provided notice.

If the need for FMLA leave is foreseeable less than 30 days in advance and the employee fails to notify the employer as soon as practicable, the employer may delay FMLA coverage of the leave. The amount of delay depends on the circumstances of each leave request and is evaluated on a case-by-case basis. Generally, the employer may delay the start of FMLA leave by the amount of delay in notice by the employee.

Unforeseeable Leave   At times, employees may be unable to notify their employers of the need for FMLA leave in advance. In these circumstances, the 2008 change to FMLA rules requires employees to provide notice in accordance with the usual and customary practice for calling in an absence, unless unusual circumstances prevent the employee from doing so. An employee's representative, such as a spouse or another responsible person, may provide the notice if the employee is unable to do so. In emergencies when employees are unable to contact employers, they're permitted to supply the notice when they're able to use a telephone.

In order for employees to provide notice in accordance with the regulations, they must be aware of their responsibility to do so. FMLA provides that proper posting of FMLA notice requirements by employers satisfies this requirement. Employers may waive FMLA notice requirements or their own rules on notice for employee leaves of absence at their discretion. In the absence of unusual circumstances, employers may choose not to waive their internal notice rules for employees who fail to follow those rules when requesting FMLA leaves, as long as those actions are consistent with practices regarding other leave requests. This is acceptable under the regulations as long as the actions don't discriminate against employees taking FMLA leave or violate the FMLA requirements described previously.

Reasons for FMLA Leave

FMLA presents covered employers with a list of circumstances under which FMLA leave must be provided if requested by an eligible employee. Passage of the 2008 NDAA added care for military personnel and their families in some circumstances to existing circumstances that qualify for leave:

- The birth of a child and caring for the infant. FMLA leave is available to both fathers and mothers; however, if both parents work for the same employer, the combined total of the leave may not exceed the 12-week total. In addition, the leave must be completed within 12 months of the child's birth.

- Placement of an adopted or foster child with the employee. The same conditions that apply to the birth of a child apply here as well; in this case, the leave must be completed within 12 months of the child's placement.

- To provide care for the employee's spouse, son, daughter, or parent with a serious health condition. For purposes of FMLA leave, a spouse must be recognized as such by the state in which the employee resides.

  A parent can be the biological parent of the employee or one who has legal standing *in loco parentis*, a Latin term that means "in place of the parent" and applies to those who care for a child on a daily basis. *In loco parentis* doesn't require either a biological or a legal relationship.

  A son or daughter may be a biological child, an adopted or foster child, a stepchild, a legal ward, or the child of someone acting in loco parentis. A child must also be younger than 18 years of age or, if older than 18, unable to care for themselves because of a physical or mental disability.

  Employers may require those employees requesting FMLA leave to provide reasonable documentation to support the family relationship with the person for whom they will be providing care.

- When an employee is unable to perform the functions of the job because of a serious health condition. According to FMLA, a serious health condition is an illness, an injury, an impairment, or a physical or mental condition that requires the following:

  - Inpatient care or subsequent treatment related to inpatient care.

  - Continuing treatment by a health-care provider because of a period of incapacity of more than three consecutive calendar days. *Incapacity* refers to an inability to work, attend school, or perform other daily activities as a result of the condition.

  - Incapacity because of pregnancy or prenatal care.

  - Treatment for a serious, chronic health condition.

- To provide care for a covered service member with a serious injury or illness sustained while on active duty. In this situation, family members are eligible to take up to 26 weeks of leave in a 12-month period.

- To provide leave for qualifying exigencies for families of members of the National Guard and Reserves. Qualifying exigencies include the following:

  - Short-notice deployments

  - Military events and related activities

  - Childcare and school activities

  - Financial and legal arrangements

  - Counseling

  - Rest and recuperation

  - Post-deployment activities

  - Leave for other related purposes when agreed to by the employee and employer

Medical Certification Process

FMLA regulations allow employers to require medical certifications to verify requests for any qualified leave as long as the employee is notified of the requirements. DOL provides the following forms for this purpose:

- WH-380-E (for employee serious health condition)
- WH-380-F (for family member serious health condition)
- WH-384 (for exigency leave for military families)
- WH-385 (for serious injury or illness to covered service member)

Employers should request initial certification within 5 business days of the employee leave request. Additional certifications may be required at a later date to verify that the leave continues to be appropriate. Employers must provide at least 15 calendar days for the employee to submit the certification but may allow more time.

FMLA regulations require employees to provide "complete and sufficient" certification for the employer. If the certification doesn't meet the complete and sufficient standard, employers may request, in writing, the additional information needed to comply. A certification isn't considered complete and sufficient if one or more of the entries on the form aren't completed, or if the information is vague or ambiguous, or the employee is nonresponsive. Employees must be allowed a minimum of 7 days to return the form with the additional information. When employers request the certification or additional information, they must advise employees of the consequences for failing to provide adequate certification of the serious illness or injury. If employees don't return the certification or fail to provide a complete and sufficient certification upon notice of deficiencies in what was submitted, FMLA regulations allow employers to deny the FMLA leave.

Employers aren't required to use the DOL forms, but may only request information that is directly related to the serious health condition necessitating the leave, including the following:

- Contact information for the health-care provider.
- Approximate date the serious health condition began and an estimate of how long it will last.
- A description of the medical facts about the health condition, such as symptoms, diagnosis, hospitalization, doctor visits, prescribed medication, treatment referrals, and continuing treatments.
- For employees with serious health conditions, the certification must establish the inability to perform essential job functions, describe work restrictions, and indicate the length of the inability to perform job functions.
- For family members with serious health conditions, the certification must establish that the patient requires care, how often, and how long it will be necessary.
- Information that confirms the medical necessity for reduced or intermittent leave with estimated dates and length of treatment.

FMLA leave certifications may be complicated when workers' compensation, ADA, or employer-provided paid leave programs are used concurrently. FMLA regulations address certifications under these circumstances as follows:

- Generally, medical certification of the need for the FMLA or workers' compensation leave may not exceed what is requested on the DOL Medical Certification Form. Visit the DOL's website to view a copy of form WH-380- E at www.dol.gov/whd/forms/WH-380-E.pdf.

- Employers may require additional information in accordance with a paid leave or disability program, but must advise employees that the additional information is required in conjunction with the paid-leave plan, not with the FMLA leave. Whatever information is collected may be used to evaluate continuation of the FMLA leave. Failure to provide the additional information doesn't affect continuation of the FMLA leave.

- When FMLA leave runs concurrently with ADA, employers may follow ADA procedures for collecting information. This information may be used to evaluate the claim for FMLA-protected leave.

Employees are responsible for providing their own medical certifications. However, if an employer disagrees with the finding of the certifying medical provider, the employer may require a second certification opinion at the employer's expense. If the opinions of the employee's and the employer's designated health-care providers differ, the employer may require the employee to obtain certification from a third health-care provider, again at the employer's expense. This third opinion will be final and binding. The third health-care provider must be approved jointly by the employer and the employee. If employees choose to do so, they may provide employers with an authorization or release to obtain information directly from their health-care providers, but employers may not require them to do so. For an excellent review of the fact sheet provided by the Department of Labor, visit at www.dol.gov/whd/regs/compliance/1421.htm.

Types of FMLA Leave

FMLA provides for three types of leave: continuous, reduced leave, and intermittent. A *continuous FMLA leave* is one in which the employee is absent from work for an extended period of time. A *reduced FMLA leave schedule* is one in which the employee's regular work schedule is reduced for a period of time. This can mean a reduction in the hours worked each day or in the number of days worked during the week. An *intermittent FMLA leave* is one in which the employee is absent from work for multiple periods of time because of a single illness or injury. When using intermittent leave, employees must make an effort to schedule the leave to avoid disruption of regular business operations. In addition, the employer may assign an employee requesting intermittent leave to a different position with equivalent pay and benefits in order to meet the employee's needs.

Calculating the FMLA Year

FMLA provides four possible methods for employers to use in calculating the *FMLA year* (the 12-month period during which employees may use the 12 weeks of leave). A FMLA year can be calculated as any of the following:

- The calendar year
- Any fixed 12-month period (such as the fiscal year or anniversary date)
- The 12-month period beginning when a FMLA leave begins
- A rolling 12-month period that is measured back from the date the FMLA leave is used by an employee

Although the most difficult to administer, for many employers the rolling 12-month period is best. Other methods are more open to abuse of FMLA by some employees, resulting in the use of 24 weeks of leave by bridging two 12-month periods, including an employee being on continuous FMLA leave for 24 weeks.

If an employer doesn't have a stated policy, the FMLA year must be calculated in the way that provides the most benefit to employees. Whichever method is selected, it must be used to calculate FMLA for all employees. Employers who decide to change the way they calculate the FMLA year must provide written notice to employees 60 days in advance of the change and obtain written acknowledgment of the change.

Tracking Reduced and Intermittent FMLA Leave

Although keeping track of the amount of FMLA leave used for a continuous leave is fairly straightforward, ensuring that accurate records of reduced and intermittent FMLA leave are maintained can be more difficult. In either case, only the amount of leave used may be deducted from the 12 weeks available to the employee. For example, an employee whose regular work schedule of 40 hours per week is reduced to 20 hours per week would be charged one-half week of FMLA leave for each week that they work the reduced schedule.

For intermittent leave, employers may charge for leave in increments of not less than 1 hour. Employees should provide at least 2 days' notice of the need to use the intermittent leave whenever possible.

Ending FMLA Leave

FMLA leave ends when the employee has used the full 12 weeks of leave, the serious illness of the employee or family member ends, or, in some cases, when the family member or the employee dies. When one of these three circumstances occurs, the employee may return to the same or an equivalent position with no loss of benefits. If the employee wants to continue the leave at that point, the company is under no obligation to grant it, unless there is a company policy in place to provide a longer leave.

Employers may require employees returning from FMLA leave to provide a *fitness-for-duty* certification from their health-care provider, attesting to their ability to return to work. If they choose to do so, employers may require the fitness-for-duty report to specify the employee's ability to perform the essential functions of the job. Employers who choose this type of certification must provide a job description or list of the employee's essential job functions with the designation notice. Similar to medical certifications, employers may contact health-care providers to clarify and authenticate information contained in the fitness-for-duty certificate but may not request information unrelated to the serious health condition that is the reason for the FMLA leave. Employees who neither provide the fitness-for-duty certificate nor request an extension of the leave are no longer entitled to reinstatement.

FMLA Implications for Employers

HR professionals need to ensure that supervisors and managers throughout their organizations are aware of the requirements for FMLA leaves and the consequences for noncompliance. FMLA requirements are complex and confusing, particularly when used in conjunction with workers' compensation or the ADA, and managers of other functional areas may not be aware of their obligations for FMLA requests.

There are some things employers can do to ensure that they comply with FMLA requirements. To start, review current leave practices to ensure that they comply with FMLA requirements and any state laws with more stringent requirements. FMLA leave policies should be included in the employee handbook; new hires must be advised of their rights to take leave under the act. It's important for HR professionals to work with supervisors and managers throughout the organization to ensure that they understand the implications for situations that may be subject to FMLA regulations and encourage them to talk to HR about potential FMLA leave situations. HR needs to take an active role in educating the management team about the interaction of FMLA, ADA, and workers' compensation requirements. Before an FMLA situation occurs, a documentation procedure and policy should be developed, and HR should take an active role in ensuring that all leaves comply with established procedures to avoid possible claims of discriminatory practices. When workers' compensation and FMLA leaves occur simultaneously, make sure to advise the employee that the leaves run concurrently.

You can find the complete text of the FMLA online at http://www. dol.gov/compliance/laws/comp-fmla.htm. The 2008 final rules are published in the Code of Federal Regulations and may be accessed at www.dol.gov/federalregister/.

Workers' Compensation

Workers' compensation laws require employers to assume responsibility for all employee injuries, illnesses, and deaths related to employment. These laws are enacted and enforced by the individual states and provide benefits for employees that cover medical and rehabilitation expenses, provide income replacement during periods of disability when employees are unable to work, and pay benefits to their survivors in the event of an employee's death.

The amount of compensation paid is based on actuarial tables that take into account the seriousness of the injury, whether the disability is permanent or temporary, whether it's a full or partial disability (such as the loss of an eye or hand), and the amount of income lost because of the injury. In most cases, employers fund workers' compensation obligations by purchasing coverage through private insurance companies or state-sponsored insurance funds. The premiums for workers' compensation coverage are based on a percentage of the employer's payroll in various job categories. The percentages are different and depend on previous claim activity in each category. The rate charged for a roofer, for example, is much higher than that for an office worker because of the inherent danger of the job and the number and severity of claims that result.

In some states, companies may self-fund workers' compensation programs, meaning that they pay the total costs of any injuries or illnesses when they occur instead of paying insurance premiums. These are known as *nonsubscriber* plans and are rare; generally, self-funded insurance plans make economic sense only for very large organizations with the financial base to support the payment of large claims when they occur.

Although increased emphasis on safety programs and training has led to a reduction in the number of nationwide workers' compensation claims filed each year, the insurance rates are increasing largely because of increased medical costs. This is most evident in California, where employers saw costs double between 2000 and 2003, but it has also led to state reform of workers' compensation programs in Florida, West Virginia, Washington, and Texas.

Implementing programs aimed at reducing the cost of workers' compensation coverage for their organizations is one way HR professionals can show a positive impact on the bottom line. Implementing safety training and injury-prevention programs as discussed in Chapter 8, "Risk Management," is one way to reduce job-related injuries and illnesses and prevent claims. The costs of individual claims can be reduced by ensuring the availability of jobs that meet light-duty medical requirements so that employees are able to return to work earlier, shortening the length of their leave.

Voluntary Benefits

Employers attract qualified candidates with different types of skills by offering cash compensation that leads or matches the labor market for those skills. They can also use the mix of their benefit packages to attract and retain segments of the labor market with characteristics that align to their particular business values and goals. For example, an organization interested in attracting employees focused on maintaining a high level of knowledge in their chosen fields may offer a generous educational reimbursement benefit and provide training opportunities as a way of attracting and retaining those employees.

Making decisions about the voluntary benefit package that is most appropriate for a particular organization's workforce requires consideration of many factors: demographics, industry standards, local area practices, the financial situation of the company, and the organizational culture among them. A needs assessment, described in Chapter 2, provides insight into which benefits are most attractive to the organization's current workforce and provides a starting point for evaluating options. There are many choices, and finding the right mix can significantly affect an employer's ability to attract and retain employees with the desired qualifications. Whatever benefits are offered, it's crucial that they meet the needs of the type of employees the organization is trying to attract and retain.

To aid in understanding the discussion of laws and benefits in this section, candidates for the PHR/SPHR examinations should be familiar with the following list of terms:

Defined Benefit   A *defined-benefit plan* is a traditional pension plan in which the employer provides a specific benefit upon retirement. The funds in these plans aren't accounted for individually.

Defined Contribution   A *defined-contribution plan* is an individual plan in which the amount of funds contributed is known, but the amount of the benefit that is eventually paid out isn't known because it depends on the investment returns that are earned. The funds are accounted for in individual accounts for each participant.

Nonforfeitable   A *nonforfeitable claim* is one that exists because of a participant's service. Nonforfeitable claims are unconditional and legally enforceable.

Party in Interest   A *party in interest* may be a fiduciary, a person or an entity providing services to the plan, an employer or employee organization, a person who owns 50 percent or more of the business, relatives of any of the above, or corporations that are involved with the plan in any of these functions.

Plan Administrator   The *plan administrator* is the person designated by the plan sponsor to manage the plan.

Plan Sponsor   The *plan sponsor* is the entity that establishes the plan. This may be a single employer, a labor organization, or, in the case of a multiemployer plan, a group representing the parties that established the plan.

Qualified Plan   A *qualified plan* meets ERISA requirements and provides tax advantages for both employees and employers. To be classified as a qualified plan, a pension plan can't provide additional benefits for officers, shareholders, executives, supervisors, or other highly compensated employees—all employees in the organization must be eligible for all plan benefits.

Nonqualified Plan   A *nonqualified retirement plan* is one in which the benefits exceed the limitations of qualified plans or don't meet other IRS requirements for favorable tax treatment. These plans aren't required to include all employees, so they may provide additional benefits to officers, shareholders, executives, supervisors, or other highly compensated employees.

As previously described in Table 6.7, voluntary benefits fall into four main categories: deferred compensation, health and welfare benefits, work-life balance benefits, and other benefits. While there are no federal laws requiring employers to provide any of these, some federal laws regulate pensions or benefits when employers choose to include them in their total rewards packages.

Federal Laws Regulating Voluntary Benefits

The most significant federal law regulating employee benefit programs is the Employee Retirement Income Security Act of 1974 (ERISA), which has been amended several times since then to keep pace with business needs and changing technology. Two of the most significant amendments, the Consolidated Omnibus Budget Reconciliation Act (COBRA) and the Health Insurance Portability and Accountability Act (HIPAA), place significant compliance requirements on employers that offer pension and health benefits. The next several sections describe requirements of ERISA, COBRA, and HIPAA and several other laws or amendments regulating benefit programs.

Employee Retirement Income Security Act of 1974

ERISA was created by Congress to set standards for private pensions and some group welfare programs such as medical and life insurance. ERISA requires organizations to file three types of reports: a summary plan description, an annual report, and reports to individual participants of their benefit rights:

Summary Plan Description (SPD)   A *summary plan description* (SPD) provides plan participants with information about the provisions, policies, and rules established by the plan and advises them on actions they can take in using the plan. ERISA requires that the SPD include the name and other identifying information about plan sponsors, administrators, and trustees, along with any information related to collective bargaining agreements for the plan participants. The SPD must describe what eligibility requirements must be met for participating in the plan and for receiving benefits, as well as the circumstances under which participants would be disqualified or ineligible for participation or be denied benefits.

The SPD must also describe the financing source for the plan and the name of the organization providing benefits. Information on the end of the plan year and whether records are maintained on a calendar, plan, or fiscal year basis must be included in the description.

For health and welfare plans, the SPD must describe claim procedures, along with the name of the DOL office that will assist participants and beneficiaries with HIPAA claims. The SPD must also describe what remedies are available when claims are denied.

A new SPD reflecting all changes made must be prepared and distributed every 5 years unless no changes have occurred. Every 10 years, a new SPD must be distributed to participants whether or not changes have occurred.

Annual Reports   ERISA requires annual reports to be filed for all employee benefit plans. The reports must include financial statements, the number of employees in the plan, and the names and addresses of the plan fiduciaries. ERISA mandates that any persons compensated by the plan (such as an accountant, for example) during the preceding year be disclosed, along with the amount of compensation paid to each, the nature of the services rendered, and any relationship that exists between these parties and any party in interest to the plan. Information that is provided with regard to plan assets must be certified by the organization that holds the assets, whether it's the plan sponsor, an insurance company, or a bank.

The annual reports must be audited by a CPA or other qualified public accountant, and any actuarial reports must be prepared by an *enrolled actuary* who has been licensed jointly by the Department of the Treasury and the DOL to provide actuarial services for U.S. pension plans.

The DOL is given authority to simplify filing and reporting requirements for plans with fewer than 100 participants.

Once submitted, annual reports and other documents become public record and are made available in the DOL public document room. The DOL may also use this information to conduct research and analyze data.

Participant Benefit Rights Reports   Participants may request a report of the total benefits accrued on their behalf along with the amount of the benefit that is nonforfeitable. If there are no nonforfeitable amounts accrued at the time the report is requested, the earliest date that benefits will become nonforfeitable must be provided. Participants are entitled to receive the report no more than once per year.

ERISA records must be maintained for 6 years from the date they were due to be filed with the DOL. In addition to requiring the preparation of these reports, ERISA regulations stipulate that annual reports are to be filed with the DOL within 210 days of the end of the plan year. The DOL may reject reports that are incomplete or that contain qualified opinions from the CPA or actuary. Rejected plans must be resubmitted within 45 days, or the DOL can retain a CPA to audit the report on behalf of the participants. ERISA authorizes the DOL to bring civil actions on behalf of plan participants if necessary to resolve any issues.

In addition to the reporting requirements it contains, ERISA sets minimum standards for employee participation, or eligibility requirements, as well as vesting requirements for qualified pension plans:

Employee Participation   A *participant* is an employee who has met the eligibility requirements for the plan. The law sets minimum participation requirements as follows:

- When 1 year of service has been completed or the employee has reached the age of 21, whichever is later, unless the plan provides for 100 percent vesting after 2 years of service. In that case, the requirement changes to completion of 2 years of service or reaching age 21, whichever is later.

- Employees may not be excluded from the plan on the basis of age; that is, they may not be excluded because they have reached a specified age.

- When employees have met the minimum service and age requirements, they must become participants no later than the first day of the plan year after they meet the requirement, or 6 months after the requirements are met, whichever is earlier.

Vesting   Qualified plans must also meet minimum vesting standards. *Vesting* refers to the point at which employees own the contributions their employer has made to the pension plan, regardless of whether they remain employed with the company. The vesting requirements established by ERISA refer only to funds that are contributed by the employer; any funds contributed by plan participants are owned by the employee. Employees are always 100 percent vested in their own money but must earn the right to be vested in the employer's contribution.

Vesting may be immediate or delayed. *Immediate vesting* occurs when employees are 100 percent, or fully, vested as soon as they meet the eligibility requirements of the plan. *Delayed vesting* occurs when participants must wait for a defined period of time prior to becoming fully vested. There are two types of delayed vesting:

Cliff Vesting   With *cliff vesting*, participants become 100 percent vested after a specified period of time. ERISA sets the maximum period at 5 years for qualified plans, which means participants vest nothing until they have completed the 5 years of service, after which they're fully vested.

Graded Vesting   *Graded vesting*, which is also referred to as *graduated or gradual vesting*, establishes a vesting schedule that provides for partial vesting each year for a specified number of years. A graded vesting schedule in a qualified plan must allow for at least 20 percent vesting after 3 years and 20 percent per year after that, with participants achieving full vesting after 7 years of service. Table 6.10 illustrates a graded vesting schedule that complies with ERISA requirements.

TABLE 6.10   ERISA graded vesting schedule

Years of Service	Percent Vested
3	20 percent
4	40 percent
5	60 percent
6	80 percent
7	100 percent

Benefit Accrual Requirements   ERISA sets specific requirements for determining how much of an accrued benefit participants are entitled to receive if they leave the company prior to retirement. Plans must account for employee contributions to the plan separately from the funds contributed by the employer because the employees are entitled to all the funds contributed by them to the plan when they leave the company.

Form and Payment of Benefits   ERISA sets forth specific requirements for the payment of funds when participants either reach retirement age or leave the company. The act also provides guidance for employers to deal with *qualified domestic relations orders* (QDRO), which are legal orders issued by state courts or other state agencies to require pension payments to alternate payees. An alternate payee must be a spouse, a former spouse, a child, or another dependent of a plan participant.

ERISA also defines funding requirements for pension plans and sets standards for those who are responsible for safeguarding the funds until they're paid to employees. Finally, ERISA provides civil and criminal penalties for organizations that violate its provisions:

Funding   An enrolled actuary determines how much money is required to fund the accrued obligations of the plan, and ERISA requires that these funds be maintained in trust accounts separate from business operating funds. These amounts must be deposited on a quarterly basis; the final contribution must be made no later than 8-1/2 months after the end of the plan year.

Fiduciary Responsibility   For purposes of ERISA, a *fiduciary* is a person, a corporation, or another legal entity that holds property or assets on behalf of, or in trust for, the pension fund. ERISA requires fiduciaries to operate pension funds in the best interest of the participants and their beneficiaries and at the lowest possible expense to them. All actions taken with regard to the plan assets must be in accord with the *prudent person standard of care*, a common law concept that requires all actions be undertaken with "the care, skill, prudence, and diligence ... that a prudent man acting in like capacity" would use, as defined in ERISA itself.

Fiduciaries may be held personally liable for losses to the plan resulting from any breach of fiduciary responsibility that they commit and may be required to make restitution for the losses and be subject to legal action. They aren't held liable for breaches of fiduciary responsibility that occur prior to the time they became fiduciaries.

ERISA specifically prohibits transactions between pension plans and parties in interest.

Administration and Enforcement   Criminal penalties for willful violations of ERISA include fines of between $5,000 and $100,000 and imprisonment for up to 1 year. Civil actions may be brought by plan participants or their beneficiaries, by fiduciaries, or by the DOL to recover benefits or damages or to force compliance with the law.

Other Laws Impacting Deferred Compensation

Changes to different aspects of federal laws regulating employee benefit programs have been made at various times:

Retirement Equity Act (REA) of 1984   The REA lowered age limits for participation and vesting in pension plans. It also required written approval from a spouse if the participant didn't want to provide survivor benefits in the plan and placed restrictions on the conditions that could be placed on survivor benefits.

Older Worker Benefit Protection Act (OWBPA) of 1990   In 1990, Congress passed the OWBPA in response to a Supreme Court decision that placed limitations on the Age Discrimination in Employment Act (ADEA) discussed in Chapter 4. The OWBPA amends the ADEA to include a prohibition on discrimination against older workers in all employee benefit plans unless any age-based reductions are justified by significant cost considerations. This amendment allows seniority systems as long as they don't require involuntary terminations of employees based on their age and extends ADEA protections to all employee benefits.

The OWBPA also defines the conditions under which employees may waive their rights to make claims under the act. To be acceptable, waivers must include the following components:

- Waiver agreements must be written in a way that can be understood by the average employee.

- Waivers must refer specifically to the rights or claims available under the ADEA.

- Employees may not waive rights or claims for actions that occur subsequent to signing the waiver.

- Employees must receive consideration in exchange for the waiver in addition to anything to which they're already entitled.

- The waiver must advise employees of their right to consult an attorney prior to signing the document.

- In individual cases, employees must be given 21 days to consider the agreement before they're required to sign; when a group of employees is involved, employees age 40 and older must be given 45 days to consider their decision.

- Once the waiver is signed, employees may revoke the agreement within 7 days.

- In cases of group terminations (such as a reduction in force or early retirement program), employees must be advised of the eligibility requirements for any exit incentive programs, any time limits for the programs, and a list of the job titles and ages of employees who have been selected or who are eligible for the program.

The federal agency responsible for enforcement of the OWBPA is the EEOC.

Unemployment Compensation Amendments of 1992   Among other provisions unrelated to pension administration, this act reduced rules for rolling over lump-sum distributions of qualified retirement plans into other plans and subjected some distributions to 20 percent income tax withholding.

Omnibus Budget Reconciliation Act (OBRA) of 1993   The parts of the 1993 OBRA with relevance to HR have to do with changes that were made to employee benefit programs in addition to the cap on executive pay discussed in the "Executive Compensation" section later in this chapter. These changes require that health plans honor court-issued qualified medical child-support orders for dependent children of employees. Other changes in this amendment require that group health plans provide coverage for dependent adopted children when those children are placed for adoption in a covered employee's home.

Small Business Job Protection Act of 1996   To relieve the costs of administering qualified plans for small businesses, this act simplified actual deferral percentage (ADP) tests for 401(k) plans and redefined highly compensated employees. In addition, it detailed minimum participation requirements and made changes to disclosure requirements for qualified plans.

Economic Growth and Tax Relief Reconciliation Act (EGTRRA) of 2001   The EGTRRA made a number of changes to contribution limits, increasing many and allowing for catch-up contributions for employees older than 50 years of age. The act provided a schedule of changes through the end of the year 2010, which were extended by Congress in the Pension Protection Act of 2006.

Pension Protection Act (PPA) of 2006   The main focus of the PPA was to require employers to fully fund their pension plans to avoid future cash shortfalls in the plans as employees retire. Beginning in 2008, companies have 7 years to bring their plans into compliance; for those that don't comply, the act provides a penalty in the form of a 10 percent excise tax. The act also specifies funding notices that must be provided by defined-benefit plans.

One of the biggest changes to pension rules made by the PPA was to allow employers to automatically enroll employees in 401(k) plans. Employees who don't want to participate must now opt out of the plan. Another change was that plan advisers may now provide investment advice to plan participants and their beneficiaries under certain conditions.

Largely as a result of the Enron scandal, the PPA included a requirement for defined-contribution plans that include employer stock to provide at least three alternative investment options and allow employees to divest themselves of the employer's stock.

When the EGTRRA was enacted, Congress increased contribution limits for 401(k) plans and IRAs and allowed catch-up contributions for taxpayers older than 50 years of age. These changes were set to expire in 2010, but the PPA made them permanent. For 2012, the maximum catch-up contribution is $5,500; combined, the general contribution limit and the catch-up contribution limit add up to a pretax maximum 401(k) contribution over 50 of $22,500 for 2012.

Finally, it's worth noting that in 2010 the Obama administration continued efforts to respond to the economic crisis. The Recovery Act provided a 65 percent tax credit to help cover the cost of health care through May 31, 2010, and made the first $2,400 in unemployment benefits tax-free, when normally 100 percent of those benefits are taxable. With the political climate rapidly changing, an HR practitioner must stay up-to-date on the extension or enactment of new employment tax law legislation.

Federal Regulation of Health and Welfare Benefits

Some ERISA requirements apply to both deferred compensation and health and welfare benefit programs. There are additional requirements for health and welfare benefits: COBRA and HIPAA.

COBRA REQUIREMENTS

Prior to 1986, employees who were laid off or resigned their jobs lost any health-care benefits that were provided as part of those jobs. ERISA was amended in 1986 by COBRA, which requires businesses with 20 or more employees to provide health-plan continuation coverage under certain circumstances. Employers that meet this requirement must continue benefits for those who leave the company or for their dependents when certain qualifying events occur.

Employers must notify employees of the availability of COBRA coverage when they enter the plan and again within 30 days of the occurrence of a qualifying event. Table 6.11 shows the qualifying events that trigger COBRA, as well as the length of time coverage must be continued for each event.

TABLE 6.11 COBRA qualifying events and coverage requirements

Qualifying Event	Length of Coverage
Employee death	36 months
Divorce or legal separation	36 months
Dependent child no longer covered	36 months
Reduction in hours	18 months
Reduction in hours when disabled*	29 months
Employee termination	18 months
Employee termination when disabled*	29 months
Eligibility for SSA benefits	18 months
Termination for gross misconduct	0 months

*An employee who is disabled within 60 days of a reduction in hours or a termination becomes eligible for an additional 11 months of COBRA coverage.

Employers may charge COBRA participants a maximum of 102 percent of the group premium for coverage and must include them in any open enrollment periods or other changes to the plans. Employers may discontinue COBRA coverage if payments aren't received within 30 days of the time they're due.

Employees must notify the employer within 60 days of a divorce, a separation, or the loss of a child's dependent status. Employees who fail to provide this notice risk the loss of continued coverage.

HIPAA REQUIREMENTS

HIPAA was another amendment to ERISA and prohibits discrimination on the basis of health status as evidenced by an individual's medical condition or history, claims experience, utilization of health-care services, disability, or evidence of insurability. It also places limits on health insurance restrictions for preexisting conditions, which are defined as conditions for which treatment was given within 6 months of enrollment in the plan. Insurers may exclude those conditions from coverage for 12 months or, in the case of a late enrollment, for 18 months.

Insurers may discontinue an employer's group coverage only if the employer neglects to pay the premiums, obtained the policy through fraudulent or intentional misrepresentation, or doesn't comply with material provisions of the plan. Group coverage may also be discontinued if the insurer is no longer offering coverage in the employer's geographic area, if none of the plan participants reside in the plan's network area, or if the employer fails to renew a collective bargaining agreement or fails to comply with its provisions.

In April 2001, the Department of Health and Human Services (HHS) issued privacy regulations that were required by the act. The regulations defined *protected health information* (PHI), patient information that must be kept private, including physical or mental conditions, information about health care given, and payments that have been made. Although these regulations were directed at *covered entities* that conduct business electronically, such as health plans, health care providers, and clearinghouses, they have had a significant impact on the way employers handle information related to employee health benefits. Many employers had to redesign forms for open enrollment periods and new hires and update plan documents and company benefit policies to reflect the changes. The regulations impact employers in other ways as well.

Although *flexible spending accounts* (FSAs) are exempt from other HIPAA requirements, they're considered group health plans for privacy reasons, so employers who sponsor FSAs must comply with the privacy requirements for them.

Employers who are self-insured or who have fully insured group health plans and receive protected health information are required to develop privacy policies that comply with the regulations, appoint a privacy official, and train employees to handle information appropriately.

Although the HIPAA regulations don't prevent employees from seeking assistance from HR for claim problems or other issues with the group health plan, they do require employees to provide the insurance provider or *third-party administrator* (TPA) with an authorization to release information about the claim to the HR department.

The new regulations include stiff civil and criminal sanctions for violations; civil penalties of $100 per violation and up to $25,000 per person each year can be assessed. There are three levels of criminal penalties:

- A conviction for obtaining or disclosing PHI can result in a fine of up to $50,000 and 1 year in prison.

- Obtaining PHI under false pretenses can result in fines of up to $100,000 and 5 years in prison.

- Obtaining or disclosing PHI with the intent of selling, transferring, or using it to obtain commercial advantage or personal gain can be punished with a fine of up to $250,000 and 10 years in prison.

MENTAL HEALTH PARITY ACT OF 1996

The Mental Health Parity Act of 1996 requires insurers to provide the same limits for mental health benefits in their plans as they provide for other health benefits.

Deferred Compensation Benefits

Deferred compensation refers to tax-deferred retirement plans, such as individual retirement accounts (IRAs), 401(k) programs, or traditional employer pension plans. This employee benefit was first offered in the late nineteenth century by business owners who wanted to reward long-term employees. Early pension plans were defined-benefit plans with all funds being provided by the employers. The payments owed to retirees weren't set aside specifically for them but were made from business operating funds. As a result, a company that went out of business was no longer able to make the pension payments, and employees didn't receive the benefits that had been promised to them. To encourage businesses to provide pension benefits, in 1935 the SSA allowed employers who provided pension plans to deduct the full amount of the payments they made to employees, but there were no laws to govern how the plans operated or to require that the funds to pay pensions be set aside to ensure their availability for retirees. In 1958, Congress made its first attempt to exert some control over private pension plans when it passed the Welfare and Pension Disclosure Act (WPDA) requiring the administrators of health insurance, pension, and supplemental unemployment insurance plans to file descriptions of the plans and annual financial reports with the DOL.

As the number of pension plans provided for employees by American businesses grew, some companies found ways to obtain tax benefits from pension plans while denying benefits to employees. There were no requirements for communicating information to plan participants, so many employees were unaware of eligibility requirements. There was also little oversight of the ways the plans were operated. Vesting schedules were inadequate, and many long-term employees found themselves ineligible to receive pension benefits as a result. There were no established standards to ensure the viability of plans to pay promised benefits. The result of this was that many employees found themselves without pensions when they were ready to retire. Furthermore, some businesses set lengthy vesting schedules to obtain tax benefits but terminated long-term employees just before they vested in the plan.

Qualified Deferred Compensation Plans

As defined at the beginning of the "Voluntary Benefits" section, a qualified deferred compensation plan is one that meets all ERISA requirements and protects employees from loss of benefits due to employer mismanagement of pension funds. Within the broad description of a qualified plan, employers have a number of options to choose from when designing a plan that meets the needs of their particular workforce:

Defined-Benefit Plans   As mentioned previously in this chapter, a defined-benefit plan is one in which the employer provides a pension for employees based on a formula. The formula looks at two factors: salary and length of service with the company. In most traditional defined-benefit plans, the retirement benefit is based on the salary earned during the last 5 to 10 years of earnings, but it may also be based on career average earnings, a flat dollar amount for each year of service, or a unit benefit plan in which the benefit payment is based on a percentage of earnings multiplied by the years of service.

 Real World Scenario

Retirement Before ERISA

In 1963, almost 7,000 employees of the Studebaker Corporation lost all or most of their pension benefits because of a plant closure in Indiana. More than 4,000 of these employees had served an average of more than 22 years with the company and, at the time of the plant's closure, were an average of 52 years old. The pension fund failed largely because there was no legal precedent requiring organizations to set aside adequate funds with which to pay retirement benefits; plans at that time were still being funded from current operating funds in the Studebaker Corporation.

Although the failure of the Studebaker Corporation fund wasn't unique, the large number of workers deprived of benefits focused national attention on the problem and led eventually to the passage of the Employee Retirement Income Security Act. ERISA replaced the WPDA, increasing the reporting requirements, requiring that pension funds be separated from the operating funds of the business, establishing vesting schedules for plan participants, requiring employers to provide summary plan descriptions of the plans to employees, and setting minimum standards for fund management.

In these plans, the company is committed to pay a specified benefit amount when an employee retires. How much the company must accrue each year may fluctuate based on the return earned on the invested funds. If the funds are invested in high-growth investments, the company will need to transfer less cash from its operating funds to the pension trust; but if the return earned on the investment drops, the company may have to play catch-up with larger-than-anticipated transfers of cash to maintain the viability of the plan. During the stock-market boom of the late 1990s, many companies didn't need to transfer large sums to fund their pension accounts; but when the stock market dropped, much of the value of the pension funds was lost. This required larger transfers to be made to maintain availability of the pension funds for employees. In defined-benefit plans, employers take the risk for paying out the promised benefit at retirement.

Cash-Balance Plans   *Cash-balance plans* (CBPs) have become increasingly popular since they were approved by the IRS in 1985—between 1996 and 2000, the percentage of CBPs nationwide grew from 4 to 23 percent. Although some companies see them as a hybrid of the defined-benefit and defined-contribution plans, they're subject to the regulations placed on defined-benefit plans. CBPs are less costly for employers: in 1999, IBM revised its defined-benefit plan to a CBP and projected savings of $500 billion over 10 years as a result of the change.

In a CBP, benefits are determined by using a hypothetical personal pension account (PPA); each month, this account is increased by a set rate—for example, 5 percent of the employee's salary. The account also accumulates interest, typically related to the interest rate on Treasury bills.

For employees, the benefit of the CBP is that it's portable: when an employee resigns, the funds may be withdrawn in a lump-sum payment, may be converted to an annuity, or may remain in the employer's account and be withdrawn at a later time. The downside to these plans is that they significantly reduce pension benefits for older workers when traditional defined-benefit plans have been converted to CBPs. A number of lawsuits challenging these plans have been filed, alleging that the plans discriminate against older workers in violation of ERISA. Because of the controversy, the IRS suspended approval of conversions in 1999, pending resolution of the issue in the courts or by Congress. The federal district courts have been split in their rulings on this issue; but a case decided on July 31, 2003, *Cooper v. IBM Personal Pension Plan and IBM Corporation*, in which the Court found that the plan did discriminate, reached the 7th Circuit Court of Appeals, which reversed the district court's finding in August 2006.

Defined-Contribution Plans   A defined-contribution plan relies on contributions from employees and employers to fund IRAs. In these plans, the amount of the contribution is fixed, but the amount of the benefit available upon retirement can vary based on the type of investments made and the returns earned on them. In these plans, the employee takes the risk for having funds available at retirement. There are several types of defined-contribution plans:

Profit-Sharing Plans   Also known as *discretionary contributions, profit-sharing plans* allow employers to contribute deferred compensation based on a percentage of company earnings each year. A maximum contribution of 25 percent may be made for an individual employee each year. The maximum contribution amount was indexed to inflation in increments of $1,000 beginning in 2003. For 2012, the maximum contribution is the lesser of $50,000 or 25 percent of compensation. When calculating contributions, employers may only use the first $245,000 of an employee's compensation; this amount is also indexed to inflation and adjusted annually in increments of $5,000. The percentage of the contribution may vary from year to year, and the company may elect to make no contributions in some years. The maximum tax deduction for contributions that can be taken by the employer is 25 percent of total employee compensation. Because the contributions may vary from year to year, profit-sharing plans work well for companies with erratic profit levels.

Money-Purchase Plans   A *money-purchase plan* uses a fixed percentage of employee earnings to defer compensation. This type of plan works well for organizations with relatively stable earnings from year to year because the percentage is fixed and, once established, contributions must be made every year. The contribution limits are the same as the limits for profit-sharing plans.

Target-Benefit Plans   A *target-benefit plan* is a hybrid plan with similarities to a defined-benefit plan and a money-purchase plan. Instead of using a fixed percentage of employee salaries to determine annual contribution amounts, actuarial formulas calculate the contribution amount needed to reach a predetermined benefit amount at retirement. Because this amount takes into consideration the current age of each employee, different amounts will be contributed for employees with equal compensation packages. As with other deferred-contribution plans, the amounts are distributed to individual employee accounts, and the contribution limits are the same as the limits for profit-sharing plans.

401(k) Plans   A common type of deferred compensation is the *401(k) plan*, established by the Revenue Act of 1978. A 401(k) plan allows for contributions from both employees and employers. Employees may defer part of their pay before taxes up to limits established by the EGTRRA. Employers may make contributions as well; the limits for these are the same as those for profit-sharing plans. Plans similar to the 401(k) are available for nonprofit workers [403(b) plans] and for public employees (457 plans). Any earnings or losses that accrue in the account impact the funds available for retirement, and employees are ultimately responsible for ensuring that the funds are properly managed and available for use when they're ready to retire.

One requirement of 401(k) plans is that they may not provide greater benefits to *highly compensated employees* (HCEs) than other employees. An HCE is defined as a plan participant who, during the current or prior year, earned $115,000 or more, owns 5 percent or more of the company, and, at the company's discretion, is one of the top-paid 20 percent of employees. Each year, an *actual deferral percentage (ADP) test* must be conducted to ensure that the plan is within limits set by IRS regulations. When the ADP test indicates that HCE participants are realizing greater benefits from the plan than non-HCE participants, the company must take action to correct this or lose the tax benefits of the plan. To correct the problem, a company may refund the excess contributions to HCE participants, which will increase their taxable income for the prior year; or the company may increase matching contributions to non-HCE employees in order to pass the test. Another option to correct imbalances is to aggregate the plan with other plans sponsored by the employer, if available.

Nonqualified Deferred Compensation

Nonqualified deferred-compensation plans aren't protected by ERISA and are generally made available only to a limited number of employees at the executive level. Known as *top-hat plans*, these benefits provide retirement funds that supplement qualified retirement benefits and aren't subject to ERISA discrimination testing requirements. These plans allow highly compensated employees to defer income in excess of limits placed on qualified plans. Two types of nonqualified plans are as follows:

Grantor or Rabbi Trusts   Commonly known as *rabbi trusts*, *grantor trusts* are nonqualified deferred-compensation plans established to provide retirement income for officers, directors, and HCEs. The funds are unsecured and therefore subject to claims made by the organization's creditors. Benefits are taxable as ordinary income at the time they're paid to beneficiaries.

Excess Deferral Plans   An excess deferral plan allows the organization to make contributions to a nonqualified plan in order to reduce the impact of discrimination testing on HCEs. This is done by making up the difference between what the executive could have contributed to the plan and what was actually allowed because of limits required by the qualified plan.

On October 22, 2004, President George W. Bush signed into law the American Jobs Creation Act. It created Section 409A of the Internal Revenue Code of 1986, which provides material changes to the tax treatment of nonqualified deferred-compensation plans and arrangements. For a deferral to escape current taxation, it must be subject to a substantial risk of forfeiture and must follow limited deferral and distribution rules, which apply to amounts deferred after December 31, 2004.

Health and Welfare Benefits

Health and welfare benefits have come to be expected by most American workers. The benefits that fall into this category were listed in Table 6.7 earlier in this chapter and are described here in more detail.

Medical Insurance

The cost of medical insurance is substantial for employers and employees. The costs can be controlled to a certain extent by the type of plan selected. These are some plans to consider:

Health Maintenance Organizations (HMOs)   HMOs are a type of managed-care plan that focuses on preventive care and controlling health costs. HMOs generally use a *gatekeeper*, most often the patient's primary care physician (PCP), to determine whether patients need to be seen by a specialist.

Preferred Provider Organizations (PPOs)   PPOs use a network of health-care providers for patient services and don't require patients to be referred by a gatekeeper. Employees who use health-care services in the network make copayments and must also pay the difference between the fees negotiated by the plan and those charged by the physician.

Point of Service (POS) Plans   POS plans include network physicians but allow for referrals outside the network. Like HMOs, these plans require employees to select a PCP from doctors in the network. The PCP generally refers employees to specialists in the network when needed, but employees may see specialists outside the network as well. When employees see physicians outside the network, they must submit reimbursement claims to the insurance company themselves. Payment is covered by the plan, but when the employee sees a care provider outside the POS network, the employee usually pays a higher percentage of the cost than for in-network physicians.

Exclusive Provider Organizations (EPOs)   An EPO consists of a network and includes a hospital. Unlike physicians who participate in a PPO, EPO physicians may see only those patients who are part of the EPO. Patients in an EPO may see only those health-care providers in the network; they receive no reimbursement for health care obtained outside the network.

Physician Hospital Organizations (PHOs)   In a PHO, physicians join with a hospital and together rely on the PHO structure to develop and market their services and to negotiate and sign contracts. PHOs are unique in that they contract directly with employer organizations to provide services.

Fee-for-Service (FFS) Plans   An FFS plan is typically the most expensive to employers and employees because it places no restrictions on the doctors or hospitals available to the patient. These plans require patients to pay for services out-of-pocket and submit claims to be reimbursed for expenses.

In managed-care settings, providers often determine premiums based on the costs incurred by the group during the current coverage period. The costs are analyzed by type, and premiums for the following period are adjusted based on this *experience rating*. Some organizations have implemented wellness programs to improve the experience rating and lower premiums.

Most carriers use a standard coordination of benefits (COB) process when an employee is also covered as a dependent on another plan, such as that of a spouse or parent. When this occurs, the employee's primary coverage pays according to the plan benefits. The secondary coverage will then pay up to 100 percent of the allowable expenses, including deductibles and copayments for the claim. The secondary plan will pay only up to the amount it would have paid as the primary carrier, so the total insurance payout may still be less than 100 percent of the claim.

Other Health Benefits

In addition to medical insurance benefits, many companies offer other health-related benefit options. These include dental, vision, and prescription coverage insurance, among others:

Dental Insurance   Employers may choose dental insurance plans to provide varying levels of coverage for preventive or restoration work such as fillings, major restoration work such as bridges, and orthodontia.

Vision Insurance   One of the lowest-cost benefits available, vision insurance provides employees with reduced costs for eye examinations and contact lenses or glasses.

Prescription Coverage   Even though most medical plans include some form of coverage for prescription drugs, these plans are also offered separately. The cost of the plans is managed by controlling the amount of the required copayment and requiring the use of generic drugs instead of name brands.

Life Insurance   Many insurance companies bundle basic life insurance with medical or dental insurance for a very low rate and offer supplemental insurance for employees who are willing to pay an additional premium for the coverage.

It's important to keep in mind that the IRS views group life insurance in excess of $50,000 as *imputed income* (any indirect compensation paid on behalf of employees) when the premiums are paid by employers. The calculation of imputed income for group life insurance is based on a table provided by the IRS. The table assigns a small amount per month for each $1,000 of coverage that exceeds $50,000 based on an employee's age. The amounts range from $.05 for employees who are 25 years old to $2.06 per month for employees age 70 and older.

You can find a complete discussion of imputed income at www .cpadvantage.com/articles/imputedincomesection79.aspx?LNC=_4_5.

Accidental Death and Dismemberment Insurance (AD&D) Insurance   AD&D insurance can provide insurance for employees and their dependents in the event of an accident that results in the death of the covered person or the loss of a bodily function. AD&D doesn't pay benefits in the event of death due to an illness.

Short- and Long-Term Disability Insurance   Disability insurance protects employees from income loss because of disability caused by illness or accident. Disability protection generally begins with sick leave provided by employers. When employees exhaust their sick leave, they may become eligible for short-term disability insurance, which can be in effect for anywhere between 3 and 6 months. Employees still disabled when short-term disability ends become eligible for long-term disability coverage, which can last for anywhere from 2 years until age 65.

Because these benefits are so common, businesses seeking to use them as recruiting and retention tools must find some way to differentiate their plans from those of their competitors. This need must be balanced with the skyrocketing cost of medical insurance and its impact on the bottom line. Companies looking for a way to increase the attractiveness of their benefit packages may want to reduce or eliminate the employee contribution toward premiums for themselves or for their families or include coverage for domestic partners in the package. A *domestic partnership* is a legal or personal relationship between two people who aren't legally married or in a legally recognized civil union. State and local governments vary in how they view and recognize domestic partnerships.

Health Benefit Cost Management

Regardless of the health plan selected, it's crucial for HR professionals to manage the cost of benefits by selecting the most cost-effective method for funding those benefits. There are several choices, and determining the most appropriate choice for a particular organization depends on factors such as the size of the organization and claim history.

One common funding method for smaller organizations is to purchase insurance coverage for the plan. The organization pays premiums for all participants in the plan, and the insurance company manages payment to the service provider and manages claims issues. In this funding method, the insurer assumes the risk for any unusual claims that may result in claim costs exceeding premiums received. Insurers keep track of the claim history and adjust premiums in subsequent years to recover any losses.

In larger organizations, it may make sense to self-fund the insurance plan. A *self-funded plan* is one in which the employer creates a claim fund and pays all claims through it. Self-funded plans must conduct annual discrimination tests to ensure that HCEs aren't using the plan disproportionately to non-HCEs. In this case, the employer assumes the risk for unusual claims that may exceed the amount budgeted for the plan.

Another option is for organizations to implement a *partially self-funded plan*. These plans use *stop-loss insurance* to prevent a single catastrophic claim from devastating the claim fund. The employer agrees on a preset maximum coverage amount that will be paid from the claim fund for each participant before the insurance company begins to pay the claim.

Self-funded organizations may decide to contract with an insurance company to manage and pay claims, which is known as an *administrative services only (ASO) plan*. A TPA, which provides claim-management services only and isn't part of an insurance company, may also be used for self-funded plans.

To take advantage of economies of scale, smaller employers may form *health purchasing alliances* (HPAs) with other employers in the geographic area. The HPA negotiates and contracts for the plans on behalf of all members of the group.

Work/Life Benefits

Work/life benefits help employees manage the conflict between work demands and family responsibilities and develop a healthful balance for the many areas of their lives. Some of the benefits in this category include time-off programs, wellness benefits, and assistance with childcare or eldercare needs.

Time-off Programs

Paid time off, like health insurance coverage, is a benefit that employees have come to expect. Over the years, businesses have developed different programs to accommodate various needs for time off, such as those described here:

Vacation Pay   Vacation pay is generally earned as employees complete time on the job. Many companies require employees to work a specific period of time, usually 3 to 6 months, before they're eligible to use any accumulated vacation pay. Some companies allow employees to accumulate vacation pay year-to-year; others have a "use it or lose it" policy, although some state laws prohibit companies from forcing employees to forfeit time off that has been earned. In those cases, companies may decide to pay employees for the leave that would otherwise be forfeited.

Most vacation-pay policies require employees to schedule time off in advance and obtain approval from their supervisors before scheduling vacations.

Sick Pay   Sick pay is provided for employees to use when they're ill or when they need to care for a sick child or other family member.

Holiday Pay   Many companies provide paid time off for a variety of national holidays including New Year's Day, Presidents' Day, Martin Luther King's birthday, Memorial Day, Independence Day, Labor Day, Columbus Day, Veterans Day, Thanksgiving, and Christmas.

Paid Time Off (PTO)   Many companies have combined all forms of time off into a single PTO bank that employees can use as they see fit to handle illnesses, personal needs, vacations, and other matters. This provides greater flexibility for employees but can add to employer costs because of the way state laws view vacation and sick pay. Vacation pay is usually viewed as earned leave, meaning that employees must be paid for the leave if they don't use it (for example, if they resign from the company). Sick leave is usually viewed differently, and employees aren't compensated for sick time they don't use. Because PTO combines the two, it's viewed as earned leave, and employees must be compensated for all leave they have earned but not used.

Sabbaticals and Leaves of Absence   In educational institutions, sabbaticals are a long-standing benefit provided for educators in which, after working for a specified period of time, they receive a year off with pay to pursue further education, conduct research, or write books in their field of study. Some companies have adopted this benefit for long-term employees to encourage professional development.

Jury Duty Pay   Employers are required to provide time off for employees who are called to jury duty, although most states don't require employees to be paid for this time. Many employers pay the difference between the employee's regular earnings and the amount they're paid for performing jury duty.

Bereavement Leave   Most companies allow employees time off with pay to attend funeral services for close relatives.

Parental Leave   Some companies provide paid leave for parents of newborns or newly adopted children.

Wellness Benefits

Some employers have developed *health and wellness programs* to prevent employee illnesses and to lower health-care costs. As with any program proposal, it's essential that HR professionals show management how the company will benefit from the program, how much it will cost, and what return the company can expect on its investment. Being able to provide specific costs and savings demonstrates HR's ability to develop programs that serve the long-term strategic goals of the business. Table 6.12 illustrates some of the benefits and costs to consider in analyzing the advantages of a wellness program for the company.

TABLE 6.12   Costs and benefits of wellness programs

Benefits	Costs
Increased productivity	Program implementation
Reduced turnover	Ongoing vendor costs
Reduced medical costs	Administrative costs
Reduced absenteeism	Liability issues
Enhanced ability to attract top-quality employees	
Reduced workers' compensation premiums	

A typical wellness program must be voluntary for employees and includes a physical screening to assess each employee's current fitness level and needs. The program may include nutrition counseling; education programs for weight control, smoking, and stress reduction; and a program of physical exercise. Other programs could include education about substance abuse, spinal care, and prenatal care, depending on the needs of the particular employee population. Health and wellness programs can take many forms, depending on the budget of the employer, the needs of the employees, and the availability of services in the local area.

Employees like wellness programs because they provide convenient opportunities to make healthful lifestyle choices that result in more energy and less stress, both on and off the job.

The size of the budget available for a wellness program will obviously dictate how the program is offered. Some large companies provide fitness centers on site, along with employee cafeterias that serve healthful meals. Smaller organizations may engage a wellness vendor to provide the educational piece of the program and offer employees subsidies for gym memberships or develop walking or sports programs for employee participation.

An important consideration for programs that include on-site fitness centers will be to analyze the total costs, including not only the space and equipment but also fitness personnel and liability for injuries suffered while an employee is working out. Recommendations for on-site programs should therefore include an assessment of the possible risks involved as part of the cost analysis.

Childcare and Eldercare

Depending on an employer's size and resources, on-site childcare opportunities may be available for employees. Although this is an ideal situation for parents, not all companies have the resources to provide this service. If this isn't an option, HR can identify resources that help parents find suitable childcare arrangements, by developing the resources internally or by contracting with an *employee assistance program* (EAP) that may have broader access to information in the commute area for the company.

Eldercare support is generally provided in the form of resources made available to employees so they can find suitable programs for elderly parents requiring ongoing care.

Other Voluntary Benefits

Other voluntary benefits available to employers are limited only by the creativity of the workforce and willingness of the employer to provide. They can include commuter assistance, onsite gourmet meals, concierge services, relocation assistance, flowers, chair massages, adoption assistance, Section 529 educational savings programs, "bring your pet to work" programs, game rooms, and pool tables—there is no limit to what some employers provide. Some of the more common benefits are described here.

Flexible Spending Accounts

FSAs were authorized by the Revenue Act of 1978. Also known as *Section 125 plans*, they allow employees to set aside pretax funds for medical expenses they plan to incur during the calendar year. Employees should be cautioned to be conservative when projecting the amounts they plan to spend during the year because any funds left in the FSA after all expenses for the year have been paid will be forfeited and may be used by the employer to pay the administrative costs of the plan. For employers, a downside to offering an FSA account is that employees may be reimbursed for expenses before the funds have been withheld from their paychecks. If they leave the company before the funds have been withheld, they aren't required to reimburse the company for those expenses.

Expenses that may be included for reimbursement are the costs of any copayments and deductibles from medical, dental, or vision-care plans and other medical expenses approved by the IRS for reimbursement. Other allowable expenses include acupuncture treatments, orthodontia, psychiatric care, wheelchairs, physical therapy, Braille books and magazines, and a variety of other medical expenses. Some expenses that aren't included are memberships to fitness clubs or gyms, elective cosmetic surgery, weight-loss programs, and over-the-counter medications. To receive reimbursement for covered expenses, employees must provide receipts for expenditures.

A similar *dependent-care account* is authorized by Section 129. Employees may set aside a maximum of $5,000 to be used to care for dependent children or elders. To obtain reimbursement for dependent-care expenses, employees must provide an itemized statement of charges from the caregiver. Unlike the FSA for medical expenses, employees may not be reimbursed for expenses in excess of the amounts that have been withheld from their paychecks.

For employees to use either of these accounts, they must sign up at the beginning of the year, at the time they join the company, or during an open enrollment period. Once the contribution amount has been set for the year, it may be changed only if a qualifying event occurs, such as the birth or adoption of a dependent, death, divorce, or a change in employment status for the employee or the employee's spouse.

The IRS requires employers to conduct annual discrimination tests to ensure that FSA plans are being used consistently. Two types of tests are used to determine this: eligibility tests and utilization tests such as the key-employee-concentration test and dependent-care test. A plan that doesn't pass the test may lose its favorable tax treatment.

As mentioned previously, there are no federal laws requiring employers to offer any of these benefits; when they're offered, amendments to ERISA, COBRA, HIPAA, and the Mental Health Parity Act (MHPA) of 1996 have implications for administering them.

Cafeteria Plans

Large employers with diverse employee populations may offer cafeteria plans with a wide variety of benefit options in response to various needs of different employee groups. At the beginning of each plan year, employees select the benefits that best meet their needs. For example, a parent with young children may select dependent coverage as a benefit to cover daycare needs. Once children no longer need daycare, another benefit, such as 401(k) matching, may be selected.

Employee Assistance Programs

An EAP is sponsored by the employer as a benefit. EAPs are often as advantageous for employers as they are for employees because they're generally a low-cost benefit that provides a resource for employees with problems that aren't work related and can't be solved in the work context. In some cases, this assistance allows people who might not otherwise be able to remain employed to stay on the job.

EAPs offer a variety of counseling services for problems ranging from alcohol and drug abuse to legal assistance or financial counseling. Many EAPs are a source for outplacement counseling during a layoff, and some programs offer on-site smoking cessation. During times of crisis, such as after the death of an employee or an incident of workplace violence, the EAP can be a resource for employees to come to grips with their feelings so they're able to continue with their jobs.

EAP services are most often provided through a third party to ensure the confidentiality of employee information, but some employers have in-house programs with counselors on staff. Smaller businesses may join together in a consortium and jointly contract with an EAP to lower costs.

Payroll

In many organizations, payroll is administered as a function of the finance department, but in others it's an HR responsibility. Although an in-depth knowledge of payroll systems and administration isn't required for the PHR/SPHR exams, candidates should have basic knowledge of payroll activities and how they interact with HR responsibilities.

Payroll Systems

Whether an organization employs one person or hundreds of thousands, a payroll system must meet some basic requirements:

- It must accurately calculate payments that are due to employees.
- It must accurately calculate statutory and voluntary deductions.

- It must track payroll tax payments owed to federal and state agencies.
- It must provide accurate reports of payroll costs to management.
- It must provide security for payroll information.

In a small organization with a few employees, all of these requirements may be met with a manual system in which a qualified bookkeeper manually calculates the payments that are due to employees, uses federal and state tax publications to look up withholding information, and prepares checks. This process can be streamlined with the addition of an off-the-shelf accounting software program that makes the calculations, prints the checks, and tracks tax payments owed to federal and state agencies. As organizations grow, manual systems are no longer feasible and may be replaced by a service bureau, which performs the necessary calculations, prints the checks or deposits them electronically, and submits payroll tax payments on behalf of the organization. Very large organizations may develop proprietary software designed to handle their specific needs.

Because payroll systems collect some of the same information that is entered into human resource information systems (HRISs), HR managers can benefit from systems that are able to interact and share information to reduce or eliminate the double entry of information into separate systems.

Payroll Administration

Payroll administration is the function in the company that is responsible for calculating employee earnings and deductions and maintaining records of those payments. Administering payroll is one of the most visible functions performed in any organization because it affects every employee from the CEO to the most junior assistant. Not only is it visible to everyone, but a payroll error has the potential to profoundly affect an employee's life, if only until the error can be corrected.

Employee Earnings

The payroll department is responsible for preparing employee paychecks and ensuring that earnings are calculated correctly. To calculate nonexempt earnings, the payroll department must know the employee's base pay rate, shift differentials, tips, and bonuses; how many hours the employee worked during the pay period; and whether any paid leave was used. With this information, the *gross pay*, or earnings before taxes, can be calculated.

To calculate earnings for exempt employees, payroll needs to know the base salary, any bonus amounts, and any paid leave used during the pay period.

Statutory Deductions

Before employees receive their paychecks, various deductions are made from the gross earnings. These deductions include the following:

- Social Security
- Medicare
- Federal income tax

- State income tax
- Unemployment insurance (in some states)
- Disability insurance (in some states)
- Other state and local taxes

These amounts are withheld from employee earnings. As explained earlier in the "Social Security and Medicare" section, employers match the amount of Social Security and Medicare taxes that are withheld from employees. These amounts, along with the federal income tax withheld, are remitted to the IRS at regular intervals. Failure to remit taxes on time results in substantial penalties for employers. State and local taxes are remitted separately to the appropriate government agency according to payment schedules established by each agency.

At the end of each calendar quarter, reports of gross payroll and withheld taxes are filed with the federal, state, and local taxing authorities. These reports reconcile the amount of tax withheld to the amounts deposited during the quarter. At the end of the year, W-2 forms are prepared for each employee and submitted to federal and state tax agencies.

Voluntary Deductions

A number of other deductions may be made from an employee's paycheck. These include medical, dental, and other health benefit contributions; 401(k) contributions; union dues; and, in some cases, contributions to charities designated by employees.

Involuntary Deductions

From time to time, employers may be required by a court order or tax levy to withhold additional funds from employee paychecks. These withholdings are known as *wage garnishments* and are issued to satisfy a debt owed by the employee. Garnishments may come in the form of a court order (for example, an order to pay child support or another debt) or from a government agency such as the IRS or other taxing authority to collect unpaid back taxes. Wage garnishments aren't voluntary, and employers have no discretion as to whether to honor them.

The Federal Wage Garnishment Law is found in Title III of the Consumer Credit Protection Act (CCPA) of 1968 and applies to all employers and employees. Employers are required to withhold funds from an employee's paycheck and send the money to an entity designated in the court order or levy document.

Title III of the CCPA protects employees in three ways:

- Prohibits employers from terminating employees whose wages are garnished for any one debt, even if the employer receives multiple garnishment orders for the same debt
- Sets limits on the amount that can be garnished in any single week
- Defines how disposable earnings are to be calculated for garnishment withholdings

The law doesn't protect employees from termination if the employer receives garnishments for more than one debt.

Disposable earnings are what is left in an employee's paycheck after all legally mandated deductions have been made, such as federal and state income tax, Social Security, state and local taxes, disability insurance, and so on. Title III provides separate garnishment calculation methods for debt garnishments and child-support orders:

Debt Garnishment Calculations   Title III defines two methods for calculating the maximum weekly garnishment. The first method allows garnishment of up to 25 percent of disposable earnings. The second method is calculated by multiplying the federal minimum wage ($7.25 per hour as of July 2011) by 30 ($217.50). The total is subtracted from the disposable earnings. Any disposable earnings that exceed that amount must be sent directly to the recipient designated in the order and not to the employee.

The maximum amount of garnishment allowed is the lesser of those two calculations.

Child-Support Garnishment Calculations   Title III allows child-support garnishments of up to 50 percent of an employee's disposable earnings if the employee is currently supporting a spouse or child and up to 60 percent if not. If support payments are more than 12 weeks in arrears, wages may be garnished an additional 5 percent. There are no restrictions on child-support garnishments.

Depending on the nature of a violation, employers who violate the CCPA may be required to reinstate a terminated employee, pay back wages, and refund any improper garnishments. Whenever possible, the DOL tries to resolve garnishment violations informally. If that isn't possible, they may take legal action. Willful violators are subject to criminal prosecution and may be fined up to $1,000 and/or face imprisonment for up to 1 year.

Record Keeping

The FLSA requires employers to keep accurate records that identify employees, such as their name, address, and Social Security number, along with their birth date if they're younger than 19 years of age, their sex, and their occupation. For nonexempt employees, the employer's records must include the work week (for example, 12 a.m. Sunday through 11:59 p.m. Saturday). Nonexempt records must also include the hours worked each day, the total hours for the week, and the basis for payment (dollars per hour, per week, or per piece), as well as any differentials, bonuses, and other additions described previously. Finally, the records must include the pay-period dates, how much straight time and overtime pay was earned for the pay period, any deductions withheld, and the date of payment.

A more recent record-keeping and reporting requirement was enacted by Congress to aid state and federal welfare agencies in collecting child support from parents who neglect to pay it and is known as the Personal Responsibility and Work Opportunity Reconciliation Act of 1996.

> ### Personal Responsibility and Work Opportunity Reconciliation Act of 1996
>
> This legislation requires employers to report all new hires within 20 days of their hire date to the State Department of New Hires. The law requires only that employers forward the W-4 form to the state, but some states have developed their own forms for this purpose. As a side benefit for employers, the new hire reporting database has reduced and prevented fraudulent or erroneous unemployment payments that would otherwise be charged to the employer's unemployment insurance account. The database also crosschecks against workers' compensation claims, which has reduced fraud and errors in those programs as well.

As long as employee paychecks are processed accurately and delivered on time, payroll administration is often taken for granted. HR professionals contribute to a smooth payroll process by providing accurate information to those responsible for processing payroll. Working with payroll to establish a procedure that meets the needs of both can ensure that employees are paid correctly and on time.

Payroll-Related Information

The data collected throughout the life cycle of the employee's tenure with the organization must be adequately accounted for and managed. This data generation begins at the time of hire when basic information is gathered, such as tax withholdings, and continues with pay adjustments to account for benefits enrollment, wage increases, or exceptions such as garnishments. It ends at the time of termination when accrued benefits are calculated, health insurance and retirement benefits are rolled over or cancelled, and final wages are paid to the employee.

Outsourcing Compensation

Many organizations are turning to outsourcing groups to help navigate the complexities of managing the various components of compensation and benefits plans. In fact, one of the most common outsourced HR functions is that of processing payroll. The services offered by various companies include payroll, COBRA administration, quarterly reporting, tax filings, and HR expertise in other functions. Outsourcing payroll is a strategic decision that allows the internal talent to focus on the core competencies required for successful operations. However, managing the vendors is still an important function of HR, because the hiring company typically retains liability in the case of errors or omissions in compliance.

Finding the right provider(s) is the first step toward effectively managing the outsourcing process. Clearly defining expectations and needs, clarifying the frequency of contact, and agreeing on set deliverables are all methods of effective vendor management.

Communicating Compensation and Benefits Programs

Taking the time to develop a compensation philosophy, participate in salary surveys, and develop new compensation programs doesn't help the organization unless results and objectives are clearly communicated to employees and managers.

For example, when rolling out the annual merit-increase process, it's important to have timely, effective, and frequent communication geared toward both management and employee populations. Management typically receives different or additional information designed to facilitate their role as evaluators. Sharing salary survey results with management continues the dialogue about attracting, retaining, and motivating talent through existing or new programs. Furthermore, training management in corporate policies and compensation philosophies allows them to properly respond to employees when questions arise. Emotions can run high when employees have questions about their pay or benefits, so it's important that front-line supervisors have the information necessary to meet employee needs. Answering questions about deductions, understanding leave policies, and justifying pay rates are all examples of information that can be shared through systematic management training.

Communicating compensation programs or philosophy involves a series of written communications. Updating the company intranet, the employee handbook, and plan documents are a few examples of written information that serve as great resources for employees.

Employee self-service options are gaining in popularity. These interactive, online services allow employees to gather relevant data based on their specific needs. Forms requests, online benefits enrollment, and access to payroll data are all examples of the convenience of robust self-service programs for employees. Benefits for employers also exist through the use of self-service programs. Time is saved by allowing employees to update their own personal information; reports such as benefit-utilization reviews can be gathered, wage statements including the value of employee benefits can be generated and communicated, and surveys and polls can be conducted to identify the needs of the real-time workforce.

Ultimately, communication of compensation programs should be simple, and the alignment to compensation philosophy should be visible.

SPHR
ONLY

Executive Compensation

As the complexity of managing organizations in a global environment increases, the need to attract and retain executives with the skills and talent to lead a company is even more critical for success. Executive compensation is a controversial subject for shareholders and, with the collapse of major corporations in the finance industry in late 2008, the focus of increasing scrutiny by federal and state regulators.

The responsibility for negotiating executive compensation packages belongs to the board of directors (BOD). The BOD is expected to negotiate with executive candidates and incumbents "at arm's length," meaning that the negotiations are conducted with objectivity and in the best interest of the company. Because executive candidates and incumbents are, almost by definition, skilled negotiators, the conventional wisdom is that they will push hard for packages that they view as competitive and in their own interests. In practice, many boards develop close relationships with executive staff, particularly CEOs, which has called into question the degree to which the negotiation can realistically be viewed as objective. Shareholders are increasingly active in challenging excessive compensation, particularly when executives receive massive compensation when business results are falling or employees are being laid off in large numbers as the result of poor decisions made by executives.

There have been many suggestions about how to develop compensation packages in a way that attracts and retains qualified, talented executives while maintaining the objectivity necessary to satisfy shareholder concerns. Some that are being considered or implemented include the following:

- Reporting transparency of executive compensation packages in annual reports and SEC filings
- Board compensation committees that consist only of outside directors (those without paid positions in the company) and establish internal guidelines for executive compensation
- Use of independent data on competitive executive pay practices in developing internal guidelines
- Linking executive pay to long-term business results instead of quarterly or annual results (performance-based pay)
- Tying a significant piece of total compensation to achievable stretch goals that include profit goals in addition to share price
- Shareholder approval of executive stock-option plans
- Inclusion of nonmonetary performance goals, such as "green" goals, ethical behaviors, or community investment in the rewards package

A typical compensation package for an executive can include elements from five categories: base salary, bonuses or short-term incentives, long-term incentives, employee benefits, and executive perks.

The composition of packages for individual executives varies by industry and company culture, with some having more pay at risk than others. In an effort to motivate executive performance and address shareholder concerns, BODs construct packages that place the majority of executive compensation at risk in the form of short- and long-term incentives. The main theory at play in the use of incentive pay for executives is that, because they will benefit personally from decisions that achieve positive results for the company, they're more likely to act in ways that benefit the company than in ways that benefit them personally. One way this connection is achieved is that the size of the executive bonus pool is usually related to the profitability of the company, which by definition ties executive pay to business results.

Executive benefits often include benefits available to employees throughout the organization, such as flexible work schedules, deferred compensation, tuition-reimbursement programs, or health club memberships. In some cases, benefit levels for executives may be expanded; for example, a flexible work arrangement for an executive may provide reimbursement for travel between the corporate office and the family home in another state, while the benefit available to nonexecutive employees allows telecommuting several days each week.

One unique element of executive compensation is *perquisites*. Perquisites, often referred to as *perks*, are additional benefits that provide comfort and luxury to the work and/or personal environment, usually intended for senior management and executives. The following are some of the perks provided to executive employees:

- Stock options
- Personal/spouse travel expenses
- Personal use of company aircraft
- Tax preparation and financial counseling
- Tax payments for benefits
- Supplemental retirement plans
- Housing allowances
- Home security services
- Company cars/chauffeurs
- Life insurance, above company plan
- Medical plans above worker coverage
- Annual physicals
- Interest free loans
- Company-paid legal advice

This element of an executive compensation package is often the least transparent and an area of increased interest to shareholders and regulators. At the beginning of 2007, the SEC requirements for reporting executive perks were reduced from $50,000 to $10,000, forcing companies to provide detailed lists of perks received by their executives. In some cases, the resulting exposure of payments outraged stockholders and employees and embarrassed BODs. As a result, there is a growing trend of eliminating or reducing the numbers and types of perks previously provided. For example, in 2006, the Lockheed-Martin BOD eliminated perks including club memberships and fees and company-paid financial counseling and tax services for executives and adjusted executive salaries to reflect the cash value of the perks to maintain the value of their compensation packages.

Federal legislation has also impacted executive pay. In 1993, OBRA was an attempt to reduce executive compensation by limiting tax deductions for executive pay to $1,000,000 annually. This led to an increase in the use of perks and stock options that were less visible to shareholders and regulators.

Other benefits that can be found in executive compensation packages include the following:

Golden Parachute   A *golden parachute* provides significant benefits to an executive whose employment is terminated, usually under specific conditions such as a change in control of the company. Benefits can include severance pay, bonuses, options, continuation of medical coverage, and other types of benefits.

Golden Handshake   A *golden handshake* is most often used when a CEO takes a position that entails a high risk of termination due to restructuring or a change in direction, or sometimes as an incentive to retire early.

Golden Handcuffs   *Golden handcuffs* are a form of retention pay designed to keep key employees from leaving a company. They can take the form of stock options that vest over a period of years or a written agreement to pay back bonuses or other types of compensation if the employee resigns within a specified period of time.

Golden Life Jacket   A *golden life jacket* is sometimes offered to executives of a company being acquired, to ensure that they remain with the reorganized company.

Stock Options

A *stock option* is the right to purchase an employer's stock at a certain price (the strike price), at a future date, within a specified period of time. Options provide an employee with an opportunity to purchase shares but don't require that the employee do so. The *grant price* or *strike price* of the stock is based on the market price at the time the options are issued. It's common to find stock options vesting over a 3- to 5-year period as a retention tactic; they can be exercised for up to 10 years. Stock options are valuable only if the stock price rises over time, so their value to employees depends on the company's financial performance. Although stock-option plans vary between companies, all plans must be operated within parameters established by the SEC or IRS.

 Real World Scenario

Executive Pay Trends

In June 2003, New York Stock Exchange (NYSE) Chairman Richard Grasso was forced to resign from his position amid outrage over his $140 million pay package (which included $48 million in special benefits). Grasso's situation at the NYSE is just one example of how executive-ranked businesspeople manage to be paid extraordinary amounts of money even during poor economic times.

According to *USA Today*, the median pay for CEOs of the 100 largest companies in America in 2005 was $17.9 million—a 25 percent increase over 2004. Several CEOs earned more than $100 million in total compensation. The American Federation of Labor–Congress of Industrial Organizations (AFL-CIO), which keeps track of U.S. executive pay trends on its Executive Paywatch website (www.aflcio.org /corporateamerica/paywatch/), calculates the ratio of executive to employee pay for 2005 at 411:1. Although this ratio has dropped from the peak of 525:1 in 2000, it has increased tenfold since 1980. Even CEOs who were fired from their positions managed to exit organizations with large payouts—one executive received a payout of $52 million.

It's surprising to some that even in the face of tighter regulation from the SEC as a result of the scandals at Enron, MCI WorldCom, and other major corporations, executive pay continues to rise—this is the second year in a row in which executive pay increased by 25 percent. This trend has been difficult for many employees and shareholders to accept. The debate continues as stockholders scrutinize executive compensation packages and compensation committees of BODs take an active role in monitoring those packages.

With the "Wall Street bailout" signed into law in 2008, the Congress has renewed its interest in scrutinizing executive compensation, particularly for executives of companies such as AIG and the banks that accepted federal funds to avoid bankruptcy. As with many labor law trends, it is important to note that outcomes are significantly influenced by national party leadership at both the presidential and congressional levels.

There are two types of stock options: *incentive stock options* (ISO) and *nonqualified stock options*. The difference between the option types is the tax treatment for the employer and employee:

Incentive or Qualified Stock Options   ISOs are stock options that can be offered only to employees; consultants and external members of the BOD aren't eligible. The tax treatment for ISOs is often favorable for employees because they don't face taxes at the time the stock option is exercised—they don't have income to report until the stock is sold at a later date. When an ISO is sold, however, it's likely that capital gains taxes will be due and subject to the alternative minimum tax under certain conditions. Use of ISOs isn't as favorable to employers because the company receives a tax deduction only if certain conditions are met.

Nonqualified Options   Nonqualified stock options can be used for consultants and external members of the BOD as well as for employees. The organization receives a tax deduction when the options are exercised, and employees pay tax on any gain they realize from the sale. Income from the stock is treated as compensation, and when the stock is sold there are further tax implications.

Two other types of stock ownership employers provide to employees are restricted stock and phantom stock:

Restricted Stock   *Restricted stock* is common stock offered to employees, typically executives or employees who demonstrate outstanding performance. Restricted stocks are actual shares, not the option-to-buy shares, like stock options. Restricted stock usually follows a vesting schedule designed to reward retention. Employees may be motivated to stay with the organization to realize the full benefit of their restricted stock, which is why employees perceive these as golden handcuffs, or a financial benefit that will be lost if they leave the organization. For example, in a broad yet creative move to motivate its employees, Microsoft Corporation gave 600 employees restricted stock plans tied to their achievement of certain performance targets.

Phantom Stock   *Phantom stock* is used in privately held companies to provide the benefits of employee ownership without granting stock. Organizations use phantom stock to motivate and retain employees without granting equity or sharing ownership in the company. Phantom stock can generate the kind of payoffs that stock options or restricted stock can yield. Executives and outside members of the BOD are the most common recipients of phantom stock. There is usually a vesting schedule based on length of service and performance (individual or company). Like common stock, phantom stock follows the company's market-price movements. A valuation formula determines the value of the stock. When the phantom stock yields a payout, the employer is eligible to receive a tax deduction for the amount paid.

Board of Directors/Outside Directors

The BOD is elected by shareholders to oversee the management of the corporation on behalf of its stockholders. Members of the BOD can be executives of the organization (known as *inside directors*) or external to the organization (known as *outside directors*).

Inside directors receive executive compensation packages consisting of stock options, benefits, and base pay, to which they're entitled based on their roles as corporate executives. Outside directors commonly receive cash for meeting fees and retainers.

 Real World Scenario

Stock Options and Compensation

Stock options have been a key part of employee compensation packages for decades, but they were never so popular as during the time of the dot-com boom. Employees at all levels, especially in the high-tech sector, were receiving stock options as part of their compensation packages. This was attractive for many reasons to both employers and employees. The alignment between employee, company, and market performance provided the upside opportunity for employees to profit if the company performed well in the stock market. During the dot-com boom, many average employees realized great wealth because of the performance of the stock market. Employers enjoyed this too, because there was the potential to create wealth for employees without dipping into the company's cash flow. When the dot-com industry became unable to sustain itself in a declining economy, the opportunity for upside potential with stock options went away.

Some employees believed so wholeheartedly in the value of their organizations that they declined salaries in exchange for more stock options. This outlook backfired on employees who lost their jobs when the bubble burst and had nothing but worthless paper to show for their hard work.

Some executives wrongly tried to create value in options by backdating them—setting the option price at an earlier date when the stock price was lower than the current market. Such backdating isn't unlawful in itself, provided sufficient disclosure is made and appropriate penalties and taxes are paid on the discounted shares. Backdating becomes unlawful when shareholders are misled as to the practice. HR executives have found themselves under investigation and have indeed been prosecuted by the SEC for such activities.

Although stock options are no longer the highlight of a typical offer package, they're still a key component of total compensation. Because of financial abuses committed by companies such as Enron, regulators and legislators worked to change the way options were expensed, requiring that the expense be recorded when the options were issued instead of when they were exercised. While many companies objected to this change because of concern that it would adversely affect their net profits, companies that voluntarily implemented this reporting change found it had little effect on their profits. Beginning in 2006, accounting rules required all stock options to be expensed in the financial statements at the time they're granted to employees.

The requirement for expensing options has opened the door for companies to consider other types of equity grants that have always been expensed. For example, companies are now granting restricted stock more often and driving a close tie between employees and other shareholders by replacing time-based vesting with performance-based vesting.

Metrics: Measuring Results

As mentioned earlier in this chapter, compensation and benefits costs are significant in virtually all organizations. Using metrics to monitor whether total rewards programs are delivering the type of qualified employees needed by the organization is therefore key to demonstrating how HR professionals add value to their organizations:

Business Impact Measures   One of the clearest indications that there is a problem with the total rewards package in an organization is an increase in turnover and exit interviews that indicate employees are easily able to find higher compensation and/or a richer, more appropriate benefits package with other employers.

Tactical Accountability Measures   Two metrics that may provide useful information about compensation and benefits programs are as follows:

Compensation as a Percent of Operating Expenses   This metric provides information about the cost of human capital relative to other operating expenses for an organization. The higher the compensation costs are, the more impact HR programs can have on the bottom line. To calculate this metric, divide the total compensation costs (base salary, variable pay, and any deferred compensation) by the total operating expenses.

Benefits as a Percent of Operating Expenses   This measure helps view increased benefit costs in the context of other expenses. Tracking the cost of benefits relative to other operating expenses can help organizations make decisions about the appropriate mix of benefits to offer as costs rise and to view increasing benefits costs in the context of other expense increases. This metric is calculated by dividing the cost of benefits (health and welfare, paid time off, and so on) by the total operating expenses.

SPHR ONLY Global Considerations

International compensation laws and practices vary widely from country to country and are often subject to heavy regulation, particularly in Europe. A significant consideration when crafting a compensation package for a third-country national or expatriate is the effect on the tax situations for the employee and employer. In some countries that are highly unionized, unions have significantly more influence on compensation practices than employers find in the United States.

Expatriate employees often receive some type of pay differential to ensure that their pay remains equitable with their peers and to equalize tax burdens and living costs unique to their specific situations. Many assignments include housing allowances and COLAs that help employees maintain their standard of living while out of the country. It isn't uncommon to find total expatriate compensation that exceeds three times the base pay. It may be helpful for both parties to the employment contract to have a choice-of-law clause. This clause allows the parties to agree on which laws—home or host country—will apply, should a contract dispute arise. It can help protect both the employer and employee who want to exercise or retain certain rights in the employment relationship. Globally operating organizations make increasing use of home-country and third-party nationals to relieve some of this financial pressure.

Summary

Compensation and benefits packages are a key factor in virtually every organization's quest to attract and retain employees who are best qualified to achieve its goals. The total rewards package is guided by the corporate mission and goals and reflects its organizational culture. The culture in particular impacts the intrinsic and extrinsic rewards that employees derive from their work. TR philosophy drives the organization's ability to attract, retain, and motivate its employees to meet strategic objectives.

TR philosophy is impacted by internal considerations such as an organization's willingness and ability to provide compensation and benefits that lead, meet, or lag the market. Whether an organization chooses a performance culture that rewards employee contributions or an entitlement culture that rewards employee service impacts the motivation and loyalty of employees.

The first mandatory benefits, Social Security, Medicare, and unemployment insurance, were developed to provide a safety net for American workers. More recent benefits such as FMLA and COBRA require employers to actively participate in and administer programs.

The mix of voluntary benefits chosen by an organization can help it attract and retain employees with particular characteristics; for example, a generous educational reimbursement benefit will help the company attract employees who are committed to continuous learning and skill development.

Exam Essentials

Be aware of the federal laws that govern compensation and benefit programs. The Fair Labor Standards Act in 1938 was the first to impact compensation in private businesses in America, and it continues to do so today. ERISA and its amendments, COBRA and HIPAA, require employers who offer benefits to meet minimum standards of fairness in benefit programs. IRS regulations often impact decisions on benefits that are offered.

Understand the provisions of the FLSA. The FLSA established a minimum wage, overtime requirements, laws protecting American children against labor exploitation, criteria for exempt and nonexempt employees, exemption tests to determine exemption status, and payroll record-keeping requirements.

Be aware of the components of compensation. Base pay is the foundation of an employer's compensation program because it reflects the value placed on individual jobs by the organization. Differentials such as overtime and hazard pay motivate employees to spend longer hours at work or to accept assignments that may be unpleasant or hazardous. Incentive pay motivates and rewards employees when they achieve corporate goals.

Understand the job-evaluation process. Job evaluation is an objective mechanism used to determine the worth of different jobs to the company. Compensable factors distinguish jobs from each other and are used in determining their value to the organization.

Understand the purpose of salary surveys and how they're conducted. Salary surveys are used to determine current market trends and competition for different skills and knowledge and assist the employer in setting pay levels that lead, meet, or lag the market. Surveys are conducted by gathering information about specific jobs in a large number of companies in an industry, a profession, or a geographic area and summarizing the data by job.

Understand how HR interacts with payroll systems.   Whether HR interacts with or administers payroll, HR professionals are involved in ensuring that changes to employee pay and deductions are accurate.

Be able to communicate the compensation and benefits program to employees.   An effective communication program informs employees about the total rewards package so they're able to take advantage of benefits that are offered and have an understanding of the full cost to the employer of providing the different programs.

Be aware of the wide variety of benefits that are available.   With an awareness of the various and sometimes unusual benefits that are available, employers are able to develop a benefit mix that meets the needs of employees at the lowest cost to net profits.

Be aware of mandatory benefits.   Mandatory employee benefits are determined by Congress and affect employers with varying minimum numbers of employees. Social Security, Medicare, unemployment insurance, FMLA leave, and COBRA continuation benefits are required by statute.

Understand how voluntary benefits influence employees.   Voluntary benefits fall into four categories: deferred compensation, health and welfare, work-life balance, and other benefits. Some benefits, such as medical insurance and paid time off, have come to be expected by employees, while others will attract and retain different types of employees with different needs.

Be aware of FMLA leave requirements.   FMLA requires unpaid leave to be provided by companies with 50 or more employees within 75 miles of the worksite. Employees who meet the eligibility requirements are entitled to unpaid leave for the birth or adoption of a child or a serious illness of an immediate family member or themselves.

Review Questions

You can find the answers in Appendix A.

1. The Federal Insurance Contributions Act requires employers to do which of the following?
    A. Contribute to a defined-benefit plan
    B. Contribute to a deferred-compensation plan
    C. Withhold Social Security tax from pay
    D. Provide health insurance for all employees

2. Employers are required to provide a portable retirement plan to employees based on which of the following?
    A. Employee Retirement Income Security Act.
    B. Omnibus Budget Reconciliation Act.
    C. Older Worker Benefit Protection Act.
    D. Retirement benefits are not required by federal law.

3. Which of the following is an example of an intrinsic reward?

    A. Recognition of accomplishments

    B. The satisfaction of a job well done

    C. A great supervisor

    D. An exciting assignment

4. A Total Rewards philosophy can help achieve an organization's strategic goals by doing which of the following?

    A. Attracting and retaining employees with the necessary KSAs

    B. Establishing a pecking order for jobs in the organization

    C. Positioning the company to lead the competition for employees

    D. Maintaining an entitlement culture

5. An entitlement culture is appropriate for a business that needs what type of workforce?

    A. One that continues to show productivity increases over time

    B. One that has a line of sight to retirement

    C. One that is highly competitive in completing daily assignments

    D. One that has a skill set that's in high demand

6. A company that wants to reduce the cost of its unemployment insurance should do which of the following?

    A. Aggressively fight unjustified claims for unemployment

    B. Establish an effective performance-management program

    C. Terminate employees who violate company policy

    D. All of the above

7. A reduced FMLA leave schedule means which of the following?

    A. The employee is absent from work multiple times for the same illness or injury.

    B. The employee works fewer hours each day or week.

    C. The employee's leave schedule is disruptive to the work schedule.

    D. Accurate records of time off are maintained.

8. The Older Worker Benefit Protection Act requires that an employee age 40 or older who is asked to waive their rights under the act must be given what?

    A. 7 days to consider the agreement before signing it

    B. 21 days to consider the agreement before signing it

    C. 45 days to consider the agreement before signing it

    D. 60 days to consider the agreement before signing it

9. The Omnibus Budget Reconciliation Act of 1993 does *not* require which of the following?

    A. Group health coverage be offered for children placed for adoption before the adoption is final

    B. Group health plans honor qualified medical child-support orders

    C. Tax deductions for executive pay be capped at $1,000,000 per year

    D. Income tax be withheld from some distributions to rollover accounts

10. A summary plan description is not required for which of the following?

    A. Defined-contribution plans

    B. Defined-benefit plans

    C. Flexible spending accounts

    D. AD&D insurance

11. Molly is the Director of HR at a large multinational corporation. She extended the open enrollment period for benefits in order to accommodate her spouse, who needed a different plan. This is an example of what?

    A. Breach of fiduciary responsibility

    B. Exercising a choice-of-law clause

    C. Breaking the law

    D. Unethical conduct

12. ESOPs, ESPPs, and profit-sharing are all examples of which of the following?

    A. Deferred compensation

    B. Gainsharing strategies

    C. Group incentives

    D. Sales bonus options

13. James is a highly productive salesperson who is required to share a team bonus with his co-workers if certain sales goals are met each month. He is frustrated with this compensation structure, because he believes his teammates do not contribute as much as he does to the final numbers. This is an example of what?

    A. Pay disparity

    B. Procedural justice

    C. Distributive justice

    D. Wage inequity

14. Tax withholding is to the _____ stage of the employment life cycle as COBRA benefits are to the _____ stage of the employment life cycle.

    A. Pre-, post-

    B. Pre-, mid-

    C. Beginning, middle

    D. Beginning, ending

15. In which of the following situations was the HR manager incorrect in their handling of FMLA medical certification?

   A. The employer disagreed with the certification by the employee's doctor, so it paid to have the employee seen by a second provider.

   B. The employee was given 5 calendar days to provide medical certification.

   C. The employer had its own medical certification that it used, but it contained information identical to the DOL's WH-380 form.

   D. None of the above options were incorrect.

16. The Economic Growth and Tax Relief Reconciliation Act of 2001 allows for catch-up contributions for employees age _____ and older.

   A. 40

   B. 50

   C. 60

   D. 63

17. Which of the following is *not* an example of a voluntary benefit?

   A. Medicare

   B. Vision insurance

   C. Qualified pension plan

   D. Sick pay

18. Which of the following would be the best choice of a profit-sharing plan if the employer wishes to improve organizational productivity through shared management and employee efforts?

   A. Employee Stock Purchase Plan

   B. Bonuses

   C. Gainsharing

   D. Improshare

19. Job fulfillment from working with a talented peer group is an example of which of the following types of compensation?

   A. Monetary

   B. Intrinsic

   C. Extrinsic

   D. Total rewards

20. For which of the following is "the highest standards of care and professionals in a legal context" a key component?

   A. Code of conduct

   B. Breach of contract

   C. Conflict of interest

   D. Fiduciary responsibility

Chapter

7

Employee and Labor Relations

THE HRCI TEST SPECIFICATIONS FROM THE EMPLOYEE AND LABOR RELATIONS FUNCTIONAL AREA COVERED IN THIS CHAPTER INCLUDE:

✓ Ensure that employee and labor relations activities are compliant with applicable federal laws and regulations.

✓ Assess organizational climate by obtaining employee input (for example: focus groups, employee surveys, staff meetings).

✓ Develop and implement employee relations programs (for example: recognition, special events, diversity programs) that promote a positive organizational culture.

✓ Evaluate effectiveness of employee relations programs through the use of metrics (for example: exit interviews, employee surveys, turnover rates).

✓ Establish, update, and communicate workplace policies and procedures (for example: employee handbook, reference guides, or standard operating procedures) and monitor their application and enforcement to ensure consistency.

✓ Develop and implement a discipline policy based on organizational code of conduct/ethics, ensuring that no disparate impact or other legal issues arise.

✓ Create and administer a termination process (for example: reductions in force [RIF], policy violations, poor performance) ensuring that no disparate impact or other legal issues arise.

✓ Develop, administer, and evaluate grievance/dispute resolution and performance improvement policies and procedures.

✓ Investigate and resolve employee complaints filed with federal agencies involving employment practices or working conditions, utilizing professional resources as necessary (for example: legal counsel, mediation/arbitration specialists, investigators)

✓ Develop and direct proactive employee relations strategies for remaining union-free in non-organized locations.

The Employee and Labor Relations (ELR) function includes the tasks and responsibilities necessary to sustain effective employment relationships in both union and nonunion environments. This chapter reviews the rights and responsibilities of both employers and employees in this relationship and HR's role in those processes.

To be fully prepared for the PHR/SPHR exams, candidates must be well versed in the basic knowledge for this functional area as well as the core knowledge requirements covered in Chapter 2, "Core Knowledge Requirements for HR Professionals," that pertain to ELR. The *2012 PHR/SPHR Certification Policies and Procedures Handbook* described in the introduction to this book provides the detailed list of ELR knowledge requirements and should be reviewed prior to studying this area of the *BOK*.

> The HRCI core knowledge requirements that will be particularly helpful in understanding this functional area include assessment methods, change-management methods, communication skills, motivation and leadership concepts, the ways in which interpersonal and organizational behavior affect employee-relations programs, the impact of diversity on employee-relations programs, methods to measure and analyze employee satisfaction, types of organizational structures, risk management, and, finally, the implications of employee-relations programs on HR programs in other functional areas.

Both employers and employees have rights that have been either granted through the legislative process or developed over time as the result of court decisions and common-law practices. Along with these rights come associated responsibilities to act in a lawful and equitable manner in the relationship.

> For up-to-the-minute updates for this chapter, please see www.sybex.com/go/phr4e.

Federal Employment Legislation

The federal employment legislation covered in detail in Chapter 4, "Workforce Planning and Employment," is equally applicable for this functional area of the *BOK*. In addition, Congress has enacted labor legislation that significantly impacts employment relationships. Table 7.1 summarizes the legislation that impacts ELR activities.

TABLE 7.1   Federal legislation governing ELR activities

Type	Enforcement Agency	Chapter Reference
Civil rights	Equal Employment Opportunity Commission (EEOC) and/or Office of Federal Contract Compliance Programs (OFCCP)	4
Executive orders	OFCCP	4
Mass layoffs	Department of Labor (DOL)	4
Polygraph	DOL	7
Privacy	Department of Justice	7
Veterans' rights	DOL, Veterans Employment and Training Service	7
Labor relations	National Labor Relations Board (NLRB)	7

This chapter summarizes some of the significant case law related to these statutes and discusses the common-law doctrines that impact employment relationships. The legal statutes are discussed in two sections: this section covers the statutes, cases, and common law governing employment relationships, such as employment at-will, sexual harassment, veteran's rights, and so on; the "Labor Relations" section covers employment issues related to the National Labor Relations Act (NLRA).

Employment relationships are affected both by common-law doctrines and by statutory requirements that protect employers and employees and require certain actions and behaviors. Employers (whether individuals or stockholders represented by a board of directors) have the right to structure organizations in the most cost-effective way necessary to fulfill their vision, strategy, mission, and goals. They also have the right to determine how to run their organizations to achieve that outcome and to develop the policies, procedures, and work rules necessary to make it happen. With those rights comes the responsibility to provide safe working conditions, pay wages for all work done by employees, and reimburse employees for expenses incurred on behalf of the employer.

Employment relationships are generally covered either by the common-law doctrine of employment at-will or by employment contracts that were discussed in Chapter 4. Employment disagreements may result in legal action based on a breach of the terms of a contract, a violation of a statute such as Title VII, or a tort action. The consequences of Title VII violations are discussed later in this chapter. A *tort* is a civil action based on a duty or obligation that has been breached by one party, causing an injury of some kind to the other. Organizations face tort actions for many reasons, such as customers who spill hot coffee on themselves and sue the restaurant for damages because they were burned. Employment-related torts are often based on obligations found in common-law doctrines.

These doctrines apply to employment relationships in the absence of an employment contract or employment related legislation.

Common-law Doctrines

Common-law doctrines are the result of legal decisions made by judges in cases adjudicated over a period of centuries. A number of doctrines have implications for employment relationships, the most common of which is the concept of employment at-will. Other common-law issues that affect employment relationships are respondeat superior, constructive discharge, and defamation. Another common-law doctrine of interest in employee relations issues, that of negligent hiring, was discussed in Chapter 4.

Employment At-Will

In *Payne v. The Western & Atlantic Railroad Company* in 1884, Justice Ingersoll of the Tennessee Supreme Court defined employment at-will in this way: "...either party may terminate the service, for any cause, good or bad, or without cause, and the other cannot complain in law." This definition allowed employers to change employment conditions, whether it was to hire, transfer, promote, or terminate an employee, at their sole discretion. It also allowed employees to leave a job at any time, with or without notice. In the absence of a legally enforceable employment contract, this definition was unaltered for more than 70 years.

Although there have always been exceptions to at-will employment based on employment contracts, beginning in 1959 the doctrine began to be eroded by both court decisions and statutes. This erosion resulted in several exceptions to the at-will concept, including public policy exceptions, the application of the doctrine of good faith and fair dealing to employment relationships, and the concepts of promissory estoppel and fraudulent misrepresentation:

Contract Exceptions   Employment at-will intentions may be abrogated by contracts, either express or implied. An *express contract* can be a verbal or written agreement in which the parties state exactly what they agree to do. Employers have been known to express their gratitude for a job well done with promises of continued employment, such as "Keep doing that kind of work and you have a job for life" or "You'll have a job as long as we're in business." Statements such as these can invalidate the at-will doctrine.

An *implied contract* can be created by an employer's conduct and need not be specifically stated. For example, an employer's consistent application of a progressive discipline policy can create an implied contract that an employee won't be terminated without first going through the steps set forth by the policy. A disclaimer can offset the effects of an implied contract; however, there is little agreement in the courts as to what and how the disclaimer must be presented in order to maintain at-will status. It is generally agreed, however, that the goal of a disclaimer is to be fair and honest with the employee about their expectations, and to remind employees that no statement may alter the at-will status of employment.

Statutory Exceptions   The at-will doctrine has been further eroded by legislation. At-will employment may not be used as a pretext for terminating employees for discriminatory reasons as set forth in equal-opportunity legislation or other legislation designed to protect employee rights.

Public-Policy Exceptions   Erosion of the doctrine of at-will employment began in 1959 when the California Court of Appeals heard *Petermann v. International Brotherhood of Teamsters*, in which Mr. Petermann, a business agent for the union, alleged that he was terminated for refusing to commit perjury on behalf of the union at a legislative hearing. The court held that it is "...obnoxious to the interest of state and contrary to public policy and sound morality to allow an employer to discharge any employee, whether the employment be for a designated or unspecified duration, on the ground that the employee declined to commit perjury, an act specifically enjoined by statute."

The public-policy exception to employment at-will was initially applied conservatively by the courts, but over time, its application has been expanded. In general, the public-policy exception has been applied in four areas:

- Employees who refuse to break the law on behalf of the employer, as exemplified by the *Petermann* case
- Employees who report illegal acts of their employers (whistle-blowers)
- Employees who participate in activities supported by public policy, such as cooperating in a government investigation of wrongdoing by the employer
- Employees who are acting in accordance with legal statute, such as attending jury duty or filing a workers' compensation claim

Although the public-policy exception to at-will employment originated in California, it has been adopted by many, although not all, states.

Duty of Good Faith and Fair Dealing   This tenet of common law provides that parties to a contract have an obligation to act in a fair and honest manner with each other to ensure that benefits of the contract may be realized. The application of this doctrine to at-will employment issues varies widely from state to state. The Texas Supreme Court, for example, has determined that there is no duty for good faith and fair dealing in employment contracts. On the other hand, the Alaska Supreme Court has determined that it's implied in at-will employment situations.

Promissory Estoppel   Promissory estoppel occurs when an employer entices an employee (or prospective employee) to take an action by promising a reward. The employee takes the action, but the employer doesn't follow through on the reward. For example, an employer promises a job to a candidate who resigns another position to accept the new one, and then the candidate finds that the offered position has been withdrawn. If a promise is clear, specific, and reasonable, and an employee acts on the promise, the employer may be required to follow through on the promised reward or pay equivalent damages.

Fraudulent Misrepresentation   Similar to promissory estoppel, fraudulent misrepresentation relates to promises or claims made by employers to entice candidates to join the company. An example of this might be a company that decides to close one of its locations in 6 months but, in the meantime, needs to hire a general manager to run the operation. If, when asked about the future of the company during the recruiting process, the company tells candidates that the plant will be expanded in the future and withholds its intention to close the plant, the company is fraudulently misrepresenting the facts about the position.

In addition to employment at-will, the common-law doctrines of respondeat superior, constructive discharge, and defamation can have serious and costly implications for employers.

Respondeat Superior

The Latin meaning of *respondeat superior* is "let the master answer." This means an employer can be held liable for actions of its employees that occur within the scope and course of assigned duties or responsibilities in the course of their employment, regardless of whether the act is negligent or reckless. This concept has implications for many employment situations; one is sexual harassment, which will be discussed later in this chapter. Another could be an auto accident where a third party is injured when an employee hits another vehicle while driving an employer's delivery truck. Respondeat superior could also come into play if a manager promised additional vacation time to a candidate and the candidate accepted the position based on the promise. Even if the promise wasn't in writing and was outside the employer's normal vacation policy, and the manager made the promise without prior approval, the employer could be required to provide the benefit based on this doctrine.

Constructive Discharge

Constructive discharge occurs when an employer makes the workplace so hostile and inhospitable that an employee resigns. In many states, this gives the employee a cause of action against the employer. The legal standard that must be met varies widely between the states, with some requiring the employee to show that the employer intended to force the resignation, while others require the employee only to show the conditions were sufficiently intolerable that a reasonable person would feel compelled to resign.

Defamation

Accusations of defamation in employment relationships most often occur during or after termination. *Defamation* is a communication that damages an individual's reputation in the community, preventing them from obtaining employment or other benefits. When an employer, out of spite or with a vengeful intent, sets out to deliberately damage a former employee, the result is malicious defamation.

Concerns about defamation have caused many employers to stop giving meaningful references for former employees, in many cases responding to reference requests only with dates of employment and the individual's last title. Employers are generally protected by the concept of *qualified privilege* if the information provided is job-related, truthful, clear, and unequivocal. Obtaining written authorization prior to providing references and limiting responses to the information being requested without volunteering additional information can reduce the risks of being accused of defamation.

Legal Statutes

Legal statutes are laws that have been enacted by the legislature, as with the Civil Rights Act of 1964, or pronounced by the president in the form of executive orders. Chapter 4 discussed extensively the requirements of equal employment opportunity legislation as it relates to hiring and terminations. Those legal statutes govern the employment relationship as well. The following sections cover those aspects that apply more specifically to existing employment relationships.

Sexual Harassment

Title VII of the Civil Rights Act of 1964 (covered in depth in Chapter 4) and its subsequent amendments require employers to furnish a workplace that is free from sexual harassment. There are two forms of sexual harassment that must be prevented: quid pro quo and hostile work environment.

Quid pro quo is a legal term that means, in Latin, "this for that." Quid pro quo harassment, therefore, occurs when a supervisor or manager asks for sexual favors in return for some type of favorable employment action. *Sexual favors* is a broad term that covers actions ranging from unwanted touching to more explicit requests.

A *hostile work environment* has been defined by the EEOC as one in which an individual or individuals are subjected to unwelcome verbal or physical conduct "when submission to or rejection of this conduct explicitly or implicitly affects an individual's employment, unreasonably interferes with an individual's work performance, or creates an intimidating, hostile, or offensive work environment." When investigating these charges, the EEOC looks at many factors. In most cases, a single incidence of inappropriate and unwelcome behavior doesn't rise to the level of a hostile work environment, but in some cases when the actions or behavior are particularly offensive or intimidating, the EEOC may find that harassment has occurred. A hostile work environment can also be found to exist for victims who have been affected by unwelcome offensive conduct toward someone other than themselves.

 Unlike the quid pro quo form of harassment, a hostile work environment can be created by co-workers, suppliers, customers, or other visitors to the workplace.

Courts have held employers responsible for the harassing actions of their employees, whether or not the employer was aware of the harassment. Beginning in 1986, the Supreme Court issued a number of rulings to clarify employer responsibilities in the prevention of sexual harassment. The most commonly cited of these for HR purposes are *Meritor Savings Bank v. Vinson* (1986), *Harris v. Forklift Systems* (1993), and two cases decided at the same time in 1998, *Burlington Industries v. Ellerth* and *Faragher v. City of Boca Raton*:

Meritor Savings Bank v. Vinson (1986)   Mechelle Vinson applied for a job at a branch of Meritor Savings Bank in 1974 when Sidney Taylor was a vice president and manager of the branch. Taylor hired Vinson, who worked at the branch for 4 years starting as a teller trainee and working her way up to assistant branch manager, based on her performance in the jobs she held. Once she passed her probationary period as a trainee, Vinson claims that Taylor began to harass her, requesting that they go to a motel to have sexual relations. Although Vinson refused Taylor's advances initially, she gave in eventually because she believed she would lose her job if she didn't. Vinson claims that Taylor's harassment escalated to the point that she was fondled in front of other employees and expected to engage in sexual relations at the branch both during and after work. In September 1978, Vinson took an indefinite medical leave, and the bank terminated her in November 1978.

The Supreme Court issued its opinion in June 1986, finding that a claim of "hostile environment" sex discrimination is actionable under Title VII. The Court rejected the idea that the "mere existence of a grievance procedure and a policy against discrimination" is enough to protect an employer from the acts of its supervisors. The opinion indicated that a policy designed to encourage victims of harassment to come forward would provide greater protection.

Harris v. Forklift Systems (1993)   In April 1985, Teresa Harris was employed by Forklift Systems, Inc. as a manager, reporting to the company president, Charles Hardy. Hardy insulted Harris frequently in front of customers and other employees and made sexually suggestive remarks. When Harris complained in August 1987, Hardy apologized and said he would stop the conduct. But in September of that year, Hardy once again began the verbal harassment, and Harris quit on October 1.

Harris then filed a lawsuit against Forklift, claiming that Hardy had created a hostile work environment on the basis of her gender. The District Court found that although Hardy's conduct was offensive, it didn't meet the required standard of severity to seriously affect her psychological well-being.

The Supreme Court agreed to hear the case in order to resolve conflicts in the lower courts on what conduct was actionable for a hostile work environment. The Court found that the appropriate standard is one that falls between that which is merely offensive and that which results in tangible psychological injury. Although this isn't a precise guideline, it does allow courts to take into consideration a number of factors about the work environment, the frequency and severity of the conduct, the level of threat or humiliation to which the victim is subjected, and whether the conduct interferes unreasonably with performance of the employee's job.

Faragher v. City of Boca Raton (1998)   Beth Faragher and Nancy Ewanchew were 2 of about 6 females out of more than 40 lifeguards for the City of Boca Raton in Florida from 1985 to 1990. During their tenure, they were verbally and physically harassed by two supervisors, Bill Terry and David Silverman. They both complained to a third supervisor, Robert Gordon, about the harassment but didn't file a formal complaint, and no corrective action was taken. Ewanchew resigned in 1989 and wrote to the city manager in 1990 to complain about the harassment. The city investigated and (when it found that both Terry and Silverman had acted inappropriately) reprimanded and disciplined both supervisors.

The Supreme Court found that employers are responsible for actions of those they employ and have a responsibility to control them. Going further, the Court determined that a supervisor need not make an explicit threat of an adverse *tangible employment action* (TEA), which the Court defined as "a significant change in employment status, such as hiring, firing, failing to promote, reassignment with significantly different responsibilities, or a decision causing a significant change in benefits" in order for harassment to be actionable. The Court determined that subordinates know that the possibility of adverse supervisory actions exists whenever requests are made, even if the adverse actions aren't stated.

Burlington Industries v. Ellerth (1998)   Kimberly Ellerth worked for Burlington Industries in Chicago as a salesperson from March 1993 to May 1994. During that time, Ellerth claims that she was subjected to ongoing sexual harassment by Ted Slowick, who wasn't her direct supervisor but did have the power to approve or deny a TEA with regard to her employment. Although Ellerth was aware of Burlington's policy prohibiting sexual harassment during her employment, she didn't complain about the harassment until after she resigned. After resigning, she filed a complaint with the EEOC and, when she received a right-to-sue letter in October 1994, filed suit against Burlington.

A key issue in this case was that of *vicarious liability* (an element of the legal concept of respondeat superior), which, in this context, means an employer may be held accountable for the harmful actions of its employees, whether or not the employer is aware of those actions. The Supreme Court decided in part that "An employer is subject to vicarious liability to a victimized employee for an actionable hostile environment created by a supervisor with immediate (or successively higher) authority over the employee."

The costs to employers for sexual harassment can be substantial, as the following partial list of cases illustrates:

$34,000,000   In June 1998, Mitsubishi agreed to a consent decree and the largest sexual-harassment settlement in the history of the EEOC to date. This case was brought on behalf of women on the assembly line in an Illinois factory who were subjected to a hostile work environment by co-workers and supervisors.

$9,850,000   In February 1998, Astra USA agreed to a settlement and consent decree with the EEOC on behalf of female employees who were subjected to both quid pro quo and hostile work environment harassment. Astra fired the president, who had been aware of the activities, and took action against other employees and customers who had taken part in the harassment.

$7,750,000   In 1999, Ford Motor Company agreed to settle a case regarding harassment of women in two plants in the Chicago area. The women were subjected to crude remarks, groping, and sexually explicit graffiti. As part of the settlement, Ford also agreed to conduct sensitivity training in its plants nationwide, promote more women into management positions, and hold supervisors accountable by making them ineligible for promotion and bonuses when they fail to take action against harassment they observe and allow to continue.

The courts have been divided on the question of same-sex harassment. Because sexual orientation doesn't constitute a protected class under federal law, some courts have been reluctant to classify cases of same-sex harassment as unlawful. In 1997, the first case of same-sex harassment reached the U.S. Supreme Court. In the majority opinion issued for *Oncale v. Sundowner Offshore Services, Inc.* (see the related sidebar), Justice Antonin

Scalia observed that "… male on male sexual harassment was assuredly not the principal evil Congress was concerned with when it enacted Title VII. But statutory prohibitions often go beyond the principal evil to cover reasonably comparable evils…." A number of cases following Oncale resulted in substantial awards or settlements in cases of same-sex harassment:

$1,900,000 In 1999, the EEOC reached a settlement with the Long Prairie Packing Company in Minnesota in the amount of $1.9 million, along with a consent decree that required the company to establish a zero-tolerance policy for sexual or disability harassment, and to conduct mandatory sexual-harassment training for all employees in the company.

$1,748,500 In 2000, $1.75 million was awarded to the plaintiff in *Jones v. Yellow Freight Systems, Inc.* in a civil law suit.

 Real World Scenario

Oncale v. Sundowner Offshore Services, Inc.

In late October 1991, Joseph Oncale was a roustabout employed by Sundowner Offshore Services on an oil rig in the Gulf of Mexico. During the time he worked on the rig, three of his male co-workers, including two who had supervisory authority over him, humiliated him in front of other employees on the rig using sexually explicit words and actions. At one point, Oncale was physically assaulted and threatened with rape. When Oncale complained to other supervisors about the harassment, no corrective action was taken, and one of them, the company's safety-compliance clerk, told him that he too was subjected to similar treatment by the three. When Mr. Oncale quit his job, he gave his reason for leaving as being "due to sexual harassment and verbal abuse."

Mr. Oncale filed a complaint against Sundowner, alleging discrimination on the basis of his sex. The district court denied the complaint, and on appeal, the Fifth Circuit Court of Appeals upheld the district court. Oncale then appealed to the U.S. Supreme Court. The Court heard oral arguments in the case in December 1997, and comments of the justices during the arguments gave a rare early indication of the way they were leaning: Chief Justice Rehnquist commented, "I don't see how we can possibly sustain the holding."

In March 1998, Justice Scalia wrote the majority opinion, referencing in part the Court's opinion in an earlier sexual-harassment case that "When the workplace is permeated with discriminatory intimidation, ridicule, and insult that is sufficiently severe or pervasive to alter the conditions of the victim's employment and create an abusive working environment, Title VII is violated" (*Harris v. Forklift Systems, Inc.*).

Scalia went on to say that even though the intent of Title VII was to protect harassment of women in the workplace, "sexual harassment of any kind that meets the statutory requirements" must be covered as well.

$500,000   The EEOC obtained a $500,000 settlement in August 2000 on behalf of a complainant who was harassed at a Chevrolet dealership in Denver, Colorado. As part of the settlement agreement, the dealership also agreed to provide mandatory sexual-harassment training to its employees.

EEOC Guidelines for the Prevention of Sexual Harassment

The EEOC has developed detailed guidelines entitled "Enforcement Guidance: Vicarious Employer Liability for Unlawful Harassment by Supervisors" to assist employers in developing policies that clearly express the employer's prohibition against harassment and conducting investigations that meet EEOC standards.

To summarize the guidelines, employers are encouraged to develop antiharassment policies, along with complaint procedures for those who believe they have been harassed. The policy should clearly explain unacceptable conduct and reassure employees who complain that they will be protected against retaliation. The complaint process should describe multiple avenues for reporting harassment and provide assurances of confidentiality to the extent it's possible. Investigations of allegations should be prompt and impartial, and if the investigation finds that harassment did indeed occur, the policy should provide for immediate corrective action.

These guidelines are fully described at `www.eeoc.gov/policy/docs/harassment.html`.

 Real World Scenario

Medina Rene v. MGM Grand Hotel, Inc.

Even though federal law doesn't expressly prohibit discrimination based on sexual orientation, the courts have applied Title VII protections to complainants in these cases.

For 2 1/2 years, Medina Rene worked as one of a group of male butlers for high-profile guests of the MGM Grand Hotel in Las Vegas. He alleged he was subjected to a hostile work environment by his supervisor and co-workers, and he provided extensive documentation of inappropriate behavior over a 2-year period. According to the evidence he provided to the court, the behavior included inappropriate touching, caressing, and being forced to look at sexually explicit photographs. At one point, Mr. Rene was asked why he thought his co-workers were behaving that way toward him, and his answer was that it was because he was gay.

Attorneys for the MGM Grand argued that this case was different from Oncale because Mr. Rene was openly gay and Title VII didn't provide protection for sexual orientation. The District Court granted summary judgment for the hotel, and Mr. Rene appealed to the Ninth Circuit Court of Appeals. The appellate court found that sexual orientation wasn't a pertinent fact in this case and remanded the case because Mr. Rene was singled out and subjected to offensive sexual conduct, the conduct was sexual in nature and discriminatory, and he was treated differently based on his sex.

As described previously in the discussions of the *Ellerth* and *Faragher* cases, the Supreme Court found that employers always have vicarious liability for unlawful harassment by supervisors when it results in a TEA, but when there is no TEA, liability may be avoided with an affirmative defense including two elements:

- The employer exercised reasonable care to prevent and correct promptly any harassing behavior.

- The employee unreasonably failed to take advantage of any preventive or corrective opportunities provided by the employer or to avoid harm otherwise.

Glass Ceiling Act

In 1991, Senator Robert Dole introduced legislation known as the Glass Ceiling Act, which was eventually signed into law as an amendment to Title II of the Civil Rights Act of 1991. An article in the *Wall Street Journal* in 1986 had coined the term *glass ceiling* to describe the limitations faced by women and minorities when it came to advancing into the senior ranks of corporate management. The act established a commission whose purpose was to determine whether a glass ceiling existed and, if it did, to identify the barriers to placing more women and minorities in senior management positions. The commission found that although CEOs understood the need to include women and minorities in the ranks of senior management, this belief wasn't shared at all levels in the organization. The study went on to identify three barriers that prevented women and minorities from advancing to senior levels:

Societal Barriers   These result from limited access to educational opportunities and biases related to gender, race, and ethnicity.

Internal Structural Barriers   These encompass a wide range of corporate practices and shortcomings over which management has some control, including outreach and recruiting programs that don't try to find qualified women and minorities, as well as organizational cultures that exclude women and minorities from participation in activities that will lead to advancement, such as mentoring, management training, or career-development assignments.

Governmental Barriers   These are related to inconsistent enforcement of equal-opportunity legislation and poor collection and dissemination of statistics that illustrate the problem.

The commission also studied organizations that have successfully integrated glass-ceiling initiatives into their operations and found some common traits that can be adopted by other organizations. Successful initiatives begin with full support of the CEO, who ensures that the initiative becomes part of strategic planning in the organization and holds management accountable for achieving goals by tracking and reporting on progress. These comprehensive programs don't exclude white men but do include a diverse workforce population. Organizations implementing programs to increase diversity benefit from improved productivity and bottom-line results for shareholders.

As a result of the study, the EEOC conducts glass-ceiling audits to monitor the progress organizations make toward including women and minorities at all levels.

Uniformed Services Employment and Reemployment Rights Act (USERRA) of 1994

Congress enacted the Uniformed Services Employment and Reemployment Rights Act (USERRA) in 1994 to protect the rights of reservists called to active duty in the armed forces. The act provides reemployment and benefits rights and is administered through the Veterans Employment and Training Service (VETS) of the DOL. USERRA applies to all public and private employers in the United States, including the federal government. The DOL issued revised rules for employers that became effective on January 18, 2006. These revisions clarified some of the requirements previously issued. Some of its stipulations include the following:

Coverage

- All employers, regardless of size, are required to comply with USERRA regulations.

- Members of all uniformed services are protected by USERRA.

- USERRA prohibits discrimination due to past, current, or future military obligations.

- In addition to service during times of war or national emergency, USERRA protects any voluntary or involuntary service such as active duty, training, boot camp, reserve weekend duty, National Guard mobilizations, and absence due to required fitness-for-duty examinations.

Notice Requirements

- In most circumstances, employees must give verbal or written notice to the employer that they have been called to active service. If an employee is unable to give notice, a military representative may provide the notice.

- If military necessity prevents advance notice, or if giving notice is impossible or unreasonable, employees are still protected by USERRA.

- To be eligible for reemployment rights, service members must report back to work within time frames that vary according to the length of service. Table 7.2 shows the reporting time requirements established by USERRA for returning to work based on varying lengths of service.

Duration

- The employer must grant a leave of absence for up to 5 years, although there are several exceptions that extend coverage beyond 5 years.

- Types of leave protected without limits include the following:
  - Boot camp
  - Initial service period
  - Waiting for orders
  - Annual 2-week mandatory training

- Employees are permitted to moonlight during off-duty hours without losing reinstatement rights.
- Employees don't lose reinstatement rights if they leave their jobs to prepare for mobilization but the mobilization is canceled.

Compensation

- USERRA doesn't require employers to pay employees during military absences, unless the employer has an established policy of doing so.
- Employers may not require employees to apply accrued vacation pay to their military leaves, but employees may choose to do so.

Benefit Protection

- Employees on military leave are entitled to the same benefits employers provide for others on a leave of absence.
- Employees continue to accrue seniority and other benefits as though they were continuously employed.
- For leave greater than 30 days but less than 240 days in duration, the employer must offer COBRA-like health coverage on request of the employee; for service less than 31 days, and at the employee's request, the employer must continue health coverage at the regular employee cost.
- Returning service members are entitled to participate in any rights and benefits provided to employees returning from nonmilitary leaves of absence.

Pension Protection

- Employee pension rights are protected by USERRA.
- Vesting and accrual for returning service members are treated as though there were no break in employment.
- Employer pension contributions must be the same as though the military leave didn't occur.
- For defined-contribution plans, service members must be given three times the period of the military leave absence (not to exceed 5 years) to make up contributions that were missed during the leave. Plans with an employer matching component are required to match the makeup funds.

Reinstatement

- The employer must "promptly" reinstate regular employees to positions that the employees would have earned had they remained on the job, referred to as an *escalator position*. The Act doesn't specify a definition of "promptly," because the timing will depend on the length of the leave. For example, an employee on leave for annual 2-week training would be expected to be reemployed on the first workday following the end of leave. On the other hand, someone who has been serving on active duty for 5 years may be promptly reemployed after notice to vacate the position is given to the incumbent.

- Temporary employees don't have reinstatement rights.
- Seasonal or fixed-term contract employees aren't entitled to reinstatement.
- Reemployment rights are forfeited if the employee has been discharged dishonorably or other than honorably from the service, has been expelled as a result of a court martial, or has been absent without leave (AWOL) for 90 days.

Continued Employment

- Employees returning to work from leaves of more than 30 but less than 181 days may not be discharged without cause for 6 months after the date of reemployment.
- Employees returning to work from leaves of 181 days or more may not be discharged without cause for 1 year from the date of reemployment.

 Real World Scenario

Velazquez-Garcia v. Horizon Lines of Puerto Rico, Inc.

Burden of Proof for USERRA Discriminatory Actions

For 6 years, Carlos Velazquez-Garcia worked as a marine supervisor at Horizon Lines of Puerto Rico. During that time, he enlisted in the Marines and took a 6-month leave required for basic training, annual 2-week training periods, and monthly service weekends. Horizon adjusted Velazquez's work schedule to accommodate the leaves, but the company made it known that the rescheduling was difficult for them. Horizon continued to pay Velazquez's full salary during his military leaves, requiring him to reimburse them when he returned to work. The salary repayment took almost 2 years, and during that time, Velazquez started a check-cashing business for his co-workers, conducting most of the business on his own time but admittedly cashing "one or two" checks during work hours.

After 7 months of operating his business, and only 3 weeks after Horizon recovered the salary paid to him during his leaves, Velazquez was fired by Horizon. The written termination didn't provide a reason, but he was told that the check-cashing business violated company policy, although Horizon had never informed him of the policy or warned him to stop running the business.

Velazquez filed suit, claiming the termination was discriminatory based on USERRA protections. The case was dismissed by the district court; but on appeal, the court determined that the lower court erred by requiring Velazquez to prove that Horizon's actions were discriminatory. The appeals court found that USERRA requires employers to prove that a TEA would have occurred regardless of the employee's military status and remanded the case for jury trial.

The finding of the appeals court had a broad implication for all employers attempting to remain compliant with USERRA guidelines. It is clear that the employer bears the burden of proof to demonstrate that they would have taken the same adverse action against the employee regardless of his or her military status.

Disabled Veterans

- The employer must make reasonable accommodation to provide training or retraining to reemploy a returning service member disabled as a result of service. If reasonable accommodation creates an undue hardship, reemployment can be made to a position "nearest approximate" in terms of status and pay and with full seniority to which the person is entitled.

Visit www.dol.gov/vets/whatsnew/uguide.pdf to view the full text of USERRA.

TABLE 7.2   USERRA reemployment reporting times

Length of Service	Reporting Time
1 to 30 days *or* absence for "fitness for service" exam	The first regularly scheduled full workday that begins 8 hours after the end of the service completion.
31 to 180 days	Submit application for reemployment no later than 14 days after the end of service, or on the next business day after that.
181 or more days	Submit application for reemployment no later than 90 days after the end of service or on the next business day after that.
Disability incurred or aggravated	Reporting or application deadline is extended for up to 2 years.

Employee Rights and Responsibilities

As discussed earlier in the chapter, employment rights developed over time from legal statutes and common-law doctrines. Just as these doctrines and statutes establish rights and responsibilities for employers, they provide employees with protection.

The statutory laws governing the employee relations (ER) function provide employees with the right to fair treatment and the expectation of equal opportunity in a workplace free from discrimination or harassment, and they protect employees' rights to join together in negotiating the terms and conditions of employment. Another legal concept with relevance to employee relations is the constitutional guarantee of due process.

Due process as a legal concept was established in the Magna Carta in 1215 and incorporated into the U.S. Bill of Rights to protect citizens from arbitrary acts of the federal and state governments. As such, it isn't a legal requirement for private employers, but the concept is a practice that is in the best interest of employers. *Due process* in the employment context means that employment actions are taken in accordance with established procedures, including notifying employees of pending actions and providing the opportunity to respond to any allegations prior to making a final adverse employment decision.

The common-law doctrine of employment at-will provides employees with the right to leave a job at any time, with or without notice. Other common-law doctrines place responsibilities on employees in the employment relationship as well:

- The *duty of diligence* requires an employee to act "with reasonable care and skill" in the course of performing work for the employer.

- The *duty of obedience* requires employees to act within the authority granted by the employer and to follow the employer's reasonable and legal policies, procedures, and rules.

- The *duty of loyalty* requires that employees act in the best interest of the employer and not solicit work away from the employer to benefit themselves.

Employee Relations

The employment relationship has broad implications for both employers and employees. Employers rely on those they hire to produce the goods and services that bring money into the organization to operate the company, compensate employees, and produce a profit for the owners. Employees, particularly in the United States, spend the majority of their waking hours at work, which means the effects of the employment relationship, good or bad, can spill over into other areas of the employee's life. The goal of ER programs is to maximize employee productivity through various means, including organization climate and culture, programs designed to build morale and encourage retention, workplace policies and procedures, performance-improvement programs that build positive communication, and dispute-resolution programs that resolve issues successfully.

Organization Climate and Culture

For many, the terms *organization climate* and *culture* are used interchangeably. Researchers trying to identify and describe how organizations work and what influences productivity and other organizational behaviors define the difference as one between a quantitative description (climate) and a qualitative one (culture).

The *organizational climate* describes how people feel about an organization based on a number of factors, including observable practices and employee perceptions. Climate is strongly influenced by organization structure as reflected in the organization chart—is it hierarchical and bureaucratic or flat and open? The management style of organization leaders also has significant influence over its climate. Are employees encouraged to take risks or punished for doing so? How are employees held accountable for their successes and failures? Are there opportunities for growth? The climate is built on the way leaders manage and interact with employees.

If climate is reflected by *how* people feel, culture reflects *why* they feel the way they do. *Organizational culture* is based on the values and beliefs shared at all levels and reflected by interactions between employees in the organization as well as with customers and vendors. Culture includes the workplace atmosphere and the way newcomers are integrated into "how we do things around here."

The level of employee involvement and communication in an organization influences and can play a part in changing the culture that is created.

Employee-Involvement Strategies

A significant factor in effective employee relations is the extent to which employees are involved in making decisions that affect them on a day-to-day basis. This requires a commitment from senior management to both ask for and listen to what employees have to say and, whenever possible, implement changes suggested by employees. It's also important that management communicate to employees that the changes were implemented. Employee involvement can be very simple, such as a suggestion box, or more complex, such as a self-directed work team. The next section discusses a number of communication strategies that are a key aspect of effective employee-involvement programs. Other strategies for involving employees include the following:

Suggestion Boxes   A suggestion box provides an anonymous means by which employees can provide management with ideas for improvements. As with any method of soliciting information from employees, it's important that suggestions be acted on in a timely manner, or the concept of the suggestion system loses its credibility.

Delegating Authority   Management demonstrates respect for its employees by trusting them to make the decisions necessary to do their jobs. To do this effectively, management needs to delegate a sufficient level of authority to employees for making decisions or incurring expenses so they're free to act without waiting for approval to take necessary action.

Task Force   A task force is brought together to research and recommend solutions for a significant undertaking or problem; once the solution has been determined, the task force disbands. A task force might be created to analyze technological improvements in a manufacturing plant and recommend improvements that will meet the long-term strategic objectives of the organization.

Committees   Committees are often formed to address ongoing issues in the organization and may be permanent, such as a safety committee, or ad hoc, such as a group appointed to plan a company function.

Work Team   A work team consists of employees who work together each day to accomplish their assignments. The team can be composed of members in a single functional area, or it can have members from several functions that are needed to accomplish the goal. A functional work team might consist of employees in the marketing department who develop collateral pieces for company products. A cross-functional work team might consist of employees from the research and development, manufacturing, marketing, operations, and accounting departments who are responsible for developing, launching, and marketing a specific product.

Virtual Work Team   A virtual work team operates in much the same way as a work team, with one major exception: team members aren't located in the same building but may work anywhere in the world and connect through the Internet to accomplish team assignments.

Employee-Management Committees   Employee-management committees are used to solve problems in a variety of areas, such as production schedules, safety, and employee social events. The inclusion of employees on these committees helps to bring all the information to the table for making decisions and provides employees with input into how they do their jobs. From this point of view, they make positive contributions to operations.

Employers should use care when creating committees to address issues related to any terms and conditions of employment such as wages, safety, training, scheduling, and overtime, because they can by viewed as "employer-dominated unions" by the NLRA. The NLRA prohibits employers from creating mock unions with no real power to bargain on behalf of employees. In 1992, the National Labor Relations Board (NLRB) found that committees established by Electromation, Inc. were employer-dominated unions. There is more information about the Electromation case in Appendix D, "Federal Employment Legislation and Case Law."

Self-directed Work Team   A self-directed work team is a group of employees who are jointly responsible for accomplishing ongoing assignments. Team members set the work schedules, determine who will do which jobs, and hold each other accountable for accomplishing goals.

Communicating with Employees

The role of open and honest communication in organizations can't be underestimated. Communication must be both top-down and bottom-up: management must be willing to hear and act on information that may be contrary to its decisions. To be effective, management needs to solicit information from those employees closest to the issue being discussed in order to make fully informed decisions. Employees must feel comfortable in approaching management with relevant information when they're aware it has not been included in the decision-making process.

Effective communication programs incorporate multiple and repeated methods of providing information to employees. Depending on the size of the organization, communication may be as simple as an "all-hands meeting" in which the owner talks to the whole company about issues, or it may be as complex as a simultaneous web broadcast for a multinational corporation. The most effective communication methods are those that occur between employees and their direct supervisors because these provide the best opportunities for a meaningful exchange of information. Some common communication methods include the following:

Open-Door Policy   Open-door policies are an effective means for managers to keep their fingers on the pulse of operations and stay in touch with employee concerns. Giving employees access to the decision makers who can provide support, answer questions, and address concerns also shows a commitment from management to the needs of employees.

Management by Walking Around   Publicized in the 1980s by Tom Peters in his book *In Search of Excellence*, management by walking around (MBWA) is a practice first used at Hewlett-Packard in which management provided employees with goals and then spent time with them observing their progress and listening to their concerns or ideas.

Department Staff Meetings   Regularly scheduled meetings in which direct supervisors meet with their staff for updates and coordination of activities, as well as to disseminate information about organization policies and changes, provide a vehicle for employees to voice their questions and concerns and have input into their schedules.

All-Hands Staff Meetings/Town-Hall Meetings   From time to time, employees like to hear from senior management to find out what's really going on with the company. The all-hands meeting is a means by which executives can update employees on the state of the company and answer questions about its future direction, new products, or stock prices. Depending on the size of the company, these meetings can occur in person, via video tele-conferencing, or as a web broadcast.

Brown-Bag Lunches   A brown-bag lunch program provides an informal setting for a small group of employees to meet with a senior manager to learn more about the company or a specific goal and ask questions. These informal meetings get their name from the fact that they occur over a lunch period on company premises, with employees bringing their own lunches.

Newsletters   Newsletters can provide employees with regular updates on company projects, profits, and goals. They're an effective means for introducing employees to other areas of the organization, reporting on financial issues, and soliciting input for changes in the employment relationship.

Intranet   An employee intranet can be an effective, easily updated source of information for employees. In many organizations, the employee handbook is available on the intranet, as are the company newsletter and updates on company goals.

Word of Mouth   In many organizations, word of mouth is the main means by which employees obtain information. This, of course, has drawbacks. Although word-of-mouth communication based on accurate information from management can be an effective way to "get the message out," the information tends to be distorted by the employee grapevine.

Email   Email provides a virtually instantaneous means of communicating information to large groups of employees at the same time. However, email, by its very nature, can be the source of problems: for example, when an executive inadvertently sends a confidential communication about pending layoffs to all staff instead of to the executive team. Particularly with regard to human resource issues, email should be used cautiously to avoid embarrassment and legal complications, because it's discoverable in the event of legal action.

Employee Feedback

A key component of effective ER programs is staying in touch with how well those programs are meeting the needs of employees. *Employee engagement*—attitudes and feelings toward work—is a critical measure of overall organizational success. Employees who are engaged report higher levels of job satisfaction, accountability for outcomes, and, most important, a desire for their company to succeed. Measuring the needs of the employees and their levels of engagement can be achieved by gathering feedback from employees.

Some of the communication techniques previously described gather this information in an informal way; however, there are also several more structured methods to do this:

Employee Surveys   As you recall from Chapter 2, employee surveys can be used to gather information on any number of issues and are often the most effective means for obtaining information from large numbers of employees.

Exit Interviews   According to a study commissioned by the Society for Human Resource Management (SHRM), 71 percent of the companies polled use exit interviews to measure employee engagement. Generally, an exit interview can be used to gather information from the departing employee related to their "real" reason for leaving the organization. The findings—better pay elsewhere, a difficult manager, the perception of stalled career growth— can help an organization direct its ER programs toward meaningful results.

See the SHRM survey in its entirety at www.shrm.org/Research/ SurveyFindings/Articles/Pages/EmployeeRecognitionPrograms SurveyFindings.aspx.

Employee Focus Groups   As discussed in Chapter 2, an employee focus group consisting of a cross-section of employees from various departments and levels in the organization can be used to involve employees in decisions.

Skip-level Interviews   A *skip-level interview* process in which employees are interviewed by their manager's manager provides insight into employee goals and job satisfaction, as well as an opportunity for career counseling.

When an organization undertakes a feedback initiative, it's critical that the results be reported to both management and employees. The HR professional should carefully review the data to ensure that it's accurate. If the results are quantified, they should be viewed critically to make sure they make sense and accurately reflect what is truly happening in the organization. Any quantitative analyses should be carefully reviewed for data-entry errors or inadvertent misrepresentations of the information. For example, if only a representative sample of the employee population was surveyed, are the results skewed because the members of the group weren't truly representative of the entire population? If the entire workforce was surveyed, did the phrasing of the questions influence the results? There are many ways in which statistical data can be misinterpreted, intentionally or unintentionally. Before reporting any survey results, it's important to ensure that they're accurate. Chapter 2 discusses quantitative and qualitative data-collection methods in more detail.

Employee Relations Programs

The ER function is, by definition, concerned with relationships in the workplace: how employees interact with each other and with management, how they feel about the work they do, and whether they think they're treated fairly. Although employee relations as a concept is difficult to quantify, the impact it has on the organization can be considerable. During times of organizational downsizing, if employees are unsure about the future of the organization and of their continued employment, they spend work time worrying about the future instead of doing their jobs, which reduces productivity. When employees feel supported and fairly treated, they're able to concentrate fully on their work, and productivity increases.

While the law, as previously discussed, governs some aspects of employee relations, the fact is that employers who want to have a profitable organization will increase the chances of doing so by treating their employees with dignity and respect. Senior and executive management may not always recognize the connection between fair treatment and profitability, and it's up to the HR professional to build the business case for implementing effective ER programs by showing the connection.

Positive Employee Relations Strategies

An effective ER program is based on mutual respect, open and honest communication, fair and equitable treatment, and mutual trust. These characteristics begin at the top. If the executive team behaves autocratically, expecting adherence to strict and restrictive policies, procedures, and work rules, this demonstrates a lack of trust in the ability of employees to do competent work. When the executive team supports employees in making decisions and taking risks, it demonstrates trust in the competence of its employees. Employees who are empowered to take ownership of the work they do, accepting the rewards of good work and consequences of errors, are more productive.

An organization characterized by mutual respect is one in which management listens to employee ideas and concerns and acts on them, and in which employees feel they're partners with management in the workplace. Management can demonstrate respect for the workforce by actions such as promoting from within, providing training for employees to prepare them for increased responsibility, and providing opportunities for employees to demonstrate their capabilities. Employees demonstrate respect for management and each other by listening to differing points of view and supporting decisions that are made.

As previously discussed in this chapter, open communication is essential to establishing productive work relationships, and the most effective communication programs use multiple methods of conveying and receiving information.

The concept of fair and equitable treatment goes beyond that which is required by legal statute and common-law doctrine. An effective ER program is one in which favoritism doesn't exist and where employees can see that employment decisions, even the ones they may not agree with, are based on objective criteria and equitable treatment. When disputes occur, an effective ER program has a nondiscriminatory process for adjudicating them, and it provides a means for employees to appeal unfavorable decisions to an impartial party. Dispute-resolution methods are discussed later in this chapter.

Finally, none of the preceding concepts work effectively in the absence of an atmosphere of mutual trust in the organization. Trust is built over time, when management continuously demonstrates that its actions are based on fairness and equity and gives employees input into decisions that affect them. A key element of building trust occurs when management communicates not only the "rosy scenario" but an honest evaluation of problems and challenges being faced by the organization. This accomplishes two goals: it encourages employees to come up with creative solutions to the problem or challenge, and it demonstrates that management both respects and values employees and trusts them to handle the information appropriately. As discussed in Chapter 2, Edward Lawler's high-involvement organization (HIO) strategy is built on the premise of positive ER programs. It allows for decision-making from the bottom up, data-sharing from the top down, and a pay-for-performance system that clearly links employee behavior to rewards. The role of the HR professional in employee relations is to provide the change-management expertise needed to develop programs containing these elements and to develop methods for measuring the impact of ER programs on the bottom line. Examples of programs that promote a positive organizational culture include the following:

Recognition   Employee-recognition programs are designed to acknowledge the efforts of employees and encourage that same behavior in the future. Length of service, safe work practices, and going "above and beyond" the expectations of the job are common behaviors acknowledged through these programs. One challenge in administering employee-recognition programs is that the measures of success continually change, making the return on investment (ROI) difficult to evaluate. However, programs that are designed to be closely aligned with desired organizational outcomes tend to be the most effective behavior management/employee relations technique.

Special Events   "Events coordinator" is a common job responsibility of the HR department. From organizing the company holiday party to sending emails on employee birthdays, these activities can be important in supporting the culture of an organization. While coordinating a company BBQ or planning a holiday party may seem relatively simple, it can be fraught with pitfalls such as sexual harassment, the role of alcohol, and the need to include all employees. For this reason, many companies have shifted from celebrating specific holidays or events to hosting an annual or quarterly all-employee meeting where recognition and achievement awards are given, and business details such as forecasted sales are shared.

Diversity Programs   The concept of *diversity* is often represented as simply the cultural differences between employees. This strict interpretation limits an employer's ability to establish meaningful ER programs using diversity as the stimulus. True diversity programs recognize the different levels of knowledge, talent, perspectives, problem-solving skills, and customer-service techniques that naturally exist in a diverse workplace. Mentoring programs, peer-recognition systems, brainstorming groups, and employee committees are all examples of programs that can help improve an organization's culture of inclusiveness.

One goal of effective ER programs is to retain employees. An effective ER program that includes the components discussed in this chapter—mutual respect, open and honest communication, fair and equitable treatment, and mutual trust—contains the building blocks for retention. In addition to these components, employee-friendly or work/life balance policies and programs can enhance the employer's ability to retain employees. These tools recognize that employees have obligations outside the workplace that they must balance with work responsibilities and provide them with flexibility so that they can be more productive when they're working. Some of the tools that add to flexibility include the following:

Telecommuting   Employees who telecommute connect to the company network via the Internet and communicate with co-workers and managers via email, fax, and telephone, all from their homes. The telecommuting solution for organizations that are willing to embrace it has many benefits for the organization, the employee, and the community. The organization is able to hold on to employees who might otherwise choose to leave, maintaining the knowledge, skills, and abilities (KSAs) and training that have been invested in the individual. The employee is able to continue working while remaining available to handle personal needs, such as caring for an ill child or parent. The community benefits from reduced rush-hour traffic congestion.

Flextime   Flextime allows employees to work the hours that enable them to take care of personal business, such as taking children to school, attending classes, or avoiding heavy commute traffic. Many organizations set core hours during which all employees are required to be at work but other than that allow employees to determine what hours meet their needs.

Compressed Workweeks   Some organizations allow employees to work four 10-hour days or a 9/80 schedule in which the employee works nine 9-hour days in each 2-week period and has a day off every other week. There are a number of variations to these schedules; employers must be aware of FLSA overtime requirements for nonexempt employees and ensure that the compressed workweek doesn't violate those requirements.

Part-Time Work   Occasionally, employees may want to reduce their hours for a variety of reasons such as attending school or caring for elderly parents or young children. Employers who agree to a regular part-time schedule will retain qualified employees who would otherwise need to leave the organization.

Job Sharing   Job sharing is a situation where two part-time employees share one job. The employer can benefit from this practice in several ways. First, it allows accommodation of an employee's request for a part-time schedule yet maintains full-time coverage for the job. Second, it can allow the employer to hire two people with complementary skills that enhance results.

Nontraditional work arrangements such as these that weren't possible in the past are available now because advances in technology have made them feasible.

Workplace Policies and Procedures

Employers need a consistent and understandable means to communicate important information about how the company operates and what is expected of employees. This is best done through *policies*, which are broad guidelines developed by the employer to guide organizational decisions. *Procedures* provide further explanation and more details on how the policy is to be applied, and *work rules* state what employees may or may not do to comply with the policy. For example:

Policy   Employees will conduct business in a manner consistent with the highest standards of business ethics.

Procedure   Employees should avoid situations in which the best interest of the company conflicts with the employee's self-interest.

Work Rule   Employees may not own, in whole or in part, any venture that seeks to do business with, or is a competitor of, this organization.

Some employment policies are required by law, such as the sexual-harassment policy previously discussed. Other policies help ensure the consistent application of employment practices throughout the organization, and still others serve to motivate employees, such as education reimbursement, recognition, or telecommuting policies. The number and type of policies in each organization should be reflective of the mission, values, and culture of the organization and seek to promote successful employment relationships. Regardless of how policies are used in any organization, it's important that they be reviewed and updated periodically to ensure that they're still relevant for the organization.

HR policies, procedures, and work rules are developed in conjunction with line management. The role of HR in this process is to advise management on current best practices and legal requirements and work with management to develop policies that are consistent with organizational goals, easily communicated, and viewed by employees as equitable. Once developed, HR is responsible to advise management on appropriate ways to administer the policies, procedures, and work rules, as well as provide training when needed.

Employee handbooks can be useful as a way of communicating policies, procedures, and work rules to employees in an organized fashion and providing a reference. However, poorly worded handbooks have, in some cases, been found by the courts to create implied contracts. When this happens, courts have required employers to abide by the contract implied in the handbook. If the organization wants to maintain its status as an at-will employer, it's important to clearly state this in the handbook and, more important, to have the handbook reviewed by legal counsel to ensure that it accomplishes the purpose intended without a negative impact.

Handbooks generally begin with a welcoming statement from senior management and a statement of the organization's ER philosophy. Some handbooks provide a history of the organization to give new employees a feel for the type of organization they have joined. Handbooks also contain legally required policies, such as statements of the organization's compliance with equal employment opportunities, prohibitions against unlawful harassment, and information about federally mandated leaves such as the Family and Medical Leave Act (FMLA). The employer then has the opportunity to describe the terms and conditions of employment in the organization, including such things as work hours, safety, ethics, employment status, eligibility for benefits, and benefit programs. The handbook is a good place to inform employees of workplace privacy considerations; if the organization has a policy of monitoring the workplace or places restrictions on Internet usage, clear descriptions of those policies can prevent future problems.

It's advisable to include a tear-out acknowledgment form for employees to sign, or, if the employer uses an online handbook, an electronic acknowledgment. The acknowledgment should include statements that employment is at-will, that the employer has the right to unilaterally change the terms and conditions described in the handbook, and that the employee has received, read, and understands the contents of the handbook. Although some of this language may be viewed negatively by employees, it provides documentation for the employer in any future disciplinary or legal actions that may occur.

Two other methods of communicating the more functional of the employer expectations are reference guides and standard operating procedures (SOPs). A reference guide is a tool used to organize large amounts of data into a single source document. Reference guides can be as simple as an employee phone list or company product list or the more elaborate user guides and troubleshooting manuals. SOPs are tools used to capture processes that typically follow a sequence of events. Capturing step-by-step procedures through the use of definitions, charts, and screen shots allows for the application of uniform business activities regardless of who is doing the work. Both reference guides and SOPs are tools that help to reduce errors, streamline processes, communicate employer expectations, and serve as an effective means of managing the knowledge of the organization.

Many employers are able to effectively address the current needs of the company through the use of handbooks, reference guides, SOPs, and other communication tools but fail to update them as the business evolves. Therefore, regularly verifying, updating, and communicating the changes is just as important as the initial effort.

 Real World Scenario

Pharakhone v. Nissan North America, Inc.

Viengsamon Pharakhone, a production technician at a Nissan plant, applied for, and was granted, FMLA leave when his wife gave birth. Because his wife owned a restaurant, during this leave he managed the restaurant while she recovered. Nissan's employee handbook prohibited employees from engaging in unauthorized work while on any type of leave, and Pharakhone was aware of this prohibition (although there is a dispute between the parties as to when he was made aware of the prohibition). Nissan advised him verbally and in writing that work of any kind during this leave, without prior approval, would be grounds for termination. Nissan learned that he was working at the restaurant during the leave and, when he returned to work, terminated him for violating company policy.

Pharakhone sued, claiming he had been terminated for taking FMLA leave. Nissan moved for summary judgment, and the court granted the motion. When Pharakhone appealed to the Sixth Circuit Court of Appeal, the appeals court upheld the decision. In the decision, the Appeals Court cited prior decisions that "an employer need not reinstate an employee if application of a 'uniformly-applied policy governing outside or supplemental employment'— i.e., a rule against working while on leave—results in the employee's discharge."

Performance Improvement

As in any relationship, there are times when disagreements occur; in the employment relationship, these disagreements are usually related to some form of performance issue and can result in a disciplinary action. Much has been written about this topic, because it can become a source of legal action if the employer doesn't act appropriately. HR's role in the disciplinary process is to provide the expertise needed to set up a fair and equitable process that is applied consistently throughout the organization.

Real World Scenario

Weingarten Rights

Leura Collins was employed by J. Weingarten, Inc., a company that operated a chain of retail stores. Collins worked at the lunch counter at store #2 for about 9 years and was then transferred to store #98. After Collins had been working at the second store for about 2 years, an undercover member of Weingarten's security department investigated a complaint that Collins was stealing money by observing her at work for 2 hours; during this time he found nothing to substantiate the complaint. He met with the store manager, who told the investigator that a co-worker reported that Collins had just underpaid for a box of chicken. Collins was called to the office and interrogated by the investigator and the store manager. Collins asked several times that her union representative be included in the meeting, but each time her request was denied. Collins explained what had happened. The investigator confirmed her story with the co-worker, found that the complaints were caused by a misunderstanding, and determined that Collins had not violated any company rules. Collins informed the shop steward of the incident, and the union filed an unfair labor practice complaint with the NLRB.

The NLRB found that employees are entitled to have a union representative present at any investigatory interview that the employee believes could result in disciplinary action. Employers aren't required to inform employees of this right, but if an employee requests that a co-worker be present, the employer has three options:

- Discontinue the interview until the co-worker arrives.

- Decide not to conduct the interview at all, and make any disciplinary decision based on other facts.

- Give the employee the choice of voluntarily waiving the Weingarten rights and continuing the interview or having the employer make disciplinary decisions without an interview.

Weingarten appealed the finding, and the case was eventually heard by the Supreme Court. In 1975, the Court upheld the NLRB's decision.

The NLRB has extended Weingarten rights to and withdrawn them from *non*union workers several times since then. The rights were first extended in 1982 and withdrawn in 1985. In July 2000, the NLRB reinstated Weingarten rights to nonunion employees based on a case involving the Epilepsy Foundation of Northeast Ohio. In its decision, the Board determined that nonunion employees invoking Weingarten rights are entitled to the presence of another co-worker but aren't entitled to have a family member or attorney present. In a case involving IBM Corp. in June 2004, the board reversed its Epilepsy Foundation decision, once again denying Weingarten rights to nonunion employees.

So, what should nonunion employers do? First, understand that employees still have the right to *ask* for a co-worker's presence, so employers should not take disciplinary action based on such a request. Although employers currently have no obligation to allow co-workers into these meetings, it may be prudent to act cautiously in this area given the unsettled nature of the law.

Organizations with effective ER programs work to prevent the need for disciplinary action. The establishment and publication of clear policies, procedures, and work rules combined with clearly communicated expectations for individual employees are the cornerstones of prevention. With regular feedback, both positive and negative, employees are better able to improve performance issues when they're easily remedied. If a performance problem can't be resolved at this level, the supervisor moves into a formal progressive disciplinary process.

Discipline is a performance management tool that is designed to modify employee behavior through the use of negative consequences. Many companies have a formal code of conduct that is used to communicate examples of expected employee behavior, and when an employee fails to behave in accordance with policy, discipline may be used. HR is responsible for creating the discipline policy, communicating the code of conduct, and ensuring that the administration of the policy doesn't violate the law. A good discipline policy doesn't necessarily have to tie an employer to specific steps in the discipline process, but rather makes a statement about the employee's responsibilities and the consequences for failing to execute those responsibilities in accordance with company guidelines. With wrongful-termination and wrongful-discipline lawsuits on the rise, it's imperative that HR is up to date on the standards pertaining to employee discipline. A seemingly neutral code of conduct that negatively impacts a protected-class group may be found to be discriminatory. Furthermore, disciplining or terminating an employee for exercising their leave rights, for reporting harassment, or to avoid paying a sales commission are all examples of wrongful discipline/discharge.

No-Beard Policy

A pizza-delivery restaurant has an inflexible no-beard policy. The restaurant fires Jamal, one of its African American drivers, for failing to remain clean shaven. Jamal has a severe case of pseudofolliculitis barbae (PFB), an inflammatory skin condition that occurs primarily in African American men and that is caused by shaving. The severity of the condition varies, but many of those who suffer from PFB effectively can't shave at all. If Jamal or EEOC were to challenge the no-beard policy as unlawful because it has a significant negative impact on African Americans, the employer would have to prove the policy is job-related and consistent with business necessity.

Chapter 2 contains a complete discussion of the steps in a disciplinary process.

Disciplinary Terminations

In progressive disciplinary situations, if informal coaching and the initial stages of the disciplinary process don't remedy the performance problem, it's time to move to the termination stage. When this becomes necessary, the manager should work with HR to ensure that, to the extent possible, all necessary steps have been taken to prevent legal action as a result of the termination. As discussed earlier in this chapter, due process isn't required in employment actions taken by private employers, but ensuring that employees are informed of the issues and given the opportunity to tell their side of the story demonstrates that the employer treats them in a fair and equitable manner.

In cases where employee actions create a dangerous situation for the employer, as in theft of company property or violence in the workplace, the employer should move immediately to the termination phase of the disciplinary process. When this occurs, the best course of action is to suspend the employee pending an investigation, conduct the investigation in a fair and expeditious manner, and, should the results of the investigation support termination, terminate the employee. Terminations are always difficult situations, and HR professionals need to be able to provide support for managers who must take this action. There are two areas in which HR's expertise is critical: counseling supervisors before the termination meeting and providing information so that managers avoid wrongful-termination claims.

The Termination Meeting

Termination meetings are among the most difficult duties any supervisor has to perform. When termination becomes necessary, HR should meet with the supervisor to ensure that there is sufficient documentation to support the action and to coach the supervisor on how to appropriately conduct the meeting. By this stage in the process, the employee should not be surprised by the termination, because it should have been referred to as a consequence if improvement didn't occur. The meeting should be long enough to clearly articulate the reasons for the termination and provide any final papers or documentation. Managers should be counseled to be professional, avoid debating the action with the employee, and conclude the meeting as quickly as possible.

The timing of termination meetings is a subject of disagreement as to the "best" day and time. Taking steps to ensure that the termination occurs with as little embarrassment for the employee as possible should be the guiding factor in making this decision.

Once the meeting is completed, and, of course, depending on corporate policy and the circumstances surrounding the termination, the employee may be escorted from the building. Company policies differ on this part of the process: some companies have a security officer escort the employee from the building; others allow the employee to pack up personal items from the desk with a supervisor or security officer present. While the supervisor is conducting the termination meeting, facilities and IT personnel are often simultaneously taking steps to prevent the employee from accessing the company network or facilities once the termination has been completed.

In any situation with the possibility of the employee becoming violent, HR should arrange for security personnel to be nearby or, in extreme cases, ensure that the local police department is advised of the situation.

Wrongful Termination

Wrongful terminations occur when an employer terminates someone for a reason that is prohibited by statute or breaches a contract. For example, an employee may not be terminated because they're a member of a protected class. If an employer gives a different reason for the termination but the employee can prove that the real reason was based on a discriminatory act, the termination would be wrongful. Similarly, an employee may not be terminated as retaliation for whistle-blowing activity or for filing a workers' compensation claim.

Workplace Behavior Issues

Employees are human beings whose behavior at work is influenced by many factors, including experiences and situations that exist outside the context of the workplace. Regardless of the source, these factors influence the way employees behave while they're at work. Employee behavior and management's response (or, in some cases, lack of response) affects the productivity and morale of the entire workgroup and may spill into other parts of the organization. Some employee behaviors that can lead to disciplinary action include the following:

Absenteeism   Employees call in sick for many different reasons—sometimes they themselves are ill or perhaps a child or parent needs care. Some employees have been known to call in sick to go surfing, hang out with friends, go shopping, or have a "mental health" day. Regardless of the reasons employees give for absences, more often than not the unanticipated absence causes problems for the work group. At the very least, another employee usually must take on additional tasks or responsibilities for the duration of the absence. When one employee has an excessive number of absences that aren't protected under FMLA, an absentee policy provides the basis for disciplinary action. An effective policy includes a clear statement of how much sick leave is provided, whether each day off work is counted as one absence, or whether several days off in a row for the same illness is considered one absence. The policy should also tell employees whether the absences are counted on a fiscal, calendar, or rolling-year basis, and when a doctor's note is required before sick leave may be used.

Dress Code   Dress-code policies let employees know how formal or informal their clothes need to be in the workplace. Some types of clothing may not be appropriate for safety reasons (such as to prevent a piece of clothing from getting caught in a machine) or to ensure a professional appearance throughout the organization. A policy should describe what type of clothing is appropriate for different jobs, give examples to clarify, and let employees know the consequences for inappropriate attire. If appropriate, the policy may also describe functions or situations in which employees are expected to dress more formally than normal.

Real World Scenario

Jespersen v. Harrah's Operating Co.

Darlene Jespersen worked for more than 20 years as a bartender with an exemplary performance record at Harrah's Reno casino. In February 2000, Harrah's implemented a comprehensive uniform, known as the "Personal Best" program, with revised standards for all its bartenders, male and female. The standards established a standard work uniform: black pants with white shirt and bow tie and comfortable black shoes. In addition, women were required to wear facial makeup, and men weren't permitted to do so. Men's hair length was required to be above the collar, while women were allowed to have long hair. The standards also included other gender-specific requirements for appearance, jewelry, and nail care.

Jespersen objected to the makeup requirements, stating "that it would conflict with her self-image." She complied with all the other requirements but was unwilling to wear makeup and left Harrah's when there were no other openings for which she qualified. She obtained a right to sue notice from the EEOC in July 2001 and filed suit, claiming that the "Personal Best" policy discriminated against women by "(1) subjecting them to terms and conditions of employment to which men are not similarly subjected and (2) requiring that women conform to sex-based stereotypes as a term and condition of employment." Harrah's requested summary judgment based on its defense that the standards created by the new policy imposed similar requirements for males and females and that the differences in the requirements placed similar burdens on both sexes. The district court granted the motion.

The appeals court upheld the summary judgment, agreeing with the lower court that Jespersen didn't demonstrate that the policy was motivated by stereotyping based on sex.

Insubordination   Insubordinate behavior can be as blatant as employees refusing to perform a legitimate task or responsibility when requested by their managers. It can also be subtler, such as employees who roll their eyes whenever a manager gives them direction. It's not only disrespectful to the manager or supervisor on the receiving end of the behavior, but it can also create morale problems with other members of the work group. Although few organizations have specific policies for insubordination, a code of conduct that describes the organization's expectations for appropriate behavior, such as treating all employees with dignity and respect, provides managers with the tools they need to correct unacceptable behavior.

When discussing performance issues with employees, managers should be encouraged to focus on describing the unacceptable behavior as specifically as possible instead of using general terms such as *bad attitude*, *insubordinate*, or *poor performance*. The more specific the description, the easier it will be for the employee to understand and improve. Specific descriptions of performance issues make any adverse actions easier to defend if an employee decides to take legal action.

Dispute Resolution

Most employment disputes are resolved within the organization, but on some occasions that isn't possible. Complaints can be filed with federal agencies such as OSHA and the EEOC, with the burden of proof often falling on the employer to demonstrate that it didn't violate a law related to working conditions of terms of employment. Using impartial third-party resources such as legal counsel and investigators is often the first step toward avoiding a court-ordered resolution—a very long and expensive process for all parties.

Alternative dispute resolution (ADR) covers a range of methods used to solve disagreements without litigation. These alternatives are often able to resolve problems with less animosity than occurs when a lawsuit is filed, and at far less cost to the parties.

Several different ADR methods can be used in resolving disputes before they reach the level of court action. Initially, the parties involved in a dispute may attempt a cooperative problem-solving meeting, where they work together to find a solution to the problem. Another internal ADR technique is known as a *peer-review panel*, which consists of management and nonmanagement employees who are trained in company policies, procedures, and work rules. The panel hears disputes and makes decisions that, depending on the individual program, can be final and binding on both parties to the dispute. Some companies establish an *ombudsman* or ombuds, an impartial person not involved in the dispute, who speaks with both parties and suggests alternative solutions. An ombudsman can be someone in the company or an outsider.

Arbitration

Arbitration is a means of resolving conflicts without the expense of a lawsuit. *Voluntary arbitration* occurs when both parties to a disagreement agree to submit the conflict to an arbitrator for resolution. *Compulsory arbitration* can be a contract requirement or may be mandated by a court system as a means of reducing the backlog of civil lawsuits or by legal statute, as with public employee unions, which are prohibited from striking. If arbitration is part of an employment contract, it's important to have such agreements periodically reviewed by legal counsel; the law regarding validity of arbitration clauses in employment agreements continues to evolve through judicial decisions.

Arbitration decisions may be either binding or nonbinding. In *binding arbitration*, the parties agree to accept the arbitrator's decision as final. In *nonbinding arbitration*, either party may reject the decision and continue the dispute by filing a lawsuit.

A number of organizations throughout the country offer arbitration services; most of them have a roster of individuals with expertise in a variety of business and legal disciplines so that the arbitrator assigned to a particular case will be knowledgeable in its requirements and common practices. These organizations develop standards for those selected as arbitrators to ensure that they have the qualifications necessary to make fair and impartial decisions in the matters they hear. For example, the oldest of these organizations, the American Arbitration Association (AAA), requires that its arbitrators have a minimum of

10 years of senior-level experience and educational degrees and/or professional licenses in their area of expertise as well as training in arbitration or dispute resolution. In addition, the AAA wants its arbitrators to demonstrate professional recognition for excellence in their field and memberships in professional associations.

Arbitration proceedings begin by selecting the arbitrator. The arbitration service provides a list of individuals with relevant expertise, and each party to the arbitration has an opportunity to eliminate those who may have a conflict of interest in the proceedings.

There are three types of arbitrators:

- An *ad hoc arbitrator* is selected to hear only a single case.

- A *permanent arbitrator* is one who both parties agree is fair and impartial to resolve any disputes arising between them.

- A *tripartite arbitration panel* consists of three arbitrators who hear the issues and reach a joint decision in the matter.

In an arbitration proceeding, each party makes an opening statement describing its case for the arbitrator. The parties then present evidence, in the form of documents or witnesses, to support their case. The arbitrator asks questions of both sides to obtain additional information, and then each side makes a closing statement to sum up the evidence that was presented. The arbitrator then weighs the evidence and renders a decision, notifying the parties by mail.

Mediation

Mediating a grievance involves having the parties work together with the aid of a mediator to devise a solution for a problem. The decisions of a mediator aren't binding on the parties, and if the process fails, the parties may continue to the arbitration process. Mediation is an informal undertaking without evidentiary rules, and no formal record of the proceedings is retained. Mediators assist the parties by using a variety of problem-solving skills to move the disagreement to a resolution.

 Real World Scenario

Davis v. O'Melveny & Myers

In June 1999, Jacquelin Davis began working as a paralegal at the firm of O'Melveny & Myers, LLP. Three years later, in August 2002, O'Melveny implemented an ADR program, stating the following: "This dispute resolution program ... applies to and is binding on all employees (including associates) hired by—or who continue to work for—the firm on or after November 1, 2002." The document included contact information for employees who had questions about the program. Davis continued to work for the firm until July 14, 2003, and during that time asked no questions about the program.

Seven months after leaving the firm, Davis filed a lawsuit claiming that O'Melveny had violated the FLSA as well as other federal and state employment laws by withholding overtime pay and denying breaks and meal periods. O'Melveny responded by claiming that the ADR program required Davis to submit her claim to arbitration. The district court sided with O'Melveny, upholding the ADR program, and Davis appealed to the Ninth Circuit Court of Appeals.

In its finding, the Ninth Circuit found the ADR program to be procedurally unconscionable because it didn't allow employees to opt out of the program—basically requiring them to "take it or leave it." Another clause in the agreement, prohibiting mention of the mediation or arbitration "to anyone not directly involved," was also found to be unfavorable to the employee because it restricted the employee, for example, from "contacting other employees to assist in litigating (or arbitrating) an employee's case." The Court also ruled that the company's unilateral ability to enforce such confidentiality requirements was "one-sided and unconscionable."

Finally, the Court held that the agreement's preclusion of employee complaints to agencies such as the DOL was contrary to public policy and therefore again unconscionable.

Because arbitration agreements continue to be challenged in court and continue to evolve over time, it's important that legal counsel periodically review any form agreements to ensure that they will pass muster with the courts' latest rulings.

The mediation process has several steps, described in the following list:

Structure   Before the parties meet, the mediator develops a structure for the mediation, deciding on the time, place, and attendees for the session.

Introductions   The mediator makes introductions, explains the mediation process, and sets expectations and goals for the mediation.

Fact-Finding   During the mediation, each party presents its side of the issue in a joint session. Generally, the mediator meets with each party individually as well, to ask questions and ensure that everyone has the same facts and that the issues are clearly identified.

Options   As the parties present their facts and listen to those of the other side, alternative solutions may become clear; the mediator may guide the parties to these options as well.

Negotiating   Once the possible alternatives are on the table, the mediator facilitates negotiations during which the parties come to an agreement. Depending on the steps identified in the employer's policy, binding arbitration is often the next step taken in the ADR process.

Writing the Agreement   The mediator or the parties write the agreement that has been reached, and the parties sign it.

Mediation is a cost-effective solution that successfully resolves many employment disagreements. In mediation, the parties are in control of the decision-making process and resolving the conflict; the mediator facilitates the process that allows this to occur.

In either mediation or arbitration (unless it's a binding arbitration), either party may choose to continue the dispute by taking the matter to court if they're dissatisfied with the decision. In most cases, the use of either of these methods results in an agreement that is acceptable to both sides.

The implications of arbitration and mediation in a union environment are discussed in the section "Contract Enforcement."

Constructive Confrontation

Constructive confrontation is a form of mediation developed by Guy Burgess, PhD, and Heidi Burgess, PhD, to resolve long-standing, deep-rooted conflicts about difficult, significant issues in organizations. This method is based on the idea that conflict can be healthy and is designed to move those in conflict from a focus on solving a large problem to removing the nonessential elements from the conflict until only the core issue remains.

Constructive confrontation begins with identifying the fundamental issue causing the conflict, the stakeholders, and their positions about the issue. The process then looks at other conflicts that arise as a result of the fundamental disagreement and how interactions between the parties, including their beliefs about the problem and how to handle it, limit their ability to resolve the conflict. These ancillary issues usually serve to increase the level of hostility surrounding the conflict without adding any benefit. The ancillary issues, when separated from the core issue, can be more easily resolved when treated as single issues. Once the ancillary issues are resolved, the core issue can be seen objectively and resolved more easily. Sometimes, the way the core problem or facts about the problem are stated causes one party to react harshly, further limiting resolution of the conflict. One party to the conflict may not like the process being used; others may believe that their points of view are being ignored. These and other issues can cause misunderstandings between the parties, escalating hostility, or can force participants to take sides, making it increasingly difficult to have meaningful discussions about the core issues. Constructive confrontation identifies ways in which the parties are exacerbating the problem and provides tools to help the parties work through the conflict, such as training, mediation, and facilitation.

Once the ancillary issues have been resolved, the parties can move on to the core issue. At this stage, the core issue can be seen more clearly, and the parties can seek alternative solutions that weren't readily apparent earlier in the process. The goal of constructive confrontation isn't necessarily to have the parties agree but to find a way to work together.

Labor Relations

The history of American labor relations begins with the formation of the Knights of Labor in 1869. This organization was an advocate of the 8-hour workday when 12 or 14 hours per day was the norm. By the end of the nineteenth century, unions became powerful enough to threaten business profitability, and federal anti-trust laws were used to hinder their growth. In reaction, Congress enacted labor legislation that supported union growth. The pendulum swung back and forth until the 1960s, when the political focus turned to civil rights legislation. Although labor unions grew in importance for more than a century, in recent years they have lost some of their appeal to working people. The various labor laws that were enacted had a significant impact on business-labor relations in the United States.

Labor Laws and Organizations

The first piece of legislation to impact the labor movement was the Sherman Antitrust Act, passed in 1890. This legislation was originally intended to control business monopolies that conspired to restrain trade in the United States. The act allowed *injunctions*, court orders that either require or forbid an action by one party against another, to be issued against any person or group that conspired to restrain trade. It was first used against a labor union to obtain an injunction against the American Railway Union in 1894 to end its strike against the Pullman Palace Car Company.

The Clayton Act, passed in 1914, limited the use of injunctions to break strikes and exempted unions from the Sherman Act.

In 1926, Congress enacted the Railway Labor Act, the intention of which was to avoid interruptions due to strikes, protect the rights of employees to join a union, and allow for a "cooling-off" period of up to 90 days if the president deemed a strike to be a national emergency. Originally intended to cover the railroad companies, today this act applies to airlines as well.

The Norris-La Guardia Act was passed in 1932 and protected the rights of workers to organize and strike without the interference of federal injunctions. It also outlawed *yellow-dog contracts*, which employers had used to prevent employees from joining unions by requiring them to sign an agreement that the employee wasn't a member of a union, that the employee wouldn't become one in the future, and that joining a union would be sufficient grounds for dismissal.

In 1935, the NLRA, or Wagner Act, was passed as part of President Franklin Roosevelt's New Deal. At the time, it was referred to as *labor's bill of rights* and represented a marked change in government attitudes toward unions. The NLRA allowed employees to organize, bargain collectively, and engage in "concerted activities for the purpose of collective bargaining or other mutual aid or protection." The right to engage in concerted activities applies not only to union employees but to nonunion employees as well. The NLRA went on to identify five employer unfair labor practices and created the NLRB to enforce provisions of the act. The NLRB is charged with conducting elections and preventing and remedying unfair labor practices. The NLRB doesn't instigate actions on its own; it only responds to charges of unfair labor practices or petitions for representation elections filed in one of its offices.

In 1947, when a Republican majority was elected to Congress, the Taft-Hartley Act, or Labor-Management Relations Act (LMRA), was passed in response to employer complaints about union abuses. Not surprisingly, union leaders decried the act as a "slave labor" law. The LMRA prohibits closed shops and allows union shops only with the consent of a majority of employees. It also provides that states have the right to outlaw closed and union shops by passing "right to work" laws. Jurisdictional strikes and secondary boycotts were also prohibited. When employers bring replacement workers in during an economic strike, the LMRA allows that they may permanently replace union workers; however, if the strike is in response to unfair labor practices committed by the employer, the union members will be reinstated when the strike ends. The LMRA established the Federal Mediation and Conciliation Service to "prevent or minimize interruptions of the free flow of commerce growing out of labor disputes" by providing mediation and conciliation services.

An important feature of Taft-Hartley is the power granted to the president to obtain an injunction ending a strike or lockout for an 80-day cooling-off period if, in the president's estimation, the continuation of the strike could "imperil the national health or safety." This power is rarely invoked because its record of leading to successful long-term agreements is mixed.

The Labor-Management Reporting and Disclosure Act (LMRDA) of 1959, also known as the Landrum-Griffith Act, placed controls on internal union operations. Congress said this was necessary because of "a number of instances of breach of trust, corruption, disregard of the rights of individual employees, and other failures to observe high standards of responsibility and ethical conduct" on the part of union leadership. The act provided a bill of rights for union members that required equal rights for all members to participate in the union, granted freedom of speech and assembly for union members to gather and discuss union issues, and restricted increases in dues and assessments to those that were approved by majority vote of the union. Landrum-Griffith gave employees the right to sue the union and provided safeguards against retaliatory disciplinary actions by the union. The act also prohibited "extortionate picketing" by unions and required that union leadership elections be conducted no less often than every 3 years for local unions and every 5 years for national or international officers.

Employee Rights

The NLRA grants employees the right to organize, join unions, bargain collectively, and engage in other "concerted activities" for mutual aid or protection, as well as the right to refrain from doing so.

The NLRA also protects the right of employees to strike and identifies lawful vs. unlawful strikes:

Lawful Strikes   One type of lawful strike is an economic strike in which the union stops working in an effort to obtain better pay, hours, or working conditions from the employer. In an economic strike, employers may hire permanent replacements for striking employees and aren't required to rehire the strikers if doing so means the replacement workers would be fired. If employees make an unconditional request to return to work, they may be recalled at a later time when openings occur.

The other type of lawful strike is one that occurs when the employer has committed an unfair labor practice and employees strike in protest. In this case, strikers may not be discharged or permanently replaced.

Unlawful Strikes   Strikes can be characterized as unlawful for several reasons:

- Strikes are unlawful if they support union unfair labor practices.
- Strikes are unlawful if they violate a no-strike clause in the contract.
- Lawful strikes can become unlawful if the strikers engage in serious misconduct.

Unfair Labor Practices

An *unfair labor practice* (ULP) is an action by an employer or a union that restrains or coerces employees from exercising their rights to organize and bargain collectively. As discussed previously in this chapter, Congress has identified ULPs for both employers and unions.

Employer Unfair Labor Practices

Employers who attempt to restrain or otherwise interfere with the right of employees to organize and bargain collectively can, in a worst-case scenario, be ordered by the NLRB to bargain with a union even if an election didn't take place or if the union loses an election. For that reason, it's extremely important for employers to be certain that all supervisory personnel are aware of what constitutes an unfair labor practice. An acronym that is helpful in avoiding prohibited activity is *TIPS*: employers may not threaten, interrogate, promise, or spy on employees.

Employer ULPs defined by the NLRA are as follows:

Interfere with, Restrain, or Coerce Unionization Efforts   Employers may not interfere in any way with attempts to unionize the workplace, including organizing activity, collective bargaining, or "concerted activity" engaged in by employees for mutual aid or protection. Interfering also includes inhibiting the free speech of employees who advocate unionization.

Dominate or Assist a Labor Organization   Employers are precluded from forming company unions that are controlled by management and, therefore, don't allow employees an independent representative. Employers are also prohibited from showing favoritism to one union over another.

Discriminate Against Employees   Employers may not discriminate against union members in any of the terms and conditions of employment. This includes taking disciplinary action against employees for participating in union activities.

Discriminate Against NLRB Activity   Employers may not retaliate against employees who have filed charges or participated in an investigation conducted by the NLRB.

Refuse to Bargain in Good Faith   Employers must bargain with a union once it has been designated by a majority of the employees and the union has made a demand to bargain.

Enter into a Hot-Cargo Agreement   It's unlawful for employers and unions to enter into a *hot-cargo agreement* in which, at the union's request, employers stop doing business with another employer.

Union Unfair Labor Practices

The LMRA identified the following union actions that were considered ULPs:

Restrain and Coerce Employees   Union conduct that interferes with an employee's right to choose a representative or to refrain from participating in organizing or collective bargaining activity is a ULP. The act identifies some of the coercive behavior that is unlawful, including assaults, threats of violence, and threats to interfere with continued employment. Unions are also held responsible for coercive acts committed by union members in the presence of union representatives if the representatives don't renounce the actions.

Restrain or Coerce Employers   Unions may not refuse to bargain with representatives chosen by the employer to negotiate with the union, or fine or expel from the union a supervisor based on the way the supervisor applies the contract during the course of business. Unions may not insist that employers accept contract terms the union has negotiated with other bargaining units.

Require Employers to Discriminate   Unions may not require the employer to terminate an employee for working to decertify the union, or require employers to hire only union members or others of whom the union approves.

Refuse to Bargain in Good Faith   Unions must meet and confer with employer representatives at reasonable times to negotiate the terms and conditions of the contract.

Engage in Prohibited Strikes and Boycotts   Unions may not engage in hot-cargo actions or secondary boycotts.

Charge Excessive or Discriminatory Membership Fees   Membership fees must be reasonable and in line with the members' wages and industry standards.

Featherbedding   Unions may not require employers to pay for services that aren't rendered. For example, unions may not require employers to continue to pay employees to do jobs that have been rendered obsolete by changes in technology. An example of this is the fireman on a train who fed coal into the fire on a steam engine to keep the water hot enough to run the train. When diesel trains came along, the fireman was no longer needed to run the train. If a union insisted on keeping the firemen on the trains even though they weren't necessary, this was known as *featherbedding*.

Organizational and Recognitional Picketing   Although sometimes organizational and recognitional picketing are done lawfully, there are three instances in which they're unlawful:

- When another union has been lawfully recognized as the bargaining representative for the organization
- When a representation election has been held within the previous 12 months
- When a representation petition isn't filed within 30 days of the start of the picketing

Picketing is discussed more fully later in this chapter in the "Union Campaign Tactics" section.

Consequences of Unfair Labor Practices

If, as the result of an investigation, an employer or a union has been found to have committed a ULP, the NLRB can order remedial actions to be taken. The NLRB goal is to eliminate the ULP and to undo the effects of the illegal action to the extent possible. One of the requirements is that the offending party post notices in the workplace advising employees that the ULP will be discontinued and describing the actions to be taken to correct the offense:

Employer Remedies   The NLRB may require that the employer disband an employer-dominated union, reinstate employees to positions they held prior to the ULP, or engage in the collective-bargaining process and sign a written agreement with the union.

Union Remedies   Unions may be required to agree to reinstatement of employees it caused to be terminated or rejected for employment, refund excessive dues with interest to members, or engage in the collective-bargaining process and sign a written agreement with the employer.

Filing an Unfair Labor Practice Charge

ULP charges can be filed by an employee, an employer, or a union representative (the charging party) on a form available from the NLRB. Charges may be filed in person, by fax, or by mail at the regional office of the NLRB where the alleged violation occurred. The statute of limitations for ULPs requires that they be filed within 6 months of the incident.

Once the case has been received by the NLRB, the charged party is notified, invited to submit a written statement of the facts and circumstances about the case, and advised that they have the right to counsel. The case is then assigned to a board agent for investigation.

The board agent conducts interviews with all parties to the action, as well as with any witnesses, and makes a recommendation to the regional director for the disposition of the case. At this stage, the charges may be dismissed if unwarranted or result in a complaint if valid. Depending on the nature and severity of the offense, the complaint may result in an informal or formal settlement agreement. An informal settlement agreement requires that the charged party will take specified actions to remedy the ULP and doesn't involve a board order or court decree. A formal settlement involves a complaint issued by the NLRB against the charged party and results in a board order or court hearing.

An administrative law judge (ALJ), who conducts a hearing on the evidence, reviews the record and issues a "decision and order" for charges that aren't settled. If a party isn't satisfied with the order of the ALJ, they have 28 days to file an exception with the NLRB office in Washington, D.C., which will issue a final order concurring with or amending the finding of the ALJ.

If the charged party isn't satisfied with the NLRB findings, an appeal can be filed with the U.S. Court of Appeals in the appropriate jurisdiction.

Union Organization

At the initial stages of a union-organizing campaign, signs of union activity are difficult to detect. By the time management notices something unusual is taking place, the organizing process may already be well underway.

One early indication that an organizing campaign has begun is a noticeable change in employee behavior. For example, employees may begin to challenge management decisions using union terminology related to benefits or employee rights. The earliest signs of a union presence are characterized by sometimes subtle changes in workforce relationships. First-line supervisors, those closest to rank-and-file employees who are the target of organizing efforts, are the ones most likely to notice that something about those relationships is different. How these changes manifest themselves is different in every company, but some signs that raise concern include the following:

- Groups of employees begin to congregate in unlikely places, scattering or ending their conversation when a supervisor or another manager appears.

- Employee behavior during meal and rest periods changes noticeably; instead of "hanging out," some employees are obviously occupied with nonwork activity.

- Absenteeism increases significantly in a short period of time for no apparent reason.

- Groups of employees challenge supervisors or managers with questions about benefits and employment practices in an uncharacteristically antagonistic manner.

- Former employees or newcomers approach employees in the parking lot or at public entrances to the building.

- People are observed taking down license numbers on employee cars.

- Employees who normally hang out with one group of co-workers befriend others, jumping from one group to another during meal or rest periods.

- Union slogans in the form of graffiti begin to appear in locations where employees congregate.

As organizing activity intensifies, the union may instigate a confrontation with the employer by coaching one or a group of employees to defy by coaching one or a group to defy instructions for reasons that are protected by the NLRA, such as refusing to work because they aren't paid enough to do a particular job. If the refusal is based on an activity protected by the NLRA, employees may not be fired and must be treated as lawful strikers. An uninformed or unaware supervisor may unknowingly commit a ULP by disciplining employees for this behavior.

What Can an Employer Do?

To begin with, employers can make truthful statements about the consequences of unionization in response to union claims—as long as the TIPS guideline is followed. Just as union organizers work to convince employees to join the union, management may communicate their reasons for opposing unionization. During any organizing campaign, an experienced labor attorney should review management statements about the union before they're disseminated. All members of the management team should be coached on ULPs and how to avoid them, particularly first-line supervisors because they interact most frequently with rank-and-file employees. First-line supervisors also have more influence with their direct reports than any other member of management, and employers should use this relationship by providing them with the information they will need to effectively represent the management view to employees.

Finally, organizers understand that enthusiasm and support for the union peaks at a certain point and then support begins to dwindle. For that reason, unions like to schedule elections to coincide with the peak of interest, and they gear their organizing activities to that goal. If an employer can delay the election, the chances of prevailing against the union are improved.

The Organizing Process

The recognition process has seven basic elements, but not all of them occur in every situation. The process consists of authorization cards, a demand for recognition, a petition to the NLRB, an NLRB conference, a preelection hearing, a campaign, and finally the election.

Authorization Cards

The goal of the union during the organizing process is to obtain signed authorization cards from employees. An *authorization card* is the means by which the NLRB determines that there is sufficient support for a union to hold an election. The NLRB will hold an election if 30 percent of the eligible employees in the anticipated bargaining unit sign the authorization cards. In practice, the union would like to have far more signed cards before submitting a petition for an election—generally it would like to have signed cards from at least 50 percent of the eligible employees.

Demand for Recognition

When the union has a sufficient number of signed authorization cards, it's ready to approach the employer with a demand for recognition. This usually comes in the form of a letter to the employer in which the union claims to represent a majority of workers and demands to be recognized by the employer as the exclusive bargaining agent for employees. The demand may also be made in person when a union representative approaches any member of the management team, including a first-line supervisor, offering proof that a majority of employees want the union to represent them. It's crucial that whoever is approached doesn't respond in a way that could be construed as recognition by the union, politely referring the union to the HR department or a senior member of the management team.

Union representatives may also approach employers requesting a neutrality agreement or a card-check election. In a neutrality agreement, an employer agrees not to say or do anything in opposition to the union. A card-check election means that the employer agrees to recognize the union based on signed authorization cards. At a minimum, agreeing to either situation limits the employer's ability to resist unionization efforts. Agreeing to one of these alternatives may be interpreted as voluntary recognition of the union.

An employer may choose to recognize a union voluntarily under some circumstances, but this should be done only after conferring with legal counsel. One way unions may seek voluntary recognition is to approach management with signed authorization cards to have management witness its majority status by accepting the cards. A number of NLRB cases have involved union claims that management has witnessed majority status by counting the authorization cards, so supervisors and management should be made aware of the consequences of handling the cards.

Petitioning the NLRB

If management refuses to grant voluntary recognition, the union files a petition for an election with the NLRB, along with evidence of employee interest in union representation. The NLRB reviews the petition to determine that it represents an appropriate level of interest in union representation and that signatures on the petition or authorization cards are valid.

NLRB Conference/Preelection Hearing Issues

When the NLRB is satisfied with the legitimacy of the petition, it schedules a conference with the employer and employee representatives. During the conference, an NLRB representative reviews any jurisdictional issues, the makeup of the bargaining unit, the eligibility of voters in the proposed unit, and the time and place of the election. If either party disputes issues related to the bargaining unit, legitimacy of the authorization cards, or timing of the election, a formal hearing is held by the NLRB to resolve those issues.

Bargaining Units

The makeup of the bargaining unit is a critical factor to both union and employer points of view. The union wants the unit to be as large as possible and include a majority of employees who are in favor of the union. Management, of course, wants to limit the size of the unit and include a majority of employees who choose to remain union-free.

The NLRA grants broad discretion for bargaining unit determinations to the NLRB. Guidance in the act is that "…the unit appropriate for the purposes of collective bargaining shall be the employer unit, craft unit, plant unit, or subdivision thereof." Aside from that, the only specifics provided are that a bargaining unit may not consist of both professional and nonprofessional employees unless the professional employees vote to be included in the unit, and that individuals hired as guards to protect the employer's premises or property may not be included in a unit with other employees. The NLRB looks at several objective criteria to devise a bargaining unit that is appropriate for the individual situation, beginning with determining whether there is a "community of interest" in the unit—that is, that the interests of members of the unit are sufficiently similar to preclude disagreements during the bargaining process. The NLRB looks as well at factors such as how the employer administers its business (whether it uses standard policies across the entire company or diverse policies in different locations), geography (how far apart the locations are in the proposed unit), whether the unit is made up of employees involved in a major process of the company, whether employees are cross-trained or frequently transfer between locations, what unit the employees want to be part of, and any relevant collective bargaining history. Finally, the NLRB considers the extent to which employees are already organized, although the act makes it clear that this may not be the determining factor.

Bargaining units may consist of two or more employees in one employer location or employees in two or more locations of a single employer. If there is an employer industry association, the bargaining unit may include employees of two or more employers in several locations.

Some employees aren't eligible for inclusion in a bargaining unit. These include confidential employees, supervisors, and management personnel. The act also excludes independent contractors and some agricultural laborers from bargaining units.

Temporary Workers

In August 2000, the NLRB made a significant change to its previous rulings on the inclusion of temporary workers in an employer's bargaining unit in a case involving M. B. Sturgis, Inc. Sturgis is a gas hose manufacturer in Missouri that was the target of an organizing campaign. When the union petitioned for an election, Sturgis wanted to include the temp workers on its site in the bargaining unit, but the union didn't want them included. The NLRB reversed two longstanding positions in this case by deciding that the determining factor in this decision is whether a community of interest in wages, scheduling, and working conditions exists between the regular employees and the temp workers, and that a unit including temp workers isn't considered a multi-employer unit needing the consent of both employers.

Union Campaign Tactics

At their peak in 1953, unions represented 35.7 percent of the private sector workforce. According to the Bureau of Labor Statistics, unions represented only 7.8 percent of the private sector workforce in 2005. However, unions are far more prevalent in today's public sector: 36.5 percent of public sector employers are unionized. As unions struggle to maintain membership levels, they have had to reexamine their strategies for attracting new members.

As the economy in the United States moved from a manufacturing to an informational base, the workforce changed from predominantly blue-collar workers who were the traditional union members to white-collar workers who haven't traditionally been attracted by union membership. Although the strategies vary with each union, the general trend is to find ways of attracting white-collar workers to union membership. Once potential members indicate interest in unionizing their place of work, a number of methods are used to organize the employees:

Internet   Many unions have sophisticated websites that provide information for employees who are interested in forming a union. The sites contain information on labor laws, information on unfair labor practices, advice on beginning a campaign, and opportunities for interested workers to contact union personnel.

Home Visits   This tactic is most often used when the union is trying to gain initial supporters in the company. It provides an opportunity for organizers to have private conversations with potential inside organizers. Because home visits are expensive for the union and can be viewed as an unwanted invasion of privacy, they aren't widely used.

Inside Organizing   The most effective organizing process occurs when one or more employees work from within the organization to build support for the union. Insiders can use their influence on co-workers, identify those most likely to respond to the effort, and encourage participation.

Salting   *Salting* occurs when a union hires a person to apply for a job at an organization they have targeted. Once hired, the employee acts in much the same way as an inside organizer who was already employed by the company.

Meetings   Union-organizing meetings bring together experienced organizers, inside organizers from the company, and employees who are undecided about supporting the organizing process. Meetings provide opportunities to communicate the benefits of membership and exert peer pressure on potential members.

Leafleting   The goal of union leaflets is to point out the advantages the union will bring to the workforce and to counter information that management provides to employees about the benefits of remaining union-free. Leaflets are generally used when the organizing campaign is well underway.

Media   Unions have developed expertise in getting their message out. When management commits a ULP or takes any action the union perceives as unfavorable, the union will issue a press release that interprets the action in the most favorable way for the union. For example, in 1999, the Union of Needletrades, Industrial, and Textile Employees (UNITE) was conducting an organizing campaign at Loehmann's Department Store in New York City. With little more than a month before the scheduled NLRB election, the store fired one of the leaders of the organizing campaign. UNITE issued a press release that concentrated on the fact that the employee had an exemplary work record at the store and was a single mother. The union went on to allege that the store had spied on the employee during her lunch break in order to find a reason to fire her. The union used this as the basis for encouraging the public to boycott the store.

Picketing   *Picketing* occurs when a group of employees patrols the entrance to a business in order to inform customers and the public about disputes or to prevent deliveries to a business that the union is trying to influence in some way. It can also occur to advise the public about ULPs the union believes the employer has committed. The NLRB recognizes three types of picketing:

> **Organizational Picketing**   *Organizational picketing* occurs when the union wants to attract employees to become members and authorize the union to represent them with the employer.
>
> **Recognitional Picketing**   *Recognitional picketing* occurs when the union wants the employer to recognize the union as the employees' representative for collective-bargaining purposes. The NLRA places a limit of 30 days on recognitional picketing, after which a petition for an election must be filed.

Informational or Publicity Picketing   *Informational or publicity picketing* is done to truthfully advise the public that an employer is a union-free workplace.

As noted earlier, there are three instances when picketing is prohibited: when another union has been lawfully recognized as the bargaining representative for the organization; when a representation election has been held within the previous 12 months; and when a representation petition isn't filed within 30 days of the start of the picketing.

NLRB Elections

The purpose of an NLRB election is to determine whether a majority of employees in the unit desire to be represented by the union. If issues between the parties are resolved during a conference, the NLRB schedules a *consent election* to take place within 30 days. A *directed election* occurs when a preelection hearing is required to resolve those issues prior to scheduling the election. Within 7 days of the consent to or direction of an election, the employer must provide an *Excelsior list* containing the names and addresses of all employees in the bargaining unit to the union.

During the time between the NLRB decision and election day, both management and the union present the case for their point of view to employees in the bargaining unit. The employer is required to post notices of the election in prominent locations frequented by employees in the bargaining unit. In the 24 hours immediately preceding the campaign, the NLRB prohibits the employer from holding company meetings for the purpose of influencing the vote.

On the day of the election, neither the employer nor the union may conduct campaign activities in or around the polling area.

To be eligible to vote in the election, an employee must have worked during the pay period prior to the election and must be employed by the business on the day of the election. Employees who are sick, are on vacation, are on military leave, or have been temporarily laid off may vote subject to rules established by the NLRA. Economic strikers who have been replaced by bona fide permanent employees may vote in any election that takes place within 12 months of the beginning of the strike.

During the election, representatives of the employer and the union may challenge the eligibility of any vote before it's placed in the ballot box. These votes are set aside, and if it's possible that the challenged votes would change the result of the election, the NLRB will determine whether they're valid after the election ends.

The NLRB representative counts the votes at the end of the voting period and provides the vote count to the parties at that time. If the union receives 50 percent plus one vote, the union is certified as the bargaining representative for the unit. In the event of a tie vote, the union isn't certified.

After a vote, the party that lost the election may file charges that the prevailing party interfered with the election results by committing ULPs. The NLRB will investigate the charges in accordance with its administrative procedures and, should they be justified, will take remedial action against the offending party.

Norma Rae

For those unfamiliar with the organizing process, the 1979 movie *Norma Rae* provides dramatic insight into the unionization of a garment factory in the South. Based on a true story, the movie follows the efforts of a union organizer from New York to build support for a union in a textile factory in a small southern town. The organizer begins by visiting the homes of some of the workers, distributing leaflets at the front gate of the factory, and enlisting the support of one of the workers who becomes the inside organizer. This insider lends credibility to the union representative by introducing him to co-workers, sponsoring organizing meetings, and obtaining signed union-authorization cards. In the course of the campaign, management commits several ULPs. One of the final scenes dramatizes the vote count: as the NLRB official observes, representatives for management and the union count each vote.

Bars to Elections

The NLRA won't allow elections in some circumstances. The following are known as *election bars*:

Contract Bar   Except in very limited circumstances, the NLRB won't direct an election while a bargaining unit is covered by a valid collective-bargaining agreement.

Statutory Bar   The NLRA prohibits an election in a bargaining unit that had a valid election during the preceding 12-month period.

Certification-Year Bar   When the NLRB has certified a bargaining representative, an election won't be ordered for at least 1 year.

Blocking-Charge Bar   An election petition will be barred when there is a pending ULP charge.

Voluntary-Recognition Bar   If an employer has voluntarily recognized a union as the representative for a bargaining unit, an election will be barred for a reasonable period of time to allow the parties to negotiate a contract.

Prior-Petition Bar   When a union petitioning for an election withdraws the petition prior to the election, then no elections will be approved for 6 months.

Union Decertification

Employees may petition the NLRB for *decertification* if they're dissatisfied with the union's performance. A decertification petition requires signatures of at least 30 percent of the employees before the NLRB will act on it. Employees may want to decertify the union for a variety of reasons, including poor performance by the union in its representation of the employees or the desire of the employees to be represented by a different union.

Decertification may also occur because the employee relationship with management is a good one and employees no longer feel the need for union representation. It's critical for HR professionals and management to understand that the employer may not encourage or support employees in the decertification process. Doing so constitutes a ULP and may well result in employees being compelled to continue to be represented by the union.

Union Deauthorization

Employees may want to maintain the union but remove a union security clause, such as union-shop, dues check-off, or maintenance of membership clause (discussed in the next section). The NLRB will approve *deauthorization* based on a petition by 30 percent or more of the members of the bargaining unit. As with decertification, employers must not participate in the effort to deauthorize the union, because doing so is considered to be a ULP.

Collective Bargaining

The NLRA imposes a duty to bargain on employers and unions. Mandatory subjects for the bargaining process include wages, hours, terms and conditions of employment, the agreement itself, and any questions that arise from the agreement. Bad faith in the bargaining process can be evidenced by a lack of concessions on issues, refusing to advance proposals or to bargain, stalling tactics, or withholding information that is important to the process. Evidence of bad faith by management in the bargaining process can also be evidenced by attempts to circumvent the union representative by going directly to employees with proposals before they have been presented to the union. Another indicator of bad faith bargaining by management occurs when unilateral changes are made to working conditions. An indication of bad faith by the union would be failing to notify management of the intent to renegotiate the contract within 60–90 days before it expires.

Collective-Bargaining Positions

Before discussing the components of collective bargaining, it's important to understand the different bargaining positions that can be taken and how each position affects the bargaining process. There are two basic approaches to negotiating:

Positional Bargaining   *Positional bargaining* is a strategy represented by demands made by each side. During positional negotiations, each side views the object of the negotiation as something finite that must be shared, stakes out the position they believe is in their own interest, and concentrates on "winning" that position for their side. This makes the process an adversarial, competitive one. Also known as *hard bargaining* or *distributive bargaining*, positional bargaining is a zero-sum game: in order for one side to gain something, the other side must lose something.

Principled Bargaining   *Principled bargaining* as a negotiating strategy is characterized by parties who are more interested in solving a problem than they are in winning a position. In doing so, the parties remain open to looking at the problem in new ways, brainstorming for ideas, and often coming up with an agreement that solves the original problem in a way that wasn't originally contemplated by either side. The most common forms of principled bargaining are the following:

Integrative Bargaining   In *integrative bargaining,* the parties look at all the issues and are able to make mutually agreeable trade-offs between those issues.

Interest-Based Bargaining (IBB)   *Interest-based bargaining* (IBB) is based on the concept that both sides in the negotiation have harmonious interests. In labor-management negotiations, for example, both labor and management have an equal interest in the continuing viability of the business—for management to earn profits and for labor to have continued employment.

Collective-Bargaining Strategies

In addition to collective-bargaining positions, HR professionals should be aware of the four basic negotiating strategies used in union environments:

Single-Unit Bargaining   The most common strategy, *single-unit bargaining,* occurs when one union meets with one employer to bargain.

Parallel Bargaining   In *parallel bargaining,* also known as *pattern bargaining, whipsawing,* or *leapfrogging,* the union negotiates with one employer at a time. After a contract has been reached with one employer, the union uses the gains made during the negotiation as a base for negotiating with the next employer.

Multi-employer Bargaining   In *multi-employer bargaining,* the union negotiates with more than one employer in an industry or region at a time. This situation can occur when temporary workers are part of a client employer's bargaining unit and the union negotiates with both the temp agency and the client employer on employment issues.

Multi-unit Bargaining   *Multi-unit bargaining,* or *coordinated bargaining,* occurs when several unions represent different bargaining units in the company. An example of this occurs in the airline industry, when the employer negotiates with the unions representing pilots, flight attendants, and mechanics or other employee classes. This allows the employer to coordinate negotiations on mandatory and permissive bargaining subjects while allowing the unions to cooperate on issues that have similar meaning to their various members.

Collective-Bargaining Subjects

The subjects open for negotiation during the collective-bargaining process fall into four areas:

Mandatory Subjects   The NLRA defines the subjects that are mandatory in the collective-bargaining process. These are wages, hours, other terms and conditions of employment, and the negotiation of the agreement and bargaining related to questions that arise from the agreement. Both parties must bargain on mandatory subjects, and unresolved issues on them are the only ones that may be the subject of a strike or lockout.

Illegal Subjects   The NLRA also identifies topics that are unlawful for inclusion in a collective-bargaining agreement, including hot-cargo clauses and closed-shop security agreements.

Voluntary Subjects   Voluntary or permissible subjects for negotiation would be any lawful topic other than those identified as mandatory by the NLRA. These generally include management rights, such as production scheduling, operations, and selecting supervisors.

Reserved-Rights Doctrine   Management generally includes a clause in the contract that states that any rights not covered specifically in the agreement are the sole responsibility of management.

Collective Bargaining Agreement (CBA)

The *collective bargaining agreement* (CBA) is a contract governing the employment relationship for a specified period of time. The clauses contained in the CBA will, of course, be reflective of the bargaining topics in individual companies. Some of the clauses found in many contracts include the following:

Wages, Hours, Terms, and Conditions of Employment   The clauses that describe the wages, medical and other benefits, overtime, hours, and other conditions of employment are the backbone of the CBA.

Union Security Clauses   The union security clause requires members of the union to provide financial support to the union. A security clause helps ensure that the union will be financially able to carry out its bargaining obligations:

- A *union shop* clause requires that all employees join the union within a grace period that is specified by the contract but is no fewer than 30 days, or, in the construction industry, 7 days.

- An *agency shop* clause specifies that all employees must either join the union or pay union dues if they choose not to join the union.

- A *closed shop* clause requires that all new hires be members of the union before they're hired. The closed shop is illegal except in the construction industry.

- A *maintenance of membership* clause allows employees to choose whether to join the union, but once they join, they must remain members until the expiration of the contract. The employee must notify the union that they wish to discontinue membership within 30 days of the contract expiration.

No Strike/No Lockout Clause   These clauses are considered very important to both unions and management because they provide economic protection from work stoppages on both sides. Strikes and lockouts are discussed more fully in the "Lockouts and Boycotts and Strikes ... Oh My!" section of this chapter.

Contract Administration   This clause covers the nuts and bolts of how the contract will be administered over its duration. Procedures for disciplinary actions, grievance resolution, and arbitration, as well as agreements on how clauses may be modified during the contract term, can be included in this clause.

Dues Check-off   Most unions prefer to have employees agree to the automatic deduction of their union dues. To be enforceable, employees must give written authorization for the deductions.

Zipper Clause   A *zipper clause* or *totality of agreement* clause is an agreement between the parties that the CBA is the entire agreement between them and that anything not in the agreement isn't part of the agreement. The purpose of this clause is to prevent the reopening of negotiations during the term of the contract.

Contract Enforcement

Disagreements that arise during the course of the contract may take many forms; some are easily resolved through the grievance process established in the CBA, and others may go to arbitration before they're resolved.

Grievance Procedure

When disagreements occur in a union environment, the grievance process described in the CBA provides the framework for resolving them. The framework describes the steps to be taken and the time frames in which actions must be implemented to either resolve or reply to the grievance. Many grievances can be resolved at the first step in the process with the immediate supervisor, grievant, and union steward working together. If resolution isn't possible at that level, a union official takes the dispute to the next level of company management, where the grievant generally doesn't attend but is represented by the union. If the dispute isn't resolved at the second level, a member of the union grievance committee meets with the next level of management in the company. Grievances that are serious enough to be unsolved at the highest management level in the process then go to a third party for resolution. Depending on the terms of the CBA, this may involve binding arbitration, as is the case in the majority of contracts, or it may use mediation or another form of alternative dispute resolution.

Binding Arbitration

As discussed previously in the section "Dispute Resolution," arbitration is one method of resolving disputes without litigation. In the union environment, binding arbitration is used to resolve conflicts without resorting to work stoppages. Compulsory arbitration is mandated by legal statute to resolve disputes in the public sector where labor strikes are prohibited.

Mediation

The process used to mediate disputes in a union environment is the same as it is in a non-union environment. With the aid of the mediator, the parties to the disagreement work to develop a solution that is acceptable to both of them.

Court Injunctions

As explained earlier in this chapter, injunctions are sought when immediate action is needed to temporarily prevent something from occurring. One example of the use of injunctions in the collective-bargaining process is the national emergency strike. The Taft-Hartley Act empowers the president to seek an injunction to stop a strike or lockout for an 80-day cooling-off period.

Duty of Successor Employers

In the event that a company with CBAs is acquired by a new company, the new management may be required to maintain the union contract. Whether the NLRB will consider an acquiring owner to be a successor employer is based on the following factors:

- Substantial continuity in operations

- The number of employees assimilated into the new company

- Similarity of operations and products

- The agreement with the previous employer

Although the terms and conditions may be changed by the new employer, the changes are required to be made through the collective-bargaining process and can't be made unilaterally by the employer.

Lockouts and Boycotts and Strikes ... Oh My!

For a variety of reasons, such as when communication between the union and management breaks down and tempers flare or when workplace conditions become so hazardous that employees are afraid they will be maimed or seriously injured on the job, one party or the other may determine that the only course of action left to them is a work stoppage.

Lockouts

A *lockout* occurs when management shuts down operations to keep the union from working. This can happen for several reasons. For example, union members may be engaging in a work slowdown, and it may be costing management more to have the employees working slowly and producing a limited number of goods or services than it would cost to shut down the operation.

Boycotts

Boycotts occur when the union and the employees in the bargaining unit work together against an employer to make their dissatisfaction with the employer's actions known or to try to force the employer into recognizing the union or conceding to the demands of the union. Boycotts occur in several ways:

Ally Doctrine   The *ally doctrine* states that when an employer whose workers are on strike contacts a neutral employer and asks the neutral employer to produce the work that would normally be performed by the striking workers, the neutral employer becomes an ally of the struck employer and is therefore a legitimate target of a picket line.

Alter Ego Doctrine   The *alter ego doctrine* developed originally as a means to protect creditors from frauds perpetrated by shareholders. Its application has been extended to labor relations to preclude employers from dodging their collective-bargaining responsibilities. An alter ego employer consists of two or more businesses with substantially identical management, business purposes, operations, equipment, customers, supervision, and ownership. In 1965, the Supreme Court heard a case, *Radio Union v. Broadcast Services, Inc.*, in which it identified four criteria that determine whether a single employer exists: interrelation of operations, central control of labor relations, common management, and common ownership. When these four criteria are present, the NLRB may determine that employees of the alter ego employer are part of the bargaining unit.

Double Breasting   *Double breasting* refers to a common owner of two businesses, one of which is a union shop and the other a nonunion shop. Unions would like to include both businesses in a bargaining unit because of their common ownership. Historically, as long as each business had different management, equipment, and customers, and a legitimate business purpose separate and apart from the other company, the union was prohibited from striking the second business because that was considered a secondary boycott by the NLRB. More recently, the NLRB has determined that unionization of both businesses may be a legitimate topic for contract negotiation, and if the owner refuses to bargain, the union may strike.

Secondary Boycott   A *secondary boycott* occurs when a union tries to compel an employer who isn't involved in a dispute (such as a supplier) to stop doing business with another employer that is part of a dispute with the union. For the most part, secondary boycotts are defined as ULPs by the Taft-Hartley Act.

Straight-Line Operations   A *straight-line operation* is one in which two businesses perform operations that complement each other's operations. If one business is struck, the other may be as well because they're engaged in a single economic enterprise.

Strikes

A *strike* occurs when the union decides to stop working. An earlier section in the chapter discussed the difference between unlawful and lawful strikes. Whether a strike is lawful depends on the purpose of the strike. The NLRA identifies several specific strikes:

- A strike in support of a ULP committed by the union is a ULP and therefore unlawful.

- A strike that occurs in violation of a no-strike clause in a CBA isn't a protected activity, and employees engaging in this type of activity may be terminated or disciplined.

- Strikers who engage in serious misconduct during a strike, including violence, threats of violence, physically blocking someone from entering or leaving the place of business, or attacking management personnel will cause a strike to be deemed unlawful.

- Work slowdowns are considered unlawful strikes and may result in disciplinary action, including termination.

- A *wildcat strike* is one that occurs in violation of a contract clause prohibiting strikes during the term of the contract.

- A *sit-down strike*, in which employees stop working and stay in the building, is considered an unlawful strike.

- Strikes in support of a hot-cargo clause are prohibited.

Picketing

As discussed in the section "Union Campaign Tactics," picketing can be a lawful activity and a way for unions to advertise their message. Although picketing often occurs in connection with a strike or work stoppage, it isn't the same thing as a strike. The difference is that picketing occurs to simply inform other parties about issues under dispute, whereas a strike occurs when employees stop working. Even in the public sector where strikes are prohibited by law, picketing can be used to inform the public about issues. The three kinds of picketing that PHR/SPHR candidates should be familiar with are the following:

Common Situs Picketing   *Common situs picketing* happens when an employer shares a building with other employers. Because picketing a common business location can interfere with the ability of secondary businesses to operate, the union must ensure that picket signs clearly state the name of the business they're striking and, where possible, restrict picketing to an entrance that is used only by the primary employer.

Consumer Picketing   *Consumer picketing* is done to advise consumers that goods have been produced by a business whose workers are on strike.

Hot-Cargo Pickets   Hot cargo was described earlier in the chapter. Because it's an unlawful activity, picketing against hot-cargo issues is prohibited.

Union Avoidance Strategies

Most employers prefer to operate in a union-free environment. An effective ER program and organization culture that treats employees with dignity and respect is more likely to remain union-free because employee needs are being met without a union. Some characteristics of organizations that are less vulnerable to unionization attempts include the following:

- An open, inclusive work environment
- Clear communication about organization goals and successes
- Consistent, equitable application of organization policies, procedures, and work rules
- An established conflict-resolution or complaint process that provides an outlet for solving problems so that employees feel heard and appreciated
- Disciplinary procedures that include an impartial, complete review of facts prior to taking action, particularly for termination decisions

When employees are treated poorly, are overworked, are stressed about their jobs, and don't have management support, union promises of better pay and working conditions are attractive, and employees often turn to unions with the hope that the union will be able to improve their work situation. Unions also offer leadership opportunities as shop stewards and union officers for members who may otherwise not have those opportunities.

SPHR ONLY Nonunion Philosophy

A carefully worded statement of an employer's philosophy regarding unions can be a useful strategy to help avoid union-organizing activities. While employees have the right to organize, an employer also has the right to communicate its desire to maintain an environment of close management-employee relations. Many employers fear that if they discuss unions with their employees, the employees will be motivated to begin organizing.

However, open communication about the factual limitations of unions serves to educate employees, enabling them to respond favorably to the employer if approached by a union. For example, it's prudent for the employer to remind employees that a union can't provide for them anything the employer doesn't agree to through the collective-bargaining process, and that if they need or desire specific working conditions or benefits, the employer is open for discussion with the employees directly. A nonunion philosophy statement can't threaten retaliation or promise benefits, but it may discuss the employer's desire to avoid third-party relationships. A nonunion philosophy statement should be properly vetted by a labor attorney to ensure compliance with the NLRA.

Climate Assessments

The best opportunity to identify and respond to labor/management communication deficiencies is before the relationship deteriorates. Assessing the organizational climate through employee surveys, committees, and third-party facilitation can provide the information necessary to get in front of issues before they grow into large-scale morale problems—a climate ripe for promises by unions of better working conditions. Building trust through open and honest communication and problem-solving will help reduce the likelihood of successful union authorization.

Management Training

Managers need to be trained to recognize union organizing activities such as the following:

- Increased interest in policies and benefits
- Surge of complaints against managers
- Unusual/excessive grouping of employees, such as in the parking lot
- Excessive strangers or visitors on site with no clear purpose
- Open talk about unions, or the use of union terms when discussing working conditions or policies

These are just some examples of behavioral indications that a union may be attempting to organize. Further training of managers should include enforcement of open-door policies, fair and proper treatment of employees, responsiveness to complaints, and what they can/can't do if they suspect union organizing.

Metrics: Measuring Results

The ultimate measure of success in employee relations is the satisfaction level of employees. Although satisfaction as a concept is difficult to measure, the results achieved by satisfied employees (longevity, customer satisfaction, and absenteeism, for example) are quantifiable and measurable:

Business Impact Measures   Two indicators of employee satisfaction that *can* be measured are absenteeism and turnover. Excessive, unplanned absences can be an indication of employee stress, dissatisfaction with job requirements, supervisory conflicts, and a feeling of being undervalued by the employer. Measuring absence rates over time can provide feedback on the success of ER programs, as well as provide indicators of supervisory issues that may be resolved through coaching or training. As discussed in Chapter 4, the turnover rate is the ultimate indicator of dissatisfaction with the supervisor, company, and/or ER programs.

Employee surveys, over time and conducted on an annual or other regular schedule, can also measure more subjective employee-satisfaction metrics. With a baseline established, positive or negative trends can be identified and ER programs adjusted or implemented to reverse negative trends.

Another important measure of employee satisfaction is the level of satisfaction customers have with products or services. An increase in customer-service complaints or a survey that indicates a lack of customer satisfaction can indicate that employee performance is affecting business results. These results must, of course, be viewed in context with other factors that may affect customer satisfaction, such as higher prices due to increased transportation costs.

Depending on the nature of the business, another indication of employee satisfaction is the presence or absence of union-organizing activity. If the business is already unionized, the success of ER programs can be measured by the frequency of strikes, slowdowns, boycotts, or lockouts.

Tactical Accountability Measures   One way to measure the effectiveness of ER programs is by tracking legal-compliance issues, such as the number of claims filed with the EEOC, the number of lawsuits filed, the cost of settlements reached, and other consequences of poorly designed or communicated programs.

In the area of performance management, HR can track its effectiveness against the timeliness of performance reviews (measured against an established timeline) and their quality (measured against established criteria, such as comments that provide meaningful feedback or training plans developed) or the number of positions with written goals and objectives.

Global Considerations

From an ELR point of view, when considering the question of whether to fill a position with an expatriate from the United States, a host-country national, or a third-country national, employers must weigh the answers to several questions:

- Does the host country restrict the number of expatriates allowed in the country?
- How does the legal system view an employee handbook, and is it advisable to create one?
- Does the legal system recognize at-will employment? Or is an employment contract required?
- What is the plan for the employee's repatriation and job assignment after the international assignment is over?

As global business operations continue to expand, these and other questions specific to particular countries must be answered. To avoid costly errors, HR must be able to provide executives with accurate, specific information about the differences in employment laws and practices that exist in the countries where the business operates.

Summary

Effective management of ELR is a critical element of a successful business. Employees who are treated with dignity and respect and given the tools they need to succeed in turn reward employers with increased production, fewer sick days, and a loyal and committed workforce. Organizational culture begins with management attitudes toward employees and ranges from those that are based on an autocratic philosophy characterized by top-down communication and interactions to those of employee empowerment where individuals and work teams make the decisions necessary to get their jobs done.

Effective dispute-resolution programs that solve employment disagreements without the need for legal action are both cost-effective and more successful than lawsuits. HR professionals can add value to their organizations by establishing programs that resolve issues and give employees who feel they have been mistreated an opportunity to be heard before the situation escalates and a lawsuit is filed.

The management of the employment relationship is subject to the laws prohibiting discrimination in all terms and conditions of employment, as well as to common-law doctrines. HR professionals must be aware of the requirements of these statutes and doctrines in order to provide sound advice to management in making employment decisions and to ensure that the programs and policies developed by HR are in compliance with them.

Labor relations are governed by a number of laws designed to protect the rights of employees. The unionization process is strictly regulated by the NLRB, which conducts union-recognition elections and adjudicates charges of ULPs by both unions and employers. Unions, whose membership has steadily declined over the past 50 years, are now seeking to expand their organizing efforts by targeting nontraditional union members and developing sophisticated methods for attracting new members. The most effective way for management to avoid unionization of the workplace is to treat employees fairly and give them a voice in decisions that affect their day-to-day work.

Exam Essentials

Be aware of the requirements of equal employment opportunity legislation on the employment relationship.   EEO legislation requires employers to provide equal opportunities and a safe workplace that is free from harassment. Federal EEO legislation established protected classes for race, color, religion, sex, equal pay/compensation, national origin, age, genetic information, pregnancy and disability. Employers must ensure that all employees are aware that the business doesn't tolerate harassment on the basis of any protected category, and they must create written policies that clearly state the employer's position and consequences that will occur if employees violate the policy.

Be aware of the impact of an effective employee relations program on the bottom line.   An effective ER program provides a workplace environment in which employees are treated with dignity and respect, are involved in making decisions that affect them each day, and have work that is satisfying and challenging. This benefits employers because employees who feel respected and valued are more productive and loyal to the company and, in the long run, have a positive impact on the bottom line.

Be aware of employer unfair labor practices.   Employers may not interfere with attempts of employees to organize unions or assist a union in organizing, and they can't discriminate against employees who advocate for the union or who engage in protected NLRB activities.

Be able to establish fair and effective disciplinary processes.   The most effective disciplinary process is one that prevents performance problems by providing clear performance expectations and regular feedback, both positive and negative, on how the employee is meeting those expectations. A fair and effective process tells employees clearly what the problem is, allows the employee to respond, and involves the employee in developing a solution to the problem.

Be able to identify various methods for alternative dispute resolution.   Lawsuits are costly and time-consuming for employers and generally disruptive to operations. Establishing alternative methods of resolving employment disputes demonstrates that an employer has provided due process to employees. An effective ADR program involves successively higher levels of management in resolving disputes.

Know how to identify and respond to union-organizing activity.   Union-organizing activity is most effective when conducted by employees in the organization. Some signs that an organizing effort is underway include employees who begin challenging management in staff meetings, employees who start talking with employees they haven't had contact with before, and newly hired employees who are very vocal about perceived management abuses toward employees.

Understand the collective-bargaining process.   The collective-bargaining process is required by the National Labor Relations Act and provides that employers must bargain in good faith with the union representative chosen by the employees. Employers have a duty to bargain in good faith on mandatory subjects, which include wages, hours, and other terms and conditions of employment.

Review Questions

You can find the answers in Appendix A.

1. A supervisor has called an employee in for an interview about an inventory shortage. When the supervisor begins asking questions, the employee invokes his Weingarten rights. The supervisor has the option to do which of the following?

    A.   Stop the discussion while the employee calls an attorney.

    B.   Stop the discussion until the shop steward is available upon return from vacation in 4 days.

    C.   Discontinue the interview, and make the determination based on other evidence and documentation.

    D.   Continue the interview while waiting for a co-worker to return from lunch.

2. An employee has resigned. During the exit interview, the employee tells HR that the reason for the resignation is that for the last 3 months the supervisor has been hostile, refused to provide instructions on work assignments, given the employee all the most unpleasant tasks in the department, and verbally reprimanded the employee in front of co-workers and customers. The employee may have a cause of legal action based on which of the following?

    A.   The employer's duty of good faith and fair dealing

    B.   Constructive discharge

    C.   Promissory estoppel

    D.   Fraudulent misrepresentation

3. All of the following statements about employment at-will are true except which one?

    A.   The employer may terminate the employee at any time for any reason.

    B.   The employee may resign at any time, with or without notice.

    C.   The employer may terminate the employee for cooperating with an SEC investigation.

    D.   The employer may withdraw an offer of employment after the employee has accepted the position and resigned another job.

4. During a unionizing campaign, management may do which of the following in response to union allegations?

    A.   Point out the consequences of unionization based on past facts.

    B.   Encourage nonunion employees to talk about the reasons they don't want the union.

    C.   Tell employees that the company will have to move the jobs to another country if the union is elected.

    D.   Ask employees what the union is saying about the company.

5. As a result of the Sturgis case, which of the following is true?

    A.   Temporary employees may form a union but bargain only with the temporary agency.

    B.   The temporary agency must agree to bargain with a client company's union.

C. Temporary employees who work side by side with regular employees may be part of the bargaining unit.

D. Temporary employees may not be unionized.

6. If employees no longer want the union to represent them, they may petition the NLRB for which of the following?

   A. Decertification

   B. Deauthorization

   C. Contract bar

   D. Statutory bar

7. A union security clause that requires all employees to join the union after they are hired is called what?

   A. An agency shop clause

   B. A union shop clause

   C. A closed shop clause

   D. A maintenance of membership clause

8. When does double breasting occur?

   A. An employer has two companies that are substantially identical.

   B. A neutral employer performs work that is normally done by striking employees.

   C. An employer has two businesses, one union and one nonunion, that do substantially the same work but have different management, equipment, and customers.

   D. Two businesses perform operations that are part of the same product.

9. During a representation election, votes can be challenged by whom?

   A. By management or the union at any time

   B. By management or the union before the votes are cast

   C. By management only

   D. By the union only

10. Which of the following describes salting?

   A. The union hires an individual to publicize its reasons for targeting an employer for unionization.

   B. The union hires an individual to distribute leaflets to employees as they are leaving work at the end of the day.

   C. The union hires an individual to picket the employer's business.

   D. The union hires an individual to apply for a job with an employer and begin to organize the company.

11. Which of the following communication strategies would be best used to measure employee job satisfaction?

   A. Exit interviews

   B. Brown bag lunches

   C. Employee committees

   D. Suggestion boxes

12. An employee with a bachelor's degree, an employee who speaks English as a second language, and an individual over the age of 40 are all examples of what?

   A. A diverse work group

   B. Protected class groups

   C. Non-discriminatory hiring practices

   D. Effective knowledge management programs

13. Which of the following is an example of a reference guide?

   A. An SOP

   B. A policy manual

   C. A troubleshooting manual

   D. An employee handbook

14. Which of the following is *not* a sign of union organizing activity by employees?

   A. An employee complaining of harassment by a co-worker

   B. An increase in employee groupings in the parking lot

   C. The use of union terms at an all-employee meeting

   D. An increase in requests for copies of the employee handbook

15. A union philosophy statement may have all of the following *except* which?

   A. A statement of the company's desire to remain union free

   B. Factual statements about the disadvantages of unions in the labor/management relationship

   C. A description of what a union cannot do for the employees

   D. A promise of extended benefits if the company remains union free

16. The Occupational Safety and Health Administration is to the Occupational Safety and Health Act as the National Labor Relations Board is to which of the following?

   A. The Labor-Management Relations Act

   B. The Labor-Management Reporting and Disclosure Act

   C. The National Labor Relations Act

   D. The Norris-La Guardia Act

17. "When the workplace is permeated with discriminatory intimidation, ridicule and insult that is sufficiently severe or pervasive to alter the conditions of the victim's employment and create an abusive working environment, Title VII is violated." This is a statement made with regard to which of the following sexual-harassment court cases?

   A. *Oncale v. Sundowner Offshore Services*

   B. *Harris v. Forklift Systems, Inc.*

   C. *Faragher v. City of Boca Raton*

   D. *Burlington Industries v. Ellerth*

18. Employee pension rights are protected by which of the following acts or regulations?

   A. The Sherman Antitrust Act

   B. Executive Order 11246

   C. Uniformed Services Employment and Reemployment Rights Act

   D. The Equal Employment Opportunity Act

19. Employee Weingarten rights established which of the following?

   A. Employers have the right to deny the presence of a co-worker in an investigatory interview.

   B. Employees have the right to consult with an attorney post-discipline.

   C. Union employees have the right to have a union representative present at an investigatory interview.

   D. Employers may not deny a nonunion worker's request for representation during an investigatory hearing.

20. Which of the following is *not* a form of alternative dispute resolution?

   A. Mediation

   B. Discipline

   C. Arbitration

   D. Peer-review panel

Chapter

8

Risk Management

THE HRCI TEST SPECIFICATIONS FROM THE RISK MANAGEMENT FUNCTIONAL AREA COVERED IN THIS CHAPTER INCLUDE:

✓ Ensure that workplace health, safety, security, and privacy activities are compliant with applicable federal laws and regulations.

✓ Conduct a needs analysis to identify the organization's safety requirements.

✓ Develop/select and implement/administer occupational injury and illness prevention programs (i.e., OSHA, workers' compensation). **SPHR ONLY**

✓ Establish and administer a return-to-work process after illness or injury to ensure a safe workplace (for example: modified duty assignment, reasonable accommodations, independent medical exam).

✓ Develop/select, implement, and evaluate plans and policies to protect employees and other individuals, and to minimize the organization's loss and liability (for example: emergency response, workplace violence, substance abuse).

✓ Communicate and train the workforce on security plans and policies.

✓ Develop, monitor, and test business continuity and disaster recovery plans.

✓ Communicate and train the workforce on the business continuity and disaster recovery plans.

✓ Develop policies and procedures to direct the appropriate use of electronic media and hardware (for example: email, social media, and appropriate website access).

✓ Develop and administer internal and external privacy policies (for example: identity theft, data protection, workplace monitoring).

Risk Management (RM) activities touch all functional areas of human resources (HR) as well as activities in virtually all other business functions. The function is so intertwined with HR activities, in fact, that it's addressed in three areas of the *HR Certification Institute PHR/SPHR Body of Knowledge (BOK)*. Chapter 3, "Business Management and Strategy," introduced the concept of enterprise risk management and briefly touched on the use of HR audits to identify risks in HR activities. In Chapter 2, "Core Knowledge Requirements for HR Professionals," the RM section presented an overview of the risk-management process, which consists of four steps:

1. Identify risks.

2. Assess/analyze risks.

3. Manage risks.

4. Review/monitor risks.

This chapter provides an in-depth look at identifying, assessing/analyzing, and managing risks in the HR function. For HR professionals, the focus of these activities is on managing those aspects of risk that impact the people in an organization.

To be fully prepared for the PHR/SPHR exams, candidates must have the basic knowledge needed to fully understand, develop, implement, and evaluate programs related to the activities detailed in the Risk Management test specifications. Knowledge of the Occupational Safety and Health (OSH) Act, Sarbanes-Oxley Act (SOX), and other federal laws in this area is key to understanding these requirements. Candidates should understand safety and security risks for the company and its employees, be aware of potentially violent behaviors and conditions in the workplace, and understand processes for preventing or reducing the impact of violence in the workplace. The exams require a thorough knowledge of health and safety practices and the ability to develop and implement response plans. Questions on the exams will also require knowledge of internal investigation and surveillance techniques, as well as employee privacy practices. PHR/SPHR candidates will need to be able to recognize the signs of substance abuse and dependency and be aware of the legally appropriate ways to respond to situations involving unlawful drug use.

The HRCI core knowledge requirements that will be particularly helpful in understanding this functional area include needs assessment and analysis, communication strategies, documentation requirements, adult-learning concepts, training techniques, motivation, and risk-management techniques.

For up-to-the-minute updates for this chapter, visit www.sybex.com/go/ phr4e.

Risk Identification

An argument could be made, and often is, that risk is inherent in any activity. The magnitude of the risk often determines whether an activity is pursued, and this of course is true for human resource activities. HR risks can be classified into one of the following five areas:

Legal Compliance   Employers are at risk for potential lawsuits arising from employment practices that are out of compliance with laws and regulations designed to protect employees from unlawful activities such as discrimination, wrongful termination, sexual harassment, and others. As described in earlier chapters, failure to comply with legal requirements has the potential to cost employers millions of dollars in legal expenses, judgments, penalties, and fines.

Safety and Health   Risks for illness and injury exist in virtually every workplace, not just those involving the operation of heavy equipment or dangerous situations such as those faced by first responders. Employees who work in pleasant climate-controlled environments face the possibility of repetitive stress injuries (RSI), emotional and physical stress, and ergonomic strains.

Security   Security risks can affect financial operations and practices, physical assets such as buildings and equipment, information assets such as documentation and data storage, and the people who work in organizations. At times, people may be the source of risk, as in the case of a hacker or an embezzler; at other times, they may need to be protected from a risk, such as a fire or natural disaster.

Business Continuity   The ability to continue operating a business can be adversely affected by environmental disasters, organized or deliberate disruptions, loss of utilities and public services, equipment or system failures, serious information-security incidents, or other emergencies. The HR responsibility for mitigating risks in this area is to develop programs that protect human assets.

Workplace Privacy   In most organizations, HR is responsible for maintaining the privacy of highly confidential employee information. Risks to this information range from identity theft to the release of private health information and improper workplace-monitoring procedures.

The process of identifying and assessing risks makes it possible for organizations to take steps to mitigate or prevent losses. The next section examines the assessment of risk in each of these areas. Following the "Risk Assessment" section, the "Risk Management" section discusses methods for managing and reducing risks in each area.

HR Tools to Identify and Assess Risk

One way for HR professionals to identify and assess risks is to ask questions of executives, managers, and employees and to learn what challenges they face in the course of doing their jobs. Often, informal conversations provide a wealth of useful information that can improve HR services as well as provide insight into potential risks facing the organization. Two more formal HR tools are used to identify and assess potential HR risks: the HR audit and the workplace investigation. Both tools have multiple purposes but easily adapt to RM purposes.

HR Audits

An HR audit is one of the most useful and versatile tools available for HR professionals. An audit can be used to see what HR functions need to be done, to identify opportunities for improving business results, and to identify organizational risks. A comprehensive audit reviews HR activities in all functional areas. The following is a brief overview of some components included in an audit:

Organization of HR Function   An audit begins by looking at the structure of the HR department and reviewing the organization chart. It verifies the existence of current job descriptions for all department positions and ensures the existence of clear accountability for different functions. The audit should evaluate the size and effectiveness of the HR team, ratio of HR staff to total employees, commitment to professional development for the team, and how well the team meets ongoing customer needs.

The audit examines whether HR programs align to organization goals, reviews the human capital management plan if one exists, evaluates the department mission statement, and analyzes the budget.

Workforce Planning and Employment   An HR audit examines the recruiting philosophy and process, whether the company promotes from within, job-posting and candidate-sourcing procedures and the approval process, and the existence and status of affirmative-action and diversity programs. A review of the staffing needs analysis and its use in projecting the availability of candidates for future needs is based on labor market demographics. The audit verifies the job-analysis process and determines whether job descriptions include essential job functions.

The selection process is examined for HR's level of involvement and how interviews are conducted, whether there are seasonal or other periodic hiring cycles, how many people interview candidates, and whether interviewers receive training. The audit also analyzes any pre-employment tests that are used and ensures that they're valid and reliable. The use of alternative staffing methods and hiring cycles is reviewed as well. The existence, accuracy, consistency, and legality of reference and background checks are examined.

HR Development   An HR audit looks at learning and development practices and programs, the existence of regular training programs, and performance-management practices. The performance-evaluation process is assessed for adequacy, equity, and content.

Compensation and Benefits   The compensation philosophy is reviewed for consistency with the practices and level of communication of the organization. The adequacy of compensation procedures is examined, and the frequency of salary survey comparisons is analyzed. Salary administration practices, including pay ranges, compression, salary budgets, and incentive pay practices, are reviewed.

The benefits program philosophy and policies are reviewed for comparability to competitor programs. Health-care programs are analyzed for cost containment and plan content. Programs for controlling absenteeism, unemployment, and other costs are analyzed. Time-off policies and accrual practices are also examined as part of the audit.

Employee Relations   An HR audit assesses the organization's employee relations (ER) philosophy for alignment with corporate goals and reviews practices for conflict-resolution and disciplinary procedures. The existence of an employee communication philosophy is reviewed, and written communication tools, such as the handbook, policies, procedures, work rules, code of conduct, and behavior expectations, are examined. Orientation programs are assessed for content and frequency.

Absentee rates and turnover demographics are analyzed; exit-interview practices and reporting are examined. Procedures for voluntary and involuntary organization exits are reviewed. Diversity practices are analyzed.

Labor Relations   The existence of labor unions, collective-bargaining agreements, and union-avoidance practices are examined.

HR Risk Management   Legal compliance for all applicable federal, state, and local governments is reviewed. Safety, health, and wellness programs are analyzed.

HR audits result in a comprehensive review of current practices and can highlight areas in need of improvement. Audits can also identify opportunities to design service improvements that align HR programs with organizational goals and add value to the business.

Workplace Investigations

When management receives complaints about inappropriate or unlawful behavior; identifies a potential financial loss from embezzlement or pilferage; receives accusations from co-workers, customers, or members of the public about an employee; or becomes aware of some other type of loss, one important tool for assessing the risk is a prompt and thorough *workplace investigation*. When the loss involves employees or an issue of noncompliance with employment laws or regulations, the responsibility for conducting investigations often falls on HR professionals. It's important for investigations to be seen as credible by all stakeholders, so they must be conducted in a way that protects the employees who make accusations and the individuals accused or suspected of wrongdoing. It's equally important that workplace investigations are conducted in a way that protects the organization from liability.

The best way to prepare for an investigation is to establish a procedure at a time when no investigation is pending so that when it's necessary, the HR professional has a guide to ensure that all necessary steps are taken. Using the same protocol for all investigations provides consistency in the process and assures the subjects of investigations (and the courts, if an employee takes legal action) that the investigator acted with integrity and the process treated everyone involved in a fair manner. An effective, prompt, thorough workplace investigation includes the following steps:

1. Begin planning the investigation immediately upon receiving the complaint.

2. Determine whether an employee or third-party investigator would be the most appropriate for the situation. For example, if the situation involves executives, or employees on the HR team are too close to the parties or situation to remain objective, a third-party investigator may be required.

3. Develop a clear strategy before beginning to collect evidence or conduct interviews.

4. Compile a list of individuals to be interviewed and documentation to be collected.

5. Prepare a list of questions based on the information presented by the complainant.

6. Conduct interviews, taking contemporaneous notes; ask each interviewee to provide a signed, written statement, or have them review and sign notes at the conclusion of the interview:

   - Interview the complainant first, and obtain names of possible witnesses.
   - Interview witnesses.
   - Interview the accused.

7. At the conclusion of each interview, make note of the interviewee's demeanor and openness, keeping the notes free from personal opinions and judgments.

8. With each interviewee, stress the importance of confidentiality for the integrity of the investigation, and reiterate company policy with regard to retaliation against accusers and witnesses.

9. At the conclusion of the interview with the accused, clearly state that retaliation or intimidation of those interviewed during the investigation isn't acceptable and that the accused shouldn't attempt to discuss the situation with the complainant or witnesses.

10. If the accused provides an alternate description of events, completely investigate the new information, re-interviewing witnesses as necessary.

11. Conclude the investigation:

    - Make a finding of fact based on the evidence obtained and observations during the interviews.
    - Include any relevant documentation that supports the finding.
    - Evaluate possible reasons for false accusations and the credibility of those involved.
    - Notify the complainant and the accused of the results of the investigation.

12. As appropriate, take disciplinary action consistent with organizational policy.

13. In some cases, there will be no clear finding; when that occurs, explain this to the complainant and accused, and document the finding.

14. Compile and close the investigation file, including signed statements from witnesses, complainant, and accused; relevant documentation; and the original handwritten notes with transcribed copies.

15. Communicate resolution only to those who have a need to know the information, and maintain the investigation file in a secure location.

16. If necessary, and without violating confidentiality of those involved, take appropriate action to subdue rumors about the situation.

Workplace investigations, properly conducted, document actions taken by the employer to respond to accusations of wrongdoing. Particularly in sexual-harassment investigations, this can make the difference in whether the employer will be held liable if a lawsuit is filed.

Taking clear, relevant notes in investigations is crucial, but it's essential that those notes be free from any comments or observations that could be construed as prejudicial. It's important to keep in mind that investigatory notes are discoverable in lawsuits unless they involve communication with legal counsel.

Risk Assessment

Risk is inherent in virtually any area of HR practice, so how does an HR professional ensure that those risks are minimized? *Risk assessment* is the process used to determine the likelihood that an organization will be affected by a particular risk, such as an employee injured as the result of unsafe working conditions or a case of identity theft resulting from a breach of confidential employee information. An assessment estimates the cost of the loss if one should happen and the impact it would have on the ability of the organization to continue operations. With this knowledge, it's possible to identify which losses are most likely to occur and what controls must be in place to prevent them. Identifying and ranking risks provides organizations with the opportunity to be proactive and implement controls to prevent losses.

Assessing Legal Compliance Risks

Mitigating or preventing losses occurring as the result of noncompliance with the legal requirements for employment practices isn't solely the responsibility of the HR function, but it's HR's responsibility to ensure that members of the management team are aware of the laws, regulations, and potential costs to the organization for failing to comply. Many risks associated with noncompliant human resource programs were discussed in previous chapters. For example, unlawful sexual-harassment risks are discussed in Chapter 7, "Employee and Labor Relations," and the risks of unlawful hiring practices are discussed in Chapter 4, "Workforce Planning and Employment." The consequences of failing to comply with those requirements are evident from the examples of actual court cases filed against employers who, whether intentionally or unintentionally, didn't comply with the requirements.

This chapter explores noncompliance issues arising from the Americans with Disabilities Act (ADA), SOX, and the growing risks from work-life and caregiver discrimination claims. Health and safety legislation, particularly the OSH Act, is also discussed in this chapter.

Table 8.1 summarizes the federal legislation that affects risk-management activities.

TABLE 8.1   Federal legislation governing risk-management activities

Type	Enforcement Agency	Chapter Reference
Civil rights	Equal Employment Opportunity Commission (EEOC) and/or Office of Federal Contract Compliance Programs (OFCCP)	4
Corporate governance	Securities and Exchange Commission (SEC), Occupational Safety and Health Administration (OSHA)	3
Health and safety	OSHA, Mine Safety and Health Administration (MSHA)	8
Privacy	Civil litigation	8
Security	SEC	8
Substance abuse	Contracting government agency	8

Let's begin by assessing risks in equal opportunity, security, and health and safety legislation.

Americans with Disabilities Act (ADA)

As discussed in Chapter 4, Congress intended for the ADA to be applied broadly, not only protecting individuals who acknowledge disabilities but also extending the same protections to individuals who aren't disabled but who are perceived to be disabled by employers. The broad nature of these protections increases the range of potential risks for employers. A number of employers have faced EEOC investigations or litigation based on their perception that an employee has a disability. One such case concerned Randal Brooks, a firefighter for the city of Tulsa, Oklahoma.

Brooks had a knee condition that the fire department believed limited his ability to perform his job duties, endangering himself and his fellow firefighters. As a result of this belief, the department transferred Brooks to a clerical position and informed him they intended to terminate his employment. In fact, the knee condition didn't prevent him from performing his firefighting duties at the same level as other firefighters. Brooks sued the city of Tulsa for discriminating on the basis of a perceived disability. Brooks prevailed in the suit and was reinstated to his position as a firefighter and awarded damages of $5,000.

In another case, the EEOC filed suit against Potlatch Corp. on behalf of a female employee in one of its paper mills. The employee fainted while she was on a rest break, explaining to supervisors that she was hot and hadn't eaten, which caused her to faint. A company doctor examined her and declared there was nothing wrong with her. The paper mill's management interpreted ADA regulations to allow the termination of employees who created a direct threat to the safety of themselves or co-workers and terminated her on that basis. During the trial, Potlatch argued that the employee's tendency to faint unexpectedly created a danger to co-workers. The jury disagreed and found in favor of the employee, awarding her $20,000 in compensatory damages and $1,300 in back pay.

Employers also face potential ADA compliance risks if they fail to engage in a sufficiently interactive process when searching for a reasonable accommodation for an employee. Minimizing and managing risks associated with failure to provide a reasonable accommodation for individuals with disabilities is discussed in detail later in this chapter.

Work-Life Discrimination

Employees face multiple responsibilities every day, from multitasking projects at work to caring for children or elderly parents and finding time to take care of other personal needs. These multiple demands increase stress levels and distract employees from concentrating on their job duties. These stresses can be compounded by organizational cultures and management attitudes that employees should leave family concerns in the parking lot when they come to work. These attitudes can have a chilling effect on solid performers who are afraid to come forward with requests for flexibility that will help them concentrate on work and manage their family responsibilities because they know the culture (or their manager) doesn't support those needs.

The stress of these multiple demands and limited time available to manage them, combined with an inflexible culture or management attitude, leads to workforce risks such as the following:

- Reduced productivity
- Increased absenteeism or tardiness
- Increased health-care costs resulting from stress-related illnesses
- Increased turnover as employees find jobs with more flexible options
- Reduced engagement, morale, and loyalty from employees
- Higher recruiting and replacement costs

If these costs don't present enough of a risk, there is also a growing area of concern regarding legal action by employees alleging what is known as *caregiver discrimination*, sometimes referred to as *childcare discrimination* or *family-responsibility discrimination*. According to WFC Resources, a consulting group that researches and publishes information concerning work-life issues for employers, the number of cases filed on this basis increased more than 450 percent between 1990 and 2005.

Although there is no federal legislation designating caregivers as a protected class, the EEOC recently published guidelines for employers in which it describes circumstances that constitute unlawful disparate treatment of caregivers, including the following:

- Disparate treatment of female caregivers when compared to male caregivers (for example, a policy of not hiring women with preschool children but hiring men with preschool children)

- Stereotyping female caregivers (for example, denying a promotion to a woman with young children based on the assumption that she wouldn't want to move)

- Pregnancy discrimination

- Discriminating against male caregivers (for example, providing childcare leave for women but denying it to men)

- Discriminating against employees providing care for disabled persons

Changing attitudes about the necessity for balancing work and life responsibilities make work-life balance and discrimination related to family responsibilities an area of risk to be managed.

Sarbanes-Oxley Act (SOX)

Although the main focus of SOX compliance is the reporting of financial transactions and activities, HR professionals may be called on to participate in SOX reporting requirements. SOX requires information that materially affects an organization's financial status to be reported to the SEC, in some cases immediately, when the organization becomes aware of the information. Some instances where this would apply to HR management include the following:

- Ensuring that material liabilities from pending lawsuits or settlements of employment-practices claims are reported in the financial statements.

- Participating in the review and testing of internal controls for hiring, compensation, and termination practices.

- Reporting immediately any material changes to the organization's financial condition. Although in most cases this wouldn't be an HR responsibility, the settlement of a large class-action lawsuit could potentially reach the threshold of a material change.

Failure to provide this information within the time frames required by SOX can result in criminal penalties, including incarceration, for employees who obstruct legal investigations into financial reporting issues. As discussed further in Chapter 3, SOX also prohibits employers from retaliating against whistle-blowers who report financial conduct that they reasonably believe violates federal laws designed to protect shareholders from fraudulent activity.

A recent case illustrates OSHA's response when it finds retaliation. In a whistle-blower complaint filed on June 15, 2007 against Charles Schwab & Co., two employees alleged they were terminated because they objected to and refused to participate in a scheme at a branch office to falsify entries in Schwab's database system. An investigation conducted by OSHA determined that there was merit to the allegations. An order issued by OSHA awarded the two employees reinstatement to their former positions, back pay, interest, compensatory damages, attorneys' fees, and other relief.

Drug-Free Workplace Act of 1988

The Drug-Free Workplace Act applies to businesses with federal contracts of $100,000 or more each year. Contractors subject to the act must take the following steps to be in compliance:

Develop and Publish a Written Policy   Contractors must develop a written policy clearly stating that they provide a drug-free workplace and that illegal substance abuse isn't an acceptable practice in the workplace. The policy must clearly state what substances are covered and clearly indicate the consequences for violating the policy.

Establish an Awareness Program   The employer must develop a program to educate employees about the policy and communicate the dangers of drug abuse in the workplace, discuss the employer's policy, inform employees of the availability of counseling or other programs to reduce drug use, and notify employees of the penalties for violating the policy. The program can be delivered through a variety of media—seminars, brochures, videos, web-based training—whatever methods will most effectively communicate the information in the specific environment.

Notify Employees About Contract Conditions   Employees must be made aware that a condition of their employment on a federal contract project is that they abide by the policy and inform the employer within 5 days if they're convicted of a criminal drug offense in the workplace.

Notify the Contracting Agency of Violations   If an employee is convicted of a criminal drug offense in the workplace, the employer must notify the contracting agency within 10 days of being informed of the conviction by the employee.

Establish Penalties for Illegal Drug Convictions   The employer must have an established penalty for any employees convicted of relevant drug offenses. Within 30 days of notice by an employee of a conviction, the employer must take appropriate disciplinary action against the employee or require participation in an appropriate drug-rehabilitation program. Any penalties must be in accordance with requirements of the Rehabilitation Act of 1973.

Maintain a Drug-Free Workplace   Contractors must make a good-faith effort to maintain a drug-free workplace in accordance with the act, or they're subject to penalties, including suspension of payments under the contract, suspension or termination of the contract, or exclusion from consideration from future contracts for a period of up to 5 years.

Occupational Safety and Health Act of 1970

For more than 100 years beginning in 1867, sporadic legislation was enacted by different states and the federal government to address specific safety concerns, usually in regard to mine safety or factory conditions, but there was no comprehensive legislation requiring employers to protect workers from injury or illness. That changed with the Occupational Safety and Health Act of 1970 (the OSH Act), a comprehensive piece of federal legislation that continues to impact employers in virtually every company in America.

Although normally this law is referred to as OSHA, this chapter talks at length about the act and the agency that is known by the same initials. For the sake of clarity, the law is referred to as the OSH Act throughout the chapter.

In the years prior to passage of the OSH Act, there was a growing recognition that employers were largely unwilling to take preventive steps to reduce the occurrence of injuries, illnesses, and fatalities in the workplace. On December 6, 1907, 362 miners died in an explosion at the Monongah coal mine in West Virginia—the single worst mining disaster in American history. In that year alone, a total of 3,242 coal miners lost their lives. As a result, in 1910 Congress established the Bureau of Mines to investigate mining accidents.

Annual fatalities in the railroad industry also peaked in 1907 when there were 4,218 work-related deaths. Railroad safety technology began developing at the end of the nineteenth century, but most railroad owners didn't implement these preventive measures until much later, partially as a result of federal legislation requiring safety improvements.

The connection between work and health was first studied in sixteenth-century Europe when two traveling physicians, Philippus Aureolus (writing under the name Paracelsus) and Georgius Agricola, wrote about mine conditions and advocated changes to protect workers. One treatise by Paracelsus, entitled "On the Miners' Sickness and Other Miners' Diseases," investigated the relationship between mining and an illness identified as the Miners' Sickness, which today we know as silicosis, a disabling and often fatal disease that still takes the lives of more than 250 American workers each year. Between that time and the advent of the Industrial Revolution, however, work done for hire was largely agrarian, and the potential for large-scale injury or illness didn't exist in the way it does today.

When steam-powered machinery and equipment took the place of animals and hand tools in the workplace and workers moved from agricultural to industrial jobs, lung diseases were the first to be noticed and addressed by government regulation. Early safety legislation in the United States was enacted by state governments and focused on conditions in factories and mines, often spurred as the result of a tragic accident. In 1869, the federal government established the Bureau of Labor to study and report on job-related accidents, but it had no ability to require changes in safety practices.

There was a long period of time in America when it was cheaper for employers to fight lawsuits filed on behalf of workers killed or injured on the job than it was to implement safety programs. Because the courts rarely held employers accountable for worker injuries, many chose this approach. Employer attitudes in this regard didn't change until the shortage of skilled workers during World War II gave employees plentiful options for places to work—and they opted to work for employers that provided safe environments over those that didn't.

The tragic nature of large accidents in the railroad and mining industries captured public attention and created pressure on the federal government to take action. This led Congress to enact legislation requiring safety improvements in the coal mining and railroad industries, but these measures were specifically targeted to those industries. Little attention was paid to equally dangerous workplace safety and illness issues that didn't produce the spectacular accidents prevalent in mines or on railroads. By the late 1960s, 14,000 American workers lost their lives each year due to injuries or illnesses suffered while on the job. The federal government had been working on solutions but was mired in bureaucratic turf battles over which agency should have control of the process. The Department of Health, Education, and Welfare wanted legislation that applied only to federal contractors; and the Department of Labor (DOL), spurred by Secretary Willard Wirtz's personal interest in the subject, wanted to protect *all* American workers. After several years of this infighting, the proposal by the DOL was sent to the Congress and enacted as the Occupational Safety and Health Act of 1970. A key component of this legislation was the creation of the *Occupational Safety and Health Administration* (OSHA), which now sets safety standards for all industries. OSHA enforces those standards with the use of fines and, in the case of criminal actions, can call on the Department of Justice to file charges against offenders.

The intent of Congress, as stated in the preamble to the OSH Act, is to ensure safe and healthful working conditions for American workers. To accomplish this purpose, the act establishes three simple duties:

- Employers must provide every employee a place to work that is "free from recognized hazards that are causing or are likely to cause death or serious physical harm."

- Employers must comply with all safety and health standards disseminated in accordance with the act.

- Employees are required to comply with occupational safety and health standards, rules, and regulations that impact their individual actions and behavior.

As mentioned previously, the OSH Act created OSHA and gave it the authority to develop and enforce mandatory standards applicable to all businesses engaged in interstate commerce. The definition of interstate commerce is sufficiently broad to cover most businesses, excepting only those sole proprietors without employees, family farms employing only family members, and mining operations, which are covered by the Mine Safety and Health Act (to be discussed later in this chapter). The act encouraged OSHA to work with industry associations and safety committees to build on standards already developed by specific industries, and it authorized enforcement action to ensure that employers comply with the standards. OSHA was charged with developing reporting procedures to track trends in workplace safety and health so that the development of preventive measures would be an ongoing process that changed with the development of new processes and technologies.

The OSH Act also created the *National Institute of Occupational Safety and Health* (NIOSH) as part of the Department of Health and Human Services. NIOSH is charged with researching and evaluating workplace hazards and recommending ways to reduce the effect of those hazards on workers. NIOSH also supports education and training in the field of occupational safety and health by developing and providing educational materials and training aids and sponsoring conferences on workplace safety and health issues.

The NIOSH website (`www.cdc.gov/niosh/homepage.html`) provides a wealth of information that may be of assistance to PHR and SPHR candidates looking for additional study resources.

In 2011, OSHA celebrated 40 years in the business of protecting American workers. Its focus in the coming years includes increasing enforcement of the standards through additional hiring, and making sure "vulnerable" workers, such as those who speak English as a second language, are heard. How this translates into the workforce remains to be seen, but we can infer from the statements several key points:

More Inspections   With OSHA pushing for an increased budget, it stands to reason that the hiring of additional enforcement officers means more inspections and fines.

Emphasis on Safety Communication   The 2010 National Action Summit for Latino Worker Health and Safety helped to launch OSHA's Diverse Workforce Limited Proficiency Outreach program, designed to "enhance (vulnerable) workers' knowledge of their workplace rights and improve their ability to exercise those rights." Conducting training and providing material in a language all workers can understand is a logical outcome from this focus.

Reporting of Injuries   OSHA is aware that incentive programs can result in the under-reporting of injuries and is preparing to address this issue. This means OSHA will increase the scrutiny of incentive programs to ensure that they actually reduce injuries and don't simply reduce reporting. Furthermore, OSHA's intended efforts will convert paper reporting to electronic reporting for more efficient and streamlined results.

 Visit www.osha.gov/dsg/topics/safetyhealth/ for more information and to see a video from OSHA regarding workplace injury and illness prevention programs.

Finally, the OSH Act encourages the states to take the lead in developing and enforcing safety and health programs for businesses within their jurisdictions by providing grants to help states identify specific issues and develop programs for enforcement and prevention.

Employer Responsibilities

As discussed earlier in this chapter, the OSH Act has three requirements, two of which pertain to employers. Not only must employers provide a workplace that is safe and healthful for employees, but they must also comply with established standards. OSHA has established other requirements for employers as required by the law:

- Employers are expected to take steps to minimize or reduce hazards; ensure that employees have and use safe tools, equipment, and personal protective equipment (PPE); and ensure that they're properly maintained.

- Employers are responsible for informing all employees about OSHA, posting the OSHA poster in a prominent location, and making employees aware of the standards that apply in the worksite. If employees request a copy of a standard, the employer must provide it to them.

- Appropriate warning signs that conform to the OSHA standards for color coding, posting, or labels must be posted where needed to make employees aware of potential hazards.

- Compliance with OSHA standards also means employers must educate employees about safe operating procedures and train them to follow the procedures.

- Businesses with 11 or more employees must maintain records of all workplace injuries and illnesses and post them on form 300A from February 1 through April 30 each year.

- Within 8 hours of a fatal accident or one resulting in hospitalization for three or more employees, a report must be filed with the nearest OSHA office.

- An accident report log must be made available to employees, former employees, or employee representatives when reasonably requested.

- When employees report unsafe conditions to OSHA, the employer may not retaliate or discriminate against them.

Employer Rights

Employers have some rights as well, including the right to seek advice and consultation from OSHA and to be active in industry activities involved in health and safety issues. Employers may also participate in the OSHA Standard Advisory Committee process in writing or by giving testimony at hearings. Finally, employers may contact NIOSH for information about substances used in work processes to determine whether they're toxic.

At times, employers may be unable to comply with OSHA standards because of the nature of specific operations. When this happens, they may apply to OSHA for temporary or permanent waivers to the standards along with proof that the protections developed by the organization meet or exceed those of the OSHA standard.

Employee Rights and Responsibilities

When the OSH Act was passed in 1970, employees were granted the basic right to a workplace with safe and healthful working conditions. The act intended to encourage employers and employees to collaborate in reducing workplace hazards. Employees have the responsibility to comply with all OSHA standards and with the safety and health procedures implemented by their employers. The act gave employees the specific rights to do the following:

- Seek safety and health on the job without fear of punishment

- Know what hazards exist on the job by reviewing the OSHA standards, rules, and regulations that the employer has available at the workplace

- Be provided with the hazard-communication plan containing information about hazards in the workplace and preventive measures employees should take to avoid illness or injury, and to be trained in those measures

- Access the exposure and medical records employers are required to keep relative to safety and health issues

- Request an OSHA inspection, speak privately with the inspector, accompany the inspector during the inspection, and respond to the inspector's questions during the inspection

- Observe steps taken by the employer to monitor and measure hazardous materials in the workplace, and access records resulting from those steps

- Request information from NIOSH regarding the potential toxic effects of substances used in the workplace

- File a complaint about workplace safety or health hazards with OSHA and remain anonymous to the employer

OSHA Enforcement

OSHA's success is the result of strong enforcement of the standards it has developed. As demonstrated in the nineteenth and twentieth centuries, without the threat of financial penalty, some business owners would choose to ignore injury- and illness-prevention requirements. Construction and general industry continue to be the source of the most frequently cited OSHA standards violations through 2011. That being the case, OSHA established fines and penalties that can be assessed against businesses when violations occur. Table 8.2 describes the violation levels and associated penalties for noncompliance.

TABLE 8.2   Categories of OSHA violations

Violation	Description	Fine
Willful	Evidence exists of an intentional violation of the OSH Act or "plain indifference" to its requirements.	$5,000 to $70,000 per violation
Serious	Hazards with substantial probability of death or serious physical harm exist.	Up to $7,000
Other-than-serious	An existing hazard could have a direct and immediate effect on the safety and health of employees.	Up to $7,000
Repeat	OSHA previously issued citations for substantially similar conditions.	Up to $70,000 per violation
Failure to abate	The employer failed to abate a prior violation.	Up to $7,000 per day past the abatement date
De-minimus	Violations exist but have no direct or immediate relationship to safety or health.	$0

Source: www.osha.gov/doc/outreachtraining/htmlfiles/introsha.html

During fiscal year 2010, federal OSHA conducted more than 40,000 inspections. Tables 8.3 and 8.4 provide a breakdown of the numbers and reasons for inspections.

TABLE 8.3   OSHA inspections during fiscal year 2010

Number	Reason for Inspection
8,027	Complaints
804	Fatalities
4,634	Referrals
3,559	Other

Source: www.osha.gov/dep/2010_enforcement_summary.html

TABLE 8.4   Violations and penalties from 2010 inspections

Violations	Type
1,519	Willful
74,885	Serious
2,758	Repeat
288	Failure to abate
17,244	Other than serious

Source: www.osha.gov/dep/2010_enforcement_summary.html

OSHA Recordkeeping Requirements

OSHA requires employers to record health and safety incidents that occur each year and to document steps they take to comply with regulations. Records of specific injuries and illnesses are compiled, allowing OSHA and NIOSH to identify emerging hazards for research and, if warranted, create new standards designed to reduce the possibility of similar injury or illness in the future. These records include up-to-date files for exposures to hazardous substances and related medical records, records of safety-training meetings, and OSHA logs that record work-related injuries and illnesses.

As of January 1, 2002, OSHA revised the requirements for maintaining records of workplace injuries and illnesses in order to collect better information for use in prevention activities, simplify the information-collection process, and make use of advances in technology. Three new forms were developed:

- OSHA form 300, Log of Work-Related Injuries and Illnesses
- OSHA form 300A, Summary of Work-Related Injuries and Illnesses
- OSHA form 301, Injury and Illness Incident Report

Completion of the forms doesn't constitute proof of fault on the part of either the employer or the employee and doesn't indicate that any OSHA violations have occurred. Recording an injury or illness on the OSHA forms also doesn't mean that an employee is eligible for workers' compensation benefits. Detailed guidance about completing the forms is available at www.osha.gov/recordkeeping/detailedfaq.html#1904.0.

The following list covers the basic requirements for OSHA recordkeeping, including who should file OSHA reports, which employers are exempt from filing, and what injuries are considered work related:

Who must complete and file OSHA forms?   All employers with 11 or more employees are required to complete and file the OSHA forms just discussed.

Are there any exemptions?   Employers with 10 or fewer employees aren't required to file the forms. In addition, OSHA has identified industries with low injury and illness rates and exempted them from filing reports. These include the retail, service, finance, insurance, and real-estate industries. Unless OSHA has notified a business in writing that reports must be filed, they're exempt from the requirement.

What must be recorded?   OSHA regulations specify which employees are covered for reporting purposes. Injury or illness to any employee on the employer's payroll must be recorded, regardless of how the employee is classified: full or part time, regular or temporary, hourly or salary, seasonal, and so on. Injuries to employees of temp agencies, if under the employer's direct supervision on a daily basis, must also be recorded. The owners and partners in sole proprietorships and partnerships aren't considered employees for OSHA reporting purposes.

Privacy concern cases are new protections developed by OSHA to protect employee privacy by substituting a case number for the employee name on the OSHA form 300 log. Cases where this is appropriate include injury or illness that involved an intimate body part or resulted from a sexual assault; HIV infection, hepatitis, or tuberculosis; needle-stick injuries involving contaminated needles; and other illnesses when employees request that their names not be included on the log.

An injury or illness is generally considered to be work related if it occurred in the workplace or while performing work-related duties off-site. The basic OSHA requirement records any work-related injury or illness that causes death, days away from work, restricted or limited duty, medical treatment beyond first aid, or loss of consciousness. Diagnoses of an injury or illness by a physician or other health-care professional, even if it doesn't result in one of the circumstances listed, must also be reported. Table 8.5 provides guidance in determining when an injury or illness isn't considered to be work related.

Once the employer has determined whether the injury or illness is work related, the employer must determine whether this is a new case or a continuation of a previously recorded case. To a certain extent, this decision is left to the employer's common sense and best judgment. OSHA considers a new case to have occurred when an employee hasn't had a previous injury or illness that is the same as the current occurrence or when the employee has recovered completely from a previous injury or illness of the same type.

TABLE 8.5   Injuries and illnesses not considered work related

OSHA Standard 1904.5(b)(2)	Employer Not Required to Record Injuries and Illnesses If...
(i)	At the time of the injury or illness, the employee was present in the work environment as a member of the general public rather than as an employee.
(ii)	The injury or illness involves signs or symptoms that surface at work but result solely from a non-work-related event or exposure that occurs outside the work environment.
(iii)	The injury or illness results solely from voluntary participation in a wellness program or in a medical, fitness, or recreational activity such as blood donation, physical examination, flu shot, exercise class, racquetball, or baseball.
(iv)	The injury or illness is solely the result of an employee eating, drinking, or preparing food or drink for personal consumption (whether bought on the employer's premises or brought in). For example, if the employee is injured by choking on a sandwich while in the employer's establishment, the case wouldn't be considered work related. Note: If the employee is made ill by ingesting food contaminated by workplace contaminants (such as lead) or gets food poisoning from food supplied by the employer, the case would be considered work related.
(v)	The injury or illness is solely the result of an employee doing personal tasks (unrelated to their employment) at the establishment outside of the employee's assigned working hours.
(vi)	The injury or illness is solely the result of personal grooming or self medication for a non-work-related condition, or is intentionally self-inflicted.
(vii)	The injury or illness is caused by a motor vehicle accident and occurs on a company parking lot or company access road while the employee is commuting to or from work.
(viii)	The illness is the common cold or flu. Note: Contagious diseases such as tuberculosis, brucellosis, hepatitis A, or plague are considered work related if the employee is infected at work.
(ix)	The illness is a mental illness. Mental illness wouldn't be considered work related unless the employee voluntarily provides the employer with an opinion from a physician or other licensed health-care professional with appropriate training and experience (psychiatrist, psychologist, psychiatric nurse practitioner, and so on), stating that the employee has a mental illness that is work related.

Source: OSHA Regulations Section 1904.5

http://www.osha.gov/pls/oshaweb/owadisp.show_document?p_table=STANDARDS&p_id=9636

Annual Summary   At the end of each year, employers must review the OSHA form 300 log and summarize the entries on form 300A, which must then be certified by a company executive as correct and complete and posted as previously mentioned in February of the following year.

Retention   The OSHA form 300 log and annual summary, privacy case list, and form 301 Incident Report forms must be retained for 5 years following the end of the calendar year they cover.

Employee Involvement   Employers are required to provide employees and employee representatives, former employees, or a personal representative of an employee with information on how to properly report an injury or illness, and they're also required to allow employees or their representatives limited access to the records of injury and illness.

The OSHA form 300 log must be provided to these requestors by the end of the following business day.

The OSHA form 301 Incident Report must be provided by the end of the next business day when the employee who is the subject of the report requests a copy. When an employee representative requests copies, they must be provided within 7 calendar days, and all information except that contained in the "Tell Us About the Case" section must be removed.

OSHA Assistance

OSHA provides many sources for employers and employees to obtain information about workplace health and safety issues. Chief among these is an extensive website (`www.osha.gov`) that provides access to the laws, regulations, and standards enforced by OSHA as well as general information on prevention. In addition to the website, OSHA publishes a number of pamphlets, brochures, and training materials that are available to employers. While OSHA exists to protect workers safety rights, there are services such as Consultation and Voluntary Participation programs that exist specifically to aid employers in complying with the standards:

OSHA Consultants   Educating employers and employees about workplace health and safety issues is key to preventing injuries and illnesses in the workplace. OSHA provides training programs for consultants who work with business owners in establishing effective health and safety programs. These free consultation services give employers an opportunity to learn which of the standards apply in their worksite, involve employees in the safety process, and correct possible violations without a citation and penalty. Once the consultant becomes involved, the employer must abate any violations, or the consultant will refer the violation to an OSHA inspector.

The *Safety and Health Achievement Recognition Program* (SHARP) recognizes small, high-hazard employers that have requested a comprehensive OSHA consultation, corrected any violations, and developed an ongoing safety-management program. To participate in the program, the business must agree to ask for additional consultations if work processes change.

Partnerships and Voluntary Programs   The *Strategic Partnership Program* is a means for businesses and employees to participate in solving health and safety problems with OSHA.

Partnerships currently exist in 15 industries, including construction, food processing, logging, and health care, to develop solutions specific to their businesses.

The *OSHA Alliance Program* provides a vehicle for collaboration with employer organizations interested in promoting workplace health and safety issues. The program is open to trade and professional organizations, businesses, labor organizations, educational institutions, and government agencies, among others.

The *Voluntary Protection Program* (VPP) is open to employers with tough, well-established safety programs. VPP participants must meet OSHA criteria for the program and, having done so, are removed from routine scheduled inspection lists. The program serves to motivate employees to work more safely, reduce workers' compensation costs, and encourage further improvements to safety programs. Acceptance into the VPP is an official recognition of exemplary occupational safety and health practices.

Health and Safety Inspections

The OSH Act authorizes both OSHA and NIOSH to investigate health or safety hazards in the workplace. The majority of OSHA inspections are focused on industries with higher hazard risks based on injury and illness rates. Some inspections occur at the request of an employer or employee in a specific organization. Less than 1 percent of OSHA inspections occur as part of the agency's Enhanced Enforcement Program that monitors employers with a history of repeat or willful violations.

NIOSH inspections, known as *health hazard evaluations*, always occur in response to the request of an employer, an employee, or a government agency.

No matter which agency conducts an investigation, employees who request or participate in them are protected from retaliation or adverse employment actions by the OSH Act:

OSHA Inspections   Most OSHA inspections are conducted without notice by a Compliance Safety and Health Officer (CSHO) who has been trained on OSHA standards and how to recognize safety and health hazards in the workplace. OSHA has established a hierarchy of situations to give priority to inspection of the most dangerous workplace environments. Table 8.6 describes the priorities OSHA uses in allocating time for inspections.

TABLE 8.6   OSHA inspection priorities

Priority	Hazard	Description
First	Imminent danger	There is a reasonable certainty that immediate death or serious injury from existing workplace hazards will occur before normal enforcement procedures can take place.
Second	Catastrophes and fatal accidents	Employers must report fatal accidents or serious injuries resulting in the hospitalization of three or more employees within 8 hours. OSHA will inspect to determine whether any safety violations contributed to the accident.

(Continued)

TABLE 8.6   *(Continued)*

Priority	Hazard	Description
Third	Complaints and referrals	Employees may request inspections when they think violations exist that threaten physical harm; OSHA also investigates referrals about hazards from any other source.
Fourth	Programmed high-hazard inspections	Based on statistical analysis, OSHA conducts planned inspections of industries or jobs that have high incident rates for death, injury, and illness.
Fifth	Follow-up inspections	CSHOs follow up on previously issued citations to ensure that the employer has taken action to correct the violation.

During an inspection, OSHA follows a distinct procedure. In advance of the inspection, the CSHO prepares by reviewing records related to any previous incidents, inspections, or employee complaints. The inspector also determines what, if any, special testing equipment will be necessary for the inspection. Upon arrival at the worksite, the inspection commences with an opening conference, proceeds to a workplace tour, and ends with a closing conference:

1. The CSHO arrives at the worksite and presents credentials. If the credentials aren't presented, the employer should insist on seeing them before the inspection begins. It's critical that any employee who may be the first person approached at the worksite be instructed as to whom should be contacted when a CSHO arrives. Employers have the right to require the inspector to have a security clearance before entering secure areas. Any observation of trade secrets during the inspection remains confidential; CSHOs who breach this confidentiality are subject to fines and imprisonment.

2. The CSHO holds an *opening conference* during which the inspector explains why the site was selected, the purpose of the visit, and the scope of the inspection, and discusses the standards that apply to the worksite. The CSHO requests an employee representative to accompany the CSHO on the inspection along with the management representative. If no employee accompanies the inspector on the tour, the CSHO will talk to as many employees as necessary to understand the safety and health issues in the workplace.

3. The next step is a tour of the facilities. During the tour, the inspector determines what route to take, where to look, and which employees to talk to. During this part of the inspection, the CSHO may talk privately to employees, taking care to minimize disruptions to work processes. Activities that can occur during an inspection include the following:

   - Reviewing the safety and health program

   - Examining records, including OSHA logs, records of employee exposure to toxic substances, and medical records

- Ensuring that the OSHA workplace poster is prominently displayed

- Evaluating compliance with OSHA standards specific to the worksite

- Pointing out unsafe working conditions to the employer and suggesting possible remedial actions

4. The inspector holds a *closing conference* where the inspector, the employer, and, if requested, the employee representative discuss the observations made and corrective actions that must be taken. At this time the employer may produce records to assist in resolving any corrective actions to be taken. The CSHO discusses any possible citations or penalties that may be issued, and the OSHA area director makes the final determination based on the inspector's report.

Should the OSHA area director determine that citations are necessary to ensure employer compliance with OSHA, the director will issue the citations and determine the penalties to be assessed according to established guidelines that consider various factors, including the size of the company. The OSHA area director also determines the seriousness of the danger, how many employees would be impacted, and good-faith efforts on the part of the employer to comply with the standards, among others. OSHA regulations allow for adjustments to penalties based on the above criteria as well.

During the course of an OSHA inspection, an employer may raise an affirmative defense to any violations observed by the inspector. Possible affirmative defenses include the following:

- An isolated case caused by unpreventable employee misconduct. This defense may apply when the employer has established, communicated, and enforced adequate work rules that were ignored by the employee.

- Compliance is impossible based on the nature of the employer's work, and there are no viable alternative means of protection.

- Compliance with the standard would cause a greater hazard to employees, and there are no alternative means of protection.

The employer has the burden to prove an affirmative defense exists. If successfully proven, the OSHA area director may decide that a citation and penalty aren't warranted.

Employers have specific responsibilities and rights during and after the inspection:

- Employers are required to cooperate with the CSHO by providing records and documents requested during the inspection and by allowing employees or their representatives to accompany the inspector on the worksite tour.

- Should a citation be issued during the inspection, the employer must post it at or near the worksite involved, where it must remain for 3 working days or until the violation has been abated, whichever is longer. It goes without saying, of course, that the employer is required to abate the violation within the time frame indicated by the citation.

- Employers may file a *Notice of Contest* within 15 days of a citation and proposed penalty. If there will be an unavoidable delay in abating a violation because the materials, equipment, or personnel won't be available, the employer may request a temporary variance until the violation can be corrected.

Within 15 days of receipt of a citation by an employer, employees have the right to object in writing to the abatement period set by OSHA for correcting violations. Employees who have requested an inspection also have the right to be advised by OSHA of the results of the inspection.

NIOSH Evaluations   The NIOSH mandate contained in the OSH Act is to identify and evaluate potential workplace hazards and recommend actions to reduce or eliminate the effects of chemicals, biological agents, work stress, excessive noise, radiation, ergonomics, and other risks found in the workplace. NIOSH established the *Health Hazard Evaluation* (HHE) program to respond to concerns about these and other risks expressed by employers, employees, unions, and government agencies. Employers and employees have protections and rights during an HHE, as explained in Table 8.7.

TABLE 8.7   Employer and employee rights during an HHE

Employers Have the Right To...	Employees Have the Right To...
Receive a copy of the request for an HHE (without identifying or personal information about the requestor)	Participate in the initial NIOSH workplace inspection
Receive verbal reports from NIOSH during opening and closing conferences	Provide information to NIOSH privately
Participate in the initial NIOSH workplace inspection	Receive verbal reports from NIOSH during opening and closing conferences
Observe NIOSH investigative procedures during the HHE (except for confidential interviews and medical tests)	Receive copies of all interim and final reports
Identify trade secrets disclosed to NIOSH during an HHE and require safeguarding of the information	
Require NIOSH to conduct investigations with minimum disruption and to comply with all workplace safety and health rules	

NIOSH has an established process for responding to requests for assistance:

1. A written response acknowledging the request is provided within a few weeks.
2. NIOSH reviews the request and, depending on the nature and severity of the hazard being described, responds in one of three ways:
   - NIOSH may have written materials that address the concern or may refer the request to another government agency better equipped to respond. If written materials aren't available, a project officer is assigned to assess the need for further assistance.

- The project officer telephones the requestor to discuss the request. In some cases, the request is resolved during the call.

- The project office may determine that the appropriate response is a site visit.

If an on-site visit is required, NIOSH will conduct an investigation, gathering information by touring the site, meeting with management and employees, and reviewing relevant records maintained by the employer. The project office may also use other investigative procedures, such as sampling devices or medical tests to gather information. During an on-site visit, employees, employee representatives, and NIOSH project officers have seven legal rights considered non-negotiable by NIOSH:

- NIOSH has the right to enter the workplace to conduct an HHE.

- NIOSH has the right to access relevant information and records maintained by the employer.

- NIOSH has the right to meet privately with management and employees for confidential interviews.

- An employee requestor or other employee representative has the right to accompany NIOSH during the evaluation inspection. NIOSH may also request participation from other employees if necessary to complete the evaluation.

- Employee representatives have the right to attend opening and closing conferences.

- Employees and managers have the right to participate in the investigation by wearing sampling devices and to take part in medical tests or in the use of sampling devices.

- The interim and final HHE reports must be made available to employees; the employer must either post the final report in the workplace for 30 days or provide NIOSH with employee names and addresses so the report can be mailed to them.

Once the information-gathering phase is complete, NIOSH analyzes the data collected during the HHE and compiles a written report that is provided to the employer, employee, and union representatives.

Many activities that occur during either an OSHA consultation or NIOSH HHE seem similar and may cause confusion about which type of assistance is appropriate for any given situation. Table 8.8 provides guidelines for determining which agency should be involved.

Mine Safety and Health Act of 1977 (MSH Act)

The MSH Act established the *Mine Safety and Health Administration* (MSHA) to ensure the safety of workers in coal and other mines. The act establishes mandatory safety and health standards for mine operators and monitors operations throughout the United States. MSHA has developed a comprehensive website (www.msha.gov/) that is a resource for miners and mine operators, providing access to information on preventing accidents, information on year-to-date fatalities, and guidance on specific mine hazards. The site also contains a link to the complete text of the act.

TABLE 8.8   OSHA consultation vs. NIOSH HHE

An OSHA Consultation Is Needed To...	A NIOSH HHE Is Needed To...
Identify workplace hazards	Identify the cause of employee illness
Suggest ways to correct hazards	Evaluate the potential for hazard from exposure to unregulated chemicals or working conditions
Assist in creating an effective safety and health program	Investigate adverse health effects from permissible exposures to regulated chemicals or working conditions
Assist in reducing workers' compensation costs	Conduct medical or epidemiologic hazard investigations
Assist in improving employee morale	Investigate higher-than-expected occurrences of injury or illness
	Evaluate newly identified hazards
	Investigate the possible hazard of exposure to a combination of agents
	Evaluate the potential for hazard from exposure to unregulated chemicals or working conditions

Other Health and Safety Legislation

Although the OSH Act of 1970 is the major piece of federal safety legislation that impacts employers, other legislation has less well-known requirements related to occupational health and safety. This additional legislation includes the following:

Fair Labor Standards Act   Components of the Fair Labor Standards Act (FLSA), more fully discussed in Chapter 6, "Compensation and Benefits," apply to children in the workforce. Minors between the ages of 16 and 18 may not be employed in jobs considered particularly hazardous to them, including those that expose them to explosives, logging operations, power-driven tools, radiation, and mining operations, as well as those that require the use of equipment that poses a significant danger to the child. In 2008, as part of the Genetic Information Nondiscrimination Act (GINA), the FLSA was amended to increase the civil penalties imposed for child-labor violations to $50,000 for each violation that resulted in the death or serious injury of a child; employers that repeatedly or willfully violate child-labor protections are subject to maximum penalties of $100,000 per violation.

Needlestick Safety and Prevention Act of 2000   This law was enacted in response to the ongoing public health issue of exposure to blood-borne pathogens by health-care workers subjected to accidental needlestick or sharps injuries. The act mandates that all needlestick and sharps injuries be recorded, requires involvement of front-line employees in finding safer devices to replace needles and sharps, and protects employees who have endured needlestick injuries.

Assessing Safety and Health Risks

Any discussion of managing safety and health risks must begin with OSHA, because it sets standards that exert overwhelming influence on those issues in the workplace. OSHA statistics, developed through the recordkeeping requirements of the OSH Act, show significant improvements in workplace safety and health since 1971: fatalities have been reduced by 62 percent, and injury and illness rates have been reduced by 42 percent, even though the workforce has more than doubled during the same time period. These improvements in working conditions are a result of many factors—the change from a manufacturing to a service economy and improvements in technology among them—but underlying them all has been OSHA, with its unwavering focus on establishing standards to improve health and safety in the American workplace.

OSHA estimates business costs for occupational illness and injury to be $170 billion a year. The purpose of assessing risk for environmental health and safety issues is to prevent those illnesses and injuries from occurring in the first place, to protect workers, and, in the long run, to reduce the costs of turnover and workers' compensation, as well as to increase productivity and eliminate OSHA fines and penalties.

Environmental Health Hazards

Environmental health hazards in the modern workplace come in many forms, from physical hazards such as noise and extreme temperatures to chemicals used for everything from making copies to manufacturing products to biological hazards from viruses and bacteria. The effects of these various hazards differ between individual employees—some are more affected than others—so employers must take steps to prevent serious health consequences in the workplace. Table 8.9 lists some of the more common environmental health hazards.

TABLE 8.9 Examples of environmental health hazards

Chemical	Physical	Biological
Asbestos	Ergonomic design	Bacteria
Battery acid	Stress	Contaminated water
Corrosives	Extreme temperatures	Dusts
Gas fumes	Light, noise	Fungi
Pesticides	Electrical currents	Molds
Polyurethane foam	Radiation	Plants
Solvents	Vibrations	Viruses

Chemical Health Hazards

Many of the OSHA standards deal with specific *chemical health hazards* in the workplace. Every chemical present in the workplace should have a *material safety data sheet* (MSDS) from the chemical manufacturer to provide information on how to both prevent and treat an injury. The MSDS identifies the ingredients in the substance, how the substance reacts to changes in the atmosphere (such as at what temperature it will boil or become a vapor), and information about its explosive and flammable qualities. The MSDS tells employees whether the substance is stable or unstable, what materials it must not be in contact with, and what additional hazards are present when it decomposes or degrades.

Most importantly for safety programs, the MSDS provides information about how the chemical may be absorbed by the body; whether it can be inhaled, can be ingested, or can enter through the skin; whether it's carcinogenic; and what protective equipment is required to prevent illness when handling the substance.

Some chemicals, known as *teratogens*, have no effect on a pregnant woman but do affect an unborn child. Some employers, concerned about the health of the employee and her child as well as about potential liability, have developed policies to protect the fetus. These policies, although well-intentioned, violate the Pregnancy Discrimination Act (PDA), which prohibits sex-specific fetal protection policies.

Physical Health Hazards

Many *physical health hazards* are easy to identify and remedy. One such hazard would be an open hole without any warning signs or barriers to prevent someone from accidentally falling. Another would be an electrical or telephone cord that isn't covered or secured to prevent someone from tripping. Another physical hazard would be a walk-in freezer storage unit that couldn't be opened from inside the unit. Other physical hazards occurring in the workplace are less obvious, such as ergonomics and stress:

Ergonomics In 1700, Bernardino Ramazzini published his "Discourse on the Diseases of Workers," which sought to connect illnesses with environmental conditions in the work-place. One of the connections he made was to identify "irregular" or "unnatural" body movements that affect the safety and health of workers. We know this concept today as *ergonomics*—the science that addresses the way a physical environment is designed and how efficient and safe that design is for the people in the environment.

Poor ergonomic designs can cause *musculoskeletal disorders* (MSDs). An MSD is the result of repeated stress to various parts of the body (including the back, arms, shoulders, and other areas) that is caused by the way tasks are performed. MSDs are referred to by several other names as well, including *repetitive stress injuries* (RSIs) and *cumulative trauma injuries* (CTIs). MSD injuries that can result from poor ergonomics in the workplace include tendonitis, bursitis, and carpal tunnel syndrome. According to the Bureau of Labor Statistics (BLS), these and other MSD injuries account for one-third of workplace injuries and illnesses each year, which makes them the largest job-related health and safety problem in the United States. Factors that contribute to MSDs include awkward postures; forceful lifting, pushing, or pulling; prolonged repetitive motions; contact stress; and vibration, such as that which occurs while using power tools for an extended period of time.

Real World Scenario

Automobile Workers v. Johnson Controls, Inc.

Johnson Controls, Inc., manufactures batteries, a process in which lead is a primary ingredient. Occupational exposure to lead can have serious health consequences, including posing a risk to the health of an unborn child. Prior to 1964, Johnson Controls didn't employ women in any of the battery-manufacturing jobs in its plant. After passage of the Civil Rights Act in 1964, women were given the opportunity to work in those jobs.

In June 1977, Johnson developed its first fetal-protection policy, which stated, "Protection of the health of the unborn child is the immediate and direct responsibility of the prospective parents. While the medical profession and the company can support them in the exercise of this responsibility, it cannot assume it for them without simultaneously infringing their rights as persons." Although this policy didn't exclude women from the manufacturing jobs, the company discouraged women who wanted to have children from taking these jobs and required them to sign a statement that they had been advised of the risks of lead exposure to a fetus.

In 1982, after eight women became pregnant while maintaining high levels of lead in their blood, the policy changed: "Women who are pregnant or who are capable of bearing children will not be placed into jobs involving lead exposure or which could expose them to lead through the exercise of job bidding, bumping, transfer, or promotion rights." The policy went on to define lead levels that would make a job inaccessible to women and required that women who wanted to work in those positions supply medical proof of their inability to bear children.

In 1984, a class-action petition challenging the fetal-protection policy was filed. Among the individuals in the class were Mary Craig, who had chosen to be sterilized so that she could keep her job; Elsie Nason, a 50-year-old divorcee who had been transferred out of a job where she was exposed to lead to a job that paid less; and Donald Penney, who had requested and been denied a leave of absence so that the lead level in his blood could be lowered in order for him to become a father.

Johnson Controls argued that its policy was a business necessity.

Both the District Court and the Federal Court of Appeals found for Johnson Controls. The case was then appealed to the U.S. Supreme Court in 1990, where the lower court decisions were reversed. The Supreme Court found that there was clear bias because the policy required only female employees to prove that they weren't capable of conceiving children, and it was therefore in violation of the PDA.

The Supreme Court ruled that "Decisions about the welfare of the next generation must be left to the parents who conceive, bear, support, and raise them, rather than to the employers who hire those parents."

Development of an ergonomics program provides a means by which employers can determine whether MSDs are a problem in their workplaces. An effective ergonomics program requires management support and involves employees in the process. After a review of OSHA logs and workers' compensation claims for injury patterns, an analysis of job tasks, beginning with an observation of the work area while work is being done, is needed to determine whether the risk factors for potential injury exist. Jobs with poor ergonomics may be redesigned to make them less hazardous and reduce injuries.

OSHA has developed tools to assist employers in reducing potential ergonomic hazards. The tools are provided in a checklist for various activities that are statistically prone to ergonomic injury, including handling baggage, sewing, and working at a computer workstation. The checklists provide guidance in the form of basic principles that can be used to reduce ergonomic injuries. For example, the computer workstation checklist provides guidelines for the placement of the monitor, keyboard, mouse, desk, chair, and telephone and discusses some common problems that can occur. You can view the checklists online at www.osha.gov/dts/osta/oshasoft/index.html#eTools. In addition to those currently available, OSHA is in the process of developing similar checklists for specific industries and jobs.

Job-Related Stress   In 1999, NIOSH published the results of a study entitled *Stress at Work*, which defined job *stress* as "harmful physical and emotional responses that occur when the requirements of the job do not match the capabilities, resources, or needs of the worker." When job stress is added to personal factors in an employee's life, such as a sick child or financial concerns, the effect on job performance can be magnified. Dr. Hans Selye, an endocrinologist, is generally credited with identifying stress as an influencer of health and well-being. He identified three stages of stress: arousal, resistance, and exhaustion. Table 8.10 describes the three stages of stress and some of the related symptoms.

TABLE 8.10   Stages and symptoms of stress

Stage	Physical	Emotional	Mental
Arousal	Teeth grinding Insomnia	Irritability Anxiety	Forgetfulness Inability to concentrate
Resistance	Fatigue without a cause	Mood swings Social withdrawal Resentment Indifference Defiance	Procrastination Indecision
Exhaustion	Headaches Chronic fatigue Indigestion Intestinal problems	Chronic depression Hostility Isolation	Disorganization Poor judgment Disillusionment

Stress-related illnesses such as allergies, heart disease, panic attacks, and other diseases affect productivity, as does burnout, which can be the result of long-term, unrelenting job stress.

High levels of job stress can result in increased turnover, low morale, increased tardiness and absenteeism, reduced productivity, poor product quality, and increased accidents on the job. All of these negatively affect the bottom line.

The NIOSH study identified six circumstances that can lead to job stress. Table 8.11 explains these circumstances.

TABLE 8.11 Job stressors identified by NIOSH

Stressor	Characteristics
Task design	Heavy workloads and infrequent rest breaks
	Long, hectic hours
	Shift work
	Routine tasks with little inherent meaning
	Tasks that don't use employee skills
	Little or no control over daily work
Management style	Lack of participation in decisions that affect employees
	Poor organizational communication
	Lack of family-friendly policies
Interpersonal relationships	Poor social environment
	Lack of support or help from co-workers and supervisors
Work roles	Conflicting or uncertain job expectations
	Too much responsibility
	Too many "hats to wear"
Career concerns	Job insecurity
	Lack of opportunity for growth, advancement, or promotion
	Lack of preparation for rapid changes
Environmental conditions	Unpleasant or dangerous physical conditions such as crowding, noise, or air pollution
	Ergonomic problems

Source: NIOSH "Stress at Work" booklet

The NIOSH study recommends a two-pronged approach to reducing job stress: organizational change and stress management. Organizational changes can take the form of employee-recognition programs, career development, a culture that values individual employees, and employer actions consistent with the organization's stated values. Stress-management programs are, to a certain extent, dependent on the needs of individual employees, because people react differently to job stressors. These programs include training for employees about the sources of stress and how it affects health and teaching stress-reduction skills. Managers can encourage employees to reduce the effects of stress by balancing their work with private activities, maintaining an exercise program, and building a support network at work and at home.

The full NIOSH study mentioned earlier is available free of charge at `http://www.cdc.gov/niosh/topics/stress/?`.

Biological Health Hazards

Biological health hazards come in many forms, from unsanitary conditions in a food preparation area to serious diseases contracted through needlestick injuries. Infectious diseases are spread by different means to employees, but the resulting impact on the health of the workforce or the community can be substantial. Although the health-care and food-preparation industries are at greater risk than other industries, HR professionals should understand the implications of infectious disease in all workplaces:

HIV/AIDS   Human immunodeficiency virus (HIV) and acquired immune deficiency syndrome (AIDS) are blood-borne pathogens transmitted through blood or other bodily fluids. For this reason, transmission to co-workers in workplaces other than in the health-care industry is relatively unlikely. Persons with HIV/AIDS are protected by the ADA; as long as they're able to perform their essential job functions, they're entitled to remain employed.

HBV   The hepatitis B virus (HBV) is another blood-borne pathogen posing risks to health-care workers. Because transmission chiefly occurs as the result of an accidental needle stick, health-care workers are at the greatest risk of infection in the workplace. The CDC recommends that health-care workers at a high risk of infection be vaccinated to prevent them from contracting the disease.

Tuberculosis   Tuberculosis is a lung disease that is spread through the air. Exposure occurs when someone with TB coughs or sneezes, expelling pathogens. Those at higher risk for contracting TB in the workplace are people who share the same breathing space, such as co-workers or health-care workers, particularly in nursing homes.

Severe Acute Respiratory Syndrome (SARS)   According to the CDC, there have been no outbreaks of SARS since 2004. Between the initial outbreak in November 2002 and the last known outbreak in April 2004, it affected business travel and had a negative effect on some industries, particularly the travel industry. SARS appears to be transmitted by close person-to-person contact when an infected person coughs or sneezes. Preventing the spread of SARS in the workplace requires frequent hand washing and the use of common household cleaners to frequently clean surfaces.

Avian Influenza   Avian influenza (H5N1) is a more current a global health concern. At this time, H5N1 mainly affects wild and domesticated birds in parts of Asia, Europe, the

Near East, and Africa, with only a small number of cases of human infection. A few cases in Asia have been the result of human-to-human transmission, and health-care practitioners are concerned that if this type of transmission increases a global pandemic will ensue. The CDC advises travelers to avoid contact with live birds, wash their hands often with soap and water, and cover their noses and mouths when coughing or sneezing.

Preparing for a Pandemic   HR professionals can play a role in preparing their organizations to cope with a pandemic by establishing plans to maintain essential functions if a large number of employees are absent from work. The CDC encourages employers to prepare guidelines for minimizing face-to-face contact; secure vaccines for employees to prevent outbreaks; modify sick-leave policies to allow ill employees time to recover so they don't spread the disease; use telecommuting, flexible work hours, and work shifts to minimize contact; and establish knowledge-management programs to ensure business continuity during a health crisis. Additional information on preparing for a pandemic is available at www.pandemicflu.gov.

Employees with infectious diseases who don't pose a threat to co-worker health and safety are protected by ADA requirements for reasonable accommodation and may not be subjected to adverse employment actions because of their disease.

Environmental Safety Hazards

Although the OSH Act didn't clearly define workplace hazards, it did empower OSHA to define *occupational safety and health standards* that would result in improved workplace safety and health as quickly as possible. Wherever possible, the act encouraged OSHA to use previously existing federal standards or industry standards that already had substantial agreement in the industry. The resulting standards range from those that are job and industry specific, such as standards for handling toxic chemicals used in manufacturing processes, to those that apply to businesses in many different industries.

Let's review some of the more generally applicable standards. Each standard is identified here with the OSHA title and the number assigned to it in the Code of Federal Regulations (CFR):

The General Duty Standard, Section 5   The *general duty standard* requires employers to provide jobs and a workplace environment that are free from recognized safety and health hazards that could potentially cause death or serious physical harm. This standard also requires employers to comply with all OSHA rules, regulations, and standards.

Employees are required to comply with OSHA standards and rules that apply to their own conduct in the course of performing their duties.

Emergency Action Plans, 1910.38   Employers are required to have *emergency action plans* in place to inform employees of appropriate procedures to follow during a fire or evacuation. The plan must designate employees who will remain behind during an evacuation to maintain or shut down critical operations. Employers must also develop a process to account for all employees after an evacuation and identify those employees who are responsible for carrying out rescue and medical duties in the event of an emergency. Employers must provide training for employees when the plan is first developed, when new employees are hired, and when an employee is assigned new responsibilities for execution of the plan.

The plan must also identify the person responsible for maintaining it who can be contacted by employees when they have questions about the plan.

Fire Prevention Plans, 1910.39   An OSHA-required fire-prevention plan must describe the major fire hazards and appropriate procedures for handling and storing hazardous materials to prevent fires. The employer must develop and implement procedures to control the accumulation of flammable or combustible refuse and ensure that devices on heat-producing machinery designed to prevent ignition of fires are adequately maintained.

The fire-prevention plan must also inform employees about any fire hazards they will face when first assigned to a new job and what actions they should take to protect themselves in the event of a fire.

Occupational Noise Exposure, 1910.95   This standard establishes permissible noise levels for the workplace, establishes measurement procedures, requires implementation of hearing-conservation programs when average noise levels reach 85 decibels or greater, and requires audiometric testing for employees who work in environments with noise at those levels. Audiometric test results indicating a hearing loss of 10 decibels must be reported on OSHA form 300.

Personal Protective Equipment, 1910.132   OSHA established standards for personal protective equipment (PPE) to be used for jobs in which employees come in contact with hazardous materials, compressed gases, explosives and blasting agents, liquid petroleum, and ammonia. The standard requires PPE to protect the eyes and face, respiration, head, feet, and hands. It also requires employers to provide gear that protects employees from electrical shocks or other injuries. The standard requires that PPE be provided, used, and maintained in working condition. Employers are required to train employees in the appropriate use of PPE and are responsible for ensuring that employee-owned equipment is adequately maintained for use in hazardous situations.

Sanitation, 1910.141   This standard requires that the workplace be clean to the extent the type of work allows and sets forth specific guidelines for maintaining sanitary conditions.

Specifications for Accident Prevention Signs and Tags, 1910.145   OSHA has developed specifications for hazard signs and tags and requires that all workplace signs conform to the OSHA specifications. These specifications describe the colors to be used for different levels of warning and, in some cases, such as biohazard and slow-moving vehicle signs (among others), provide specifications for size, color, and design of the sign.

In general, OSHA defines red as the background color for danger, yellow for caution, orange for warning, and fluorescent orange or orange-red for biological hazards. Lettering or symbols on the signs is specified as being of a contrasting color to the background.

Permit-Required Confined Spaces, 1910.146   OSHA requires permits for employees to enter spaces that may become filled with a hazardous atmosphere that is immediately dangerous to life or health. The atmosphere in confined spaces must be tested prior to an employee's entrance into them, and other personnel are required to be in close proximity to the entrance to render assistance if needed. Employees who will be entering the space have the opportunity to observe the testing process if they desire to do so.

The Control of Hazardous Energy (Lockout/Tagout), 1910.147   The lockout/tagout standard applies to machinery that may start unexpectedly when a guard or other safety device must be removed to perform a service or maintenance process and any part of an employee's body may be subjected to injury in the course of the process.

Medical Services and First Aid, 1910.151   OSHA requires that employers provide adequate first-aid supplies and either have medical personnel available or ensure that one or more workers are trained in first aid to assist injured employees in an emergency.

General Requirements for All Machines (Machine Guarding), 1910.212   OSHA requires that woodworking machines; cooperage machinery; abrasive wheel machinery; mills; power presses; forging machines; portable power tools; welding, cutting, and brazing tools; and tools for specific industries such as paper, textile, bakery, and sawmill, among others, use guards to protect employees from injury. These guards can be barrier-type guards, two-hand tripping devices, electronic safety devices, or other guards or devices that effectively prevent injuries.

Selection and Use of Electrical Work Practices, 1910.333   Employers must ensure that employees who work on or around electrical equipment or circuits are protected from injury that could result from direct or indirect contact with electrical currents.

Blood-Borne Pathogens, 1910.1030   Blood-borne pathogens are pathogenic microorganisms in human blood that can cause disease in humans. HBV and HIV are examples of blood-borne pathogens but are not by any means the only ones. Workers in the health-care industry are those most at risk for exposure to blood-borne pathogens, and OSHA regulations require employers to take steps to prevent exposure, including a written exposure-control plan that informs employees of preventive steps, post-exposure evaluation and follow-up, recordkeeping, and incident evaluation procedures.

Hazard Communication Standard (HCS), 1910.1200   The HCS requires employers to provide employees with information about physical and health hazards related to the use of any chemicals in the workplace. Employers must develop and maintain an ongoing written HCS plan that is to be updated as changes occur in the materials used in the workplace. The material safety data sheets (MSDSs) provided by chemical manufacturers provide sufficient information for communicating to and training employees.

You can access the comprehensive list of OSHA standards at http://www. osha.gov/law-regs.html.

Assessing Security Risks

Security in the workplace covers a broad spectrum of topics related to protecting the company from threats of one kind or another, including fires, earthquakes, hurricanes, tornadoes, and other natural disasters and manmade threats such as terrorist attacks, computer hackers, workplace violence and theft, or unintentional release of trade secrets or confidential information. Many of these threats aren't ultimately the responsibility of HR professionals, but a working knowledge of the impact they have on the workforce is essential to understanding the ways HR interacts with other business functions in the organization.

As you will recall from an earlier description in this chapter, risk assessment is the process used to evaluate the likelihood that losses will occur. Before an employer can put plans in place to reduce security risks, the threats (external forces) and vulnerabilities (internal weaknesses) must be evaluated for the degree of risk to the organization. This knowledge is needed to determine appropriate controls to protect the company and which emergencies are most likely to occur so that preventive measures can be taken.

A security risk assessment is most often a collaborative effort between internal managers and outside consultants with expertise in security issues. Depending on the nature of the business, consultants with different types of expertise will be required; for example, a software company developing a new product will have significantly different needs than a manufacturing plant whose employees belong to a labor union and may go on strike. Risk assessments are most frequently accomplished using a qualitative analysis, where all the possible emergencies are listed along with the potential financial costs and impact on operations. The emergencies can then be prioritized to address those with the greatest possible impact on the business first.

Identifying and ranking risks provides management with the opportunity to be proactive and implement controls to prevent damage to the assets of the business. There are four basic types of company assets: financial assets, such as cash, securities, and accounts receivable; physical assets, such as buildings, machinery, and equipment; information assets; and human assets, including the effects of workplace violence and substance abuse. Table 8.12 displays some of the common risks associated with each of these asset types.

Let's examine the asset types and associated risks in more depth:

Financial Assets   Financial assets, including cash, inventory, accounts receivable, and securities, are vulnerable to theft and embezzlement. Implementing policies and procedures to protect financial assets is generally the responsibility of a company's chief financial officer (CFO).

Physical Assets   Physical assets consist of buildings, manufacturing machines and equipment, vehicles, furniture, and office equipment. HR responsibility for risk assessment on these assets is related to how people are impacted by risks associated with them. For example, a possible risk to physical assets could be fire. HR assessment of risks for physical assets focuses on protecting people from these risks. In most cases, these risks are managed through the safety plans described in the "Injury and Illness Prevention Programs" section of this chapter.

Information Assets   Risks to information assets come in different forms. Employees may release confidential information to an unauthorized person unintentionally or, in some cases, intentionally. Information stored on servers may be compromised because of unauthorized access by hackers or unintentional release by employees. Regardless of the cause, the risks from information loss can range from a minor disruption of operations to a catastrophic loss of trade secrets or financial records that damage an organization's credibility in the marketplace or its ability to continue operations.

TABLE 8.12 Types of risks and assets impacted

Type of Risk	Financial	Physical	Information	Human
Accidents	x	x	x	x
Computer hackers	x	x	x	
Corporate espionage	x	x	x	
Embezzlement	x			
Fire	x	x	x	x
Human error	x	x	x	x
Identity theft			x	x
Lawsuits	x	x	x	x
Loss of confidential information			x	x
Natural disasters	x	x	x	x
Pilferage		x		
Breach of private information			x	x
Sabotage		x	x	x
Substance abuse				x
Terrorism	x	x	x	x
Theft	x	x	x	
Workplace violence				x

Human Assets Providing protection for employees takes many forms. Many of the security measures that protect physical assets also protect employees; in addition, an ongoing safety training program can include information on ways in which employees can protect themselves in different situations. Protecting employees working outside the United States presents different issues for employers. Issues of political stability and animosity toward American companies and citizens require programs and vendors that specialize in protecting them abroad. Large corporations must often take special security precautions to prevent executives from kidnapping, particularly when they travel overseas. Executive security may take several forms, including bodyguards and vendors that specialize in corporate protection.

Employees must also be protected from the effects of workplace violence and substance abuse in the workplace.

Assessing Business Continuity Risks

Ensuring an organization's ability to continue despite a disruption is one of the many challenges facing business leaders today. Whether the threat to operations is natural or manmade, accidental or intentional, the goal of business continuity planning is to protect the organization from unforeseen emergencies and other circumstances. Risks to business continuity can generally be classified as natural, manmade, or biological. In some cases, disasters such as fires or floods can be either natural or manmade, but response is similar in either situation:

Environmental Disasters   Environmental disasters come in many forms, from extreme weather conditions as in hurricanes, tornadoes, or blizzards, or from other causes such as floods, earthquakes, fires, volcanic eruptions, toxic gas releases, chemical spills, and so on. For some environmental disasters, such as volcanic eruptions and floods, there is usually some advance warning, such as rising water levels in a river or gradually increasing volcanic activity. In these cases, businesses are able to take precautionary steps to secure people, data, and physical assets. At other times, natural disasters are unexpected, such as a major earthquake or toxic gas release. At those times, people must react instantly to save lives and business assets; the best way to do this is with a pre-established plan for people to follow so they don't have to make decisions under stressful conditions.

Organized or Deliberate Disruptions   Organized and/or deliberate disruptions can be the result of acts of terrorism, major thefts, sabotage, or labor disputes. Major thefts and acts of sabotage come with little or no warning and can disrupt operations and, in the case of sabotage, potentially injure people. Terrorism also comes with little or no warning. In addition to the devastation to people and infrastructure, this disruption has the additional element of creating fear in people who may not have even been on the same continent where the attack occurred. In addition to the loss of life and infrastructure, management must be able to calm employee fears to continue operating the business.

On the other hand, labor disputes generally occur after a period of notice by a union and provide an opportunity to plan for continued operations. Even so, the disruption is costly and can be dangerous for employees who cross picket lines.

Loss of Utilities and Public Services   The loss of utilities can occur as the result of a demand for electricity that exceeds the capacity of the power grid, as the result of an oil shortage, or as the result of a failure of the communication system, any of which can be caused by an environmental disaster or an organized disruption. In some cases, such as excessive demand on the power grid, the utility company may have a system in place to notify business owners of a potential loss of power prior to the loss. At other times—as the result of a terrorist act, for example—the disruption could be immediate and unexpected.

Equipment or System Failures   Equipment breakdowns, such as a failure of production equipment or water pipes bursting and causing a flood, can halt production and disrupt operations unexpectedly. Other internal systems such as the company's Internet service, communication system, or building power can fail as well, disrupting operations.

Serious Information Security Incidents   Cyber attacks by hackers, or the unleashing of a major email virus, can compromise sensitive and confidential information, shut down the customer-ordering website, or cause the IT system to fail.

Other Emergencies   Other emergencies vary widely in the amount of disruption caused to business operations. At one extreme, a biological disaster such as a serious epidemic could affect much of the workforce, reducing the ability of the company to function. Biological disasters can be either natural, such as the SARS outbreak in 2002–03, or manmade, as the result of a bioterror attack. These types of disasters pose different challenges than some others because they affect the people who would otherwise be available to reduce the impact of the emergency. The unexpected loss of a key employee might not have an immediate impact but could cripple an organization's forward movement, regardless of the cause. In some cases, such as a resignation, there is some opportunity for transitioning to a replacement including the transfer of essential knowledge. At other times, because of an accident, terrorist attack, or other type of disaster, the circumstances would rule out any time for transition, and remaining employees would need to reconstruct critical information in order to move forward. A public-transportation strike or gas shortage is another situation that could either prevent employees from getting to work at all or significantly increase commute times.

Assessing Workplace Privacy Risks

Many employees are surprised and angry when subjected to electronic monitoring, physical property searches, or video surveillance of their activities in the workplace. Employers use electronic surveillance to monitor email, voice mail, and telephone conversations and to access call logs, monitor Internet use, or inspect computer files. Organizations may conduct property searches in cubicles, offices, file cabinets, employee lockers, or in some circumstances personal employee belongings. In some cases, employers may conduct video surveillance by installing cameras in the workplace to protect employees or monitor behavior. There can be compelling reasons for employers to monitor employee activities, including concerns about theft, employee safety, improper use of equipment, loss of confidential proprietary information, productivity, and other issues. Employers may be accused of knowingly allowing employees to disseminate harassing or inappropriate communication, and implementing some form of electronic monitoring may protect them from liability. Add to this mix concerns about identity theft, and employers have legitimate reasons to take protective actions. In doing so, it's important to balance these concerns with the effect monitoring has on employee rights, morale, and productivity and then assess the risks inherent in those programs.

Risk Management

The factors considered in making the decision for handling specific risks are discussed in Chapter 2, which describes options for managing risk in an organization. To summarize here, risks can be managed in one of the following ways:

- *Mitigation:* The company minimizes the risk.

- *Acceptance:* The company manages the risk if it occurs.

- *Avoidance:* The company eliminates the risk.

- *Transfer:* The company uses insurance to cover the risk.

Now that we've identified and assessed many of the risks related to the workplace, the following sections describe some of the possible choices for minimizing, managing, transferring, and even eliminating HR risks.

Managing Legal Compliance Risks

Members of the management team look to the HR function for guidance in complying with employment laws and regulations. HR also takes the lead in establishing compliant policies and procedures and is responsible for ensuring that members of the management team are aware of laws and regulations governing employment practices and the potential costs to the organization for failing to comply.

Americans with Disabilities Act

Preventing losses from the mishandling of ADA claims can be accomplished by developing and implementing guidelines for employees to follow when requesting an ADA accommodation. Documenting the steps in this process demonstrates an employer's good-faith participation in an interactive process to provide a reasonable accommodation for a disabled employee. Some employers develop accommodation request forms to facilitate this process:

Employee Requests an Accommodation   Making sure managers and employees know what kind of information is needed to assess a requested accommodation can save time and indicate the employer's good-faith participation in a discussion of the request. Supervisors shouldn't assume they know the best solution or know what the employee needs or wants. Instead, the first step for supervisors to take when an employee asks, or indicates the need for, an accommodation is to request information from the employee.

At this stage, an accommodation request form guides employees in providing the information needed to proceed with the interactive process. The form requests a description of the limitation and how it affects their ability to perform one or more essential job functions. It also requests their suggestions for accommodation that would allow them to perform the functions.

Employee Obtains Physician Certification   Employees take the written accommodation request to their physicians for review, along with a copy of their job descriptions, to obtain medical certification of the need for an accommodation. The request, job description, and certification are submitted to human resources when completed.

HR Obtains a Supervisor Response   With the employee's request and physician's certification, HR and the supervisor discuss the requested accommodation. The supervisor assesses whether the employee is performing essential job functions satisfactorily and whether the accommodation is reasonable. If needed, additional approvals are obtained from management.

HR Facilitates a Meeting with Employee and Supervisor   Once all necessary approvals have been obtained, HR engages the employee and supervisor in an interactive discussion of the request and response by management.

Management Review   Once an agreement has been reached (or not), management is made aware of the result. Particularly when the accommodation is denied, this is a critical step.

Employee Appeal Process   As further evidence of good-faith participation in an interactive process, if employees disagree with the result of an accommodation request, it's important that they have the opportunity to appeal the decision. This can be done through the organization's conflict-resolution process.

Sarbanes-Oxley Act

Chapter 3 described the background and intention of SOX to ensure the accuracy and fairness of financial reporting for public companies and its specific requirements for key executives and board members. This section discusses the requirements that are relevant to HR practice.

So that employees may raise possible violations without fear of retaliation, SOX Section 301 requires the board of directors (BOD) audit committee to establish procedures to receive and address complaints regarding accounting practices, internal accounting controls, and auditing matters, including confidential or anonymous complaints submitted by employees. Methods for submitting anonymous complaints that companies have established involve a variety of avenues including intranet- or Internet-accessible forms, a toll-free telephone number specifically for such complaints, the ability to contact the company's general counsel either by telephone or by email, and providing information on how to contact the audit committee directly either via email or regular mail.

Section 401 requires that financial statements for public companies include all material liabilities, obligations, or transactions that aren't reflected in the balance sheet. From the HR function, this could include potential lawsuit judgments or pending employee settlements.

As mentioned earlier in this chapter, *section 404* requires organizations to review and test their internal controls for financial transactions. For HR, this includes activities that result in financial transactions, such as procedures for ensuring that employment offers conform to internal requirements for approvals and are consistent with established guidelines or salary ranges and that exceptions are approved in accordance with corporate signature policies. Another area requiring internal controls is the documentation of salary increases. For example, if the organization conducts focal reviews, the approved increases must be signed in accordance with signature approval policies, and the increases implemented in the payroll system must agree with the approved amounts.

Section 406 establishes requirements for public companies to either implement a code of ethics and regularly train key officers on its requirements or disclose why they haven't done so. The SEC final rule defined a code of ethics for these purposes as written standards designed to deter wrongdoing and to promote the following:

- Honest and ethical conduct, including the ethical handling of actual or apparent conflicts of interest between personal and professional relationships

- Full, fair, accurate, timely, and understandable disclosure in reports and documents that a registrant files with, or submits to, the SEC and in other public communications made by the registrant

- Compliance with applicable governmental laws, rules, and regulations

- The prompt internal reporting to an appropriate person or persons identified in the code of violations of the code

- Accountability for adherence to the code

SEC rules allow these standards of financial ethics to be incorporated into an expanded code of ethics or code of conduct, such as those described in Chapter 3, that applies to a broader group of employees than just the key executives and members of the BOD covered by the SEC regulation.

Section 409 requires organizations to report "on an urgent basis" material changes to its financial condition. The filing of an employment-practices lawsuit with a significant demand for damages could be considered a material change to the financial condition and require an immediate report to comply with this section.

Section 802 provides criminal penalties, including up to 20 years in prison, for actions that obstruct or otherwise attempt to influence an investigation into allegations of fraudulent financial reporting practices.

The section 806 whistle-blower prohibitions that protect employees who report questionable financial transactions are covered in some detail in Chapter 3.

Work-Life Discrimination

Risks in the area of work-life balance and discrimination need to be managed in two ways. The first is to reduce costs that result from employee distractions caused by family responsibilities, such as decreased productivity, absenteeism, turnover and related recruiting costs, lower morale, lack of employee engagement, and increased health insurance premiums that occur because of increased employee stress. The second is to reduce the likelihood of caregiver discrimination lawsuits.

Employers have built work-life balance programs into their benefit packages to provide "family-friendly" services such as on-site childcare, health and wellness programs, paid parental leave, and many others to ease the stresses employees face from conflicting responsibilities. Some organizations also implement benefits such as flextime, telecommuting, paid time off, and others to assist employees in maintaining productivity at work while managing family responsibilities. These programs are covered in detail in Chapter 6. From a risk-management perspective, these and similar programs can reduce family responsibility distractions that draw employee focus away from job duties.

The second area of concern, demonstrated by the examples of disparate treatment described in the earlier "Risk Assessment" section, is generated by the organizational culture and management attitude toward employees with family responsibilities. The solution to this problem begins with educating management about the connection between EEO discrimination protections and employees with family-care responsibilities and the costs associated with discrimination claims.

Managing Safety and Health Risks

Previous sections in this chapter have described various laws, regulations, and standards that govern workplace safety. So, what exactly is workplace safety? In a word (or two), it's accident prevention. *Safety* is about identifying possible hazards in the workplace and reducing the likelihood that an accident will happen by correcting the hazard. Management and employees are partners in this process. Because employees are close to the possible hazards, they should feel empowered to take the steps necessary to reduce hazards that are within their control, whether that means correcting the hazard themselves or reporting the hazard to management with suggestions on how to correct it.

Workplace accidents negatively impact the bottom line in many ways. They reduce productivity because an injured employee must be given time to recover from an injury. A high accident/injury rate increases insurance costs and, when employees sense that management is unconcerned about their safety, lowers morale and increases turnover. Employees who aren't satisfied with their work care less about what kind of job they do, which has a negative impact on quality. Poor quality products tarnish the company's reputation, which makes it more difficult for the company to compete against other products. All of these consequences of poor safety policies reduce the company's ability to earn a profit, which reduces the value of the company to its owners. All of this can happen when employers don't think safety matters!

Accident prevention begins with a commitment from the top that safety does matter and that the health and well-being of employees is important to the company. Employers need to provide safe operating procedures, train workers to use those procedures, and then enforce the procedures by rewarding positive safety actions and disciplining employees who fail to comply with procedures.

Because the employees doing the job know best what is safe and what is unsafe, they must be involved in developing safe operating procedures. Working in partnership, management and employees can identify the hazards present in the workplace and develop strategies to reduce or eliminate them. An added benefit of including employees in this process is that they will have a greater stake in maintaining safe operations that they were part of creating. As safe operating procedures are identified, they become part of a safety and health-management plan.

Employers that have developed effective safety-management programs have safer work environments for their employees. Over the past 30 years, through workplace investigation and analysis of injury and illness statistics, OSHA has determined that effective safety and health-management plans have four common characteristics:

- Senior management is committed to a safe work environment, and employees are involved in the decisions and activities to make it happen.

- The company is engaged in an ongoing worksite analysis to identify potential safety and health hazards.

- The company has active hazard-prevention and -control programs in place to correct hazards before injury or illness occurs.

- Safety and health training is an ongoing process in the company.

An effective plan identifies the person who is responsible for its overall implementation and creates a safety committee with representatives from both management and labor to address safety concerns and develop workable solutions to safety problems. An effective plan identifies hazards that exist in the work environment, whether they're physical, chemical, or biological, and provides guidance, in the form of OSHA safety standards, on the appropriate way to work with each hazard. The plan provides a mechanism for employee complaints so they reach the appropriate management level for speedy resolution to prevent injuries. If the work environment requires the use of machinery, equipment, tools, or PPE, the plan spells out the appropriate methods for using and maintaining them and includes consequences for failing to comply with the standards.

The plan describes how to report accidents, who must be notified, and the time frames in which the notifications must occur and provides an accident investigation procedure, identifying who will conduct the investigation, what records must be kept, and how and where they're filed. When an investigation takes place, the plan should include a process that ensures all employees are advised of the accident circumstances and what steps should be taken to avoid similar accidents in the future.

Part of an effective plan is ongoing training for employees that addresses previous accidents and ways to prevent similar occurrences in the future.

PHR ONLY Injury and Illness Prevention Programs

Injury and illness prevention plans (IIPP) are required by OSHA and designed to protect employees from preventable workplace injuries and illnesses. OSHA describes several plans with different purposes. This section describes each of these plans. Some elements are present in all of the plans, and others are related only to individual plans. OSHA requires the following plans:

- Safety and health management plan (also known as an *injury and illness prevention plan*)

- Emergency action plan (also referred to as an *emergency response plan*)

- Fire-prevention plan

Generally, employers with 10 or fewer employees aren't required to provide written plans unless they have been notified by OSHA to do so.

To ensure the safety of employees and business assets, an emergency action plan, combined with ongoing employee training, is essential. By developing a plan and having regular drills to reinforce the steps to be taken, employers can improve the chances that all employees will be safe in an emergency.

The OSHA emergency action plan standard requires, at a minimum, that the employer define the preferred method for reporting fires and other emergencies, an evacuation policy and procedure, and floor plans or maps that define escape procedures and assign evacuation routes. The plan must have contact information for individuals who can provide additional information during an emergency and provide procedures for employees who will remain behind to perform essential services during the emergency. Employees who will perform rescue and medical duties are to be included in the plan as well. The plan requires alarm systems to notify all employees, including those who are disabled, of the need to evacuate.

 Real World Scenario

Sample Emergency Action Plan

Section 1: Responsibilities   In this section is a description of everyone who has a role to play during an emergency. Who will make the decision to evacuate the building? If critical machinery must be shut down, who will do that? Who is responsible to "take roll" and ensure that all employees have been safely evacuated from the building? Which employees are certified to perform first aid until medical personnel arrive on the scene? How will the emergency be reported to authorities, and who is responsible for doing that? Finally, this section should include the names of those who have been designated to answer questions and explain duties required by the plan.

Section 2: Emergency Escape Procedures   This section of the plan identifies the emergency escape procedures that employees are to follow and provides a diagram of the building showing escape routes from each floor and each area. In this section, special procedures for evacuating persons with disabilities, visitors to the building, and others with special needs should be spelled out. A safe meeting area should be designated so that all employees know where they should go in the event of an evacuation.

Section 3: Critical Plant Operations   Particularly in manufacturing operations, there are processes that must be shut down according to specific protocols. This section should identify these processes, along with instructions for employees on recognizing when they must evacuate themselves, even if the operation is not yet complete.

Section 4: Accounting for Employees   In the event of an evacuation, it's critical that rescue personnel know whether people are trapped in the building. Equally important is that rescue personnel not endanger themselves if everyone has been

---

(Continued)

successfully evacuated. This section of the plan should describe the procedures to be followed, including where employees will meet and who will account for employees and visitors to the area.

Section 5: Reporting Emergencies This section describes how emergencies are to be reported to the appropriate authorities.

Section 6: Identifying Emergency Contacts In this section, the plan should identify who should be contacted for specific information. This may be a single person, or it may be several individuals who are responsible for different sections of the plan.

Section 7: Alarm System This section of the plan should describe how employees will be notified of an emergency, where alarms are located, if there are different alarms for different emergencies, what they sound like, and whether the alarm system automatically notifies emergency personnel.

Section 8: Types of Evacuations If the building is located in an area in which the potential for different types of emergencies exists, such as fires, tornadoes, and floods, this section of the plan describes the evacuation plan for each type of emergency.

Section 9: Training Requirements In this section, the plan should describe how employees will be trained in emergency procedures and how often. The person responsible for training employees should be identified, along with a schedule for emergency drills.

Section 10: Recordkeeping In this section, the plan should include documents that might be required in an emergency. This could include information on MSDSs for chemicals in the worksite, maintenance records for safety equipment, equipment inspection records, building plans, and OSHA forms.

Elements Common to All Plans

Some elements are important enough for inclusion in each of the plans:

- A clear statement of the company policy regarding the program
- The commitment and full support of senior management
- A process for including employees in the process, whether through the establishment of a safety committee or some other means
- Identification of those with responsibilities under the plan, including employees, vendors, and public health and safety officials, and contact information for those individuals
- A clear, unambiguous process for reporting hazards or concerns to the responsible parties
- A description of the process to be used in training employees
- Procedures for maintaining records required by OSHA

Safety and Health Management Plan

In addition to the elements common to all plans, a safety and health management plan will also include the following:

- A process to ensure two-way communication between management and labor
- An assessment of known hazards
- Procedures to correct known hazards
- A procedure to ensure that the company engages in an ongoing analysis of workplace hazards and conducts updated training on changes
- Maintenance procedures for any equipment, machinery, tools, or PPE used in the workplace
- An accident investigation procedure
- An accident reporting procedure

Emergency Action Plan

The emergency action plan begins with the common elements described previously and adds the following:

- Emergency escape procedures, including a floor plan or diagram for employees to follow
- Procedures for shutting down critical plant operations
- A process to account for employees after an evacuation
- A description of the alarm system that will notify employees of an emergency, including how persons with disabilities, visitors, and temporary employees will be notified
- Procedures to follow for different types of emergencies, such as fires, tornadoes, earthquakes, and terrorist attacks

Fire-Prevention Plan

The fire-prevention plan may be included as part of the emergency action plan. Whether the plan is included with it or separate, it must provide information about the following:

- All major fire hazards, how they should be handled and stored, a description of possible causes of igniting them and how to prevent that from happening, and a description of the appropriate equipment to suppress each hazard
- The location of fire-extinguishing systems or portable fire extinguishers
- The procedure describing how waste materials that are flammable or combustible will be stored before disposal

Injury and Illness Compensation Programs

As long as there have been workers and employers, there has been a debate about financial responsibility for injuries suffered on the job. The first written record of this is in the Hammurabic Code, written some 4,000 years ago by the king of Babylon. Of course, at that time, the workers were slaves, and compensation for injuries was paid to their masters, but nonetheless, there was recognition of financial liability when injuries occurred.

Over time, three common-law doctrines developed that were applied to workers who were injured on the job:

- The *fellow servant rule* absolved employers of responsibility if a co-worker's actions caused the injury.

- The *doctrine of contributory negligence* was used to mitigate the employer's responsibility if the worker's actions contributed in any way to the injury.

- *Voluntary assumption of risk* said that workers who knew the dangers of the job when they took it assumed the associated risks, and the level of pay they accepted reflected the amount of danger involved, so the employer had no responsibility when death or injury occurred.

For workers, these doctrines presented many problems. First, they assumed the employer and the worker were equals in the labor market, so the law treated employment relationships the same as it did contracts between business owners. They also assumed that if the terms and conditions of employment weren't agreeable to the worker, the worker could simply seek other employment.

Second, these doctrines required workers injured on the job to seek recompense through the court system. Employers for the most part could afford the best attorneys to represent them, whereas few employees could afford a lengthy legal battle.

These common-law doctrines became known as the *unholy trinity* because the results were almost always in favor of the employer: only 50 percent of cases brought on behalf of workers killed or injured on the job resulted in any kind of compensation; of those who did receive compensation, it was rarely more than a few months' pay. As governments recognized the blatant unfairness of the lopsided way these doctrines were applied, states began enacting workers' compensation laws to level the playing field for workers. Wisconsin was the first state to pass a workers' Compensation Act in 1911, and New Jersey followed in the same year.

Federal Workers' Compensation Requirements

Workers' compensation laws for private employers are in most cases the purview of state government; however, there are a few industries with federal legislation to protect injured workers. These include the federal government, the longshoring industry, coal mines, and the Department of Energy. Legislation pertaining to these industries is covered by the following laws:

Federal Employees Compensation Act (FECA) of 1916   FECA is administered by the DOL and is the federal employees' equivalent of workers' compensation, providing similar benefits for workers injured during the course of performing their jobs.

The Longshore and Harbor Workers' Compensation Act (LHWCA) of 1927   LHWCA provides workers' compensation benefits for maritime workers whose injuries occur on the navigable waters of the United States or on piers, docks, or terminals.

Black Lung Benefits Act (BLBA) of 1969, amended in 1977   The BLBA provides benefits to coal miners who have been disabled by pneumoconiosis as a result of their work in the mines. Benefits are also paid to surviving dependents if the miner dies from the disease.

Energy Employees Occupational Illness Compensation Program Act (EEOICPA) of 2000   This act was created to provide compensation for employees and contractors of the Department of Energy who were subjected to excessive radiation while producing and testing nuclear weapons.

Safety Training Programs

OSHA has developed guidelines to assist employers in developing effective training programs that reduce work-related injury and illness. The following guidelines can be modified to fit the specific industry and work site requirements for individual businesses:

1. Determine whether training is needed. In other words, is the safety problem something that can be corrected with training, or is another correction necessary?

2. Identify the training needs. What should employees be doing that they aren't doing? The program should inform them of appropriate methods for doing the job.

3. As with any other training program, develop objectives for the training.

4. When the learning needs and objectives have been identified, methods for delivering the training can be developed. Will classroom training be best? One-on-one training with an experienced employee? Demonstration and practice? This will depend on the specific training needs for the organization.

5. Conduct the training.

6. Evaluate how well the training worked, using the methods discussed in Chapter 5, "Human Resource Development."

7. Based on the evaluation, adjust the training to improve its effectiveness.

Managing Security Risks

HR professionals must provide the expertise to appropriately handle suspected inappropriate conduct by employees in order to protect the company from liability.

Workplace security measures are those taken by employers to ensure the safety of the people and assets of the business and begin with assessing the possible risks. When the potential risks have been identified, plans for protection of the people and the assets of the organization can be made and implemented. The following sections briefly review security issues with which HR professionals may become involved.

Financial Assets

CFOs are responsible for implementing *internal controls* to ensure that cash and negotiable securities aren't mishandled, along with inventory controls to reduce employee pilferage or customer theft. In most organizations, CFOs implement processes to ensure that purchase commitments at certain dollar levels are reviewed and approved by senior-level managers to prevent the misappropriation of funds. One common control used to ensure the security of financial assets is to define accounting jobs so that more than one person handles different aspects of transactions. For example, the job with responsibility for preparing customer invoices would not also be responsible for opening the mail or making bank deposits. Separating these duties makes it more difficult for an employee to embezzle money.

The internal control requirements of SOX (described later in this chapter) have a major impact on finance operations. These more stringent reporting requirements affect other business functions, including HR, where business processes must be more consistent, reliable, and efficient to conform to internal controls. HR also plays a role in helping companies manage the cultural transformation to higher levels of transparency and financial accountability with change initiatives discussed in Chapter 5.

Physical Assets

HR responsibility for managing physical asset risks focuses on two areas: protecting people from injury and protecting assets from theft or damage. Managing risks from injuries caused by physical assets was described earlier in the chapter. Methods for protecting physical assets from theft or damage can include building security measures such as guards, security cameras, keys or card-key lock systems, and entry barriers such as fences or security gates. The size, nature, and cost of the asset, along with the budget of the organization, determine appropriate methods for protecting these assets.

Information Assets

Managing risk for information assets includes maintaining the confidentiality of information and protecting the loss of personal employee data.

Protection of Confidential Information

The most effective way to protect confidential information from intentional or unintentional distribution by employees is to ensure that they know what the company considers confidential before they're hired. An *intellectual property agreement* (IPA) and/or *nondisclosure agreement* (NDA) is used for this purpose. Because the types of confidential information vary widely between different organizations, it's important that an attorney develop an agreement to meet specific needs. An IPA should identify what the company considers to be confidential information (such as customer lists, financial information, or trade secrets) and how its use is limited by the agreement, as well as how long the information must remain confidential after the agreement expires. The agreement may contain a "nonsolicitation" clause limiting the ability of employees who leave the organization to hire co-workers. IPAs should contain clauses that require employees to describe any discoveries or inventions they may have made prior to entering into the agreement and require that they don't share confidential information from other companies with the new employer or disclose who owns the inventions or discoveries made during the course of employment. Finally, the agreement should state that materials containing confidential information are the property of the company and may not be removed from a given location.

These agreements help prevent employees from sharing confidential proprietary information with other companies or individuals. For these documents to be effective, the organization must advise employees on a regular basis that even inadvertently sharing this information can cause damage.

Although this discussion has been limited to the use of IPAs and NDAs in employment relationships, these documents are equally important when sharing proprietary information with others outside the organization. This can include business partners or others with whom the company shares the information in the course of doing business, such as candidates for jobs during the interview process.

Preventing Data Loss

Data loss can occur as the result of an intentional act (such as hacking, data theft, or sabotage); through the failure of equipment (storage media or hardware), software errors, or inadequate operating procedures; or by accident. Preventing the loss of critical data is the responsibility of the IT function, which ensures the safety of the hardware and software systems used in an organization. The use of enterprise-wide databases that store massive amounts of data from all functions can make data protection a complex process. Many organizations use data-sharing technology to streamline operations internally and, in some cases, to share data externally. This efficiency carries with it greater risk for the unauthorized release of data and has led to the creation of security measures, such as firewalls, that ensure the integrity of the data. A *firewall* is a hardware device or a software program that restricts access to an organization's computer network based on criteria established by the IT function.

Human Assets

Many of the risk-management activities that protect human assets have already been described, including health and safety plans, injury- and illness-prevention plans, and emergency-response plans. Two areas of risk apply almost exclusively to people for discussion here: workplace violence and substance abuse.

Workplace Violence

Workplace violence occurs when an employee with poor behavior control becomes highly stressed. The stress may or may not be work related, but it's often set off by an incident in the workplace. Under OSHA's General Duty Clause, employers are required to be aware of employees exhibiting the signs of possible violent behavior and take steps to prevent its occurrence. Employees who commit acts of violence in the workplace frequently show recognizable signs of stress before they commit the acts. It's up to employers to train managers and supervisors to identify these signs so that employees who are having difficulty can be referred to an employee assistance program (EAP) for counseling or directed to social services if needed. Training managers to recognize and prevent workplace violence is becoming a more common topic for inclusion in management training curricula, along with supervisory skills, sexual-harassment prevention, and other issues.

Some of the more common signs of stress include a change in work habits, a decline in productivity, conflicts with co-workers, depression, and refusing to take responsibility for individual actions.

Even though not everyone who exhibits signs of stress is likely to become violent, any employee who exhibits these signs should be counseled and referred to appropriate professional assistance. As part of the emergency response plan described in the "Managing

Business Continuity Risks" section, a plan for responding to an incident of workplace violence should be developed and communicated to employees. This plan, in addition to other requirements, can include code words to be used when employees feel threatened so they can alert co-workers to call for help, along with a resource book for managers and supervisors that contains referral agencies for different types of issues to assist employees who are troubled.

Substance Abuse

Government statistics indicate that more than 70 percent of substance abusers have jobs. They're all working in someone's business—some of them might work in your organization. Substance abusers increase costs for employers due to tardiness and absenteeism, increased errors, accidents, and increases in health-care costs and workers' compensation claims. When a substance abuser's job is to drive a semi-trailer or operate heavy equipment, an employer also faces increased costs for injuries or damages that occur as a result of an accident. If the employer is a federal contractor subject to the Drug-Free Workplace Act, continued substance abuse at the workplace could result in the loss of the contract.

There are six components for an effective substance abuse program in the workplace:

- Support for the substance-abuse policy from top management. (As with any policy, this is the most important component.)

- A written policy clearly stating that substance abuse won't be tolerated in the workplace.

- Training for managers and supervisors to ensure that they understand and can explain the policy, are able to recognize the signs of substance abuse, understand the importance of documenting poor performance, and know what steps to take when they become aware of a substance abuser.

- Education programs for new hires and employees to inform them of the policy and explain the consequences for violations. If the organization has a drug-testing program, it should be explained prior to employment and during orientation. Employees should be made aware of resources in the community or through the EAP, as well as the effects of substance abuse on themselves, their families, and the costs to the employer.

- An EAP that provides confidential counseling for substance abusers as needed.

- An ongoing, fair, and consistent drug-testing program that complies with federal, state, and local laws and union contracts. The program should identify who will be tested, when tests will occur, which drugs will be tested for, and what happens if the test is positive.

Drug-testing Programs

There are several decisions to make when a company decides to implement a drug-testing program. First, the program must be implemented in a fair and consistent manner to avoid charges of discrimination. Next, the company must decide what type of testing will be done:

Pre-employment Testing   Lawful only after an offer of employment has been made. Before beginning a testing program, the employer must decide which applicants will be tested. This decision may be based on the type of work done in different jobs; for example, a company may decide to test all employees who operate machinery. The test must be conducted fairly and consistently on all applicants for the designated jobs.

Random Drug Testing   Done on an arbitrary, unscheduled basis. To make the testing truly random and reduce the risk of legal challenges, employers may want to use a computer program that randomly selects employees. Random drug testing should be implemented with legal counsel to avoid violating privacy rights unnecessarily.

Scheduled Drug Testing   Can be useful when monitoring the rehabilitation progress of employees but has limited value because employees who may be currently using drugs are generally able to stop long enough before the test to clear their systems of the drugs.

Reasonable-Suspicion Drug Testing   Can be used any time there has been an accident in which an employee's actions contributed to the cause of the accident in the workplace or when a supervisor suspects, based on behavior, that an employee is under the influence of drugs.

Regardless of the substance-abuse testing schedule that is used, it's important to keep in mind that implementation must be fair and equitable to avoid charges of discrimination. If employers choose to test specific job categories, then all employees in those categories must be subjected to the testing process. If random testing is used, all employees in the selected category must be included in the selection group.

HR professionals must also keep in mind that, under the ADA, current users of illegal drugs are specifically excluded from protection, while current abusers of alcohol aren't automatically denied protection. Regardless, employers may take adverse action if the behavior negatively affects an employee's ability to do the job. Entering recovery is a trigger for protection under the ADA for both groups. For more information on the ADA and substance abuse, visit its question and answer page at `www.ada.gov/qandaeng.htm`.

Return-to-Work (RTW) Programs

Whether the absence was the result of a work-related illness or injury or another cause, a return-to-work policy can reduce the risk of re-injury. Some organizations develop a comprehensive policy that includes accident reporting procedures, definitions of various terms, types of leaves covered by the RTW program, and administrative procedures in their procedures, while others develop separate policies and procedures for different aspects. Organizations will develop policies tailored to their specific needs, but all should include a clear statement of compliance with specific legal requirements of Family and Medical Leave Act (FMLA) medical certifications, workers' compensation, or other laws that may apply. The procedure should answer basic questions for supervisors and employees, such as the following:

- What is the goal or objective of the RTW program?
- Who is eligible?

- Are there policy or procedure differences between a work-related medical leave of absence (MLOA) and a non-work-related MLOA?

- What is the impact of an MLOA on employee compensation and benefits?

- Under what conditions will the organization accommodate modified work assignments that allow employees to transition back to work before they have recovered completely?

- What are the employee's responsibilities with regard to the leave and RTW?

- What are the employer's responsibilities with regard to the leave and RTW?

- What are the responsibilities of the HR department with regard to the leave and RTW?

- What type of medical release does the organization require prior to accepting workers back on the job?

Elements of an RTW Program   Once the previous questions have been adequately addressed, designing the elements of a RTW process becomes necessary. Examples include the following:

Modified Duty Assignment   Because many injured workers are quite willing and able to perform some but not all of the essential duties of a job, modifying specific tasks or functions may be necessary to allow an employee to return to work. In fact, workers' compensation studies have shown that employees who are offered modified/light duty assignments return to full duty more quickly than injured workers who incur lost time. This translates into a lower overall injury cost and allows the employee to get back into the routine of work much more quickly. Modified duty may include eliminating essential functions or creating a short-term job for the employee until they're able to return to full duty.

Having accurate job descriptions is necessary to engage in this process, as the employee and doctor will use them to return the employee to work with the proper restrictions.

Reasonable Accommodations   Reasonable accommodation is similar to modified duty, with two very major distinctions. Modified duty is typically a short-term option used for injured workers who are expected to be able to return to full duty, and an employer need not create a light-duty position for a "non-occupationally injured employee" as part of reasonable accommodation efforts. The process of identifying reasonable accommodation includes discussing options such as a reduced schedule, additional unpaid time off, and reassignment to a vacant position for which the disabled individual is qualified. It very well could also be modifying the essential functions of the job if that action wouldn't impose undue hardship on the employer.

Independent Medical Exam (IME)   Fit-for-duty exams are effective tools to use to determine if an employee is capable of returning to work without causing harm to themselves or others. These types of exams allow for an impartial review of the injured employee's medical status. For employers, IMEs can help to prevent fraud and deal with excessive extensions of time off due to lack of a proper diagnosis or treatment. For employees, these types of exams are helpful when there are conflicting reports of their needs or an employee doesn't agree with a doctor's findings.

A clear, legally compliant RTW policy mitigates the risk of inadvertent errors by managers and helps ensure that all employees are treated equitably when returning from medical leaves. In addition, requiring a medical release prior to an employee's return reduces the risk of reinjury.

Managing Business Continuity Risks

As noted throughout this chapter, many identified risks have the potential to disrupt business operations. Planning for these eventualities is a process known as *business continuity planning* (BCP), which results in a written document used to describe possible disruptions to operations and actions to be taken to minimize those disruptions and assign responsibility for executing the plan to specific individuals.

A BCP is often an umbrella that includes other emergency plans, such as the emergency-response plan and disaster-recovery plan. In some organizations, these terms are interchangeable, while in others each describes a specific process. For the purposes of this discussion, the BCP is treated as an umbrella covering different aspects of the business-continuity process.

A successful BCP begins with a commitment from the CEO so that sufficient resources are provided for the process. When the CEO is committed to the process, a planning committee that includes representatives from each business function is appointed and defines the scope of the plan. At this point, the committee assesses the risks facing the organization:

Assess and Prioritize Organizational Risks   By their very nature, emergencies occur with little or no warning and can devastate individuals, single organizations, or whole communities. As presented earlier in this chapter, there are several different types of emergencies to consider when planning response, recovery, and continuity processes:

- Environmental disasters such as earthquakes, fires, tornados, hurricanes, toxic gas releases, chemical spills, and so on

- Organized and/or deliberate disruptions such as theft, labor disputes, sabotage, terrorism, and so on

- Loss of utilities and services caused by power failures, oil shortages, communication-system failures, and so on

- Equipment or system failure such as a breakdown in the production line, equipment failure, or internal loss of power

- Serious information security incidents such as loss of customer data to hackers or failure of the IT system

- Other emergency situations such as workplace violence, legal problems, the unexpected loss of key employees, public-transportation strikes, violations of health or safety regulations, and so on

The BCP planning process identifies those risks most likely to occur based on the organization's location, industry, and other considerations. The risks are then assessed for the level of disruption each would cause and the impact on different business functions, as well as an estimate of the cost to reestablish or maintain them in the event of each risk. Information systems are so integral to operating ability that most businesses will need to assess the impact of each risk on information and communication systems. Finally, each identified risk is evaluated and prioritized for its impact on operations.

Identify Vital Processes and Key Employees Another element of the BCP is a review of each functional business area. This review identifies vital business processes, key employees necessary to maintain operations in each critical area, and records essential for the continuation of the business. If emergency plans currently exist, the planning team will review them at this time and determine what revisions are needed for different risks. At this stage, the BCP team will identify critical vendors and suppliers and how to move forward if one or more of them are incapacitated. Alternative locations and equipment resources for use in the event that the building is destroyed are also identified.

Emergency-Response Plan An important piece of the planning process is to develop an *emergency-response plan* (ERP) describing how the organization will react to different emergency situations or natural disasters if they occur. The OSHA emergency action plan (previously described) will be part of the ERP, describing how employees and visitors who are on-site during an emergency will be evacuated or, in cases where it's safer to remain at the workplace, sheltered in place until it's safe to leave the worksite. The ERP identifies a response team, assigning specific responsibilities to each team member, describes how vital records and information will be protected, and establishes an emergency communication plan. Depending on the type of emergency, the communication plan can include a public-relations component and identify individuals who will represent the organization to customers, vendors, suppliers, and the media.

The ERP describes how computer systems and information will be protected and accessible. Prudent business practice includes ongoing off-site storage system backups and copies of records and legal documents needed to maintain operations in an emergency.

Disaster-Recovery Plan A *disaster-recovery plan* (DRP) describes activities that take place once the initial response to the emergency is over.

Planning for this phase develops alternatives for reestablishing operations when property, processes, information systems, and people have been disrupted. If the building is unusable, what are the arrangements for temporary facilities? If the computer systems are inoperable, how and where will the off-site backups be reinstalled to continue operations? If transportation systems and roadways are damaged, how will employees get to work?

One important factor to consider in the DRP is compliance with SOX requirements for information safety. This requirement is discussed in Chapter 3.

Another element to include in the DRP is a list of alternative vendors, suppliers, and service providers that can provide materials or support when normal sources are affected by emergencies and unable, either temporarily or permanently, to continue in the aftermath. This may make the difference in an organization's ability to continue servicing customers after an emergency.

Continuity of Operations Plan   The *continuity of operations plan* (COOP) generally refers to plans created to move from the disaster-recovery phase, during which critical business functions are maintained but normal operations may not be taking place, back to pre-emergency service operating levels.

Maintaining Business-Continuity Plans   Too often, organizations go through the process of creating plans and, once completed, never look at them again, assuming that the plans will work when needed. A critical component of a BCP is the need to test the plan, train employees to use the plan, and revisit it annually to keep the information current. An evaluation of the test results provides information about any necessary changes so the plan can be refined.

Many of the threats to continued business operations described throughout this chapter can be managed in the framework of the BCP process. A few of the threats may be handled in different ways or require additional consideration:

Unexpected Loss of Key Employees   Ensuring that the business survives the unexpected loss of a key employee is the point of a *succession plan*. These plans identify employees with leadership potential and prepare them for senior and executive management roles through the use of high-potential employees (HiPo) programs or other development plans. These programs are fully discussed in Chapters 4 and 5.

Biological Threats   An additional consideration for a plan to maintain operations during a serious pandemic is that many of the people who would, in other disasters or emergencies, be the ones called on to maintain the business may themselves be incapacitated. One strategy that was used during the SARS outbreak of 2002–03 to reduce the impact of SARS on the workforce was to create redundant employee teams and isolate them from each other, assigning each team to a different work location and rotating the teams between sites on a schedule that coincided with the incubation period of the virus. For the duration of the threat, personal contact between members of the different teams was prohibited to enhance the chances that at least one of the teams would survive intact during the outbreak without one or more members being subject to quarantine.

Terrorism   In the aftermath of a terrorist attack, many employees may be fearful of returning to normal activities such as commuting or traveling. A company that is the target of a terrorist attack or is directly affected in another way may want to include some form of counseling for employees who lost friends or co-workers during the attack or who live or work where the attack occurred.

Clearly, a wide range of situations will benefit from the preplanning of the BCP process. HR professionals can play a key role in managing emergencies by participating in planning activities and maintaining accurate employee information that will be needed during the execution of the plans.

Once the risks have been identified and plans have been developed, it's imperative that the affected employees have a clear understanding of the plan components through communication and training. Effective and frequent communication of the BCP allows the employees to respond to emergency situations properly, mitigate the risks associated with the crisis, and handle emergency situations when the owner/manager isn't present. Methods include classroom training of the procedures, hands-on training such as drills, and simulation of disasters such as data breaches and loss of power.

Managing Workplace Privacy Risks

As described earlier in this chapter, there are many legitimate reasons for employers to monitor workplace activities—to ensure the safety of employees, for example, or to maintain security of trade secrets. There are risks to doing so, including lower morale among employees, abuses of the surveillance by unethical employees, and damage to personal employee belongings from physical searches. Employers must balance security needs against employee privacy concerns to avoid an atmosphere of distrust that negatively impacts productivity. Creating this balance requires employers to communicate with employees about the need for any type of monitoring activity and to clearly explain what activities are subject to monitoring, when they will occur, and how the information will be used.

Whatever type of monitoring program is established, it's important for employers to preserve employee dignity. This may not make monitoring popular with employees but should help reduce the lack of trust that may be created by the program. To avoid legal issues, a written policy describing the employer's practices is needed, and should include compliance measures identified through court interpretations and the Electronic Communications Privacy Act of 1986.

Electronic Communications Privacy Act of 1986 (ECPA)   The ECPA updated Title 18 of the U.S. code to bring an older law current with technology by adding electronic communication to the list of prohibited interceptions. Although the original law was enacted to control law-enforcement wiretaps, the ECPA amendment added civil penalties that affect an employer's ability to monitor employee communication. The law permits employers to monitor communication that occurs in their normal course of business and when employees give consent.

Reasonable Expectation of Privacy   A key consideration for courts in cases involving workplace searches is whether employees had a *reasonable expectation of privacy* based on factors such as whether there was a privacy policy in place and how an employer handled similar situations in the past. The combination of a legitimate business reason to conduct the search and a clearly stated policy that the employer can demonstrate was communicated to employees will help justify a search.

Privacy Policies   An effective privacy policy makes an unambiguous statement that the employer reserves the right to search, describes the activities and resources the organization will monitor, and tells employees that there should be no expectation of privacy. Specific information about what could trigger a search and how the employer will proceed should be included as well. The policy should be specific about the following:

   Monitoring Telephone Calls   Generally, employers aren't required to provide notice before monitoring business-related calls (although some states require that both parties to a call be aware of any monitoring that occurs). The monitoring must terminate as soon as the employer becomes aware that the call is personal.

Monitoring Email or Instant Messages   When accessing employee emails or instant messages (IMs), it's best to have a legitimate business reason for doing so. Policies should make it clear that email and IMs sent using the employer's equipment are the property of the employer and may be monitored or reviewed at any time. In addition, protecting customer data and information should be one component of an email privacy policy. For example, the ability of an employee to forward confidential financial or medical information should be controlled.

Some attorneys consider an email policy important enough to be a separate policy that is signed by every employee.

Monitoring Internet and Computer Use   Many issues affect employee use of the Internet, including demand for bandwidth during peak hours of operation, access to inappropriate websites, and downloading viruses, spyware, or other potentially harmful files. The Internet use policy should include a statement of acceptable uses, reasons to restrict access or use, and whether the employer allows personal use. The policy should also state that the employer reserves the right to review data stored on hard drives and require that employees provide any current password information to a designated employee.

Monitoring the Use of Social Media   Prohibiting use of social media while employees are at work is difficult at best. Smartphones allow near-instant access, so making a statement to employees about their reasonable expectation of privacy (or lack thereof) on company-issued phones and laptops is a step toward control. Furthermore, it's important to issue guidelines for acceptable social media site use, both on and off the job. For example, discouraging the use of company-specific information or the sharing of confidential corporate data in posts is reasonable. The key is to be clear on what the expectations are for the employee.

Monitoring the Use of Cell Phone Cameras   The use of personal cell phones in the workplace can be disruptive and difficult to monitor in general, and the advent of camera phones presents even more challenges for employers. Cell phone cameras can be used surreptitiously to take inappropriate photographs of co-workers that expose the employer to harassment claims, make copies of confidential documents, or photograph proprietary work processes or new product development.

An outright ban of cell phone cameras in the workplace is difficult to enforce, but stating clearly situations the employer considers inappropriate (such as in bathrooms, on customer premises, or in sensitive work areas) can be effective.

Video Surveillance   In some workplaces, installing cameras may be viewed as a necessity: for example, in small, all-night retail stores where one employee works alone late at night. In other situations, the need for video surveillance may not be as clear. Employers who determine that video surveillance is necessary for their business operation should clearly state the reasons for the surveillance, the circumstances in which tapes will be reviewed, and how the information will be used.

Video surveillance of bathrooms or locations where employees may change their clothes isn't appropriate.

Searching Property   As with other privacy policies, searches should be conducted for a legitimate business reason, because random searches conducted for no apparent reason are difficult to justify in court. Narrowing a search to employees suspected of theft, or to those who had an opportunity to commit the theft based on other information such as video surveillance tapes, is preferable. Although some employers may be tempted to search an employee's body, this is inappropriate. If this is believed to be necessary, law enforcement should be brought in to conduct the search.

A search policy should clearly state what types of situations will trigger a search, how it will be conducted, what types of property are liable for search (for example, company property such as a desk, an office, a cubicle, a locker, and so on, or personal property such as a purse or car).

Table 8.13 provides some questions to consider before conducting a search.

TABLE 8.13   Questions to ask before searching

Question	Yes	No
Is there a legitimate business reason to search this employee?	X	
Does the employee have a reasonable expectation of privacy?		X
Is there another way to find out if this employee engaged in an improper activity?		X
Is there a workplace search policy in place?	X	
Are all employees aware of the search policy?	X	
Is this a random search?		X

If the answer to any of these questions is different in a particular situation, it may be advisable to look for another way to collect the information needed.

🌐 **Real World Scenario**

Email Monitoring: *Fraser v. Nationwide Mutual Insurance Company*

Richard Fraser was employed as an independent insurance agent for Nationwide Mutual Insurance when he was terminated in September 1998. Nationwide claimed it terminated Mr. Fraser for disloyal activities—contacting competitors and asking whether they would be interested in acquiring some of Nationwide's policyholders. When it learned of the contacts, Nationwide searched Mr. Fraser's email records on its main file server and found evidence of additional disloyalty. On the basis of this information, Nationwide terminated him.

Mr. Fraser filed an action claiming the search was a violation of two restrictions of the ECPA. First, he claimed that interception of email is prohibited by the act. The court found that because the email wasn't intercepted during transmission, no violation occurred. He also claimed that the search of his email violated ECPA prohibitions against access of electronically stored communication. The court found in this instance as well that because Nationwide provided and administered the email service on which Mr. Fraser's email was stored, the search of the email was allowable.

The Third Circuit Court of Appeals upheld summary judgment in favor of Nationwide.

Employers must be aware of legal restrictions on workplace-monitoring policies. In addition to the federal ECPA controls (described previously in this chapter) and state laws enacted to protect individual privacy rights, common-law torts for invasion of privacy must also be considered when making the decision to implement a monitoring program. These common law torts use the "reasonable person" standard to measure whether an intrusion is highly offensive and causes harm, is publicized without a legitimate reason, or knowingly puts an individual into a false light in public. The courts often support an employer's right to monitor their employees in the workplace.

NOTE   As discussed in Chapter 6, the Health Insurance Portability and Accountability Act (HIPAA) imposes requirements on some employers to protect the privacy of personal health information for employees.

Metrics: Measuring Results

Measuring the effectiveness of risk-management activities can be challenging. The key, as with measurement in all other HR functional areas, is to determine what kind of meaningful information can be provided to management in order to improve the effectiveness of risk-management programs:

Business Impact Measures   The effectiveness of RM programs can be measured with a return on investment (ROI) calculation to validate the program's benefits.

Evaluating risk-management programs can be a relatively simple matter: compile statistics on a regular basis, and compare them over time. For example, if employees are lax about following safety procedures, establishing a baseline number of violations occurring before implementing a training program and then compiling statistics on a regular basis to determine whether the training reduced violations indicates whether the training was successful. The same metric can be used to keep track of whatever RM issues are of greatest concern in any organization. Whether it's incidents of sexual harassment before and after a prevention program, the number of cyber attacks before and after improvements to the network firewall, or warehouse losses before and after installing a surveillance system, these simple measures validate the benefits of the program or indicate areas requiring adjustment or further prevention activities.

Another useful measurement for risk-management purposes might be to track the reasons for employee resignations from the company. This provides information for improvements to whatever area is the source of resignations by valued employees to reduce future recruiting and training costs and prevent unwanted turnover.

Another example of a useful metric that measures program effectiveness is OSHA's recordable case rate formula to calculate the incidence rate of ergonomic injuries before the program is implemented and taking periodic measures as the program progresses to determine the reduction in injuries. The recordable case rate formula uses a base of 100 full-time employees working 40 hours per week, 50 weeks per year, or 200,000 hours. Figure 8.1 illustrates the formula for calculating the ergonomic injury rate before implementation of the program, when 53 injuries occurred, and after implementation, when the injuries were reduced to 35. The example assumes that an individual employee works 2,000 hours per year (40 hours per week times 50 weeks per year).

FIGURE 8.1   Quantitative analysis of ergonomic injury program

$$\text{Ergonomic Injury Rate} = \frac{\text{Number of Ergonomic Injuries} \times 200{,}000}{\text{Total hours worked by all employees during the period}}$$

Total number of employees: 350 FTE
Number of Ergonomic injuries = 53

$$\text{EIR} = \frac{53 \times 200{,}000}{350 \times 2{,}000} = \frac{10{,}600{,}000}{700{,}000} = 15.15\%$$

Total number of employees: 350 FTE
Number of Ergonomic injuries = 35

$$\text{EIR} = \frac{35 \times 200{,}000}{350 \times 2{,}000} = \frac{7{,}000{,}000}{700{,}000} = 10\%$$

Tactical Accountability Measures   Areas for HR accountability in the RM function could include a measure of the number of job descriptions that include ADA physical and mental requirements to total job descriptions in the company as a predictor of risk for ADA discrimination claims.

Global Considerations

Organizations operating in a global environment must be aware of risks their operations face in locations outside the United States and comply with occupational safety and health laws that may differ significantly from the OSH Act and other federal requirements. Although those laws are country-specific, there is a movement to improve working conditions on a global level, and several organizations focus on the issues. Two of them, the World Health Organization (WHO) and the International Labour Organization (ILO), have established programs with this goal in mind.

The WHO uses a global collaboration network to promote its strategy for improved occupational safety and health throughout the world. The strategy provides evidence of the extent of occupational illness and injury and related costs to governments and businesses, supports the development of infrastructure to improve workplace safety and health, and supports labor organizations in the quest to improve worker health. More information is available on the WHO website at www.who.int/occupational_health/en/.

The ILO is an agency of the United Nations with a broad mandate to promote social justice and human rights in addition to establishing internationally recognized standards for labor rights, including occupational safety and health. The ILO issues policy conventions that set standards for safe practices in this area. In addition, the agency collects and disseminates statistics used to promote safe workplace conditions. Information about ILO programs is available at www.ilo.org.

Managing global risks requires an understanding of what risks are endemic to the regions and countries in which organizations operate, as well as the risks that occur without regard to national boundaries, such as information security, terrorism, and the spread of contagious diseases. The OSHA website provides links to several international agreements the federal government has made with other countries at www.osha.gov/international/index.html.

In addition to the differences in health and safety compliance requirements, American corporations employing workers around the globe must also be aware of differences in data privacy management. Data-privacy regulations are much stricter in other countries than they are in the United States. Employers shouldn't assume that if they're in compliance with U.S. data-privacy regulations, they're compliant in other countries. For example, managers of American organizations who access certain personal information about employees in the United Kingdom could find themselves in violation of U.K. data-privacy laws.

Summary

As an HR function, Risk Management identifies, assesses, manages, and reviews people-related organizational risks related to legal compliance, safety and health, security, business continuity, and workplace privacy. A number of tools are available for assessing and managing risk, such as HR audits, workplace investigations, and plans such as safety and health-management plans that provide guidance for workplace hazards. Occupational health and safety has been a source of concern to workers and physicians for centuries, but until relatively recently, employers weren't required to protect workers from dangerous environments and were rarely held accountable when death, injury, or illness occurred as a result of hazards in the businesses they managed. The OSH Act of 1970 was the first comprehensive, effective legislation that required employers to provide safe and healthful workplaces for their employees and provided an enforcement process that penalized employers who didn't comply with safety standards. OSHA has been successful where other attempts to do the same thing have failed because Congress provided strong enforcement powers to the agency.

In the past, employers were also not willing to compensate workers who were injured during the course of their jobs and made full use of the "unholy trinity" of common-law doctrines to avoid financial responsibility for injured workers. In 1911, Wisconsin was the first state to provide workers with a more equitable process for determining compensation due to them for injuries suffered during the course of their work by passing the first workers' compensation law. This enabled workers to receive compensation for injuries and illnesses without having to use the court system, which was, at that time, heavily weighted in favor of employers.

OSHA has been a key proponent and motivator in identifying workplace health and safety hazards and in developing processes designed to protect workers in a variety of situations. Once employers realized the financial benefits of creating safer working environments, they developed employee benefits designed to enhance health and safety programs, such as employee assistance and wellness programs that serve employee needs as well as add value to the business bottom line.

Security—of information, individuals, and organizations—becomes more complex and challenging each day as new technologies are developed. HR professionals must be able to provide employers with the tools needed to protect them without infringing on employee privacy rights. In the aftermath of devastating natural disasters and acts of terror, preparing to continue business operations is an essential responsibility of leadership teams in every organization. HR professionals contribute to this process through their awareness of the issues involved and participate by providing information necessary to respond, recover, and return to normal operations.

Exam Essentials

Understand the risk-management process.   Risk-management activities begin with identifying potential risks; each identified risk is then assessed for the level of risk to the organization and cost of mitigation, transfer, or avoidance. Risks are prioritized and managed to reduce exposure and financial impact in the event a loss occurs.

Be familiar with federal legislation and regulations for workplace health and safety. The major federal legislation for this functional area is the Occupational Safety and Health Act of 1970. This law created OSHA, which develops and enforces workplace health and safety standards.

Understand the safety needs of organizations, and be able to design, implement, and evaluate a safety program; train employees; and evaluate program effectiveness. Employers are responsible for ensuring that those who work for them have a workplace that is free from danger. To provide this, employers must be committed to a safe workplace, involve employees in meeting safety standards by giving them the information they need to be safe in the workplace, and provide training for the equipment and materials employees will use to perform their jobs.

Understand business-continuity plans, and be able to contribute HR's perspective when creating a plan. Being prepared to protect organizational assets during natural or manmade disasters can mean the difference between an organization's survival or demise when an emergency occurs. One of the key assets to be protected during an emergency is the workforce. HR can contribute valuable input with regard to employee communication plans and develop training programs that will help to keep the workforce intact in an emergency.

Understand the purpose of an emergency-response plan, and be able to design and implement one and evaluate its effectiveness. The emergency-response plan is created in advance of an emergency. It describes what roles are to be played in the emergency and who will play them, communicates to all employees a place to meet in the event of an evacuation, and assigns responsibility for implementing the plan in the event of an emergency.

Understand organizational and workforce security needs, and be able to develop, implement, and evaluate workplace security plans. Both employers and employees must feel secure in the work environment. Employees must be safe in order to work productively; employers must feel secure that the assets of the business will continue to be available for use in the business.

Review Questions

You can find the answers in Appendix A.

1. An OSHA violation with substantial probability of death or serious physical harm as the result of a workplace hazard is which of the following?

    A. Willful

    B. Serious

    C. Repeat

    D. De-minimus

2. Under OSHA regulations, employers do *not* have the right to do which of the following?

    A. Refuse to allow an OSHA inspector on the premises

    B. Request a variance to an OSHA standard while waiting for repairs

    C. Consult with OSHA to correct hazards without fear of a citation and penalty

    D. File a *Notice of Contest* within 30 days of the citation

3.   What is the *best* way to ensure that employees comply with the Drug-Free Workplace Act?

    A. Develop and publish a written policy.

    B. Notify employees about contract conditions.

    C. Establish penalties for drug arrests.

    D. Establish an awareness program.

4.   The 16-year-old son of one of your friends is looking for a summer job and has been offered a job at a coal mine. Which of the following makes this illegal?

    A. Mine Safety and Health Act

    B. Occupational Safety and Health Act

    C. Fair Labor Standards Acts

    D. Hazard Communication

5.   The company receptionist has always been cheerful and warm when greeting customers and has taken the initiative to do what needed to be done without waiting to be told. She has always kept the front desk tidy and presentable for visitors. Over the last few weeks, the receptionist has become moody and called in sick several times complaining of headaches, and the reception area looks disorganized all the time. This receptionist is showing classic signs of which of the following?

    A. Stress

    B. Job dissatisfaction

    C. Substance abuse

    D. SARS

6.   The union rep has requested copies of all the incident reports filed during the last year. You are required to do what?

    A. Furnish the copies by the end of the day

    B. Furnish copies within 15 calendar days but only of the "Tell Us About the Case" section

    C. Furnish the copies by the end of the next business day

    D. Furnish copies of the "Tell Us About the Case" section within 7 calendar days

7.   An employee-assistance plan will *not* assist employees with what?

    A. Outplacement counseling

    B. Substance abuse

    C. Gambling problems

    D. Legal assistance

8.   Which of the following injuries or illnesses is considered work related?

    A. An employee twisted an ankle at an aerobics class the company sponsored.

    B. An employee fell while taking a shower in the dressing room after a work shift.

    C. An employee is hit by a car in the parking lot while walking toward the building.

    D. An employee disregards the safety procedures and is cut by a table saw.

9. An effective safety and health-management plan does *not* include which of the following?

    A. Senior management support

    B. Ongoing worksite analysis

    C. Regular OSHA inspections

    D. Active hazard-prevention program

10. How can an employer determine whether a job creates an ergonomic hazard for an employee?

    A. Review and analyze the OSHA logs.

    B. Review and analyze the workers' compensation records.

    C. Review the MSDS.

    D. Observe the incumbent performing the job duties.

11. An emphasis on bilingual safety communication represents which of the following OSH objectives?

    A. An outreach objective of OSHA's Diverse Workforce strategy

    B. An emphasis on safety training required under OSHA's general industry standard

    C. Compliance with a model program

    D. Requirement for enrollment in the voluntary protection program

12. Which of the following groups have *not* been identified for protection under the Americans with Disabilities Act as it relates to substance abuse?

    A. Current abusers of alcohol

    B. Current users of legal drugs

    C. Current users of illegal drugs

    D. Recovering addicts

13. Millie is an injured worker who has been back to work on modified duty for approximately 13 months. Which of the following return-to-work strategies would best help Millie get back to full duty?

    A. Reasonably accommodating her into a more permanent position

    B. Paying to have her evaluated by an independent medical examiner

    C. Continuing the modified duty assignment until she is released to full duty

    D. Terminating her employment as she is no longer qualified to do the work for which she was hired

14. Which of the following standards is the most frequently cited type of OSHA violation?

    A. Construction

    B. Maritime

C. Whistle-blower

D. Agriculture

15. Which of the following standards requires employers to provide employees with information about physical and health hazards related to chemical use in the workplace?

   A. The control of hazardous energy

   B. General duty clause

   C. Hazard communication

   D. Personal protective equipment

16. Which of the following injuries would be considered work-related for purposes of reporting?

   A. An employee fell in the parking lot while playing a voluntary game of basketball on his lunch break.

   B. An employee sprained his ankle while loading a truck on the dock.

   C. An employee choked on a sandwich while eating her lunch.

   D. An employee caught a cold from a co-worker.

17. A key consideration for courts in cases involving workplace searches is which of the following?

   A. Whether the employer had a policy regarding workplace searches

   B. How the employer handled similar situations in the past

   C. The specific laws of the state where the employer is conducting business

   D. Whether the employee had a reasonable expectation of privacy

18. Which of the following is *not* an example of an environmental health hazard?

   A. Electrical currents

   B. Workplace violence

   C. Biological hazards

   D. Gas fumes

19. Poor ergonomic design would result in which of the following types of injury?

   A. Stress

   B. Musculoskeletal disorder (MSD)

   C. A nonrecordable injury

   D. A recordable injury

20. If an employee files a complaint with OSHA, under which of the following would they be protected?

   A. Emergency action

   B. Physical environmental hazard

   C. General-duty clause

   D. Whistle-blower protection

Appendix A

Answers to Review Questions

Chapter 2: Core Knowledge Requirements for HR Professionals

1. A. A needs assessment is conducted to determine what is required to solve a problem, including whether training is the appropriate intervention. If, for example, network crashes are the cause of the low productivity, training will not solve the problem. Lesson plans (B) are created during the design stage of training discussed in Chapter 5. Talking to other managers to validate the situation (C) may be included in the needs assessment along with other factors. The training method is selected (D) during the development phase discussed in Chapter 5.

2. C. A talent-management program is a comprehensive strategy to workforce management. This approach includes planning for future needs, recruiting qualified candidates, creating compensation and retention strategies, developing employees, managing performance, and cultivating a positive culture. A succession plan (A) is part of the workforce-planning element of a talent-management program. Knowledge management (B) focuses on building systems that retain corporate knowledge accessible as needed by the organization.

3. B. A business case lays out the desired result of an action or program, presents alternative solutions, describes possible risks from both implementing and not implementing the action, and defines the criteria used to measure success. ROI (A) and CBA (C) may be included as part of the business case, and a SWOT analysis (D) may have identified the need for a program or action.

4. C. Maslow's hierarchy of needs is a theory developed to explain what motivates workers. The levels are physiological, safety, social, esteem, and self-actualization. Growth is a need level identified by Alderfer in the ERG theory, which is based on Maslow's work. Social, safety, and self-actualization are all from Mazlow; growth is Alderfer.

5. B. Assuming that the nature of the previous conversations with Rachel has been informal, the first step is a verbal warning, where Rachel is advised that this is the first step in the disciplinary process and failure to improve will lead to further disciplinary action, up to and including termination. The first written warning (A) takes place after a verbal warning. A decision-making day (C) is usually the final step prior to termination. Coaching (D) is an

informal means of talking to employees about performance problems and generally occurs prior to a verbal warning.

6. B. A diversity initiative is designed to increase diversity in an organization. Diversity training educates employees about the cultural and social differences in other cultures and is designed to increase the comfort level of employees (A and D). A benefit of diversity is increased organizational creativity (C).

7. C. Data for employee expense reports is maintained by the accounting department. An HRIS system can be used to collect and track employee data for various uses, including EEO-1 reporting, time and attendance, and other employee records.

8. B. The median is the middle value when values are arranged from high to low. Half the numbers are higher than the median; half are lower. The mean (A) is calculated by adding up the values and dividing by the number of values. The mode (C) is the value that occurs most frequently in a set of numbers. The moving average (D) keeps data current by dropping the oldest data when new data is added.

9. A. The correct focus of a job analysis is the job itself, not the incumbent in the job. Performance management focuses on the person in the job (B). An analysis may use a number of sources in addition to task inventories and questionnaires (C), including interviews, observation, and supervisory input. The required qualifications should be related to the essential functions of the job to avoid complaints of discrimination (D).

10. B. As part of the risk assessment, inconsistent policies have been identified (A), a plan for reducing risk has been developed (C), and management has reviewed the plan for reducing risks (D). After the assessment is complete, the company may decide to purchase insurance, self-insure, or mitigate the risk by making operational changes.

11. C. Cultural competence considers the diversity efforts necessary to achieve corporate aims such as reflecting the population and increasing the applicant candidate pool. It measures the ability of a company to function effectively in the context of these diverse beliefs. Conflict management training is one example of an HR behavior that addresses an organization's cultural competency.

12. A. The ability to interpret and apply information related to internal sources allows HR to respond to specific elements of an organization's strategic plan. For example, understanding how an HRIS system can integrate with an accounting database is one example of cross-functional strategic decisions. Scanning the legal and regulatory environment (B), analyzing industry changes (C), and staying abreast of technological advances (D) are all examples of external forces that impact a strategic plan.

13. D. A multigenerational workforce is one example of the diversity represented in the workplace today. Bringing in new points of view for strategic decision making and needs identification (A), the ability to access the knowledge of a broad range of workers (B), and reflecting the ever-changing face of the customers (C) are three of the benefits of having an older workforce. A multi-generational workforce does not directly impact organizational productivity.

14. C. Electronic or e-learning encompasses many forms of synchronous and asynchronous training (D). Mobile and self-directed learning (A and B) are two examples of e-learning principles. E-learning is discussed in more detail in Chapter 5.

15. D. The use of a variety of tools to gather employee feedback enables employers to measure employee levels of engagement. The use of anonymous surveys, topical focus groups, and employee interviews all provide insight into both individual and organizational needs. Intuition is rarely a legally defensible methodology for use in HR, and focus groups are not the best choice for measuring individual needs.

16. A. An income statement, also referred to as a profit and loss statement, provides financial information about revenue and expenses in a set reporting period. The statement of cash flow (B) communicates the ways in which monies came in and out of the organization, and the balance sheet (C) is a thumbnail sketch of assets, liabilities, and equity at a certain time.

17. B. A product-based structure is useful for an organization with multiple well-defined product lines. The structure and subsequent job responsibilities are divided by product line, rather than shared company-wide. The functional structure (A) is the more traditional format where the organization is divided by departments such as production and sales. A divisional structure (C) groups the company based on market or industry, useful for decentralized divisions. A flat line structure (D) is a different term for a seamless organization, one in which hierarchies do not exist.

18. D. Manufacturers, importers, processors, and distributors of toxic chemicals must keep records related to hazardous material exposures, including claims of occupational diseases, for 30 years from the report date.

19. C. Job analysis and the subsequent job descriptions provide the building blocks for all other HR activities. Clearly identifying the output and skills necessary to accomplish each job allows for proper EEO compliance (D), job pricing, recruiting, and other HR functions (A and B).

20. B. Measures of central tendency such as mean average, moving average, and weighted average are useful when an organization must include outdated information in its analysis. Typically, more weight is assigned to the more current data; or, as new data is added, older criteria are dropped. This allows for a more accurate reflection of the current condition. A trend analysis (A) compares the movement of a single variable over time, for example, the hiring rate from a single recruiting source. Simple linear regression (C) measures the relationship between two variables, such as how many units employees can produce. All techniques can be used for planning and forecasting purposes.

Chapter 3: Business Management and Strategy

1. C. HR participates in the strategic planning process by providing expertise on attracting, retaining, and managing a qualified workforce. Organization strategies (A) are formulated by the executive team. Each business function participates in the environmental-scanning process (B), gathering information about its area of responsibility. Strategic goals (D) are identified by the executive team during the strategy-formulation phase.

2. A. Corporate restructuring examines individual business units to eliminate redundancy, reduce costs, and increase production. Employee assimilation (B) is accomplished with new-hire orientation and similar programs. Reengineering looks at the entire organization to improve efficiency and increase customer satisfaction (C). In an acquisition, one corporation purchases or trades stock to gain controlling interest in another (D).

3. D. The mission statement describes who the organization is, what it does, where it is going, and how it is different from others. The corporate values statement (A) communicates the executive team's expectations for the way the organization conducts business. Corporate goals (B) describe what the organization plans to achieve in the future. The vision statement (C) is a short, inspirational statement of what the organization will accomplish in the future.

4. C. As an organization becomes more successful during the growth phase, it can afford to provide competitive compensation and benefits for employees. Executive benefit packages (A) are often enhanced during the maturity stage of organizational growth. During the maturity stage, the organization is able to hire new employees with less experience (B) and train them to grow into positions requiring additional experience. Employees work the closest with organization founders (D) during the startup phase.

5. B. The greatest effect of technology is increased worker productivity. Employee morale (A) may be affected positively or negatively by technological improvements but is not the main impact. The cost of living (C) is a function of the cost of consumer goods and is a factor in an environmental scan. Span of control (D) may also be affected by technological improvements, allowing managers to directly supervise a larger number of employees, but it is not the main effect.

6. B. The balanced scorecard ties objectives to performance measurements (A), sets targets (D), and measures how the objectives contribute to organization goals (C). The elimination of unnecessary processes to increase customer satisfaction (B) is the purpose of reengineering.

7. C. An HR audit examines HR policies and procedures for compliance and to determine whether the department is successfully meeting the organization's needs. Evaluating employee skills (A) is part of a SWOT analysis during the strategic planning process. Employee productivity and turnover rates (B) are metrics used to diagnose potential workforce problems. A timeline for changes in the HR department (D) would be included in an HR plan.

8. A. The four *p*'s of marketing are product, price, placement, and promotion, which summarize the responsibilities of the marketing team.

9. A. A SMART goal is specific, measurable, action-oriented, realistic, and time-based.

10. B. Once Congress forwards a bill, the president has 10 days to sign it. A pocket veto occurs when Congress adjourns before the 10 days are up and the president does not sign it. When the president vetoes a bill (A), Congress may try to override it with a two-thirds vote of a quorum in each house. If the bill does not pass, the veto stands. If Congress cannot raise a

quorum to override a veto (C), the veto stands. If Congress submits a bill to the president and stays in session (D), the bill becomes law if the president does not sign it within 10 days.

11. C. Mentoring programs are a valuable training tool but do not necessarily reflect a corporate mission, vision, or values when the mentor is outside of the organization. Written policies (A) help an organization mitigate risk by identifying employee rights and responsibilities. Modeling appropriate behavior from the top down (B) shows employees how to act and contributes to the corporate culture. Coaching (D) gives the employee the opportunity to modify and correct behavior in accordance with company guidelines.

12. A. Employee handbooks are one tool used to compile written policies that aid in compliance with various state and federal laws but are not specifically required by any one law or standard.

13. D. An HR audit can serve many strategic and operational purposes. In all three of the other answers, the HR audit allows for a comparison of the current environment to the future desired state.

14. B. Sustainability is behavior that does not deplete the resources used to achieve an outcome. Viable sustainability programs are those that are able to have a regular, systematic impact on resource depletion, thereby reducing waste and increasing efficiencies.

15. D. Corporate responsibility has influence across all HR functions. Examples of CR concepts explored throughout the strategic planning process include worker rights, legal compliance, company culture development, and corporate governance (A, B, C).

16. A. When funding is low due to startup conditions, a decision must be made regarding obtaining the talent necessary to do the work. Because organizations at this stage do not typically have the funds to develop employees from within such as in the growth and maturity stage (B, C), they often must choose which positions are critical to day-to-day operation and outsource the rest.

17. A. An HR budget reflects how many and what types of resources are necessary to accomplish a goal. The addition of employees, costs to train, and the purchase of new equipment are all examples of items that require cash to achieve strategic goals.

18. B. Just-in-time inventory is an inventory-management strategy that purchases smaller amounts of inventory more frequently to reduce inventory and ensure a steady supply of products for distribution.

19. D. A *prima facie* violation of whistle-blower protection must demonstrate that an employee was engaged in a protected activity, that the employer knew or suspected that the employee was engaged in a protected activity, that the employee suffered an unfavorable employment action, and that the unfavorable action was the result of engaging in a protected activity.

20. B. Creating an HR budget takes into account standard expense items associated with having employees. They include salaries, taxes, benefits, training, travel, and equipment costs, to name a few. A compensation strategy defines pay equity both internally and externally (C) and the cost of recruiting is a measurement of HR activities return on investment (D) and can be a measurement of business impact.

Chapter 4: Workforce Planning and Employment

1. D. The candidate profile is developed after the job requirements have been determined, beginning with the job description and developing the competencies (broad requirements of the position) and the specifications necessary for successful performance. Job competencies (A) identify skills and qualities beyond tasks and responsibilities specific to the position that help determine how well a candidate will fit into the work group, such as team orientation vs. individual contribution or ability to learn new skills quickly. The job description (B) provides the tasks and responsibilities that must be accomplished. Job specifications (C) define the job-specific KSAs that will be needed for success in the position.

2. C. According to the EEOC, there are no circumstances where race or color are a BFOQ. (A) is incorrect because Title VII specifically allows religious organizations to give preference to members of the religion. (B) and (D) are incorrect because Title VII specifically allows sex as a BFOQ if it is "reasonably necessary" for business operations.

3. A. *Griggs* identified adverse impact to mean that discrimination need not be intentional to exist; *Albemarle Paper* (B) extended the concept to require that tests must be validated in accordance with the EEOC Uniform Guidelines for Employee Selection Procedures. *Washington* (C) determined that employment tests resulting in adverse impact are acceptable if they predict future success on the job. *Taxman* (D) found that employment decisions made on the basis of race are discriminatory.

4. A. A staffing needs analysis begins with an assessment of the KSAs needed to achieve future goals along with those that are currently available within the organization. Although the tasks, duties, and responsibilities (B) are used to determine what the KSAs are, it is possible for individuals with the same or similar KSAs to perform different jobs, so (B) is not used in a needs analysis. KSAs available in the local labor market (C) will be used to develop the recruiting strategy and plan but are not relevant to the staffing needs analysis. The organization's core competencies (D) are factors that make the organization unique but are not generally part of the staffing needs analysis.

5. C. The GM could be influenced by his similar experience working his way through college. Knowledge-of-predictor bias (A) is a factor when the interviewer knows that a candidate scored particularly high or low on an assessment test. The halo effect (B) occurs when interviewers allow one positive characteristic to overshadow other, less positive attributes. The gut feeling bias (D) occurs when interviewers rely on intuition to make hiring decisions.

6. B. To calculate the selection rate, divide the number of applicants hired by the total number of applicants in each group:

Black	23 ÷ 140 = 16%
Asian	21 ÷ 120 = 18%
Hispanic	19 ÷ 145 = 13%
Caucasian	35 ÷ 230 = 15%

7. C. To determine whether adverse impact has occurred, multiply the highest selection rate, which is Asian, at 18%, by 4/5 or 80%. (18% × .80=14%)

8. D. Government contractors with 50 or more employees and contracts of $50,000 or more each year must complete Affirmative Action Plans. (A) was the original compliance requirement for Title VII and was changed to 15 employees by the EEOA of 1972. The criteria in (B) apply to employers that must comply with the Rehabilitation Act and federal contractors that must take affirmative action for all terms and conditions of employment based on executive orders. (C) is not a compliance requirement.

9. C. ADEA waivers are valid during a reduction in force only if the employee has 45 days to consider the agreement. Once employees sign a RIF-related waiver, the ADEA requires that they have 7 days (A) to revoke it. Terminations that are not part of a RIF require only 21 days (B) for consideration. An employee has 180 days (D) to file a charge with the EEOC in states that do not have their own EEO enforcement agency.

10. D. IRCA allows, but does not require, employers to make copies of documents presented for employment eligibility. The employee section of the I-9 must be completed by the end of the first day of employment (A). The employer section must be completed and documents checked by the end of the third day of employment. Employers who make a good faith effort to comply with IRCA (B) have an affirmative defense to inadvertently hiring an unauthorized alien. IRCA requires that I-9 forms be maintained and available for audit (C) by the USCIS for 3 years from date of hire or 1 year after the date of termination.

11. C. E-Verify is a system-wide approach to helping employers comply with post-hire documentation regulations. Recertifying (B) and requesting updated documents (D) may be appropriate on a case-by-case basis but neither is a long-term solution to the problem.

12. B. Although the decision to store employment records online is influenced by all of these factors, the ability to limit access is a strong element of labor law and privacy compliance.

13. C. Strategic staffing and recruitment involves taking a picture of the company at a 30,000-foot level, rather than from an operational perspective. Identifying recruitment sources such as employee referrals may prove to be valuable once the strategies have been defined. Conducting a labor market analysis allows HR to identify the availability of a qualified workforce for use in the achievement of strategic objectives. Total rewards packages include conducting wage surveys and utilization reviews to understand compensation and benefits trends, designed to compete with internal and external market conditions. Defining the employer brand not only creates an employer identity, but helps to differentiate a company from their competition.

14. B. Any tool used to select employees must be job related and a valid predictor of success on the job. If a selection tool results in discrimination against an individual who is a member of a protected class (A), the criteria used must be shown to be job related and valid. For example, a bona fide occupational qualification occurs when religion, sex, or national origin is "reasonably necessary to the normal operation" of the business.

15. D. State employment agencies are required under VEVRAA to give priority to Vietnam-era veterans when providing referrals to job openings. The act further requires that contractors and subcontractors meeting certain criteria list all job openings with these same state agencies. The Rehabilitation Act of 1973 prohibits discrimination against individuals with disabilities, and the executive orders prohibit discrimination in employment by federal contractors, sub-contractors and the government.

16. B. Negligent hiring occurs when an employer knows or should have known about an applicant's prior history that endangered customers, employees, vendors, or others with whom the employee comes into contact. While this behavior may be classified as a criminal act (D), it is not a violation of the employee privacy (A) but rather a function of workplace violence that may have been prevented through proper screening at the time of hire.

17. C. A major life activity under the ADA defines major life activities under two categories: general activities such as caring for oneself and major bodily functions such as breathing. A physical or mental impairment in and of itself does not constitute a disability (A, C) qualified for protection under the ADA. Mitigating factors (B) are considered if they allow an otherwise qualified individual to perform the essential functions of the job.

18. A. The EEO-1 report requires employers to group jobs into job categories based on average skill level, knowledge, and responsibility. Exempt workers are defined by professional, executive, and administrative exemption criteria (B), and these are not examples of the protected class groups under federal law (D).

19. C. Job bidding allows internal candidates to express interest in a job prior to it becoming available. It gives employees the opportunity to develop the skills necessary to successful compete for the position once it becomes available. A job posting is an internal job announcement (A); RFP's (B) are typically used to allow outside vendors to bid on project work and the ranking of job applicants is a function of the selection process used to identify the most qualified individual for the job.

20. B. Any inquiries into an applicant's citizen status must be specific to the requirements of the job. In this example, it is not necessary for the employer to know specifically whether the applicant is a U.S. citizen, but rather, whether the applicant is authorized to work in the United States.

Chapter 5: Human Resource Development

1. C. Systems thinking refers to the characteristic of a learning organization that uses a variety of information-gathering techniques to acquire knowledge about new technology, determine its value, and convert this knowledge into new and improved practices and procedures. Assessment centers (A) are used to determine what kind of training an individual needs. Massed practice (B) is a form of practicing job tasks during training in which all tasks are practiced at the same time. Programmed instruction (D) is a type of self-instruction that requires trainees to complete each step in the training before moving on to the next step.

2. A. Supervisory training programs concentrate on topics related to interactions with employees, such as conflict-resolution skills. Budgeting skills (B) and internal control training (D) are included in management development programs. Rotation through various divisions (C) is part of a leadership development program.

3. B. The learning evaluation method focuses on how well the training resulted in learning new skills. The reaction evaluation method (A) focuses on participant reactions. The behavior evaluation method (C) measures on-the-job behavior changes as a result of training, and the results evaluation method (D) measures organizational results. Of the four methods, the results evaluation method is considered the most valuable for the organization.

4. B. A lack of job reinforcement can adversely affect transfer of training. Other adverse impacts are the result of interference from the immediate work environment and a nonsupportive organizational climate. The trainer's expertise (A) could affect how well trainees learn information but does not specifically affect transfer of training. The subject of the training (C) affects how receptive trainees are to the information but not necessarily how the information transfers to the job.

5. A. The positively accelerating learning curve begins with smaller increments but increases in pace and size as learning continues. The negatively accelerating curve (B) begins with larger increments that decrease as learning continues. The S-shaped learning curve (C) is a combination of the positively and negatively accelerating learning curves, whereas a plateau (D) occurs when no learning seems to take place.

6. D. The most common reason for the failure of change initiatives is that people were not prepared for the change and given time to assimilate the reasons for the change. Failing to communicate a change in strategic direction (A) as the basis for organization changes in and of itself will not lead to failure of a change initiative. Leaders who do not support change (B) do have an influence on employees, but that factor alone is not the most common reason for failure. The absence of a training system (C) may negatively impact the change process, but it is not the most common reason for failure.

7. B. An Ishikawa diagram is an effective tool for organizing information about a problem when brainstorming with a group. A Pareto chart (A) graphically represents the 80/20 rule. A stratification chart (C) shows the individual components of a problem in addition to the total or summary. A histogram (D) provides a way of looking at random occurrences to find out if there is a pattern.

8. C. The first three choices are all employee growth and assessment programs. Behavioral-based performance assessment (A) focuses on behaviors, whereas skills-based performance assessment (B) focuses on skills. MBO programs measure the successful attainment of objectives. The continuous-feedback program (D) is a performance management program.

9. C. The BARS system is used most effectively in organizations when a number of jobs have similar duties. Because it is expensive and time-consuming to implement, an organization must have enough resources available to develop the program. Critical-incident appraisal tools (A) are most effectively used by managers who have daily interaction with subordinates. Forced ranking (B) is best for use in organizations with fewer than 100 employees because it becomes unwieldy for large groups. Field reviews (D) are conducted by someone other than a direct supervisor.

10. C. A mentor is someone who takes a personal interest in an employee's career and who guides and sponsors them. Although a supervisor may be a mentor, mentors are usually individuals who are outside the chain of command and may even be from outside the organization. The functions in A, B, and D are not generally performed by mentors.

11. D. Formative evaluation is a technique used prior to the commencement and during the design phase of training. It is used to gather data that will be used in training to ensure that the objectives are met and that the training meets the needs of the workgroup. This is different from summative evaluation (A), which occurs after the training has taken place. Knowledge banking (B) and an attitude assessment (C) are not used in the evaluation of training.

12. B. The ADDIE model is a process that begins with an analysis of the specific training needs. In this example, management may believe that the negative reviews are the result of lack of training, but until a thorough needs analysis is conducted—including the gathering of relevant data—it is not possible to create specific training objectives that will result in the desired outcomes. While training design (A), participant identification and scheduling (C, D) are components of training, they do not launch the ADDIE model.

13. A. Job design is made up of several factors related to how the work gets done, broken into two categories: job enrichment and job enlargement (B). Task identity, task significance and feedback are examples of job-enrichment activities that can significantly influence job satisfaction through design. KPI's (C, D) can be used as performance appraisal criteria, but are not directly related to job enrichment activities.

14. B. Performance feedback bias such as the halo/horn effect, leniency, and central tendency can (but don't always) exist whenever managers are asked to make a discriminatory judgment, including in rating performance and selecting new hires. Note that not all discrimination is unlawful; it is in fact necessary to make distinguishing decisions on the job. Discrimination becomes unlawful when the performance is not rated according to neutral, job-related standards.

15. C. Asynchronous training is self-paced training that typically occurs using computer-based tools. Although timelines for completion may be preestablished (such as specifying that all assignments must be submitted no later than 11:59 p.m. Sunday evening), students typically are able to set their own schedule for when they engage in learning the material. Vestibule training is a form of OJT (A), mobile learning (B) is a type of e-learning that occurs typically through mobile devices, and the Delphi technique (D) is a decision making or forecasting activity that relies on a group of experts to reach a consensus.

16. B. Formative evaluations are designed to gather information prior to the design of training to measure the needs of the participants. This allows the designer to include content and exercises that will aid in the participant transfer of the training to the job. Summative evaluations (A, C) are used after the training has taken place, and often include a measure of participant reactions and trainer evaluations (D).

17. A. Peer-to-peer coaching is useful when a management work group has shared values or objectives. Assigning a one-on-one peer coach or using a team approach maximizes the diversity of skills available in any particular peer group. A mentor relationship (B) implies a hierarchy (the mentor and a subordinate), an executive coach (C) is used for more one-on-one upper level management development, and strategic planning (D) is a broad organization-wide string of activities related to the planning the direction of the company.

18. B. Training cost per employee is calculated by dividing the total of all associated training costs by the number of full-time equivalent employees. The proper calculation is $4,500 divided by 25 full-time equivalent employees.

19. B. A case study allows participants to review real-world scenarios related to their topic of study. Practical application and transfer of training are typically more successful when participants can see how it's done in the work environment. Vestibule training (A) occurs "on the job," facilitation (C) uses an individual to create an interactive training experience, and a Socratic seminar (D) is a type of training that welcomes opposing viewpoints in a problem-solving setting.

20. D. Comparing employee performance is a non-narrative style of performance review involving comparing one employee to another in the same job category.

Chapter 6: Compensation and Benefits

1. C. FICA requires employers to pay Social Security and Medicare for employees and to withhold an equal amount from employee paychecks. There is no federal law requiring employers to provide pension plans (A) and (B). No federal law requires employers to provide health insurance (D).

2. D. No federal law requires employers to provide a retirement plan to employees. If employers do provide retirement benefits, ERISA (A) regulates how the plans are offered and administered. OBRA (B) capped executive pay, required health plans to honor qualified medical child-support orders, and required that group health plans provide coverage for dependent adopted children of employees. The OWBPA (C) amended the ADEA to prohibit discriminating against older workers in benefit plans and defined requirements for employee waivers of their rights under the act.

3. B. Intrinsic rewards are those in which esteem is achieved from within oneself. A, C, and D are examples of extrinsic rewards that come from external sources.

4. A. A Total Rewards philosophy helps determine what kind of employees will be attracted to the organization. Developing a philosophy to target employees with the KSAs needed by the organization can help advance the organization's mission. The pecking order for jobs (B) is based on the value of those jobs to the organization. The philosophy defines leading the competition as a strategy; positioning the company to do so (C) is a result of creating the compensation structure. An entitlement culture is maintained (D) by continuing to pay employees for time on the job instead of for performance.

5. A. An entitlement culture rewards longevity in the job. If increased productivity is a function of time on the job, an entitlement culture will encourage employees to stay with the company. Line of sight (B) occurs when employees know that their performance impacts their pay. A highly competitive workforce (C) is more likely to exist in a pay-for-performance culture. A workforce with a highly desired skill set (D) would be better served by a pay-for-performance culture.

6. D. A and B are both obviously correct. Although C may seem counterintuitive to some because many employers are hesitant to terminate employees for policy violations, those terminated for cause generally aren't eligible for unemployment insurance. Because retaining an employee who is not contributing to the organization is a poor business decision, maintaining adequate records to demonstrate the reasons for termination provides the tools to fight claims that are unjustified.

7. B. A reduced FMLA leave is one in which the employee's regular work schedule is reduced by some number of hours per day or days per week. An intermittent FMLA leave (A) is one in which an employee is absent from work multiple times for the same illness or injury. Disruption to the work schedule (C) is not a factor in the type of FMLA leave. Although accurate records of time off (D) should be maintained for all FMLA leaves, they are most critical for intermittent leaves.

8. B. Workers age 40 or older who are asked to sign a waiver of their rights must be given 21 days to consider the agreement before signing it, unless they are part of a group termination or layoff. In that case, they must be given 45 days to sign the agreement (C). In both instances, they may revoke the agreement within 7 days (A). The OWBPA does not require 60 days to consider the agreement (D).

9. D. The Unemployment Compensation Amendments of 1992 required 20 percent withholding from some distributions. OBRA capped executive pay (C), required that group health coverage be offered when children are placed for adoption before the adoption is finalized (A), and required health plans to honor qualified medical child-support orders (B).

10. D. Summary plan descriptions are required only for group health plans, and not for defined contribution plans, defined benefit plans, or FSAs.

11. A. As the Director of HR, Molly is in a position of control over the administration of HR policies, procedures, and rules. As such, she is held to a high standard of responsibility that goes beyond unethical conduct (D). Fiduciary responsibility requires that the HR professional act without regard for their own self interests. A choice of law clause (B) applies in the administration of expatriate agreement, and extending pen enrollment is not necessarily illegal (C).

12. C. Group incentives share common elements including the reward of individuals based on their collective efforts. Employee Stock Ownership Plans, Employee Stock Purchase Plans, profit-sharing, and gainsharing (B) are all examples of group incentives. Deferred compensation (A) refers to tax-deferred retirement plans, and a sales bonus (D) is a type of commission paid to workers.

13. C. Distributive justice is a concept that speaks to perceived inequity in the distribution of outcomes. It is the result of the belief that an employee puts more into the system than they receive as an outcome when compared to the efforts of other organizational members. Procedural justice (B) is a perception of inequity in the procedures used to design or apply the pay structure. Wage inequity and pay disparity (A, D) are essentially the same thing, occurring when employees are either paid outside of current external position market value or internally based on compensable factors shared between jobs.

14. D. The life cycle of all compensation-related employment records is marked by specific data collection and documentation. Understanding what documents are required at each stage will allow HR to properly plan for security, updates, retention, and destruction. The other answers are not reflected in the organizational life cycle.

15. B. Under the FMLA, employees must be given at least 15 calendar days to obtain appropriate medical certification. Under certain conditions, employers may request a secondary exam, and employers are allowed to use their medical certification form provided it conforms to the requirements of the DOL's form WH-380.

16. B. EGTRRA made a number of changes to existing contribution limits, including the allowance for older workers to catch up on their retirement savings.

17. A. Medicare is a type of involuntary benefit introduced by the Social Security Act of 1935. Along with retirement (Social Security), these mandated benefits are subsidized by a tax on both the employer and the employee called FICA (Federal Insurance Contribution Act). Vision, retirement and sick pay (B, C, D) are all examples of voluntary benefits that employers may choose to offer their employees.

18. C. A key component of a gainsharing plan is the shared responsibility of outcomes between management and employees. Productivity is reviewed, new performance is measured, and both work groups share in the gain. ESPPs, bonuses and improshare (A, B, D) all could be used, but are not specifically grown around the concept of shared responsibility between management and employees.

19. C. Intrinsic rewards are driven by internal versus external factors. Job fulfillment based on work relationships, the opportunity to use strengths, and career growth are examples of nonmonetary compensation. Extrinsic rewards (C) are those rewards that are driven by external factors, usually in the form of monetary (A) or benefit rewards (components of a total rewards system (D)).

20. D. Fiduciary responsibility implies a greater legal obligation to act with great care and responsibility on behalf of a company. Acting in one's own self-interest, conflicting duties, and profiting from a role are all examples of how HR could breach this obligation. Code of conduct, breach of contract and conflict of interest are certainly components of HR standards, but in terms of ranking, they fall below the concept of fiduciary responsibility.

Chapter 7: Employee and Labor Relations

1. C. Weingarten rights give all union members the right to request that a co-worker or shop steward be present during an interview if the employee believes the interview could lead to disciplinary action. The employer may decide to use other facts available without interviewing the employee. The Weingarten ruling does not entitle employees to have an attorney present (A). Employers are not required to wait for a lengthy period of time until the co-worker returns (B). The interview must be discontinued while waiting for the co-worker (D). As of 2004, employers are required to honor Weingarten requests only for union members.

2. B. Constructive discharge occurs when the employer forces an employee to resign by creating a work environment that is so unpleasant a reasonable person would resign. The duty of good faith and fair dealing (A) applies to contracts, requiring both parties to act in a fair and honest manner with each other to ensure that benefits of the contract are realized. Promissory estoppel (C) occurs when an employer entices an employee to take an action by promising a reward but then does not follow through on the reward. Fraudulent misrepresentation (D) occurs when an employer makes untrue promises or claims to a candidate.

3. C. The public-policy exception to the at-will doctrine prevents an employer from terminating an employee who is cooperating in a government investigation of wrongdoing. Options A and B are elements of at-will employment. Option D would also be allowed based on the at-will doctrine but could be affected by other common-law doctrines.

4. A. The company may make truthful statements about a unionized environment during an organizing campaign, such as pointing out that employees will have to pay dues to the union. Although nonunion employees are free to talk about their reasons for not wanting a union (B), it is an unfair labor practice for the employer to encourage them to do so. Telling employees that the company will have to move the jobs to another country if the union is elected (C) is also a ULP, because it constitutes a threat. Employers may not threaten, interrogate, promise, or spy on (TIPS) employees during an organizing campaign (D).

5. C. Temporary employees who have a community of interest with regular employees of the client company may become part of the bargaining unit whether or not the temp agency agrees to bargain with the union.

6. A. The NLRB will conduct a decertification election if the employees present a petition signed by 30 percent of the employees in the bargaining unit. Management may not participate in or encourage employees to circulate the petition or provide any support in the process. Doing so is considered an unfair labor practice. A union can be deauthorized (B) if employees want to remove a union security clause, such as dues check-off. If there is a valid CBA in place (C), the NLRB will not direct an election. The NLRA prohibits an election if one took place during the preceding 12 months (D).

7. B. A union shop clause requires all new employees to join the union within a grace period specified by the contract: no less than 30 days, except in the construction industry, where the grace period must be 7 days. An agency shop clause (A) requires all employees to pay union dues whether or not they join the union. A closed shop clause (C) requires all new hires to be members of the union before they are hired. Closed shops are illegal except in the construction industry. A maintenance of membership clause (D) allows employees to choose whether to join the union, but once they join, they must remain members until the expiration of the contract.

8. C. Double breasting occurs when an employer has two companies that are separate and distinct from each other but do the same type of work, and one company is union while the other is nonunion. This occurs most often in the construction industry when contractors have two different crews for bidding on union and nonunion jobs. An alter ego employer has two substantially identical businesses (A). The ally doctrine describes work that is done by a neutral employer while another business is shut down by a strike (B). A straight-line operation is one in which two businesses perform operations that complement each other's

operations (D). If one business is struck, the other may be as well because they are engaged in a single economic enterprise.

9. B. Votes can be challenged by the union representative or by management only before the vote goes into the ballot box.

10. D. Salting occurs when a union hires an individual experienced at organizing tactics to apply for a job with a company that has been targeted for an organizing campaign (D). Options A, B, and C are tactics used by unions during organizing campaigns.

11. A. Exit interviews are one method used to gauge employee job satisfaction or lack thereof. Brown bag lunches (B), employee committees (C), and suggestion boxes (D) are all employee communication tools, but they are not necessarily conducive to measuring overall employee job satisfaction in a consistent, measurable way.

12. A. Diversity simply means "the differences among people." Although diversity encompasses protected-class characteristics (B) and can be a measure of non-discriminatory hiring practices (C), it represents the differences of all employee behaviors and classifications. Knowledge management programs (D) refer to the ability of the employer to retain and apply the collective knowledge of their workers to achieve strategic aims.

13. C. Collecting large amounts of data into one coherent document can be done through the use of an employee handbook that references policies (D), standard operating procedures (A), or reference guides. A troubleshooting manual (C) best represents the type of document designed for short-term reference of a specific nature.

14. A. Unusual activity related to employee meetings (B), complaints against supervisors, the sudden use of union terms (C), and an increased interest in employee benefits (D) are all signs of potential union activity.

15. D. A company cannot threaten employees or make promises to them contingent on the workforce remaining union free. A philosophy statement should be geared toward communicating the company's desire to work directly with the employees in discussions about working conditions or benefits. If a union does attempt to organize, it is important for the employer to work directly with outside council to determine the strategic benefits of discussing the desire to remain union free and the disadvantages/limitations of unions as employee representatives.

16. C. The NLRB was established by the NLRA to enforce provisions of the act related to conducting elections and preventing unfair labor practices. The LMRA, LMRDA and the Norris-La Guardia Act (A, B, D) are all examples of legislation influencing the application of unions in the workplace.

17. B. *Harris v. Forklift Systems Inc.* was referenced in the case of same-sex harassment brought to the Supreme Court in *Oncale v. Sundowner* (A). *Oncale* helped determine that gender is of little consequence when harassment meets the statutory requirements defined in *Harris. Faragher v. City of Boca Raton* (C) and *Burlington Industries v. Ellerth* (D) were also important cases aiding in interpreting the concept of sexual harassment in the workplace.

18. C. USERRA protects the rights of reservists called to active duty in the armed forces and applies to all public and private employers in the United States. It includes pension protection for returning service members related to vesting, accrual, and employer contribution continuity. The Sherman Anti-Trust act is legislation used to control business monopolies, and Executive Order 11246 (B) prohibits employment discrimination. The Equal Employment Opportunity Act (D) provided litigation authority to the EEOC back in 1972.

19. C. Weingarten rights were upheld by the NLRB, establishing that union workers have the right to representation in any meeting that may amount to an investigatory interview that could lead to disciplinary action. These rights do not currently apply to nonunion workers (D). Any employee has the right to consult with an attorney post-discipline, and employers do not have the right to deny representation to union workers (A, D) in a meeting that may result in discipline.

20. B. Wrongful discipline and wrongful termination are two actions that can lead to the need for ADR methods. Mediation (A), ad hoc arbitration (C), peer-review panels (D), constructive confrontation, and the use of an ombudsman are all examples of dispute methods that are an *alternative* to court action. A peer review panel, mediation and arbitration represents the continuum of elevating through the alternative dispute methods.

Chapter 8: Risk Management

1. B. A serious violation is the second level of violation. Willful violations (A) are, in addition to having the potential for serious harm or injury, done intentionally or with "plain indifference" to the requirements. Repeat violations (C) are violations for which an employer has been previously cited and have recurred. *De-minimus* violations (D) are unlikely to cause serious harm or injury.

2. D. A *Notice of Contest* must be filed within 15 days of the citation. The OSH Act requires employers to allow the CSHO to inspect the workplace (A). Employers may request variances until repairs are made (B) or for processes that provide equal or greater safety for workers. Employers may consult with OSHA to identify possible hazards without fear of a citation or penalty (C); but once a consultant becomes involved, the employer must abate any violations, or the consultant will refer the violation to an OSHA inspector.

3. A. Although all of these are steps in the process, the *best* way to ensure that employees will comply with the Drug-Free Workplace Act is to develop and publish a written policy.

4. C. The FLSA defines a list of jobs not suitable for children between the ages of 16 and 18. OSHA regulates worker safety through standards related to mine safety and hazardous communication.

5. A. The receptionist is exhibiting symptoms of all three types of stress: physical, emotional, and mental. SARS (D) is a type of disease, and while her symptoms could be attributed to job dissatisfaction (B), there must still be a root cause.

6. D. The employee representative is entitled to receive copies of incident reports with the identifying information omitted. Employers have 7 calendar days to provide the information to an employee representative. Copies of the OSHA form 300 log must be provided by the end of the following business day (C) when requested by employees or their representatives. Options A and B do not apply to OSHA requirements.

7. C. EAPs provide counseling for a variety of employee needs, including financial and legal counseling (D), substance abuse (B), and help to quit smoking. Outplacement counseling (A) is often, but not always, included in an EAP. The plans typically do not cover gambling.

8. D. Injuries that occur while performing the job are reportable, whether or not the employee was at fault. OSHA regulations exempt injuries that occur as a result of voluntary participation in fitness activities (A), those from personal grooming activities (B), or those caused by motor vehicles in a company parking lot (C).

9. C. OSHA inspections are conducted at the request of an employee based on a safety violation, as a preprogrammed high-hazard inspection, or on a random basis. The four characteristics of a safety and health-management plan are senior management support (A), ongoing worksite analysis (B), active hazard-prevention and -control programs (D), and ongoing safety and health training.

10. D. Although a review and analysis of OSHA logs (A) or workers' compensation records (B) can be used to determine any injury patterns occurring in the workplace, observing the incumbent (D) performing the work is necessary to determine whether there is an ergonomic hazard in the job. An MSDS (C) describes chemical hazards unrelated to ergonomics.

11. A. Raising awareness about safety and health is the responsibility of employers covered by *all* standards. Providing safety and health information in a language all employees can understand is part of the Diverse Workforce Limited Proficiency Outreach strategy. It is not specifically required by its own standard, nor is it an element of creating a model program (C) or enrolling in a VPP. Employers are however required to effectively communicate the safety rules to all employees.

12. C. Current users of illegal drugs are specifically excluded from protection under the ADA. The ADA, however, does not require that an employer retain any employee whose substance abuse—regardless of the status or type of substance—represents a serious safety risk to themselves or others. Recovering addicts are protected by the ADA. And, depending on certain conditions, users of legal substances such as alcohol or prescription drugs may be protected by the ADA.

13. B. An IME will allow Millie to be evaluated by an impartial third party. Modified duty is a short-term solution to be used when an injured worker is able to return to work but not to full duty (C). A reasonable accommodation strategy (A) may become necessary, but only after Millie's diagnosis and treatment plan is clearly understood. Terminating her employment (D) prior to identifying the extent of her qualifications and limitations is not advisable.

14. A. The construction and general industry standards are the most frequently violated—and therefore the most frequently cited—of the four major areas for which OSH provides standards. These areas include general industry, construction, maritime (B), and agriculture (D). Whistle-blower protection (C) is granted under the Sarbanes-Oxley Act.

15. C. While the use of PPE (D) could certainly be used to mitigate the exposure of hazardous chemicals in the workplace, it is the Hazard Communication Standard that requires employers to inform employees of the risks associated with chemical use in the workplace. The general-duty clause (B) is used for safety hazards that are not specifically identified through an existing standard. The control of hazardous energy (A) is part of the lockout/tagout standard.

16. B. Generally, injuries are not work-related if the employee is engaged in a voluntary wellness activity (A), eating food prepared for personal consumption (C), or has the common cold/flu (D). This is important for two reasons: to determine OSHA recordability and to determine compensability under workers' compensation.

17. D. The courts will determine whether the employee had a reasonable expectation of privacy based on the employer policy (A), how situations have been handled in the past (B), and state-by-state regulations of employee privacy laws (C).

18. B. Environmental health hazards are those hazards that include physical (A), chemical (D), or biological exposure (C) in the workplace. Workplace violence is a security risk more than a physical exposure in the workplace.

19. B. The recordability of an MSD injury is based on many factors, including the general recording criteria and the severity/description of the symptoms. Injuries from poor workplace or ergonomic design typically fall into an MSD classification, and include injuries to the back, arms, and shoulders. An MSD can be caused by a repetitive stress injury (A), although this is not always the case.

20. D. Whistleblower standards protect an employee's right to file a complaint to OSHA about a workplace safety or health hazard. It is considered a basic employee right granted under the OSH act in 1970. Emergency action (A) is a type of plan required by OSHA, and the general duty clause (C) states that employers have a general duty to provide a safe and healthy workplace for employees.

Appendix B

Case Study: Where the Green Glass Grows

Where the Green Glass Grows (WGGG) is an eco-friendly glass manufacturer located in California. It services the numerous wine producers of the coastal region, manufacturing glass wine bottles in various sizes and colors. Starting with four employees in a small manufacturing facility in 1964, the company went through a major growth initiative 10 years ago. This resulted in a renovation of its manufacturing facility, bringing the company to its current four-line production configuration. Output is approximately 24 million bottles annually, working with a single shift of workers. WGGG's current sales volume peaked 3 years ago at $1.2 million. Now at 42 employees, the company has committed in 2012 to undergo a series of strategic interventions to respond to the rapid growth of international wine sales. Figure B.1 shows the organizational chart for the company.

FIGURE B.1   WGGG organizational chart

The Company

Sustainability and innovation became corporate objectives for WGGG long before they were considered trendy.

"At WGGG, our mission is all about growth. Growing our talent, growing our resources, and growing our financial stability are at the heart of everything we do," said Emerald Cyan, CEO and granddaughter of the founder, Forrest Gumby.

Furthermore, WGGG has an established business practice of using a minimum of 85 percent recycled glass for all products as evidence of its commitment to sustainable business practices and the environment.

WGGG's competitive advantage is significant: the ability to manufacture glass bottles that weigh 20 percent less than those produced by industry counterparts. WGGG's technology enables the company to melt down an existing glass bottle, remove a portion of the glass, and replace it with an injection of a patented gel solution, re-forming it into a new mold. The result is a lighter-weight bottle that is more durable (and thus shatter-resistant) than what is currently available on the market. Because the weight of the bottle accounts for up to 49 percent of the cost to ship wine, producers took notice.

The Customer

The United States surpassed France as the nation that consumes the most wine in 2010. California wine accounted for a 61 percent volume share of the total U.S. wine market with sales at 199.6 million cases, up 1 percent from the previous year. Retail value was $18.5 billion. In addition, since the reversal of an 80 percent import tax to Hong Kong, wine imports into China from across the globe saw a record $491 million in sales, 8 percent of which was from America. It is anticipated that over the next 3 years, American wine imports to the region will reach as much as 138 percent of existing sales. Combine that with the growth of homeland consumption, and American wine producers are near giddy with anticipation. If WGGG wants to service wine producers across the United States, it needs to grow again.

Exercises

1. Using Table B.1, complete a thumbnail SWOT audit for WGGG using all available data.

TABLE B.1   SWOT audit

Internal	**Strengths**	**Weaknesses**
External	**Opportunities**	**Threats**

2. Using Table B.2, match the internal HR activity to its proper function.

TABLE B.2 Internal HR activities

Effectively recruit for and select a sales and marketing department.	A. Business Management and Strategy
Conduct a cost-benefit analysis on running a second shift.	B. Workforce Planning and Employment
Develop the leadership to effectively manage the rapid changes that will occur.	C. Human Resource Development
Assess the security levels of trade-secret data.	D. Compensation and Benefits
Conduct wage surveys by geographic location where potential new facilities are being considered.	E. Employee and Labor Relations
Increase the use of new versus recycled glass.	F. Risk Management
Measure the ROI of projected growth due to the increase in staff.	
Engage in planning activities to map out strategic short-term and long-term goals.	
Design training for sales staff across multiple geographic locations through the use of mixed media.	
Plan and prepare for the regulatory compliance required of 50 employees.	

3. Using Table B.3, match WGGG's activity with the correlating driving external force.

TABLE B.3   WGGG's activities

Compliance with the regulation of chemical use in food storage by various governmental agencies	A. The political/legal climate
Accounting for the cost of production in the wine coast region	B. Geographic limitations or opportunities
Evaluating the quality of the labor force population	C. The economic climate
Accounting for the cost of labor in the wine coast region	D. The competition
Establishing the rate of pay required for a second shift	
Evaluating the strength of WGGG's trade patent	
Procuring and evaluating the availability of additional glass suppliers	
Monitoring the status of trade relations with China	
Mitigating the threat of new market entrants	

Answer Key and Additional Exercise

1. A SWOT audit allows a company the opportunity to see where it excels and where it's deficient. Although we provide only a snapshot here, you can see how taking a 50,000-foot approach via a SWOT audit will allow the company to create a 5,000-foot operational plan, taking into consideration its internal strengths and weaknesses and external opportunities and threats. See Table B.4.

TABLE B.4   SWOT audit

Internal	**Strengths**	**Weaknesses**
	Competitive advantage	Under-staffed
	Longevity	Doesn't have the facilities necessary to produce forecasted demand
	Existing customer base	Doesn't have a functioning sales and marketing department
External	**Opportunities**	**Threats**
	Cross-functionality of the product, diversifying the product line	Competition and copy-cat technology
	The global market	Possible limits on glass procurement
	The potential for decreased overhead via a relocation	Cost of capital improvements or relocation
		The rise of alternative sources, such as plastic

2. Clearly assessing the need for HR activities in strategic interventions is the first step toward contributing to organizational development. This case study gives you a sampling of the types of activities to consider, ordered by functional HR area. See Table B.5. *Can you identify at least three more examples of HR activities WGGG will need to undertake?*

TABLE B.5 Internal HR activities: answers

B	Effectively recruit for and select a sales and marketing department.	A. Business Management and Strategy
A	Conduct a cost-benefit analysis on running a second shift.	B. Workforce Planning and Employment
C	Develop the leadership to effectively manage the rapid changes that will occur.	C. Human Resource Development
F	Assess the security levels of trade-secret data.	D. Compensation and Benefits
D	Conduct wage surveys by geographic location where potential new facilities are being considered.	E. Employee and Labor Relations
A	Increase the use of new versus recycled glass.	F. Risk Management
B	Measure the ROI of projected growth due to the increase in staff.	
A	Engage in planning activities to map out strategic short-term and long-term goals.	
C	Design training for sales staff across multiple geographic locations through the use of mixed media.	
B	Plan and prepare for the regulatory compliance required of 50 employees.	

3. Porter's 5 Forces (Chapter 2) reflect on the drivers that exist in the external business climate. Being able to anticipate which of those forces will impact strategic initiatives and how they will do so is critical to putting mitigation or risk-management measures into place. Table B.6 provides a sampling of the considerations relevant to the case study. *Can you identify at least three more examples of external forces WGGG will need to consider?*

TABLE B.6   WGGG's activities: answers

A	Compliance with the regulation of chemical use in food storage by various governmental agencies	A. The political/legal climate
B	Accounting for the cost of production in the wine coast region	B. Geographic limitations or opportunities
C	Evaluating the quality of the labor force population	C. The economic climate
B	Accounting for the cost of labor in the wine coast region	D. The competition
C	Establishing the rate of pay required for a second shift	
A	Evaluating the strength of WGGG's trade patent	
D	Procuring and evaluating the availability of additional glass suppliers	
A	Monitoring the status of trade relations with China	
D	Mitigating the threat of new market entrants	

Appendix

C

Federal Employment Legislation and Case Law

This appendix provides a brief overview of the federal employment legislation and case law that is required knowledge for HR professionals. All of the legislation has been covered in detail in the appropriate chapters, as have most of the cases.

Legislation and Case Law Summary

In addition to the cases discussed in the book, the following table includes some additional cases that exam candidates may find useful during their review. This information isn't presented as or intended to replace legal advice. Please consult your employment attorney for advice on specific employment situations.

 NOTE *USSC* refers to decisions made by the U.S. Supreme Court.

Year	Name	Significance	Chapter
1884	*Payne v. The Western & Atlantic Railroad Company*	Defined employment at-will.	7
1869	Bureau of Labor Statistics (BLS)	Established to study industrial accidents and maintain accident records.	8
1890	Sherman Antitrust Act	Controlled business monopolies; allowed court injunctions to prevent restraint of trade. Used to restrict unionization efforts.	7
1914	Clayton Act	Limited the use of injunctions to break strikes; exempted unions from the Sherman Act.	7
1916	Federal Employees Compensation Act (FECA)	Provided benefits similar to workers' compensation for federal employees injured on the job.	8

Year	Name	Significance	Chapter
1927	Longshore and Harbor Workers' Compensation Act	Provided workers' compensation benefits for maritime workers injured on navigable waters of the United States or on piers, docks, and terminals.	8
1926	Railway Labor Act	Protected unionization rights; allowed for a 90-day cooling-off period to prevent strikes in national emergencies. Covers railroads and unions.	7
1932	Norris-La Guardia Act	Protected the right to organize; outlawed yellow-dog contracts.	7
1935	National Labor Relations Act (NLRA; Wagner Act)	Protected the right of workers to organize and bargain collectively; identified unfair labor practices; established the National Labor Relations Board (NLRB).	7
1935	Federal Insurance Contributions Act (FICA)/Social Security Act	Required employers and employees to pay Social Security taxes.	6
1936	Federal Unemployment Tax Act (FUTA)	Required employers to contribute a percentage of payroll to an unemployment insurance fund.	6
1936	Public Contracts Act (PCA; Walsh-Healey Act)	Required contractors to pay prevailing wage rates.	6
1938	Fair Labor Standards Act (FLSA)	Defined exempt and nonexempt employees; required and set the minimum wage to be paid to nonexempt workers; required time-and-a-half to be paid for nonexempt overtime hours; limited hours and type of work for children; established record-keeping requirements.	6
1947	Labor-Management Relations Act (LMRA; Taft-Hartley)	Prohibited closed shops; restricted union shops; allowed states to pass "right to work" laws; prohibited jurisdictional strikes and secondary boycotts; allowed employers to permanently replace economic strikers; established the Federal Mediation and Conciliation Service; allowed an 80-day cooling-off period for national emergency strikes.	7

(Continued)

Year	Name	Significance	Chapter
1947	Portal-to-Portal Act	Clarified the definition of "hours worked" for the FLSA.	6
1952	Patent Act	Established the U.S. Patent and Trademark Office.	5
1959	Labor-Management Reporting and Disclosure Act (LMRDA; Landrum-Griffin)	Controlled internal union operations; provided a bill of rights for union members; required a majority vote of members to increase dues; allowed members to sue the union; set term limits for union leaders.	7
1963	Equal Pay Act	Required that employees performing substantially similar or identical work be paid the same wage or salary rate.	6
1964	Title VII of the Civil Rights Act	Established the Equal Employment Opportunity Commission (EEOC); prohibited employment discrimination on the basis of race, color, religion, national origin, or sex.	4
1965	Executive Order (EO) 11246	Prohibited employment discrimination on the basis of race, creed, color, or national origin; required affirmative steps for all terms and conditions of employment; required a written *Affirmative Action Plan* (AAP) for contractors with 50 employees.	4
1965	Immigration and Nationality Act (INA)	Eliminated national origin, race, and ancestry as bars to immigration; set immigration goals for reunifying families and preference for specialized skills.	4
1965	Service Contract Act	Required government contractors to pay prevailing wages and benefits.	6
1967	Age Discrimination in Employment Act (ADEA)	Prohibited discrimination against persons 40 years of age or older; established conditions for bona fide occupational qualification (BFOQ) exceptions.	4
1967	EO 11375	Added sex to the protected classes in EO 11246.	4
1968	Consumer Credit Protection Act (CCPA)	Limited garnishment amounts on employee wages; prohibited discharge of employees for a single garnishment order.	6

Year	Name	Significance	Chapter
1969	EO 11478	Included disabled individuals and those 40 years of age or older in the protected classes established by EO 11246.	4
1969	Black Lung Benefits Act (BLBA)	Provided benefits for coal miners suffering from pneumoconiosis due to mine work.	8
1970	Occupational Safety and Health Act (OSH Act)	Required employers to provide a safe workplace and comply with safety and health standards; established the Occupational Safety and Health Administration (OSHA) to enforce safety regulations; established the National Institute for Occupational Safety and Health (NIOSH) to research, evaluate, and recommend hazard-reduction measures.	8
1970	Fair Credit Reporting Act (FCRA)	Required employers to notify candidates that credit reports may be obtained; required written authorization by the candidate and that the employer provide a copy of the report to the candidate before taking an adverse action.	4
1971	*Griggs v. Duke Power*	USSC: Required employers to show that job requirements are related to the job; established that lack of intention to discriminate isn't a defense against claims of discrimination.	4
1972	Equal Employment Opportunity Act (EEOA)	Established that complainants have the burden of proof for disparate impact; provided litigation authority for the EEOC; extended the time to file complaints.	4
1973	Rehabilitation Act (RA)	Expanded opportunities for individuals with physical or mental disabilities; provided remedies for victims of discrimination.	4
1974	Privacy Act	Prohibited federal agencies from sharing information collected about individuals.	4
1974	Vietnam Era Veterans Readjustment Assistance Act (VEVRAA)	Provided equal opportunity and affirmative action for Vietnam veterans.	4
1974	Employee Retirement Income Security Act (ERISA)	Established requirements for pension, retirement, and welfare benefit plans including medical, hospital, accidental death and dismemberment (AD&D), and unemployment benefits.	6

(Continued)

Year	Name	Significance	Chapter
1975	*Albemarle Paper v. Moody*	USSC: Required that employment tests be validated; subjective supervisor rankings aren't sufficient validation; criteria must be tied to job requirements.	4
1975	*NLRB v. J. Weingarten, Inc.*	USSC: Established that union employees have the right to request union representation during any investigatory interview that could result in disciplinary action.	5
1976	*Washington v. Davis*	USSC: Established that employment-selection tools that adversely impact protected classes are lawful if they have been validated to show future success on the job.	4
1976	Copyright Act	Defined "fair use" of copyrighted work; set the term of copyright effectiveness.	5
1977	Mine Safety and Health Act (MSHA)	Established mandatory mine safety and health standards and created the Mine Safety and Health Administration (MSHA).	8
1977	*Automobile Workers v. Johnson Controls, Inc.*	USSC: "Decisions about the welfare of the next generation must be left to the parents who conceive, bear, support and raise them, rather than to the employers who hire those parents."	8
1978	Uniform Guidelines on Employee Selection Procedures (UGESP)	Established guidelines to ensure that selection procedures are both job related and valid predictors of job success.	4
1978	Pregnancy Discrimination Act (PDA)	Required that pregnancy be treated the same as any other short-term disability.	4
1978	Civil Service Reform Act	Created the Senior Executive Service, the Merit Systems Protection Board (MSPB), the Office of Personnel Management (OPM), and the Federal Labor Relations Authority (FLRA).	6
1978	Revenue Act	Established Section 125 and 401(k) plans for employees.	6
1979	EO 12138	Created the National Women's Business Enterprise Policy; required affirmative steps to promote and support women's business enterprises.	4

Year	Name	Significance	Chapter
1980	Guidelines on Sexual Harassment	Assisted employers to develop antiharassment policies, establish complaint procedures, and investigate complaints promptly and impartially.	4
1984	Retirement Equity Act	Lowered the age limits on participation and vesting in pension benefits; required written spousal consent to not provide survivor benefits; restricted conditions placed on survivor benefits.	6
1986	Consolidated Omnibus Budget Reconciliation Act (COBRA)	Provided continuation of group health coverage upon a qualifying event.	6
1986	Tax Reform Act	Reduced income tax rates and brackets.	6
1986	Immigration Reform and Control Act (IRCA)	Prohibited employment of individuals who aren't legally authorized to work in the United States; required I-9s for all employees.	4
1988	Drug-Free Workplace Act	Required federal contractors to develop and implement drug-free workplace policies.	4
1988	Employee Polygraph Protection Act (EPPA)	Prohibited the use of lie-detector tests except under limited circumstances.	4
1988	Worker Adjustment and Retraining Notification Act (WARN Act)	Required 60 days' notice for mass layoffs or plant closings; defined mass layoffs and plant closings; identified exceptions to the requirements.	4
1990	Americans with Disabilities Act (ADA)	Required reasonable accommodation for qualified individuals with disabilities.	4
1990	Older Worker Benefit Protection Act (OWBPA)	Amended ADEA to prevent discrimination in benefits for workers 40 years of age and older; added requirements for waivers.	6
1990	Immigration Act	Required the prevailing wage for holders of H1(b) visas; set H1(b) quotas.	4
1991	Civil Rights Act (CRA)	Allowed compensatory and punitive damages; provided for jury trials; established defenses to disparate impact claims.	4

(Continued)

Year	Name	Significance	Chapter
1991	Glass Ceiling Act	Established a commission to determine whether a glass ceiling exists and identify barriers for women and minorities. As a result, the Office of Federal Contract Compliance Programs (OFCCP) conducts audits of the representation of women and minorities at all corporate levels.	4
1992	Unemployment Compensation Amendments	Reduced rollover rules for lump-sum distributions of qualified retirement plans; required 20 percent withholding for some distributions.	6
1992	Energy Policy Act of 1992	Allowed employers to provide a non-taxable fringe benefit to employees engaged in qualified commuter activities such as bicycling and mass transit.	6
1993	Family and Medical Leave Act (FMLA)	Required qualifying employers to provide 12 weeks of unpaid leave to eligible employees for the birth or adoption of a child or to provide care for defined relatives with serious health conditions or to employees unable to perform job duties due to a serious health condition.	6
1993	*Taxman v. Board of Education of Piscataway*	Found that in the absence of past discrimination or underrepresentation of protected classes, preference may not be given to protected classes in making layoff decisions.	4
1993	*Harris v. Forklift Systems*	USSC: Defined an actionable hostile work environment as that which falls between merely offensive and that which results in tangible psychological injury.	7
1993	Omnibus Budget Reconciliation Act (OBRA)	Revised rules for employee benefits; set the maximum deduction for executive pay at $1,000,000; mandated some benefits for medical plans.	6
1994	Uniformed Services Employment and Reemployment Rights Act (USERRA)	Protected the reemployment and benefit rights of reservists called to active duty.	7
1995	Congressional Accountability Act (CAA)	Required all federal employment legislation passed by Congress to apply to congressional employees.	4

Year	Name	Significance	Chapter
1996	Illegal Immigration Reform and Immigrant Responsibility Act (IIRIRA)	Reduced the number and types of acceptable documents used to prove identity and employment eligibility, and launched the E-Verify pilot programs.	4
1996	Mental Health Parity Act (MHPA)	Required insurers to provide the same limits for mental health benefits that are provided for other types of health benefits.	6
1996	Health Insurance Portability and Accountability Act (HIPAA)	Prohibited discrimination based on health status; limited health insurance restrictions for preexisting conditions; required a Certificate of Group Health Plan Coverage upon plan termination.	6
1996	Personal Responsibility and Work Opportunity Reconciliation Act	Required employers to provide information about all new or rehired employees to state agencies to enforce child-support orders.	6
1996	Small Business Job Protection Act	Redefined highly compensated individuals; detailed minimum participation requirements; simplified 401(k) tests; corrected qualified plan and disclosure requirements.	6
1996	Small Business Regulatory Enforcement Fairness Act (SBREFA)	Provided that a Small Business Administration (SBA) ombudsman act as an advocate for small-business owners in the regulatory process.	8
1998	EO 13087	Expanded coverage of protected classes in EO 11246 to include sexual orientation.	4
1998	*Burlington Industries v. Ellerth*	USSC: Established that employers have vicarious liability for employees victimized by supervisors with immediate or higher authority over them who create an actionable hostile work environment.	7
1998	*Faragher v. City of Boca Raton*	USSC: Established that employers are responsible for employee actions and have a responsibility to control them.	7
1998	*Oncale v. Sundowner Offshore Services, Inc.*	USSC: Extended the definition of sexual harassment to include same-sex harassment.	7

(Continued)

Year	Name	Significance	Chapter
2000	NLRB: Epilepsy Foundation of Northeast Ohio	Extended Weingarten rights to nonunion employees by allowing employees to request a co-worker be present during an investigatory interview that could result in disciplinary action.	7
2000	NLRB: M. B. Sturgis, Inc.	Established that temporary employees may be included in the client company's bargaining unit and that consent of the employer and temp agency aren't required to bargain jointly.	7
2000	Needlestick Safety and Prevention Act	Mandated recordkeeping for all needlestick and sharps injuries; required employee involvement in developing safer devices.	8
2000	Energy Employees Occupational Illness Compensation Program Act (EEOICPA)	Provided compensation for employees and contractors subjected to excessive radiation during production and testing of nuclear weapons.	8
2000	EO 13152	Added "status as a parent" to protected classes in EO 11246.	4
2001	*Circuit City Stores v. Adams*	USSC: Arbitration clauses in employment agreements are enforceable for employers engaged in interstate commerce except for transportation workers.	4
2001	EO 13201	Applies to federal contractors and subcontractors.	7
2002	Sarbanes-Oxley Act (SOX)	Mandated improved quality and transparency in financial reporting, and increased corporate responsibility and the usefulness of corporate financial disclosure; required companies to establish and maintain an adequate internal control structure and procedures for financial reporting.	7
2003	*Pharakhone v. Nissan North America, Inc.*	Established that employees who violate company rules while on FMLA leave may be terminated.	6
2004	NLRB: IBM Corp.	NLRB reversed its 2000 decision in Epilepsy, withdrawing Weingarten rights from nonunion employees.	7

Year	Name	Significance	Chapter
2004	*Jespersen v. Harrah's Operating Co.*	Established that a dress code requiring women to wear makeup doesn't constitute unlawful sex discrimination under Title VII.	7
2005	*Smith v. City of Jackson, Mississippi*	USSC: Established that ADEA permits disparate-impact claims for age discrimination comparable to those permitted for discrimination based on sex and race.	4
2006	Pension Protection Act (PPA)	Amended ERISA financial obligations for multi-employer pension plans; changed plan administration for deferred-contribution plans.	6
2006	*Burlington Northern Santa Fe Railway Co. vs. White*	USSC: Established that all retaliation against employees who file discrimination claims is unlawful under Title VII, even if no economic damage results.	7
2006	*Sista v. CDC Ixis North America, Inc.*	Established that employees on FMLA may be legally terminated for legitimate, nondiscriminatory reasons, including violations of company policy if the reason is unrelated to the exercise of FMLA rights.	6
2006	*Bates v. United Parcel Service*	Established that when employers apply an unlawful standard that bars employees protected by the ADA from an application process, the employees don't need to prove they were otherwise qualified to perform essential job functions. The employer must prove the standard is necessary to business operations.	4
2007	*Taylor v. Progress Energy, Inc.*	Established that the waiver of FMLA rights in a severance agreement is invalid. FMLA clearly states that "employees cannot waive, nor may employers induce employees to waive, any rights under the FMLA."	6
2007	*Repa v. Roadway Express, Inc.*	Established that when an employee on FMLA leave is receiving employer-provided disability payments, they may not be required to use accrued sick or vacation leave during the FMLA absence.	6

(Continued)

Year	Name	Significance	Chapter
2007	*Phason v. Meridian Rail Corp.*	Established that when an employer is close to closing a deal to sell a company, WARN Act notice requirements are triggered by the number of employees actually employed and the number laid off on the date of the layoff, even if the purchasing company hires some of the employees shortly after the layoff.	4
2007	*Davis v. O'Melveny & Myers*	Established that arbitration clauses in employment agreements won't be enforced if they're significantly favorable to the employer and the employee doesn't have a meaningful opportunity to reject the agreement.	7
2007	*Velazquez-Garcia v. Horizon Lines of Puerto Rico, Inc.*	Established that the burden of proof that a termination wasn't related to military service is on an employer when an employee protected by USERRA is laid off.	7
2008	Genetic Information Nondiscrimination Act (GINA)	Prohibits employment discrimination on the basis of genetic information. Prohibits employers from requesting, requiring, or purchasing genetic information, and describes exceptions.	4
2010	Patient Protection and Affordable Health Care Act	Created new requirements for employer-sponsored healthcare plans. Amended the FLSA to require large employers to provide lactation breaks and facilities for employees who are breastfeeding.	6

Additional Cases

A great deal of case law impacts human resource management. This book has included many of those significant cases in the chapters where they have the most impact, but numerous others affect HR practice on a daily basis. You should be prepared to see some of these included in questions on the exam.

1968: *Rosenfeld v. Southern Pacific*

Leah Rosenfeld began working for Southern Pacific (SP) in 1944 and was a member of the Transportation Communication Employees Union, which represented employees at that location. As part of its collective bargaining agreement (CBA) with SP, the union had negotiated a clause that stated, "Employees shall be regarded as in line for promotion, advancement depending upon faithful discharge of duties and capacity for increased responsibility. Where ability is sufficient, seniority shall govern."

In 1966, Ms. Rosenfeld applied for the position of agent-telegrapher at the SP office in Thermal, California, and was the most senior employee bidding for the opening. She was fully qualified for the position based on all the standards established by the CBA and was fully qualified to perform the services of the position, including required overtime and the physical duties required by the position. The company didn't perform any tests or evaluation of her abilities for requirements of the job.

A male employee with less seniority was selected for the position.

SP gave two reasons for refusing the job to her:

- The California Labor Code limited the number of hours of work per day that could be performed by women and placed a limit of 25 pounds on the weight that could be lifted by a woman.

- Hiring Ms. Rosenfeld was contrary to SP's discretion as an employer.

Rosenfeld filed suit, claiming that the labor code sections were discriminatory on the basis of sex based on Title VII and that the requirements weren't BFOQs.

The Ninth Circuit Court of Appeal determined that the labor code didn't create a BFOQ and was, in fact, discriminatory; that SP did violate Title VII; and that the refusal of SP to assign her to the position wasn't a lawful exercise of SP's discretion as an employer. SP was ordered to consider her for future openings.

1969: *Weeks v. Southern Bell Telephone Co.*

In 1947, Lorena Weeks began working for Southern Bell (Bell) in Georgia and was a member of the union that represented the workers. The union had a CBA with the company including a clause that seniority would be the deciding factor in determining which job bidders were placed in positions if they otherwise met all the requirements for an opening.

In 1966, Ms. Weeks and one other employee applied for an opening as a switchman. Bell refused her application, telling her it had decided not to place women in this position. The other applicant, a man, had less seniority than Ms. Weeks.

Ms. Weeks filed a complaint with the EEOC, claiming that the company had discriminated against her on the basis of her sex and later filed suit against the company on the same basis. Bell admitted a *prima facie* violation of Title VII but claimed that sex was a BFOQ for the position, basing this claim on the Georgia Commissioner of Labor's Rule 59, which prohibited women and minors from lifting over 30 pounds. Ms. Weeks argued that the limit was unreasonably low, that it was arbitrary, and that it both violated the Equal Protection Clause of the Fourteenth Amendment and was contrary to Title VII.

In 1969, the Fifth Circuit Court of Appeal ruled that Bell had not proven that sex was a BFOQ for this position. The fact that by then Georgia had repealed Rule 59, replacing the specific weight limit with a requirement that the weight of loads be limited to avoid strains or undue fatigue, was noted by the court in its decision.

1973: *McDonnell Douglas Corp. v. Green*

Percy Green was an African-American man working as a mechanic for McDonnell Douglas Corp. in St. Louis, Missouri, from 1956 until he was laid off at the end of August 1964 as part of a general reduction in the company's workforce. Mr. Green claimed that his termination and the company's hiring practices in general were racially motivated. To protest this alleged discrimination, Mr. Green, a member of the Congress of Racial Equality (CRE), participated in a "stall-in" with other members of the group that was designed to block access to the company's plant during the morning rush hour. Mr. Green was arrested for his part in the action and pled guilty to obstructing traffic. Some time later, the CRE conducted a "lock-in" at the plant that prevented some McDonnell Douglas employees from leaving the building.

When McDonnell Douglas advertised for mechanics a few weeks after the lock-in, Mr. Green applied and was turned down based on his participation in the stall-in and lock-in. He filed a complaint with the EEOC, claiming that he was turned down because of his race and his participation in the civil rights movement. Mr. Green sued McDonnell Douglas in 1968 for violations of Title VII, and the case was heard by the U.S. Supreme Court in 1973.

In issuing its findings in 1973, the Supreme Court and subsequent court interpretations that followed defined the requirements for a finding of a *prima facie* case of discrimination as follows: "The complainant in a Title VII trial must carry the initial burden under the statute of establishing a prima facie case of racial discrimination. This may be done by showing (i) that he belongs to a racial minority; (ii) that he applied and was qualified for a job for which the employer was seeking applicants; (iii) that, despite his qualifications, he was rejected; and (iv) that, after his rejection, the position remained open and the employer continued to seek applicants from persons of complainant's qualifications."

1978: *Regents of California v. Bakke*

Although the Bakke case was based on a college admissions program, its results impacted the use of affirmative-action programs in general.

The Medical School at the University of California–Davis used two admissions programs to qualify students for the medical program. Both the regular and special admissions programs evaluated applicants based on a number of criteria and ranked them with a "benchmark score" based on the results. Applicants for both programs were rated on similar criteria, but those in the special admissions program weren't rated against those in the regular admission program when decisions were made as to which applicants would be offered admission. In addition, a specific number of spots were allotted to applicants from the special admissions program.

In 1973 and 1974, Allan Bakke's applications for admission to the medical program through the regular admission process were rejected, while applicants from the special admissions program who ranked lower than he did on the admission criteria were accepted. Mr. Bakke filed suit, claiming that the special admissions program was in violation of the Equal Protection Clause of the Fourteenth Amendment to the Constitution, as well as Title VI of the Civil Rights Act of 1964 and a provision of the California constitution. The Supreme Court handed down its decision in 1978, finding that Mr. Bakke's rights had indeed been violated by the special admissions program, which operated as a quota for admitting minorities to the medical program.

The Court's decision acknowledged the need to consider race in admission decisions when it was necessary to correct prior discriminatory practices but ruled that quotas weren't an acceptable method to accomplish this.

1979: *United Steelworkers v. Weber*

This case began with an AAP that had been negotiated by the United Steelworkers of America (USWA) and Kaiser Aluminum & Chemical Corp. (Kaiser) as part of a CBA. The AAP had been negotiated to "eliminate conspicuous racial imbalances" in skilled craft positions at 15 Kaiser plants by reserving 50 percent of openings in the in-plant training programs for black employees until the percentage of black craft workers in each plant corresponded with the percentage of blacks in the local labor force. Employees were selected for the program based on their seniority, as long as 50 percent of the trainees were black.

Brian Weber filed suit against Kaiser and the USWA when he was rejected for a spot in the training program in favor of black employees who had less seniority than he did. Mr. Weber claimed that this was a violation of Title VII of the Civil Rights Act of 1964. The Supreme Court found that the AAP was permissible because it allowed that half of the participants would be white, that it had been designed to remedy prior discrimination, and that it was a temporary measure designed to eliminate a racial imbalance.

1981: *Texas Department of Community Affairs v. Burdine*

In 1972, Joyce Ann Burdine was hired by the Texas Department of Community Affairs (TDCA) as an accounting clerk in the Public Service Careers (PSC) division whose mission was to train unskilled workers for public-sector jobs. Six months later, Ms. Burdine, who had previous training experience, was promoted to the position of field service coordinator. The project director (her supervisor) resigned a few months later, and Ms. Burdine applied for the position, but it wasn't filled and remained open for another 6 months. At that point, the U.S. Department of Labor (DOL), which funded the PSC and was concerned about the quality of its operations, decided to cease funding in 30 days. Based on the efforts of the TDCA, with input from Ms. Burdine, the DOL was convinced to continue funding for the PSC if it was reorganized and a permanent director was hired.

The TDCA reassigned a male from another division to the project director position. He terminated three employees, including Ms. Burdine, retaining one male employee. Shortly after the termination, Ms. Burdine was rehired by the TDCA in another division at the same salary as was paid to the project director of the PSC.

Ms. Burdine filed this suit, claiming gender discrimination had motivated both the refusal of TDCA to promote her and her subsequent termination from PSC. The District Court determined that gender had not been a factor in either decision. The Fifth Circuit

Court of Appeals found that the male hired for the project director position may have been better qualified than Ms. Burdine for the position but that the TDCA had not proved that there were legitimate, nondiscriminatory reasons for Ms. Burdine's termination.

The Supreme Court held that employers aren't required to prove the nondiscriminatory reasons for an employment action but are required only to explain the nondiscriminatory reasons for the action.

1987: *Johnson v. Santa Clara County Transportation Agency*

Paul Johnson, a male employee of the Santa Clara County Transportation Agency (SCCTA), was passed over for a promotion in favor of a female employee, Diane Joyce. Both candidates were deemed to be well qualified for the position of road dispatcher, a job classified as a Skilled Craft Worker by the EEOC. The director of the agency made the final decision based on a number of factors, including the qualifications of both candidates, the selection committee recommendation, and affirmative-action issues, among others.

The affirmative-action issues included the fact that the agency had established a voluntary AAP in 1978 that had as one of its goals increasing the participation of women in the Skilled Craft Worker category. At the time Ms. Joyce applied for this position, none of the 238 SCCTA positions classified as such was held by a woman.

Mr. Johnson filed a complaint with the EEOC, received a right-to-sue letter in 1981, and filed suit against the agency for violating Title VII. The Supreme Court handed down its decision in 1987.

The Supreme Court held that the SCCTA acted appropriately in promoting Ms. Joyce into the position. The Court stated that the plaintiff has the burden to prove a *prima facie* case of discrimination. Once that occurs, the employer has the burden to prove that there is a nondiscriminatory rationale for the decision (that is, the AAP). At that point, the burden once again shifted to the plaintiff to show that the AAP is invalid.

The agency's AAP was determined to be "a moderate, flexible, case-by-case approach" consistent with Title VII requirements. Key elements in this finding were that the AAP was flexible and temporary, designed only to correct an existing workforce imbalance. That being the case, it's acceptable for an employer to place a less qualified member of a protected class in a job.

1987: *School Board of Nassau v. Arline*

Gene Arline contracted tuberculosis in 1957 and was hospitalized until the disease went into remission. In 1966, Ms. Arline became an elementary school teacher in Nassau County, Florida, where she taught for 13 years. In 1977, the TB became active again and was active off and on through the 1978–79 school year. The school board suspended her with pay twice to accommodate her recovery but in 1979 decided to terminate her employment due to the contagious nature of her ongoing illness.

Ms. Arline sued the district, alleging that her dismissal was a violation of Section 504 of the Rehabilitation Act of 1973 because its terms qualified her as a handicapped person based on her illness.

Section 504 is based on Title VI of the Civil Rights Act of 1964 and defines a handicapped individual as "any person who (i) has a physical or mental impairment which substantially limits one or more of such person's major life activities, (ii) has a record of such an impairment, or (iii) is regarded as having such an impairment." Regulations formulated by the Department of Health and Human Services define "major life activities" as "functions such as caring for one's self, performing manual tasks, walking, seeing, hearing, speaking, breathing, learning, and working."

The case centered around whether a person with a contagious disease could be considered a handicapped individual under Section 504 of the Rehabilitation Act.

In 1987, the Supreme Court handed down its decision that a person afflicted with tuberculosis can be a handicapped person as defined by Section 504.

Justice Brennan, writing for the majority, stated, "The fact that some persons who have contagious diseases may pose a serious health threat to others under certain circumstances does not justify excluding from the coverage of the act all persons with actual or perceived contagious diseases." The decision also stated that the determination of whether someone with a contagious disease poses a serious health threat to others should be left to the medical judgments of public health officials.

1989: *Martin v. Wilks*

The basic issue in this case was whether an employee can sue for reverse discrimination when hiring and promotion decisions are made pursuant to a consent decree.

The city of Birmingham, Alabama, and the Jefferson County Personnel Board were sued by Martin and six other black individuals in 1974, alleging that the city and the board had unlawfully discriminated against blacks when making hiring and promoting decisions for public service jobs. The case was resolved when the parties entered into consent decrees that established AAPs intended to increase the hiring and promotion of black firefighters.

At a public fairness hearing and in other subsequent actions, objections and a request for injunctive relief to prevent enforcement of the decrees by the Birmingham Firefighters Association (BFA) and white firefighters were denied by the District Court.

A third group of firefighters (including Robert Wilks) then filed suit against the city and the board, alleging that they were being denied promotions in favor of less-qualified blacks and that this was a violation of Title VII. Martin and the other black individuals sought to have the Wilks suit dismissed, claiming that the consent decree precluded any claims of reverse discrimination.

The Supreme Court held that, because the white firefighters weren't involved in the original litigation that resulted in the consent decrees, they couldn't be held to employment decisions based on them and were entitled to challenge the validity of the consent decrees.

1992: *Electromation, Inc. v. NLRB*

This case resulted from an unfair labor practice (ULP) charge filed against Electromation by the Teamsters union.

Electromation was a small company with 200 employees that was having financial problems in late 1988. As a result, management decided to eliminate the employee attendance bonus policy and the wage increase for 1989. Instead, it made lump-sum payments to employees based on each individual's length of service. Shortly after this decision was made, the president received a petition signed by 68 employees objecting to the change in policy. The president first met with supervisory personnel to discuss the complaints and then decided to meet directly with a group of employees to discuss their concerns. After meeting with the employees, the president realized that the employee issues were unlikely to be resolved without employee participation. The company decided to create five action committees, one for each area of concern:

- Absenteeism/infractions

- No-smoking policy

- Communication network

- Pay progression for premium positions

- Attendance bonus program

The committees met weekly, beginning in late January 1989, and included management personnel as well as employees as members. Although employees were allowed to sign up for the committees, management determined how many were allowed and limited employees to serving on one committee. Management communicated to the committee members that they were expected to talk with their co-workers to get ideas that could be incorporated into the work of the committees. Management also expected committee members to inform co-workers about "what was going on."

On February 13, 1989, the Teamsters union made a demand for recognition to Electromation; at that point, management advised the committees that management was no longer able to participate but that the committees could continue their work if they wanted to do so.

The NLRB Administrative Law Judge determined that the action committees were unlawful employer-dominated labor organizations for the following reasons:

- They included employees, supervisors, and management as members, and management personnel had the ability to reject recommendations.

- Management expected committee members to represent co-workers by soliciting ideas from them to be presented to the committee.

- They included discussions about conditions of employment. The formation of the committees was a direct result of the company's unilateral change to the attendance bonus policy.

- Management organized them by establishing their goals, determining what each committee would work on, deciding how many employees would be allowed on each committee and how they would operate, and determining their functions.

- The company provided support in the form of a place to meet, supplies, materials, and payment for time spent on committee work.

In its decision, the NLRB indicated that not all employee-participation committees are employer-dominated organizations and that they can serve a useful purpose if they aren't employer-dominated. It also determined that paying employees who participate in committees at work doesn't in and of itself violate the NLRA.

1993: *E. I. DuPont & Co. v. NLRB*

This case was initiated by the Chemical Workers Union, which represents clerical workers, production personnel, and maintenance employees at DuPont's plant located in Deepwater, New Jersey. The union claimed that six safety committees and a fitness committee established by DuPont were company-dominated labor organizations and that the company was bypassing the union by dealing with the committees on bargainable issues. DuPont claimed that the committees were "a management vehicle to enhance the safety of employees through labor-management communication or to carry out similar management functions."

The NLRA established three conditions that must be met in order for a labor organization to exist:

1. Employees participate in the organization.

2. A function of the organization is dealing with the employer.

3. The function of the organization is concerned with some form of "conditions of work," including grievances, labor disputes, wages, rates of pay, or hours of employment.

The purpose of this case was to determine whether DuPont was using these committees to bypass the union in dealing with the employees, because clearly employees were participating in them and they dealt with safety issues, which are a mandatory subject for collective bargaining.

Some of the reasons the NLRB found these to be employer-dominated labor organizations include the following:

- Each committee included at least one member of management who set the weekly agenda and had veto power over any decisions or recommendations made by committee members.

- DuPont controlled the number of members on each committee.

- DuPont determined how many and which employees served on each committee.

- DuPont could unilaterally restructure the committees.

The board also found that DuPont was using the committees to circumvent the union. For example, the union had repeatedly requested that changes be made to the ventilation system in the welding shop. Until one of the committees made the suggestion, DuPont took no action; but once the committee suggestion was acted on, DuPont constructed a new shop. In another instance, DuPont had consistently refused the union's request for employee fitness facilities, but when the committee made the suggestions, management acted on them.

DuPont was required to disband the action committees and to post a notice at the plant that read, in part, "We will not deal with these committees or their successors. We will not bypass the Chemical Workers Association as your bargaining agent. We will not unilaterally implement these committees' proposals concerning safety awards and fitness facilities without affording the union an opportunity to bargain."

1993: *St. Mary's Honor Center v. Hicks*

St. Mary's Honor Center is a halfway house run by the Missouri Department of Corrections and Human Resources (MDCHR), which hired Melvin Hicks as a correctional officer in 1978 and, in 1980, promoted him to one of the six shift commander positions at St. Mary's. Mr. Hicks' work performance during this time was deemed to be satisfactory by his supervisors. As the result of an investigation by MDCHR, the supervisory structure of St. Mary's was reorganized in January 1984, at which time Mr. Hicks' immediate supervisor was replaced, as was the superintendent of the facility. Shortly after this change, his new supervisors singled out Mr. Hicks for disciplinary actions that his peers weren't subjected to. In fact, they were more lenient with his peers even with regard to more serious violations, in some cases disregarding them entirely. At one point Mr. Hicks was suspended, and he was later demoted from his supervisory position. In June he was terminated for threatening his supervisor during a heated argument.

At this point, Mr. Hicks filed suit, alleging discrimination on the basis of his race in violation of Title VII of the Civil Rights Act of 1964. Mr. Hicks was able to convince the District Court that a *prima facie* case of discrimination existed. St. Mary's then provided evidence of legitimate, nondiscriminatory reasons for its actions (the rules infractions for which Hicks had been disciplined). Once that occurred, the burden fell once again to Mr. Hicks to show that those reasons were actually a pretext, designed to hide the racial motivation of St. Mary's. The District Court found that, although the court didn't believe the reasons given by St. Mary's, Mr. Hicks had not proved that his termination was racially motivated. Based on the evidence offered, there was no way to determine whether the termination had been racially motivated (unlawful) or based on personal dislike for Mr. Hicks (lawful).

The Eighth Circuit Court of Appeals determined that since Mr. Hicks had proved the reasons were a pretext, he was entitled to a judgment in his favor.

When the case reached the Supreme Court, it relied on two prior cases in making its decision: *McDonnell Douglas Corp. v. Green* and *Texas Dept. of Community Affairs v. Burdine*. Based on *Green*, Mr. Hicks was required to establish that a *prima facie* case of discrimination existed. (He did.) Once that happened, according to *Burdine*, St. Mary's needed to provide a lawful explanation for the adverse employment actions taken against Mr. Hicks. (It did.) Once St. Mary's provided a nondiscriminatory reason for the employment actions, it was once again up to Mr. Hicks to prove that those reasons were racially motivated and not based on some other, lawful motivation.

1995: *McKennon v. Nashville Banner Publishing Co.*

Christine McKennon was employed by Nashville Banner Publishing Company (Banner) for 30 years. At age 62, Ms. McKennon's employment was terminated as part of a workforce reduction that was needed to reduce costs. Ms. McKennon believed that the termination was in fact unlawfully based on her age and filed suit claiming that this violated ADEA. During a deposition, she admitted copying confidential documents that she had access to in the course of her employment. Within a few days of the deposition, Banner notified her that removal of the documents was in violation of her job responsibilities and once again terminated her employment. Banner claimed in the letter that, had Banner known of this wrongdoing, her employment would have been terminated immediately based on this fact alone. The District Court then granted summary judgment for Banner, finding that her misconduct was grounds for her termination and that she wasn't entitled to any remedy in light of her actions.

The Supreme Court agreed to hear the case in order to resolve the question of whether all relief must be denied when an employer has violated the ADEA in its discharge of an employee but later discovers employee conduct that would have justified a lawful termination. The Court ruled that after-acquired evidence of employee misconduct that would have resulted in a termination doesn't relieve the employer for liability in discharging the employee for an unlawful, discriminatory reason.

2001: *Circuit City Stores v. Adams*

In 1995, Saint Clair Adams applied for and was hired as a sales counselor at a Circuit City store in Santa Rosa, California, after signing an employment application that contained a condition requiring that all employment disputes be settled through binding arbitration based on the Federal Arbitration Act of 1925 (FAA). In 1997, Mr. Adams filed a discrimination claim against Circuit City in state court, and the store responded with a federal suit seeking to stop the state action and force Mr. Adams to arbitration per the agreement he had signed. The District Court agreed with Circuit City, and Mr. Adams appealed the decision to the Ninth Circuit Court of Appeals, which ruled that the FAA doesn't apply to employment contracts. Because this ruling conflicted with all other circuits of the Federal Court of Appeals, the Supreme Court granted certiorari in 2000.

The Supreme Court reversed the Ninth Circuit, finding that mandatory arbitration agreements in employment contracts are enforceable under the FAA except for transportation workers, who are specifically exempted from the FAA.

Appendix D

Resources

Thousands of references are available for every aspect of human resources, so it's just not possible to include every great resource here. The resources included in this appendix are those that add dimension or different perspectives to the information presented in this book. Although the best preparation for both the PHR and SPHR examinations is diverse generalist experience, these resources will provide a more in-depth refresher than is possible in this guide:

A Word About the Internet   A wealth of information is available on the Internet that is current and easily accessible. The best way to access this information is through a search engine such as Google (www.google.com). If you haven't used a search engine before, you can get instructions on how to search by clicking the Help button on each search page. When you type in the phrase you want to research, you will get a list of websites to check out.

Information About the Test   For information about eligibility requirements and test dates, the best source is the Human Resource Certification Institute (HRCI). There are two sources for information from HRCI. The first is the *PHR/SPHR/GPHR Certification Handbook* (described in the introduction of this book), which is free of charge and published annually. The handbook provides all the information necessary to apply for the exams and includes pricing, deadlines, and general information. The second source is the HRCI website (www.hrci.org). The website contains a great deal of information about the exams and also allows you to view the handbook online, download a copy, or request that a hard copy be mailed to you. Another helpful information source is the *HRCI Certification Guide*, published by the Society for Human Resource Management. This inexpensive guide explains the testing process, discusses various study methods, and contains sample questions and answers; it can be purchased from several national online booksellers.

Professional Associations   Professional associations are often a great source of information about current trends in a particular practice area. Some of them are member-only sites, but even those often have useful information available to nonmembers.

As mentioned earlier, many sources of HR information are available. The inclusion of these resources is not an endorsement of the information contained in them. They are provided only as suggestions for further reading should you feel the need for more detail in one of these areas. For ease of use, the list is organized according to functional area.

At the time of publication, the URLs included in the following sections were operational; given the changing nature of the World Wide Web, though, some of them may have been changed or no longer exist.

Business Management and Strategy

Resources included with Business Management and Strategy cover general human resource books and resources for other business disciplines with which HR professionals interact on a daily basis.

Books

Chase, Richard B., F. Robert Jacobs, and Nicholas J. Aquilano. *Operations Management for Competitive Advantage*, 11th ed. Boston: McGraw-Hill/Irwin, 2006.

Fitz-Enz, Jac. *The 8 Practices of Exceptional Companies: How Great Organizations Make the Most of Their Human Assets*, 3rd ed. New York: AMACOM, 2005.

Hiam, Alexander. *Marketing for Dummies*, 3rd ed. Indianapolis: John Wiley & Sons, Inc., 2009.

Kaplan, Robert S., and David P. Norton. *The Balanced Scorecard: Translating Strategy into Action*. Boston: Harvard Business School Press, 1996.

Losey, Mike, Dave Ulrich, and Sue Meisinger. *The Future of Human Resource Management: 64 Thought Leaders Explore the Critical HR Issues of Today and Tomorrow*. Hoboken, NJ: John Wiley & Sons, Inc., 2005.

Mathis, Robert L., and John H. Jackson. *Human Resource Management*, 12th ed. Mason, OH: Thomas South-Western, 2008.

Phillips, Jack, Ron Stone, and Patricia Phillips. *The Human Resources Scorecard: Measuring the Return on Investment (Improving Human Performance)*. Boston: Butterworth-Heinemann, 2001.

Tracy, John A. *How to Read a Financial Report: Wringing Vital Signs Out of the Numbers*, 7th ed. Hoboken, NJ: John Wiley & Sons, Inc., 2009.

Weill, Peter, and Jeanne Ross. *IT Governance: How Top Performers Manage IT Decision Rights for Superior Results*. Boston: Harvard Business School Press, 2004.

Professional Associations

American Institute of Certified Public Accountants, www.aicpa.org

American Management Association, www.amanet.org

American Marketing Association, www.marketingpower.com

HR People & Strategy, www.hrps.org

The Institute for the Management of Information Systems, www.imis.org.uk

The Institute of Operations Management, www.iomnet.org.uk

International Association for Human Resource Information Management, www.ihrim.org

Society for Human Resource Management, www.shrm.org

Workforce Planning and Employment

These resources are some of the many related to planning for workforce recruiting and employment. In addition, Chapter 4, "Workforce Planning and Employment," includes links to government agencies enforcing employment laws, should you want to read more about them.

Books

Ahlrichs, Nancy S. *Competing for Talent: Key Recruitment and Retention Strategies for Becoming an Employer of Choice*. Palo Alto, CA: Davies-Black Publishing, 2000.

Bechet, Thomas P. *Strategic Staffing: A Comprehensive System for Effective Workforce Planning*, 2nd ed. New York: AMACOM, 2008.

Bradt, George B., and Mary Vonnegut. *Onboarding: How to Get Your New Employees Up to Speed in Half the Time*. Hoboken, NJ: John Wiley & Sons, Inc., 2009.

Manning, Paula, and Jennifer Brugh. *Recruiting and Retaining Employees for Dummies*. New York: Hungry Minds, 2001.

Phillips, Jack J., and Adele O. Connell. *Managing Employee Retention: A Strategic Accountability Approach*. Boston: Butterworth-Heinemann, 2003.

Steingold, Fred S. *The Employer's Legal Handbook*: *Manage Your Employees and Workplace Effectively*, 10th ed. Berkeley, CA: Nolo Press, 2011.

Truesdell, William H. *Secrets of Affirmative Action Compliance*, 9th ed. Walnut Creek, CA: Management Advantage, 2010.

Professional Associations

American Staffing Association, `www.staffingtoday.net` (look for the issue papers)

International Labour Organization, `www.ilo.org`

International Public Management Association for Human Resources, `www.ipma-hr.org`

Worldwide ERC, `www.erc.org`

Human Resource Development

These resources provide additional information about developing talent within organizations.

Books

Anderson, Dean, and Linda Ackerman Anderson. *Beyond Change Management: How to Achieve Breakthrough Results Through Conscious Change Leadership*. San Francisco: Pfeiffer, 2001.

Becker, Brian E., Mark A. Huselid, and Dave Ulrich. *The HR Scorecard: Linking People, Strategy, and Performance*. Boston: Harvard Business School Press, 2001.

Carliner, Saul. *Designing e-learning*. Alexandria, VA: ASTD Press, 2002.

Fitz-Enz, Jac. *The ROI of Human Capital: Measuring the Economic Value of Employee Performance*, 2nd ed. New York: AMACOM, 2009.

Grote, Richard. *Discipline Without Punishment: The Proven Strategy That Turns Problem Employees into Superior Performers*, 2nd ed. New York: AMACOM, 2006.

Hodell, Chuck. *ISD from the Ground Up: A No-Nonsense Approach to Instructional Design*, 3rd Ed. Alexandria, VA: ASTD Press, 2011.

Knowles, Malcolm S., Elwood F. Holton, and Richard A. Swanson. *The Adult Learner: The Definitive Classic in Adult Education and Human Resource Development*, 6th ed. Boston: Butterworth-Heinemann, 2005.

Marquardt, Michael J. *Building the Learning Organization: Achieving Strategic Advantage Through a Commitment to Learning*, 3rd ed. Boston: Nicholas Brealey, 2011.

Philips, Jack, and Ron D. Stone. *How to Measure Training Results: A Practical Guide to Tracking the Six Key Indicators*. New York: McGraw-Hill, 2002.

Robbins, Stephen, and Timothy Judge. *Organizational Behavior*, 14th ed. Upper Saddle River, NJ: Prentice Hall, 2011.

Senge, Peter M. *The Fifth Discipline: The Art and Practice of the Learning Organization*, rev. and updated ed. New York: Doubleday/Currency, 2006.

Professional Associations

American Society for Training & Development, www.astd.org

Compensation and Benefits

Additional information about compensation and benefit issues and processes is available in the following resources.

Books

Beam, Burton T., Jr., and John J. McFadden. *Employee Benefits*, 8th ed. Chicago: Real Estate Education, 2007.

Berger, Lance A., and Dorothy R. Berger, eds. *The Compensation Handbook: A State-of-the-Art Guide to Compensation Strategy and Design*, 5th ed. New York: McGraw-Hill, 2008.

Plachy, Roger J., and Sandra J. Plachy. *Building a Fair Pay Program: A Step-by-Step Guide*, 2nd ed. New York: AMACOM, 1998.

Professional Associations

American Payroll Association, www.americanpayroll.org

Employee Benefit Research Institute, www.ebri.org

International Foundation of Employee Benefit Plans, www.ifebp.org

International Society of Certified Employee Benefits Specialists, www.iscebs.org

WorldatWork (formerly American Compensation Association), www.worldatwork.org

Employee and Labor Relations

These resources provide additional information on labor and employee relations.

Books

Brounstein, Marty. *Coaching and Mentoring for Dummies*. New York: IDG Books Worldwide, 2000.

Costantino, Cathy A., and Christina Sickles Merchant. *Designing Conflict Management Systems: A Guide to Creating Productive and Healthy Organizations*. San Francisco: Jossey-Bass, 1996.

DelPo, Amy, and Lisa Guerin. *Dealing with Problem Employees: A Legal Guide*, 6th ed. Berkeley, CA: Nolo Press, 2011.

Holley, William H., Kenneth M. Jennings, and Roger S. Wolters. *The Labor Relations Process*, 9th ed. Mason, OH: South-Western, 2008.

Grazier, Peter B. *Before It's Too Late: Employee Involvement… An Idea Whose Time Has Come.* Chadds Ford, PA: Teambuilding, 1989.

Kaye, Beverly, and Sharon Jordan-Evans. *Love 'Em or Lose 'Em: Getting Good People to Stay*, 4th ed. San Francisco: Berrett-Koehler Publishers, 2008.

Larkin, T.J., and Sandar Larkin (contributor). *Communicating Change: Winning Employee Support for New Business Goals*, 2nd ed. New York: McGraw-Hill, 1994.

Cassel, Robert M. Charles S. Loughran. *Negotiating a Labor Contract: A Management Handbook*, 4th ed. Washington, D.C.: BNA Books, 2010.

Sheridan, Kevin, *Building a Magnetic Culture: How to Attract and Retain Top Talent to Create an Engaged, Productive Workforce.* New York: McGraw-Hill, 2012.

Spitzer, Dean R. *Supermotivation: A Blueprint for Energizing Your Organization from Top to Bottom.* New York: AMACOM, 1995.

Professional Associations

National Public Employer Labor Relations Association, www.npelra.org

Recruiting and Staffing Focus Area, www.shrm.org/hrdisciplines/staffingmanagement/

Risk Management

These are some of the many resources available for workplace health, safety, and security issues.

Books

Blanco, James A., and Dave Evans. *Business Fraud: Know It & Prevent It.* Huntington, WV: Humanomics Publishing, 2001.

Fay, John J. *Contemporary Security Management*, 3rd ed. Burlington, MA: Butterworth-Heinemann, 2011.

Geller, E. Scott. *The Psychology of Safety Handbook*, 2nd ed. Boca Raton, FL: CRC Press, 2001.

Greenspan, Amy. *Employer's Guide to Workplace Privacy*, 7th ed. New York: Aspen Publishers, 2007.

Levy, Barry S., David H. Wegman, Sherry L. Baron, and Rosemary K. Sokas. *Occupational and Environmental Health: Recognizing and Preventing Disease and Injury,* 6th ed. New York: Oxford University Press, 2011.

Mitroff, Ian I., Christine M. Pearson, and L. Katharine Harrington. *The Essential Guide to Managing Corporate Crises: A Step-by-Step Handbook for Surviving Major Catastrophes.* New York: Oxford University Press, 1996.

Professional Associations

The American Society of Safety Engineers, www.asse.org

National Association of Safety Professionals, www.naspweb.com

National Safety Council, www.nsc.org

Appendix
E

About the Additional Study Tools

IN THIS APPENDIX:

✓ Additional study tools

✓ System requirements

✓ Using the study tools

✓ Troubleshooting

Additional Study Tools

The following sections are arranged by category and summarize the software and other goodies you'll find from the companion website. If you need help installing the items, refer to the installation instructions in the "Using the Study Tools" section of this appendix.

 The additional study tools can be found at www.sybex.com/go/phr4e. Here, you'll get instructions on how to download the files to your hard drive.

Sybex Test Engine

The files contain the Sybex test engine, which includes two bonus practice exams, as well as the assessment test and the chapter review questions, which are also included in the book itself.

Electronic Flashcards

These handy electronic flashcards are just what they sound like. One side contains a question, and the other side shows the answer.

PDF of Glossary of Terms

We have included an electronic version of the glossary in .pdf format. You can view the electronic version of the glossary with Adobe Reader.

Adobe Reader

We've also included a copy of Adobe Reader so you can view the PDF files that accompany the book's content. For more information on Adobe Reader or to check for a newer version, visit Adobe's website at www.adobe.com/products/reader/.

System Requirements

Make sure your computer meets the minimum system requirements shown in the following list. If your computer doesn't match up to most of these requirements, you may have problems using the software and files. For the latest and greatest information, please refer to the ReadMe file located in the downloads:

- A PC running Microsoft Windows 98, Windows 2000, Windows NT4 (with SP4 or later), Windows ME, Windows XP, Windows Vista, or Windows 7
- An Internet connection

Using the Study Tools

To install the items, follow these steps:

1. Download the .zip file to your hard drive, and unzip it to an appropriate location. Instructions on where to download this file can be found here: www.sybex.com/go/ phr4e.

2. Click the Start.EXE file to open the study tools file.

3. Read the license agreement, and then click the Accept button if you want to use the study tools.

The main interface appears. The interface allows you to access the content with just one or two clicks.

Troubleshooting

Wiley has attempted to provide programs that work on most computers with the minimum system requirements. Alas, your computer may differ, and some programs may not work properly for some reason.

The two likeliest problems are that you don't have enough memory (RAM) for the programs you want to use or you have other programs running that are affecting installation or running of a program. If you get an error message such as "Not enough memory" or "Setup cannot continue," try one or more of the following suggestions and then try using the software again:

Turn off any antivirus software running on your computer. Installation programs sometimes mimic virus activity and may make your computer incorrectly believe that it's being infected by a virus.

Close all running programs. The more programs you have running, the less memory is available to other programs. Installation programs typically update files and programs; so if you keep other programs running, installation may not work properly.

Have your local computer store add more RAM to your computer. This is, admittedly, a drastic and somewhat expensive step. However, adding more memory can really help the speed of your computer and allow more programs to run at the same time.

Customer Care

If you have trouble with the book's companion study tools, please call Wiley Product Technical Support at (800) 762-2974 ext. 74 or email them at `http://sybex.custhelp.com/`.

Index

Note to the reader: Throughout this index **boldfaced** page numbers indicate primary discussions of a topic. *Italicized* page numbers indicate illustrations.

The Best Study Tools for the PHR and SPHR Certifications

Readers have access to the most comprehensive study tool package on the market, including the Sybex test engine, electronic flashcards, and a database of key terms and definitions.

Get ready for your Professional in Human Resources (PHR) or Senior Professional in Human Resources (SPHR) exam with the most comprehensive and challenging sample tests anywhere!

The Sybex test engine features

- All the review questions, as covered in each chapter of the book

- Challenging questions representative of those you'll find on the real exam

- Two practice exams: one for PHR candidates and one for SPHR candidates

Use the electronic flashcards to jog your memory and prep last-minute for the exam:

- Reinforce your understanding of key concepts with these hardcore flashcard-style questions.

An assessment test to narrow your focus to certain objective groups

glossary for instant reference:

through the PDF of the glossary to terms you'll need to be familiar e exam.

Readers can access the companion study tools for the PHR/SPHR: Professional in Human Resources Study Guide, Fourth Edition at www.sybex.com/go/phr4e.